D0759537

DATE DUE

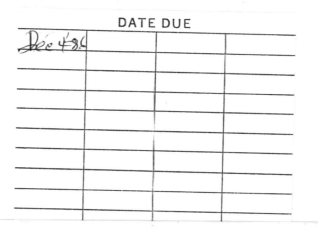

Dec 4 86			

Cherokees and Missionaries, 1789–1839

Cherokees
AND
Missionaries,
1789–1839

WILLIAM G. McLOUGHLIN

Yale University Press

NEW HAVEN AND LONDON

Published with assistance from the Louis Stern Memorial Fund.

Designed by James J. Johnson
Set in Caslon Old Style type by Northeast Typographic Services, Meriden, Connecticut.
Printed in the United States of America by Edwards Brothers, Inc., Ann Arbor, Michigan.

Library of Congress Cataloging in Publication Data

McLoughlin, William Gerald. / 922~
  Cherokees and missionaries, 1789–1839.

  Bibliography; p.
  Includes index.
    1. Cherokee Indians—Missions. 2. Indians of North America—Southern States—Missions. 3. Cherokee Indians—Cultural assimilation. 4. Indians of North America—Southern States—Cultural assimilation. 5. Missions—Southern States. I. Title.
  E99.C5M39 1984   303.4'82'08997   83–11759
  ISBN 0–300–03075–4

10   9   8   7   6   5   4   3   2   1

To Carol and Michael Wreszin,
good old friends

Contents

Acknowledgments

During the ten-year course of gathering material for and writing this book, I have run up numerous debts to institutions and people who have helped me along the way. First I wish to gratefully acknowledge the financial assistance of the National Endowment for the Humanities, the American Council of Learned Societies, and the Newberry Library. Then I want to thank the many librarians and archivists who have been of invaluable help in tracking down materials: Dan McPike and Marie E. Keene of the Gilcrease Institute; Bill Towner and John Aubrey of the Newberry Library; Rella Looney and Louise Cooke of the Oklahoma Historical Society; Marty Shaw of the Houghton Library; William H. Brackney of the American Baptist Historical Society; Mary Creech and Elizabeth Marx of the Moravian Archives in Winston-Salem, North Carolina; Lother Madeheim of the Moravian Archives in Bethlehem, Pennsylvania; Pat Bryant of the Secretary of State's Office in Georgia; Dean R. Kirkwood of the American Baptist Foreign Missionary Society; Jack D. Haley of the Western History Collections of the University of Oklahoma; Elma S. Kurtz of the Atlanta Historical Society; Marilyn Bell and Dawnene Matheny of the Tennessee State Library and Archives; Janet S. Fireman and John M. Cahoon of the Natural History Museum of Los Angeles County; David A. Jonah, Dorothy Day, and Janet Draper of the Brown University Library. I also wish to thank numerous scholars in the field of Native American history whose works I have cited and particularly those who have gone out of their way to provide me with specific answers to queries: Thurman Wilkins, Douglas Wilms, Edwin A. Miles, and A. D. Lester. Several colleagues and graduate students at Brown have also assisted me with statistical collaboration: Walter H. Conser, Jr., R. Burr Litchfield, Steven Hochstedt, and Morey Rothberg. And finally, as always, I wish to express my enduring appreciation to my wife, Virginia W. McLoughlin, for her assistance in research, her editorial advice, her typing skill, and, above all, her endless patience and consideration.

Abbreviations and Short Titles

ABCFM   American Board of Commissioners for Foreign Missions, papers indexed by name in the Houghton Library, Harvard University

Annual Reports, ABCFM (date)   Reports of the American Board of Commissioners for Foreign Missions. These were published annually in Boston from 1810 and are numbered accordingly.

ASP I, ASP II   *American States Papers*, Class II, Indians Affairs, 2 vols., *Documents, Legislative and Executive of the Congress of the United States*. ed. Walter Lowrie, Walter S. Franklin, and Matthew Clarke (Washington: Gales and Seaton, 1832, 1834)

Bangs, *Methodist Missions*   Nathan Bangs, *An Authentic History of the Missions Under the Care of the Missionary Society of the Methodist Episcopal Church* (New York 1832)

Baptist Missionary Magazine   Published in Boston originally as *The American Baptist Magazine* and later as *The American Baptist Magazine and Missionary Intelligencer*

BFMB   Baptist Foreign Mission Board Papers; later called the Baptist Mission Union. American Baptist Historical Society, Rochester, New York. These consist of "Letters Sent" and "Letters Received." Native American missions, though technically "Foreign," are classified separately from overseas missions.

BIA (see also OSW, below)   The prefix referring to Record Group 75 of the microfilm series published by the Bureau of Indian Affairs. RG75 consists of many different sets of papers. The following are used in this volume:

BIA, M-15, Letters Sent by the Secretary of War Relating to Indian
Affairs, 1800–1824
BIA, M-21, Letters Sent by the Office of Indian Affairs, 1824–1832
BIA, M-208, Records of the Cherokee Indian Agency, Tennessee,
1801–1835
BIA, M-234, Letters Received by the Office of Indian Affairs,
1824–1880
BIA, M-271, Letters Received by the Secretary of War Relating to
Indian Affairs, 1800–1823. Letters for M-15 and M-21 are in
letterbooks, and I have cited the page numbers; papers in M-208 are
listed only by date sent or received; all others have frame numbers in
each roll and I have given frame numbers, e.g., #1124.

Brainerd Journal   The official journal kept by the missionaries of the
ABCFM at Brainerd mission in the Cherokee Nation; entries are not
attributed to any single individual. Houghton Library, Harvard, under
this title.
Cherokee Laws   *The Laws of the Cherokee Nation* (Tahlequah, C.N.,
1852). I have used this edition because it is the most readily available to
scholars.
Cherokee Phoenix   Later *Cherokee Phoenix and Indian Advocate*, New
Echota, C. N., 1828–34
Christian Advocate   *The Methodist Christian Advocate and Journal and
Zion's Herald*, a quasi-official paper of the Methodist Episcopal Church
published in New York City
Clauder, Diary   The diary kept by Henry G. (Heinrich Gottlieb)
Clauder during the years 1828–31, when he was a Moravian missionary
at Springplace, Georgia. Moravian Archives, Bethlehem, Pennsylvania
Clauder, Journal   The journal kept by Henry G. Clauder for the year
1837, when he was at Red Clay, Tennessee, as a Moravian missionary.
Moravian Archives, Bethlehem, Pennsylvania
Fries   Adelaide L. Fries, ed., "Records of the Moravians in North
Carolina," published in various volumes of the *Publications of the North
Carolina Historical Commission*, Raleigh, North Carolina
McCoy Papers   The Papers of Isaac McCoy at the Kansas State
Historical Society, Kansas City, Kansas. Microfilm
MAB   Moravian Archives, Bethlehem, Pennsylvania
MAS   Moravian Archives, Salem (Winston-Salem), North Carolina
Missionary Herald   Originally called *The Panoplist;* adopted this title in
1821. The official monthly magazine of the ABCFM, published in
Boston
Missionary Intelligencer   *The United Brethren's Missionary Intelligencer
and Religious Miscellany*, published in Philadelphia starting in 1822. The
official journal of the Moravian mission agencies
Mooney, *Myths*   James Mooney, *Myths of the Cherokees*, Bureau of

American Ethnology, 19th Annual Report, part I (Washington, 1900). Also available in a reprint by the Aldine Press, 1975.

OSW   The prefix referring to Record Group 107, Records of the Office of the Secretary of War, published in various microfilm series, of which I have cited:

OSW, M-22, Register of Letters Received, Main Series, 1800–1870
OSW, M-221, Letters Received by the Secretary of War, Main Series, 1801–1870
OSW, M-222, Letters Received by the Secretary of War (Unregistered), 1789–1861

Payne Papers   The John Howard Payne Papers, Newberry Library, Chicago. Unless otherwise noted I have given volume and pagination for the typescript rather than for the originals, although the typescripts are not always accurate and have to be checked against the originals.

Schwarze, *Moravian Missions*   Edmund Schwarze, *History of the Moravian Missions among the Southern Indian Tribes of the United States* (Bethlehem, Pa.: Times Publishing Co., 1923)

Springplace Conference, 1802–14   "Minutes of the Mission Conference Held in Springplace [1802–14]," trans. and ed. Kenneth G. Hamilton, *The Atlanta Historical Bulletin* (Winter, 1970): 9–87

Springplace Conference, 1819   "Minutes of the Mission Conference Held in Springplace [1819]," trans. and ed. Kenneth G. Hamilton, *The Atlanta Historical Bulletin* (Spring, 1971): 31–59

Watchman   *The Christian Watchman*, quasi-official organ of the Baptists, published in Boston

Introduction

This story of the failure of the first Indian policy of the United States between 1789 and 1839 is not told through the eyes of white and Cherokee political leaders but through the eyes of the missionaries and those Cherokees who were in closest contact with them.[1] It is not an analysis of federal and state Indian policies in terms of treaties, trade and intercourse acts, debates in Congress or in Cherokee councils. The external aspects of Indian–white policy have been well described already.[2] By focusing upon the missionaries' efforts to alter the behavior and world view of the Cherokee people (and upon the resistance of the Cherokees to those efforts), I have had to put political and economic developments somewhat in the background. It would be difficult in one book to do justice to the total pattern of Cherokee acculturation in these years. I have concentrated upon ideological and social reorientations as seen by those Cherokees who came face to face with the missionaries. I am also concerned to show the effect of the Cherokees upon conscientious white missionaries. While white Americans in general could, and did, treat the Indians as little more than temporary impediments to the development and expansion of the new nation, the missionaries, living in intimate daily contact with the

1. While I am aware that many anthropologists and historians now prefer the collective word *Cherokee* as the plural form rather than *Cherokees*, there is by no means a consensus on this. I have used the latter throughout because it still seems to be preferred by most writers and because it was the form used by the Cherokees and whites in the years 1789 to 1839 (thereby making quotations consistent with the text).
2. The best studies of Indian policy in this period are Francis P. Prucha, *American Indian Policy in the Formative Years*; Bernard W. Sheehan, *Seeds of Extinction*; and George D. Harmon, *Sixty Years of Indian Affairs, 1789–1850*.

Indians, were forced to make critical reevaluations of their own culture. The impact upon the missionaries of Andrew Jackson's reversal of George Washington's original Indian policy has not been adequately told, although it is well documented in missionary archives. In addition, therefore, to examining how the Cherokees made their own selective adaptations to white culture, I will explore how white culture itself changed during its struggle with the Indians. Anthropologists have always recognized that the clash of cultures is a two-way street, but historians have not yet fully examined what happened to the religious idealists who were trying to interpret our original revolutionary principles to those whom they at first considered "savages."

Because the War Department left the internal affairs of the Cherokees up to their own councils, Cherokee acculturation inside the nation seemed within their own control. Externally, in formal dealings with the United States, the Cherokee leaders struggled to preserve their boundaries, regulate their land use, sustain their right to internal self-government, prevent removal of their people west of the Mississippi, obtain federal economic and technical assistance. Internally, in their relations with the federal agents and the missionaries (and among factions of their own people), the Cherokees tried to sustain as much as possible of their traditions, beliefs, and customs. The two aspects of the struggle, external and internal, were of course closely related, but this book is written from within the nation looking out rather than from outside looking in. Externally, the initiatives for change came from the whiteman's desire to acquire Cherokee land and to force the Cherokees to become fee-simple farmers. Internally, the pressure came from the necessity for drastic social and political restructuring and the divided tribal responses to this. The missionaries, by strongly supporting economic and social change, were soon caught up in tribal factionalism.

The drama of this double effort for economic reorganization and cultural survival was heightened by the extraordinary skill of the Cherokees. Over this half century they proved so adept at sustaining their political rights and their cultural integrity that they provided a model both to the leaders of other Indian nations and to the missionaries. By the 1820s they had become, in the missionaries' eyes, "the most civilized tribe in America." But what did that mean?

When George Washington inaugurated the nation's policy of Indian assimilation in 1789, he expected all of the Indians east of the Mississippi (roughly 125,000 in eighty-five different tribes) to be acculturated within fifty years. His goal was to teach them English, make them farmers, divide their land among them "in severalty" (that is, as individuals). Once they could support themselves individually as farmers, they were to be admitted into the republic as full and equal citizens. The Indian nations would then be denationalized and their land not actually under cultivation would be ceded to the federal or state governments. The missionaries were an integral part of the government's civilization and Christianization program (although the government provided no funds to assist the missionaries on a sustained basis until

1819).[3] Most white citizens in the frontier states doubted that Washington's policy was either desirable or feasible. "You can't tame a savage" remained the frontier outlook. The Cherokees were never asked if this policy and goal were agreeable to them. From the inception of Washington's "civilization program" many Cherokees and frontier whites strongly resisted it and sought other ways to deal with their respective cultural goals. The missionaries, by persisting longer than most in sustaining the policy, aroused increasing hostility both from frontier whites and traditionalist Cherokees. Because the policy was bound to impede the whites' desire for Indian removal, frontier politicians engaged in persistent efforts to thwart missionary programs and ultimately tried to expel the missionaries from the Indian nations. By so doing, these whites helped to drive the missionaries and Cherokees closer together while at the same time they stimulated a new sense of Cherokee nationalism. By 1828 "the Indian question" had become a three-way battle over whose sovereignty would prevail—that of Congress, that of the frontier states, or that of the Cherokee Nation (sustained by the treaty power and the Supreme Court).

This story could be told, as John Witthoft, Michael Rogin, Mary Young, and others have demonstrated, simply in terms of economic determinism. Native American "culture complexes" were, Witthoft says, "destroyed not by the interaction of traits and ideas but by economic and social determinism, by processes of economic competition and by social ranking."[4] I am not interested in reducing this complex issue to a single cause, and I do not think the Cherokee culture was destroyed. It persists today, but like white American culture in the years 1789 to 1839 it was drastically transformed. It is the process of transformation which concerns me. I have framed the controversy between Euro-Americans and Native Americans in terms of a question with which both were equally concerned: What does it mean to be an American? The competing economic and political interests of the two cultures were important, and it would be foolish to ignore them, just as it would also be foolish to ignore the importance of demographic and geographic expansionism. But I have focused primarily on cultural ideology and attitudinal changes both among white Americans and among Cherokees because they seem to me to be the least understood. By culture I mean, to quote Clifford Geertz, "a set of symbolic devices for controlling behavior" or "an historically transmitted pattern of meanings embodied in symbols"[5] which give order, direction, and meaning to life. Missionaries and Cherokee religious leaders were particularly concerned with these symbols.

3. Small federal grants were made to the Presbyterian missionaries from 1803 to 1810 and to the Moravian missionaries from 1809 to 1819, but only on an ad hoc basis out of the contingency funds of the federal agent. Until Congress passed the Civilization Act in 1819, missionary societies provided the bulk of the funds for voluntary benevolence. See Prucha, *American Indian Policy*, pp. 220–22.

4. John Witthoft, "Eastern Woodlands Community Typology and Acculturation," in *Symposium on Cherokee and Iroquois Culture*, ed. William N. Fenton and John Gulick, p. 73

5. Clifford Geertz, *The Interpretation of Cultures* (New York: Basic Books, 1973), pp. 52, 89.

"Missionaries," as Robert Berkhofer and others have noted, "represented a subculture within American life, for they emphasized theology and morality more than other people. They adhered more vigorously to the sexual code, were more honest (or were supposed to be), propounded the theological system more seriously, and were more concerned with the minor taboos of drink and verbal prohibitions against obscenity, profanity, and blasphemy."[6] They also adhered more strictly than most white Americans to the biblical view that "God hath made of one blood all nations" and that all men were by nature equal. They tended to exalt the federal constitution over states' rights because of the new nation's peculiar covenant with God. They sympathized neither with the "barbaric" behavior of frontier whites toward the Indians nor with the "benighted" ignorance of the Cherokees in resisting assimilation into what (in Ernest Tuveson's words) they considered "the Redeemer nation."[7] After 1828 most missionaries found it difficult to defend the policies of their government, although ostensibly they were working as its agents in Indian affairs. Jackson seemed to them to be a covenant-breaker, an unrighteous man. The very ground upon which they had undertaken their costly humanitarian effort—costly both in money and personal sacrifice—seemed to be cut out from under them by Jackson's coercive removal program. They were astounded and appalled by Jackson's claim in 1833 that the Cherokees were "established in the midst of a superior race and without appreciating the causes of their inferiority or seeking to control them, they must yield to the force of circumstances and ere long disappear."[8]

Starting as dedicated emissaries of the War Department, most of the missionaries ultimately moved either toward a strained political neutrality or toward outright opposition to its policies. Some of them ultimately taught the Cherokees the meaning of civil disobedience in the name of a law higher than those of Congress. While most confined their direct opposition to private letters and diaries, a few openly defied federal authority and encouraged political resistance among the Cherokees. Over the years, their attitude toward the Cherokees shifted from one of paternalistic pity for these wayward "children of the forest" to increasing respect for their capabilities, their persistence, and their courage. They found Cherokee children "as apt to learn as any white child," and their leaders as discerning, wise, and judicious as the best white statesmen. They discovered that Cherokee civil society was

6. Robert F. Berkhofer, Jr., *Salvation and the Savage*, p. 9. See also G. Gordon Brown, "Missionaries and Cultural Diffusion," *American Journal of Sociology* 50 (November 1944): 214. Significantly, Leonard Bloom has also identified "frontier culture" as a "sub-culture" which held almost opposite views from those of the missionaries. Leonard Bloom, "The Acculturation of the Eastern Cherokee: Historical Aspects," pp. 348–49.

7. See Ernest L. Tuveson, *Redeemer Nation: The Idea of America's Millennial Role* (Chicago: University of Chicago Press, 1958).

8. Andrew Jackson, "Message to Congress, December 3, 1833," *Congressional Serial Set, House Executive Documents*, 23d Congress, 1st session, vol. 254 (Washington, D.C.: Gales and Seaton), 1833, doc. #1, p. 14.

more stable, orderly, just, and concerned for the general welfare than most of the surrounding white settlements and frontier state governments. They deplored the racial prejudice of white Americans. Some missionaries married Cherokee women and defended the right of Cherokee men to marry white women. One missionary teacher, Delight Sargent, married a Cherokee leader, Elias Boudinot, after his first wife (also white) died. Missionaries educated their children in the same classrooms as Cherokee children and shared the hospitality of their homes with Cherokee families. In their letters they often noted how mistaken were the stereotypes they had brought with them, although they never totally overcame their ethnocentric conviction that whitemen (especially of Anglo-Saxon background) were at the forefront of human progress while redmen had far to go before they could catch up.[9] Although a few missionaries persistently characterized the fullblood traditionalists as inherently lazy, dirty, superstitious, and ignorant, they tended to blame this on their culture, not on their nature. Most were impressed at the speed with which Cherokees adopted white ways and concluded that potentially (especially for the young) there was nothing a white man could do that an Indian could not. Ultimately, when their mission boards instructed them to withdraw from any defense of Cherokee rights and to acquiesce silently in Jackson's removal policy, some missionaries became openly critical of the pious laymen and ministers who employed them.

The acculturation of the Cherokees had already advanced considerably by 1794 when the last of their warriors in Alabama and Tennessee made peace with the United States, and I have devoted little space to their precontact structure or to the changes in their beliefs and customs which preceded 1776. The works of James Mooney, Charles Hudson, Fred Gearing, Raymond Fogelson, and William Gilbert have treated this early phase of acculturation from the viewpoint of anthropology, while the works of Charles Royce, David Corkran, Henry Malone, John Haywood, Rennard Strickland, and John Reid have treated it from the historical viewpoint. Ever since Ralph Linton made the important distinction between "non-directive" (or voluntary) and "directive" (or compulsory) acculturation in 1936, anthropologists and historians have recognized that a crucial watershed in the history of any tribe is the point at which it loses control over its own affairs.[10] As Robert Berkhofer puts it in *Salvation and the Savage*, "Probably the most significant turning point in the acculturative history of any Indian tribe was the loss of political autonomy. . . . Before this point the Indian tribal members enjoyed a traditional way of life free of outside interference. . . . After . . . the members of the Indian society were under the effective control in some form of the agents of Anglo-American civilization."[11] This point, Berkhofer continues, "was usually marked by

9. See Michael C. Coleman, "Not Race but Grace." For the general ethnocentricity of American culture in these years, see Reginald Horsman, *Race and Manifest Destiny*.

10. See Edward H. Spicer, ed., *Perspectives in American Indian Culture Change*, p. 518.

11. Berkhofer, *Salvation and the Savage*, Introduction, n.p.

the commencement of reservation life." For the purposes of this study, I have chosen the date 1794 to mark the turning point in Cherokee acculturative history, even though the precise limits of their autonomy remained a major question until 1832. The Cherokees were by no means on a reservation after 1794, but they had lost most of their hunting grounds and were almost surrounded by whites. They retained the right of local self-government, but they were under constant pressure from federal agents, factors, and missionaries to alter their ways and beliefs. They recognized the need for reorganization of their economy and their political structure, and most of them availed themselves of useful acculturative opportunities offered to them.[12]

What makes 1794 a significant date in Cherokee history was the signing of a treaty which finally ended their last effort to make war upon white Americans, and thereby ended twenty years of terrible suffering, dislocation, and disorientation resulting from their decision in 1776 to remain loyal allies of the king of England. Most anthropologists agree with Raymond Fogelson that "the rhythm of Cherokee economic life was shattered after the American Revolution" and that "Cherokee strength was so sapped by constant bloodshed and the razing of their villages" from 1777 to 1794, that the old pattern of Cherokee culture was thoroughly disrupted.[13] Charles Hudson states in his fine study of the Southeastern Indians that after 1794, as a result of repeated invasions by white armies "burning towns, destroying crops, and killing men, women, and children," the Cherokees "were never the same."[14] After the Revolution, Fogelson writes, "the Cherokees embarked on a path of 'conscious acculturation.' " My concern is with that process of conscious acculturation and the remarkable renascence of the Cherokees under new forms of government and a new social order which was largely the result of their own determined effort. I write, however, as a historian, not as an anthropologist. I am aware of, and greatly indebted to, the work of social anthropologists and ethnographers, and I believe that no historian can ignore their work. But the historian is concerned with the specific, the contextual, the detailed progress of social change in an historical framework, while the anthropologist is concerned with abstracting general laws and principles common to all peoples, times, and places.[15] Social

12. Fred Gearing noted that after 1730 heavy dependence upon European firearms and trade goods forced the Cherokees to try drastic important changes in their governing structure, though none of them was very successful. Fred O. Gearing, *Priests and Warriors: Social Structures for Cherokee Politics in the 18th Century.*

13. Raymond D. Fogelson and Paul Kutsche, "Cherokee Economic Cooperatives: The Gadugi," in Fenton and Gulick, Symposium, p. 98. Fred Gearing states that after 1780 Cherokee society "slipped into virtual anarchy." Gearing, *Priests and Warriors,* p. 104.

14. Charles Hudson, *The Southeastern Indians,* p. 443.

15. Robert Berkhofer provides an astute analysis of the differences in methods and interests between historians and anthropologists in writing about native Americans. Robert F. Berkhofer, Jr., "The Political Context of a New Indian History," in *The American Indians,* ed. Norris Hundley, Jr. (Santa Barbara: Clio Press, 1974), pp. 101–26.

anthropologists could probably find examples of acculturation among the Cherokees from 1789 to 1839 which would fit most of the categories defined by Edward Spicer in his seminal essay, "Types of Contact and Process of Change" (that is, additive, incorporative, fusional, assimilative or replacive, isolative, bicultural), but this is not my subject. I am interested in the more specific ways in which Cherokees and missionaries looked at the need for, and means of, modifying social, institutional, familial, and individual behavior, beliefs, and customs. Why did the Cherokees make some changes and not others? Why did they make them when they did? Why did the missionaries urge more changes in some directions than in others? How did particular groups of Cherokees feel about these changes and to what extent were they accepted or rejected by these groups? Most of the changes I shall discuss fall within the types of acculturation which anthropologists describe as "protective" or "preservative innovation" and "selective adaptation." I agree with Anthony F. C. Wallace and Robert Berkhofer that "the history of a tribe can be seen as a series of renascences according to varied forms of activity which revitalize and reorient Indian life . . . by grafting what he [the Indian] wants of white culture to his own values and attitudes."[16] In one sense, this is a history of Cherokee revitalization from 1794 to 1832 in terms of what the missionaries offered and what the Cherokees took or rejected from white culture, and why.

I am also concerned with factionalism as a useful means of trying to explain the choices which the Cherokees made in acculturation. Berkhofer has noted that the study of Indian factions is one of the more fruitful ways historians have to explain the Indians' position. Factionalism, he writes, "can both facilitate and delay change."[17] Factionalism is a "creative response" to internal pressures. It articulates and promotes options. Factions also provide continuity, as Berkhofer explains, even though the issues upon which the factions divide may alter over time. In tracing the history of the Cherokees from 1789, I am concerned with regional and political factions (such as the divisions between the Upper and Lower Towns, the old and the young chief) and various ethnic, social, and ideological factions (the mixed bloods and fullbloods, the Christians and traditionalists, the pro- and antimission groups, the pro- and antiemigration groups, the rich and the poor, the educated and the uneducated, the pro- and antislavery groups). The most persistent of all factional disputes were those concerned with the speed and extent of acculturation needed to cope with internal and external pressures. Three times between 1789 and 1839 the Cherokee traditional religion reasserted itself so pervasively as to frighten the missionaries with its continuing power. Often the greatest pressure for rapid cultural change came from that group of Cherokees who were of mixed ancestry, better-educated, wealthier,

16. Berkhofer, "The Political Context of Indian History," p. 126. See also Anthony F. C. Wallace, *The Death and Rebirth of the Seneca* (New York: Random House, 1972).

17. Berkhofer, "The Political Context of Indian History," pp. 117–23.

and who expected personal gains in power and prestige from new laws and institutions. Because they were capable of mastering rapidly the skills of the white missionary teachers, they worked hard to earn their praise; in accepting the ways of their conquerors, they overcame the insecurities of defeat. But by grasping at this new source of dignity and self-worth, they had to reject their identity with the values and customs of their own people. Unfortunately these ambitious mixed bloods were not always conscious of this. They thought they were proving themselves to be good Cherokees by becoming good whitemen and white women. The reversal of Washington's policy of Indian integration forced terribly self-destructive choices upon many in this particular group. Yet these mixed bloods could never ignore the force of tradition exerted by the overwhelming majority. The mixed bloods, sometimes referred to as "the elite" (as opposed to "the peasantry") by recent historians and as "the forward-looking" by the missionaries, were strongly committed to sustaining Cherokee control over their own affairs and skeptical about assimilation. Although Cherokee political structure was moving away from consensus decision-making and toward majority rule as well as away from decentralized town government and toward a strong central government, the traditional emphasis upon harmony and consensus inhibited simple majority rule. The elite were powerful and persuasive, but they could not act without the support of the fullbloods. Cultural persistence and Cherokee initiatives for reformation provided the counterparts to alternatives presented by white agents and missionaries.

Cultural transformation took place in six major areas during these fifty years. These areas provide the general background of missionary—Cherokee interaction discussed in this book:

1. *Economic transformation* from fur trading to farming (including the rise of an elite who profited from owning slaves and developing commercial activities such as trading stores, taverns, ferries, gristmills, cotton gins, turnpikes, etc.);

2. *Familial roles and kinship transformations* (particularly the shift from a matrilineal, exogamous clan system to a patriarchal nuclear family system with a concomitant shift from communal cooperation to individualism);

3. *Social and ethical transformations* (the decline of the hospitality and harmony ethics, the accumulation of private family wealth through patrilineal inheritances, the development of class and educational distinctions);

4. *Political transformation* (particularly centralization of authority and the adoption of an elective, bicameral legislative system with courts and police able to coerce all individuals to conform to tribal laws);

5. *Religious transformation* (particularly the shift to religious pluralism and the adaptation of Christian views and practices while retaining certain traditional beliefs, customs, and ceremonies, especially in the medical and conjuring arts);

6. *The transformation from an oral to a written tradition* (especially after Sequoyah found a way of writing Cherokee, though it began earlier among those familiar with English).

In and through all of these transformations I am concerned with the changing sense of personal identity, the redefinition of what it meant to be a good Cherokee. Could one be a good Cherokee and speak English, dress as whitemen did, and attend Christian religious services? Was it enough to defend the nation's political independence and territory or did being a good Cherokee require also a Cherokee view of the world—of man's relationship to nature and the supernatural? Did a Cherokee have to reside in the ancestral homeland or could he withdraw to live west of the Mississippi? Did being a Cherokee have anything to do with the color of one's skin or racial ancestry? What was the status of a white who married a Cherokee and of their children?

When the missionaries first came among the Cherokees they frequently heard a story about the creation of man which answered these questions and which, for some Cherokees, increased in significance as contact with whites intensified: In the beginning the Great Spirit created three kinds of men out of three different colors of clay—the red, the black, and the white. He then placed each of them in different parts of the world, separated by vast bodies of water, and gave them different ways of life specifically suited for each. The red man was the favorite of the Great Spirit and he was angry with whites for invading the redmen's continent, taking their land, and interfering with their way of life. In response to this story, the missionaries told the Cherokees their creation myth: God had created only one pair of human beings in the beginning, and from them all men and women had descended and were thus brothers and sisters. These descendants had been dispersed around the earth (after God destroyed the Tower of Babel), their complexion had changed, their languages differed, their ways of life diverged, but nevertheless all men were still brothers under the skin. Since God governed the universe by natural laws, mankind would someday learn those laws and be reunited to live according to them as one people. Then there would be peace, harmony, and justice throughout the world. Republicanism, the natural law of political science, was one great discovery which would reunite mankind; agriculture, free enterprise capitalism, and commerce were other aspects of God's laws; the moral philosophy of the Scottish Common Sense school was another; the physical, chemical, psychological, and biological laws discovered by Newton, Harvey, Locke, Priestley, and Boyle were others. While English-speaking, Protestant Americans were at the forefront of these discoveries and were therefore the vanguard of human progress in the pursuit of happiness, other nations and peoples could join with them. Happiness in this world and the next depended upon man- and womankind's following the spiritual laws revealed by God in the Bible. For their own good, the Indians should model their lives upon those of white Americans.[18]

18. The basic myths of nineteenth-century Euro-American culture with regard to race are fully described in Horsman, *Race and Manifest Destiny*. Changing theories of racialism in America in the early nineteenth century are traced also in William Stanton, *The Leopard's Spots* (Chicago: University of Chicago Press, 1960).

The concepts of American manifest destiny and Americans as God's chosen people played a significant part in shaping Indian—white relations in these years, helping to confirm the frontier view that Indians were a different and unassimilable race and that Anglo-Saxon displacement of the Indians (ineradicably doomed to be roaming hunters) was the will of God (or "the nature of things" or "the force of circumstance.") If Cherokee nationalism or separatism was born in part out of a desire to sustain their cultural identity, it was also a response to the claim of Euro-Americans that this was "a whiteman's country."

While it has been argued that missionary activity proved a divisive and therefore destructive force in Indian affairs, it can also be shown that the shift from religious homogeneity to religious pluralism had certain advantages. Just as British Americans had found separation of church and state a source of unity, so too did the Cherokees after 1789. Increasing contact with whites inevitably produced strains and doubts about the power of their traditional religious system. The variety of missionary denominations (Moravian, Presbyterian, Congregationalist, Baptist, Methodist) offered different ways of transition to a new world view. Each missionary society had its own methods of explaining Christian theology and each had different forms and styles of Christian ritual and worship. Heterodoxy thus became a preservative innovation, enabling some Cherokees to select one alternative and some another. In addition, some chose a skeptical secularism and some a syncretic melding of old and new religious ideas and practices. The old rituals and the new world view were not mutually exclusive; as Raymond Fogelson noted in his field research on Cherokee medico-magical beliefs, "today's conjurors consider themselves to be good Christians and feel that their work is completely consistent with Christian doctrine."[19] Furthermore, missionaries differed not only on denominational grounds but also in regional attitudes and political outlooks. New England Baptists and Congregationalists, for example, deplored slavery and preached that those Cherokees who owned slaves should treat them as equals. Southern Methodists and Baptists taught that God had ordained blacks to slavery and offered "redmen" a means of distinguishing themselves (as "a people of color") from the African outcasts.

Missionaries helped Cherokees to adapt to new necessities. Their schools offered vocational skills for men and women, the ability to read and write English, the understanding of the whiteman's way of counting and measuring. Missionary science and philosophy provided a more sophisticated sense of history and nature, new treatments for sickness, a clearer perception of their place in a larger world, a new set of personal values (especially the Protestant ethic of hard work, internal self-discipline, and delayed gratification). All of these were immensely helpful both in practical terms and in enabling Cherokees to obtain a renewed sense of their self-worth and

19. Raymond D. Fogelson, "Change, Persistence, and Accommodation in Cherokee Medico-Magical Beliefs," in Fenton and Gulick, Symposium, p. 219.

potential. While the Cherokees produced no native prophets like Handsome Lake among the Senecas, among the Cherokees "there may have been a counterpart in the missionary," as Fred W. Voget says.[20] On the other hand, missionary ethnocentrism and smugness often humiliated the Cherokees by ridiculing their theory of nature, deriding their religious beliefs, criticizing their family system, and describing their priests and doctors as charlatans. Three general studies of missionaries to the Indians have been of great use to me: those of Robert Berkhofer, R. Pierce Beaver, and Henry Bowden. Like the studies of acculturation by anthropologists, they have provided me with general concepts of religious interaction with which to analyze the Cherokees.

A chronological outline of the major events affecting Cherokee acculturation and religious revitalization from 1776 to 1839 (as I see it) will provide a rough overview of the structure of this book:

I. *1776 — 1794:* War, tribal division, cultural disruption, and defeat
   A. Severe loss of population, land, towns (cultivated areas)
   B. Shift of population center 100 miles to the south and west
   C. End of fur trade economy with the loss of adequate hunting grounds
   D. Disruption of religious ceremonies and festivals

II. *1794 — 1812:* Cherokee rebirth as farmers, herders, traders
   A. Federal agents, factors, and first missionaries enter the nation
   B. Regional friction, near civil war, first removal crisis (1808 — 11)
   C. Reunion of Lower and Upper Towns and passage of new laws (1808 — 11)
   D. Revival of Cherokee religion (Ghost Dance movement, 1811 — 12)

III. *1812 — 1832:* Cherokee renaissance and nationalistic fervor
   A. Alliance with United States in Creek War (1812 — 14)
   B. Second removal crisis and increased political centralization (1817 — 24)
   C. Extensive missionary activity by four denominations (1819 — 30)
   D. Traditionalist reaction against rapid acculturation (White Path's Rebellion, 1824 — 27)
   E. Cherokee constitutionalism and the Christianized commercial elite (1824 — 32)

IV. *1832 — 1839:* The fight for national survival in the East
   A. Tribal division over the third removal crisis (the Ross vs. the Ridge factions)
   B. Missionary divisions over removal
   C. Nativist and Christian revivalism as responses to the crisis

While my narrative progresses in terms of this chronology, I have devoted some chapters to specific missionary activities and others to specific Cherokee activities rather than to let dates dictate the exposition. It is the inner life of the Cherokees that I am trying to portray. Those interested in

20. Fred W. Voget, "Comment on Robert K. Thomas's 'The Redbird Smith Movement,' " in Fenton and Gulick, *Symposium,* p. 171.

the political details of Cherokee history in these years or in specific aspects of Cherokee life (such as Cherokee politics, jurisprudence, or slaveholding) should turn to the works of Henry Malone, Thurman Wilkins, Rennard Strickland, Theda Perdue, Rudi Halliburton, Gary Moulton, Grace Woodward, Marion Starkey, Dale Van Every, and others listed in the bibliography. This is essentially a study of Cherokee religious history and the role the missionaries played in it. Much that the missionaries did, and tried to do, for the Cherokees deserves more credit than has been given. Much that the Cherokees did for their own revitalization has been unduly neglected. I have tried to redress the balance in both cases. Whether the missionaries were, in the long run, the friends or enemies of the Indians has to be left to the individual judgment of those who sift the conflicting evidence. I see no simple answer, but I have tried to provide arguments for both positions. In any case, the answer does not lie in a simple statistical table of Christian conversions, for what the Cherokees took from the missionaries they took on their own terms and adapted to their own needs and perspectives.

CHAPTER ONE

When the Missionaries Arrived, 1799

Many Cherokees think that they are not derived from the same stock as the whites, that they are the favorites of the great spirit and that he never intended they should live the laborious lives of the whites. These ideas, if allowed to have a practical effect, would undoubtedly opperate their extinction.

Colonel Return J. Meigs,
federal agent to the Cherokees, 1805

When the American Revolution was over and the guerrilla war between the Cherokees and the frontier settlers had finally ended, missionaries began to bring the religion of the conquerors to the conquered. With that religion came a new way of life.

Some Cherokees, finding that they were to provide land for permanent settlements for these friendly whitemen, suspected them of ulterior designs. Others saw them as teachers of new skills which would be useful to them and their children. None was aware of the profound impact these somber, black-suited men and earnest, bonneted women would have upon every aspect of Cherokee society.

The United Brethren (or Moravians) took the first steps toward establishing a permanent mission station within the Cherokee borders in 1799, five years after the Cherokees had made permanent peace with the United States. Twenty years of war had devastated their towns, killed or maimed hundreds of their warriors, brought death, famine, and poverty to their women and children, totally disrupted their pattern of existence.[1] In 1776 they had sided with their ally, the king of England, as most Indian peoples west of the Appalachians did. The king ceased fighting in 1783, but many of the Cherokees and their Indian allies continued the war against white invaders beyond the Appalachian Ridge for another decade. At various points in their long and bloody guerrilla war, the Cherokees had been forced to make treaties with the rebellious colonies. These treaties cost them over half

---

1. The Cherokees' long war against the United States from 1776 to 1794 is told in most histories of the Cherokees. See esp. John P. Brown, *Old Frontiers;* Mooney, *Myths;* John Haywood, *Natural and Aboriginal History of Tennessee* (Jackson, Tenn.: McCowat-Mercer Press, 1959).

of the 40,000 square miles of territory in which they had cultivated fifty to sixty towns and over the rest of which their hunters had freely roamed. Prior to 1776 their territory stretched from West Virginia and the Ohio River southward to the Coosa River in Georgia and from the upper reaches of the Savannah River in South Carolina westward to the Tennessee River. (Some of the area they ceded was also claimed by their neighbors, the Shawnees, the Chickasaws, and the Creeks, particularly their common hunting grounds in Kentucky and Tennessee. Border lines were indistinct between Indian peoples.)[2] By 1799 the Cherokees had lost most of their hunting ground in Kentucky and most of their oldest and most sacred town sites (including Tugaloo in western South Carolina and Echota in northeastern Tennessee). Their population had diminished from 16,000 to 10,000.[3] As a result of white depredations and forced land cessions, their displaced population had moved westward and southward until the tribe's demographic center was now one hundred miles southwest of where it had been in 1776. The refugees from the ceded areas of the East and North had started a dozen new towns in northwestern Georgia and southeastern Tennessee.[4]

The various treaties entered into with the individual states, with transient states (like the states of Franklin and Transylvania), and with the United States from 1777 to 1798, as the Cherokees understood them, had at least guaranteed the boundaries of what was left of their territory and also their right of internal self-government. The federal government had promised to evict whites who intruded on their land, and they had promised to let legal disputes between Cherokees and white citizens be settled in the whiteman's courts. For the land they had ceded and their pledges of loyalty to the United States, they received an annuity of several thousand dollars every year in trade goods. The government also agreed by the treaty of 1791 to provide them with hoes, ploughs, spinning wheels, and looms "from time to time" to facilitate their economic transformation from the fur trading system to self-subsistent farming. While permitted to elect their own town chiefs and national councils to govern their internal affairs, the Cherokees lost their power to declare war or to make treaties of trade and alliance with European nations. A federal agent appointed by the secretary of war lived among them after 1792 and (utilizing government-paid interpreters) guided their relations with the federal and state governments. A government trading post (or factory) and a factor (or storekeeper) came in 1798 to provide a yardstick for fair prices and quality with respect to traveling white traders from nearby white settlements.[5] Most Cherokees clung to the fur trade, which had since

2. For "Henderson's Purchase" in 1775 and other early land cessions and treaties, see Charles C. Royce, *The Cherokee Nation of Indians.*

3. For Cherokee population estimates, see Royce, *Cherokee Nation*, p. 14; William N. Fenton and John Gulick, eds., Symposium on Cherokee and Iroquois Culture, p. 89; Fred O. Gearing, *Priests and Warriors*, pp. 1–3.

4. For the Chickamauga towns, see Mooney, *Myths*, p. 44.

5. For good studies of the federal government's early Indian program, see Francis P. Prucha, *American Indian Policy in the Formative Years*, and George D. Harmon, *Sixty Years of Indian Affairs.*

1700 constituted their primary economic activity—trading skins and pelts for clothing, guns, powder, traps, and axes. However, after 1794, there were too few deer and beaver left in their diminishing hunting grounds and too much competition from white hunters to enable the Cherokees to sustain this way of life. Often whitemen in their hunting areas stole their winter catches or cheated them of their true worth after plying them with whiskey.[6]

The cultural disorientation caused by the war years was thus exacerbated by the difficulty of adjusting from the hunting to the farming economy. In addition, warfare had been a prime activity in Cherokee life, and now that too was over. In the past, to be a good hunter and a brave warrior had been the essential ways by which a Cherokee man established his sense of dignity and status.[7] In peacetime, status had derived from skill in the ballplay (a surrogate for war) or from oratorical and diplomatic skills in council affairs. A few attained prestige as priests or medicine men familiar with the spiritual relationships between man and nature. Women's status was sustained through the matrilineal clan system, which dictated that husbands settled in the wife's locality, where her brothers and uncles protected her and her children; if she and her husband did not get along, separation or divorce was simple, but their home, the household goods, and their children remained with the wife, and her husband had to leave.[8] Women also played some role in tribal affairs, but primarily their status came from their crucial economic contribution. They cultivated the corn, beans, melons, and pumpkins; they gathered wild fruits, nuts, and berries to supplement the hunter's venison, bearmeat, and turkeys; they tanned the hides and made them into hunting jackets, leggings, mocassins, skirts. In council and clan affairs the women had a voice although ultimate political power rested with the men.

But what did it mean, after 1794, to be a Cherokee when war activities were gone, the fur trade was failing, the women could not grow enough food to sustain them, and the old counselors and medicine men did not know which way to turn? Some Cherokees decided to move westward, across the Mississippi, where game was still plentiful and war was still possible. Several hundred Cherokees did migrate to the banks of the St. Francis River in Arkansas between 1782 and 1800, but most were too deeply attached to their families and ancestral land to consider this.[9] Having lived in the region of the Great Smokies from time out of mind, the Cherokees had adjusted to the climate and to the plant and animal life there. Every river, waterfall, spring, cave, and natural wonder had sacred meaning; their battlefields and graves had historical significance. Who could tell whether in the West there would

6. For the difficulties the government had trying to regulate the Indian fur trade after 1794, see Prucha, *American Indian Policy*, pp. 66–101.

7. The best study of the social organization of the Cherokees and other Southeastern Indians is Charles Hudson, *The Southeastern Indians*.

8. Some Cherokee women also became conjurors. For the Cherokee kinship system of seven exogamous clans (following the Crow-type matrilineal organization), see Gearing, *Priests and Warriors*, pp. 15–18, and Hudson, *Southeastern Indians*, pp. 184–96.

9. For early migrations of the Cherokees to the west, see Mooney, *Myths*, p. 91.

be the same kinds of herbs, mosses, and plants needed to remedy their wounds and cure their sicknesses? Who knew whether in the West (traditionally the land of darkness) their priests could call so effectively upon the benevolent spirits of the Upper World (with whom they lived on such intimate terms) in order to thwart malevolent spirits, ghosts, and witches? Besides, other Indian peoples already had claims to those western lands, and Cherokees were ill-prepared for further wars at that moment. The great majority preferred to stay where they were if only the whites, who now almost surrounded them, would treat them with fairness and let them go their own way.

Except for the mountainous areas and the sandy or clay hills, most of the Cherokees' land was fertile, especially along the river banks where they preferred to live. The climate was moderate, the growing season long.[10] Plentiful forage and pasturage existed for cattle, sheep, horses, and hogs; and herding livestock proved to be the first step toward a new way of life. Some were ready to try the whiteman's intensive form of farming and to take advantage of the technical assistance the government offered them through its agent. In the expanding white settlements around them they might sell or trade livestock, poultry, and corn and melons to obtain the manufactured goods to which they had become accustomed. In 1792, one of their chiefs, Bloody Fellow (renamed Clear Sky by George Washington for his new peaceful intentions), reminded the president about the promises he had made a year earlier: "The treaty mentions ploughs, horses, cattle and other things for a farm; this is what we want; game is going fast away from us. We must plant corn and raise cattle. . . . In former times we bought of the traders' goods cheap; we could then clothe our women and children; but now game is scarce and goods dear. We cannot live comfortably."[11] However, federal assistance was not only meager but unreliable. It came "from time to time," and what there was went to those chiefs nearest to the federal agent geographically and politically.[12] Moreover, few Cherokee women knew how to use spinning wheels and looms, and few men knew how to manage a farm and plough a field. The agent had to provide teachers whenever he distributed "wheels and looms." To become farmers and farmer's wives required far more basic changes than simply learning how to weave or plough. To the whiteman, the transition from hunting to farming to commerce seemed simple and natural. It was the ordinary course of human history and progress. To the Cherokees this concept of progress required an almost total reorientation of his spiritual, social, and psychological understanding of the

10. For Cherokee land use and agriculture, see Douglas C. Wilms, "Cherokee Indian Land Use in Georgia, 1800–1838" (Ph.D. diss., University of Georgia, 1973), and Douglas Wilms, "Cherokee Settlement Patterns in Nineteenth Century Georgia."

11. ASP I, 205.

12. For the uneven distribution of federal agricultural assistance in these years, see Mooney, *Myths*, pp. 72–73, and Henry T. Malone, *Cherokees of the Old South*, pp. 49–53.

world. For example, by Cherokee tradition, women were the cultivators of the soil. The Creator had endowed them particularly with the power to grow things. Men did not have this power, and for men to assume women's role in the division of labor established by Nature and the Great Spirit was to turn the world upside down.[13]

One of the oldest sacred legends of the Cherokee religious system explained how the Creator had made the first man, Kanati, to be a hunter, and the first woman, Selu, to provide food. The word *Selu* meant corn. And "in ancient time," when social order began, "No matter when Kanati went into the woods, he never failed to bring back a load of game," and "Every day when Selu got ready to cook the dinner, she would go out to the storehouse with a basket and bring it back full of corn and beans."[14] When her two sons discovered that she produced corn in the storehouse by leaning over a basket and rubbing her stomach and made beans by rubbing her armpits, so that this food simply flowed from her body into the basket, they thought she was a witch and decided to kill her. But because she was their mother (the Earth Mother) she taught them, before she died, how to grow corn. Corn sprang from the blood of Selu after her wicked sons had killed her, and for their laziness in not following her planting instructions, corn grew only after very hard work and long cultivation. Thereafter, while Cherokee men cleared fields for cultivation and helped with planting and harvest, the task of growing or cultivating corn and vegetables rested upon Cherokee women. The sons inherited Kanati's powers of hunting. In this same sacred legend, Kanati (whose name meant Lucky Hunter) taught his sons how to hunt after they wickedly spied out his secret hiding place for game and carelessly let all the animals loose into the forest. Thus a sexual division of labor based on what Cherokees considered the sacred order of things inhibited the adoption of the whiteman's agricultural system. A Cherokee man lost status by assuming the woman's role as cultivator of the earth. As Charles Hudson has noted,

> Southeastern Indians conceived of men and women as two radically different forms of humanity, and they consequently assigned to them contrasting roles in subsistence activities. . . . The activities of men and women varied according to the two divisions of the year—the cold season and the warm season. The men made their primary contribution to subsistence in the cold season, when they hunted, while the women made theirs in the warm season, when they cultivated the crops. . . . Indeed, the roles of men and women were so different that the two sexes were almost like different species. Consistent with this basic assump-

13. See Raymond D. Fogelson and Paul Kutsche, "Cherokee Economic Cooperatives," in Fenton and Gulick, Symposium, p. 116. For the survey of Cherokee religion which follows I am indebted to works by the following authors which are listed in the bibliography: Charles Hudson, James Mooney, Raymond Fogelson, Rennard Strickland, Jack and Anna Kilpatrick, John Philip Reid.

14. This myth is quoted in full in Hudson, *Southeastern Indians*, pp. 149–55.

tion, men and women kept themselves apart from each other. During the day women worked with each other around their households, while the men resorted to their town house or square ground. Separation was the most important in activities which in their view epitomized sexual identity.[15]

Conversely, of course, white Americans considered it a mark of Cherokee barbarity that the women were made to till in the fields, "doing a man's work," while Cherokee men engaged in talk, games, or ceremonies all summer long.

For women as well as men, the new system of agricultural subsistence pressed upon them by white authorities created profound difficulties. The Cherokee method of farming was totally different. Women had worked together cultivating a common village plot near the center of each village; using wooden hoes, they barely scratched the surface of the earth. To adopt the white woman's way of life, the Cherokee wife would have to give up working together with other women in the common field or nearby households of their clan; they would have to move away from the village and onto a larger plot of ground after clearing a space in the forest; they would be alone in their log cabin while their husband worked constantly alone in his field. They would have to learn how to milk cows, churn butter, make cheese, spin and weave. In time of trouble there would be no one near to help. Loneliness would make the drudgery harder. The sense of community and of extended family would diminish. With each family struggling to survive on its own, the old ideal of sharing and the hospitality ethic would disappear.

The missionaries came to offer the Cherokees a new set of beliefs and values to fit this new way of life, one based upon enlightened self-interest, internalized self-discipline, and competitive individualism. They preached a wholly different view of human nature and of the fundamental order of things. The Cherokees could scarcely make sense of it, and what they did understand they rejected.[16] The key values in the Cherokee religious ethic were harmony, balance, order, and sharing.[17] The essence of good conduct lay in the careful moral ordering of human life in relation to the natural and spiritual worlds of which man was an integral part. Their sacred myths explained the fundamental relationships and categories of the cosmos—the relations between man and the earth, between man and the animals, between the sun and the moon, between sickness and health. Social order prevailed when man was in proper harmony with his fellowmen and with all other aspects of nature; in village affairs this meant the avoidance of any open confrontation, anger, quarreling, or hostility and the utmost effort to achieve consensus in decision-making. It also required absolute honesty, loyalty,

15. Ibid. p. 260.
16. For the federal agent's view of the difficulties of acculturation, see Return J. Meigs to Benjamin Hawkins, February 13, 1805, BIA, M-208.
17. See Hudson, *Southeastern Indians*, chap. 3, "The Belief System," pp. 120–83.

trust, and keeping one's word. The ability to sustain these fundamental relationships defined the values which gave honor, respect, and dignity to a good Cherokee.

One of their important sacred myths concerned the origin of bears, a very human kind of animal who often stood on his hind feet, who defended his young, who used his paws like hands. The bears were once a group of dissident Cherokees who went off into the woods, separating themselves from the tribe. After a while they grew hair all over their bodies, began to walk on all fours, forgot how to speak Cherokee, and failed to avenge the death of their clansmen murdered by hunters. The point of the story was to stress not only the necessities of clan responsibilities but the necessity of close communal interaction to sustain humanity. It also taught that bears, like other animals, had sacred spiritual attributes which must be respected, for the bears had, in the end, offered the sacrifice of their own lives as food for man when needed.[18]

Another basic sacred myth told of the decision of the animals, because of excessive hunting by man which threatened to exterminate them, to fight back by inflicting various diseases upon the hunters who so heedlessly slaughtered them. Each animal chose its own particular form of disease to inflict upon man. Then the reptiles and insects did the same. However, the plants took pity on man, and for every disease caused by vengeful animals, reptiles, or insects, the plants agreed to provide a special antidote or remedy.[19] From this sacred parable the Cherokee child learned that he must not kill indiscriminately but must kill only what he needed and say a prayer of thanks and respect to the spirit of the deer or bear he shot. He learned also that nature had provided medicinal herbs which, with proper study (by the specialists who became their doctors), could be applied to restore health whenever some omission of respect to animal spirits brought sickness (which was a disruption of the natural order). Also he learned to respect those doctor-priests whose secret skills enabled him to preserve the critical balance between man and the spirits that animate nature.

A wide variety of other sacred myths explained the harmonious relationships among the distinct spheres and categories of the cosmos. Their universe was divided into three parts—an Upper World, a Lower World, and the world on which human beings, animals, and plants lived. The Upper World existed above the stone hemisphere which constituted the sky or dome over the earth (and under which the Sun and Moon moved, disappearing behind the western edge of the dome and reappearing on the opposite side of the dome). The superior beings or spirits who lived in the Upper World

18. This myth is discussed in Hudson, *Southeastern Indians*, pp. 61–62.

19. This myth is discussed in Hudson, *Southeastern Indians*, pp. 157–59. It was generally believed that Indian medical and religious rites worked only for Indians and not for whites. In prophetic visions, however, the Great Spirit sometimes told the Indians that he would use his power to drive back or destroy the whites, who had disturbed the cosmic order of things.

resembled in superior form and power those who existed on earth—the spirit of the bear, the deer, the eagle, etc.; they were the upholders of order and harmony. From the sky dome, at the four cardinal points of the compass, long, invisible ropes held up the earth. The earth was flat and circular. It rests upon a great ocean into which it might sink if the four ropes ever broke. Beneath the earth was the watery Lower World where the malicious forces of disorder dwelt. The earth was thus precariously suspended between order and disorder. Life was a constant struggle to sustain order. The demons and monsters who dwelt in the Lower World were able to intrude upon the earth through various holes in it—deep springs and dark caves. The superior spiritual beings in the Upper World were available to assist man. So long as men sustained the proper relationships among the three worlds and among all categories of life, and so long as he performed all the necessary prayers, ceremonies, and responsibilities respecting the spirits and his fellowman, harmony would prevail. But men and women were not perfect, and trouble came because through carelessness they failed to perform their proper spiritual and social duties. Sometimes trouble came to one individual alone, but most often it came to a whole group—a family, a clan, a village, or in the case of epidemics, droughts, pestilence, storms, and earthquakes to the whole tribe. Wars themselves were abnormal and resulted from some failure to act properly or from someone's getting out of his or her properly assigned sphere. All life was thus closely interwoven with all other life, natural and spiritual. The utmost circumspection, caution, and vigilance were necessary to avoid or correct mistakes.

The priests, doctors, or conjurors (a word transcribed as adonisgi, didahnesigi, or didahnewisgi) played a crucial role in helping people to comprehend the sources of disorder and to provide the remedies to restore harmony.[20] In early adolescence, talented Cherokees were apprenticed to those priests and doctors in whose footsteps they would follow. The priests presided over the seasonal ceremonies which kept the village and tribe in harmony with nature (the feasts of first planting and harvest thanksgiving to express respect to the Earth Mother), in harmony with superior spirits (the feast of the new fire), and in harmony with each other (the feast of purification and forgiveness for trespasses). They also presided at dances (hunting dances, war dances, scalp dances) to make sure that honor and respect were paid to the spiritual forces which controlled such activities. Priests were major members of war parties; they interpreted the dreams of the war leader and foretold whether they augured victory or defeat (dreams

20. Because of the different ways in which the Cherokee term for conjuror or sorcerer is transcribed, I have used simply the word *conjuror* throughout. Fogelson transcribes it "didahnesigi" in "An Analysis of Cherokee Sorcery and Witchcraft," in *Four Centuries of Southern Indians*, ed. Charles M. Hudson, p. 123; Charles Hudson transcribes it "didahnewisgi" in *Southeastern Indians*, p. 337; Jack and Anna Kilpatrick transcribe it "adonisgi," in *New Echota Letters*, p. 33, n. 38. I have found that most missionaries at the time transcribed it as "adoniski" or "adoneeskee."

were a prime means of communication from the spirit world). They presided over ballplays (an early form of lacrosse) on which whole towns wagered. They were called upon in times of catastrophe to bring rain to withering cornfields, to stave off hailstorms, to stop epidemics, to explain what pollutions had invoked disorder and then to invoke the proper superior spirits able to reassert the harmony of nature in each case. They also performed a variety of private services—curing sickness, warding off death, finding lost objects, keeping wives or husbands faithful, bringing happiness to the lovesick. Their most serious problem was to identify witches, for w tches were wild spirits bent on bringing death and disorder. A witch in human form was a selfish, self-centered person who had no respect for clan or communal harmony. As enemies to everyone, they must be summarily put to death before they brought anarchy. Cherokee religious ceremonies and rituals were both private and public, daily and seasonal. Each Cherokee learned from childhood his or her own various roles and responsibilities to sustain harmony. Charles Hudson has summarized this spirtual climate: "the Southeastern Indians believed that if a person mixed things from opposite categories [fire and water, male and female, clean and unclean] the result was sure to be some form of chaos. Therefore many rules ("tabus") in Cherokee society had to do with avoiding the mixing of categories, or pollution, while many of their ceremonies were intended to dispel pollution once it had occurred."[21] Annual festivals, on the other hand, were to assure that what was going well would continue to go well. War dances put warriors in the proper spiritual frame of mind to overcome enemies and retaliate for harm to their tribe.

Few missionaries who came to the Cherokees bothered to learn much about the Cherokee belief system. What little they heard struck them as childish superstition, the primitive concepts of the infancy of the human race. At best, Cherokee religion seemed foolish to missionaries; at worst it was sacrilegious or profane—contrary to Christian Truth. They were oblivious to most of the daily religious activity around them, but did notice the general festivals, ballplays, all-night dances. The missionaries were pleased to find no large religious temples for regular worship and no graven images. While aware of the conjurors, the missionaries noted that they were not organized into any general ecclesiastical order under a high priest. The Cherokees, so far as most missionaries were concerned, had no real religion or priesthood worthy of notice. "It is impossible," an early missionary wrote, "to obtain any tolerable understanding of the Cherokee religion. I suspect . . . there was nothing among them which would be called a system of religious beliefs" even in former times, or, if there were, it had long since disappeared.[22] This was, from the missionaries' viewpoint, a great blessing,

21. Hudson, *Southeastern Indians*, p. 148.
22. Report from Brainerd mission, April 1828, ABCFM. Some missionaries, as will be noted later, believed the Indians to be descended from the lost tribes of Israel and claimed to have

for it meant that "They have not . . . a system of false religion handed down
. . . which must be overturned," as in the elaborate religious systems that
other foreign missionaries found in China, Burma, and India.[23]

On the other hand, comparatively few Cherokees found the Christian
religion particularly relevant or helpful when they first heard it. It lacked the
sense of balance and harmony between man and nature which was so central
to their sort. Christianity had a dualistic view of nature and the supernatural;
an unbridgeable gap separated this world and the next, man from the
Creator, human beings from animals. Christians did not seem to see how
integrally related man, animals, and plants were and were ignorant of the
constant, reciprocal interactions among the spirits of the Upper World, the
Lower World, and this world. Whitemen said they had crucified their God.
Christians waged ruthless wars of conquest against each other and then
divided up the land among individuals. They said that the Creator told them
to "have dominion" over nature, to plough deeply into Mother Earth, to dig
up the minerals beneath the earth, to chop down the forests, dam up the
rivers, dig canals, recklessly kill or drive off all of the animals, and plant
acres and acres of land with the same crop only to sell it to others. "The
Cherokees recognized," as Charles Hudson says, "that man had to exploit
nature in order to live," but they also knew "that man should do so carefully,
and that nature was not infinitely forgiving. If mistreated, nature could
strike back."[24]

However, the Cherokees could understand the Christian concepts of a
universal law in nature, of a Creator who instituted order in the cosmos, of
rewards and punishments for good or bad behavior in a different world after
death. An old woman, asked by a missionary whether she believed in God,
said "she thought there was somewhere above a good man and woman who
would make good people happy."[25] Cherokee religion recognized something
like the concept of a soul, the spirit of every person, which continued to
sustain the personality and bodily form after death. Those who had led a
good life and whose relatives had performed all the rituals required at their
deaths would enjoy a life of contentment with other good souls in the next
world. As one chief said, "I have lived long enough; now let my spirit go; I
want to see the warriors of my youth in the country of spirits."[26] Another

found evidence for this in certain Cherokee myths, rituals, and historical accounts. The
Cherokees themselves, as will also be noted, came to doubt whether it was to their advantage to
be described as descendants of the Israelites, given the prejudice against Jews that they
discovered among many whites.

23. Brainerd Journal, April 9, 1818, ABCFM. Mooney, Adair, and other historians
note that prior to the smallpox epidemic of 1738–39 there seems to have been an organized order
of priests and doctors among the Cherokees. However, their inability to cope with this new
disease caused the tribe to reject them. See Payne Papers, I, 34; III, 34; VII, 8; Mooney,
Myths, p. 26.

24. Hudson, *Southeastern Indians*, p. 159.
25. Brainerd Journal, July 26, 1818, ABCFM.
26. Fenton and Gulick, Symposium, p. 92.

Cherokee told a missionary that he believed that "in the other world they shall live in the same manner in which they live here—that they shall find there the same pleasures which they enjoy on earth; that they shall attend ballplays and all-night dances and find various amusements in which they take delight."[27]

Like all religious systems, the Cherokee world view included a sense of justice. This was not simply a world of haphazard chance. "Many of the things which went wrong," Hudson notes, "they explained as having come about because people in their communities broke rules of ritual separation [of the basic orders] and propriety; when such rules were broken, men suffered. This was the working of supernatural justice, in which good men were rewarded and evil men punished by gods and spirits."[28] This sense of justice required the punishment of lawbreakers. Clans had to punish murderers, adulterers, and those who married within a clan and thus were guilty of incest.[29] Theft had to be scorned, and "when a man was caught in an immoral act his fellows would reproach and ridicule him so unmercifully he might contemplate or resort to suicide."[30] Missionaries, while recognizing that the Cherokees had high standards of justice, honesty, and fair-dealing, were disconcerted to discover that there were no courts of law, no written laws, no police system, no jails or whipping posts, hence no overt form of public coercion to duty that they could see. Whites drastically underestimated the power of communal ostracism and ridicule in sustaining law and order because in their social system individualism and confrontation were the norms while in the Cherokee social organization, cooperation and conformity were the norms. A Cherokee was taught never to pit his will or interests against those of the group or to try to impose his wishes upon others. The white taught that men often advanced in power by confrontations, inflexibility, self-assertion. Cherokees reached agreement through consensus gradually arrived at through long and dignified discussion; whites favored majority rule (often with boisterous haranguing) but with certain private rights which even the majority could not gainsay. A good Cherokee always quietly withdrew from an argument and peacefully opted out when he could not accept the consensus. A whiteman argued, shouted, and did his best to force his own way upon the group. No council decision ever coercively bound any Cherokee to obey it, and whole towns might decline to abide by a tribal council's decision. The constant tensions between good and evil which pervaded Cherokee life resulted, in Hudson's terms, in "a morally intense community,"[31] whereas to the casual white observer, the Cherokees' dislike of confrontation and their absence of tribal coercion presented an appearance of anarchy, indifference, and unconcern.

27. Robert S. Walker, *Torchlights to the Cherokees*, p. 127.
28. Hudson, *Southeastern Indians*, p. 173.
29. For a good discussion of clan revenge, see John P. Reid, *A Law of Blood*.
30. Hudson, *Southeastern Indians*, p. 173.
31. Ibid., p. 174.

It is hardly surprising then that Cherokees listened skeptically (though politely) to the white agents of the government and to the missionaries who offered them a different way of life and belief system. Most of them agreed with the woman who told a missionary that "It was her belief that the Cherokees were an entirely different race of people from whites and that a religion for the whites was not intended for the Cherokees,"[32] Different peoples had different ways. They could learn to tolerate each other, to live together in peace, but they would always be different. The white and red and black peoples were brothers and sisters in some respects: "We are," said the Cherokee chief Tickagiska to George Washington, "made by the same hand and in the same shape as yourselves."[33] Nevertheless, it was too much to expect that they would all act and think alike.

The missionaries were, however, aided in their efforts to "civilize" the Cherokees by the fact that twenty years of havoc and trouble had greatly weakened the Cherokees' sense that they understood how to cope with a world dominated by the whiteman. Discouraged by their defeats and devastation, they ceased to practice many parts of their old traditions. Of the six annual tribal festivals, only two were sustained with any regularity after 1794—the Green Corn Dance and the Purification ceremony. The hunting and war dances became irrelevant. A few Cherokees were ready to abandon all their rituals because they had failed to sustain the tribe in its time of need. Even the basic kinship patterns and responsibilities were giving way. A sense of confusion descended upon them; agnosticism and skepticism became common.

Despite their aversion to becoming "husbandmen" or "cultivators," as the government wished, the Cherokees did take some important steps in acculturation in the decade after 1794. Federal agents reported that many of the women were raising cotton (a crop seldom raised before) and were willing to take lessons to learn how to spin and weave. They noted that the Cherokee men were supplementing their diminishing income from the fur trade by raising black cattle, hogs, and sheep for sale. When the council allowed the first federal road to be built through the nation from Georgia to Tennessee in 1804, it also asked the government to provide (as part of the price for the right of way) blacksmiths and wheelwrights, gristmills, sawmills, and cotton gins. A most critical aspect of social change was a tribal decision in 1798 to form a small, mounted police organization (called the Lighthorse) to be paid for by the War Department and charged with catching and whipping horsethieves. As early as 1802 the federal agent reported that the more important chiefs of the tribe realized that clan revenge or "personal retaliation" for murder was disadvantageous to the tribe since it simply provoked similar retaliation (especially where whites were involved), but it was not until 1808 that the council was able to persuade the elders of the

32. Walker, *Torchlights*, p. 178.
33. ASP I, 57.

seven clans to abolish this fundamental clan responsibility and turn it over to
the Lighthorse. (However, the law was ignored by many Cherokees.) By
1804 some Cherokee men were asking the agents to draw up written wills so
that they could leave their property to their children and not have it go "in
side way manner" to the older brothers or to uncles on the mother's side as
clan tradition dictated. However, as the federal agents reported, it was usually "the half-breeds" who took the lead in these matters. The fullbloods, or
"real Indians," agents said, were much slower to change their ways, partly
because most of them lived in mountainous districts remote from the main
lines of commerce.[34]

Social changes took place most rapidly where there was regular contact
with whites. From 1776 onward, there was a constant influx of whites into
the nation. The first to enter were revolutionary Loyalists fleeing (temporar-
ily they thought), the wrath of American patriots. Some of these brought
black slaves with them. Others married Cherokees and settled down to farm
on good land in the nation. During the course of the war, a number of army
deserters from both the British and patriot ranks took refuge in the nation,
and many of these took Cherokee wives. Once a white had a Cherokee wife
he was entitled to settle on and farm any piece of ground not already
occupied. After the peace white traders came to open stores, and white
craftsmen, usually too incompetent to find employment in white communities, opened blacksmith, tinsmith, and cooper's shops. Some Spanish
and French deserters came into the nation, and numerous white renegades
escaping the clutches of the law in nearby white communities found sanctuary in the federally protected Indian territory. The shortage of white
females on the frontier increased intermarriage with Cherokees—though
such couples lived primarily in the Cherokee nation. The children of such
marriages were usually raised by their white fathers according to white
standards and spoke more English than Cherokee. Because white frontier
communities had little use for "half-breeds," the children of these mixed
marriages identified themselves as Cherokees. By 1825 missionaries estimated that as many as one-quarter of the Cherokee population had some
white ancestry. Although the tribe officially recognized white husbands as
having the civil rights of any Cherokee, and while technically, in a matrilineal system, the children were members of the mother's clan, the whites
and their mixed blood offspring adopted the patriarchal system of white
society. They seldom acknowledged any clan responsibilities or connections.
White fathers, for example, did not allow their wives' brothers to discipline
their children, and if they separated from their wives, they did not acknowl-

34. These early steps in acculturation are noted in the letters from the federal agent to the
War Department. See BIA, M-208, letters from Return J. Meigs dated July 13, 1801,
December 10, 1801, April 12, 1802, September 21, 1802, December 3, 1802, December 28,
1802, January 1, 1803, March 27, 1804, July 25, 1804, August 28, 1804, February 13,
1805, August 4, 1805.

edge the wife's right to the house, household property, or children. A woman who married a whiteman was thus often cut off from her familial relationships and her clan rights despite efforts of the tribal council to sustain a Cherokee woman's right to her own property.

Because they grew up under the father's training, the mixed bloods dressed, ate, talked, and thought more like whites than like Cherokees, even though politically they identified themselves as Cherokees and often rose to high ranks in town and tribal affairs. Caught between the two cultures, they provided valuable assistance to the Cherokees in relationships with white officials and traders. Many of them became traders and many were owners of black slaves. They were more apt than fullbloods to welcome the missionaries, for they saw the benefit of free schools in which their children could be educated; some of the wealthier intermarried whites and mixed bloods hired itinerant schoolteachers to tutor their children before missionaries were available in their region of the nation. It was much easier for those of mixed ancestry to see the advantages of the whiteman's ways and even of his religion, though some were so resentful of the racist attitudes of frontier whites that they were more hostile to whites than many Cherokee fullbloods. In any case, it was clear to the mixed bloods that as the Cherokee people went, so must they. It behooved them to assist in making the critical tribal decisions in those years, and the federal agents often went out of their way to befriend them.[35]

As a nation the Cherokees had only one small advantage left in their political relationship with their conquerors. The United States was too weak to assert complete control over its long western border on the Mississippi River in 1794. Beyond the scattered white settlements in eastern Ohio, Kentucky, Tennessee, and western Georgia, lay a vast valley filled with Indian tribes more or less subdued for the moment but ready for assistance in defending their land from further attrition, whether offered by the British in the North or by the French and Spanish in the South. Although the Battle of Fallen Timbers in 1794 served to open up Ohio to white settlement (just as the end of the Cherokee-Creek-Shawnee guerrilla war opened Tennessee and Kentucky that same year), the British, French, and Spanish were not yet ready to relinquish all hope of gaining control of the Mississippi Valley. Fearful of this, President Washington and his successors felt compelled to treat the western Indians gingerly. All the states turned over their western lands to the federal government, and the state governments also agreed to leave political relations with the Indians to the federal government; only federal funding could finance the treaties, pay for land cessions, and support

35. Federal agents spent so much time among mixed bloods who lived near the federal agency and factory that they greatly underestimated the proportion of fullbloods. For example, Return J. Meigs told the secretary of war in 1805 that "the numbers of the real Indians and those of Mixed blood are nearly equal," when probably at that time the mixed bloods were less than 10 percent of the tribe. July 27, 1805, BIA, M-208.

trading posts and army garrisons, federal agencies, and annuities which would convince the border tribes that they were better off allied to the United States than to any European nation. White frontier communities bridled under the restrictions this put upon their efforts to acquire Indian land, but until 1815 they had no choice; they had to let the federal government call the tune in Indian affairs because it provided the military protection and footed the bills.

By promising the ultimate incorporation of Indians as full citizens, Washington's policy maintained that they were the equals of whites even though frontier whites saw them only as conquered savages encumbering good land. Federal agents, while persistently asking the tribes to cede more land for white settlement, admitted that the Indians had the right to refuse such cessions and therefore tried to make payments for them attractive. Most Cherokees soon realized that tribal ownership of their land was the key to their cultural survival as a people. Once they agreed to parcel it out to individual Cherokee families in fee simple, it would easily be bought or stolen by white speculators. So long as the threat of European war in the Mississippi Valley remained, the Indians were able to assert some resistance to the demands for cessions of their "vacant" or "waste" hunting grounds (as the whites described unsettled Indian land). However, "the anaconda of civilization," to use Charles Royce's famous metaphor, was gradually squeezing the life out of tribe after tribe.

Next to the mixed bloods, the Cherokee women were the most likely to be attracted to—or forced to—try new ways. They had always been farmers; they had always provided the basic sustenance and made the clothing; they tended the children. Furthermore, the women could no longer depend upon their hunters' income from the fur trade to provide them with the necessities. Consequently they were among the first to accept suggestions for planting cotton or tending sheep and then to ask the agent for teachers to show them how to spin and weave. "The raising and manufacturing of Cotton is all done by Indian women," the Cherokee agent reported in 1802; "they find their condition so much bettered by this employment that they apply for wheels, cards, etc. with great earnestness."[36] The agent explained this in terms of the basic human desire to "better their condition" because according to the philosophy of the whiteman, it was a simple fact of human nature that men and women sought happiness in terms of improving their material condition. This was part of the belief system the missionaries described as "civilization," "progress," and "Christianization." According to the psychological and social laws of cosmic order ("the laws of nature" and "the laws of God") which whites learned from reading John Locke, William Paley, Lord Kames, Adam Smith (laws integrated and popularized in eighteenth-century America by Benjamin Franklin and college presidents like John Witherspoon and Timothy Dwight), self-interest or self-love was

36. Return J. Meigs, Journal, December 1802, BIA, M-208.

the essential motive of all human action. In order to find happiness, men prudently sought pleasure and avoided pain. This required hard, persistent work, delayed gratification, and attention to profit in order to accumulate property. Private ownership of property (and the right of profiting from that property) was a "natural right" deriving from human labor. Private property converted into money enabled a man to purchase whatever would improve his condition, increase his happiness, decrease his pain. Enlightened self-interest (foresight or prudence) led men to take a long-range view of happiness and to recognize that after this life there was an even longer life of the soul. Consequently, moral and spiritual happiness entered into this utilitarian measurement. Even the most self-interested person could see that some benevolence toward others was part of the law of the Creator; otherwise this would be a world of might makes right. As William Paley, the British moral philosopher, wrote, altruism grew from prudent self-interest because the rational man would always consider "what we shall gain or lose in the world to come" by our actions in this world.[37] Alexander Hamilton expressed a prudent whiteman's view of human nature when he said, "Every man ought to be supposed a knave and to have no other end, in all his actions, but private interest."[38] Benjamin Franklin's "Poor Richard" stories explained the whiteman's view that hard work was virtuous because it was "the way to wealth" and hence to power, honor, influence, and happiness. The power and wealth of nations, Adam Smith declared, stemmed from the accumulated wealth of individuals each seeking their own self-interest. The new American nation had based its revolution on the rights of the individual to life, liberty, property, and the pursuit of happiness in terms of this "acquisitive nature of man."

Federal Indian agents saw the gradual acculturation of the Cherokees through this perspective. They told a story of one such Cherokee which had all the elements of a parable from "Poor Richard." (The missionaries later reprinted the story in their journals to inform their supporters of the scientific and scriptural inevitability of Cherokee progress.) This allegedly true story concerned a respected old chief who was noted for his ability as a hunter. Every spring he returned from six months in the hunting grounds with a large cache of deerskins and beaver pelts, sufficient to obtain from white traders all the goods he needed to provide for his large family (clothes, pots, pans, kettles, knives, salt, blankets, axes, powder, flint, lead, etc.) But after 1794, he discovered that the game was disappearing and, despite his best efforts, he returned from the hunt one year with such a meager supply of skins that he knew it would not be able to provide for the necessities of his family. As he entered the cabin dejectedly to tell his wife the bad news, he

37. D. H. Meyer, *The Instructed Conscience* (Philadelphia: Pennsylvania State University Press, 1972), p. 8.

38. Herbert W. Schneider, *History of American Philosophy* (New York: Columbia University Press, 1946), p. 52.

discovered to his amazement that all the necessities for the family were already provided for. His faithful wife informed him that she and his daughters, following the instructions of the federal agent, had planted cotton the previous spring and during the fall and winter had carded, spun, and woven it into long bolts of cloth. They had then cut and sewn the cloth to make new clothing for him and the rest of the family and found they had sufficient cloth left to barter with a trader to acquire all the other goods they needed for the coming year. The chief was so impressed that he vowed to change his way of life. According to the story, he "came to the agent with a smile, accusing him for making his wife and daughters better hunters than he."[39] Then he asked the agent for a plough, a mattock, and a hoe, took the seeds from his wife's cotton and corn, and planted large crops. Tending it carefully all summer, he found himself with such a large surplus in the fall that he was able to provide for his family without going hunting. Thus agricultural commerce and domestic industry started this once savage family on the way to wealth and happiness. The story concluded by noting that the chief's example was followed by all the people in his village, and soon, in place of rundown hovels, a community of neat and tidy farms with barns, stables, fences, pastures, and orchards had blossomed in the wilderness. The agent reported to the secretary of war, "The Cherokees are rapidly becoming a civilized people."

This Cherokee success story, retold many times by whites, allegedly took place in 1795 in a remote Cherokee village in Tennessee. But it was apocryphal. Although a few Cherokees of mixed ancestry made a living as herders and cash-crop farmers by 1800, the vast majority did not. They lacked not only the desire to do so, but also the skills and the tools. The government did not have enough ploughs, spinning wheels, and looms for every family nor were there sufficient blacksmiths, carpenters, and other craftsmen to repair such tools. Few Cherokees could speak English or measure by American terms with sufficient skill to engage in private barter. There were no wagons and no wagon roads, no ferries and no bridges to get back and forth to any market. Most trading was done by whites with pack-horses. Frontier traders were notoriously corrupt and sharp in dealing with Indians. In frontier states Indians were not allowed to testify in courts of law against a whiteman, and they had no recourse if they were cheated, or even if their goods were stolen outright, unless they had white witnesses to testify for them.

Although more and more Cherokee men did, out of sheer necessity, take up farming after 1794 and more and more Cherokee women did learn to spin, weave, and sew, most of them did so at a bare subsistence level and most still had to supplement their diet of corn and vegetables by hunting deer, turkey, or rabbits. So marginal was the Cherokee agricultural system at the turn of the century that any prolonged drought or early frost could

39. John Ridge to Albert Gallatin, February 27, 1826, Payne Papers, VIII, 114.

produce widespread famine. "We are likely to perish for Bread," wrote the chief of one small town in Tennessee to the Indian agent in 1804, "oweing to the hand of the Great Spirit above not sending Rain."[40] They begged him to send them 360 bushels of corn so they could survive until the next harvest. The agent wrote to the War Department to say that since a council was taking place soon at which the government hoped to wheedle more land from the Cherokees, he thought it both benevolence and good policy to supply the corn. Such famines in various parts of the nation were common in these years as the Cherokees made the difficult transition from a hunting to an agricultural economy. It was not unknown in some bad years for a Cherokee to kill his only plough horse in order to provide food for his family.

In the critical years from 1794 to 1812, the Cherokees' cultural dis-orientation was reflected in a deep-seated political division which came close to erupting into civil war. The roots of this division lay in their reluctance to adopt a strong, centralized tribal government under national leaders.[41] Even after 1794 they were divided into forty to sixty towns or villages. A town usually stretched along a river bank near a council house and a squareground in which they performed their dances, festivals, and ballplays. The average town contained 300 to 350 persons (about 80 families).[42] Each town chose its own chiefs or headmen, had its priests and doctors, its seven clan leaders, and it various ranks of warriors. Politically each town was independent—a source of constant difficulty from 1720 onward when the advancing Euro-pean settlers were able to concentrate far more firepower in their armies than any town or small group of towns could muster. The lack of tribal unity meant that sometimes part of the tribe was at war while part was not. War was basically a town decision, not a tribal decision; wars were traditionally fought for retaliation against the raids of other tribes and not for conquest. Efforts to unify the nation after 1720 largely failed. There were ostensible "kings" or "emperors" from time to time who claimed to speak for the whole nation and sporadic tribal councils attended by the headmen from all (or most) of the towns, but they could not overcome the ancient practice of town autonomy.[43]

In 1775, three elderly chiefs who claimed to speak for the nation made

40. Doublehead to Return J. Meigs, March 27, 1804, BIA, M-208.

41. See Gearing, *Priests and Warriors*, for a discussion of this. Hudson notes that the difference between tribal political order and an Indian nation-state is that the former relies on clan authority for unity while the latter relies on centralized civil coercion. Hudson, *Southeastern Indians*, p. 202.

42. Gearing, *Priests and Warriors*, p. 3. Gearing estimates the average village as "350 to 600 souls" and chooses 400 as the average or typical village. Fogelson says "the typical Cherokee town numbered between 200 and 325 persons" in the eighteenth century. Fogelson and Kutsche, "The Gadugi," in Fenton and Gulick, Symposium, p. 90.

43. See the works by Gearing, Mooney, Corkran, and Malone listed in the bibliography for discussion of Cherokee politics in the eighteenth century.

a major mistake when they agreed to sell a large part of the tribe's hunting ground in central Kentucky over the bitter objections of the younger chiefs. When the Revolution broke out the following year, the old chiefs made another mistake by commencing attacks upon white settlements before the king's agents were able to establish effective supply lines to provide guns and powder. After major defeats in battles with large American armies (1,500 to 2,000 strong) these Cherokee chiefs were forced to make a disastrous peace in 1777 with more land cessions, including several of the areas in which their oldest and most sacred towns were located. The younger chiefs refused to accept the peace and moved farther west with their own families and with many other families who were evicted from the newly ceded lands. Between 1777 and 1781 hundreds of these dissidents—perhaps half the population—settled along the Tennessee River between present-day Chattanooga and Muscle Shoals and refused to accept the peace treaties of the old chiefs in the Upper Towns. The new settlements were known as the Chickamauga, or Lower Towns (because they were lower down in the Tennessee Valley than any Cherokees had previously lived). Here, allied with the Creeks and Shawnees, the dissident Cherokees kept up a bitter guerrilla warfare with white settlers (despite various treaties in 1785, 1791, and 1792 which the old Upper Town chiefs signed). During the war, from 1781 to 1794, the whiteman's armies, claiming they could not tell the friendly Upper Town Cherokees from the hostiles in the Lower Towns, frequently invaded and destroyed Upper Towns, thereby turning even more young warriors into guerrillas. The old, Upper Town chiefs were unable to stop the war until the whites had decimated the Lower Towns.

When peace came in 1794 a loose form of tribal unity was achieved under a chief named Little Turkey, who lived in the Lower Town area, in northeastern Alabama. But in fact the Upper Town region and the Lower Town region continued to hold separate regional councils in addition to the annual national council. In effect the regional division of the war years remained a political fact of Cherokee life until 1810. The federal agents, finding that the Lower Town chiefs were the more dominant force in the nation, did their best to increase the strength of this faction. The Upper Town chiefs complained that the agent never attended their regional councils, that he gave the majority of the annuities and agricultural implements to the Lower Towns, that he made special gifts and credit arrangements for the Lower Town chiefs. In 1805 and 1806, large cessions of land were made in treaties for which the Lower Town chiefs received bribes. When this became known, a group of Upper Town chiefs murdered the leader of the Lower Towns, a chief named Doublehead.[44] This led the other Lower

44. All the political histories of the Cherokees in the nineteenth century discuss this schism and regional rivalry. The best account of the political assassination of Doublehead, the leader of the Lower Towns faction, on August 9, 1807, is contained in Thurman Wilkins, *Cherokee Tragedy*, pp. 36–38.

Town chiefs to make a secret agreement with the agent to exchange all of their part of the nation for an equal tract of land in Arkansas Territory, to which they planned to remove. The vast majority of the tribe repudiated this agreement when they learned of it and branded those who had made it traitors. Nonetheless, over 1,100 Cherokees did move to Arkansas between 1810 and 1811, even though the federal government was unable to conclude a treaty which would complete the agreement by ceding the Lower Town region to the United States. As a result of this first removal crisis, the Cherokee finally reunited under Black Fox and Path Killer, formed a thirteen-member executive committee which acted for the nation between councils, and agreed to abandon the regional councils and act as one people under a centralized national council which met annually with representatives from all of the towns.[45]

Between 1794 and 1810 the Cherokees were a confused, disheartened, and disunited people. The first missionaries to establish stations among them, the Moravians and the Presbyterians, were inevitably caught up in their political factionalism and were accused of taking sides in it. Because they came with a message of hope and a new way of life for those who were lost, they expected to be welcomed. However, the Cherokees were struggling so hard to cope with their political, economic, and social problems that they had little time to listen to Christian sermons. Some Cherokees were ready to send their children to mission schools so that their sons might learn enough English and arithmetic to help them do business with whites and their daughters might learn spinning and weaving in order to provide better for their families. But most of those who did this were intermarried whites or of mixed ancestry. The great bulk of the Cherokees were still believers in the old ways, but they were frustrated in their efforts to apply them under the changing circumstances. As whites began to travel regularly through their country, numerous angry confrontations, robberies, fights, and murders took place. The federal agent and the chiefs found it almost impossible to settle the issue of clan revenge and the endless round of retaliations it created every time a Cherokee was killed by a white. Under the treaties, the chiefs were obliged to hand over to the federal agent any Cherokee accused of a crime against a whiteman. But frontier courts would never convict a white-man for a crime against a Cherokee. Consequently, Cherokee murderers, practicing the code of clan revenge, were judicially hung while white murderers went scot-free. Clan elders found it hard to restrain the next of kin from taking their own vengeance as tradition required. When the chiefs allowed the agent to inaugurate a process of monetary compensation to the relatives of murdered Cherokees in lieu of justice, they lost face, and so did the agent.

45. For a discussion of the first removal crisis and its role in stirring Cherokee political nationalism, see W. G. McLoughlin, "Thomas Jefferson and the Beginning of Cherokee Nationalism," *William and Mary Quarterly*, 3d ser., 32 (October 1975): 547–80.

Equally shattering for traditionalists was the inability of fathers and uncles, those responsible for training and disciplining the young, to sustain their positions of respect. The skills they knew were the old skills of hunting and war, which were of little use to the rising generation.[46] They could not teach them how to be herders, farmers, traders, blacksmiths. Some of the more attractive and ambitious Cherokee women preferred to marry whitemen or men of mixed ancestry, who could provide better for their children in the transitional years. The more mettlesome young men, unable to become warriors and hunters and ignorant (or scornful) of farming, found adventure in stealing horses from the white settlements. Horse stealing had many of the aspects of war; it took courage and daring and it could easily lead to gun battles and sudden death. The horsethief required much the same cunning and skill as the warrior. A successful raid on a white settlement, even if only to steal horses, was a form of vengeance for hurt pride. Moreover, the traffic in stolen horses was very lucrative. Horsethieves made more money than hunters or farmers and were secretly admired, even by many who publicly disavowed them.

The prevalence of horse stealing was a mark of the social breakdown of Cherokee order. The chiefs and council officially opposed it, though some chiefs secretly abetted it and profited from it. The institution of the Lighthorse police force in 1798 was not very effective, and it operated only sporadically. The federal government had added a clause to one of its treaties requiring the tribe to reimburse from its annuity any settlers who could prove that they had lost horses to Indian thieves, but the Cherokees insisted that whites as frequently stole from them and demanded federal recompense in those cases. Attempting to adjudicate such claims, the federal agent became a self-appointed court of justice for the whole tribe and thereby further usurped and undermined the authority of the town and tribal chiefs. Honesty had always been a prime virtue among the Cherokees, and theft was almost unheard of in former days. Now almost everyone stole, told lies, and cheated, justifying it by saying the whiteman did the same to them. Circumstances beyond their control forced the Cherokees into shameful behavior; many took to drinking excessively. They were losing their own self-respect as they lost any sense of how to be a good Cherokee.

The missionaries hoped to bring a new sense of order to these desperate people. Though missionaries had originally been part of George Washington's plan for Indian civilization, the government did nothing to implement mission work or schools. Henry Knox, Washington's secretary of war, had said in 1789 that the United States government should lead the Indians from barbarism to enlightenment by imparting "our knowledge of cultivation and the arts. . . by which the source of future life and happiness"

46. For a discussion of Cherokee dislocation in these years, see W. G. McLoughlin, "Cherokee Anomie, 1794–1809, " in *Uprooted Americans*, ed. Richard L. Bushman et al. (Boston: Little, Brown, 1979), pp. 125–60.

would be extended.[47] Congress had implemented part of this program in
1792 by providing money for agricultural assistance and for teaching Indian
women "the domestic arts." Knox had also advocated sending missionaries,
who would not only "effect the civilization of the Indians" by teaching them
Christian morality, but would also act as agents of government policy.
Missionaries, he said, "of excellent moral character, should be appointed to
reside in the nation" (he referred specifically here to the Cherokees). They
"should be well supplied with all the implements of husbandry and the
necessary stock for a farm. These men should be made the instruments to
work on the Indians; presents should commonly pass through their hands or
by their recommendations. . . . They should be their friends and fathers."[48]
As Knox saw it, missionaries would be the religious counterparts of the
federal agents and factors. They should appear to the Indians as benevolent
and disinterested father figures, though in fact they were to be government
"instruments to work on the Indians." From the outset, federal Indian
policy assumed this partnership in paternalism. Indians were considered as
children or wards of the government; the president was "the Great White
Father" in Washington; the agents, factors, treaty commissioners, and missionaries were "white fathers" among the tribes.

   Knox was from Puritan New England and Washington from an Episcopal background. Neither seemed to doubt that the church should act as an
arm of the state in Indian matters.[49] Equally odd, no denomination ever
doubted the propriety of this collaboration, even those, like the Baptists, who
had been staunch advocates of the separation of church and state. But Congress had appropriated no specific funds for missionaries or schools (and was
not to do so until 1819). The initial Christian impulse to save the Indians'
souls came from the pietistic fervor of the great religious awakening which
began in the 1790s and extended throughout the United States for almost a
generation. Revivalism generated that pious concern for converting the
heathen which inaugurated new efforts both in domestic and foreign mission
agencies and the volunteers and donations to sustain them. No one asked
whether the Cherokees needed or wanted Christianity. That seemed like
asking whether a starving man needed food or a drowning woman a boat.
The Cherokees themselves were ambivalent when the Moravians suddenly
appeared in their country in 1799 offering free schools for their children and
a better way of life.

   47. ASP II, 53.
   48. ASP II, 54.
   49. For a good general discussion of this issue, see R. Pierce Beaver, *Church, State and
the American Indians.*

CHAPTER TWO

The Cherokees and the Moravians, 1799–1803

I believe that you have been inspired by the Great Sp rit to be willing to come to us and to teach us.

Arcowee of Chota to the Moravians, November 8, 1799

When the Cherokees decided to admit permanent mission stations in their nation, they did so because they expected the missionaries to teach their children to read and write and to provide them with other useful information in their effort to cope with a rapidly changing social order. The ability to read and write was a gift which the Great Spirit had, for some reason, given to the whiteman long ago. Now, in his own good time, the Great Spirit had inspired the whiteman to share this skill with the redman. Nevertheless, most Cherokees were wary of the Moravians' offer, for, like every connection with whites, this one began by asking them for land.

Prior to 1799, the Cherokees had rejected visiting miss onaries without giving them much thought. Anglican, Presbyterian, and Moravian missionaries had traveled to the Cherokee towns on several occasions between 1740 and 1799, but found them so apathetic or bemused by their sermons that they never pursued their work. For example, the Presbyterian John Martin, who preached among them in 1758–59, was asked to leave because "he had so long plagued them with that they no ways understood" or cared to know more about.[1] The most famous story of Cherokee dubiety over the validity of Christianity concerns Chief Yonaguska (or Junaluska), who refused to let missionaries circulate among his townspeople in the North

---

1. Henry T. Malone, *Cherokees of the Old South*, p. 96. The only missionary who seems to have made a serious impression on the Cherokees in the eighteenth century was the mysterious Christian Gottlieb Priber. He lived among them from 1736 to 1743, when he was captured by the British and jailed on suspicion of being a Jesuit in league with the French. He died in prison in 1745, and the large manuscript dictionary of the Cherokee language which he had compiled was lost. Ibid., pp. 26–27.

Carolina area of the nation until they had translated the Gospel of Matthew
for him. When he had heard it, he remarked, "It seems to be a good book;
strange that the white people are not better after having had it so long."[2]
Even in the midst of their severe cultural disorientation in the 1790s, few
Cherokees showed any interest in the Moravians' theology.

The Moravians were a small, pietistic and pacifistic, German-speaking
sect formed after the Reformation as the Unitas Fratrum, or United Brethren, in northern Europe.[3] They had suffered much persecution until they
found sanctuary for a time in Moravia. Since coming to America in 1735,
they had clung tightly together in self-subsistent farming communities, first
in Savannah, Georgia, later in Bethlehem, Pennsylvania, and Salem, North
Carolina. Though happy to be in America and eager to save the souls of the
Indians, they did not wish to lose their own identity as a separate, German-
speaking Christian fraternity. Prior to 1776, they were ostracized noncon-
formists in the Anglican colonies, and in Pennsylvania they kept apart from
the rest of the Christian community from choice. However, their separatist,
apolitical stance was advantageous to their preaching among the Indians. So,
too, was their pacifism (though that did not endear them to the American
revolutionists in 1776). The Moravians could honestly say to the Indians
that no one in their sect had ever killed an Indian, tried to subjugate them, or
broken a treaty. They shared neither the chauvinism nor the expansionism of
the English-speaking American, though they were deeply concerned to
spread God's word among the heathen. Uninterested in the nationalistic
movement among the British colonies or in accumulating wealth or political
influence, the Moravians saw themselves as a small band of pilgrims on their
way to a better world. They were in this world but not of it. Their chief aim
was to sustain and spread God's revelations.

The Moravians had sent ministers to the Cherokees in 1735, in 1753,
and in 1783, but lack of Cherokee interest and the incipience of frontier
wars on each of these occasions had thwarted their efforts. Their missionaries had, however, been more successful among the northern tribes,
particularly among the Delawares. When the deacons of the Society of the
United Brethren for the Propagation of the Gospel among the Heathen read
in a Knoxville newspaper in 1798 a statement by a minister of the New York
Missionary Society that some Cherokees had told him that their nation
would welcome missionaries, they persuaded the managing board in Bethlehem, Pennsylvania, to make another effort to Christianize that tribe. In
the fall of 1798 the mission board sent Abraham Steiner and Frederic de
Schweinitz to meet with the Cherokee Council to discuss the matter. They
arrived at the federal agency in Tennessee late in October, a month after the
Council had concluded its annual meeting. All the able-bodied males had
moved out to their hunting grounds for the winter.

2. Mooney, *Myths*, p. 163.
3. The standard history of the Moravians and their Indian missions is Schwarze,
Moravian Missions.

Steiner and de Schweinitz discussed their plans with various government agents in the vicinity: Major Thomas Lewis, the federal agent to the Cherokees at Southwest Point, Tennessee; Colonel David Henley, the superintendent of Indian affairs in Knoxville, and Captain Edward Butler, commander of the United States Army garrison at Tellico. These officials promised to assist the missionaries but said nothing could be done until the national council met the following October.[4] Before returning to Bethlehem, Steiner and de Schweinitz toured some of the Cherokee towns near the federal agency in eastern Tennessee. They noted that some Cherokees had already adopted an agricultural economy and that in 1798 the government had distributed "300 ploughs, 300 pairs cotton cards," and some spinning wheels. "Now," wrote the missionaries in their detailed report on the Cherokees, "they begin to apply themselves to the cultivation of the land and the raising of cotton. . . . [B]esides that, they had begun to spin and weave some of it themselves," for the government had also supplied looms and hired weavers to teach them to make cloth.[5] But the missionaries also noted that the Cherokees were justifiably suspicious of whites. As a previous Moravian visitor, the Reverend Martin Schneider, had reported when he visited in 1783, most whites in the West wanted only to "extirpate" the Indians: "They scarce look upon them as human creatures."[6]

Interested in the Cherokee religious system, Steiner and de Schweinitz spoke (through interpreters) with some of the women and older men, who had not gone out to hunt. One of the interpreters, James Carey, "informed us that there are many deceivers among the Cherokees who go by the name of sorcerers or conjurors." But they were pleased to find that the Cherokees had a word for God, "Utajah," meaning, according to Carey, "the great man who dwells above." Their discussions with two old chiefs, Arcowee of Chota and Kulsatahee of Hiwassee Town, provided them with important insights into the Cherokee belief system. Their conversation also revealed that the Cherokees, through long intercourse with whites, had already incorporated some aspects of the whiteman's philosophy into their world view.

To Arcowee, a former war chief in the Upper Towns who had helped to sign peace treaties with President Washington in 1792, the Bible—"the great book" of the whites, called "God's Word"—held many powerful secrets. In this book, Arcowee believed, lay the source of the whiteman's wisdom and knowledge. Arcowee expected that in offering to live among the Cherokees and teach them from their great book, Steiner and de Schweinitz were agreeing to share that knowledge and power with the Cherokees. Their

4. The accounts of the early visits of Steiner and de Schweinitz which are quoted in the following pages are quoted also in Schwarze, *Moravian Missions*, but the originals (in German and English) are in MAB and MAS. I am indebted to the archivist at Bethlehem, Lother Madeheim, and the archivist at Salem, Mary Creech, and also to Elizabeth Marx of Salem for invaluable assistance in translating these documents and others quoted throughout.

5. The reports of Steiner's and de Schweinitz's visits in 1799 and in 1800 are in MAB.

6. Martin Schneider's report, dated December 1783–January 1784, is in MAB.

arrival, therefore, was an historic occasion of great potential importance. To acknowledge this momentousness properly, Arcowee appeared for the interview with them "decked out in all his finery and had a silver medal [from President Washington] hanging on a ribbon about his neck." To begin their talk, Steiner told the old chief that they had come "to acquaint them with their God and Creator and what he had done and suffered to save them." Steiner was talking about saving their souls, "the way of salvation" in the next world, but Arcowee may have understood this to mean the saving of his people from discouragement and social disintegration in this world.[7]

After hearing them out politely, Arcowee responded in the dignified but roundabout way common to Indian formal discussion. He provided a historical background describing the present state of Indian — white relations and indicated that he had had a premonition of the significance of the missionaries' coming to help his people:

> I heard yesterday evening that you were here and that you expected me [to speak with you]. I then looked towards heaven and saw my father there. I thought all night long what I might hear today, and now, indeed, I hear great words. The Great Father of all breathing things in the beginning directed all men, the white, the red and the black. He placed the red here toward the going down of the sun and the white men toward the rising of the sun [in Europe]. Then, after a great day long past, the white men came hither in their great canoes and received permission to build a city.

Arcowee was making it clear at the outset that the Indians had benevolently welcomed the Europeans to their part of the world. Indian hospitality, however, "had not sufficed them." The whitemen, after building towns along the coast, "had gone even further" inland, taking more and more of the Indians' territory. "This had caused conflicts between the red and white people and eventually brought on a war." Arcowee did not wish to dwell on the long period of warfare, but neither did he wish to let the Indians bear the blame for it. "Therein both had been wrong," he said graciously, "but the Father who dwells above [Utajah] does not regard this [warfare] with favor but would have it that all should be brethren." Since the war's end in 1794, whenever the two peoples came together, Arcowee noted, "the whites are now called the older brother and the red the younger." He found this ironic: "I do not object to this and will call them so, though, really, the naming should have been reversed, for the red people dwelt here first." Now, the great concern was to establish true brotherhood between them. "The Great Father of all breathing things, who has created all men, has given men also the breath of life and can take it again so soon as it please him." Arcowee was preaching humility to the white missionaries to counter the arrogance of white frontiersmen. "We have all been made of the earth and must all sooner or later return to the earth again." He was sure that "the Great Father who

7. Steiner's and de Schweinitz's report, dated October 28–December 28, 1799, is in MAB.

dwells above" was pleased at this friendly meeting. The Creator "has given us much for our profit that we do not regard."

The missionaries were impressed by the old chief's spiritual wisdom and probably expected him to express some interest in attaining the advantages of civilization which were now being offered to him. But instead Arcowee praised God for more basic gifts: "One need only look upon the water without which we could not live. He made it. The fire in the fire-place, what a little thing, yet he has created it for our benefit, and what especially would the poor red man do if there were not fire since they had not as many warm clothes as have the whites." He marveled at how cunningly the Creator had made the world: "Everywhere there is fire hidden in a subtle manner. It may be drawn even from the smallest stone," the flint, which when chipped against steel made sparks to ignite fire. "And thus it is with everything that one sees; all point to the almighty power of God." Then Arcowee came to his main point: "The whites have indeed advantage" over the Indians in their technical ability to manipulate nature. "They can make themselves clothes against the cold. The red people can only build the small canoes and cross small water; the whites, on the other hand, build enormous canoes and cross safely over the greatest waters." Today the Indians and whites lived in harmony and, being brothers, should share their knowledge. Whites have "the great book from which they can learn all things," and Arcowee welcomed the opportunity to learn those secrets. The Cherokees needed to know them in order to survive and prosper again.

Arcowee then related a legend which had grown up among the Indians since the coming of the whiteman, a legend which sought to explain the origin of the whiteman's superior technological power. "When the Great Father in the beginning created men, he had a great book. This he first extended to the red men and bade them speak to it [that is, read from it] but they were unable to do so. Then he offered it to the white people with the same command. As soon as they saw it, they were able to speak to the book at once, and thus it has come about that the white people know so much that is not known to the red."[8] This, implicitly, explained the successful conquest of the Indians by the Europeans. But Arcowee was also trying to explain to the Moravians why he had had a vision of his father the night before. It was an omen of a new era in Indian–white relations. "The time appears to have come when the red people should learn it [the book] too. When the white people first came to this land, they had the great book wherein is the Word of God [the most hidden secrets of nature], but they did not instruct the red concerning it." The blame for the Indians' ignorance of God's power lay not

8. This legend, though recited as an ancient Cherokee myth, clearly did not go back before contact with white Europeans. It is, however, similar to a legend among the Ashanti in Africa, and runaway black slaves may have told their version of it to the Cherokees. See W. G. McLoughlin. "A Note on African Sources of American Indian Racial Myths," *Journal of American Folklore* 89 (June–September, 1976): 331–36.

so much with the Indians' inability to read as with their older brothers' refusal to share his superior knowledge with them as he should have. The coming of the missionaries indicated God's will that this betrayal of brotherly responsibility should be rectified: "I believe," Arcowee said, "therefore, that you have been inspired by the Great Spirit to be willing to come to us and to teach us." That was the meaning of his vision of his father and the reason he had put on his finery and his presidential medal, pledging peace and friendship. "For my part, I will bid you welcome," the old chief said; "I believe that it will be agreeable to my people as it is to me."

The Moravians no doubt believed that they were sent by God, but they probably missed the point that they were not to come paternalistically or with ethnocentric pride toward benighted children. They would be welcome so long as they came out of a sense of regret for having neglected their duty toward their brothers and for the Europeans' aggressive reaction to the Indians' initial hospitality. The Great Spirit expected the whites to treat the Indians as equals, for they originally owned this land; the technical superiority of the whites was, after all, a gift of God and not the result of their own accomplishment.

Chief Kulsatahee of Hiwassee, to whom Steiner and de Schweinitz spoke a week later, expressed more directly what Arcowee had suggested. His primary concern was to discover whether the missionaries shared the common frontiersman's view that the Indian was by nature incapable of being civilized. Kulsatahee too had had may dealings with whites in councils and knew them well. He began by admitting that the Cherokees might at first be slow to learn the skills of the whiteman or to accept the teachings in "the Great Book." Nevertheless, schooling "would indeed be welcome" because "it was needed." Kulsatahee thought his people "would be glad to hear and know the words" of God, but "we are indeed very stupid [dull] and clumsy" about such things. "Still, it might be effective." Despite their dullness and clumsiness the Cherokees had already learned much from the whiteman: "When first it became necessary for us to learn to live as the white people and the cultivation of land and cotton culture were introduced, we thought we would never understand this; we are not intended for it; it is not for the red people." So many had said. Yet they had now begun to learn it. "I think that we shall gradually comprehend and learn to know the great words" in the Great Book, "but it goes slowly."

Part of the difficulty, Kulsatahee believed, was that the Cherokees had been made to feel more stupid than they were by the whites. "Many people think that we Indians are too evil and bad to become good people and that we are too unclean and brown." He was asking, in effect, whether the missionaries agreed with Thomas Jefferson that the Indians were innately the equal of Europeans or whether they shared the westerners' view that they were savages, like the Africans, incapable of improvement.[9] As "brown"

9. Jefferson said in 1785, "I believe the Indian then in body and mind equal to the whiteman." Winthrop D. Jordan, *White Over Black* (Baltimore: Penguin, 1969), pp. 453.

people, people of color, the Indians had been enslaved by the first colonists, and they might well be reduced to slavery again. Many Indians had accepted the theory of polygenesis, that God had created the three races separately and that they were never supposed to live together for they had different ways. If the Cherokees were to accept the government's policy of acculturation and believe in Washington's promise of ultimate "incorporation" or integration as equal citizens, they had to know what the priests of the whiteman's religion believed about this key issue.

Steiner and de Schweinitz understood the question. Their faith that all men descended from Adam and Eve and thus all were brothers inevitably led them to support the position of Washington and Jefferson and to oppose the frontier view of Indian racial inferiority. "We do not think so," the missionaries responded to Kulsatahee's question about racial hierarchy; Indians were not incapable of improvement because they were "evil," "unclean," or "brown." "We love all people, no matter what their color. God too does not think so. He is the Creator and Father of all men, be they white, brown, or black." (The Moravians, writing in German, used the word *braun* rather than *rot* to describe the color of the Indians.)

By and large the Christian missionaries of all denominations agreed with the Moravians in these early years of mission work and refused to accept the frontier view of the innate racial inferiority of the Indians.[10] As it turned out, however, their pride in the accomplishments and religion of white Euro-Americans fostered an ethnocentrism which had almost the same effect upon their relations with the Indians. They consistently treated them as inferiors, not as equals, and their unrealistic expectations of the rapidity of acculturation, their frustration over Indian cultural resistance, and their own exalted standards of proper Christian conduct ultimately caused many missionaries to have serious doubts about the success of Washington's Indian policy—or at least to doubt whether it could be accomplished within the original fifty-year timetable (by 1839). The Cherokees were wise to be wary of these idealistic whitemen, who claimed to serve God and not the white majority. Within a generation, the white majority had elected to the presidency a frontier Indian fighter who repudiated Washington's policy, seriously doubted Indian racial equality, and believed that the voice of the people was the voice of God. The missionaries then found themselves torn between their philanthropic idealism and their patriotic ethnocentrism.

Kulsatahee expressed great pleasure at the Moravians' answer to his pointed question. He said he would talk to the younger chiefs when they returned from hunting and try to persuade them to allow the missionaries enough land to establish a permanent station within the nation. However, Kulsatahee and Arcowee were chiefs of the Upper Town region, and at this

10. The missionaries in general shared the view among educated whites at the time that God created man white and that the different complexions of the human race resulted from environmental factors. See William Stanton, *The Leopard's Spots* (Chicago: University of Chicago Press, 1960), and Michael C. Coleman. "Not Race but Grace."

time the predominant power among the Cherokees rested with the chiefs of the Lower Towns. The Lower Town chiefs in 1799 were led by Doublehead, the Glass, Dick Justice, Toochalee, Bloody Fellow, Black Fox, Tolluntuskee, the Bark, and the Boot. Wise in their own ways, some of them had an inveterate hatred of whites and wanted to do all they could to thwart them. Others among them believed that the old ways were irretrievably lost and wanted only to obtain as much of the goods, technical assistance, and money from the whiteman as they could. With the connivance of the agent, they ran up large debts at the government factory in order to obtain equipment for their own farms, and with their profits they acquired gangs of black slaves to work for them. The most powerful of these chiefs— Doublehead, the Glass, Dick Justice, Tolluntuskee—thought they could outwit the whiteman at his own game. They were willing to sell parts of their old hunting ground (a little at a time) provided they got a good price for it. From such sales they expected rewards for themselves and their immediate townsmen which would make them rich and independent, able to sustain themselves as planters and traders and to use their influence with the federal government to protect their region from white intruders. In the treaties they negotiated they asked not only for ploughs and looms but for government-built gristmills, sawmills, and cotton gins. They wanted the government to build roads through the nation and to give them the franchises for ferries, tollgates, taverns, and mail horses. They were willing to lease the tribes' timberlands, salines, saltpeter caves, iron ore deposits, and other resources coveted by white entrepreneurs provided they maintained control and shared the profits. As they became wise in the ways of white politics and economics, they saw to it that their relatives and friends acquired major interests in such concessions. Their shrewdness and ambition is well illustrated in a letter Doublehead sent, through his clerk, to the federal agent in 1802:

> Sir,
>   When I saw you at the Green Corn Dance—you Desired me to come & see you and get some goods from you—My intention is to come and trade with you—But I am so Engaged in Hunting and gathering my Beef Cattle that I expect it will be a moone or two before I can come—I . . . have now one Request to ask of you—that is to have me a boat Built—I want a good Keal Boat some 30 to 35 feet in length and 7 feet wide—I want her for the purpose of Descending the River to Orlians & back—I want her to be lite & well calculated to stem the Steam—I am Determined to b[u]y the Produce of this place & then Return back by Water. . . . I shall want two of your big guns to mount on the Boat—I am Determined for to see up the White & Red Rivers in my Route & oppen a trade with the western wild Indians—Let me here from you soon—I am Ser Your Reale
>
>   friend & Brother—Doublehead[11]

11. Malone, *Cherokees*, p. 145.

Doublehead was to be one of the major opponents of the Moravian mission. He was a fullblood who could not read or write English, but he had taken a whiteman, John D. Chisholm, as his partner and secretary. He saw nothing immediate to be gained from the missionaries, so he took little interest in them.

One of the difficulties which was to plague the missionaries as they sought admission to the nation was the confusion over whether to give first priority to teaching or to preaching. In their original letter to Colonel David Henley they said they were motivated by "the importance to the whole country of the Indian's being brought to a true knowledge of religion whereof civilization is a necessary consequence."[12] Henley thought this put the process backward. The Cherokees favored schooling without religion.

Henley wrote the Moravian mission board that he thought the chiefs at their fall council in 1800 would "consent to one or more missionaries among them" in order that "their children should be instructed in Reading, etc." and that "after that," the Cherokees might "be brought to like the preaching of the Gospel."[13] How could the Indians comprehend Christianity, he asked, "unless they first became more civilized, did understand English and could read?" Steiner replied to Henley, "Our experience is of a contrary nature. We know the gospel finds an entrance among the most barbarous heathen and that they are capable to believe it and become obedient to it," simply by the power of the Holy Spirit when it is preached through interpreters.[14] Would Indians bother to send their children to obtain a Christian education if they were not first convinced that they wanted them to become Christians? Spiritual regeneration of the parent must precede education of the child. Education in a mission school would of course be Christian education.

Furthermore, the Moravians believed that once converted, an Indian must move away from his or her heathen family and friends and come to live near the mission in a Christian environment. The pietistic separatism of the Moravians had led them to a similar choice; they separated themselves from the sinful world by forming their communes in Bethlehem and Salem, where they could keep their children free of bad influences. So must it be for the Indian converts. To expect a new convert to sustain his or her faith while continuing to live among pagans was to place an impossible burden upon him or her. The Moravians planned their mission settlements as Christian enclaves within the pagan nation. All converts were to be given Christian names at baptism, to be dressed in whiteman's clothes, and then asked to build new homes for their families at the mission station. Other heathen, seeing the superior moral, social, and economic benefits of this Christian enclave, would wish to join it. Gradually the mission compound would

12. Schwarze, *Moravian Missions*, p. 44.
13. Ibid, pp. 47–48.
14. Quoted by Steiner in his report under date of November 9, 1799, MAB.

expand; a church and school would be built. As the compound grew, the pagan community would shrink. Ultimately the whole Indian nation would be encompassed in the ever-widening Christian circle.

Of course this plan would take time, but the Moravians were patient. They were willing to let the Lord work it out in his own way and his own good time, while they faithfully preached his word and set a good example. Until they had converted sufficient parents to form a community with enough children to make a school worthwhile, there would be no school and no mission church. The mission station would consist simply of the homes of the missionary families and the farm they would cultivate to support themselves. The Cherokees were to come to them to learn God's word; they would not go out and evangelize among them. The principles upon which they planned to run their Christian commune among the Cherokees can be seen in the list of rules which they had adopted in 1793 at their mission enclave among the Delawares:

> We whose names are hereunto subscribed, do solemnly and sincerely agree among ourselves on the following rules and regulations, viz.
> 1. Everyone who wants to live with us must adore and worship God above.
> 2. None shall live with us who will go to other places to feasts and dances.
> 3. None who will bring whisky into our town . . .
> 4. None who keeps a whore . . .
> 5. No man who forsakes his wife . . . nor woman who leaves her husband . . .
> 6. No son or daughter who abuses their parents . . .
> 7. None that steals.
> 8. . . . none that uses . . . witchcraft or such like things.
> 9. None that will doctor or be doctored after the wild Indian manner.
> 10. None that paint, shave, shear, or dress themselves as the heathen do. . . .[15]

Had the Cherokees known that the missionaries envisioned the establishment of such a Christian *imperium in imperio,* they would certainly have denied their admission.

Colonel Henley may not himself have realized it. Speaking to Little Turkey, Doublehead, Bloody Fellow, and other principal chiefs at a council in May 1800, he explained the Moravians' intentions rather differently. The missionaries, he said, were "good men who wish to know if the Cherokees would receive one or more of them favorably in the Nation to teach the young people to read and write, to be industrious in farming, etc., and above all, to teach both young and old to know the goodness of the Great Spirit and what He can do for them if they will follow the straight path which He will tell His servants to point out to them all."[16] This, at least, was what Henley

15. Elma E. Gray, *Wilderness Christians* (Ithaca: Cornell University Press, 1956). pp. 109–10.

16. Schwarze, *Moravian Missions,* p. 50.

expected. These chiefs agreed to bring the matter before the National Council for a full discussion in October.

When Steiner and de Schweinitz arrived for this Council, they first met informally with a group of Lower Town chiefs (Little Turkey, Bloody Fellow, Doublehead, the Boot, the Glass) near Tellico. They found these chiefs unsympathetic to their proposals. Ignoring the request of the missionaries to be allowed to preach the Gospel, the chiefs said they would consider only their request to establish a school. Then the chiefs asked whether the Moravians intended to provide free room, board, and clothing at the school? When Steiner said, "No," the chiefs told them to "go home" and reconsider the matter. Captain Butler was embarrassed and told the chiefs that he was "disappointed in finding the Cherokees so indifferent as to the future of their children and Nation." But he told the Moravians he was "quite at a loss how to advise" them to proceed.[17]

From the missionaries' viewpoint the cost of boarding, feeding, and clothing students was beyond the means of their small mission treasury. It never occurred to them to ask the federal government to subsidize them at this time. (Not till 1809 did the Moravians obtain their first federal subsidy through the efforts of the agent.) On the other hand, the Moravians did not plan to settle in one of the large Cherokee towns, where the children could attend school in the day and return home at night. They wanted to settle away from any populous area, where they could start a farm and build up their own separate and distinct Christian village.

The chiefs of the Upper Towns (perhaps influenced by Arcowee and Kulsatahee) were somewhat more sympathetic to the Moravians' proposition than those from the Lower Towns. Several of them had white fathers, particularly Charles Hicks, James Vann, Will Shorey, and Richard Fields. They lived in areas where other mixed bloods and intermarried whites wanted an education for their children—leading traders such as John McDonald, Daniel Ross, Samuel Riley, John Rogers, William Woodward. Some of these had been sending their children to schools in nearby white settlements or hiring tutors. For them, a nearby mission school would be very advantageous. The Lower Towns, farther from the white settlements and with fewer whites and mixed bloods, had less interest in education. When the National Council met at Tellico in October 1800, the Lower Town chiefs continued to raise objections and insisted that if there was a school it "would have to care for the students and provide for their food and raiment." Steiner noted that "the chiefs seemed yet to harbour a good deal of suspicion, fearing we had in view to obtain their land," and that the school was simply a pretext for gaining a foothold in the nation.

While the council was still in session, Charles Hicks and James Vann,

17. Ibid., p. 54. See also the detailed report in MAB. The federal government did not at this time assume the power to admit missionaries into Indian nations without the Indians' explicit permission.

two of the more influential mixed-blood chiefs of the Upper Towns, talked to the missionaries and said they would try to persuade the Council to give them a trial. "If the Lower Towns will not take these people," said Hicks, the Upper Towns "will receive them" (an indication of the regional division which still troubled the nation).[18] Vann noted that the missionaries could "accomplish more among them than in the Lower Towns" because there were more people in their region anxious for education. The Lower Town region lay close to the old hunting grounds in middle Tennessee and was bounded on the west by the Chickasaws and on the south by the Creeks. The Upper Town region was bounded by white settlements on all sides except the south, where it too adjoined the Creek Nation.[19]

Vann, the wealthiest of the Upper Town chiefs, was the son of a white trader and a Cherokee. He had inherited his father's trading post near Springplace, Georgia, and expanded his father's business by opening a second store in the Alabama area of the nation. Bilingual and the owner of several dozen black slaves, Vann cultivated a large plantation near his home (which he called Diamond Hill). He traded extensively in corn, horses, cattle, and hogs with white merchants in Charleston, Augusta, and Knoxville as well as with the federal agency. Charles Hicks, also the son of a white trader and a Cherokee, was an astute farmer, trader, slaveowner, and one of the official interpreters for the federal agent. He and Vann were probably the first Cherokees to build gristmills. Neither Hicks nor Vann knew or cared much about Christianity, but both believed that the Cherokees would benefit from schools. Vann belonged to that group of mixed bloods who resented the whiteman's claim to intellectual and spiritual superiority and were opposed to attempts to spread Christianity. White traders who married Indians were seldom noted for their piety, and neither were their children.

Through private conversations among the other chiefs and by promising to make themselves responsible for the good behavior of the missionaries, Hicks and Vann finally persuaded the National Council to agree to admit the Moravians "on trial." As the Council put it, in October 1800, the Moravians were permitted "to make an experiment" with a school "to instruct us and our children and improve our and their minds in the Nation."[20] The Council's approval was significantly silent about preaching. Doublehead, who was "Speaker" for the Council, said in announcing approval, "We will be the judge of their conduct and their attention to us and our children"; if they did not keep their promise to start a school, then the federal agents, as witness to the contract, would have to agree to their ejection. Doublehead, feeling that he had done the missionaries a favor by yielding to

18. Schwarze, *Moravian Missions*, p. 55.

19. The missionaries reported that the Connesauga River was the boundary between the Upper and Lower town regions, but the precise line was never clearly marked. Ibid., p. 56.

20. Ibid., p. 55.

Hicks and Vann, asked them for a bottle of whiskey after the Council as payment for his cooperation.

The Moravians had requested a plot of ground upon which they could start a farm to support themselves. The Cherokees suggested that they should live at John McDonald's place at Chattanooga, a point which was on the border between the Upper and Lower towns. However, Doublehead said that, there being two Moravians available, "if one goes to Mr. McDonald's," then the other might go "to James Vann." The Moravians took this to be advice only and not a command. They investigated McDonald's area and found it "not healthful." Major Lewis told them it was malarial. He wanted them to settle further north in Tellico, which would be closer to the federal agency, the army garrison, and the white settlements. Vann, however, wanted them near his home in northwestern Georgia, fifty miles southeast of Chattanooga. Steiner and de Schweinitz examined two other sites before returning to Bethlehem to give their report.

According to Moravian practice, when difficult choices were to be made, the final decision was "laid before the Lord." They called it "seeking the approval of the Savior," but in effect it was a spiritual lottery, and they spoke of it as "the lot." They wrote the options on slips of paper, folded them, and placed them in a box. After suitable prayers for divine guidance, one slip was drawn from the box. In this case four slips were put in the box, and the slip marked "James Vann's place" was drawn; it had "received the approbation of the Lord," they wrote.[21] Later this reliance upon "the lot" had awkward consequences for the mission.[22]

Vann arranged for the Moravians to purchase "the improvements," or farm buildings, of a whiteman named Robert Brown, who had worked for him and was now moving to another part of the nation. No title to Brown's land was given because all Cherokee land belonged to the nation; Brown was entitled to remuneration only for his efforts in clearing the fields and for his expenses in building his cabin, stable, and fences. Brown's farm was about a mile and a half from Vann's home and trading post. The trail past Vann's home became in 1804 the federal road to Knoxville. The Moravians rechristened the site Springplace because it was near a good spring. It turned out that it was a site on which traveling Cherokees often camped and when they did so, they expected hospitality from the missionaries.

Steiner and a missionary named Gottlieb Byhan were assigned to start the mission. They arrived from Salem, North Carolina, in April 1801. (The mission board in Bethlehem transferred supervision and support of the

21. For an explanation of "the lot," see ibid., p. 58. Sometimes a blank slip of paper was added to the box to allow the option of taking no action.

22. In 1805 the Reverend Gottlieb Byhan wrote of Springplace that it could never "become a missionary post" of any consequence "for we are too near Mr. Vann's" turbulent household. Byhan to Benzien, April 7, 1805, MAS. McDonald's farm, however, became in 1817 the site of the highly successful Brainerd Mission of the ABCFM.

Cherokee mission to the Moravian community in Salem because it was much closer.) First they built a cabin to replace the decrepit one left by Brown. Then they ploughed and planted the land Brown had cleared. But Steiner caught malaria that summer and in September had to return to Salem. He was replaced by Jacob Wohlfahrt and his wife. The board in Salem also designated a wife for Byhan (the Moravians had no compunctions about arranging marriages), and the four missionaries returned to Springplace in November to clear more land, build a stable, and start the other facilities for a farm upon the stolid German-American model. The labor of this enterprise was heavy and though Wohlfahrt and Byhan were good craftsmen (perhaps a bit too perfectionist), it took them three years to build an establishment which met their high standards for efficiency and order.

Under pressure from the chiefs, they agreed in the spring of 1802 to accept such students who would come to "be instructed several hours each day," but they refused to accept boarders. Vann sent his youngest daughter, Sally, and later his son Joseph; Vann's sister sent her daughter, Polly. But these day-students received very little classroom instruction, for the missionaries were too busy building, improving, and running their farm. To assist them, Vann allowed some of his slaves to work at the mission, but only on Sundays (their free time). This arrangement caused the pious Moravians some qualms at first, for they were strict Sabbatarians, but it was unavoidable. All missionaries were to find that day-laborers were very difficult to obtain in the Cherokee Nation. As everywhere on the frontier, good workers in the nation preferred to establish their own farms. The Moravians paid the slaves fifty cents a day each to split rails and perform other farm chores.

Religious services were held in their homes every Sunday for the mission families and any persons in the vicinity who cared to attend. Although they spoke German among themselves, they preached in English (and the Council had specifically said that their school must be conducted in English). Few Cherokees in the vicinity understood English, though the slaves were to some extent bilingual, and they attended with interest. The missionaries could not afford an interpreter, however, so the Cherokees who came at first out of curiosity soon ceased to attend. For various reasons, the slaves did not meet the high standards the Moravians set for Christian conversion. Though often fervent in prayer, song, and profession of belief, they were inconsistent in religious attendance and Christian deportment. Profanity and drunkenness as well as a tendency to petty theft were common among them. Perhaps also, the Moravians sensed that it would appear strange to start their mission church with black slaves as the first and most numerous members. In any case, no blacks were considered sufficiently pious to be baptized and admitted to Christian fellowship.[23]

23. Between 1800 and the time Springplace mission closed in 1833 there is mention of only one black convert, in 1827. In answer to a question from the mission board in Salem in

By 1803 the missionaries were becoming discouraged by the lack of interest shown by the Cherokees in hearing God's word, but Christian resignation was their only response. "I for my part don't let myself in for a lot of meditation about our project here," wrote one of the missionaries, "and rely only on this: the Savior has put us here and He will know how to carry out His purpose and to work out His gracious design."[24] As they saw it, their duty was to "trust Him in a child-like way." Sooner or later he would lead the Cherokees to them or lead them to other pastures.

Meanwhile, the Cherokee chiefs kept careful watch upon the mission and waited for the boarding school to open. The missionaries, however, had no intention of opening a full-scale boarding school until they had made a sufficient number of Cherokee converts who would settle within the mission compound. Tension mounted between them and the chiefs because it looked as though the missionaries were in some way connected with the government's determined effort to run a federal road through the nation from Georgia to Tennessee. James Vann was a leading figure supporting the granting of a right of way and as the patron of the Moravians it was assumed that he and they shared the same views. Nevertheless, Doublehead and most of the Lower Town chiefs bitterly opposed the road, arguing that it would simply increase the traffic of whites through the nation and thereby increase friction between them and the Cherokees—theft, drunkenness, brawls, and bloodshed. More important, the government wanted to establish inns, ferries, and stables for mail horses along the way, and they wanted land ceded so that innkeepers and ferry-keepers could have farms and pasturage to support themselves and feed the travelers. The government expected these franchises to go to whitemen, but Doublehead and his friends argued that if a road was granted, the franchise must go to the Cherokees. Vann expected the road to pass right by his trading post and ferry and wanted not only an inn franchise but the government mail franchise for the whole road. This quarrel extended from 1799 to 1804 as both sides jockeyed for advantages, and President Jefferson put increasing pressure upon the agent to gain a treaty even if it meant bribing some of the important chiefs.

The Moravians kept out of politics and knew little of these dealings, but they could see the animosity mounting against them. "The discontent" of the chiefs "concerning our not beginning a School and boarding Children

---

1819 the missionaries at Springplace stated that if they did admit any blacks they would be "assigned special seats" at communion and "the cup is given them last of all." See Springplace Conference, 1819, p. 47.

24. John Gambold to Riegel, January 19, 1806, MAS. In 1802 the managers of the Society of the United Brethren for the Propagation of the Gospel among the Heathen, located in Bethlehem, Pennsylvania, transferred care and supervision of the mission to the Cherokees to the Diacony and General Helpers Conference of the brethren in Salem, North Carolina. All papers concerning the mission after that date (and some earlier) are in MAS. Salem was four hundred miles from Springplace via Knoxville.

at our own expense had become more known than we thought," Wohlfahrt wrote to his board on April 24, 1803. He had explained to the chiefs "that we intend as soon as possible to begin one with the Children of such as imbrace the word of God and would live together [near the mission] conformable thereto," but the chiefs were not satisfied with this.[25] There had not yet been a single convert. Matters came to a head in June 1803, when a council of the Upper Town chiefs met at Oostenali (or Ustanali) and voted "that a long time has elapsed since a school was to be begun for the instruction of [our] youths. We now consider that the [Moravian] Society have fallen through [on] their good intentions toward us, as we discover no prospect of such business going on." The council gave them to the end of the year to make good on their promise of 1799 or else to leave the nation.[26] Major William Lovely, the assistant agent, brought this news to the missionaries. "We cannot describe our feelings at the receipt of this letter," wrote the disconsolate missionaries to their board. "The whole nation seems to be stirred up against us and we can, as it were, perceive it in the people around us, that they would fain see us gone. We now hear that Mr. Vann was of the same opinion" as the council. They went to Vann and "tried to tell him that we were not come to keep school to the Indians but to make known unto them the word of God." Another chief who was present at Vann's home when they explained this responded bluntly that "they had no ear to hear it [the Word of God] and that this were no sufficient cause for our stay in the[ir] Country."[27]

Wohlfahrt decided to go to Salem to discuss matters with the mission board. The board suggested that it might be expedient to offer to take three or four students as boarders while they awaited God's help in the conversion of adults. As soon as he returned, Wohlfahrt asked Vann to gather the chiefs together so he could present this option to them. The chiefs met in August, but they were angry. They said that "three years ago they had granted us at Tellico only two years time to make a trial" and four had passed with no results. The plan to start a school for three or four boarding students was unacceptable to them. "The chiefs proposed that we might take seven." After all, they noted, "the expense cannot be great. The corn grows; our children are used to it and want nothing else." To this Steiner replied stubbornly, "The corn grows, to be sure, but must however be pounded and baked and this would be for us a great trouble and waste of time. It would be best if we limited the number to four." Grudgingly the chiefs gave them a year's extension.

Colonel Return J. Meigs, the federal agent, suspecting that the chiefs thought the missionaries had ulterior motives for being there, sent a letter to the chiefs. He had heard rumors from certain Cherokees that the mis-

25. Johann Wohlfahrt to Stotes, April 24, 1803, MAS.
26. Quoted in Springplace Diary, June 10, 1083, MAB.
27. Ibid.

sionaries were there to make money off the Indians, but "they are not speculators nor merchants," Meigs told the chiefs. "They do not want your lands nor your money."[28] Still, such rumors persisted, for what else could the missionaries be doing with their constantly expanding farm, and did they not buy and sell things—taking venison from one Indian, corn from another; bartering vegetables for maple sugar? In addition, the attitude of the Moravians had rubbed the Cherokees the wrong way. Lovely, who lived at Diamond Hill with Vann, reported to Meigs that "the minister don't please the people" and that "no consideration will induce them to think of their continuance among them."[29] One great difficulty was the failure of the missionaries to learn to speak Cherokee. Chief Chulioa, a major leader in the Upper Towns, had visited the mission in June and told Lovely, "We have heard that the missionaries were too proud to converse" with the Cherokees in their own tongue.[30] The charge was not entirely fair, for the missionaries had tried to find a Cherokee couple to live with them and teach them the language, but they had been unsuccessful. Lovely remarked to Meigs, "Preaching alone, and that in an unknown tongue, will make but slow progress" in civilizing and Christianizing the Cherokees.[31]

Not knowing what the next step would be and feeling too poor and shorthanded to start a school even for four students, let alone seven, the Moravians asked "the lot" whether the Lord wanted them to continue at their station. The answer was positive, so they went on to construct a small dormitory and tried to hire a slave woman from Vann who would help the missionary women with the cooking, washing, and other household chores and also with the haying and other farm work. When the school had not opened by October, the National Council issued stern reprimands. The Moravians learned afterward that "the Chiefs—Glass, Sour Mush, Bark and Doublehead and in general all the chiefs—wanted to force us out of their country." Their decision was given added weight by the surprising appearance at this Council of a Presbyterian minister from eastern Tennessee, with a far better educational offer. The Reverend Gideon Blackburn of Maryville, Tennessee, "promised to send 3 or 4 schoolmasters each of whom would take 25 to 30 children and would furnish them with food and clothing" free of charge. The teachers would be laymen under Blackburn's supervision. Nothing was said about preaching the Gospel or starting a model farm. The Presbyterians believed that education must precede Christianization.[32]

When the Council heard this, the Moravian missionaries wrote to their board, "The chiefs said that now they stood no more in need of us; we were

28. Springplace Diary, August 27, 1803, October 30, 1803, December 15, 1803, MAB; and Schwarze, *Moravian Missions,* pp. 76–77.
29. Lovely to Meigs, June 13 and 27, 1803, BIA, M-208.
30. Chulioa and Sour Mush to Meigs, July 11 and August 27, 1803, BIA, M-208.
31. Lovely to Meigs, June 13, 1803, BIA, M-208.
32. Springplace Diary, October 30, 1803, MAB.

already four years in the Country and had as yet done nothing and now we would take only four Children which amounted to almost nothing." At the same time, the rumors were still prevalent at this Council that the Moravians had other designs. "They also pretend we were only intent upon growing rich in their Country. . . . [W]e raised so much Corn and arranged matters as if we were to stay there permanently, when [in August] only one year's time had been given us for a trial" (really for a second trial).[33] The thoroughness and stolidity with which the Germans built and farmed gave an aura of permanence to their station. On the frontier, whites did not build for permanence, and if the Moravians did, they were peculiar and must have ulterior motives.

The Cherokees had by no means turned against missionaries or education, however. They eagerly embraced Blackburn's offer. "As his plan is first to teach the Children the Knowledge of letters as introductory to the Knowledge of Christianity," the agent explained to the Moravians, "the plan very readily met with the approbation of the Chiefs. The Glass, in his speech on the occasion, desired me [Meigs] to inform you that unless your plan was enlarged so as to teach more children, that you must leave the Nation. I was sorry to hear it," Meigs said. Nevertheless, "it has always appeared to me that instruction in letters should precede preaching, or at least that it should go at the same time. This seems the general opinion." The agent felt that the government had to do as the Cherokees ordered in this matter: "You are sensible that we cannot with propriety oppose the Cherokees on any matters of which they have the right to judge."[34] The education of their children and the admission or expulsion of missionaries were considered by Jefferson's administration to be matters of internal affairs among the Indian nations and therefore within the jurisdiction of their councils.

Stoically the Moravians agreed to open a boarding school where seven students would be taught regardless of whether their parents were converted Christians or not. But it took them another year to finish the dormitory and enroll their first student. To make matters somewhat easier for them, their board in Salem purchased a black slave woman and sent her out with a new missionary, John Gambold, who replaced Wohlfahrt. The slave, named Pleasant, turned out to be a thoroughly disagreeable person and on occasion the missionaries had to whip her into obedience.[35]

It seemed, however, as though the Presbyterians would completely supplant their work. Only later did it appear that Blackburn had in fact saved them from expulsion and given them time to readjust. The Presbyterian

33. Ibid.
34. Meigs to Wohlfahrt, December 13, 1803, MAS.
35. Steiner left the mission in 1803; Wohlfahrt and Byhan remained. In 1805, Wohlfahrt asked to be relieved and Gambold replaced him. Schwarze, *Moravian Missions*, pp. 79—82. For other references to the use of slave labor at Springplace, see Springplace Conference, 1802—14, pp. 29, 37, 38, 40, 50: entries for June 22, 1804, June 22 and November 3, 1805, March 9, 1806, July 19, 1807.

schools were sixty miles to the northwest, in the Tennessee area of the nation, and were at first so successful that the Cherokee Council simply ignored the Moravians' feeble school. Only a few children in the vicinity of Springplace attended. But the Moravians' caution paid off. The Presbyterians overextended themselves, and then Blackburn became involved in some shady activities which cast the whole Christian enterprise in a bad light. But the important point about this initial confrontation between the Cherokees and the missionaries is that the Cherokees knew better what they wanted and how to get it than the missionaries did. Moreover, they felt in a strong enough position to demand that the missionaries yield to their wishes and not vice versa. They wanted education, not Christianity; teachers, not preachers. And they got them.

~◐(CHAPTER THREE)◑~

Presbyterian Mission Difficulties,
1803—1810

Mr. Blackburn undertook a journey . . . for which a conversation with the
Secretary of War with him is supposed to have been the inducement. . . .
[T]hey built several boats and purchased a large quantity of whiskey in order
to trade with. . . . [T]he disgrace of this venture falls in large part on
religion.

Moravian missionaries to their board, July 23, 1809

Expecting to find a simple, submissive, childlike people grateful for
their benevolence and impressed by their wisdom and self-sacrifice,
the Moravian and Presbyterian missionaries were surprised by
the Cherokees' hardheaded reactions to their efforts. The missionaries had to accept the status of guests in the Cherokee country and to avoid
giving offence. Their problems were compounded by their inevitable entan-
glement in the continuous disputes between the Cherokees and the federal
government as well as among the various Cherokee factions. It was no easy
task to separate the church from the world. Both the Moravians and the
Presbyterians suffered acute embarrassment from their mistakes in the years
1803—10, while the Cherokees were trying to find a new sense of unity and
identity.

The arrival of the young Presbyterian missionary Gideon Blackburn in
the fall of 1803, offering a different kind of school system, came at an
opportune moment for those Cherokees who were dissatisfied with the performance of the Moravians. Blackburn was not trying to replace the Moravians. He simply saw an opportunity for additional missionary work in
eastern Tennessee. The two missionary establishments, it turned out, com-
plemented each other. Where the Moravians were slow, steady, solid but
unobtrusive, the Presbyterians were slapdash, extravagant, publicity-
conscious, and highly visible. Blackburn devoted much of his time to adver-
tising his own work, and most of what we know of his schools survives in
his own colorful, self-congratulatory, optimistic, and dramatic fund-raising
publicity. A kind of pious Davey Crockett, Blackburn promised the
Cherokees more than he could deliver. He had too many irons in the fire.
While he had the audacity to ask for, and obtain, the first government

funding for missions among the Cherokees, he never established the economic base to fulfill his grandiose schemes. Missions to the Indians proved more difficult and more expensive than anyone had imagined.

Blackburn found the Cherokees as cautious toward his initial offer of help in 1803 as they had been toward the Moravians' offer in 1799. Colonel Return J. Meigs, the federal agent, attributed this to the Cherokees' traditionalism, which he described as "timidity" toward rapid change. "The Cherokees are extremely jealous of their Customs," Meigs noted, "which have descended down to them from their ancestors from time immemorial."[1] To counter this conservatism, Meigs always worked closely with the "forward-looking" mixed bloods and intermarried whites in the nation.[2] Daniel Ross, a white trader who had married a mixed-blood Cherokee in 1786 and raised his children as whites, was trying in 1803 to persuade the Council to permit him and his friends at Chattanooga to hire a private tutor to start a school there. (The Cherokee Council had to license any white who sought residence in the nation unless he married a Cherokee.) Ross suggested to Meigs that the fear of mission schools in the Council could best be overcome by deviousness: "I now find," Ross wrote early in October 1803, "the chiefs have hesitated in the admission of school education in the Nation. I take the liberty to suggest the probability of introducing the scheme although the Chiefs should be against it; that is, let one or two reputable teachers slip in, one to this quarter (if thought expedient) and others to Hiwassee or Oostenali, and make a beginning. They will find their school to increase [as white and mixed-blood parents seek their children's improvement] although the Chiefs may not choose to send their children."[3] Eventually the chiefs would have to come around. "At first the Indians could not bear the idea of planting cotton, spinning, and weaving, etc.," Ross noted, "Tho' they now see the utility of it."

Despite Ross's doubts, the Council agreed to Blackburn's impressive proposals in October 1803, saying, "We approve a school being established in our nation under the superintendence of the Rev'd Mr. Blackburn and hope much good will [be] done by it to our people."[4] As with the Moravians, their approval was only of a trial: "Two years are allowed in the first place that we may have opportunity to see what progress our Children make." They instructed Blackburn to locate his first school on the Hiwassee River in eastern Tennessee because there were sufficient families there with children to fill it. Blackburn later said (in order to play up his struggle against

1. R. J. Meigs to Valentine Geiger, June 6, 1806, BIA, M-208.

2. Meigs to Dearborn, July 27, 1805, BIA, M-208.

3. Daniel Ross to R. J. Meigs, October 10, 1803, BIA, M-208. For Daniel Ross, the father of John Ross, see Gary Moulton, *John Ross: Cherokee Chief* (Athens: University of Georgia Press, 1978), pp. 5–7. In 1809 there were 113 whitemen like Ross among the Cherokees, according to a census taken by Meigs, but there were probably ten times as many children and grandchildren of such mixed marriages.

4. Chief Glass to R. J. Meigs, October 21, 1803, BIA, M-208.

adversity) that they chose to locate him "in a part of the nation most unlikely
to be civilized," but that was untrue.[5] He found a great many more children
eager to come to his school than his first teacher could manage and many of
them already spoke some English.

Born in 1772, Blackburn had come to eastern Tennessee with his uncle
in 1787. Converted that same year, he studied for the ministry and was
licensed to preach in 1792. The Cherokees were still at war in that region,
and for two years Blackburn served as a militia chaplain. After peace came in
1794, he settled as pastor of two small churches, one in Eusebia, the other in
Maryville, Tennessee. He married and lived in Maryville, a town only a few
miles north of the Cherokee border. His congregations experienced a great
religious revival in 1800, during which 550 persons were added to his two
churches. The enthusiasm for soul winning led Blackburn to consider starting a mission to the Cherokees. His parishioners being too poor to support
the venture, Blackburn found the funds elsewhere. In the spring of 1803 he
persuaded the Presbyterian General Assembly to grant him $200 and a salary
of $33.33 a month to oversee the project. With this official endorsement, he
visited President Jefferson, who instructed Colonel Meigs to provide
$200−300 worth of assistance through the Indian funds at the agency.
Finally, Blackburn sought private donors in the East, who contributed
another $430. With these sums in hand, he approached the chiefs in the
summer of 1803, just as they were about to expel the Moravians.[6] Though
cautious at first, as Daniel Ross noted, the Cherokees decided in October to
see what he could do.

Meigs used the funds Jefferson had authorized for Blackburn to hire a
carpenter to build a boys' dormitory, a dining hall, and a house for the
schoolmaster and his wife large enough to house female students who lived at
a distance. While Blackburn had been wiser than the Moravians in offering
to establish a number of schools, all of which would provide free room,
board, and clothing, he was not interested, as the Moravians were, in starting
a model farm or a Christian enclave. Aware that he would have an attendance problem when students found the classes too confining and frustrating,
Blackburn made an agreement "with the Chiefs that if any of the children
should leave the school without permission [of the schoolmaster] or, if
permitted to go home, would stay ten days longer than allowed, without a
reasonable excuse, they should forfeit the clothing I have given them." If the
chiefs did not get the clothing back to Blackburn, they agreed "at the
distribution of the next annuity, I should have a right to deduct the amount
from the dividend of such Chief, to be applied to the use of the school."[7] If

5. *The Panoplist* 3: 85.
6. For Blackburn, see Dorothy C. Bass, "Gideon Blackburn's Mission to the
Cherokees," and V. M. Queener, "Gideon Blackburn," *East Tennessee Historical Society,
Publications* 6 (1934): 12–28.
7. *The Panoplist* 3: 85, and Jonathan Blacke to R. J. Meigs, February 13, 1804, BIA,
M-208. The "dividend" was the proportion of the annuity allotted by Meigs to each town on the
basis of its population.

the Cherokee Council had continued to play such a supervisory role in mission education, it might have given more stability and continuity to the schools, but they had too much else on their hands.

Blackburn's first school opened late in February 1804, nine months before the Moravian school at Springplace admitted its first boarders. Jonathan Blacke, a young schoolmaster and Presbyterian layman from Tennessee, and his wife were in charge. They started with eleven students (aged eight to twelve) but regular attendance soon grew to between twenty and twenty-five. Blacke was dedicated to his task of inculcating education and Christianization at the same time. His wife threw herself into the work, making clothing for all the children, cooking and managing the girls' dormitory in her home. Meigs provided blankets for the children from the government factory. Blacke supervised the boys' dormitory and conducted the one-room school with the aid of the bilingual students. Gideon Blackburn devoted his time to his own churches and to raising funds. He published regular accounts of the school in a number of religious periodicals and appeared at the school once or twice a year to conduct public exercises in which the children displayed their progress and were awarded prizes. On such occasions he made every effort to have important personages, such as Governor John Sevier of Tennessee and the federal agent, attend and solicited favorable testimonials from them. Once he arranged to march his scholars before a council of chiefs and federal commissioners who were negotiating a treaty in order to show the large throng their achievements in recitation and singing.

In March 1806, Blackburn hired a second schoolmaster, Robert Denham (later replaced by Daniel Bayles), and started a second school on Sale Creek, twenty miles south of the Hiwassee school.[8] Lacking funds to build a dormitory and dining facilities here, Blackburn made arrangements to board the students at the home of Richard Fields, a whiteman married to a Cherokee.[9] Fields enrolled five of his own children in the school, which soon had about the same number as that at Hiwassee. Blackburn later claimed that in six years, from 1804, his school taught 400−500 Cherokee children to read and write. The claim was an exaggeration; many of those were already familiar with English when they entered his schools. One pupil, Nancy Fields, a daughter of Richard, stated that of the nineteen boys and twelve girls enrolled at the Sale Creek school, all of them previously had known some English.[10] Missionary reports state that it took three to four years of regular attendance for a Cherokee child to master the rudiments of

8. Report of Sale Creek School, October 31, 1806, OSW, M-222, #0757. According to this report the school opened March 25, 1806.

9. Bass, "Blackburn's Mission," p. 214.

10. The claim of 400–500 Cherokees taught to read, write, and cipher is given in Queener, "Gideon Blackburn," p. 22, but the schools averaged only 25 students each per year, one for seven years and one for five. In addition, many of these same students returned for two to four years. A more judicious estimate would be that Blackburn helped 100 to 150 Cherokee students of mixed ancestry to improve their skills in reading, writing, and arithmetic.

reading and writing English. It seems unlikely that many of Blackburn's pupils attended that persistently. In any case, it is evident that students of mixed ancestry predominated. Charles Hicks, who later became one of the principal chiefs of the nation, said in 1819, after twenty years of personal knowledge of mission schools, that few of the Cherokees (even those of mixed ancestry) ever learned to be fluently bilingual. Those of mixed ancestry who attended schools gave up the use of Cherokee; fullbloods who spoke good Cherokee seldom spoke good English. "If a native [Cherokee] speaks good English," Hicks said, "then it is certain that he speaks broken Cherokee and similarly, the reverse."[11] Because missionary schools preferred children who already knew some English (in order that they might help the teachers with non-English-speaking students) the numerical predominance of the mixed bloods was evident in every mission school.

Blackburn's reports indicate that boys outnumbered girls at his schools three to one. Parents sent their sons, Blackburn reported, primarily to master the linguistic and mathematical skills needed to help their fathers in trading with whites. The girls who attended were trained to be proper housewives for such ambitious young men and came from the wealthier mixed-blood families. Cherokee students of fullblood parents found schooling extremely difficult. Their attendance was sporadic, and they frequently dropped out after a few months because they made such slow progress. Blackburn employed no interpreters, nor did the Moravians.

Although Blackburn's teachers were not ministers, they nevertheless permeated their teaching with Christian doctrine and piety. A Moravian who visited the Presbyterian school at Hiwassee in 1807 described Jonathan Blacke as a "kind man who really loves Jesus and who makes it his business with his whole heart to have the Indian children come to know the Savior."[12] Blacke's students began and ended the day with prayer and the singing of hymns. They were required to attend religious services on the Sabbath; they learned to read from the Bible and religious tracts; they had to memorize texts of Scripture and to recite the Shorter Catechism of the Westminster Confession of Faith. "My design," Blackburn wrote, "was to introduce Christianity as the young mind should be capable of receiving it."[13] He placed considerable emphasis on teaching hymns because he found that the Cherokees had good voices and loved to sing. "Music," he remarked, "has a remarkable tendency to *soften* the savage mind."[14]

In addition, the teachers sought the moral and social renovation of every aspect of "savage" life, including teaching "the etiquette of the table." The Hiwassee school, Blackburn said, was "an institution designed not only

11. Springplace Conference, 1819, p. 53.
12. John Gambold to Benzien, May 5, 1807, and to Reichel, May 6, 1807, MAS.
13. *The Panoplist* 3: 85.
14. Ibid. The hymns were from "Dr. Watts Divine Songs and Rippons' selection and other compositions."

to rescue the rising race from savage manners but also to light up beacons by which the parents might gradually be conducted into the same field of improvement."[15] Blackburn would disperse Christianity where the Moravians wished to concentrate it. "As soon as they are civilized," he said, "their way will be opened for the establishment of regular religious society" in those areas of the nation where the educated young Cherokees went to live and spread the message.[16]

Learning by rote was the chief method of instruction, and many of the children probably memorized the sounds of English words before they comprehended their meanings. A letter from a group of the students to Blackburn in 1807 provides a good summary of their average day at the school as well as of their growing awareness of the Christian concepts of hell, sin, guilt, and damnation, topics heavily stressed in the Calvinistic theology of the Presbyterian church:

> The moment we open our eyes in the morning we bless and thank God we did not open them in that hell which we now read of in the Bible; which we knew nothing about until we came to your school; but thought before that hell was no other place than a bad country where bad people were sent by the Great Spirit after death.[17] We then all go to our knees and say our prayers, one after the other. After this we all together sing a hymn of praises to that blessed Jesus who, as we can now all read, died for us; then attend to public prayer; then we read over our spelling lessons three times; afterwards repeat the same to our master off the book; then until noon we read the Bible and other history; then we get a spelling lesson and repeat it as before, off the book; read our lessons in the above way until the evening, then get a spelling lesson and say it off the book to our master; afterwards all sing a hymn of praises to our ever blessed Redeemer and attend to public prayer; then . . . we generally read the Shorter Catechism once over . . . then attend to public prayer; afterwards, before we lay down . . . we all go to our knees and pray, all one after the other, and so go to rest.[18]

Although Meigs considered Blackburn's training inferior to the painstaking instruction given by the Moravians, the Moravian missionary Gottlieb Byhan, after visiting Blackburn's school, wrote, "I found the school at Hiwassee better than it had been represented to us."[19] Byhan's description of one of the public performances conducted by Blackburn in 1805 noted that there were fourteen scholars who performed, eleven male and three female:

15. Ibid.

16. *The Panoplist* 4: 325.

17. For sacred myths about "the Darkening Land in the West," which the Cherokees considered the land of wicked spirits, see Mooney, *Myths*, pp. 248, 254, 297, 436–38.

18. *The Evangelical Intelligencer*, 4: 43. Letters ostensibly written by children in mission schools were probably carefully supervised by mission teachers because they were usually designed for publication in religious journals. They probably reflect what the mission teacher hoped the children were thinking as much as the actual thoughts of the writer.

19. Springplace Diary, November 15, 1807, and Gottlieb Byhan to Benzien, April 7, 1805, MAS.

"Toward 9 o'clock Mr. Blackburn kept a morning prayer. . . . Then Mr. Black kept school, after which the Children got their breakfast consisting of meat, bread and sour hominy which diet they have also for dinner and supper." After breakfast Blackburn tested each student's progress. To a young mixed-blood student named Fox Taylor he gave a medal worth two dollars. "The rest received money, knives, beads, and the like" for their performances. Then Blackburn preached for an hour on "man's fall and perdition and how they may come again into favor with God."[20]

Blackburn also endeavored to spread the word of God among the parents who came to watch the children perform. Gottlieb Byhan was present one evening when Blackburn spoke at length with the parents of one of his pupils about the fall and perdition of man and about the destruction of the Flood. "To which Kotaquaskey's wife replied, 'What a pity that all men were not made good from the beginning.' "[21]

The Moravian missionary also noted that Blackburn's schoolmaster kept very rigid discipline in the classroom: "During school no one dare look off from his book nor talk to his neighbor." Infractions of discipline were punished in various ways, including whipping, as in white schools. Nevertheless, many Cherokee parents were well pleased with Blackburn's efforts. From 1805 to 1810 his schools taught the basics of reading, writing, and arithmetic to thirty to forty students per year while Blackburn himself valiantly toured the eastern and southern states, speaking at churches and benevolent societies to raise funds to supplement the money provided by his denomination and the federal government.

The Moravian boarding school finally opened in November 1804. The missionaries were disappointed to discover that three of the first four students sent to them were the nephews of fullblood chiefs (Chulcoah, Five Killer, and Sour Mush) and that "one of them only can speak English which renders their progress in learning but slow."[22] More discouraging, the fullblood students were no help in teaching Cherokee to the missionaries. By February 1805, the missionaries reported, "They have gone through several times the little spelling book and are able to pronounce small words. . . . [E]ach of them has learned a verse [of a hymn] which at Christmas they were able to sing with us. Since that time we also sing with them a verse before and after meals as also before and after school."[23] In addition to the four boys who boarded at the mission school, they taught three or four other children, some of them girls, who boarded with James Vann.

Because they had a model farm, the Moravians included vocational training in their curriculum. The girls learned sewing, household chores, how to make butter and cheese, how to raise vegetables and care for chick-

20. Gottlieb Byhan to Benzien, April 7, 1805, MAS.
21. Ibid.
22. Jacob Wohlfahrt to Benzien, February 3, 1805, MAS.
23. Ibid.

ens. The boys helped the missionaries in ploughing, cultivating, and caring for the livestock, and did some carpentry. On the theory that the Devil found work for idle fingers, the missionaries kept the children busy from sunrise to bedtime. They were convinced that a basic cause of Cherokee poverty was their inveterate laziness, especially of the males. "I fully agree with you," wrote the Reverend John Gambold in 1809, "that where the Indians are not cured from their idleness, which is admired in their nations and deeply engrained in their nature, things must remain precarious for Christianity." On the other hand, "following Jesus and laziness are incompatible."[24] Consequently, "we make it our responsibility to inculcate in the children entrusted to us, in every way possible, the joy in work and diligence and on the other hand to present to them idleness in all its ugliness and to urge them as much as feasible to all kinds of handwork." Unfortunately, "we have, however, not been able to get very far with it." The children did not like the manual labor imposed on them, and their parents felt that the missionaries were exploiting their children. It was not the Cherokee custom to force children to work. Cultivating fields, formerly done by the women of the tribe, was now done in wealthy Cherokee families (such as these pupils came from) by black slaves. One parent, suspecting that the missionaries were working his son so hard because they were short of labor, offered to provide them with a slave to do his son's work. "When some one would wish to go so far as to put a 'free-born Indian' to work against his will," John Gambold said with bitter sarcasm, "and even insist on his continuing it when he no longer wants to do it or perhaps is a little tired—and would want to use measures to compel him" to keep at it, "such a person would soon lose the good-will of the Indian, without which it isn't very comfortable to live in their country."[25] The uncles and parents who brought their children to school "have more than once expressed the thought that they wished the children might learn not only reading and writing but also all kinds of handcrafts," but they did not want them simply working in the fields and barns.

The difference between the Presbyterian schools (with their concentration upon classroom learning) and the Moravian schools (which also included vocational training in "the agricultural and domestic arts") is evident in this description of an average day at the Moravian school written by John Gambold in 1809:

> In order to present to you a little more clearly the methods used by us up to now in order to advance industry, I will describe to you our daily routine. In our dwelling where the school is kept, they take turns by the week bringing in

24. John Gambold to Benzien, August 21, 1809, MAS. It is not clear whether Gambold means by "engrained in their nature" that the Indians were biologically lazy (and only the miracle of conversion could alter that nature) or whether he simply means that it was strongly engrained by habit and culture. Probably he meant the latter.
25. Ibid.

water, as they do also in their own house (the dormitory). Then my wife insists that they get every morning and evening a big basket full of grass, purslane, etc. for the pigs in the pen, and at times also for the others. . . . If she has to water the plants [in the truck garden] during dry weather, then she appoints the children for carrying water and also has a similar shift weekly for the washing. At every milking, two are appointed to hold the calves [away from their mothers]. . . . They have to shell corn needed for bread and take it to the mill, and then to get flour; to ride the horses to water, and also to give the pigs their daily portion of corn. We always take them along to help when we plant the welschcorn as well as for all the harvesting. . . . We don't get any wood for their dwelling but insist that they themselves cut it in the bush and bring it in. . . . [W]e give them a piece along the border of our yard, each one a plot, where they can plant corn, potatoes, melons or whatever [for their own use]. . . . [T]hey have to work during the summer themselves [on their patch]. They also have laid out a small flower garden near their house. . . . During the long winter evening we gave them cotton to pick [seeds from]. . . . [W]e cannot completely forbid the children the hunting to which they are born and which is necessary for their future well-being . . . [so my wife urges them] between their school hours to be very diligent with their bow and arrow and to shoot some birds with which she can feed her cats. . . . From this description of our daily routine and our method of treating the children, you see that we are seriously engaged to destroy, as much as lies in us, this pillow for Satan on which he lulls the people to sleep to their eternal destruction, namely, idleness.[26]

The Moravian missionary letters are filled with stories of the mischief their pupils got into, some of it childish impulse and some apparently calculated revenge or rebellion. One stole small items and sold them to passing Indians. Another took a gun and shot two of the mission's pigs. A third "goes into the bush and to the Negro children [Vann's slaves] from whom he learns the most filthy language which he then brings to the others and even writes on their slates."[27] Fearing punishment, they were often caught telling lies. The worst offense was running off to Vann's trading post, where there was always whiskey or rum available. Several returned to the school slightly tipsy and one terribly sick. More commonly, in an effort to sustain their own cultural traditions, they ran away to attend ballplays or tribal dances. "Chulcoah (probably at their request) promised to take them along to the Green Corn Dance . . . which doesn't sit well with us," wrote the missionaries, "but we don't know how to prevent it."[28]

Like the Presbyterians, the Moravians punished stealing and other "naughtiness" by scolding, denial of treats, extra chores, and whippings. Sometimes rather than whip a child themselves, they called James Vann and he "conferred a bit with him [the thief] with the interpretation of the Cow

26. Ibid.
27. Anna Gambold to Mamma Benzien, April 22, 1806, MAS.
28. John Gambold to Reigel, August 6, 1806, MAS.

Hide." However, the thieving student simply laughed afterward. It was not good form to admit that physical punishment hurt. "I wish we were rid of him," said the frustrated missionary.[29]

Parents did not agree with the missionary opposition to student attendance at ballplays, dances, and festivals. They often came to the school themselves to take their children to such traditional observances. This was a severe trial for the missionaries and to the Moravians gave further proof that only the children of converts should be given schooling. Missionary letters reflected frequent exasperation and frustration. The Moravians laid part of the blame for their pupils' insubordination upon James Vann, who seemed to enjoy perverting them and enticing them to his trading post.[30] But at bottom the missionaries blamed the students for their inability to resist temptation. They seemed unaware of the concerted efforts by the students to resist total acculturation.

Between 1804 and 1810 the Moravians taught a total of about eight students per year, some of whom stayed three or four years, some of whom lasted barely a month. "It is very painful to us," said Gambold, "that the children are taken away from us often when they are just beginning to learn something of what we tell them of our and their Savior."[31] Considering that as many as 3,000 to 4,000 children in the nation were of school age each year, the Moravians and Presbyterians were scratching the surface of educational needs.

One great stumbling block was the language barrier. Blackburn's teachers did not even try to learn Cherokee; the Moravians never found anyone to tutor them in it. Both missions admitted that bilingual children were of little help. As one Moravian noted, the children of mixed parents "know only [a] little English so that they do not understand rightly what we ask of them."[32] "A few weeks ago an Indian woman came here and offered for sale a small cake of brown sugar. We asked her through our [student] George what she wanted for it, and he told us that she wanted turnips." This was surprising, and they asked an older female student to corroborate it. "It was found that she wanted a dollar for her sugar. Such misunderstandings occur often with them, so that our hopes of learning something [of the language] from them have thus far been disappointed."[33]

Cherokee proved to be a far more complex language than the missionaries had expected. Furthermore, the Moravians discovered that within the nation "there are various dialects so totally different from each other that they sound like different languages."[34] When they tried to speak in

29. John Gambold to Reichel, September 28, 1806, MAS.
30. John Gambold to Reichel, July 30, 1808, MAS.
31. John Gambold to Reichel, December 28, 1806, MAS.
32. John Gambold to Reigel, January 19, 1806, MAS.
33. John Gambold to Reichel, March 23, 1806, MAS.
34. Henry Clauder to John G. Herman, April [n.d.] 1830, MAB.

Cherokee they found "that some of the words and syllables are pronounced through one's nose, some get stuck in one's throat; frequently it is sufficient to have the tongue touch the gums or the lips lightly. Their tones are often such that no possible combination of our vowels can produce the desired sound."[35] Even those who could speak Cherokee and English could not tell them how Cherokee words could be written in English letters. In addition, "the length or the shortness of the syllables has a certain meaning; if one of the syllables is drawn out, the meaning is changed; should the same syllable be drawn out even more, the word gets still another meaning."[36] "The slightest variation of accent changes the signification entirely."[37]

Explaining to their mission board why they were not making more rapid progress in mastering the Cherokee language, the Moravians insisted that virtually no adult white had ever been able to learn the language so as to speak it fluently. Charles Hicks, an able interpreter, told the Moravians that "with a single exception, he has never heard any white man who is not a native of the country, speak the Cherokee language perfectly." The exception was "John McDonald, who in his youth spent a number of years among the Cherokee scarcely having seen a white man."[38] When the Moravians went to McDonald in 1809 and asked him to provide them with translations of some important paragraphs of Christian doctrine, he told them it was impossible. "He assured us," they reported, "that for matters of that nature neither words nor expressions are available in this language."[39] They were appalled to find that the Cherokees had no words that could represent the concepts of sin, repentance, forgiveness, grace, redemption, perdition, damnation. "How sad it is that the Cherokee language has no words for matters which are not related to the daily life and walk of the Indians." In their opinion the fault lay with the Cherokees for "their word-poor language."[40] No Moravian missionary ever learned to speak Cherokee, though some of them lived in the nation for twenty-five years. They concluded, "their Language cannot be attained by Adults and when attained is incapable of conveying any Idea beyond the sphere of the senses; there seems to be no other way left by which the Spiritual or Temporal Good of these People can be promoted than by teaching them in our Language."[41]

35. Springplace Conference, 1819, p. 52.

36. Ibid.

37. Henry Clauder to John G. Herman, April [n.d.] 1830, MAB. Neither Blackburn nor any of his teachers refer to linguistic problems because they did not try to learn Cherokee. For some of the problems of the Cherokee language, see *New Echota Letters*, ed. Jack and Anna Kilpatrick, and *The Shadow of Sequoyah*, ed. Jack and Anna Kilpatrick (Norman: University of Oklahoma Press, 1965).

38. Springplace Conference, 1819, p. 52.

39. John Gambold to Benzien, November 5, 1809, MAS.

40. Springplace Diary, July 6, 1807. After living for twenty years among the Cherokees, Gambold said, "I have attained so little of the language that I can hardly purchase a Venison from an Indian without an interpreter." John Gambold to Schulz, September 1, 1824, MAS.

41. John Gambold to Thomas L. McKenney, January 7, 1817, MAS.

The Moravians also blamed the Cherokee language for the difficulty they encountered in identifying the parents of their students under the matrilineal clan system of relationships. The Cherokee language was precisely worded to explain all of the personal relationships within the clan system, but because the missionaries thought in terms of a nuclear family with patrilineal relationships and because they found polygamy and the loose marriage—divorce practices of the Cherokees repugnant they claimed to be unable to discover who the true parents of many of their students were (the only true parents by their standards being the man who begat and the mother who bore a child). A student who could not make clear to the missionaries precisely who his father and mother were in these terms was made to feel shame and disgrace, or at best, gross ignorance. "Among the Cherokees not only is polygamy very much in vogue," said Gambold, "but the marriage knot is tied so loosely among them that it is often untied and then knotted again in a different way. In addition to that problem, is that of the Cherokee language which is so poor in words and expressions that all close relationship are indicated with one noun." The term *father* might apply to many different relatives:

> for example, father, step-father, father's brother, mother's brother and more than one degree of close relationship are called 'Father,' and all the female relatives are called 'Mother,' and similarly the relatives of the grand-parents are all called grand-father and grand-mother. Thus we have already learned to know two fathers and three or four mothers of our Johnny, and it is only with very great difficulty that we can find out which among all these are really his actual parents, and still I do not want to answer for the correctness of the information; for since it happens not infrequently that the child of a repudiated or an abandoned wife is taken and reared by close or distant relatives as their child, there are cases when an Indian himself does not know whom he has to thank for his existence.[42]

One of the advantages of the matrilineal system (which was lost on the missionaries) was that children were never really orphaned or parentless.

Cherokees of course had similar difficulties with English customs and the English language, but apparently they were better linguists since many of them did come to master the whiteman's language. At first, however, the schoolchildren memorized the sounds of words before they comprehended their meanings. Speaking of their singing hymns, one Moravian wrote that doubtless God is "graciously pleased with the praise of these little brown ones who indeed at this time understand very little of that which they sing."[43] The slowness with which the Cherokees learned to read and speak English was attributed correctly by the missionaries to the fact that "they are not yet accustomed to think in it." After five years of schooling, Gambold reported,

42. John Gambold to Reichel, May 22, 1809, MAS. In Cherokee the word for "husband" signified, "the man I am living with."
43. John Gambold to Reichel, December 28, 1806, MAS.

some students "are still so backward in the English language that they never converse with each other in that language." (Probably this was another indication of conscious resistance to acculturation.) The mother of one pupil, Margaret Vann (James Vann's wife), told the Moravians that "she believes that the English language would have to be introduced completely among her people if they are to be given an understanding of holy things and especially of the reconciliation through Jesus because in their language the words are entirely lacking to express even in a limited way this truth."[44] Mrs. Vann, though her father was white and her mother Cherokee and her husband bilingual, was unable to help the missionaries translate their catechism into Cherokee. She tried but soon gave up because "she knew how to translate only a few of all" the words in the text, and "with all the rest she attested that not only the expression but the concept was wholly unknown to the Cherokees; for instance, the word forgiveness . . . is completely unknown among the Indians and . . . therefore there is no word to be found in their language by which this idea could be expressed." When friends or relatives brought about a reconciliation between two persons who had quarreled, they did not forgive each other, Mrs. Vann told the missionaries; they said, "We will drink whiskey together and no longer speak of what has happened." "How something like that could be applied to the forgiveness of sin," said the literal-minded missionaries, "is really not clear to me." So Gambold decried again "the wretched Cherokee language."[45] Behind the "wretched language," the missionaries believed, lay wretched ideas and habits; civilization and Christianization required the replacement of the Indians' ways of thought by Anglo-American ways of thought. Only the English language could convey truth.

Because most intermarried whites and Cherokees of mixed ancestry spoke Cherokee poorly, if at all, many of them were ready, like Margaret Vann, to confirm the missionaries' preconceptions about its uselessness. By 1808 the Moravians confessed that they were not going to bother to learn it. Anna Gambold, writing to a friend in December 1808, said that when she brought up the question of learning Cherokee, "My dear husband often said to me, 'Nothing is going to come of that; just be reconciled to it.' "[46] "It is possible," Mrs. Gambold said, "to remember individual words with effort when one strains the ears and with such we get along when we do business with the Indians, but the connecting words are missing; for the most part they consist of tones which one can neither write down nor imitate. And the Indians don't always understand each other in everything."

After seven years of futile evangelistic effort, the Moravians began to think that education might have to precede Christianization despite the miraculous powers of the Holy Spirit. "It has often occurred to me," wrote

44. John Gambold to Reichel, May 22, 1809, MAS.
45. Ibid.
46. Anna Gambold to Reichel, December 3, 1808, MAS.

one of them in 1806, "whether it may not go with this Nation as it did with the Hottentots, who had first to learn Hollandish in order to be able to hear and understand the message of the Cross for their salvation. All the hopes which we had up to now to take advantage of this or that person in [learning] the Cherokee language have been disappointed."[47] The missionaries could not learn to think in Cherokee so it was up to the Cherokees to learn to think in English.

Gideon Blackburn, who never troubled his head about the language problem because he expected the Cherokees to come to Christianization through learning English, nevertheless remained optimistic about converting the nation. For him hope lay in his young bilingual students, who would spread the message to their people. "The prospects of a future day opening the Gospel fully on this nation are apparent," he wrote in 1805; "especially the ground to hope that before long their own children will be able (and, I hope, willing) to preach Jesus, lead to this expectation." He already saw signs of this. "On the morning I last left the school, the two more forward boys, whom I used as interpreters, were bathed in tears under a sense of their sin; the same emotion has been observed at other times during morning and evening services. Should they get religion, they will be qualified to have easy access to the conscience of their friends."[48] Two years later he wrote, "Many of the important ideas necessary to the existence of religion are spreading through the nation not only by our particular instruction but by the observation of the children in their intercourse with their parents which is certainly the surest and most effectual method to gain their attention to truth."[49] On occasion the Moravians expressed a similar hope: "Our [pupil] George wrote a letter [in English] to his mother in which he also told her something about our Creator and Redeemer. The Chief [Bark] gave this letter to Mr. Charles Hicks who, surrounded by chiefs, had it read aloud at Vann's and translated it. . . . Doesn't that mean, dear Brother, that the Gospel was preached? O, yes. . . . The young people will do it. It is the children who are to proclaim the death of the Lord. . . . In these bad times the Lord will probably bring in His Kingdom through their children . . . even though the adults have no desire for it."[50]

Because there was as yet no way of writing Cherokee and since the children of the mission school were supposed to learn English, the Moravians eventually came to accept Blackburn's view that English-speaking Cherokees would be the means of converting the nation (assuming they were bilingual). "Indeed," wrote Gambold in 1809, "on the whole we can have hope only from those who understand some English, but when these are converted to the Lord, He will surely prepare some from among them as

47. John Gambold to Reichel, September 28, 1806, MAS.
48. *The Evangelical Intelligencer*, 1: 357.
49. *The Evangelical Intelligencer*, 3: 222.
50. John Gambold to Reichel, December 3, 1808, MAS.

'Apostles to their Nation,' or the rest, when they become fearful [and] in the need of comfort, will soon learn English [in order] that they can understand the Words of Life."[51] Fifteen years later, however, Gambold concluded that only when the whole nation understood English would they effectively be Christianized and civilized:

> I have been impressed with an Idea that it is indispensably necessary for their preservation that they should learn our Language and adopt our Laws and Holy Religion. . . . The Study of their language would in a great measure prove but time and Labor lost. . . . [I]t seems desirable that their Language, Customs, Manner of Thinking, etc. should be forgotten. To be brief, my Object, and I trust the object of all other missionaries, has been to rescue the Aboriginal Man himself from the Destruction which awaits his Race, rather than [to rescue] his History, Language, Customs, etc.[52]

The Cherokees who refused to learn English were in all senses irredeemable and doomed.

Blackburn's view that the older generation was probably beyond hope either of education or salvation stemmed not from any belief in Indian racial inferiority but from his conviction that the older Cherokees could not, or would not, give up their old ways of thinking and acting—"their customs and habits." "I look forward," he wrote in 1807, "to the period when the invincible ignorance and obstinacy [of] this nation . . . shall retire . . . before the improved minds of the children shaped by the hand of education. . . . Were the attempt to be made on minds already formed to habit, the case would be desperate, but with the offspring, everything is possible if we can exercise sufficient fortitude and perseverance," and if the Cherokees could be protected from "unprincipled and scape gallows whitemen" who came among them and corrupted them.[53]

The federal agent Return J. Meigs, after watching the missionary efforts for several years, reached a similar conclusion: "The savage character cannot be effaced in the real [fullblood] Indian after he has arrived to manhood."[54] Meigs placed his hope for acculturation in the mixed bloods:

> It is impossible to tell the result of all the exertions to civilize the Indians, but if the plan is to be continued, it appears to me that nothing will contribute more to it than to give as many as our means will permit some knowledge of letters; for those who are advanced in years never can be brought generally to estimate the advantages of becoming civilized; they think that our enjoyments cost more than they are worth. But the children that are growing up, especially those of the mixed blood, and they compose a very considerable part of the whole, may be brought to such a state of improvement as to become an acquisition of useful citizens by being incorporated at no very distant period with some of our State

51. John Gambold to Reichel, July 23, 1809, MAS.
52. John Gambold to Schulz, September 1, 1824, MAS.
53. Gideon Blackburn to R. J. Meigs, November 4, 1807, BIA, M-208.
54. R. J. Meigs to Benjamin Hawkins, February 13, 1805, BIA, M-208.

Governments. . . . But it seems as if the Graver of time had fixed the savage character so deeply in the native [fullblood] Indian, I mean those who have arrived to manhood, that it cannot be effaced; but where the blood is mixed with the whites, in every grade of it, there is an apparent disposition leaning toward civilization, and this disposition is in proportion to its distance from the original stock.[55]

Because the "disposition toward civilization" lay "in proportion" to the amount of white blood in any Indian, Meigs, like Jefferson and Madison, favored intermarriage between Indians and whites as one of the major steps toward their integration into the general population of the United States as citizens. "I encouraged marriages between whitemen and Cherokee women," Meigs wrote proudly in 1808; "I always have and I always will . . . because I conceive that by this measure civilization is faster advanced than in any other way—having considered the whole human race as brothers."[56]

Meigs, like the missionaries, was wrestling here, rather inconsistently, with the fundamental issues of racialism and cultural resistance. If the whole human race were brothers, then better environment and education and not racial intermarriage and blood-mixing were the fastest means to acculturation. Meigs in another place stated this clearly: "It cannot be expected that the adult real Indian will alter his habits" and because "the real Indians still hug the manners and habits of their ancestors and are unwilling to give [up] the pleasures of the shade and idleness" to work in the fields as farmers, "the real Indian will disappear"; on the other hand, the mixed bloods "are almost without exception in favor of improvements and have very much thrown off the savage habits."[57] To be a good American one had to cease to be a good Indian.

The ambivalence is obvious, and it has led Robert Berkhofer to argue that there was in fact little difference between missionary ethnocentrism and racism. Those Indians "favoring Christian civilization," Berkhofer writes, "could not reach the ideal envisaged by the missionaries and their supporters not because of the Indians' desire to retain old customs, but because of American racial attitudes. . . . By discriminating against the aborigine upon the basis of a belief of white cultural superiority, Americans . . . guaranteed the failure of the missionary program."[58] The issue was simply "white intolerance."

The debate over heredity and environment has not yet ended; so it is not surprising that there was confusion about it among the early missionaries and Indian agents. It is curious, for example, that Meigs encouraged marriage

55. Ibid.
56. R. J. Meigs to Chief Chulio and Chief Sour Mush, March 14, 1808, BIA, M-208.
57. R. J. Meigs to Henry Dearborn, July 25, 1805, and August 4, 1805, BIA, M-208.
58. Robert F. Berkhofer, Jr., *Salvation and the Savage*, pp. 159, 7–15, 151–58.

between "whitemen and Cherokee women" but apparently not vice versa.[59] The missionaries, who were more concerned to marry Christians to Christians, may have been less sexist than the federal agents.[60] Neither the agents nor the missionaries accepted the Cherokee traditionalists' reasons for resistance to intermarriage and assimilation; that is, "that they are not derived from the same stock as the white [and] that they are the favorites of the great spirit."[61] This was contrary not only to the Christian view of human history but also to the prevailing scientific theory of environmentalism as the basis of racial variations.[62] Over the years the missionaries gained the respect of the Indians because they did not share the overt racist views of most whites. Still, the fullbloods could not help noting the annoyance of missionaries regarding their slowness to learn English, to adopt white behavior, to become Christians. Missionary favoritism toward mixed bloods who were quick and eager for acculturation was patent. John Gambold noted with pleasure that the desire "to become English" was directly related to the high proportion of white blood among the Cherokees: "The Cherokee Nation is mixed with white people to a considerable degree. The offspring of whites and Indians constitutes a large part of it, and many of these completely resemble whites in color, physiognomy and conduct; yet they are considered by the Cherokees as belonging completely to their Nation. It is no wonder then that just as much English is spoken in this country as Cherokee; moreover, the Nation wishes its young people to become English."[63] Gambold was probably rationalizing his own inability to overcome the language barrier. He greatly exaggerated the number of Cherokees who spoke English just as Meigs greatly exaggerated the proportion who had white ancestry. In part this was because the agent and the missionaries lived in those parts of the nation where there was more intermarriage and in part because the Cherokees they associated with were those who were eager for such association. The fullbloods lived in the mountainous areas of North Carolina and on the southern and western borders near the Chickasaws and Creeks, where the agent seldom traveled and where there were no missionaries until the 1820s. Whenever the missionaries came in contact with the traditionalists, their prejudices against them became obvious. After attending a large council in

59. In the notable case of Clarinda Ellington, a white girl captured by the Cherokees who later married the chief named Shoeboot and bore him several children, Meigs did his best to break up the marriage and return her to her relatives in Tennessee when they finally located her. See Meigs's interview with Clarinda Ellington, October 19, 1803, BIA, M-208.

60. Examples of white Christian women marrying Cherokees were rare, but several are noted in later chapters. These marriages were not acceptable to all missionaries and certainly not to all white Christians. See, for example, Ralph H. Gabriel, *Elias Boudinot*.

61. R. J. Meigs to Benjamin Hawkins, February 13, 1805, BIA, M-208.

62. See William Stanton, *The Leopard's Spots* (Chicago: University of Chicago Press, 1960). As Stanton points out, the environmentalist theory of racial variation was under attack from 1810 onward.

63. John Gambold to Reichel, July 23, 1809, MAS.

1807, one Moravian wrote revealingly: "Many were comically painted in the face with black and red designs and likewise with rings around the eyes. Others had square black spots outlined in red on the cheeks and still others red wreaths over the nose and white rings around the eyes. Their dress was just as funny."[64] The missionaries were similarly frank about their disgust for the tattoos on women's arms, the slit ears of the men, the silver nose and ear ornaments. Blackburn, trying to impress the readers of a missionary journal in 1807 with the progress of Christianity resulting from his schools, offered the following comparison between his neat, pious students and their wild heathen friends and relatives:

> Figure, my dear friend, to yourself a lofty grove, lately the haunt of beasts of prey or resounding with the war whoop of the untamed savage. . . . But what do I hear? it is music . . . sweet music, lisped by the young Cherokees [from the mission]. . . . [T]he dear little Indian children (near twenty) marched in Indian file, singing with almost angelic sweetness. . . . [H]ere, the savage taken from the filth of the smoky hut, from the naked and untamed state of the heathen, and from the idols of the pagan world, is brought to the habits and manners of civilized life.[65]

Always the missionaries exalted their own work by contrasting the clean-cut Christian Indian with the filthy, untamed savage. By viewing the Cherokees as infants in the development of the human race, the missionaries paternalistically romanticized the relationship of red and white. White benevolent fathers would lift these children of the forest up to the ranks of "rational men." An official of the War Department once asked John Gambold to compare the task of transforming the native American into a useful citizen with the task of assimilating the foreign-born European immigrants pouring into the new nation. Gambold unhesitatingly answered that the former task was harder and more deserving of government support: "Certainly it is a greater work to *form* a Man than to receive one; [greater] to transform savage Nations into rational and useful members of Society than to admit—without any labor or expense on our Part [as Americans]—such as have already been formed elsewhere."[66] The European immigrant was a mature, civilized man, even though he might speak French or German; and even though he might be a Roman Catholic or a deist, he came from a Christian environment. The European could read and write; he understood the ideals and ethics of Christianity and the arts of civilization. But the Indian was not yet "human" in anything but biological form. The missionary had to start from zero to "form a man" out of an aborigine.

The Cherokees' responses to this persistent denigration were complex. Some came to believe the missionaries and felt themselves to be backward and inferior. Some denied the implication, said the issue was one of differ-

64. Springplace Diary, October 24, 1807, MAS.
65. *The Evangelical Intelligencer*, 4: 41–42.
66. John Gambold to Thomas L. McKenney, January 7, 1817, MAS.

ence not rank, and advocated cultural separatism. Some simply tried harder to prove they were innately able to do anything that whites could do. Comparatively few had much direct contact with missionaries in the first two decades of the nineteenth century. The Moravians and Presbyterians noted disconsolately that year after year went by with no conversions to Christianity.

Return J. Meigs, noting the rapid expansion of the white population in the west and the slow progress of Cherokee acculturation (by his standards), began after 1807 to press for a different policy toward "the Indian question." His alternative sprang from Jefferson's suggestion at the time of the Louisiana Purchase in 1803. Perhaps the Indians east of the Mississippi would be willing to exchange their present territory for an equal amount west of the Mississippi.[67] This would get around the constant friction between Indians and unruly white frontiersmen pressing into their land and would provide the "backward" Indians with more time to undergo the process of acculturation. For the more "progressive" Indians, who were already good farmers, Meigs proposed that they be allowed to remain on their farmstead, which would be granted them in fee simple along with citizenship in the state where they were located. Those not yet capable of assuming citizenship but unwilling to move west would be consolidated onto a smaller tract than they presently had and, under the guidance of white supervisors, be given simple republican laws and prepared for citizenship. Meigs assumed that the great bulk of the eastern Indians would prefer to go west, thus freeing at once millions of acres for white settlement. Agents and missionaries would immediately go west to continue the tutelage of the backward Indians on the tracts the government assigned to them. This was the germ of the reservation system adopted after 1839.

Meigs's effort to implement this plan among the Cherokees in the years 1807 – 09 was fully supported by Jefferson and his secretary of war, Henry Dearborn. It also received the support of many of the leading chiefs in the Lower Towns. But it was bitterly opposed by the vast majority of Cherokees and it plunged the nation into a political crisis in which the missionaries were unable to remain neutral. Even before this removal crisis reached its peak in the winter of 1808/09, Blackburn had been sucked into the bitter factionalism dividing the nation. His lack of neutrality became evident with the assassination of Doublehead in 1807. Blackburn had become an admirer of Doublehead, the leader of the Lower Town faction, and when he was assassinated by three men appointed by the chiefs of the Upper Towns in February 1807, Blackburn could not help expressing his disapproval. The assassination resulted from the discovery of secret treaty clauses rewarding Doublehead for supporting the cession of over ten million acres of Cherokee

67. See Annie H. Abel, "Proposals for an Indian State," and W. G. McLoughlin, "Thomas Jefferson and the Beginning of Cherokee Nationalism," *William and Mary Quarterly*, 3d ser., 32 (October 1975): 547–80.

land to the government in 1805—06. The leading opponents of Doublehead were James Vann, Charles Hicks, and the Ridge, major chiefs of the Upper Town faction. The Moravian missionaries, because of their close association with Vann and Hicks, came under suspicion from the War Department as opponents of Meigs's removal plan. Vann's faction, "the anti-government faction," according to Meigs (who had always found Doublehead easy to do business with), hoped that Doublehead's assassination would end the secret dealings between Meigs and the Lower Town chiefs. Instead it merely drove Doublehead's friends into making the final agreement with Meigs to exchange land in the east for land in the west. This secret agreement became known to the Upper Towns in November 1808, when Meigs led a delegation of chiefs to meet with Jefferson, ostensibly to honor him upon his leaving the presidency. Half of this delegation consisted of chiefs pledged to the exchange and ready to sign a treaty to effect it (behind the backs of the Upper Town delegates).

Blackburn, living close to the government agency, kept himself well informed about what was happening in these years and may even have hoped to profit from speculation in land which the Cherokees would cede in eastern Tennessee. When Doublehead was killed, Blackburn wrote to the secretary of war, calling the murder "a serious loss to the nation." To him it proved that "savage ignorance, rivetted and long practised superstition and the blackest ingratitude are to be encountered in all their horrid form" among those who had perpetrated the deed.[68] By "ingratitude" he meant the failure of the Upper Town faction to accede to the treaties of 1805—06, made with a benevolent government which had done so much to help the Cherokees (including support his mission). Doublehead, Blackburn told Dearborn, "entered more fully into the real interest of the Nation than any Indian in it, and it was because his plans interfered with the selfish designs of Van[n] and his party that he lost his life."

When the assassins in their initial assault on Doublehead merely wounded him, he found refuge in Blackburn's school building at Hiwassee. The assassins found him there the next day and completed their work. Doubtless some Cherokees suspected Blackburn's schoolmaster of having assisted the traitor by trying to hide him. In any case, Blackburn asked the War Department soon after this to let him transfer his school from Hiwassee to an abandoned army fort called Tellico Blockhouse some miles to the north and nearer to the Tennessee—Cherokee border. "This affair occasioned a great shock to my schools," he wrote, "as it was evident that their success would equally destroy the hope of improper gain."[69] He implied that the Upper Town faction was the group seeking "improper gain" and that its leaders were an antimission faction because missionary success would put an

68. Gideon Blackburn to Henry Dearborn, November 7, 1807, OSW, M-211, roll 4, #1144.
69. Ibid.

end to their corruption. "The intestine commotion at this time in the Nation," he continued, "induces me to make the following application" to obtain the old blockhouse, for should "this malicious faction [of Vann's] defeat our design, our buildings are lost without recovery." There is no evidence that the Upper Town faction planned to burn his mission buildings; nevertheless, he felt that military protection for his school was essential. The War Department agreed to let him move to Tellico Blockhouse, where he continued the school. But his problems were just beginning.

Meanwhile, the Moravians, having failed to express their disapproval of Doublehead's assassination, came under suspicion from the agent of being in league with Vann or at least of knowing more about Vann's "rebellion" than they had communicated. "The nearness of Mr. Vann to our station," the missionaries reported to their board, "and his kindness to our missionaries had made an unfavorable impression upon the leaders of the [United States] government as Vann constantly set himself against the rules laid down by government for the Cherokee nation. The secretary of war, Mr. Dearborn, complained that we did not give any information to [the] government about what we were doing."[70] Dearborn apparently expected the missionaries to spy on Vann and to acquaint the government with what the Cherokees in that area were up to. Worse than that, the missionaries said, there was fear "among members of the Government in Washington whether because of our neighborliness and friendly relationship with James Vann we might at the least be misguided [so as] to make common cause with him against the Government."[71]

Blackburn, in return for the annual government subsidy to his school, had made annual reports to the federal government. The Moravians, supporting themselves from their own funds, made no reports. Meigs and Dearborn believed (as Washington and Knox had) that all missionaries should consider themselves agents (eyes and ears) of the government. Their work was to pacify the Indians, to keep them tractable and submissive, to make them appreciate the benevolence and good intentions of the government. Meigs had told Blackburn that missions would be important, as factionalism arose, "to keep the Indians quiet."[72]

In order to obtain a better hold over the Moravians, Meigs went to Dearborn soon after Doublehead's murder and arranged for an annual financial subsidy for their mission school. In April 1809, he happily informed them that they would henceforth receive $100 a year from the government.[73] However, he reminded them, the government would henceforth expect annual reports of their work in exchange for this subsidy. In the years that followed, the Moravians were increasingly consulted by the gov-

70. Fries, 7: 3092.

71. John Gambold to Benzien, April 9, 1809, MAS.

72. R. J. Meigs to Gideon Blackburn, February 25, 1807, OSW, M-222, roll 2, #0747.

73. Springplace Conference, 1802–14, p. 61. This sum was later increased to $250.

ernment for their advice on Cherokee affairs, and they unfailingly told them that the fullbloods were the backward element in the nation and that it was necessary to stamp out all traces of Cherokee culture. They fully supported government policy on acculturation and the desirability of persuading the Indians to divide their land in severalty. They did not, in their simplicity, believe they were being manipulated by the government or that they were in any sense taking sides in the political struggle between the government and the Cherokees' effort to retain their cultural identity. They sincerely believed that the government's policy and their own coincided for the benefit of the Indians.

Although the discovery of the secret plan to exchange the Lower Town area for land in western Arkansas prevented a treaty, Meigs nevertheless believed that a bargain had been made and he intended to stick by it. During 1808 – 10, as the effort of the government to remove the Cherokees (by encouraging voluntary emigration and paying the transportation costs) mounted, so did the internal fears and tensions within the nation. Their country and people were being torn in two. The "neutrality" of the Moravians in this crisis was taken by "the patriot party" (as Meigs now began to call the Vann — Hicks — Ridge faction) to mean that they approved of the government's plan. It was a case of being damned if they did and damned if they didn't. In the end about 1,500 Cherokees did move west to Arkansas between 1809 and 1811, but Meigs eventually had to abandon his effort because President Madison became fearful that if a war ever broke out in the Mississippi Valley, a heavy-handed removal program might push the Cherokees into the hands of the British. Furthermore, once the leaders of Doublehead's faction had moved west, the patriot party was able to consolidate its leadership of the nation. In 1810 the Upper and Lower Towns united under an improved and more highly centralized form of government designed to prevent any clique or faction from acting without the consent of the whole Council (including chiefs from every town). In addition to this political reorganization, some of the most important laws in the nation's history were passed by the council in 1808 – 10. One of these regularized the previously sporadic policing of horsethieves by a mounted police force responsible to the council. Another law finally accepted by the elders of the seven clans put an end to most of the situations requiring clan revenge for murder in order to prevent endless feuding among the clans. A third law, promoted by the mixed bloods, established the beginning of patrilineal inheritance patterns.[74] While political unity and the new laws were important steps in acculturation, there is little evidence that the missionaries played any part in them. The actions of the Cherokee chiefs and people in the crisis of 1807 – 10 constituted a secular rather than a religious revitalization movement. It took place in the teeth of strong federal efforts to destabilize the

74. See Rennard Strickland, *Fire and Spirits*, pp. 58–60, and *Cherokee Laws*, pp. 3–4.

nation and indicated a resilience in the Cherokee people the missionaries had not suspected.[75]

After 1810 the Cherokees demonstrated a far more united front and a much more cohesive effort to manage their own affairs. Their successful revolution against the Lower Town chiefs gave them renewed self-confidence and hope. They had demonstrated that with unity they could resist the powerful efforts of the federal agents and the secretary of war to make them give up their homeland. It was rather ironic. For ten years the missionaries had been working for their acculturation, trying to break down their national and cultural identity, yet in 1810 that identity underwent a significant rebirth. Nationalism proved stronger than assimilation. But nationalism was not the same as traditionalism or cultural resistance. "The patriot party," which now dominated the Council, was firmly committed to encouraging an agricultural and market economy and to cooperating with missionary schools. The Council continued to welcome white school-teachers, mechanics, blacksmiths, carpenters, tinsmiths, and other artisans who had useful skills to offer (though it reasserted its own right rather than that of the agent to license such persons). The new leaders of the nation were convinced that national self-government depended upon economic self-reliance; that, in turn, depended upon learning how to deal with the white-man on his terms.

The assassination in 1809 of James Vann, one of the principal architects of this nationalistic revitalization, did not constitute the shock it might have had he been more stable and less impulsive. The Moravians believed that he was shot by members of the mounted police force which he was leading in his region of the nation. The police had turned upon him because of his excessive cruelty in punishing horsethieves and other criminals.[76] A wealthy man who had often been robbed by whites, Indians, and blacks, Vann had a vicious temper. He frequently drank too much and when drunk engaged in brawls which often ended in stabbings and shootings of those who affronted him. He had tortured a white female servant and burned one of his slaves to death for participating in a plot to rob his store. In 1808 he was arrested by the agent for stabbing a white citizen and shooting another when drunk. Meigs hoped Vann's conviction for these crimes would undermine "the rebellious party."[77] While Vann escaped conviction for lack of evidence, the other members of his party viewed him thereafter as a liability rather than an asset. In any case, his murder was not considered a political act; the finger did not point to anyone in Doublehead's faction. Some thought the murderer was a clan relative of a man whom Vann had

75. McLoughlin, "Beginning of Cherokee Nationalism," pp. 575–80.

76. John Gambold to Benzien, February 23, 1809, MAS. Gambold said the murder was generally attributed to Alex Sanders.

77. R. J. Meigs to John Sevier, October 23, 1808, BIA, M-208. "If Vann is properly brought to justice, it will have a very good effect, will silence his partizans—negotiations with the Cherokes will be conducted with ease." See also Meigs's letter to Dearborn of the same date.

killed in a duel some years earlier, but whoever did it was never caught.

"Our friendship with Mr. Vann," wrote the Moravians shortly before his death, "goes no further than a quiet and modest demeanor toward him."[78] They owed him much for his help in establishing their mission, but he had always repulsed their efforts to convert him and members of his family. Once, in 1805, when he was very ill, the missionaries came to his bedroom and tried to reprove him for his drunkenness, fornication, and wife-beating, hoping for a deathbed conversion. After hearing them out, he rose up, "jumped from his bed, seized a bottle and drank as much as he could in one gulp and said in anger that it was his house and he could drink as much as he pleased, dance, fornicate and what not and that it was none of our business." When they said they would nevertheless pray for Jesus to save his soul, "Vann left the room saying that he did not believe there was a Jesus Christ." The missionaries concluded that "the Devil has so possessed and bound Vann" that he was beyond human help.[79]

After his death, the Cherokee executors appointed by the Cherokee Council to settle his large estate found it too complex for their abilities. Vann's holdings were so extensive and intricate that the executors asked the Moravians to assist them. Reluctantly, they obliged, but it took them many weeks to straighten it all out.[80] Vann, breaking the matrilineal tradition, had made a will leaving all of his property to his oldest son, Joseph, except his large two-storey brick mansion, which he left for the use of his second wife. His two sisters maintained that he had cheated them out of some slaves left to them by their father; they claimed the eighteen "issue" of these slaves. Because he had married two wives (sisters) he had two sets of children; the children of the wife who had left him were omitted from the will and so was she. Various creditors were eager to seize parts of his holdings—his two trading posts, his ferry, his cattle, his plantation, his seventy to eighty slaves.[81] To the Moravians the Vann estate was an abomination of sharp dealing, polygamy, female property inheritance, and outright fraud (but, owning slaves themselves, the Moravians were not upset by his slaveholding). Consequently, after settling the estate as best they could, they wrote to the federal agent suggesting that some effort should be made to convince the Cherokee Council to enact more suitable laws governing the inheritance of property. As they put it, they wished to "do the Nation a real service" by telling Meigs "to introduce a law which would regulate the settling of estates."[82] Apparently their financial connection with the federal government had given them a sense of responsibility for shaping the economic and political transformation of Cherokee society. In addition to saving souls,

78. Fries, 8: 3092.
79. Springplace Diary, June 6, 1805, and June 20, 1805, MAS.
80. John Gambold to Reichel, March 27, 1809, MAS.
81. Ibid.
82. John Gambold to Benzien, April 9, 1809, MAS.

they now saw themselves as partners with the agent and the secretary of war in the task of secular reform of the nation.

Blackburn too had become active in trying to influence Cherokee politics. His letters regarding the noble work of Doublehead had not been publicly known, however much his sympathy for him may have been suspected. His desire, like that of the Moravians, to shape the affairs of the nation was known, however. "I have labored with some of the chiefs," he wrote to Meigs in November 1807, "to have an attempt made to have a few simple laws passed by their Nation and reduced to writing and have some one of themselves to act as Secretary of State and that no law should be in force unless committed to record."[83] He did not specify what laws he favored at this time, but from other letters it appears that they related to polygamy, infanticide (or self-induced abortion), divorce, inheritance, and the protection of private property. He had written for publication in a missionary journal in 1805, "I have reason to believe that marriage will soon be introduced with some significant ceremony" and that the Cherokee custom of matrilineal inheritance will be "altered in favor of the issue" of the father. He also hoped that soon "the marriage contract [would] be perpetuated by preventing easy divorce," and he was happy to report that "Several of the mixed blood have been lately regularly married" by clergymen. "Should marriage and the observance of the sabbath be obtained [by law], I should flatter myself a sufficient palisade would be raised to prevent a recurrence to their forms of barbarism."[84] He was also happy to see "the thirst of this people for the acquisition of property is rapidly increasing" and that the "procuring of abortions" was rapidly declining.[85] However, to sustain the rights of private property, he believed "more regulations for its adjustment" would be needed. Presumably it was these kinds of laws that he labored with the Lower Town chiefs to have enacted over the next two years. It seems doubtful that they were much interested. No such laws were passed until long after Blackburn had left the nation (with the exception of the law of 1808 regarding the right of a man's widow and children to share in his estate, and the Lower Town chiefs were not behind this).

However, it was not Blackburn's effort to push new laws upon the Cherokees which finally led to his disgrace. According to Cherokee oral tradition, Blackburn destroyed his reputation by clandestinely engaging in the selling of whiskey to Indians contrary to the United States Trade and Intercourse Act. Others said he was secretly speculating in land which as yet belonged to the Cherokees but which he thought would soon be ceded to the United States (by Doublehead's old faction). Most likely he was trying to

83. Gideon Blackburn to R. J. Meigs, November 4, 1807, BIA, M-208.

84. *The Evangelical Intelligencer*, 1: 408.

85. Ibid. Blackburn took credit for the laws passed by the Cherokee Council in 1808 and said, "I suspect their next step will be the partitioning out their lands and entering into regular habits of husbandry" on farms owned in fee simple. *The Panoplist* 1: 325—26.

help the government obtain control of Cherokee waterways by finding a route from eastern Tennessee to the Gulf of Mexico. As early as 1807 the Moravians had heard from James Vann that Blackburn was concerned with more than schooling in the nation. Vann had told them confidentially, shortly before his death, "Blackburn is not so disinterested as he wishes to appear; he is a secret Speculator."[86] This rumor was given substance when, after moving his school to Tellico, Blackburn requested that the government help him to obtain "a mile or two square" of Cherokee land "for the purpose of supplying the school with wood"; when the timber was gone, he said, he would use the land "to supply it [the school] with food."[87] The land was to be located north of the Little Tennessee River, close to the edge of the Cherokee border on a tract which Blackburn undoubtedly knew the government was negotiating for. Meigs had reported to the War Department that this land would probably be ceded, and Blackburn wanted to have a prior claim upon a mile or two square of it. After the cession, he would be able to obtain personal possession by sale from the government at two dollars an acre (the minimum price) and then he would resell it for many times that sum. It is hardly conceivable that his school needed so much land for firewood, and if it did, the school was south of the river and the land was north of it. The War Department did not grant the request (which could properly have been granted only by the Council). When the patriot party gained control of the nation in 1810, it blocked the cession of land north of the Little Tennessee.

The stories about "Parson Blackburn's whiskey," however, were based upon fact, not rumor.[88] Blackburn owned a distillery in Maryville and traded regularly in whiskey in Tennessee. He knew, of course, that it was illegal to sell it to the Indians, but in 1808 he entered into a complex scheme with his brother, Samuel, to hire a young Cherokee (James McIntosh, son of Quotaquskee and formerly one of the most promising students in Blackburn's school) to carry a boat loaded with 2,226 gallons of Blackburn's whiskey (and other goods) from Maryville to Fort St. Stephen on the Tombigbee River. Blackburn gave his note to secure the credit of the cargo; it was to traverse the rivers though the Cherokee and Creek nations to reach its destination. Blackburn later asserted that the whole venture was designed simply to test whether a water route could be found (with short portages). He also obtained permission from some of the leading Cherokee chiefs for this venture, but he failed to obtain permission from the Creeks. The Creeks having at this time refused to grant a water right-of-way through their nation, the War Department was ready to claim that trade along navigable rivers must be open to commerce regardless of the Creeks' opposition. Blackburn, it appears, was acting for the government to test the practicability of the route.

86. John Gambold to Reichel, July 23, 1809, MAS.

87. Gideon Blackburn to R. J. Meigs, February 3, 1808, BIA, M-208.

88. See W. G. McLoughlin, "Parson Blackburn's Whiskey," *Journal of Presbyterian History* 57, no. 4 (Winter, 1979): 427–45.

After journeying safely through the Cherokee Nation, James McIntosh and his boats were stopped on March 1, 1809, when they entered the Creek Nation on the Coosa River. The Creek chief, Big Warrior, declared that McIntosh did not have a proper pass to go through his nation, confiscated his cargo, and charged that some of the whiskey had been sold during its passage through the Cherokee Nation and more was to be sold to Indians as it passed through the Creek Nation. McIntosh, Blackburn's brother, and all others concerned in the enterprise denied these allegations, but the charge neverthe-less stuck in the minds of both the Cherokees and the Creeks. The fact that Blackburn just happened to be in Turkeytown (miles from his school) on the border between the Cherokee and Creek nations when the cargo reached that crucial juncture contributed to the belief that he was watching over the venture because he stood to profit by it. In any case, as the Moravians heard the story shortly thereafter, the whiskey was Blackburn's and therefore he was implicated. The Moravians believed the story and considered that Black-burn had brought the whole missionary effort into disgrace:

> Even in this land where in truth very little Gospel light has appeared, the opponents [of the Gospel] have received a reason for slander. In fact, Mr. Blackburn undertook a journey through the land principally to reconnoiter the waterways here as far as the Bay of Mobile, for which a conversation with the Secretary of War with him is supposed to have been the inducement. For this purpose he entered into a sort of company with one of his own brothers and two or three others; they built several boats and purchased a large quantity of whiskey in order to trade with that on their journey, and thus they traveled down the Connesauga River. . . . To be sure, they had prepared themselves a little . . . by taking along a half-breed Indian who claimed that the freight was his property, only nobody believed him. . . . Now the whole matter would not cause so much commotion and would even be quickly forgotten if Blackburn, a man well-known far and wide, described as having great gifts and also known among other things for the blessed preaching of the Gospel, had not been at the head of this undertaking; but just because of that, the disgrace of this venture falls in large part on religion.[89]

The more cynical antimission Cherokees at last had a handle with which to indict the whole mission enterprise. Blackburn's actions confirmed the wide-spread belief that the missionaries had other motives for entering their nation than saving their souls. The Moravians rightly concluded that "now that his credibility has gone down very much, he may find it difficult to keep" his schools going. The schools, they said, were already "decreasing greatly" in enrollment a few months after the event. By January 1810, the Moravians learned that "Mr. Blackburn's school at Tellico Blockhouse has gone to pieces."[90] The second school at Sale Creek kept up a desultory performance for several more months but by August it too had been "given up." The

89. John Gambold to Benzien, July 23, 1809, MAS.
90. John Gambold to Benzien, January 8, 1810, and August 15, 1810, MAS.

Moravian school, with eight students, was now the only mission activity in the nation and remained so for another seven years.

The Moravians became very discouraged. "My God," wrote one of them in April 1809, "is Satan to remain on the throne here and have it in his power to keep everything away from us?"[91] Were they never to make a convert? That year they received a tempting offer from Major W. P. Anderson near Nashville, who said that if they would transfer their school to the white settlements near Nashville, he could assure them warm support. Was it not time, Anderson asked, to admit failure?[92] The Moravian missionaries wrote to their board in Salem for advice. But just at that moment Providence intervened. James Vann's widow, Margaret (who now called herself Peggy Scott, her maiden name), told the missionaries on June 13, 1810, that she felt she was ready to believe in Jesus Christ and follow God's ways. The daughter of a white trader, Margaret Scott Vann had always been sympathetic to the mission. She not only sent her children to the school but often visited it, attended its services, acted as an interpreter. After carefully examining her spiritual state, the elated Moravians concluded that she had indeed been converted by the Holy Spirit and was ready to be baptized as their first Cherokee convert. Margaret's mother-in-law and other Cherokee relatives stoutly opposed her decision and constantly harassed her. Yet she remained faithful, and, after duly consulting the lot, John Gambold baptized her on August 13, 1810.[93]

Convinced that God was encouraging them to stay and that Mrs. Vann's conversion was the start of more serious spiritual concern among the Cherokees, the missionaries gave up any thought of moving to Nashville. Yet during the next eight years they received only one other convert (in 1813). Instead of a great wave of conversions to Christianity, a tremendous outburst of traditionalist religious fervor arose in 1811. This revival of the old Cherokee religion, in the wake of the nation's political revitalization, was led by a new school of prophets, who received visions that the nation must return to the ways of its forefathers.

91. John Gambold to Benzien, April 9, 1809, MAS.

92. W. P. Anderson to John Gambold, December 13, 1809, MAS. The mission board in Salem shared the pessimism of the missionaries, replying in February 1810 that "doubts have already been expressed concerning the mission establishment at Springplace" and that serious consideration was being given to moving the school to Nashville. See Fries, 7: 3118.

93. Mrs. Vann's baptismal date was twice rejected by "the lot," and she also had difficulty moving from baptism to communion because of the lot. See Springplace Conference, 1802–14, pp. 69–70.

~⊚{ CHAPTER FOUR }⊚~

Cherokee Religious Revival, 1811–1813

> The Mother of the Nation has forsaken you. . . . She will return to you, however, if you put the white people out of the land and return to your former manner of life. You yourselves can see that the white people are entirely different beings from us; we are made of red clay; they out of white sand. You may keep good neighborly relations with them, just see to it that you get back from them your old Beloved Towns.
>
> Ancestral vision to three Cherokees, January 1811

The revival of the old Cherokee religion in 1811–13 was not, as James Mooney thought, a Ghost Dance movement urging a rejection of acculturation.[1] It was an assertion of Cherokee nationalism and a profound expression of their desire for cultural autonomy —their desire to be left alone to manage their own affairs in their own way. No single prophet emerged to lead the movement, however, as had happened among the Senecas in 1800 and among the Shawnees in 1807, nor did it halt the movement toward Cherokee political centralization and economic adaptation. It simply asserted that acculturation could and should take place within the traditional social and religious philosophy of the Cherokees rather than under the alien theology and political dominance of the whiteman. While the outbreak of the War of 1812 and then the Cherokees' participation in the Creek War of 1813–14 obscured this revival from general public attention, nevertheless for three years a resurgence of Cherokee dances, customs, and festivals took place which astonished the missionaries, frightened the neighboring whites, and puzzled the federal agent.

During this revival many Cherokees were visited in dreams and visions by the spirits of their ancestors. These spectres delivered messages confirming the prevailing opposition to the intrusions of whites, expressing concern over the loss of sacred land, and calling for a return to traditional

---

1. James Mooney gave this movement the name Cherokee Ghost Dance in 1896, but his chief information came from James Wafford, who was a young boy in 1811. James Mooney, *The Ghost Dance Religion*. See also W. G. McLoughlin, "New Angles of Vision on the Cherokee Ghost Dance Movement," *American Indian Quarterly* 5 (November 1979): 317–46.

82

religious observances. To missionaries and other whites the religious concern had a simple explanation: the superstitious savages were frightened by a series of earthquakes which began on December 11, 1811, and rocked the nation for four months off and on, shaking buildings off their foundations and opening huge potholes in the ground which slowly filled with green water. However, the revival began before the earthquakes and the earthquakes were to the Cherokees the symptoms of far more profound problems. To many Cherokees the earthquakes indicated that the Great Spirit and the Mother of the Nation were angry at their forgetfulness of their religious duties and might punish them if they did not repent and worship as they should. To other Cherokees the earthquakes were a warning addressed to the whitemen that the Great Spirit would no longer tolerate their injuries and insults to his favorite children. After all, the earthquakes could destroy the white nation as easily as the Cherokee nation.

As in most traditionalist revivals, the mystical messages and signs from the spirit world were ambiguous, even contradictory, symbolic of both fear and hope. Some Cherokees received messages from spectral figures telling them to give up everything they had learned or borrowed from the whiteman and to return totally to their old ways; some received messages saying that they had now acquired all they needed from the whites and should accept no more. Still others heard the spirits say that there were yet some skills which whites could teach them but that this must be only on their own terms. Clearly the nation had reached a turning point in its cultural identity. The people were trying to find a coherent alternative world view—to correlate their new way of life with their old values, customs, and beliefs. Had war not interrupted this revitalization movement, it might have produced a spiritual leader capable of coalescing the deeply felt hopes and fears into a coherent program similar to that which Handsome Lake was at this time developing among the Senecas.[2] On the other hand, it is apparent that the secular leadership which had emerged between 1807 and 1811 was itself supplying a powerful source of order and direction. Some of the new national leaders were drawn toward a Christian interpretation of the world though they hesitated to embrace it openly. Chiefs like Charles Hicks, the Ridge, David Watie (Oowatie), John Lowery, for example, had sent their children

---

2. See Anthony F. C. Wallace, *The Death and Rebirth of the Seneca* (New York: Random House, 1969). Thomas L. McKenney writing about the movement in 1833 from information obtained from the Ridge, spoke of a prophet named Charlie from the town of Coosewatee, who was the leader of it, but there is no contemporary evidence about him. Thomas L. McKenney and James Hall, *Biographical Sketches and Anecdotes of Ninety-Five of 120 Principal Chiefs from the Indian Tribes of North America*, vol. 2 of the 1838 edition, reprinted by the U.S. Department of Interior, Bureau of Indian Affairs (Washington: Government Printing Office, 1967), pp. 191–92. Robert K. Thomas argues that "Cherokee culture does not allow for a prophet no matter how much stress the society is under. One man just does not initiate action this way." "The Redbird Smith Movement," in *Symposium on Cherokee and Iroquois Culture*, ed. William N. Fenton and John Gulick, p. 165.

and nephews to the Moravian school or to Blackburn's school, had attended mission services, and been impressed with the honesty of the missionaries and the power of their faith. For them a combination of Christian regeneration and internal political reorganization seemed the best path for the nation. Other leaders, like Chulioah, the Warrior's Nephew, Big Bear, felt the pull of the old religion but remained cognizant of the nation's need for the whiteman's assistance to restore self-sufficiency and order.

Many other Cherokees thought the nation was now self-sufficient and needed nothing more from the whites. They had learned to become farmers, herders, and weavers; they had reunited the Lower and Upper towns; they had found able and honest leaders, and they had frustrated the federal government's effort to remove them to the west to Arkansas. If the whites would now return to them some of their most sacred places and if their own people could revive their religious harmony with the spirit world, then the nation could survive on its own.

In important respects this Cherokee religious revival was similar to the Christian religious revivalism sweeping across the United States from 1800 to 1830. It contained millennial and apocalyptic predictions; it groped for a transformation in religious thought; it expressed a yearning for national unity; it was torn between reverence for the past and hope for the future. Both the Cherokee and the white awakenings gained power through successful armed battles — for the Cherokees it was the Battle of Horseshoe Bend in 1814, for white Americans it was the battle of New Orleans in 1815. Symbolically, General Jackson led the troops in both portentous victories. Just as the Americans exulted in a new sense of national prowess following their second victory over the British, so did the Cherokees after their victory over the Creeks. For a brief moment during the war years the two peoples — Cherokees and white Americans — were joined in the euphoric fervor of nationalistic exuberance, each believing the Creator was smiling particularly upon their country, that he had renewed a special relationship with his chosen people. Yet, as the Cherokee prophets warned more than once during the period 1811 — 1813, the destinies of the two nations were not the same but separate.

The first prophetic vision of the Cherokee revival of 1811 — 13 occurred on Rocky Mountain in northern Georgia late in January 1811. Reported first to a council at Oostenali by the three Cherokees who experienced it (but whose names have not survived), it was later told to the Moravian missionaries at Springplace by Chief Keychzaetel (the Warrior's Nephew), a highly respected leader who, like the other chiefs at the council, was deeply impressed by the message received from their ancestors.[3] "The old chief was very eager to hear our ideas about this story," the missionaries

<hr />

3. Springplace Diary, February 10, 1811, MAS. In other accounts the Moravians described Keychzaetel as "Koy,ch,z,o,te,li" and identified him by his English name, the Warrior's Nephew.

reported. He had no desire to conceal the new revelations from whites nor did he come to them with threats or warnings. Chief Keyzhzaetel's revelation was, for him, as valid within his cosmography as the revelations of the Christians regarding the millennium or Judgment Day were within Christian cosmography. To him the vision conveyed matters of significant import both for whitemen and red, for the same Great Spirit ruled over both.

The three unnamed Cherokees who had received the message on Rocky Mountain and who delivered it to the council at Oostenali in early February had failed to impress the Ridge. The Ridge, who had been a guerrilla warrior of the Lower Towns as a young man, had been one of the first to adopt farming and herding after 1794 when he settled at Oochgelogy (in Georgia) in the Upper Town region. Intelligent and capable, he gradually acquired a dozen or more black slaves and established an efficient and profitable plantation. An able orator, the Ridge rose rapidly in the nation and joined the faction of Vann and Hicks against Doublehead. According to most accounts, he was the one chosen to assassinate Doublehead in 1807 because of his courage and because of the high regard in which he was held by the people. Oochgelogy was not far from Springplace and the Ridge sent his son John to the school and persuaded his brother Stand Watie to send his son Buck (Galagina). Ridge and his wife talked often with the missionaries; though Ridge could understand English and speak brokenly in it, he could not read or write it. Some accounts say he was a fullblood; some say he had a Spanish grandparent.[4]

When, at the Oostenali council in January 1811, Ridge heard the report of the vision which had appeared to the three Cherokees on Rocky Mountain, he scoffed at it. This so offended those present by its sacrilege that they attacked him not only verbally but physically. His insensitivity to the nation's religious traditions did not lessen respect for his political leadership, but it left him outside the spiritual fervor of the revival. In the account of the assault upon him at the council which Ridge told to Thomas L. McKenney in 1833, he said he had almost been killed for defying a threat that nonbelievers in the prophecy would be struck dead.[5] But he was rescued from the assailants by some of his relatives.

The three Cherokee travelers who saw the vision were not conjurors or medicine men but ordinary people, a man and two women, on a journey to visit friends. As it grew dark early that January afternoon, they were looking for a place to spend the night and "came to an unoccupied house near a hill

4. The best account of the Ridge and his family is Thurman Wilkins, *Cherokee Tragedy*, pp. 51–61.

5. McKenney's account of this movement telescopes it into a short period and makes the Ridge the hero of "progressive" opposition to a backward-looking reaction. McKenney states that Ridge's opposition to the Rocky Mountain vision at this council destroyed the credibility of the movement and ended the revival. In his version the prophet who reported the vision was trying to draw the Cherokees into a war against the United States. McKenney, *Biographical Sketches*, pp. 191–92.

called Rocky Mountain." They had just entered the house when "they heard a violent noise in the air and wondered whether a storm was brewing." They went out of the house to see. When they looked up in the air "they saw a whole crowd of Indians arriving on the hill from the sky; they were riding on small black horses and their leader was beating a drum." (The beating of a drum was central to most Cherokee religious ceremonies, and the drummer was a person of key spiritual importance because he invoked the spirits.) The three Cherokees were frightened as the ghost riders approached, but the one with the drum reassured them:

> Don't be afraid; we are your brothers and have been sent by God [*"Gott"* in the Moravian transcript; probably "Great Spirit" in the oral version] to speak with you. God is dissatisfied that you are receiving the white people in your land without distinction. You yourselves see that your hunting is gone—you are planting the corn of the white people—go and sell that back to them and plant Indian corn and pound it in the manner of your forefathers; do away with mills. The Mother of the Nation has forsaken you because all her bones are being broken through the grinding.[6]

This segment of the message in part reflected Cherokee guilt over their abandonment of the old ways and in part anxiety over the many bad harvests and frequent famines resulting from their unfamiliarity with the new agricultural system. It also indicated a dislike of the complex machinery (mills, cotton gins, wagons, smithies, looms) of white civilization, which required them to hire white men to build and keep in repair. The Mother of the Nation, Selu (goddess of corn), was calling them back to a simpler form of agricultural life which they understood better. Perhaps she was also warning them against the complexities of the staple-crop system and the new market economy with its individualistic, competitive, profit-oriented ethic. She was upset by the loss of their communal ethic, by their loss of a sense of harmony among themselves and with nature, and by the decline of their hospitality ethic.

A critical aspect of the remainder of the spectral drummer's message was that the Great Spirit did not want the Cherokees to admit good and bad white people into the nation "without distinction." They must discriminate between those who came to help them and those who came to corrupt them, to take their land, to change their ways. Too many whites were being admitted into the nation because they claimed to have skills which the new economic order required: millers, carpenters, blacksmiths, schoolteachers, traders, tanners, tinsmiths, even sharecroppers who purported to teach them how to farm but who used their land and its profits for themselves, leaving the Cherokees with a pittance. Many of these mechanics and croppers were renegades, outlaws, drunkards, and "scape gallows" who could not make a living in white communities or who thought it easier to cheat the Indians.

---

6. Indian corn, or maize, was being replaced in the Cherokee Nation by the new hybrid corn developed by whites. Unfamiliarity with this new species may have contributed to some of the crop failures which caused famines.

With a shortage of skilled labor in the white frontier, few honest and able artisans or teachers would come into an Indian nation to earn a living. The Great Spirit and the Mother of the Nation were providing advice on a fundamental problem of their economic and social adjustment; they had sent the drummer to tell the Cherokees that they were going too fast and too far in their reliance upon the whites and might soon lose their bearings. But the Great Spirit did not suggest that they reject the whiteman's help entirely and return to the old hunting economy. He suggested only that the Cherokees should stick with the simplest kind of subsistence farming and herding, which they could manage by and for themselves.

The drummer went on to inform the three astonished Cherokee travelers that the Mother of their nation would "return to you, however, if you put the white people out of the land and return to your former manner of life." By "former manner of life" she referred to the nonexploitative, noncompetitive harmonious relationship of man to nature and to the community; she did not mean a return to the fur trade economy or to the bow and arrow. The drummer's message made no mention of returning to a hunting economy. Throughout the revival other spectral visions expressed a longing to return to the old communal ethic but never for a specific return to hunting and war. Like all religious revivals, this was concerned primarily with a reaffirmation of old values.

To explain why total assimilation to the whiteman's ethic and way of life could not be useful to Indians, the drummer reminded them of their creation myth, which spoke of the different colored people's being assigned different vocations. "You yourselves can see that the white people are entirely different beings from us; we are made from red clay; they out of white sand." The Great Spirit intended them to live apart; the whites would develop technology and live in cities; the reds would live close to nature in their quiet valleys and woodlands. The Rocky Mountain vision spoke to a rising desire for withdrawal and separation from the whites, who were pressing in so hard upon them. The vision was posing an alternative to the total assimilation policy of the government and the missionaries, which so many of the mixed-blood leaders and intermarried whites favored. One of the significant actions taken by the Cherokee Council during the revival (and spurred by it) was to pass a law requiring all whites who entered the nation to obtain a license from the Council which limited specifically the duration of their stay; the Council also demanded in May 1811 that the federal agent expel from the nation all those whites who had no such license.[7] It was this last requirement which convinced the Moravians that

7. There is much correspondence between the Council and the federal agent over the removal and licensing of whites in the nation in 1811–12, but Meigs never linked this to the revival. The debate consisted of defining how many and what kinds of white traders, teachers, mechanics, and sharecroppers should be allowed to enter or remain in the nation and for how long. Meigs recognized the need for some regulation of these whites but thought the Council might be too restrictive in its licensing and thereby hinder their acculturation. See Meigs to Col. Alexander Smyth, February 27, 1811, and the Council at Oostenali to Meigs, May 5, 1811, BIA, M-208.

the Cherokee revival was directed against them, although there is no indication that the Rocky Mountain vision was alone responsible for the new law.
A general concern over acculturation and white intruders inspired both the
vision and the licensing act.

Another key element in the message delivered at Rocky Mountain
concerned cooperation with whites. The drummer explained that the Great
Spirit did not oppose such cooperation; he simply expected the Cherokees to
assert its limits. "You may keep good neighborly relations with them, just
see to it that you get back from them your Beloved Towns." Their spiritual
mother and father did not suggest driving the whites back to the other side of
the Appalachians or exterminating them. The Cherokee revival contained
none of the virulent hostility toward whites expressed by the Shawnee
Prophet Tenkswatawa, brother of Tecumseh, in these years. Indian prophets
in the Great Lakes region declared that the white man was made from "the
white scum" on the shores of the lakes and that the Great Spirit hated the
whiteman.[8] Tecumseh would, in the autumn of this very year, come to the
Southern Indians with some of his angry prophets to try to persuade them to
join a confederacy of western Indian nations which would agree to sell no
more land to the whites without a general agreement among them all.
Eventually Tecumseh planned to ally this confederacy with Great Britain in
an effort to win back the Mississippi Valley by force of arms. If any rumors
of Tecumseh's program or any knowledge of Tenkswatawa's religious message had reached the Cherokees by January 1811, there is no record of it.
This early vision contains no indication of Shawnee influence; it seems to
have been wholly indigenous. The spectre's reference to getting back their
"Beloved Towns" from the whites was not phrased in warlike terms. The
Mother of the Nation expressed essentially a concern for the spiritual integrity and heritage of the Cherokees.

The call to get back their beloved towns from the whites is the closest
the vision came to being overtly political, but it seems to have been presented
as a subject for peaceful negotiation, not for war. "Beloved Towns" were
traditional sacred places. This particular vision did not mention any towns by
name, but other visions during the next two years specified the towns of
Chota in northeastern Tennessee and Tugalu in western South Carolina.
The nationalistic spirit of the revival is indicated by this irredentist impulse.
Significantly, the ghost rider said nothing of revoking treaties or attempting
to reclaim all the land which had been sold to the whites or fraudulently
taken from them. For example, he said nothing about getting back their old
hunting grounds. He spoke only of those spots of special religious significance without which the nation's spiritual rejuvenation could not be

8. See the discussion of the Shawnee vision and message from the Great Spirit in
Mooney, *Ghost Dance*, p. 665. The Great Spirit told the Shawnees that the whitemen were "the
children of the Evil spirit" and not his creation: "I hate them." See also the statement by the
Shawnee Prophet, the Trout, in 1807 in OSW, M-222, roll 2, #0859.

fulfilled. The whites by their presence and activities in these sacred places were desecrating Cherokee holy ground. By tradition and legend these beloved towns were places where the Great Spirit had made some special revelation or to which he had ascribed some special religious function. Chota, the old capital of the nation on the upper Tennessee River, had been "a city of refuge" where, under certain circumstances, sanctuary was granted to murderers. Tugalu, on the upper Savannah River, was said to be the spot where the Great Spirit first gave them fire. Kituwah, another sacred town in the Great Smoky Mountains of North Carolina, was considered the place of first settlement by Cherokees in the South, the mother town of the nation. Somehow these places must be returned and regain their important places in tribal affairs.

The Rocky Mountain prophecy went on to speak of the political changes taking place in the nation. The spirit drummer referred specifically to the law of 1808 which had regularized the Lighthorse Patrol. Because the nation had then no courts or jails, the mounted police constituted a frontier *posse comitatus*, acting as judges, juries, and executioners. But where white posses regularly hung horsethieves, the Cherokees, fearing clan revenge, simply gave them a severe whipping. Sometimes these whippings of one hundred lashes or more brought a thief close to death. On several occasions in 1808 – 10, thieves seeking to avoid such punishment had fought back, been wounded, and even died in the course of arrest. The Cherokee nation had never known this kind of public law and punishment. Whipping was particularly repugnant to the Cherokees (as missionaries learned when they first whipped errant schoolchildren). Much as they recognized the need to curtail horse stealing, they were upset by this drastic revision of their tradition of communal control of crime.

The spirit drummer therefore tried to instruct his auditors to proceed with more caution in their modernization: "Furthermore, your Mother is not pleased that you punish each other so hard; you even whip until [you draw] blood." This produced hard feelings between Cherokee families and clans at a time when they needed to affirm their solidarity and brotherhood. However, the spirit did not call for the abolition of all the new laws; it simply said they should not punish each other "so hard." The essence of the revelation was to suggest that the nation should stop and think about how far and how fast it wished to go with change and in imitation of the whiteman's concepts of law and order. The tone of the message was cautionary, not reactionary; mediative not fanatical. In effect, it expressed a maturation in acculturation, not a total rejection of it. Having reached a new plateau of stability and prosperity after 1810, the Cherokees were asked to think more seriously about what they were losing and what it meant to be a Cherokee under this new order of things. Did survival require abandonment of all traditional beliefs, values, behavior or could they rest now where they were, keeping the best of the old and the new?

The first part of the Rocky Mountain vision ended with the words, "Now I have told you what God's will is, and you are to pass it on." Significantly, the drummer told the three Cherokees to pass his message on not only to the other Cherokees but also to the whites: "You are to report everything which you have just heard to Colonel Meigs," and through him, of course, it would be reported to the secretary of war, the Congress, and the president. The revivalists were asserting a declaration of cultural independence and political self-government. No longer should they passively react to white initiatives. The revival prophets urged a new program for political action as well as spiritual renewal. As the missionaries realized, this reassertion of the traditional religion constituted a rejection of the white American's concept of the separation of church and state. In effect, Cherokees were not free to adopt any religious viewpoint they chose if they were to be true patriots.

To add weight to the message, the drummer informed the three Cherokee travelers that "if there is someone who does not believe it, then know that it will not be well with him." This was not exactly the threat of imminent death which the Ridge later said he had challenged by his expression of disbelief. It is in the nature of prophecies to promise good to those who heed them and harm to those who do not; several other revelations which occurred during this revival contained such warnings and promises. The Rocky Mountain vision ended with a final prophetic revelation: "If you do not believe my words, then look up at the sky." When they looked up, they "saw the heaven open and an indescribably beautiful light and in it four white houses." The mysterious drummer explained that "such houses you are to build in your Beloved Towns, one for Capt. Blair, the rest are to be for other white men who can be useful to the Nation with writing, etc." Captain James Blair was a Georgian who had performed many helpful services for the Cherokees, particularly by helping James Vann to remove white intruders and to apprehend white criminals who had stolen from them or injured a Cherokee. The fact that he and other true friends (apparently nonproselyting teachers) were to be given fine houses in the Sacred Towns and that these whites were to encourage the Nation to learn to read, write, cipher, and acquire other useful skills marks the cultural ambivalence of the whole religious movement from 1811 to 1813. It was not explicitly antiwhite, antimission or antiacculturation. Nevertheless, it was an affirmation of cultural integrity.

The Moravians, who were the first to hear of the momentous vision which had so astonished the council of chiefs at Oostenali in early February 1811, found it threatening. In the first place, it acknowledged a spiritual power which they did not accept. "Since we are well aware," the Moravians wrote to their board, "that the Indians have already considered in many council meetings how to get rid of the many white people who have penetrated [intruded into the nation], have also made various resolutions in that regard but have not carried anything out until the present time, so we could easily think for what purpose this story had been thought up." Its purpose was, in their view, to warn all whites, including themselves, to leave the nation. Tactfully the Moravians declined to comment on Keychzaetel's story beyond the remark that "it might have been a dream."

Keychzaetel may have realized that the Moravians were frightened by the message, for six months later, in July, he returned to Springplace after another Council meeting and tried to assure them that they were among those, like Captain Blair, who would always be welcome among the Cherokees because they were honest and helpful friends.[9] "He said he had come to bring us a report from the Council at which he is the most famous speaker. 'It is true," he said, 'the white people must all go out of the Nation,' " but the Council had not been so foolish as to order the removal of those whose help it needed. "Four [black]smiths, some school teachers [private tutors] and those who are building mills for us, are to be tolerated" for the time being; "later, they too must return to their own country." But while they were serving the Cherokees, "No one shall put anything in their way." (Apparently the Mother of the Nation's complaint that gristmills were grinding her bones had not weighed heavily with the Council in May 1811.) As for the Moravian missionaries, Keychzaetel was happy to report, "We do not consider *you* as *white people* but as *Indians*. God has sent you to teach our people. You don't want our land. You are here only out of love for us." The Cherokees were able to discriminate between their white friends and their white enemies and to accept their friends as "brothers."

That there were other visions or prophecies between January and October 1811 seems very likely, but there is no record of them. In October, however, Tecumseh, with some of his prophets (though not Tenkswatawa), visited the Creeks, bringing his call for a pan-Indian confederacy. The Shawnee prophets taught the Creeks the songs and dances of the Great Lakes Indians, which evolved after a prophetic message to the Shawnees from the Great Spirit several years before. Some Cherokees were present at these meetings with Tecumseh at Tuckabatchee and may have heard that the Great Spirit wished them to drive all the whitemen back across the mountains. There is no record that Tecumseh ever visited the Cherokee nation or sent anyone to enlist their participation in his movement.[10] Some Cherokees, no doubt, were sympathetic to Tecumseh's proposals but no formal action on them was ever taken by a Cherokee council.

9. Springplace Diary, July 10, 1811, MAS. Keychzaetel came at this time to report that the Council had voted in May to ask the agent to use the United States Army to round up and expel all whites from the nation with a few exceptions specified by the Council.

10. According to Mooney's informant, the dances and doctrines of the Ghost Dance movement among the Cherokees "first came to them through the Creek about 1812 or 1813." Mooney, *Ghost Dance*, p. 676. This does not square with the reports made by the Moravians at the time.

On December 11, 1811, a month after Tecumseh left the South, a tremendous earthquake shook the whole region around the Cherokees, a phenomenon which some Creeks attributed to Tecumseh's magical power over the spirit world and a demonstration of the havoc the Great Spirit might wreak on those who would not join the Shawnee confederacy. Among the Cherokees the earthquake provided evidence that the Great Spirit and the Mother of the Nation were still uneasy with their spiritual and political development. A host of new visions and prophecies occurred after the first earthquake and during the ten or twelve subsequent tremors which rocked the nation between December 1811 and April 1812. Colonel Meigs, who evidently knew nothing of the Rocky Mountain vision, attributed the whole Cherokee revival solely to the earthquakes. "They have revived their religious dances of ancient origin," he wrote to the secretary of war in March 1812, in order to "appease the Anger of the great Spirit." This religious activity, he continued, was "occasioned by the late shocks of the earth" for which they sought supernatural explanations. Meigs was one of the few contemporaries to record any of the rituals and ceremonies associated with the Cherokee revival: "They have revived their religious dances of ancient origin with as much solemnity as ever was seen in worship in our churches. They then repair to the water, go in and wash. These ablutions are intended to show that their sins are washed away and that they are cleansed from all defilements."[11] Meigs knew of the old Purification ceremony, which the Cherokees performed at the end of each year. He gave it Christian connotations which it did not have, but he was correct in seeing it as a ritual of renewal and harmony among the people. The mere revival of old ceremonies did not bother him, but he learned that there were "some fanatics" among the Cherokees who used these occasions to whip up animosity toward all aspects of acculturation. These fanatics or prophets, Meigs reported, "tell them that the Great Spirit is angry with them for adopting the manners, customs, and habits of the white people who, they think, are very wicked." "In some few instances," after dancing and chanting all night around a council fire, "some have thrown off their clothing into the fire and burned them up." The whites being wicked, deceitful, treacherous, those who imitated them and wore their style of clothing were in a sense condoning their wickedness. To put away wickedness one must also put away the symbols of wickedness. Meigs did not express it in these terms, however. He described such acts as the foolishness of superstition. Meigs did not see any of this himself, but from what he heard, these actions were not taken simply by the uneducated or "backward" fullbloods; nor did only males participate. "Some of the females are mutilating fine muslin dresses and are told they must discontinue dancing reels and country dances which have become very common amongst the young people." Fine muslin dresses were worn by the

11. R. J. Meigs to Secretary of War William Eustis, March 19, 1812, BIA, M-208. This is a long memo which Meigs headed "Some Reflections on Cherokee Concerns."

well-to-do; country reels were danced to the tunes of fiddles, not to drums and rattling gourds. Some of the more acculturated mixed bloods, it seems, as well as the poorer fullbloods, felt the urge to sustain the nation's spiritual identity and back off from assimilation.

While Meigs found these actions regrettable, he did not consider them dangerous to the peace and did not connect them with Tecumseh. At worst, "I think probable for a short time" this might "have a partial retrograde effect as respects civilization," he reported. However, once "the present frenzy has subsided," he expected the result would be to "accellerate improvement" and civilization among them. His confidence was based on information that not all those present at such ceremonies were swept up in them: "At a late [revival] meeting when a man burned his hat as a sacrifice, he called on a young chief present to follow his example. The young chief told him that he would not and, putting his hand to his Breast, said, 'It is not a matter of what cloaths I wear while my heart is straight.' " It did not occur to the informant or to Meigs that the symbolic act of burning the hat was meant in its way to inaugurate the very moral reformation this young chief thought was needed. The issue for all Cherokees was how to keep their hearts straight in an era of social transition. The revivalists wanted to get their hearts straight in Cherokee terms, not in white or Christian terms. That the issues at stake were moral as well as spiritual is evident in the reaction of one Cherokee woman whom Meigs heard about: "A young Cherokee woman told me that she was told that the Cherokees ought to throw away the habits of the white people and return to the ancient manners, and that she told them that was nothing, that they ought to become good people and leave off stealing horses and drinking whiskey instead of destroying their clothes." "Becoming good people" was the essence of the movement. Or, looked at in another way, the problem was how to find the power to *remain* good people. The Cherokee nation divided over the answer. Did greater support for honesty and morality rest in adopting the whiteman's religious beliefs and values or in strengthening their own religious and moral traditions? Horse stealing and whiskey drinking were symptoms of the social disruption brought upon them by imitating bad whitemen, by trying too hard to get rich fast without respect for others or for themselves. The revivalists felt that the best way to halt personal and social disintegration was to revive their dances and their traditional supplications for health and tribal solidarity. A Cherokee who remained true to Cherokee spiritual and communal ideals would have the power to resist temptations and corruptions suggested by wicked whites. However, the young chief and the young woman whom Meigs praised for resisting the revival frenzy thought the answer to the nation's moral confusion lay in personal self-discipline and rational morality of the sort offered by the missionaries and better-educated whites. They favored change, and they believed in self-reliant individualism, whereas the Cherokee revivalists called upon faith in the spiritual resources of the community. Meigs said of the revivalists, "They deserve some pity and compassion because they are looking from the effect to the cause." But in fact the Cherokees were closer to the cause and Meigs to the effect; trying to change (or being forced to change) too rapidly from a communal to an individualistic ethic had confused their sense of right and wrong. They realized that the problem lay deeper than wearing the whiteman's clothes or dancing his dances. The revival prophets asked, in fact, whose tune will the Cherokees be dancing to tomorrow?

The earthquakes affected Cherokees in different ways. They were for some a symbol of the Great Spirit's wrath, for others a symbol of earthly decay. For some they were a warning to the Cherokees, for others a rebuke to the whites. The absence of a central, charismatic prophet to mold these visions and revelations into a coherent, symbolic form and to develop from them a clear set of moral guidelines, religious rituals, and political goals which would produce both personal and social reformation stymied the spiritual revitalization underlying the revival. Following the earthquakes, the Moravians were besieged with Cherokee inquirers asking them to provide an interpretation of the cataclysm, and that in itself was an indication of their doubts about their own religious leaders as well as some respect for the religious powers of the Moravians.

On December 17, 1811, the day after the first shock, four chiefs "came to us to get information about the earthquake," said John Gambold; they were Chief Bead Eye, his brother (the Trunk), and two others. But while these chiefs were "very much disturbed," they did not look for spiritual causes of the earthquake. They hypothesized that "the earth is probably very old" and asked the missionaries whether it "would soon collapse."[12] They were aware that whitemen knew more than they about certain laws of nature. But the Moravians offered supernatural explanations: God controlled the world, they said to the four chiefs. He has "the might and power to discipline people who live on it in various ways, and for this purpose He has also used concussions of the earth from time to time." The Great Book recorded some of these instances of God's wrath. People should "thank Him that He has been so gracious to them this time and should regard it as a warning to do away with the service to sin and listen to His voice."[13] Earthquakes, they explained, were symbolic of the Day of Judgment described in the Bible: "God has destined the day on which He will judge all people. . . . At that time the earth will be consumed by fire, etc." When the chiefs heard this explanation, they "bowed their heads and seemed to be deep in thought." It raised the serious question of whose particular sins deserved punishment. Did the earthquakes mean, as they suspected, that God

---

12. Springplace Diary, December 17, 1811. According to Cherokee mythology, the earth was a flat piece of soil and rock suspended at each of four corners over a large body of water by means of ropes tied into the arch of the sky. Mooney, *Myths*, p. 239.

13. Springplace Diary, December 17, 1811, MAS.

was angry particularly with the sinful whitemen or that he might punish both redmen and white?

Other Cherokees did not seek an explanation for the earthquake from Christian missionaries but from their conjurors or revival prophets. "Some of them attribute the occurrence to the sorcerers, some to a large snake which must have crawled under their house; some to the weakness or old age of the earth which will soon cave in," the Moravians recorded.[14] Even the Ridge, who had scorned the revelations on Rocky Mountain, came to the Moravians in deep anxiety in February 1812. Thinking in terms of Christian sermons he had heard, he wished to know "whether the end of the world were not near." The Moravians' answer was not reassuring. They said that "no man knows this, but that it behooves us to be prepared and ready." Ridge, like many Cherokees, felt that God or the Great Spirit was angry with them. "It is true we are very bad," he said; "may God make us better." He wished the Moravians to tell him how God forgave those who "had spent a large part of their lives in evil." He then told them of some of the wicked deeds which he had seen in the nation recently, especially the murder of a harmless old man by a drunken Cherokee. (The act was symptomatic of the new lack of respect by the young for the old.) In the years 1811–12 Ridge came closer to Christian conversion than at any time in his life.[15] The spiritual confusion and the search for order permeated the nation, affecting even those who rejected the new visions and prophecies.

Ridge, being sympathetic to Christianity, was willing to believe the Moravians' view that the earthquakes were a warning from God about the wickedness of the Cherokees. Other Cherokees believed that the wickedness which caused the Great Spirit's anger came from the whites who had stolen their land, corrupted their people, destroyed their way of life. Chief Chulioah visited the Moravians in February 1812 and, after confessing his perplexity over the quakes, "said in a very emphatic way that many Indians believe that the white people were responsible [for God's anger] because they had already taken possession of so much of the Indian land and wanted still more. God was angry because of that and He wanted to put an end to it."[16] Chulioah did not deny that a day of judgment might be near, but he refused to believe that the Cherokees were to blame.

One of the most remarkable visions or dreams inspired by the earthquake, or growing out of its aftermath, dealt with the problem of sickness and the remedies for it. It expressed the view that the younger generation were suffering great stress which the older generation should, but could not, cure. Recorded by the Moravians on February 17, 1812, it contains some of the syncretic symbolism common to this revival. By 1812 Christian theol-

14. Ibid.
15. Springplace Diary, February 11, 1812, MAS. See also Wilkins, *Cherokee Tragedy*, pp. 55–56.
16. Springplace Diary, February 17, 1812, MAS.

ogy had become incongruously mixed with Cherokee religion. The Moravians considered this story blasphemous:

> Soon after the earth trembled for the first time, an Indian was sitting in his house in deep thought, and his children were lying sick in front of the fire. At that point a tall man, clothed entirely in the foliage of the trees, with a wreath of the same foliage on his head, who was carrying a small child in his arm and had a larger child by the hand, said to him, 'The child in his [my] arm is God. I am not able to tell you now whether God will soon destroy the earth or not. But God is not pleased that the Indians have sold so much land to the white people. Tugaloo, which is now possessed by white people, is the first place which God created. There in a hill he placed the first fire, for all fire comes from God. Now the white people have built a house on that hill. They should abandon the place; on that hill here should be grass growing, only then will there be peace. And the Indians no longer thank God before they enjoy first fruits of the land [the Green Corn Dance]. They are no longer organizing, as was formerly the custom, dances in his honor before they eat the first pumpkins, etc. Furthermore,' the messenger said to the Indian, 'you are sad because you think your children are ill; they are really not ill but have only taken in a little dust.' Thereupon he gave him two small pieces of bark from a certain tree, which he also named, and told him to cook them and to give the drink to his children, and from that they became well right then. He then also told him about other remedies for use during illness, and at the end, he said he would now take God back home.[17]

This vision, told to the Moravians by Chief Big Bear, combined some features of the earliest visions (the anger of the Creator over the sale of the sacred towns, the need to revive their sacred dances) with new concerns for the "soul sickness" of their young people and for the imminent end of the world. While telling "this silly narration," as the Moravians called it, with its strange image of an Indian carrying the Christ child, Big Bear "looked so solemn, as if he were really proclaiming God's will and word." Big Bear truly believed that the Cherokees were a sick people, out of right relationship with the world and with nature.

After telling his story and seeing the consternation on the faces of the missionaries, Big Bear assured them that he had no hostility toward them: "I love you," he said; "I have never heard anything bad about you. But there are also very bad white people." The Moravians agreed with the latter point but said they knew nothing of the meaning of such visions as he reported, for they relied wholly on the Bible for their knowledge of God's will. Chief Chulioah, who was also present, remarked sagely, "Yes, the white people know God from the Book and we, from other things."

The Cherokee religious revival seems to have reached a peak in the spring of 1812. "There is at the present time," the Moravians noted in February, "a real tumult in the Nation and a dark, heavy feeling." Now they began to hear "much about dreams and false prophets" from those friendly to

17. Ibid.

the mission. They also heard predictions of apocalyptic catastrophes which would befall the region. During February "the residents of one town fled into the hills and tried to crawl into hiding in the holes of the rocks in order to escape the danger of hail stones the size of half bushels which were to fall on a certain day."[18] An old woman called Laughing Molly told them of a prediction concerning an imminent eclipse of the moon during which "hail stones as large as hominy blocks would fall, all the cattle would die, and soon thereafter the earth would come to an end."[19] After another earthquake in March 1812, a Cherokee had a revelation "that there would be an intense darkness and that it would last three days, during which all the white people would be snatched away as well as all Indians who had any clothing or household article of the whiteman's kind." This Cherokee urged his friends to "put aside everything that is similar to the white people and that they had learned from them, so that in the darkness God might not mistake them and snatch them away forever." Anyone who did not do this "will die at once together with all his stock."[20] When an Indian named the Duck refused to believe in this prophecy and act upon it, and then died suddenly, many Cherokees became certain that the prediction was true.[21]

Some of those who had come to trust the Moravians became skeptical of these prophecies. They not only refused to give up all their clothing and whiteman's goods but went around buying up such goods at bargain prices from those who did believe.[22] These speculators were Cherokees who had sent their children to the mission school at Springplace and frequently attended its services. They had found their new ethic.

Not all the prophecies concerned death and destruction. Others told of a golden day of renewal that would come soon. One pupil at the Moravian school "said that in his neighborhood there was . . . talk that a new earth would come into being in the spring."[23] However, the student assured the missionaries that "he did not pay attention to their absurd talking."

In April 1812, Colonel Meigs thought it might help these superstitious people if the Moravian missionary John Gambold came to the Council to give the chiefs a Christian view of history "in order to calm, as much as possible, the emotions of the Indians which were made very fearful through

18. Springplace Diary, February 23, 1812, MAS. This is evidently the event (only one of many prophecies at the time) which James Wafford related in more detail to Mooney in 1888. Mooney, *Ghost Dance*, pp. 676–77. Thirty years later, when the white prophet William Miller predicted the end of the world in 1843, the editor of the *Cherokee Advocate* published a bemused account of this incident, noting that Miller, "the Catastrophe Preacher and his *enlightened* followers, are treading almost in the very footsteps of some old Cherokee Conjuror and his *benighted* followers, who have gone before them" thirty years earlier. *Cherokee Advocate*, November 16, 1844.
19. Springplace Diary, March 1, 1812, MAS.
20. Springplace Diary, March 8, 1812, MAS.
21. Springplace Diary, March 1 and 8, 1812, MAS.
22. Springplace Diary, March 8, 1812, MAS.
23. Ibid.

the oft-mentioned false prophets."[24] During this Council, Chief Sour Mush made an angry speech in Cherokee in the presence of Gambold. Then, realizing that Gambold might think the speech was directed against him, he assured him, through the interpreter, "that he was angry neither with him nor with the white people in general." Sour Mush was angry with those who had been known horsethieves and now were fearful about being swallowed up by an earthquake. He had said to these kinds of people in his tirade, "As the earth moved sometimes a short time ago, you were in great anxiety and feared you would sink down into it, but when you go among the white people to break down their stables and steal their horses, you are not afraid, and there there is much great[er] danger, for if they should catch you in such an act, they would surely shoot you down, and then you would surely be sunk [buried] into the earth."[25] Sour Mush, like the Ridge, had sent his son to the Moravian school and believed that acting rightly was the great need of his people, not burning their clothes and hats.

Charles Hicks, a strong supporter of the missionaries and of acculturation, used his influence as a chief to suppress the religious excitement. When the local chiefs of Etowah, a traditionalist area where the movement was very powerful, asked him for advice about the revival enthusiasts and their prophets, Hicks told them "not to give the liars any hearing at all," and he "showed them out of God's word"—a Bible which he was studying—what Christians said "about the end of the world."[26] A few years later, Hicks was to present himself to the Moravians for Christian baptism.

For several reasons the revival began to simmer down during the latter part of 1812. At least the Moravians and Colonel Meigs seem to have heard little about it thereafter. Probably the devout believers, finding little sympathy from the whitemen and the promission chiefs, concluded that they had better keep the movement to themselves. Nevertheless, if the revival of traditionalism went underground, it did not lead to any increase in Christianity. Apart from the conversion of Charles Hicks in 1813, there was no convert recorded by the missionaries between 1810 and 1818.[27]

As war with Britain loomed in the west in 1812, many whites, assuming that there was some connection between Tecumseh's movement, the anticivilization movement among the Creeks, and the religious revival among the Cherokees, believed that the Cherokees would soon join forces with the British and that there would be a bloody Indian war against the frontier settlements. To calm the whites, some of the Cherokee chiefs

24. Springplace Diary, April 30, 1812, MAS. The fear of witchcraft revived among some Cherokees, and a woman later reported that "all her near relatives were slain for the supposed crime of witchcraft" in 1812. She escaped death because she was pregnant. Brainerd Journal, May 28, 1822, ABCFM.

25. Springplace Diary, April 30, 1812, MAS.

26. Springplace Diary, March 1, 1812, MAS.

27. See Schwarze, *Moravian Missions*, p. 120, and Springplace Conference, 1802–14, pp. 77–79.

announced at the Council which John Gambold attended in May 1812 that they would like to gather a group of Cherokee volunteers to fight with the United States should war come. "Three young chiefs," Meigs reported to the secretary of war, "men of property and considerable information, came into the Council and observed that there would be war between the United States and the English and that they wished each to raise a number of young warriors and offer their service on [the same] terms of pay and emolument of our military corps."[28] The three chiefs were the Ridge, John Walker, and John Lowery, all of them opponents of the revival and staunch advocates of rapid acculturation.

However, the majority of the Council did not react positively to this suggestion. Their coolness arose not out of a desire to join Tecumseh but because they believed neutrality was the best course for the nation. The suggestion of raising a volunteer force was debated, but no action was taken. While Meigs encouraged the three chiefs to proceed to raise volunteers, he had some difficulty persuading the War Department to agree to give some of them appropriate officer rank and all of them pay as regular soldiers. In addition, there was some fear that because of the "retrograde movement" behind the revival, the Cherokee soldiers might not "be restrained from acts of barbarity" in a war (such as scalping British soldiers). Meigs resolved this by saying that "to employ them against the British Indians" (the Shawnees or Creeks) "would not be considered inconsistent with just principles of defense" because that would simply pit "barbarians" against each other.[29]

The United States declared war on Britain in June 1812, but the immediate issue on the southern frontier was the Red Stick rebellion of the Creek Upper Towns against the Creek Lower Towns. From May 1812 to August 1813, the Cherokees tried desperately to remain neutral toward the Creek civil war on their southern border, but as Meigs reported in August, "The civil war amongst the Creeks has placed the Cherokees in a disagreeable situation and should the insurgent Creeks get the ascendancy, they will, if possible, corrupt the Cherokees"; that is, persuade them to join the British and Tecumseh against the frontier whites.[30]

In many respects the Creeks had been going through the same religious concern over rapid acculturation as the Cherokees in these years, but in their case the conservatives were so angered by the arbitrary actions of their dominant Lower Town chiefs that they were willing to engage in open civil war against them. The leaders of this internal rebellion, called the Red Sticks, were known to be sympathetic to Tecumseh, but the Cherokees had no intention of joining Tecumseh. They did their best to remain neutral toward the warring Creek factions, as they did toward the war between

28. R. J. Meigs to William Eustis, May 8, 1812, OSW, M-22, roll 47, #1813.
29. R. J. Meigs to John Armstrong, August 23, 1813, OSW, M-221, roll 55, #9216.
30. R. J. Meigs to John Armstrong, August 6, 1813, BIA, M-208 R. J. Meigs to John Armstrong, August 6, 1813, OSW, M-221, roll 55, #9112.

Britain and the United States. However, when the Red Stick Creeks attacked the United States army post at Fort Mims, Alabama, in September 1813 and wiped out its garrison and those whites who had taken refuge there, Cherokee neutrality became impossible. The outrage of the frontier whites at this act would lead them to interpret continued Cherokee neutrality as sympathy and complicity with the Red Sticks. When President Madison placed Andrew Jackson in charge of the Tennessee and Georgia militia to put down the Creek rebels, the War Department at last agreed to allow Cherokee volunteers to enlist in Jackson's army, and the Cherokee Council silently acquiesced (though it never officially declared war on the Creeks). Meigs arranged for the Ridge to be commissioned as major and gave suitable ranks to the other chiefs, who had managed to enroll 500 to 600 Cherokees to join Jackson's command.[31]

It is almost impossible to determine how many of these volunteers were fullbloods or mixed bloods, prorevival or antirevival, traditionalists or acculturationists. Most likely there was a fair representation from all of these categories. Few Cherokee males could resist the opportunity to test their valor in war; furthermore, the War Department promised to let them keep all the personal booty they gained when they captured Creek towns. Some Cherokees were eager to obtain black slaves as booty (the Creeks owned many slaves). A few Cherokees, it later turned out, also took Creek women and children as slaves. They were ruthless in their slaughter of Creek warriors and undoubtedly scalped some of those they killed. Those chiefs who led the Cherokee volunteers believed that by demonstrating their loyalty to the United States in this crisis and fighting side by side with white frontiersmen (who had always despised them), they would obtain both gratitude toward their people and a better relationship with white Americans thereafter. Some believed their valor in war and their self-discipline as soldiers would also convince the whites that they were no longer savages. Perhaps their efforts would convince the whites that the Cherokees were capable of managing their own affairs and thus give support to the nationalistic separatism evident in the revival.

On the other hand, there were undoubtedly some Cherokee leaders, like the Ridge, who considered participation in the war essentially an effective means to overcome the divisions which the revival movement had created among them. War would redirect that excessive enthusiasm into channels which would unite the nation against external enemies (but not against whites). In short, the Creek War seemed a fortuitous occasion for the restoration of Cherokee harmony in terms which both conservatives and acculturationists could embrace.

The Cherokees fought well in the Creek War. They won the praise of their white commanders, including General Jackson. Great self-respect and

31. R. J. Meigs to William Eustis, November 17, 1813, OSW, M-221, roll 55, #9287.

pride was generated among them by their accomplishments. The revival petered out during the war years without ever integrating the various visions into a concerted, tradition-oriented revitalization movement. The Battle of Horseshoe Bend in 1814, in which the outnumbered and under-armed Red Sticks were slaughtered in large numbers, marked the climactic moment of the war for the Cherokees. They played a crucial role in that famous battle. The Creek traditionalist rebellion was put down, a treaty signed, and the Lower Town (proacculturation) Creek chiefs reassumed control.

The war did not do the Moravian mission (the only mission in the nation from 1810 to 1817) any particular good. The Moravians were pacifists, but they allowed their one male convert, Charles Hicks, to serve in the volunteer army without censure on the ground that he could not, in his capacity as a chief, refuse the request of the government to lead his people.[32]

The religious revival and the war against the Creeks combined to instill new confidence among the Cherokees and to increase their nationalistic fervor. They emerged from the war prepared for a new surge forward in social and political reorganization. At the same time, the second victory of the United States over the British renewed the zeal of white Americans for further westward expansion and created a new threat of removal for the Cherokees and the other Indians in the valley. In addition, the great religious awakening among white Americans in these same years also revived interest in the evangelization of the Indians and sent a new wave of missionaries to the Cherokees as well as to most other Indian nations after the war. The conflict between the new ways and the old took a different form in the Cherokee nation after 1816, when the small, mild, and self-contained Moravian mission at Springplace was supplemented by more aggressive, better-financed, and more numerous missionaries sent by the American Board of Commissioners for Foreign Missions in Boston.

32. Schwarze, *Moravian Missions*, p. 120.

ᕦ⊙(CHAPTER FIVE)⊙ᕤ

The New England Missionaries,
1816–1819

Mr. John Ross [a Cherokee chief] . . . has asked us how a portion of land can be secured for the benefit of the schools of the nation. He is not satisfied that the Cherokees should barely say they are *willing* to receive instruction; it is his wish that they should evince their ardent desire for it by *doing* something to promote it.

The Reverend Ard Hoyt, January 11, 1819

The arrival in the Cherokee Nation in 1816 of the New England missionaries of the American Board of Commissioners for Foreign Missions marked a new dimension in the efforts at civilization and Christianization. The American Board represented a Christian public in the Northeast not only free from much of the anti-Indian prejudice which the Cherokees faced on the southern frontier, but also opposed to the institution of black slavery. The board's publications—a monthly journal and an annual report—provided information about Cherokee progress which reached a wide audience of American voters on a regular basis. The influence of the board's members, particularly of its important business and political leaders, was to have great weight with members of Congress, who would ultimately decide upon the Indian policy of the nation; some of the board's members were themselves congressmen. The open and persistent involvement of the American Board in Cherokee political affairs made the previous actions of Blackburn and the Moravians seem minuscule. Quickly the Cherokees began to see that these missionaries represented not only a more extensive means of education in needed skills, but also a new source of friendly political power upon which they could draw.

Founded in Massachusetts by the Congregationalists in 1810, the American Board thought of itself as national in support, interdenominational in makeup, and global in mission. In 1818 its corresponding secretaries described it to the secretary of war in grandiloquent terms: "its members reside in seven states of the union . . ., it has patrons and friends in all the states of the union . . ., its members are not confined to any religious denomination . . ., it disowns all narrow, local or party views, and seeks to do good by aiding in the moral improvement of our fellow men wherever accessible who have not yet enjoyed the blessings of civilization and christianity . . ., it regards with peculiar interest the wants of the Aborigines within our own borders . . ., it will not solicit the patronage of government for any object to which the members of the society are not ready to contribute their property, their time, and their labour."[1] Nevertheless, it was dominated by New Englanders and it was essentially a New England effort to remake America in its own image. The well-to-do merchants and textile manufacturers who financed the board, the Calvinistic church members, mostly descendants of the Puritans, who contributed their mites, and the Congregational clergy who managed and worked for it were convinced that they, better than anyone else, understood the principles upon which God wished American society to be organized. Most of them had been Federalists and many defended the union of church and state in Massachusetts until 1833. Fearful that the young nation was headed for danger in its headlong expansion westward and convinced that God had chosen the people of the United States and its institutions as the instruments of his plan to redeem mankind, the leaders of the American Board decided to supervise and regulate what they could not prevent. Assisted to a small extent by the Presbyterian and Dutch Reformed churchmen of the Middle Atlantic states and the Midwest, the Congregationalists of the American Board set out to coordinate, direct, systematize, and control the elevation of the aborigines of the southern states, beginning with the Cherokees.

They raised many thousands of dollars annually for this purpose, and they obtained the generous patronage of the president and of Congress for their work. The board (and the Prudential Committee in Boston, which directed the enterprise) did not hide the fact that it considered itself a primary engine of national as well as Christian progress. Explaining the reasons for its founding in 1810, the official historian of the board wrote in 1840, "Religion, from which the struggle for national existence and the formation of the national government had partially withdrawn the minds of men, was beginning to recover its former power" through the great religious revival sweeping the country in the early years of the century. "The temporal concerns of the nation were 'in the full tide of successful experiment,' " and the "pecuniary embarrassment" of the early decades of the nation (the Critical Period of debased paper money) "had passed away." In 1810 the time was ripe for a new kind of philanthropic organization. A host of "local societies . . . were springing up in various parts of the land" to carry forward "the religion of this country" to those who had not yet heard and embraced it. But to those of enlarged vision and means in Boston, "the spirit which was spreading and strengthening the community would soon demand and create a system of operation for the management of which [the small] organizations then existing would be found inadequate."[2] In short, missions

1. Jeremiah Evarts and Elias Cornelius to John C. Calhoun, July 15, 1818, ABCFM.

2. Joseph Tracy, *History of the American Board of Commissioners for Foreign Missions* (New York: M. W. Dodd, 1842), p. 22. See also John A. Andrews III, *Rebuilding the Christian Commonwealth* (Lexington: University of Kentucky Press, 1976), pp. 1–6.

were to advance from the small-time efforts of the Moravians and Blackburn into a big business. Beyond the religious and nationalistic motivations of these New England Calvinists lay the equally potent drives of the Yankee businessman and his desire to expand the nation's economy and exploit its resources. The expansion of international commerce, republicanism, evangelicalism, and free enterprise capitalism were to be harnessed for the advance of patriotism, empire, and the millennium—all in the name of "benevolence."

Jackson's Providential victory at New Orleans in 1815 had ended all threat of British control over the Mississippi Valley and though some eighty-five Indian nations with 125,000 people still lived on the land they had owned east of the Mississippi for untold centuries, these former enemies to white expansion were rendered harmless by the defeat of Tecumseh in the North and the Red Stick Creeks in the South. Although in a piteous condition for the most part, these eighty-five Indian nations had treaties with the government which guaranteed their right to much of the most valuable land in the Mississippi Valley—the rich corn and wheat areas of the old Northwest and the black soil of the cotton belt in the old Southwest. To attain the riches of the valley, the heartland of the rejuvenated nation, the missionaries would convert the hearts and minds of the Indians to patriotic Christianity, the Protestant ethic of hard work, and individualistic free enterprise. Just as the first tariff law of 1816 offered government protection to "infant industries" in New England and New York, so federal aid to missions would provide after 1816 subsidies to large benevolent associations interested in the dramatic enterprise of transforming ignorant savages into useful citizens. The Indian policy devised by Henry Knox in 1789 was at last ready to operate on a grand scale.

"The religion of the country," in the view of the American Board, was evangelical Protestantism, a religion which transcended both sectarian and regional divisions. Joseph Tracy, the early historian of the board, spoke chiefly of his agency's positive, optimistic hopes for national unity and progress, but beneath his optimism lay deep-seated fears that without missionary evangelism (home missions to the white frontier people, foreign missions to the Indians) the nation was in grave danger of sinking into the iniquities of materialism and sectionalism. At the same time "hordes" of "foreigners" were pouring into the cities and factory towns of the East, many of whom still clung to the Church of Rome. It was an era of specialization, and in the division of Christian labor the American Board left home missions to its sister organizations and gave primary attention to the heathen abroad and the Indians in the Mississippi Valley.

The Reverend Cyrus Kingsbury, sent by the American Board as a spiritual scout to the southern frontier in 1816, concluded that the 65,000 Southeastern Indians there were ripe for missionary action on a broad scale. Writing to the secretary of war for aid on the board's behalf, Kingsbury noted that the government had too long borne alone the burden of civilizing the Indians: "the duty" to uplift them was "incumbent on individuals and societies as well as on the government." Government and benevolent voluntary societies such as the one he represented must combine forces "to extend to the Indians, as far as is practicable, the distinguished advantages which we enjoy." These advantages would not only rescue the perishing savages but prove "the most effectual means . . . to give security to our frontier settlements." Consequently he spoke to the president and then to the secretary of war to request their "liberal patronage" and partnership "in this enterprise." The board would supply and supervise the volunteer workforce of this benevolent bureaucracy if the government would provide the funds for "the erection of suitable buildings and for providing those implements of husbandry and the mechanic arts" which are essential for a "respectable and useful" vocational education. It was a project vital to "national interest and national happiness," and "probably no other means could be so successfully employed to prevent the recurrence of expensive and bloody Indian wars."[3]

The board's plans were grandiose. It expected to establish mission stations among all four of the major Southeastern Indian nations and would probably have included the Seminoles except that they lived in Florida, which until 1819 belonged to Spain. Furthermore, it believed that its resources and managerial skills were such that the United States government should give it a total monopoly over the Christianization and education of the Cherokees, Choctaws, Creeks, and Chickasaws—about 65,000 Indian souls. "There are obvious considerations," said Dr. Samuel A. Worcester of the board's Prudential Committee to Kingsbury in November 1817, "which render it highly desirable that one [mission] Station at least should be occupied in each of the four Nations with the least unnecessary delay." These would in effect stake out the board's preemptory spiritual claims to the territory. "Such an occupation would prevent either of them from thinking themselves neglected and what is of high consideration, would give us a sort of possession of the entire field and place us on 'vantage ground with the Government." It would give them first claim "with respect to any interference of others." The board considered it "of very great importance to have an unmolested possession of the field. For other [benevolent] societies other fields are open, and the way to preserve harmony in the great work is prudently to avoid and prevent interference."[4] Such monopolistic visions of Indian missionary effort proved impossible of fulfillment. The board was to have considerable competition after 1819, but the attitude was typical of its broad-ranging, self-assured zeal and its businesslike attitude.

Madison's secretary of war, William H. Crawford, informed Kingsbury in May 1816 that he and the president fully concurred with the idea of a

3. ASP II, 477–78. I have used the statistics of Jedidiah Morse, who tabulated 55,493 Indians in the North and 65,625 in the South in 1822. His figure of 11,000 for the Cherokees is probably too low by several thousand. He also lists 85 different tribes by name. Jedidiah Morse, *A Report to the Secretary of War*, pp. 361–64.

4. Samuel Worcester to Cyrus Kingsbury, November 19, 1817, ABCFM.

partnership between the government and the board. A written contract was entered into in which the War Department agreed to instruct the federal agents in the South to supply ploughs, hoes, axes, spinning wheels, cards, and looms for the board's schools as well as to provide for the erection of dormitories and schoolhouses for the board's Indian students and their teachers as well as gristmills to grind the corn for the model farms. ("The houses thus erected and the implements of husbandry . . . will remain public property to be occupied and employed for the benefit of the nation," Crawford noted in a clause which was later to become a major bone of contention between the Cherokees and the missionaries.) The missionaries were to teach "the art of cultivation" to the males and of domestic manufactures to the females. They were to provide annual reports of their progress and, implicitly, to assist in the implementation of government policies. Noting that the budget for all of this was small, Crawford said that he expected in the near future that "the attention of Congress will be attracted to the subject" and then more ample funding would be available.[5] No doubt he expected the American Board to apply political pressure and publicity toward this. Three years later Congress did pass an act specifically creating a fund for the support of Indian education—the so-called Civilization Fund—which the secretary of war thereafter divided up among the missionary agencies. The major part of this fund went annually to the American Board.

This auspicious beginning of the board's work among the Southeastern Indians ran into political difficulty almost immediately, however, when the pressure of frontier voters and their Congressmen produced a powerful demand to remove to the west of the Mississippi all Indians then living to the east of it. Land speculators, prospective farmers, and southern planters were too impatient to wait a generation or more for the civilization, Christianization, and incorporation of the Indians (a possibility they had grave doubts about anyway). Some of the smaller Indian tribes in the North may have favored removal in order to extricate themselves from untenably small reserves on which they could not subsist, but the vast majority of Indians were bitterly opposed to being shoved around, hither and yon, to make way for land-hungry whites. The five Southeastern nations (Cherokees, Creeks, Choctaws, Chickasaws, and Seminoles) who still had sufficient land to support their people (and treaty guarantees preserving it to them) were especially hostile to this policy. The Cherokees in particular could see no justification for it because of their successful transition to an agricultural economy and their loyal defense of the frontier against the Creeks and the British. To them, as to all Indian peoples, their homeland was a sacred place and so closely related to their cultural identity that to uproot them would be as destructive as trying to transplant an ancient oak tree. The Cherokees looked forward to the new assistance being offered on such a grand scale by

5. ASP II, 478.

the American Board because they were convinced that with only a little more help they would soon be fully self-sustaining.

Where the Cherokees and the American Board were to quarrel in the near future was not over removal, for both concurred in opposing that policy, but in regard to who should control the schools, how many schools there should be, where they should be located, what their curriculum should be, what standards of admission and progress should be set. The Cherokees were ready to share the cost of running a public school system, but the American Board did not believe they were ready to supervise it. It came as a shock to the board and to the government in the 1820s that many Cherokees believed the schools, being on their land, belonged to them and that the missionaries were there to do as the Cherokees thought best in educating their young and not vice versa.

But before these issues arose the more pressing problem of removal had to be settled. To the dismay of the Cherokees after 1815, the frontier whites felt no sense of gratitude for their part in the war. The number of Cherokees killed and wounded in fighting with Jackson against the rebellious Creeks was not large by white standards, but it was to the Cherokees. Besides, it was the spirit of their effort, their decision to honor their treaty obligations and fight with white Americans against other redmen that deserved recognition. The Cherokees conveniently forgot their initial hesitancy to join this conflict and their long effort to remain neutral.

In 1814 when Jackson made his peace treaty with the Creeks, he included with the tract taken from the Creek Nation as reparations 2.2 million acres of rich cotton land in northern Alabama which was claimed by the Cherokees (land, incidentally, in which Jackson and his friend John Coffee were heavily concerned as speculators).[6] Jackson justified this on the grounds that the land had never really belonged to the Cherokee Nation but had simply been loaned by the Creeks to those Cherokees of the Lower Towns who had settled there after 1781. However, this land had been confirmed to the Cherokees by the Treaty of Hopewell in 1785, and even Meigs and President Madison believed Jackson had erred in taking it from them in 1814. In an unprecedented action, the United States made another treaty with the Cherokees in March 1816 in which it overruled Jackson's treaty and returned this land to the Cherokees. It did so, however, only when the Cherokees agreed to cede their remaining land within the state of South Carolina. Jackson and the frontier whites were furious, and at another treaty negotiation in September-October 1816 Jackson, by means of intimidation and bribes, forced a tiny minority of the Cherokee chiefs (most of them from the Lower Town region) to cede this 2.2 million acres back to the United States.[7] Then, in July 1817 Jackson obtained an even more devastating

6. Charles C. Royce, *The Cherokee Nation of Indians*, pp. 78–81; Michael Rogin, *Fathers and Children* (New York: Knopf, 1975), pp. 165–205.

7. Royce, *Cherokee Nation*, pp. 69–83.

treaty, again by intimidation—one which he expected would result in the removal of the whole Cherokee Nation to Arkansas. If this were successful, the American Board's project in the South would have collapsed, for the other tribes too would be forced to emigrate.

This second removal crisis among the Cherokees derived from the first back in 1807–09. Jackson had assumed that an agreement had been formally made by a Cherokee delegation meeting with Jefferson in December and January 1808–09 to exchange land in the East for land in Arkansas and that it was on this basis that 1,100–1,500 Cherokees had moved west at government expense between 1809 and 1811. However, the government had failed to provide a tract west of the Mississippi for these emigrants. Jackson's treaty in 1817 promised to do this, but it allowed a year for other Cherokees to take advantage of it and to go west at government expense.[8] Jackson's hope was that most of the Cherokees would remove and virtually all of their eastern territory would be exchanged for land in Arkansas (those more advanced Cherokees who did not want to remove would be given their farms as fee simple "reserves" and allowed to become citizens of the states in which they resided). To this end agents were sent into the nation to encourage emigration by any and every possible means.

The confusion, turmoil, and anxiety resulting from Jackson's treaty in 1817 provided a poor climate in which to start a new effort for Christianization and civilization in the East. The American Board had barely inaugurated its first mission station among the Cherokees when Jackson's treaty was concluded. Although the board was not in favor of the removal policy, it hardly seemed proper for its missionaries to say so publicly because they were supported in part by the government and were considered its agents. On the other hand, to refuse to help the Cherokees in this critical effort to retain their homeland would be disastrous to good relations with the Cherokees. The principal chiefs opposing the treaty were Charles Hicks, Path Killer, Major Ridge, George Lowery, and John Ross. These same chiefs were also eager to encourage the American Board's plan for a nationwide school system and equally eager to establish a Cherokee school fund which would give the Council some control over education in the nation.

The Moravians, following their usual quietistic approach, took no part in the political crisis of 1817–19 other than to offer spiritual consolation to their distressed congregation at Springplace. The Congregationalists from New England had never been admirers of Andrew Jackson and his rough frontier attitudes toward national policy. They decided that in this situation they should assume the role of mediators and compromisers—"honest brokers"—able to see both sides of the question and willing to suggest solutions which would be fair and just both to the Cherokees and to the frontier whites in the South. It required all the skill of Yankee horse traders to walk the narrow line between these angry factions. Jackson's official agent

8. Royce, *Cherokee Nation*, pp. 84–91; ASP II, 129–31.

to encourage removal, Governor Joseph McMinn of Tennessee, claimed that the nation's "half-breeds," led by Hicks and Ross, were resorting to violence against would-be emigrants and told Secretary of War John C. Calhoun in June 1818 that the Cherokees had even threatened his life (a justification for bringing United States soldiers to attend a council held in November 1818). Frontier whites in the region professed to fear an armed uprising. The Cherokees, on the other hand, accused McMinn of lying and misleading unlettered Cherokees and even plying them with drink in order to register them for emigration. Though the treaty said emigration was to be entirely voluntary, some chiefs feared that unscrupulous whites on the border might provoke a violent incident in order to give the government an excuse to remove the Cherokees by force.[9]

The Reverend Elias Cornelius, the corresponding secretary of the Prudential Committee of the American Board, started his involvement in the dispute on the assumption that the government would hardly have encouraged the board's missionary enterprise in 1816 unless it had believed that there would be Indians in the South to be civilized. On July 25, 1817, less than three weeks after Jackson's removal treaty was negotiated, Cornelius wrote to the secretary of war thanking him for agreeing to support the board's schools among the Cherokees. "I am further instructed," he said, "to mention distinctly that it is the settled policy of the Committee and of the Board to form in the Choctaw, Chickasaw, and Creek Nations establishments similar to the one already commenced in the Cherokee nation. . . . In consequence of the encouragement given by the Government to expect its patronage and protection . . . I have to state that arrangements are *immediately* to be made" for that purpose. Consequently, "I have to request, dear sir, of you, a statement of your judgment as to the certain or probable patronage which may be expected from the government in the institution of these establishments."[10]

Almost nine months prior to this, when Kingsbury was first making inquiries regarding possible government patronage of the Cherokee mission, he was well aware of the dilemma the board faced due to the mounting clamor of western whites and land speculators for removal of the Indians. "I ought to observe," Kingsbury wrote to the board in November 1816, after discussing the matter with the secretary of war, "that I expect an attempt will be made at the coming session of Congress to induce the Cherokees to remove over the Mississippi. . . . If the attempt should succeed, I should blush for my country, though I am not confident that it would not be for the good of the Indian."[11] Kingsbury reflected the general feeling among New Englanders that it would be cruel and unfair of the government to abrogate

9. Details of the debate over the interpretation of this treaty can be found in ASP II, 142–48, 478–90.
10. Elias Cornelius to George Graham, July 25, 1817, OSW, M-221, roll 73, #5025.
11. Cyrus Kingsbury to Samuel Worcester, November 28, 1816, ABCFM.

treaty promises made to the Cherokees after they had made such progress as farmers. He might, in his heart, have wished the Indians would move, but he also knew that this would thwart the plans of the board. Kingsbury said the animosity of the frontier whites against the Indians was so great that the Indians might really be better off at a distance from them. Had the Cherokees known of his views on this question, they might not have been so friendly to his starting the mission in 1817. Nevertheless, once the mission started, the Cherokees realized they had at last a potential source of friendly political assistance; consequently they set out to make the most of the board's self-interest.

The Cherokee Council had agreed to admit the board's missionaries in October 1816. Within a month, Kingsbury had purchased the improvements of John McDonald at Chattanooga as the site of the mission. McDonald, now an old man, was ready to give up his farm to go to live with his grandson, John Ross (son of Daniel Ross), a few miles away at Ross's Landing. Ross was a rising young leader in the nation, twenty-seven years old; one-eighth Cherokee but married to a fullblood named Quatie, he was thoroughly loyal to the nationalistic aims of the Council and vehemently opposed to removal. Intelligent and well educated, he ran a trading post at the landing with his brother Lewis and through government contracts had become one of the wealthiest and most influential of the chiefs. He immediately established close relations with the New Englanders.

The first missionaries, Cyrus Kingsbury, Lorin Williams, and Moody Hall, who arrived in January 1817, and Ard Hoyt and Daniel S. Butrick, who arrived the following January, found Ross a valuable friend and were pleased with the welcome given them by the Cherokees.[12] They christened their mission station Brainerd and started their school there in March 1817. Overwhelmed by the number of students who enrolled, they nevertheless agreed to take all who wished to enter. Within a year they had forty-four male students and thirty-one females. When they discovered that the tuition and board fee of one dollar a week was too expensive for most fullblood families, they dropped the fee entirely in May 1818, thereby more than doubling the number of fullblood students (from twenty-four to fifty-seven) in 1819. The Reverend Ard Hoyt became superintendent of the mission in 1818 when Kingsbury moved westward to commence negotiations with the Choctaw Nation. Because the tensions in the nation increased rapidly after July 1817 the board decided not to start another mission station or school until the crisis was resolved.

Because there were no Congregational ministerial associations in the South, the American Board's missionaries eventually asked to be received as Presbyterians into the Union Presbytery of Eastern Tennessee in order to

12. For Ross, see Gary E. Moulton, *John Ross, Cherokee Chief* (Athens: University of Georgia Press, 1978); for the early years of Brainerd mission, see Robert S. Walker, *Torchlights to the Cherokees*.

establish formal ecclesiastical relations in the region. Under the Plan of Union between Congregationalists and Presbyterians in 1801, the two denominations had agreed to unite their efforts on the frontier. Nevertheless, even though they sometimes referred to themselves as Presbyterians, the Congregationalists of the American Board brought with them regional attitudes which were not similar to those of their southern frontier colleagues. The Presbyterians in the South held the common frontier views about Indian removal and in support of Andrew Jackson, and the presbytery's relationship with the New Englanders was strictly formal. The Prudential Committee and virtually all the missionaries of the American Board were decidedly Federalist and National Republican (later Whig) in their political outlook, though as a benevolent association they claimed to be above worldly affiliations of that kind. The board's political influence in Congress lay through political leaders of the anti-Jackson party. Significantly, the Cherokee leaders who opposed removal came to consider themselves Whigs as they began to master the art of manipulating American politics and public opinion. Cherokee nationalism and New England religious and business interests constituted a strange alliance after 1816 in their joint opposition to the rising tide of Jacksonian democracy. Well aware of the Cherokees' concern over Jackson's treaty of 1817, the missionaries at Brainerd let them know that they sympathized with them and shared their concern over Jackson's methods and policies. Ard Hoyt explained to the board in Boston why the Cherokees put no faith in the treaty: "This people consider the offer of taking reserves and becoming citizens of the United States as of no service to them. They know they are not to be admitted to the rights of freemen or the privileges of their oath and [they] say no Cherokee or white man with a Cherokee family can possibly live among such white people as will first settle their country."[13] By "the rights of freemen" and "the privileges of their oath" Hoyt referred to the laws of the states in which Cherokees who took fee-simple reserves would become citizens. Indians had never been given the right to testify under oath even in their own defense, ostensibly because they were not Christians but in fact because they were not white. As Governor McMinn said in 1816, Cherokees who took reserves in the state of Tennessee would be "considered as entitled to all the rights of free citizens of color," which meant racial segregation and limited civil rights.[14] The federal government, under the Constitution, could do nothing to define the qualifications for citizenship within the sovereign states of the Union. Indian "citizens" would be denied not only the right to vote and testify but even to send their children to public schools. Hoyt agreed with the Cherokees that Jackson's treaty was a mockery of justice, designed to compel them against their will to give up their homeland or become second-class citizens, and, like Kingsbury, he blushed for his country.

13. Brainerd Journal, November 25, 1818, ABCFM.
14. ASP II, 115.

The Cherokees' views of the kinds of whites who would occupy their land and surround those who took reserves were also based upon hard experience. They would be harassed until they gave up and sold their land for little or nothing, if they were not simply cheated out of it or driven away. Kingsbury had noted the intense prejudice against Indians as soon as he arrived in Tennessee. Forgetful of how similar the New Englanders' views of Indians had been a century earlier, he expressed astonishment at the unchristian attitudes of southern whites: "My residence and extensive acquaintance in Tennessee has given me an opportunity to converse much respecting the Indians, and I hope to remove some of the prejudices against them. But you cannot conceive the state [of] feeling [against Indians] even among professors [of religion] on this subject."[15] It reflected in part the memories of Indian cruelties in the guerrilla war but also a conviction that the Indians were an innately inferior race: "The sentiment very generally prevails among white people near the Brainerd mission," Hoyt wrote in 1818, "(and perhaps with some farther to the north) that the Indian is by nature radically different from all other men and that this difference presents an insurmountable barrier to his civilization." The missionaries themselves, Hoyt added, believed that "Indians are men and their children, education alone excepted, [are] like the children of other men."[16]

Having come to understand the reasons for Cherokee resistance to the treaty, the American Board did not try to keep its sympathy a secret—with unfortunate results for its relations with the War Department. For various reasons a number of Cherokee chiefs, led by John Jolly, were ready to support the removal policy. They saw nothing but trouble for the Cherokees so long as they remained in the East. Jolly lived on an island in the Tennessee River not far from Brainerd. When Sam Houston had run away from home as a boy, he had lived with Jolly, who thought of him as a son. Houston, through Jackson's influence, was appointed by the War Department in 1818 to assist McMinn in registering Cherokees for emigration. When John Jolly informed Houston that the American Board missionaries were doing their best to oppose the removal policy, Houston investigated. He discovered that the Reverend Elias Cornelius, when he had come to the nation in September 1817 to visit Brainerd, had told several gatherings of Cherokees that they need not worry much about Jackson's wicked treaty for the United States Senate would never ratify it. The Cherokees knew that Cornelius had just come from talking to the secretary of war and with various congressmen in Washington. His opinion carried great weight with those chiefs who were trying to persuade their people not to enroll to emigrate (in order to maintain the nation's hold over as much of their homeland as possible). They quoted Cornelius to those who were fearful that there was no hope of holding on to their land.

15. Cyrus Kingsbury to Samuel Worcester, November 28, 1816, ABCFM.
16. Brainerd Journal, June 24, 1818, ABCFM.

When Houston confirmed Jolly's insinuations and told McMinn, McMinn wrote angrily to the War Department. Secretary Calhoun, shocked that missionaries would try to thwart government policy, wrote to Cyrus Kingsbury for an explanation. "Lieut. Houston . . . states that Major Jolly, an Arkansaw emigrant and former chief of the Cherokee Nation . . . informed him that a Mr. Cornelius . . . had taken many opportunities of stating to the Cherokees that the Commissioners who held the treaty in July last, acted entirely without authority from the President . . . and therefore the Treaty would not be ratified." Cornelius was also alleged to have maligned the War Department by telling the Cherokees that "if they received rifles" when they enrolled as emigrants, "they would be old and good for nothing."[17] McMinn accused Kingsbury, too, of using his influence "to prevent the Cherokees from removing."

Upon receiving this angry letter from the secretary, Kingsbury went at once to see McMinn to deny the allegations. He told McMinn that Cornelius had no intention of opposing the government. He had simply mentioned, to those Cherokees who asked him, "a passage in a letter from the acting Secretary of War to Gov. McMinn and which his Excellency showed to Mr. C., in which the Secretary states that it was doubted whether the treaty would be ratified and that for three reasons, only one of which Mr. C. recollected, which was that too much stress had been laid on the former stipulations between President Jefferson and the Arkansas chiefs" back in 1809. Furthermore, Kingsbury assured McMinn, he himself "had never said any thing with a view to influence the Indians not to remove over the Mississippi. That I did not consider that the discharge of my duties called on me to interfere in that matter" in any way. He then wrote to the board to explain that "Lt. Houston is a deputy agent for this nation lately appointed and is much engaged to get the Indians away from the country. What effect this will have on our affairs is known only to him who has the hearts of all men in his hand. We have no doubt that advantage will be taken of every circumstance to destroy the influence and popularity of this mission," for that was only to be expected of Satan.[18] For Kingsbury, it was the whites and not the Indians who were antimissionary.

The board had no choice but to plead innocent to charges that it was meddling in politics if it wished to sustain its image as an honest broker mediating between the Cherokees and the government for the good of all concerned. The Prudential Committee in Boston, led by Dr. Samuel Worcester, immediately set to work to exonerate Cornelius. It assured the secretary of war that Houston's accusations were "incorrect." As for Kingsbury,

---

17. Cyrus Kingsbury to Samuel Worcester, December 11, 1817, ABCFM. According to Jackson's treaty, as an inducement to enroll for emigration, the government agreed to give to every enrollee a rifle, ammunition, blanket, and brass kettle, "as a full compensation for the improvements which they may leave."

18. Cyrus Kingsbury to Samuel Worcester, December 11, 1817, ABCFM.

"the Prudential Committee have been express in their instructions to all employed in the concerns of the Mission to withold themselves sacredly from every colour of interference" in any government policy.[19] Worcester then cautioned Kingsbury that "too much care cannot be used that no umbrage be given on this score. We wish to act as far as possible in perfect harmony with the Government."[20]

Calhoun accepted Worcester's explanation, and the matter was dropped. Evidently a more circumspect position was taken by the missionaries for a time. But this too had its problems. Some Cherokees always suspected missionaries of trying to acquire pieces of their land. "The broken state of this people," Kingsbury wrote to Boston in March 1818, "and their extreme jealousy respecting their lands, renders it necessary to proceed with prudence. Some of the emigrating party have circulated a report that it was our object to form a large settlement of white people and get possession of their land."[21] The frontier people on the border of the Cherokee Nation were also suspicious of the expanding activities of the board. "The white people" in the nearby settlements, Ard Hoyt reported in July 1818, were as "agitated" as the Indians. He had to be extremely careful "lest our good intentions [toward the Cherokees] should be misconstrued by those who think it of great importance that all the natives should be removed."[22]

Meanwhile, those chiefs who opposed removal continued to petition the government against the injustice of the treaty and against the improper methods of McMinn and Houston in promoting emigration.[23] One such memorial stressed the contradiction between the War Department's encouraging mission schools in the East while at the same time trying to remove the nation to the west. "We hope," said the Council, "by the [assistance of] the benevolent societies of our white brothers from the north, that in course of time, if we shall be allowed to keep our country, our white brothers will not blush to own us as brothers."[24] Not only the reference to *northern* philanthropy but its association with a less prejudiced attitude toward their color raised fears among southern whites of Yankee interference

19. Samuel Worcester to John Calhoun, February 6, 1818, ABCFM.
20. Samuel Worcester to Cyrus Kingsbury, January 30, 1818, and John C. Calhoun to Thomas L. McKenney, February 16, 1818, BIA, M-15, roll 4, p. 119.
21. Cyrus Kingsbury to Samuel Worcester, March 6, 1818, ABCFM.
22. Ard Hoyt to Samuel Worcester, July 25, 1818, ABCFM.
23. ASP II, 142–48, 483–90. See also Brainerd Journal, February 13, 1817, and Ard Hoyt to Samuel Worcester, July 25, 1818, ABCFM. Among the enclosures in Hoyt's letter is a copy of a "talk," or memorial, by the women of the Cherokee Nation addressed to a "Council at Oostanalee," June 30, 1818, opposing the removal or exchange of lands: "The land was given to us by the Great Spirit above as our common right, to raise our children upon and to make support of our rising generation. We therefore humbly petition our beloved children, the headmen and warriors, to hold out to the last in support of our common rights. . . . [T]he thought of being compelled to remove [to] the other side of the Mississippi is dreadful to us because it appears to us that we, by this removal, shall be brought to a savage state again."
24. ASP II, 143.

in their concerns. From this point on, the politicians of the South found it convenient to blame opposition to their policy of Indian removal upon "northern do-gooders," missionaries, and Indian-lovers, who, having exterminated red people in their own region, now demonstrated a guilt-ridden and hypocritical concern for their well-being in the South. The South had its own business interest in developing the cotton belt and wanted no northern meddling there.[25]

Had Calhoun, McMinn, or the frontier whites seen the letters that the missionaries were writing back to Boston, they would have been fully confirmed in their suspicions. On July 25, 1818, the Reverend Ard Hoyt wrote to Worcester, "We think with the Chiefs of this People that a general removal would greatly distress this people and in a great degree retard, if not ultimately defeat, the benevolent design of bringing them out of their state of darkness to the light of divine truth and the privileges of civilization: still, we hold ourselves bound not to interfere with state affairs or in any measure to become partisans in this business."[26] Kingsbury too found the government's policy contradictory. The Cherokees had the better of the argument, he thought. "The Indians say they don't know how to understand their Father, the President. A few years ago he sent them a plough and a hoe and said it was not good for his red children to *hunt*, they must cultivate the earth. Now he tells them there is good *hunting* at the Arkansas, if they go there he will give them rifles."[27] Then, realizing that many of the missionary letters were published verbatim in *The Missionary Herald*, the official organ and fund-raising mechanism of the American Board, Kingsbury added, "Perhaps it will be best not to publish the above." What he and the Cherokees were explicating here was the growing power of the west in determining American Indian policy. "Their father in Washington" was inconsistent because his political constituency was shifting from easterners, who believed the Indian was assimilable, to westerners, who believed him unassimilable.

In order to persuade the government of their willingness to be cooperative, the American Board offered to establish a mission school among those Cherokees already in Arkansas. The War Department accepted with alacrity: "As it is the wish of the President that the Arkansas should be the permanent home of the Cherokees, he would be particularly friendly to the establishment of schools among the Cherokees there."[28] The board's offer made it easier for the government to promote removal among the Cherokees who feared that in the west there would be no way to teach their children to read,

25. In later years, when the abolition movement began, southern whites began to describe the missionary opponents of removal, especially those of the ABCFM, as "northern fanatics" and to equate defenders of Indian rights with defenders of African rights, i.e., abolitionists.
26. Ard Hoyt to Samuel Worcester, July 25, 1818, ABCFM.
27. Cyrus Kingsbury to Samuel Worcester, May 25, 1818, ABCFM.
28. John Calhoun to Jeremiah Evarts and Elias Cornelius, July 15, 1818, ABCFM.

write, and become farmers. The evenhandedness of the American Board at this time did not endear it to the antiremoval Cherokees, who considered anyone who had left or might leave the homeland as at best an expatriate and at worst a traitor.

In the same letter in which the board proposed to establish a school in Arkansas, it also sought to cover its financial losses should the Cherokees be totally removed. "In case the Indian title to the land on which our schools are and shall be established," the board wrote in July 1818, "should hereafter be extinguished," it was to be hoped that "the Board shall enjoy the land occupied and improved by them," and "no man would think a mile square too great a reservation" in such a case. That is, the board wished to be given a square mile of the Cherokee Nation should the Cherokees be forced to remove and to be able to use that to recoup its losses. Although the government had paid two-thirds of the building costs and stated that all missionary buildings remained the property of the government, the board expected a full indemnity for its investments. Had the Cherokees known of this, they would have felt certain that the missionaries were essentially land speculators. However, the secretary of war declined this guarantee on the correct ground that "the public lands, after the extinguishment of Indian title," were "entirely under the disposition and control of Congress" and could not be disposed of in advance to a private organization by the executive.[29]

By the end of 1818 many of the board's missionaries as well as the Prudential Committee were convinced that the government would succeed in its removal effort. "The great part of the Cherokee nation will cross the Mississippi," the board's treasurer, Jeremiah Evarts, wrote in Boston in December. Still, he had hope that "enough will remain to furnish a good field of Christian exertion." Though he doubted that many could hold out against emigration, he nevertheless remained convinced that they were in the right. "If there were a Wilberforce in Congress, *there* would be the place to plead their cause. As the case is, I know not what can be done."[30]

Although fewer than 2,000 (out of 13,000) Cherokees in the East were enrolled for emigration (or had actually emigrated) by the end of 1818, the Council was desperate to bring some order out of the confused situation. Many Cherokees were so dubious that they could remain much longer in the East that they had done no planting in the spring of 1818; the small harvest that fall meant a severe shortage of food for the winter and probably famine conditions in the spring and summer. Yet next spring they would again not know whether it was worth planting a crop which they might have to leave for the whitemen to harvest. Consequently the Council sent another delega-

29. Jeremiah Evarts and Elias Cornelius to John Calhoun, July 15, 1818, and John Calhoun to Jeremiah Evarts and Elias Cornelius, July 15, 1818, ABCFM. Copies of these letters are also in the Tennessee State Archives, Nashville.
30. Jeremiah Evarts to Moody Hall, December 24, 1818, ABCFM.

tion to Washington in January 1819 with orders to find some resolution to the dilemma. The missionaries at Brainerd heard that the despairing chiefs instructed their delegates that if removal was inevitable, the delegation had the power to make a treaty embodying that plan—provided the government offered sufficient remuneration for their farms and guaranteed them a permanent home on equally good land in the West. "For the information of those concerned in the mission," Ard Hoyt wrote to the board on January 11, 1819, "we are told, in confidence, that the delegates have full power to negotiate an entire exchange of country if they think best after a conference with the President. If they do not agree to a total exchange, a considerable part of the country must at all events be given up as the portion of the emigrants, perhaps this may be the best time to secure the property of the Board here; but if the whole country is now given up, it may be the only time."[31] Hoyt meant to alert the board. If it wished to protect its interest, it should have a voice in any negotiations in Washington.

John Ross, one of the delegates, offered additional confidential information regarding the Council's instructions (probably calculating on its having a particular kind of impact). He dropped in at Brainerd just prior to departing for Washington for two reasons. He wished the missionaries to know that if the delegation did agree to total removal, it would do its best to make some arrangement to preserve the mission property from white land speculators. He also wanted to ask the board's help in obtaining some funds from the sale of a portion of Cherokee land to be used as a school endowment in case they did not remove. The Cherokees would need all the help they could get in Washington and Ross probably hoped that the board would send some of its members there to have a voice in negotiations. His confidential information was a warning to the missionaries that they might lose their property, while at the same time it offered them the hope of additional funding for their mission schools if the Cherokee remained in the East. By implication, the majority of the Cherokees' education fund would be at the disposal of the board, the Moravians having little claim upon it.

> Mr. John Ross, one of the delegates, without even a hint from any of us, has asked us how a portion of land can be secured for the benefit of the schools in the nation. He is not satisfied that the Cherokees should barely say they are *willing* to receive instruction; it is his wish that they should evince their ardent desire for it by *doing* something to promote it. He had not consulted the other delegates, but he did not doubt they would be all of his mind.
>
> He thought the mission families must have a reserve at least equal to the Cherokees who choose to remain, i.e., 640 acres to each family—that the grant for Chickamaugah [Brainerd] must be sufficient to include all our buildings and improvements—but the great object of his inquiry was how a large tract of good land at some place where it would sell high, could be secured in the hands of some white people (as they had no law by which it could be secured among themselves)

31. Ard Hoyt to Samuel Worcester, January 11, 1819, ABCFM.

so that the nation should hereafter have the benefit of it for the support of schools.[32]

Hoyt replied to Ross's suggestions by saying that the missionaries did not want any land for themselves but that "it would greatly encourage and rejoice the hearts of their friends at the north to know that the Cherokees were disposed to make provision for the support of schools on the plan he was proposing." After describing Ross's proposition to the board, Hoyt suggested that it would be well if Mr. Cornelius or some other influential member of the Prudential Committee would "visit the delegation at Washington and grant them friendly aid in their time of trouble." The moment seemed ripe for the board to come forward as a friendly mediator.

Fortunately for the board and for the Cherokees, McMinn seemed by then at the end of his rope as removal agent. After a year and a half in the nation, he still had not succeeded in persuading more than 15 percent of the Cherokees, if that many, to enroll for emigration. That in itself was a victory for Cherokee solidarity. The Reverend Daniel S. Butrick, one of the Brainerd missionaries, reported:

> After the late council [November 1818] Gov. McMinn adopted a measure which some think will terminate in the removal of all the Cherokees from this country. He opened an office at the Cherokee Agency for the sale of all improvements made by Arkansas emigrants to the highest bidder, thus to fill the country with whites and, as he might expect, with whites of the most abandoned character. This measure the Cherokees say was in direct opposition to the treaty of 1817. And we are sorry to learn that his Excellency kept his office open during the sabbath. . . . Unless some measure is taken by the General Government to prevent the white people from intruding, the Cherokees will probably soon be gone from this country.[33]

Hoyt added that McMinn, who in his frustration seemed to have been drinking heavily, had even put up Brainerd mission for sale to the highest bidder: "It is reported, and in a way which entitles it to some credit, that the mission farm at Brainerd has been rented in this way—that when the Governor set it up [for bids] he was told it would be displeasing to the government, as they had patronised this school, but that he proceeded, and 750 dollars were given for the place. Some say he was intoxicated when he did this." Hoyt then pointed out that this was "contrary to the express language of the treaty" and that there was some hope that "he will in some way disannul this sale in his sober moments."[34]

McMinn's mistakes may have provided the Cherokees and the American Board with the leverage needed to arrange a solution to the predicament. Congress had appropriated $80,000 for the negotiations and for emigration. McMinn had used the whole sum with very little to show for it. If the

32. Ibid. See also Hoyt's letter to Worcester dated January 8, 1819.
33. Daniel Butrick to Samuel Worcester, January 1, 1819, ABCFM.
34. Ard Hoyt to Jeremiah Evarts, March 17, 1819, ABCFM.

matter came before the Senate, there might be a public investigation and a scandal for the War Department. Perhaps out of embarrassment, McMinn did not accompany the Cherokee delegation to Washington, but he wrote Calhoun to say he was still sanguine that emigration was increasing and that if Calhoun would hold the line, "few if any [Cherokees] will remain east of the Mississippi."[35]

The delegation, which arrived in Washington late in January 1819, was headed by Charles Hicks, who since 1817 had been chosen second principal chief to Path Killer. He was assisted by John and Lewis Ross, John Martin, George Lowery, James Brown, Gideon Morgan, Jr., Cabbin Smith, Sleeping Rabbit, Small Wood, John Walker, and Currahee Dick. The American Board sent Dr. Samuel Worcester to look after its interests, but he did not arrive from Boston until February 18, when the Cherokee delegation had almost concluded the negotiations.[36] From the statement of Calhoun on February 11, it appears that the delegation never proposed a total exchange of land and emigration but asserted its determination to retain as large a portion of its homeland as possible. It did agree, for the sake of putting an end to the enrollment of more emigrants, to cede a fair proportion of its homeland in the East in order to provide an exchange of land in Arkansas to accommodate those Cherokees who had enrolled to go or were already there.

The delegation stressed to Calhoun that "after making the proposed cession," they hoped that what remained "may be to them a permanent and lasting home without further cession" at any time in the future. Calhoun refused to give the Cherokees a formal guarantee: "it will not be possible by any stipulation in the treaty to prevent future cessions."[37] Nevertheless, he left the decided impression that if the grant of land ceded in the East were sufficiently large, the government would be reconciled to a permanent homeland in the East for the Cherokees who wished to stay there and continue to acculturate. Calhoun, in agreeing to end the present removal effort, thus seemed to reaffirm Knox's original policy:

> You are now becoming like the white people; you can no longer live by hunting but must work for your subsistence. . . . Your great object ought to be to hold your land separate[ly] among yourselves, as your white neighbors; and to live and bring up your children in the same way they do, and gradually adopt their laws and manners. . . . Without this, you will find you have to emigrate, or become extinct as a people. You see that the Great Spirit has made our form of society stronger than yours, and you must submit to adopt ours.

35. ASP II, 483.
36. The board voted in December 1818 that Dr. Worcester should go "to Washington for the sole purpose of consulting with the Cherokee delegation and with our own government in regard to the best means of promoting the permanent good of the Indians.' Jeremiah Evarts to John Gambold, February 27, 1819, ABCFM.
37. ASP II, 190.

Hoping with this final cession that they would be allowed to remain forever
on their homeland to acculturate "gradually" under their own government,
the Cherokees acquiesced.

They agreed, sadly, to exchange land in proportion to the numbers of
emigrants, but there was some disagreement as to how many emigrants there
were. The Cherokee delegation insisted that no more than 3,000 to 3,500
Cherokees were in Arkansas or enrolled to go there, while 12,000 to 13,000
would remain in the East. Calhoun, relying on McMinn's figures, argued
that a total of 5,291 Cherokees were either in Arkansas or enrolled to go and
that no more than 10,000 would remain.[38] In the absence of a census, the
Cherokees reluctantly accepted Calhoun's figures, the tribal annuity was
divided, as was their homeland, so as to give one-third to the emigrants.

As John Ross had promised Ard Hoyt, the Cherokee delegates then
brought up the plan for selling a large plot of Cherokee land to provide a
permanent endowment for a school fund. Calhoun said, "The reservation
which the Cherokees wish to make . . . for a school fund must be in the
Alabama Territory, as the cession which will be made in Georgia [to be
exchanged for land in Arkansas] will belong to that state" and so would the
cessions in Tennessee and North Carolina. Only federally owned land could
be sold for the Cherokee Nation's benefit. Ultimately the school fund land
was located north of Muscle Shoals along the Tennessee River and was of
extremely high value.[39]

There is no record of precisely what part Dr. Samuel Worcester played
in the final negotiations after he arrived on February 18. Calhoun submitted
a draft of the treaty to the Cherokee delegates on February 22; they signed
the treaty for the nation on February 27. Worcester appears to have been
shown the treaty and to have assisted in its final wording. He also spoke to
the secretary of war privately and to several congressmen (probably those who
were on the board's board of directors) who would ultimately have to ratify it
over objections from the frontier states. Worcester reassured the Cherokee
delegates that they had made a wise treaty; most of them considered it a
moral victory over McMinn and Jackson. But the price they paid was heavy.
They lost over 700,000 acres of land in North Carolina; 800,000 in Georgia; 800,000 in Alabama, and over a million in Tennessee, for all of which

38. The last census by Meigs, taken in 1809, showed 12,395 Cherokees in the East, but
it did not include those in the west. The birthrate in the East increased the population faster than
emigration, however, and by 1825, despite the 4,000 to 5,000 Cherokees in the west, a census
taken by the Cherokee Council showed 14,972 Cherokees in the East. See W. G. McLoughlin
and Walter H. Conser, Jr., "The Cherokees in Transition," *Journal of American History* 64,
no. 3 (December 1977): 678–703.

39. Ard Hoyt fully expected that "the avails of this land" would be vested "in the hands of
the ABCFM." No doubt the Cherokees expected, however, to have control over it. Ard Hoyt to
Samuel Worcester, January 8, 1819, ABCFM. Through delays and bureaucratic confusion in
the War Department (if not some chicanery) the Cherokees never received any income from this
fund prior to their removal in 1838–39.

the emigrants were ultimately given an equivalent tract in western Arkansas (though it was not surveyed until 1825). When finally surveyed, the eastern cession came closer to four million acres, or slightly less than one-third of the total Cherokee land area in the East.[40]

The treaty spelled out these cessions as well as defining a tract 12 miles square for the school endowment. It also granted 342 reserves of 640 acres each to Cherokees (on the land ceded) who had chosen to become citizens on their own farms.[41] Within two weeks after it was signed, the Senate ratified the treaty. On March 6, Calhoun wrote to McMinn, "You are requested, as no further encouragement will be given to the emigration to the Arkansas, to take immediate measures to wind up the business."[42] It took somewhat longer to resolve all the illegal sales and rentals McMinn had made in the last stages of "the business."

Ard Hoyt at Brainerd mission reported the great sense of relief among the Cherokees and the missionaries: "Your kind letter of March 4th," Hoyt wrote to Dr. Worcester, "giving the joyful information that God had heard the prayers of his people in behalf of the poor, despised and afflicted Cherokees, gladdened our hearts on the 2nd instant. This deliverance, great beyond expectations, has spread joy and gladness through the nation, and we are happy to learn that some ascribe it to the true cause [God's will]."[43] Some of the more knowledgeable Cherokees were also willing to credit Dr. Worcester and the political influence of their friends in the North. John Ross wrote to Hoyt from Washington to express his gratefulness to the distinguished members of the American Board: "I have the pleasure and satisfaction of becoming acquainted with the Rev. Dr. Worcester who has been here several days and been very active in promoting much good towards our welfare and future happiness. I cannot express my feelings of gratitude in behalf of the Cherokee Nation to those religious societies who have so much softened the hearts and influenced the minds of the gentlemen of Congress, as well as the heads of departments toward the interests of the poor red children of nature."[44]

Dr. Worcester wrote to Charles Hicks to confirm the mutual effort the board had made with the delegates to resolve the nation's problems. He

40. Royce, *Cherokee Nation*, pp. 119–20; Thomas L. McKenney to Black Fox, April 11, 1828, BIA, M-21, roll 4, p. 397.

41. ASP II, 187–88. See W. G. McLoughlin, "Experiment in Cherokee Citizenship," *American Quarterly* 33, no. 1 (Spring, 1981): 3–25, for a discussion of what happened to those Cherokees who "took reserves" as a result of this treaty.

42. ASP II, 190, and Royce, *Cherokee Nation*, pp. 104–07.

43. Ard Hoyt to Samuel Worcester, April 10, 1819, ABCFM. Hoyt added later, "The success of this delegation has raised the hopes of this nation. They feel more than ever anxious to make improvement. . . . The Missionary is received and treated as an old friend." Brainerd Journal, May 11, 1819, ABCFM.

44. Ross is quoted in the letter from Ard Hoyt to Samuel Worcester, April 10, 1819, ABCFM.

wished the Cherokee people to know that an alliance was born between them
and their benefactors in Boston:

> I rejoice with you and thank the Great Spirit for his kindness to you and your
> nation. It was a day of darkness. . . . You feared that you would be compelled to
> give up your houses, your cornfields, your rivers, plains and mountains. . . .
> The Dark cloud has passed away. A good portion of your lands is secured to
> you; the wicked men who seek your hurt are to be kept from troubling you.
> You are to be allowed to sit quietly around your own fires and under your own
> trees and all things are to be set before you and your children. . . . Many have
> long been your friends and now many more are coming to be your friends . . .
> hundreds of thousands of good men and women in all parts of this country. . . .
> Brother, it is the morning of a new and happy day.[45]

Worcester referred to Hicks as a "brother" because Hicks was a Christian.
Hicks was elated that the nation had held onto its homeland and that the
American Board could now proceed, with the help of the Cherokees' own
school fund, to expand its schools and missions among them. "Hicks is
much engaged for the instruction of his people," Hoyt wrote to the board in
April 1819. "While an entire exchange of country was thought of as a
measure they might be pressed to adopt, his spirit was often greatly born
down with discouragement." Path Killer, though principal chief, could
neither read, speak, nor write English. His dedication to his people was
great, but the burden of negotiating with McMinn and the government over
the past three years had fallen upon Hicks and Ross. "Since they have
succeeded in getting a part of their country guaranteed to them anew," Hoyt
concluded, "and so many christian people are engaged for their instruction,"
it had raised Hicks's spirits enormously.[46]

The Cherokees' second removal crisis was over, although another body
of discouraged Cherokees (perhaps 2,000) had gone west and one-third of
the old nation in the East was lost forever. New Cherokee leaders had arisen
in the crisis, and the newly arrived missionaries from New England not only
presaged the start of a larger, more efficient school system, making education at last available to the whole nation, but also offered a new source of
political power in an increasingly political struggle. For better or worse,
missions were now politicized, although the missionaries often denied it.
The American Board had only begun to cope with increasing sectional
pressures (North and South, East and West) and the mounting conflict
between states' rights and federal authority which would dominate the future
of the Cherokee people. But the saviors of the Cherokees in one crisis (if that
is what the board was) could become their destroyers in the next. The
northern brother of the redman was also the brother of the southern whiteman. Moreover, as the board's schools and missionaries placed new pressures

45. Samuel Worcester to Charles Hicks, March 4, 1819, ABCFM.
46. Brainerd Journal, April 12, 1819, ABCFM.

upon the Cherokee people to assimilate and become Christians, many fullbloods and traditionalists became annoyed over this highly organized assault upon their culture. Divisions within white society were mirrored in divisions within red society, and these divisions grew apace in the 1820s.

ঞ(CHAPTER SIX)ঞ

The Missionaries and the Cherokee Bourgeoisie, 1819—1829

As they [the Cherokees] rise in information and refinement, changes [in their institutions] must follow until they arrive at that state of advancement when, I trust, they will be admitted into all the privileges of the American family . . . . It needs not the display of language to prove to the minds of good men that Indians are susceptible of attainments necessary to the formation of polished society.

Elias Boudinot, *An Address to the Whites*, 1826

The year 1819 was not only the start of the Era of Good Feelings among white Americans but also the beginning of the halcyon decade in Cherokee history. The treaty of 1819 convinced the Cherokee leaders that the threat of their removal to the West was gone and that they were now permanently secure in their homeland. The passage that same year of the Civilization Fund to provide an annual subsidy to Indian education and the treaty clause for their own school endowment persuaded the Cherokees that the government was truly serious about helping them to help themselves. When the Baptist and Methodist denominations sent their missionaries to join those of the Moravians and the American Board, who could doubt that the philanthropic interest in the Indians had reached new heights? Some of the more affluent Cherokees began to see the virtue of adopting the religion of the whiteman along with his agricultural system and his exploitation of economic opportunities in the Mississippi Valley. Those willing to join a mission church and industrious enough to take advantage of the market economy felt they had found the means to obtain the whiteman's respect. The Cherokees were given the sobriquet "The most civilized tribe in America" after 1819 because an important group among them made the most of the new climate of encouragement and hope. They may not have attained all the attributes of the white bourgeoisie in their aspirations to rise in the world, but they came as close as they could, and the missionaries were very proud of them.

The enactment by the Cherokee Council of over one hundred complex laws between 1817 and 1827, capped in 1828 by the adoption of a constitution modeled on that of the United States, provided their nation with a highly centralized, orderly, cohesive government and opened up new opportunities for internal economic growth. The nation ceased to be governed by local town chiefs loosely confederated under a national council. It adopted a bicameral, elective legislature, an executive committee which conducted daily affairs, an independent judiciary operating under written laws, jury trials, and Anglo-Saxon procedures. A national treasurer managed the annuity as the Council directed. Under a law passed in 1825, the Council instructed the treasurer to loan money from the treasury at low interest rates to Cherokee entrepreneurs who needed capital to undertake activities useful to the general welfare, such as new turnpikes, ferries, inns, saltpeter mines, trading stores, salines.[1] By 1827 the Cherokees were economically self-subsistent and actively engaged in regular trade in cotton, corn, livestock, and poultry with towns and cities as distant as New Orleans, Charleston, and Augusta. Five years before this, the federal government had ceased providing ploughs, hoes, looms, and other technical assistance on the ground that the Cherokee Nation could now generate its own capital for economic expansion.

A census conducted by the Council in 1825 indicated a population increase of over 7,000 since the census of 1809. There were now 14,972 Cherokees in "the old nation" and approximately 5,000 in Arkansas; in 1809 there had been only 12,395 in the East and 300 to 400 in Arkansas.[2] The number of black slaves owned by Cherokees had almost doubled from 583 to 1,038 in 1825 as the planting of cotton had increased. The totals of sheep and hogs had doubled. The nation now had 7,628 horses and 22,405 cattle spread among 2,500 families. Virtually every family had a plough and a spinning wheel and one out of four had a loom and a wagon. There were 31 gristmills scattered around the nation, 14 sawmills, 6 powder mills, 9 saltpeter works, 18 ferries, and 19 schools. Given the turmoil of the Creek War and of the two removal crises (1808−10 and 1817−19) this growth was truly phenomenal. No figures are available for the number of miles of roads, but there were 62 blacksmith shops, and 55 silversmiths still practiced that ancient Cherokee art. "The Cherokees," reported the American Board missionaries in 1820, "are rapidly adopting the laws and manners of the whites. They appear to advance in civilization just in proportion to their knowledge of the gospel."[3]

Confident now of their ability to run their own affairs, the Cherokees paid little attention to the federal agent except when they needed his help to remove intruders or he needed theirs to meet with federal negotiators hoping for another cession of land. They quarreled vigorously with the War Department after 1820 when the agent tried to pay their annuities in depreciated state bank notes, declining to accept any payments except in specie or federal

1. See *Cherokee Laws.*
2. See W. G. McLoughlin and Walter H. Conser, Jr., "The Cherokees in Transition," *Journal of American History* 64, no. 3 (December 1977): 678–703.
3. Brainerd Journal, November 1, 1820, ABCFM.

bank notes. In order to increase their internal revenue the Council laid a poll tax on all Cherokee citizens and a tax upon all native and white merchants doing business within the nation. The Council became closely involved with the missionaries, urging them to establish schools in various regions which wanted them, passing laws to accommodate Christian customs (honoring the Sabbath at Council sessions, for example) and adjusting frictions between the missionaries, parents, and local chiefs. As they had done for Gideon Blackburn, the Council passed a law in 1820 for the American Board which penalized parents who enrolled children in schools and then withdrew them before they had completed their training. Another law in 1820 permitted some mission stations to apprentice Indian boys to skilled artisans (blacksmiths, wheelwrights, tinsmiths) at the mission station for three to five years in order to assure the completion of training. The Council agreed to furnish such apprentices with a complete set of tools so that they could set up their own shops when they graduated.[4]

Cherokee revitalization up to 1819 had been essentially a secular movement (though the revival of 1811—13 had also played a part). After 1819 Cherokee revitalization became increasingly inspired by Christianity. However, not all Cherokees prospered equally or were equally pleased by the rapid pace of acculturation. Increasing Protestant evangelism was a divisive as well as a progressive force. But Cherokee society in the 1820s was too complex to be divided into simplistic categories such as pro- or antimission, fullblood or mixed blood. Many other factors were at work: regionalism, social class or wealth, slave ownership, kinship, and opinions regarding the optimal amount and speed of change. For example, class divisions arose because the more ambitious and better educated rapidly accumulated wealth, slaves, and credit and then took up the best land for their expanding farms, pastures, plantations; they seized the most lucrative opportunities for trade and manufacture, inns and ferries, mills and trading posts; they assumed a prominent place in politics and in effect made policies which suited their interests. Most of those in this rising Cherokee middle class were of mixed ancestry and had been the first to obtain the skills of reading and writing English and learning arithmetic. Among their symbols of prestige and respectability were not only the regular use of the whiteman's dress, language, and social manners, but also their friendship with whites, the regular attendance of their children at mission schools, the adoption of the whiteman's religious beliefs, his ethical values, and his concept of merit based upon individualistic competition and the accumulation of property. All of which they passed on to their children. "Many consider it an honor," wrote the Reverend Ard Hoyt in 1822, "to have been among the first to discern the national advantage of these [mission] institutions and that it is by many at least considered a mark of a weak mind not to see it now."[5] The size of this

4. Brainerd Journal, June 26, 1820, ABCFM.
5. Brainerd Journal, August 3, 1822, ABCFM.

aspiring middle class was small, not more than 8 to 10 percent of the Cherokee families (roughly corresponding to the 7.4 percent of the families who owned slaves), but their influence was large.

Of course, every Cherokee family adopted to some extent the behavior and dress of the whiteman. Not since the 1790s had Cherokee children made fun of those who failed to dress in buckskins and moccasins. Most Cherokee women had given up tattooing their arms, and Cherokee men had stopped plucking or shaving their heads and wearing silver earrings. Outward accommodations were accompanied by more significant inward changes in behavior and family structure. Fathers replaced uncles as the major authority figures in the home. Women were restricted to a narrow domestic sphere in their husband's homes. Family farms broke up the communal ethic. Patrilineal inheritance placed a premium on the nuclear family and accumulating property to leave for one's wife and heirs. A materialistic, acquisitive value system replaced a more easy-going ethic of sharing. Logically those who lived outside the centers of commerce in the distant valleys and mountain regions were slower to acculturate and adapted only minimally to new ways. They lived on poorer land, had smaller farms, seldom acquired slaves, saw fewer whites and missionaries, and tended to retain more of the old religious beliefs and practices. Those parts of the nation lying next to the Creeks in the southern part of the nation and those in the Great Smoky Mountains in the North were the major areas of conservatism, although as a cast of thought it could be found anywhere and in times of crisis it welled up everywhere. There was a common tendency for fullbloods to marry fullbloods and mixed bloods to marry among themselves. While everyone was aware of these differences, the assumption was that the Cherokees were one people who were all moving in the same direction although some were at different stages in the march of progress. Thomas L. McKenney, director of the Office of Indian Affairs, reported to Congress in 1825, "The Cherokees on this side of the Mississippi are in advance of all other tribes. They may be considered a civilized people."[6]

Among the leading figures of the Cherokee bourgeoisie in 1825 were men like "Rich Joe" Vann, who lived in a two-storey brick mansion, cultivated thousands of acres with scores of slaves, and raised large herds of cattle, sheep, and hogs for market; John and Lewis Ross, who managed extensive trading and credit services for Cherokees who were improving their farms or launching merchant ventures; Richard Riley, who held control over saltpeter production and sold thousands of pounds of powder to the United States Army annually; and George Sanders, who was described in the following terms by Jeremiah Evarts of the American Board in 1822: "He is one of several brothers, half-breeds, who have become rich. He early began to amass money and is now said to have bushels of silver. He has been known to lend $1000 or $2000 at a time." Sanders was one of five brothers

6. ASP II, 651–52.

descended from "a soldier from New Hampshire in the revolutionary army who deserted," came to the Cherokee Nation, and married a Cherokee. George's brother John kept "a very good house of entertainment" on the Georgia turnpike through the nation.[7] Such men were the bankers of the expanding economy. There were other affluent Cherokees who owned gristmills or sawmills or cotton gins and who shipped bales of cotton to New Orleans on riverboats and brought back manufactured goods to sell. The selling of whiskey, though illegal for whites in the nation, was legal for Cherokees. Everything that was taking place in these years along the maturing white frontier settlements was also taking place within the Cherokee Nation. By 1828 the Cherokees owned their own printing press and printed a weekly newspaper in their capital city of New Echota, where they had also built a two-storey clapboard building for their Supreme Court and were planning to establish a national academy or seminary for which several of their young mission-educated leaders were raising money by a speaking tour though the major cities of the East. Inevitably the gap between the rich and the poor, the influential and the ne'er-do-wells increased from year to year among the Cherokees as in white settlements. Sometimes all that seemed to hold the nation together was resistance to white prejudices and pressures. Occasionally the leaders praised the common people, and the common people expressed pride in their acculturated chiefs. More often, the old-fashioned Cherokees were an embarrassment to the highly acculturated, and the highly acculturated were an affront to the traditionalists.

Though missionaries tried to bring impartial assistance to all Cherokees, they inevitably tended to favor the more acculturated. They also believed that acculturation was best diffused from the top down. To some Cherokee conservatives in the 1820s, it became a term of opprobrium when they spoke of someone as "the missionaries' man." But it was not easy to decide who was the better Cherokee patriot, he who clung to the old ways or he who rushed to adopt the new. Not *whether* to preserve the nation's identity but *how best* to preserve it became the major ideological concern, and this was not really a class issue. But it was related to how much a Cherokee could acculturate and still remain a Cherokee. Neither the language nor skin color being sufficient, some other form of Cherokee identity needed to be constructed. (John Ross, who became principal chief in 1828, could easily have been taken for a whiteman and did not trust himself to speak to his people in Cherokee, but there was no stronger patriot.) The missionaries, who offered only their own Christian assimilationist and capitalist ideology as the answer, found it impossible to remain neutral within the conflicting internal factions. Nor were they able to remain neutral in the controversies between the Cherokee Nation and the state and federal governments of the United States.

As the hope-filled decade began, the missionaries of the American

7. Jeremiah Evarts, "Memorandum," April-May 1822, ABCFM.

Board were in the best position to help the Cherokees, and they were confident they could rapidly transform them into a civilized, Christian people. As Ard Hoyt wrote to the Prudential Committee in 1823: "The most influential characters in the nation appear to put unlimited confidence in your integrity and your widsom. They look to the ABCFM as the chief instrument under God which has saved them from migration, dispersion, and impending annihilation. And they look to you, more than any other [agency] to carry on the work until their people shall be so enlightened and enriched as to take it into their own hands."[8] Since 1817 the Prudential Committee of the American Board had been spending $10,000 a year on the missions in the Cherokee Nation and sending dozens of volunteers to staff them. They were by far the most highly organized, ambitious, well-equipped, and ably staffed of the four denominations who came to work in the nation—and they were easily the richest. Their school and model farm at Brainerd made such a favorable impression upon those who saw it that local chiefs throughout the nation sent requests to have similar schools established in their towns. Once the removal crisis ended, the board in Boston was happy to answer these requests. It started new schools as rapidly as it could recruit missionaries, farmers, mechanics, and teachers to staff them. The school at Taloney (later called Carmel) opened in November 1819; three months later, the school at Creek Path began. By 1824 the board had added schools at Willstown, Haweis (or Turnip Mountain), Hightower (Etowah), and Candy's Creek (Thomas Foreman's neighborhood); two years later an eighth mission station opened at New Echota: here the Reverend Samuel A. Worcester (nephew of Dr. Samuel Worcester) began the translation of the Bible into Cherokee.[9] None of these stations was as large as Brainerd, and while they included small farms and usually a blacksmith shop, they tended to conduct day schools rather than boarding schools; as time went on there seemed less need to teach husbandry and domestic manufactures to students whose parents already practiced them. On the average, each of the eight American Board schools taught 20 to 30 students annually; Brainerd averaged 75. By 1825 this meant that 200 to 250 were in school each year, but because the same students came back for three or four years, the total taught by the board from 1817 to 1833 was 355 at Brainerd and 882 for all the schools combined.[10]

In addition to instructing the children, the board's missionaries made a concerted effort to convert the parents to Christianity. In this they made better progress than the Moravians had, and within a few years after each

8. Ard Hoyt to Jeremiah Evarts, June 4, 1823, ABCFM.

9. After 1832 two other mission stations were opened by the board at Amohee and Red Clay. See Robert S. Walker, *Torchlights to the Cherokees*, pp. 69–70.

10. See the records of the ABCFM and its annual reports, from which these statistics have been compiled. I am also indebted to Morey D. Rothberg, "The Effectiveness of Missionary Education among the Cherokees," seminar paper, Brown University, 1973.

new school started, a mission church was organized at each station consisting of the white "mission family" and the local Cherokee converts. Occasionally a black slave was admitted as a member of these churches but in general the American Board, like the other missionary agencies, concentrated on converting the Cherokees. (No blacks were admitted to the schools though for a short time Brainerd conducted a Sunday school for blacks.)[11] With a mission church came a meetinghouse, regular worship services (open to the public), prayer meetings, Sunday schools, and benevolent societies. At some mission stations the schoolchildren and congregations founded temperance societies or societies to raise funds for foreign missions or for the American Colonization Society (to send freed blacks back to Africa).[12] Proud of their own accomplishments, the Cherokee students and church members were pleased to donate money to enlighten benighted pagans around the world or to help the mistreated Afro-Americans to return home. The irony of these activities escaped them.

Not only did mission churches increase self-esteem for many Cherokees and enlarge their horizons (developing a sense of noblesse oblige), but they also incorporated the converts into the larger Christian community in America. Beyond that, their connection with the American Board's worldwide activities placed them firmly in the forefront of human progress and history. A Cherokee Christian became at once an active participant in the manifest destiny of the white American republic as it strove to lead, redeem, and uplift the world. What was more, their efforts to improve

11. The annual report of the ABCFM for 1831 reported in their eight churches "219 members of whom 167 were Cherokees and the remainder were of African descent or white persons residing in the nation." No breakdown was given, however, and since there were at least 35 whites in the mission families and several others married to Cherokees, it is unlikely that there were more than 10 or 12 black members, if that many. Annual Report, ABCFM (1831), p. 60.

12. For the Cherokee American Colonization Society, see William Chamberlain to Jeremiah Evarts, January 8, 1829, ABCFM. Chamberlain wrote, "I have assisted the black people in Wills Valley in forming themselves into a society called the Wills Valley African Benevolent Society. Their object is to aid the cause of civilization and Christianization in Africa. . . . [T]hey have raised ten dollars for the American Colonization Society." This appears to have involved only blacks and does not say whether they were church members. However, mention is made of Cherokee support to the colonization society in other correspondence and in the *Cherokee Phoenix* (see, for example, no. 38, October 8, 1828). For Cherokee temperance societies, see Walker, *Torchlights*, p. 248. David Walker probably spoke for many converted Cherokees in the American Board churches when he said in 1825, "There are some African slaves among us; they have been, from time to time, brought in and sold by white men; they are, however, generally well treated and they much prefer living in the nation to a residence in the United States. There is hardly any intermixture of Cherokee and African blood. The presumption is that the Cherokees will, at no distant date, cooperate with the humane efforts of those who are liberating and sending this proscribed race to the land of their fathers." ASP II, 651. For the general view of the Cherokees toward slavery, see Rudi Halliburton, Jr., *Red Over Black*, and Theda Perdue, *Slavery and the Evolution of Cherokee Society*.

themselves and other pagan people were widely publicized in the missionary journals, where the Cherokees could read each month about their own role in the evangelical enterprises of the day. That was what it meant to be civilized and Christianized. They had risen to the forefront of man's advance. For the converts it was a heady experience, and they could scarcely contain their desire to be more Christian than the Christians, more civilized than their civilizers. It even enabled the more pious to look down with forbearance upon the unchristian behavior of their white neighbors and oppressors in the surrounding frontier communities. The editorials of the Christianized editor of the nation's newspaper were remarkable for their condescension toward uncivilized frontier ruffians, the impoverished Irish in eastern city slums, "the wretched Creeks" (to whom he did not wish the Cherokees to be compared), and "the wild savage Indians" of the West (among whom it would be inhuman to send the Cherokees).[13] Another Cherokee, Captain Spirit, converted by the missionaries at Brainerd in 1824, upon hearing of "Cherokees from our country going about in the cities of the United States with bows and arrows, shooting about, and expecting to obtain a little money" in circuses and theaters, wrote an outraged letter to the nation's newspaper about "such disgraceful" conduct; it gave the nation a bad image.[14]

The close connection between Christianizing the Cherokees and giving them a sense of their own self-esteem can be seen in the letters written by mission schoolchildren to various northern benefactors explaining why the mission schoolchildren had founded missionary societies to raise money for the board. A sense of duty, of gratitude, self-discipline, and the refusal to waste time in idle play were all part of the effort required to raise money. Their teachers "told us how they managed in charitable societies in civilized countries" and joined them in their efforts. They were helping them to develop the values and the institutions of a voluntaristic bourgeois society. This new activity made these young Cherokee girls (missionary societies seem to have been formed chiefly by females) feel that they were doing what all proper young ladies did in civilized society in order to be useful. Twelve-year-old Nancy Reece wrote earnestly in 1828:

We have a [missionary] Society among the Cherokee scholars; we are trying to

13. Elias Boudinot also filled spaces in the columns of the *Cherokee Phoenix* with ethnic jokes about Scotchmen and blacks. See the issues of May 21 and June 18, 1828. For his dislike of comparing the Cherokees to the "wretched Creeks," see July 21, 1828. For his praise of the American Colonization Society, see October 8, 1828. For an ambiguous reprint hostile to Nat Turner's Rebellion, see January 21, 1832. For a joke about a Scotchman, see April 24, 1828. For a statement by a Cherokee (who had raised himself up in the world) protesting against the view that "the Cherokees are as wretched and degraded . . . as the Hottentots of Africa and some of the Isles of the Sea," see March 13, 1828. For a reference to "the poorer classes" of Cherokees, see May 21, 1828.

14. *Cherokee Phoenix*, July 2, 1828. Captain Spirit was rechristened John Huss at his conversion; William Chamberlain to Jeremiah Evarts, July 8, 1824, ABCFM.

make some things as the Northern ladies do in their Societies to get some money for the Board so that they can send out more missionaries to the heathen. We have made several things, such as work bags, needle books, etc. and Miss Ames [the teacher] learns us to make and repair bonnets for the Cherokee women; she sets a price to the work and they pay the money to our Society. I have been thinking that perhaps we shall have enough to support a heathen child. I feel very much interested in this Society; if we had not one, we should be wasting our time; we meet on Saturdays in the afternoon in the hours that were given us to play.[15]

Money sent to the American Board for other missions, of course, freed money for the Cherokee mission. "We all ought to exert ourselves and try to do all we can to pay [back] what has been done for us," Nancy Reece concluded.

By 1825 the American Board's mission to the Cherokees was an international showpiece, attracting numerous visitors from at home and abroad (including President Monroe). But the paternalistic and elitist quality of the board's missions was bound to create tension. Their schools, though conducted on the Lancastrian method, where older pupils did much of the teaching of the younger, made few concessions to the difficulties faced by those unable to speak English. Their churches maintained the same rigid standards of faith and conduct as in New England. Christian bourgeois standards were the same world round. The missionaries saw no reason why the Indian children should not be required to master the same subject matter with the same thoroughness as white children; they believed that adult Cherokees could learn to understand Calvinistic doctrine as precisely as whites who cared about their souls. While willing to make some allowances in deportment for students and converts because of their upbringing, environment, and "ingrained habits," the American Board believed that pious teachers and pastors, loving Christian brethren, and constant exhortation would enable them to develop the same willpower and self-control which God had instilled in the Puritans. The strength of evangelical Calvinism was that it dealt equally with mankind and offered the same spiritual power of self-help to each individual who truly embraced the faith with total commitment. While God helped those who helped themselves, the fault for failure lay with the individual. "Total commitment," however, meant something different to many Cherokee converts from what it meant to the missionary. Many converts tried to keep something of their own identity and cultural outlook in reserve.

To gain admission to an American Board church was considered by the missionaries a great privilege and honor. It required long intellectual training and moral probation. First, the Cherokee concerned had to convince the

15. Nancy Reece to David Greene, Payne Papers, VIII, 25–26. Nancy Reece's father, an early convert at Brainerd, sent eight of his children (by a polygamous marriage) to the Brainerd school.

missionary that he or she had gone through a period of repentance for sin and then undergone a miraculous rebirth of the spirit. The missionary required many long conversations with those who applied for membership so that he could truly examine their hearts and feel convinced that their conversion was indeed a genuine work of God. He sought not only evidence of inner piety and conviction but also outward evidence: Had the applicant given up all sinful behavior? Had he or she engaged in regular, heartfelt prayer? Had the applicant attended services regularly and exhibited true humility and submission to God's commands? Did he or she truly understand the meaning of original sin, total depravity, limited atonement, irresistible grace, repentance, forgiveness, predestination, regeneration through grace, and the perseverance of the saints? Usually American Board missionaries required a probationary period of several months between baptism and admission to full church membership as a communicant in order to test the validity of the conversion. Satan could too easily lead people into self-deception on this important matter. Ultimately the whole membership of the mission church had to approve of the admission of any new member, so that even one's neighbors scrutinized a new convert's daily behavior during his or her probation, and afterward as well.

A sermon by a Cherokee exhorter of the American Board delivered in 1834 provides some insight into the moral code which Calvinistic Christianity supplied to the latest stage of Cherokee revitalization. John Huss (who was ordained as a "native preacher" in 1834) spoke on the text "Wide is the gate and broad is the way which leadeth to destruction and . . . strait is the gate and narrow is the way which leadeth unto life." The sins he described were all familiar to the Cherokees. Through the broad gate to hell

> go a multitude of quarrelers, who are fighters and murderers. There go a multitude of robbers . . . . There go a multitude of drunkards . . . . There go a multitude of cheats . . . . There go a multitude of thieves . . . . There go a multitude of fornicators . . . liars . . . despisers of the poor.

And through the gate to heaven go those who accepted the revealed commandments:

> Thou shalt love thy neighbor as thyself. Thou shalt not kill. Thou shalt not be contentious. Thou shalt not be a thief. Thou shalt not be a drunkard.

Those who chose the broad way would "dwell in the darkness and fire of hell. In those dreadful flames will they burn, in endless pain." But those who entered in at the narrow gate "will be no longer liable to sickness, and no longer liable to death. And no source of trouble shall exist there. No enemy shall dwell there. . . . [A]nd there they shall dwell together with their true friends" and "their Savior."[16] Such a code of conduct, demanded by such a powerful God (and the Great Book), however alien to Cherokee

16. Walker, *Torchlights*, pp. 127–32.

tradition in its individualism, was nevertheless admirably suited to the demands of their new way of life and to their difficult transition from the old to the new. While it required tremendous self-discipline, it offered also the mystical assistance of the Spirit of God, which was directly available to all who prayed to him; furthermore, fellowship among loving spiritual brethren was there to uphold them in times of trouble. Such help seemed worth some effort.

Anyone capable of sustaining the missionaries' Puritanical code of behavior was prone to develop a sense of his or her own moral and spiritual superiority over weaker mortals. The world was henceforth divided into saints and sinners, and the child of Christ became a Christian soldier, hardened and disciplined in the daily battle with Satan. A kind of self-righteousness exhibited itself in the criticisms by American Board missionaries not only of their weaker converts but also of the lower standards tolerated among other denominations in the nation. Scorn was particularly shown toward the Methodists, who were not Calvinists, and the Baptists, who, though Calvinists, did not believe in the necessity of a learned ministry, refused to baptize infants, and insisted that total immersion was the only true form of baptism. Worst of all, Methodists and Baptists had what the American Board Congregationalists considered very low standards for church membership. Only the Moravians managed to gain their respect. By 1830, after thirty years in the Cherokee Nation, the Moravians had found only 45 Cherokees worthy of membership; by the same year, the American Board, with five times as many missionaries and four times as many mission stations, had found only 167.

More important, there was an unconscious social bias imbedded in the American Board's missionary work. While they welcomed all children who seriously wished to be educated, their mission schools carefully noted in their rosters those who were fullbloods, those who were "half Cherokee," those who were "quadroon," and those who were "one-eighth" or "five-eighths" white. (Similar identifications were often made of church members.) In the beginning the Brainerd teachers also listed in the rollbooks which of the children were "lower class," which "middle class," and which were born of "influential" parents.[17] Had they been asked why these social and racial distinctions were so carefully noted, they would undoubtedly have said they were simply recording "facts" which would enable them to "place" students better. Usually, however, the missionaries noted that fullbloods were slower to learn, the poor seemed more "backward," and hence there was a correlation between the brighter pupils, their social class, and lighter skin. These were also considered simply "facts."

Students and parents took a different view of all this. Those students

17. See Elizur Butler's report for Haweis mission, April 1828; report from Brainerd mission church listing all its members, April 1828; see list of all church and school members at Creek Path mission, dated 1828, ABCFM.

who measured up to their teachers' expectations felt proud; those who did not felt inferior, angry, or frustrated. Ultimately fullblood enrollment in mission schools fell off and antagonism heightened between those Cherokees who habitually spoke English and those who did not. Despite their claim of Christian egalitarianism (God is no respecter of persons) and their genuine determination to qualify all Cherokees for equal membership in white American society, the missionaries exacerbated inequalities and social distinctions. Inasmuch as three-quarters of the Cherokees were fullbloods, the American Board missionaries (and the Moravians) permitted their unconscious elitism to work against them.[18] When Cyrus Kingsbury inaugurated the American Board's work among the Cherokees, he adopted the same plan the Moravians had tried in 1800: "Those who will be the first educated will be the children of the halfbreeds and of the leading men of the nation," he said. "On their education and influence the character of the nation will very much depend."[19] Kingsbury was thinking of the male students primarily, but eleven years later Jeremiah Evarts made the same kind of remark about the female students: "It is of great consequence to have the females in the principal families well instructed. In this way only will education become popular and fashionable."[20] The New Englanders believed that in any society the influential people set the tone of the community

The Methodists and Baptists operated under the opposite assumption. They believed that it was the generality of the people who ruled and set the tone. Among the missionaries to the Indians, as among the home missionaries in the white frontier settlements at this time, a contest was taking place between the democrats and the elitists. Among the Indians, as in the white communities, the democrats won the competition. As white Americans moved west, the Presbyterians, Congregationalists, Dutch Reform, Episcopalians, and Unitarians fell rapidly behind the Methodists and Baptists and Disciples in the quest for church members. So it was among the Cherokees. But among the Cherokees this had fatal consequences, for ultimately a handful of the elite (many of them trained in Moravian and American Board schools or members of their congregations) took it upon themselves to make a fraudulent removal treaty on the ground, as one of them put it, that "an intelligent minority had a moral right, indeed a moral

18. This is not to say that the missionaries thought fullblood children innately incapable of learning as fast as white or mixed-blood children, for they clearly denied this: "The general capacity of the Indian children and their aptness to learn we think is not inferior to the whites." Ard Hoyt, Second Annual Report to the Secretary of War from Brainerd, OSW, M-221, roll 85, #3323-3324. However, what they believed in theory was often in conflict with what they learned or came to believe from experience. For a good discussion of missionary attitudes toward race, see Michael C. Coleman, "Not Race but Grace," pp. 41–60. The parallels between the Cherokee bourgeoisie and the black bourgeoisie in America are striking, and a reading of E. Franklin Frazier's *Black Bourgeoisie* (New York: Macmillan, 1957) will provide valuable insights for anyone studying Native American history or anthropology.

19. Cyrus Kingsbury to Samuel Worcester, December 16, 1816, ABCFM.

20. Jeremiah Evarts to Isaac Proctor, January 9, 1827, ABCFM.

duty, to save a blind and ignorant majority from inevitable ruin and destruction."[21]

Much of the American Board missionaries' discrimination against fullbloods and the lower class stemmed less from conscious belief in the superiority of white blood than from the fact that fullbloods struck them as essentially slovenly, dirty, smelly people. The idea that "cleanliness is next to godliness" was deeply imbedded in the child-rearing of the missionaries. When a fullblood named Atsi (or John Arch) arrived at Brainerd from the mountains of North Carolina and sought admission to their school in 1819, the missionaries noted that "he had the dress and dirty appearance of the most uncultivated part of his tribe." His "wild and savage aspect seemed to mark him as one unfit for admission to the school."[22] However, he spoke English; he was humbly respectful; he said he was willing to make any sacrifice to get an education; he pointed out that he had sold his most valuable possession (his rifle) in order to make the journey. In the end his persistence and humility overcame their doubts about his ability. He was reluctantly admitted "on trial." John Arch proved to be an apt pupil. He was converted and ultimately became one of the first exhorters and translators of the board. When he died seven years later, he became a symbol of Christian martyrdom in the cause to which he had dedicated his life. But in all the accounts of his career, his transformation was portrayed as some kind of special miracle, a wonder past belief. John Arch, the dirty, "savage" fullblood who became a Christian exhorter was the exception that proved the rule.

Only one of the American Board missionaries, the Reverend Daniel S. Butrick, seemed fully aware of the ethnocentrism and snobbery which permeated their behavior. Born in Windsor, Massachusetts, in 1789 and ordained at Park Street Church in Boston in 1818, he left Boston a month later for the Cherokee Nation and devoted the rest of his life to the Cherokees. He was one of the few who took a genuine interest in trying to study the history and culture of the Cherokees (though he thought they were descendants of the lost Israelites), and he firmly believed that only by learning the Cherokee language could the missionaries truly perform their task. He left the comfortable life at Brainerd mission soon after his arrival and went to live in a smoky cabin with a fullblood family in order to be able to learn Cherokee. He developed a totally different view of the language from that of the Moravians. Far from its being "word poor," Butrick de-

21. Thurman Wilkins, *Cherokee Tragedy*, p. 275. Wilkins is here paraphrasing a longer statement made by Elias Boudinot defending himself and his collaborators in *The National Intelligencer*, May 22, 1838. I do not mean to imply that all those who signed the Treaty of New Echota were mixed bloods with missionary training, although the ringleaders were. Some who signed the treaty were simply convinced that they could not beat Jackson; others thought they could curry favor with Jackson and reap personal rewards. But without the support of Boudinot, John Ridge, Major Ridge, and others close to the missionaries, the treaty never could have been ratified. They gave it respectability because they were acculturated, Christianized leaders.

22. Walker, *Torchlights*, p. 84.

clared in 1819, "this language exceeds all my former expectations in richness and beauty. I think there would be but little difficulty in translating the New Testament into it."[23] Six years later, after completing the translation of the New Testament, he wrote, "In many respects their language is far superior to ours." He was convinced that all theological concepts "of every kind and degree may be communicated to this people in their own language with as much clearness and accuracy as in ours."[24]

Butrick was convinced that one reason the American Board did not make more progress in Christianizing and civilizing the Cherokees was because the board did not send its best volunteers to work there. It was thought more important to convert the millions of heathen in Burma, India, and China; so the best missionaries were sent there. "Have not the missionary societies too frequently and too long laboured under a mistake concerning the qualifications of missionaries among the natives?" he asked in 1819. "The Indians have been considered as the offscouring of all things, and it has been thought that anything was good enough for Indians and that their instruction was not worth the attention of a wise man." This was a bad mistake. "The Indians are a quick-sighted, discerning people," he had found; "they know who is wise and who is not. Perhaps there is not a native people in the world who will discover a man's real character quicker than the Natives of America."[25]

While he did not hesitate to stress the great differences between the social classes within the Cherokee Nation, Butrick was shocked at the growing gap between them. "There is a very great difference between the highest and the lowest class," he noted in 1824, and "the most enlightened scarcely know the depths of ignorance in which the great body of these people lie nor how to get down to them so as to raise them."[26] Butrick, one of the first American Board missionaries to get on horseback and itinerate to the most remote parts of the nation to preach, found it even more appalling that the missionaries themselves seemed so contemptuous of the poor. "This is the case also with many, if not most, missionaries: They will not come down far enough to take hold even of their blankets to lift them out of this horrible pit. They think they must equal [in comfort], if not surpass, the first class of Cherokees, and thus fix their marks entirely beyond the reach of all the common Indians." The Cherokees, he thought, were fast becoming two nations, and "unless peculiar caution is used, two parties will be formed which will probably be called, though falsely, the Christian and Pagan. I say falsely because objections arising from an appearance of pride and superiority cannot be said to arise from opposition to God though attended with opposi-

23. Daniel Butrick to Samuel Worcester, January 1, 1819, ABCFM.
24. Daniel Butrick to Jeremiah Evarts, September 27, 1825, ABCFM. Butrick acted as a secret advisor to David Brown, whom the Cherokee Council had appointed to translate the Bible into the Sequoyan syllabary.
25. Daniel Butrick to Samuel Worcester, January 1, 1819, ABCFM.
26. Daniel Butrick to Jeremiah Evarts, November 24, 1824, ABCFM.

tion to the cause of missions." Butrick's prediction was all too accurate. Furthermore, he rightly predicted that there were other denominations which were willing to reach down to the poor if the American Board was not: "If we will not condescend to the poorest class of Cherokees . . . they will either go to the Baptist or methodist meetings, where they can find someone who does not feel above them, or they will excite such opposition as we cannot withstand."[27]

The American Board's schools, like those of all missionary organizations, were Christian schools, designed to indoctrinate a specific religious creed in conjunction with its academic subjects. The children had no choice but to imbibe Calvinistic Christianity along with their reading and writing. They began their days at 5:30 A.M. with prayer and hymns; they were taught to read the Bible and Shorter Catechism as well as from a variety of Christian literature; they memorized Bible texts, said grace before meals, and closed their days at 9 P.M. with more prayer and hymns. The teachers constantly looked for signs of spiritual "awakening," of the moving of the Holy Spirit within their hearts. They were questioned regularly about the state of their souls and their morals. Special attention was given to any child who said he or she wished to learn more about Jesus and forgiveness for sin. God's Spirit hovered over their enterprise, and the teachers were in constant expectancy of signs of his work upon the hearts of their charges. Students ranged from eight to fifteen years old; while all were eligible for baptism, only the older ones were eligible for church membership. During the period from 1817 to 1833 when Brainerd was in operation, 20 out of 325 students who attended did join the mission church (though sometimes after they had left the school).[28]

The teachers were equally concerned to inculcate the habits of obedience, hard work, promptness, tidiness, thoroughness, and self-discipline. Infractions of rules or failure to perform duties could be punished by dismissal, whipping, denial of treats, or being made to stand in the center of the classroom and recite an appropriate text. However, the Cherokees realized that the missionaries worked selflessly, for little pay, to help them. The gratitude of parents and the desire of the children to please their teachers contributed to the building up of close personal relationships, especially between the women teachers and their female students. Females were given daily tasks to perform to assist with household chores and to learn the domestic arts. As one fourteen-year-old explained her duties, "When school hours are over the girls attend to domestick concerns and learn to make their own clothes and the clothes of the boys so they can do such work when they

27. Ibid. Butrick was not so accurate in predicting that "should the chiefs determine to support us, they would probably lose their authority."

28. Rothberg, "Missionary Education," p. 22. The Brainerd mission church admitted 104 Cherokee members in this period, so roughly 20 percent were, or had been, students. The remainder were parents of students or other adults living nearby.

go home, to assist their parents. They can then take care of their houses and their brothers and sisters and perhaps learn their parents something that they do not understand."[29] Sometimes the parents provided homespun cotton cloth for them to make into clothing; sometimes benefactors from the North sent gingham or calico, which were made into dresses "to wear on sabbath days." The female students also helped in the kitchen and with the laundry and ironing. Older girls took care of younger ones and assisted in nursing chores when there was sickness. The only vocation other than housewife for which they received training was schoolteaching, so that they could "teach to poor children who cannot come to the Missionaries school."[30] Presumably this would happen only if they became missionaries or the wives of missionaries, for there were no other schools to employ them.

Brainerd was designed as a model farm, like Springplace, and the boys received a much wider range of vocational help than the girls. They learned the principles of the three-field system of planting, how to care for horses and cattle, how to plough, harvest, and grind corn at the mission gristmill and how to saw wood at the mission sawmill. Some were apprenticed to blacksmiths or other mechanics. Because there was so much work to be done on the farm, including caring for sixty to seventy-five students plus a large staff, the students became in fact an essential part of the labor force. Even then, most missions had to hire slaves to assist in the harder or more skilled labor. Well-to-do Cherokee parents resented the amount of menial labor required of their sons and occasionally accused the missionaries of working them "like niggers."[31]

Another important aspect of mission education concerned manners and decorum. They were taught cleanliness, hygiene, table manners, and respect for authority. Missionaries were especially shocked at the sexual behavior of Cherokee children. "The intercourse between the young of both sexes was shamefully loose," when Brainerd opened in 1817. "Boys or girls in their teens would strip and go in to bathe or play ball together naked. They would also use the most disgusting indecent language without the least sense of shame. But when better instructed, they became reserved and modest."[32]

The missionaries always hoped to cull the brightest and best students for missionary work among their people. Between 1818 and 1825 ten of the Brainerd students were sent to the board's missionary academy in Cornwall,

29. Payne Papers, VIII, 22. Nancy Reece to Rev. Fayette Shepherd, December 25, 1828.

30. Payne Papers, VIII, 49. Lucy Campbell (age twenty-one) to Jane Speaker, November 18 [1829].

31. Walker, *Torchlights*, p. 140: "One of the chiefs offered to find a slave who should work all day if the missionaries would excuse his son from agricultural labor between school hours, but he was easily convinced of his mistake and apologized for his ill-judged request." Brainerd Journal, July 20, 1819, ABCFM: "Some Indians complain about boys working in the fields" and say "that was no way to learn them."

32. Jeremiah Evarts, "Memorandum," April-May 1822, ABCFM.

Connecticut, where they joined similar students from foreign mission stations around the world. Here they spent two or three years learning theology, church history, Latin, Greek, Hebrew, and other subjects necessary for entering a college or seminary. One of the ten, David Brown, spent a year at Andover Theological Seminary, and Stephen Foreman attended Union Seminary in Virginia in 1830 and Princeton Seminary in 1831; but none ever completed theological training or attended college.[33] Four Cherokees were sent to a small theological seminary run by the Presbyterians in Maryville, Tennessee, but they did not complete the course. The ministerial training required of Congregationalists and Presbyterians was arduous and far less appealing to most young Cherokees than the secular vocations available to them in the nation. Some of them gave up Christianity entirely after they returned home from these seminaries. When David Brown seemed to waver between becoming a preacher or taking up a political career on the Cherokee Council in 1824, Jeremiah Evarts wrote to him, "For you to be a minister of the Gospel among your Countrymen would be a more honorable and useful station than to be a chief, a lawgiver, or anything else."[34] After some indecision, Brown did decide to return to Andover Seminary, but he died in 1829 before completing his studies. None of the ten who went to Cornwall was ever ordained, though five of them (John Ridge, Leonard Hicks, Elias Boudinot, James Fields, and David Carter) became influential leaders in the nation.

In the long run the principal accomplishment of the American Board missionaries lay in the social models for respectability they provided. Of the 325 students who attended Brainerd from 1817 to 1833, about 100 attained significant proficiency in reading and writing English, and the rest gained enough to manage their affairs and help others. Probably the proportions were the same for the other 500−600 taught in the other American Board schools.[35] More important than academic and vocational skills were the habits and moral values instilled. They were aptly summed up in a letter to the Cherokee newspaper in 1828 by one of the Cherokee exhorters of the board. What is important to the Cherokees, he said, if they wished to maintain their independence was to

> attend to business, make themselves good houses and farms and attend well to the raising of cattle. If we all pursue this course, we shall be firmly established and those who ask of us our land will be discouraged. And if we labor well, we shall live well, for our land is valuable. This is the way the whites have done; they have labored well and pursued their business with great effort. If we pursue the same course, we shall prosper. But they who are lazy, will always be poor.[36]

33. See Walker, *Torchlights*, pp. 155–58, for summary sketches of the Cornwall pupils.
34. Jeremiah Evarts to David Brown, January 6, 1824, ABCFM.
35. See Rothberg's evaluation in "Missionary Education."
36. *Cherokee Phoenix*, July 2, 1828. In this same issue there is a remarkable obituary for "an elderly Lady, Oo-dah-less," who had died in the nation on April 22. Written by John Ridge, a Congregationalist convert, it praised her as a prime example of the success myth: "She

While the mission schools instilled the Calvinist virtues of industry and piety, thrift and sobriety with great zeal and persistence, they also developed serious anxieties among their students. In the letters written by some of the female students to northern benefactors to thank them for their gifts and support, these young Cherokees reveal considerable ambivalence about their identity and self-esteem. Respectful and genuinely fond of their teachers, they were painfully conscious that white students (the children of the missionaries) were much more successful at mastering the school tasks. Those of mixed ancestry compensated for this by noting their own superiority over the fullbloods. "I think you would be pleased," wrote one Cherokee girl, "to sit in our school room and see us attend our studies; you would see some tawny girls and some [Cherokees] who are white as any children."[37] The "tawny" girls were fullbloods; most of the letters were written by mixed bloods. In one school, where there were twenty-three female students, two of whom were white, fifteen of mixed ancestry, and six "full Cherokee," a fourteen-year-old mixed blood wrote of her teacher's unconscious bias: "When Miss Ames tells the two white girls they have done well, we [Cherokees] often say that they can do well because they are white girls, though she says people of the North think that the Cherokees have as good a genius to learn [as whites] if it was only cultivated." Another girl put it differently: "people do not know that Indian children can learn like white children." Apparently Miss Ames told them that all children were potentially equal regardless of their color, but she displayed regret that many of the Cherokees refused to take advantage of the enlightened ways which the missionaries were offering them. Students' letters often reflected the missionaries' disdain for traditionalists.

> The unenlightened parts of this nation assemble for dances around a fire . . . . Every year when the green corn, beans, etc. are large enough to eat, they dance all night and torture themselves by scratching their bodies with snakes teeth before they will eat any . . . . Their dishes are made by themselves of clay . . . . Many [Cherokees] about this [mission] station are more civilized . . . and appear as well as white people . . . . But I have learned that the white people were once as degraded as this people and that encourages me to think that this nation will soon become enlightened . . . . I hope I feel thankful for the good that missionaries are doing to bring the word of God to this people. I fear I am taking up too much paper.

---

was a woman distinguished through life for honesty and industry, habits of application to Agricultural pursuits, and the support of a large family, that would give to any of the other sex a claim for admiration. Unassisted by education, only in the knowledge of simple addition and subtraction, which is within the reach of uncultivated minds, she, by dint [of] application in farming and trading, had accumulated a very handsome property consisting of household furniture, mill, waggon, horses and cattle, sheep, Negro Slaves, and some money, all of which she has left to an only daughter and three grand children." She was not, however, a Christian.

37. This, and all the letters from schoolchildren which follow, are in the Payne Papers, VIII, 9–61. Most of them were written from the Brainerd mission school in 1828–29 by female students aged ten to fifteen.

Her belief that "white people were once as degraded" as the Cherokee fullbloods came from the teacher's effort to acquaint them with the history of western civilization. When Julius Caesar invaded Britain in 45 B.C., he found the Britons to be wild barbarians. Unfortunately, the Cherokees were expected to acquire in one generation the civilized ways which British-Americans had taken 1,800 years to acquire.

Most of the mixed-blood children had no doubt that they ought to become as much like whites as possible: "The missionaries do a great deal of good; they teach us to behave as Christian people do and how to study as white children do. . . . We ought to be thankful to the Missionaries and especially to God who sent them to us." The requirement that they express gratitude sometimes seemed to grate, but rather than express any latent hostility toward the teachers (as the male students sometimes did), they internalized it and then expressed superiority over the fullbloods. "I have a class of the younger children in Sabbath school," said one of the older girls; "I ask those children who do not talk english if they understood the sermon that was read [in English] and they say they do not . . . . I try to tell them how to spend the sabbath and tell them where they will go when they die if they are not good."

Another child compared the successful Cherokees with the unsuccessful: "I think that you would be pleased to hear about the improvement of the Cherokees. Many of them have large plantations and [the] greater part of them keep a number of Cattle and some have large buildings, but some live miserably; they don't send their children to school and don't care any thing about the Sabbath." Living decently and being Cherokee went together. Another compared the improvement in her own family since the missionaries came: "Once my father was a warrior and did not think so much about the education of his children," but then he was converted to Christianity and now "he is an Elder of the church at Brainerd . . . . I think I ought to be very thankful to God for giving me such a Father." The nonchurchgoing Cherokees went to "conjurors" when they were sick, and "some Cherokee children have parents who are drunkards and will not let them hear about God." In short, this girl believed, far too many Cherokees "have yet a great many bad customs, but I hope these things will soon be done away with." Not to be Christian was to be poor, wretched, and ignorant.

The teachers were so convinced that the mission schools were the only beacon lights in the benighted pagan world that they passed on to their students their anguish whenever a parent removed a child from the school. "We were very sorry," said a teacher, "to part with this child and have her taken back to the regions of darkness perhaps never to see the light of life."[38] A letter written to the mission from one of the students after she was taken home by her parents expressed the same uneasiness: "I am here amongst a

38. Brainerd Journal, November 22, 1818, ABCFM.

wicked set of people . . . . When I think of the poor thoughtless Cherokees going on in sin, I cannot help blessing God that he has led me in the right path to serve him."[39]

Influential chiefs, as well as mission teachers and children, felt in the 1820s that they were in a desperate struggle to achieve civilization and white respect as rapidly as possible. They not only pushed for acculturation, they seemed to favor the obliteration of all that preserved the image of the "savage" Indian. A delegation of Cherokee leaders visited John Quincy Adams in Washington in 1825 to ask him to stop pressing the nation to remove to the West. In their address to him they wrote, "For the sake of civilization and the preservation of existence, we would willingly see the habits and customs of the aboriginal man extinguished, the sooner this takes place the [sooner the] great stumbling block, [white] prejudice, will be removed."[40] One of the most notable of the American Board converts, Elias Boudinot, speaking to an audience of whites in Philadelphia in 1826, declared, "A period is fast approaching when the stale remark—'Do what you will, an Indian will still be an Indian'—must be placed no more in speech," because "as they rise in information and refinement, changes [in their institutions] must follow until they arrive at that state of advancement when, I trust, they will be admitted into all the privileges of the American family." "Indians," he said, would shortly attain a "polished society."[41]

While the missionaries and many influential chiefs told the Cherokees that to save their country they must accept the beliefs and values of Christianity and the whiteman, neither the chiefs nor the missionaries seemed to sense danger in the fact that the peak of fullblood attendance at the American Board schools was reached in 1821. Thereafter it declined rapidly. Though fullbloods constituted 75 percent of the population, they never constituted 75 percent of the student body. Those who did attend, though they tried as hard as the mixed bloods to learn, gradually fell farther and farther behind. Part of the reason they dropped out was that they had unrealistic expectations: "Many of this ignorant people," said Ard Hoyt in 1818, "appear to think their children can become learned in a few months."[42] Yet in large part it was the fault of the teachers, who spoke no Cherokee and relied upon other, presumably bilingual, children to teach the fullbloods. Suspecting that fullbloods would be bad students, the teachers probably were more ready to give up on them. The Moravians did no better.

Compared to the rapid expansion of the American Board's efforts in the 1820s, that of the Moravians was small. They too catered to the well-to-do, mixed-blood elite. Their funds, however, were far more limited, and government aid was proportionate to the resources of mission boards. The lion's

39. Rufus Anderson, *Memoirs of Catherine Brown*, p. 39.
40. ASP II, 775.
41. Elias Boudinot, *An Address to the Whites*, p. 4.
42. Brainerd Journal, December 17, 1818, ABCFM.

share of Congress's Education or Civilization Fund went to the more affluent American Board year after year.[43] In part, however, to be small, stolid, and unaggressive was the Moravian preference. They continued to believe that the Lord would direct the Cherokees to them if they labored faithfully after their fashion. While they established friendly and fraternal relations with the missionaries of the American Board, they kept their distance. They taught by example and somewhat resented the hard-driving zeal of the board's missionaries. One Moravian, in a letter to his board in Salem, dramatically explained the differences between the approaches of the two denominations:

> We preach an all-embracing salvation from sins through meritorious sacrifice of Jesus; they, predestination. We allure; they hit out. We work in all quietness; they trumpet their doings abroad. We emphasize a change of heart, [they] emphasize ceremonial matters such as the keeping of the Sabbath, etc. as the main duties. We are concerned to have those who unite with us become true disciples of Jesus, even though they be few in numbers; they are concerned with large numbers, more attention being given to paper than to reality. We guarded against ever letting the Indians become aware of any distinctions between religious factions; nevertheless, this has now become known.[44]

It was not simply a matter of money or theology, but a matter of style. Nevertheless, the competition from the American Board (and later from the Baptists and the Methodists) did compel the Moravians to make some alterations in their work after 1819. They saw no reason why they should not take advantage of the Education Fund to the extent they were able. They were pleased that several of their students were chosen to attend the American Board's seminary at Cornwall. They decided to open a second mission station.

What encouraged them most was the small religious revival which took place at Springplace in 1819–20. Perhaps as a result of the successful alleviation of the tensions over the removal crisis, there was a sudden wave of interest in attending the Moravian services. The Moravians had made only two converts in the years 1800 to 1819, so the sudden addition of twelve converts over the next two years encouraged them to believe that the tide might at last be turning in their favor. Even though these converts did not leave their homes to settle near the mission compound, nevertheless the Moravians decided it was time to organize a mission church (hitherto they had simply held family worship and public meetings). Then, at the urging of

43. When the Education Fund Act was passed in 1819, the American Board told the commissioner of Indian affairs that they could easily use the whole of it for themselves: "For obvious reasons, it seems not desirable that different societies should be engaged with the same Tribe or Tribes. The field is sufficiently wide and each Society may take its allotment. . . . We should find no difficulty in applying immediately and with good effect, the whole $10,000 appropriated by Congress." Samuel Worcester to Thomas McKenney, April 24, 1819, ABCFM.

44. Springplace Conference, 1819, p. 48.

a group of influential Cherokees living fifteen miles to the west of them at Oochgelogy, they agreed to start a second school. Several of those who persuaded them to undertake this had sent their children to the school at Springplace and were thus well known to them, such as the members of the Ridge, Watie, and Hicks families.

The Moravian mission board was not eager to start a new station and did not understand why the system which had worked so well in their missions among the Delawares and other Indians to the north was not applicable to the Cherokees. John Gambold and Abraham Steiner, the missionaries at Springplace in 1819, wrote a long report to the board in an effort to explain. The difference lay in the kind of farming which the Cherokees had adopted and the kind of farm labor. It was not possible, they said, for Cherokees who owned large plantations worked by slaves simply to give up these establishments and to reestablish them in the mission compound. "Only a few acres are to be found [near] the mission where a tract of good land exists in one place large enough for the needs of a Cherokee farming community with its present husbandry methods." Most of their converts "have extensive fields and numerous herds of horses and cattle, pigs and sheep; how could they live together in one place?" Moreover, "all of our present members, together with all of those who are connected with us and desire to be connected, own from 4 to 10 Negroes who can multiply year by year." Consequently, "it must be evident first of all that considerable space would be needed for the dwellings and maintenance of the Negroes, and further, that it would be more of a Negro town than an Indian" one.[45]

The Moravians had come to save Indian souls, not black souls. A mission compound in which there were more blacks than red people would be anomalous. This report also revealed that because of their high standards and cautious approach to evangelistic activity over the years, they had succeeded in converting primarily persons of considerable wealth and of mixed ancestry. Less than 2 percent of the Cherokee families owned four to ten slaves. "Among free heathen," Gambold and Steiner wrote (that is, among nonslaveholding Indians like the Delawares), mission compounds or "settlements [of converts] are more easily formed; but among slaves [or slaveholding Indians] this is impracticable."[46] Despite their initial success in attracting slaves to their services in 1801−04, they eventually found only one black worthy of admission to communion during their thirty-nine years in the nation.

Because their wealthy converts had become successful before they became Christian, Gambold and Steiner praised their habits of industry and attributed their success to their wisdom at having moved out of the old communal town structure early in the century to strike out on their own. "It had now [1800] become demonstrable that so long as the Indians lived

45. Ibid., pp. 32–33.
46. *Missionary Intelligencer*, 1: 10.

together in towns, they always would remain lazy, careless, miserable, and poor folk despite every effort on the part of the government officials to improve their condition, but, on the other hand, that those who lived on separate plantations constantly improved their lot and became more industrious and civilized."[47] This seemed to reverse the Moravian theory that conversion would precede the development of steady habits and therefore that Christianization must precede civilization. The Moravians attributed the success of their late converts also to their more frequent intercourse with white people, and "because of their constantly increasing association with white people, the Cherokees want their young people to learn English."[48] If the Moravian mission society was to continue to have an influence among the rising generation of the more successful Cherokees, it was necessary, Gambold and Steiner concluded, to establish a new mission where it suited such Cherokees. Because some of those at Oochgelogy were among the converts of the revival of 1819—20, a mission church could be started there, and with regular services in that neighborhood, Christianity would spread its light even farther.

Oochgelogy was close to the new Cherokee capital of New Echota, and, given their long-standing belief that Christianity would work its way down from the top of the nation to the poorer classes, it seemed logical to the missionaries to start a second station in this area. Among those who invited them to come were Major Ridge, his wife Susanna (a convert in the 1819 revival), his son John Ridge (a former Moravian student, later a member of the Brainerd Church), David Watie (brother of Major Ridge, converted in 1829), his wife Susanna (a convert in 1822), his son Elias Boudinot (a former student at Springplace and now a member of Brainerd Church), Stand Watie (a former student), William Hicks (brother of Charles Hicks), his wife Sarah (both converts in 1819), and his son Elijah (a former student at Springplace who had gone to school in Cornwall, as had John Ridge and Elias Boudinot). All in all, these constituted a very imposing group of Cherokee leaders. There was every reason to believe that their participation in the Oochgelogy school and church would attract other influential persons. It was ironic, however, that these Cherokees were attracting the Moravians to settle in their compound rather than vice versa. For many years the Moravians had hoped to convert Major Ridge and Stand Watie (brother of Elias Boudinot) and in the 1820s it seemed likely they would succeed. These two would be as important converts as Charles Hicks himself. Charles Hicks, who joined in inviting the Moravians to come to Oochgelogy, did not himself live there, but he lived closer to that spot than to Springplace, and with his lame leg would certainly attend its church more often than he had been able to attend that at Springplace.

The narrow social scope of the Springplace mission school in the years

47. Springplace Conference, 1819, pp. 32–33.
48. Fries, 7 (1809–22): 3445.

1804 to 1824 can be seen by an analysis of the 105 students educated there. Of these, 6 were whites; 29 appear to have been fullbloods; the remaining 70 were of mixed ancestry. Analysis of the families from which these students came indicates that 41 of them came from 9 families: Hicks, Watie, Ridge, McDonald, Shorey, Vann, Taylor, Burghess, and Wolf. Examination of the 65 converts who joined the two Moravian churches during their first thirty years in the nation indicates that two-thirds of them were of the same small group of families, two-thirds of them were women, two out of three were of mixed ancestry.[49]

The Moravians may also have been hampered by their reliance on the lottery system. Every candidate for baptism and then for admission to their churches had to go through this appeal to God's will. Charles Hicks, though he was in every respect an exemplary convert, had to wait two years after the missionaries were convinced of his conversion before he could take communion because the lot repeatedly came out negative. Others, seeing how difficult it was for Hicks to gain admission, could easily be discouraged from trying. In addition, the cautiousness of the Moravians plus the added stumbling block of the lottery system, probably kept down the development of a native ministry. Of all the four denominations which worked among the Cherokees, the Moravians were the only one that never ordained a native preacher. Several of their converts, like Charles Hicks, occasionally acted as interpreters, translators, or exhorters at Moravian services, but none became officially associated with the mission. The most promising candidate for such a post was Taucheechy, a convert and Springplace student whom the Moravians christened David Steiner. After attending Cornwall Academy for several years, Taucheechy returned to Springplace eager to be allowed to become a preacher to his people. "The Lot was consulted" about his request, "and several times said 'No.'" This so discouraged and angered Taucheechy that he went to Brainerd and became a member of its church, severing his connection with the Moravians.[50] The lack of a native ministry and their own failure to learn to speak Cherokee undoubtedly served to confirm the Moravians' conviction that they should concentrate their attention upon influential, English-speaking Cherokees.

The Moravians opened their mission at Oochgelogy in 1821.[51] John and Maria Gambold were sent there to take charge of the school and church. No effort was made here, as at Springplace, to create a model farm and provide vocational training, for the students all came from highly acculturated families. Maria Gambold (John's second wife) had charge of the girls and John (with the help of Johann Proske) of the boys. Their school was as

49. This analysis is based upon the Springplace Diary, MAS, and Fries, 8: 3791–92. The former lists all converts, the latter all students at the school up to 1824.

50. Schwarze, *Moravian Missions*, p. 170. Although he served for a time as an interpreter for the American Board, Taucheechy was never licensed or ordained by them.

51. Ibid., pp. 156–69, describes the mission at Oochgelogy.

painstaking in its thoroughness as the one at Springplace, but it never grew very large. Some of the girls from this school went on to attend the female seminary at Salem, North Carolina, run by the Moravians (but not as a mission school).

When the Reverend Henry G. Clauder was put in charge of Oochgelogy late in the decade, he suggested that if his denomination expected to grow and to keep up with the efforts being made by other denominations, it should consider permitting him to itinerate. "I think it is a useless expense to the Board," he wrote, to maintain a fixed mission station serving only a handful of people. "Other denominations are by far more diligent in diffusing religious knowledge among the natives than we are." Clauder noted enviously that the Methodists were gathering in hundreds of Cherokee converts through the use of circuit riders. They did not have the expense of a single permanent station. "Their entire plan and system is better adapted to this country; our congregation of 12 or 13 converts cannot possibly increase in numbers because most of the neighbors either belong to the Methodists or Presbyterians [the American Board]."[52] While the Moravians sat quietly tending their own tiny flock, others moved around them and gathered the harvest of their years of hard work. If the board were serious about saving souls, said Clauder, it would have to abandon its school, buy him a good horse, hire an interpreter, and send him out into the highways and byways to preach; "more good could be done on the itinerant plan than by the present expensive way."[53]

But the Moravian mission board considered Clauder young and impatient. Nothing was done about his proposal. The Moravians continued to preach and teach at Springplace and at Oochgelogy, waiting for the Lord to turn the tide in their favor. Meanwhile, the American Board, the Methodists, and the Baptists grew by leaps and bounds. In 1825, David Brown wrote a letter to a religious newspaper in Richmond, Virginia, *The Family Visitor,* in which he described the enormous progress his people had made in the past quarter century. In this letter he said, "The Christian religion is the religion of the nation." The letter was picked up by Thomas L. McKenney of the Office of Indian Affairs as an accurate account of the state of the Cherokees, and he included it in his report to Congress. After noting that the Cherokees were "in advance of all other tribes" and "may be considered a civilized people," he predicted that "a little time only will be required (so far at least as it regards the Cherokees) . . . when the whole tribe will, no doubt, seek to place themselves under the laws of the United States and by that act prepare the process for their extinction as a race."[54]

McKenney and Brown both exaggerated. But Brown's point about the Christian religion being the religion of the nation had some basis. By 1825

52. Henry Clauder, Diary at Oochgelogy, May 10, 1829, MAB.
53. Clauder, Diary, May 2, 1829, MAB.
54. ASP II, 651–52.

most of the Cherokee mixed bloods were prepared to accept Christianity as a viable alternative to the old religion. Equally important, many fullblood Cherokees were now ready to give Christianity a hearing. The work of the Moravians and the American Board had proven too valuable to be rejected out of hand. Upon their solid base the Methodists and the Baptists began to build a wider Christian constituency. If the board and the Moravians catered to the elite, the Methodists and the Baptists set out to reach the common man.

❦《 CHAPTER SEVEN 》❧

The Baptists and the Methodists, 1819−1829

If we will not condescend to the poorest class of Cherokees . . . they will either go to the Baptist or methodist meetings where they can find someone who does not feel above them.

Daniel S. Butrick, American Board missionary, November 4, 1824

The Baptists founded their first permanent mission in the Cherokee Nation in 1819; the Methodists began their first formal circuits within the nation in the winter of 1823/24. These denominations brought to the Cherokees, as they did to other areas of the frontier, a more democratic, informal version of Christianity than that of the Moravians and the American Board. Their missionaries were less well educated and their ecclesiastical system much less formal; they were less concerned with doctrinal preaching and more interested in a personal, spiritual commitment which would lead *toward* reformation rather than mark the culmination of it. They preached a simpler and more direct message of hope and divine assistance and placed fewer barriers between the honest "seeker" or "anxious inquirer" and acceptance into Christian brotherhood than the American Board and the Moravians did. Though no less committed to upright moral conduct and sincere piety, the Baptists and the Methodists started by winning the hearts, not the heads, of the Cherokees. A clear, earnest statement of faith sufficed to make a man or woman eligible for baptism; the willingness to seek further instruction and to yield to the Christian discipline of the faithful was sufficient for communion.

In addition, the Baptists and the Methodists displayed a social egalitarianism which was lacking in the earlier missionaries. They were willing to treat the poorest and most illiterate Cherokee with the same interest and concern as the most wealthy or influential chief. They accepted far more readily the services of ordinary Cherokees of good heart as interpreters, exhorters, missionary assistants, and they more readily licensed Cherokee preachers and ordained Cherokee ministers without worrying over

150

their ability to explicate the fine points of theological doctrine. While missionaries of all denominations believed in theory that all souls were equal before God, the Baptists and the Methodists, perhaps because of their lower status in white society, were not obsessed with the notion of converting first and foremost the influential members of Cherokee society; they did not believe this was the best or fastest way to Christianize white or Indian nations. Their mission enterprise operated from the bottom up, not from the top down. The Baptists demonstrated their democratic principles by deciding to build their schools chiefly among the conservative fullbloods in the poorest and most remote mountain districts of the nation. Methodist egalitarianism was evidenced by their willingness to work, eat, and sleep among the Cherokees wherever they found them along their circuits and by their decision to establish no permanent mission stations or compounds. Early Methodist missionaries, unlike any other missionaries, were happy to find Cherokee wives and raise families in the nation. The leader of the Baptist mission was the only missionary of any denomination to learn Cherokee well enough to preach in that language.

While they shared the common touch, the Baptists and the Methodists were in other respects very dissimilar. The Baptists were Calvinists and the Methodists, Arminians; the Baptists believed in congregational autonomy and ordination; the Methodists, in episcopacy; the Baptists practiced total immersion of adult believers only; the Methodists sprinkled whole households (including infants and slaves) upon the conversion of the head of the family; the Baptists were slow to take up itinerancy, preferring to start with the same model farm system used by the Moravians and American Board; the Methodists from the outset believed that conversion must precede education and put much more effort into Methodist classes for spiritual growth than in mission schools for secular education. Neither Methodists nor Baptists had the financial resources of the American Board, but they had more volunteers for mission work than the Moravians. The Baptists, after 1826, had their board headquarters in Massachusetts; the Methodists had theirs in Tennessee. Beyond their egalitarianism, the Baptists and the Methodists shared one other important characteristic which proved a great asset to their work. Most Baptist and Methodist missionaries in the field did not try to remain politically neutral. When the government attempted to force the Cherokees to cede their land and emigrate, these missionaries freely and publicly expressed their sympathy for the Cherokees. After 1828, their open support of social justice frequently placed the Baptist and Methodist missionaries in opposition to the boards to whom they were responsible and who took a more cautious view of mixing religion and politics, especially antigovernment politics.

For all these reasons, the Methodists first, and later the Baptists, reaped the major harvests of souls among the Cherokees. But they could hardly have done so had not the Moravians and the American Board made Christianity a live option by 1825. As the Moravian missionary Henry G. Clauder said of the Cherokees in 1830, "It is the fashion of the day to be religious."[1]

The Baptists in the South were slow to launch a missionary effort among the Indians. In part the delay was due to strong antimission sentiment among rigid predestinarians, particularly in Kentucky and Tennessee. The antimission Baptists believed that God would save the Indians in his own good time and that money for missions was wasted. When God wanted people converted, he raised up preachers among them. In addition, and perhaps reenforcing that, the Baptists consisted chiefly of poor people who had little enough surplus to support their own churches. Baptists had always opposed "a hireling ministry," believing that spiritual truth was not confined to the educated; they had also fought hard against the Anglican establishment in the colonial era because it had used the power of the state to hinder their growth. Nevertheless, a Baptist minister in Georgia or the Carolinas or Tennessee would occasionally feel the call to preach to the heathen and wander off to see whether he could save them from hellfire.

The first consistent Baptist efforts to evangelize among the Cherokees came from William Standidge (or Standige) in Georgia and Humphrey Posey in North Carolina (where antimission sentiment was less strong). Standidge began itinerating among the Cherokees in northern Georgia in 1815; he was licensed to preach by the Sarepta Baptist Missionary Society of the Sarepta Baptist Association and received some financial support from its board of managers, headed by the Reverend Jesse Mercer and the Reverend Littleton J. Meeks. Posey, a resident of Haywood County, North Carolina, began itinerating in the western part of that state in 1817 among whites and Cherokees. He started on his own initiative after his conversion that year in Greenville, South Carolina, but that summer he wrote to the board of managers of the American Baptist Foreign Mission Society in Philadelphia telling them of the work he was doing and asking if they would support him.[2]

The American Baptist Foreign Mission Society had been founded by the Triennial Convention of the Baptist denomination in 1814, but until 1817 it was concerned primarily with overseas missions in Burma. Its general agent, Luther Rice, toured the southern states in 1816–17 and returned to convince the board in Philadelphia that they should include Indian nations as part of their work. The Triennial Convention of 1817 added Indian missions to the board's charge, and in the fall of that year William Staughton, the corresponding secretary of the board, wrote to Posey saying that the board would be happy to assist him in preaching and establish-

1. Clauder, Diary, September 19, 1830, MAB.
2. For the early Baptist mission efforts, see James W. Moffitt, "Early Baptist Missionary Work Among the Cherokees"; Henry T. Malone, *Cherokees of the Old South*, pp. 106–09; the files of *The Latter Day Luminary* (Philadelphia) and the *Baptist Missionary Magazine* (Boston). The papers of the American Baptist Foreign Mission Board (later the American Baptist Mission Union) are in the Baptist Historical Society, Rochester, New York.

ing schools among the Cherokees. Posey accepted the appointment on December 1, 1817, and with the aid of a Cherokee interpreter, Edward Tucker, formed four day schools among the Cherokees at Cowee, Tillanoocy, Eastatory, and at Tucker's hometown. Posey's plan was similar to that of Gideon Blackburn; he planned to continue as a preacher while he hired lay teachers (and interpreters) to conduct his schools. He had difficulty finding teachers for $160 a year (payable quarterly), but all the schools commenced operation during the spring and summer of 1818. However, the confusion in the nation over the effort to force a removal to Arkansas soon forced Posey to suspend operations. Convinced that Calhoun and McMinn would succeed in compelling emigration of the whole nation, Posey took a trip to Arkansas in October 1818 to scout out a place for a Baptist mission. When he returned in January 1819 he discovered that most of the tribe would remain in the East. He then applied to the Cherokee Council for permission to start a permanent mission station in North Carolina. In October 1819 Path Killer and John Ross informed him that the Cherokee Council had granted permission. Meanwhile the Baptist Foreign Mission Board had voted in April not to revive the four small schools but "to make liberal appropriations for a rigorous and comprehensive school and mission establishment" which, like Springplace and Brainerd, would include vocational training on a model farm.[3] Posey then negotiated for a site with the local Cherokee chiefs in North Carolina; they allowed him a plot of seventy to eighty acres at Valley Towns on the Hiwassee River (which flowed westward into the Tennessee). The Foreign Mission Board expected to be subsidized in part by the Education Fund, but like most missionary associations it grossly underestimated the expense involved in such a project.

In January 1820 the board recruited and sent to Valley Towns Thomas Dawson, a Lancastrian schoolteacher from Georgetown, South Carolina. He was given the position of assistant missionary to help Posey. The board also authorized Posey to start erecting buildings, to have a gristmill and sawmill built, and to purchase forty cattle, three horses, one hundred hogs, and the necessary ploughs, seed, hoes, axes, and other equipment. Staughton then placed advertisements in various Baptist periodicals calling for a wide variety of volunteers to staff the establishment—female teachers, a miller, a blacksmith, a carpenter, a farmer, and some mechanics. These high hopes were realized when the Reverend Thomas Roberts, pastor of a Baptist church in Great Valley, Pennsylvania, near Philadelphia, persuaded a number of his church members with the requisite skills to join him as volunteers in this work. Among those who left Philadelphia with Roberts on September 21, 1821, in a train of covered wagons, were Evan Jones, a schoolteacher, Isaac Cleaver, a blacksmith, and John Farrier, a farmer, all with their families.

---

3. See the *Proceedings* of the Baptist General Convention, 1817, and the "Outline of a Plan for Establishing a School" in the minutes of the American Baptist Foreign Mission Society, vol. 1, January 25, 1820.

These families, plus Roberts's, included fifteen children. There were three female teachers, Mrs. Elizabeth Jones, Mary Lewis, and Mrs. Ann Cleaver. They arrived in Valley Towns in December and found that Posey and Dawson already had forty schoolchildren in the first buildings. A year later, Evan Jones reported that the school had forty-eight male students and twenty-two female, while Roberts reported that they had formed a mission church with twenty converts and had started a second school, a day school, at the town of Notley (or Nottle), sixteen miles southeast of Valley Towns.[4]

Posey was enthusiastic about the prospects for the work, and when the federal agent to the Cherokees sent him the first installment from the Education Fund ($500) he rhapsodized about this new partnership between the Baptists and the state, contrasting it with the problems of foreign missionaries abroad: "Instead of Romish Bulls or superstitious bigotry and persecution of earthly Monarchs, instead of being under the power of Juggernaut or the idolatry of Boodah, I feel myself under the better than Banyan shade of the Government of the United States."[5]

Meanwhile, the Sarepta Baptist Missionary Society in Georgia continued (until 1818) to support Standidge's work among the Cherokees and to raise funds for the Reverend Thomas Brown and two other itinerant missionaries to assist him. Then, because of the removal crisis, it suspended operations until 1820. Standidge then returned to preach among the Cherokees and in April 1821 started a day school at the town of Tinsawattee on the Etowah River, sixty miles southeast of Valley Towns. This school proved successful and reported twenty-three students that year. However, Standidge apparently asked to be relieved in 1824; the Sarepta Society hired that year the Reverend Duncan O'Briant and his wife to take charge of their mission station. O'Briant was assisted by regular visits from Jesse Mercer and Littleton Meeks as supervisors of the mission, which was not far from the white settlements in Georgia. The Tinsawattee School averaged twenty students a years until 1829, when the school was transferred to the town of Hickory Log, eight miles to the south along the river. O'Briant's wife taught the female students, and he divided his time between the church, which remained at Tinsawattee, and the teaching of the male students at Hickory Log. Most of his students and church members—of whom he reported thirty by 1828—were of mixed ancestry or whites married to Cherokees. At Valley Towns most of the students and converts were fullbloods. Until 1826 the Sarepta Society raised most of the funds and hired the staff for its ministers, but that year Jesse Mercer asked the Baptist Foreign Mission Board in Philadelphia to assume the general responsibility for the mission, although he and Meeks continued to supervise it. Thereafter the Sarepta Baptist

4. *Baptist Missionary Magazine* 3: 463; *Watchman*, December 8, 1821, July 14, 1821, March 9, 1822, August 24, 1822, April 12, 1823.
5. Humphrey Posey to R. J. Meigs, June 13, 1820, BIA, M-208.

Missionary Society sent whatever funds it raised to the denominational board.[6]

Posey's management of the funds for the Valley Towns station left much to be desired. He left the mission to return to itinerant preaching on his own after 1824. Thomas Roberts and Evan Jones continued the mission and expressed surprise at their warm reception by the Cherokees. As elsewhere, however, the Cherokees wanted schools rather than churches. They told the Baptists, "We want our children to learn English so that the white man cannot cheat us."[7] The missionaries were more interested in evangelizing, but they were also pleased to find the Cherokee children so eager to learn English: "The Cherokee children learn as fast as any Children I ever saw," Roberts reported. "They are kind, obedient, and industrious." Moreover, their "mental powers appear to be in no respect inferior to those of whites." Whites, however, were the norm by which red children were to be measured: "Though their skin is red or dark, I assure you, their mental powers are white—few white children can keep pace with them in learning."[8] The Baptists, like other missionaries, were appalled at the virulent hatred and prejudice of the surrounding frontier whites toward the Indians and their anger at the missionaries for befriending and assisting them. "The White people are constantly opposing every effort to instruct the poor benighted Indians," wrote one of the missionaries at Valley Towns. "The great objection urged by most people in these parts is the enmity of the old wars in which some of their friends have been killed by them."[9] White frontiersmen also resented the use of federal funds to help Indians when they themselves felt hard-pressed to make ends meet. Nevertheless, the Baptists slowly expanded their work at the two missions in North Carolina. "It is truly pleasing," Roberts wrote in 1824, "to see so many young immortals [that is, immortal souls] taken from abodes of vice and wickedness, assuming habits of industry and civilization, and acquiring knowledge for this life and especially the knowledge of the word of God."[10] The children behaved well and "there is seldom need of corporal punishment," he said. "Rewards and forfeits have far better effects." Under the Lancastrian system, reward tickets were given for good behavior and academic performance; the reward tickets had a small monetary value and could be saved toward the purchase of additional clothing or books. Forfeits consisted of the loss of privileges.

Heavy emphasis was placed upon prayer, piety, neatness, honesty, perseverance, and polite behavior, as at other missions. The Baptists taught

6. Jesse Mercer, *A History of the Georgia Baptist Association* (Washington, Georgia, 1838), p. 74. See also minutes of the BFMB and *Baptist Missionary Magazine* 3: 177, 185, 269, 386, 413, 463; 4: 264, 336.

7. Leonard Butterfield to Lucius Bolles, January 12, 1835, BFMB.

8. *Watchman*, March 9, 1822; *Latter Day Luminary* 3: 91.

9. Evan Jones to Lucius Bolles, April 1, 1827, BFMB.

10. *Baptist Missionary Magazine* 4: 336.

theology from the catechism of the Reverend Thomas Baldwin of Boston, history from the Bible, and reading from Philip Doddridge's *Rise and Fall of Religion in the Soul.* At the Valley Towns school, the boys learned husbandry trades; the girls, spinning and weaving. Mrs. Evan Jones conducted the girls' school. Probably among the poorer Cherokees in this part of the nation the vocational training was more important. Although the people were all farmers, they spent much time hunting in the hills; there was almost no slave labor. Still, the Baptists held the usual view of the Indians' inveterate laziness: "It is doubtless no small branch in the system of Indian reform," the mission board wrote to the missionaries, "to learn and habituate the natives to labor. Their subsequent subsistence in a civilized state depends upon it. It is expected that this habit will be commenced and somewhat matured at this school."[11] If the children were to be given room, board, and tuition free, they were expected, as at Springplace and Brainerd, to do their share of the labor.

Thomas Dawson drew up a list of regulations for the schools in 1824 to which all parents were required to assent when they enrolled their children. According to these, all parents "shall furnish their children with shoes and one blanket," and if they could afford it, "with clothes." "Every pupil shall continue at school till he has attained at least a plain English education." Pupils caught stealing would be "excluded from the school and forfeit all clothes" which the school had provided. Students were allowed to leave school only during specified vacation periods. "No scholar shall be allowed to keep a horse, dog, gun, or dirk" at the school, and "any pupils who shall attend any ball play or dance, or be guilty of getting drunk, shall be expelled from the school." The board of managers reported in its minutes in 1824 that "the new rules . . . have had a very salutary effect on both parents and children. They no longer deem it a favour conferred upon us [to patronize the school], as they formerly did when they brought their children to school, but [now see it as a favour conveyed] on themselves and their offspring" by the Baptists.[12]

The Baptists met the same difficulties that the Moravians and the American Board had encountered with the Cherokee language. "The misfortune is," Roberts reported soon after arriving, "they do not understand English and we have no good interpreter."[13] Students became frustrated. "Some of the boys who have been here for a long time trying to learn English," Roberts said in 1822, "without understanding what they read, became discouraged, went away, and we see them no more. Others seem to hang on between hope and despair."[14] In 1822 the board authorized the

---

11. Lucius Bolles to Evan Jones, November 4, 1826, BFMB.
12. Minutes of the board of managers, vol. 2, pp. 166–70, BFMB.
13. *Watchman,* March 9, 1822.
14. *Baptist Missionary Magazine,* 3: 463.

hiring of an interpreter, though urging its missionaries to learn the language. The first interpreter, James Wafford, was of mixed ancestry and had formerly been among the older pupils. However, he lived at some distance from the school. Having to manage his own farm and support his family, he was present primarily to translate the sermons on Sundays.[15] Evan Jones, who had been a teacher before coming to Valley Towns, knew Welsh, Latin, Greek, and Hebrew, but he found Cherokee very difficult to master. Hearing that the Reverend Daniel Butrick at Brainerd mission was also trying to learn the language and to find a way to write it (using roman letters), Jones went to see him. Later he corresponded with him and with the Reverend Samuel Worcester at New Echota. It took Jones almost a decade to learn the language well enough to preach in Cherokee. The conversion of a bilingual Cherokee named John Timson at Valley Towns in 1825 provided some help. Timson agreed to serve as an interpreter at the school. However, he, like Wafford, lived at a distance and had to support his family, so that even with two part-time interpreters work at the mission went slowly. By 1830 the Valley Towns mission church had sixty-eight Cherokee members, the Tinsawattee church, thirty-one. (The schools continued at Hickory Log and Notley, but no churches were formed there.) While this was more than the Moravians had converted in thirty years, it was only about half as many as the American Board had obtained by 1830. The Baptist mission board found the total far from satisfactory given the heavy expense of the four stations.

The missionaries pointed out that in addition to the language barrier, they had to overcome serious ignorance of religion among the Cherokees and considerable opposition from ungodly whites. So far as Christianity was concerned, the Cherokees "view all we said as mere legendary tales," wrote Evan Jones in 1827, "in which Indians would have no sort of concern, and the apathy and profligacy of the whites residing among them confirmed this opinion, and some [whites] have even taken the pains to endeavour to persuade them that there was no truth in the gospel doctrines."[16] Jones reported visiting a Cherokee who had some white ancestry and could speak some English but who "seemed quite ignorant of the depravity of his nature, though he has often heard the gospel." He, like most Cherokees, seemed to have no sense of sin nor fear of hellfire. Jones told him of these matters and "endeavoured to impress on him the necessity of laying to heart the awful condition of a dying Sinner," but this made little impression. "In their dark, uninstructed state they seem to have no other fear of death than that which arises from the apprehension of the bodily pain with which it may be accompanied."[17] Among many conservative fullbloods in the Great Smokies, the old religion still had a stronger appeal than the whiteman's religion.

15. *Latter Day Luminary*, 3: 213.
16. Evan Jones to Lucius Bolles, October, 12, 1827, BFMB.
17. Evan Jones to Lucius Bolles, March 2, 1828, BFMB.

In 1826 the Baptist Foreign Mission Board moved from Philadelphia to Boston, where it found more wealthy supporters and came under the direction of New Englanders whose viewpoint was very similar to that of the Prudential Committee of the American Board. The leading figures of the Baptist board became Daniel Sharpe, Lucius Bolles, and Heman Lincoln, all from the Boston area. The influence of the southern Baptists continued strong because of the work of the Sarepta Baptist Missionary Society and the contributions to the board from promission Baptists in the southern seaboard states. (After 1829, however, disagreements began to arise between the southern and northern Baptists about Indian missions.) When Roberts left Valley Towns in 1824, Evan Jones was ordained and became superintendent of the mission. He found himself more in harmony with the board in Boston than with the mission society in Georgia. Born in Wales and educated in London, Jones had emigrated to Philadelphia at the age of thirty-three. He had no sympathy for slavery and even less for the white frontier people of the South who kept trying to drive the Cherokees to the west. Jones never hesitated to let the Cherokees know where his political feelings lay, which eventually got him into difficulty with his own board and with the government.

A man of great energy and domineering personality, Jones was to head the Baptist mission to the Cherokees for forty years. His first problem as superintendent was to explain why the costs of the mission were so high and the number of converts so low. Lucius Bolles, the executive secretary of the Baptist Foreign Mission Board, tried to be understanding, but he demanded results: "The Indian stations have been kept up at very great expense," he wrote to Jones in 1826, "considering the small number of persons who are instructed or are in a situation to derive advantage from them." "Something must be done effectively to lessen expenditures or the Station cannot be maintained."[18] Even with federal assistance, the board had already provided $42,000 of its own funds to the mission; even so, mission expenses exceeded the budget by large sums each year. The board suggested several ways of cutting costs. The missionaries must do without all luxuries, such as tea, coffee, and sugar, which had to be imported into the nation at great expense. The missionaries had to learn Cherokee so as to cut down on the expense of interpreters. The burden of labor on the farm should be borne by the students, and no outside labor should be hired. The Cherokee parents and others in the vicinity of the schools were to bear more of the financial burden by contributing food and paying for the children's clothes.

Jones and his brethren were chagrined at the first of these suggestions. They did not feel that they were living in luxury; those in Boston could scarcely imagine their sacrifices and hardships. As for the students' performing more labor, some of them were too young and none of them was skilled. Learning Cherokee was far more difficult than learning Greek or Hebrew.

18. Lucius Bolles to Evan Jones, November 4, 1826, BFMB.

The cost of all tools, supplies, and labor on that remote frontier was exorbitant. Jones considered the board's budgetary expectations wholly unrealistic as well as unfair. In order to try to reconcile their differences, Bolles and Jones agreed to ask a respected Baptist minister from South Carolina, the Reverend Iveson L. Brooks, to visit the mission and render his impartial judgment. Meanwhile, the board suggested that the mission cease to board children and "substitute a day school to be kept four days in the week." At the same time, Bolles suggested that the missionaries should devote less time to running the farm: "so much secular business tends to injure the spirituality and heavenly mindedness of a Missionary and therefore lessens his ministerial usefulness very much."[19]

Without quite realizing it, the Baptist board, like the American Board, was moving toward a major shift in the nature of mission work because of financial constraints. They had formerly thought civilization should precede Christianization. By 1827 they were ready to put Christianization first, not only to increase "ministerial usefulness," but also, by winning converts, to enable the board to offer stronger evidence that the gifts of donors were producing the results intended. Mission supporters tended to measure results by conversion statistics. After some hesitation, Evan Jones, perhaps as a result of the recommendation of Iveson Brooks after he visited Valley Towns, seems to have reached the same conclusion himself in the spring of 1827. Jones now concluded that the Cherokees had advanced further toward civilization (in the form of self-sufficient farming) than he and most other white Americans had realized. "All the Indians around here," he told the board in May 1827, "are used to farming" and "some of them understand the business better than the Missionaries do" because they had been farming in that soil and climate for over twenty-five years.[20] Jones therefore concurred with the recommendation of Brooks and the inclination of the board, which was to shift their principal effort from the model farm and its educational program to itinerant evangelism.

In October 1827 Bolles wrote to Jones that the board had voted "that the School at Valley Towns be reduced to twenty scholars which are expected to be mostly, if not all, female children, boarded by you and taught chiefly by Mrs. Jones. This will leave you at liberty to visit other places . . . and preach to many the unsearchable riches of Christ." The school at Notley should be continued provided that "the Indians complete, at their charge, the school house commenced by them, give towards the support of a teacher 500 lbs. of pork and 120 bushels of Corn per annum, and provided also that you can provide a native Cherokee competent to take charge of the school and at a salary not exceeding ten dollars a month." In addition, the missionaries were instructed to sell half of their hogs, cattle, and horses at the farm in order to pay off the outstanding debts. To assist in spreading the gospel, the board

19. Lucius Bolles to Evan Jones, May 11, 1827, BFMB.
20. Quoted in letter from Lucius Bolles to Jesse Mercer, May 11, 1827, BFMB.

agreed to hire an interpreter to accompany Jones until he could learn to speak the language himself. In conclusion, Bolles wrote, "I do hope we are now arrived at a point when the hands of our Missionary will not be filled with secular concerns but when he will be at liberty to promote by his whole powers the spiritual improvement of the Indians."[21] Bolles spoke of "our missionary" at Valley Towns in the singular because by October 1827 Jones was the only minister left at that station. For one reason or another the others had dropped out and had not been replaced. Only the Reverend Duncan O'Briant, dividing his time between Tinsawattee and (after 1829) Hickory Log, remained to assist Jones in the Cherokee Nation. But O'Briant was supported and supervised less by Jones and the board in Boston than by the Reverend Jesse Mercer and the Sarepta Baptist Missionary Society in Georgia.

The Baptists' change in operations did not please the Cherokees. They had welcomed them to their remote villages because they wished their children to learn English. Over the next few years Jones was to meet some resistance to his itinerant evangelism (as did itinerants of other denominations) from those Cherokees who could not help but see in the reduced emphasis on education another promise broken by the whiteman. Jones also met increasing opposition from the conjurors and supporters of the traditional religion. Nevertheless, Jones was pleased by the new plan. It freed him from the daily routine of classroom work, and it enabled him to mount his horse and go out in the more exciting quest of saving souls from Satan. But for this he needed help. He needed an interpreter and he needed an assistant to take charge of the converts in each town as he traveled around the nation. Here the Baptists' traditional preference for a spirit-filled rather than a learned ministry proved to be crucial. Starting from the proposition that a zealous heart was a more powerful instrument for God's work than any other attribute, Jones collected an ever-expanding team of Cherokee converts and exhorters to assist him in the work of spreading Christianity and combating heathenism. The Baptist (and the Methodist) emphasis upon emotional preaching intersected with a similar oratorical tradition in Cherokee culture—the honor and respect paid to the man who was eloquent and persuasive in speaking. Cherokees had always admired good public speakers, just as they had honored prophets with new visions. The Baptists, by opening their missionary ranks to young Cherokee men who possessed the talent and earnestness to preach from the Great Book, were providing a new avenue for advancement and influence. The opportunity for dedicated young men to assert a new kind of message and leadership came at a moment in Cherokee cultural transformation when the message of Christianity carried some weight within the nation. Its message of divine assistance, of miraculous personal change, and of ultimate social justice on earth (as it is in heaven)

21. Lucius Bolles to Evan Jones, October 22, 1827, BFMB.

offered its followers new hope, dignity, and courage. To some it made as much sense as the old religion. The Cherokees needed a religion of change and individual initiative. The old religion was made for a more static order. Now Christianity could become a significant force in Cherokee revitalization because it was being preached and interpreted by their own people in their own language and idiom. By utilizing Cherokee exhorters, the Baptists and the Methodists found a hearing and a following which the conservative and elitist Congregationalists and Moravians did not. A native ministry was the key to giving vital new power to God's word among the Cherokees.

Significantly, several of those whom Evan Jones was willing to trust as his assistants spoke no English at all and had virtually no academic training. Because very little of the Bible had been translated into Cherokee, its message became at first an oral tradition (once again, a form with which the Cherokees were familiar). Jones had developed by 1827 sufficient familiarity with the language to be able to judge when a convert had caught the spirit of his message, whether he could state it in English or not. It was this faith in their converts—the willingness to take a chance on their spiritual power regardless of their doctrinal knowledge—which marked the Baptists and the Methodists off from the Moravians and the Congregationalists. It also helped to make Christianization into a social movement. If Moravians and Congregationalists promoted the older Federalist–Jefferson ethic of rule by the elite, the Baptists and the Methodists promoted the new Jacksonian ethic that the voice of the people may be the voice of God. The political dimension of this split was to divide the nation more deeply between integrationists and separatists, both of whom claimed to have the true solution to the nation's destiny.

James Wafford, in 1822, became the first native Cherokee to act as an interpreter and exhorter for the Baptists. In 1823 John Timson began to preach for them. That same year Roberts described the conversion and baptism of Wasadi, "a full breed and a member of the National Council" from Valley Towns. Wasadi, though "totally ignorant of the English language," got the message and began to tell others of the spiritual comfort he had experienced. "He feels great concern for his people," Roberts said, "and thinks if they only knew the gospel of the Saviour, all would believe. He asked whether the ungodly white people ever heard the gospel? When answered that they did, he was astonished that they could continue in sin and unbelief."[22] Though he was not officially appointed a preacher by the board, Wasadi nevertheless was encouraged by the missionaries to take every occasion he could to spread the new religion. In 1828 another fullblood, Kaneeda, was baptized. He too was inspired to preach the new religion and Jones encouraged him. He proved so effective as an exhorter that Jones persuaded the board to make him a licensed Baptist preacher and to pay him

22. *Baptist Missionary Magazine* 4: 264.

ten dollars a month so that he could devote himself to this work. Later Kaneeda was ordained and christened John Wickliffe. In 1830 a bilingual fullblood, Dsulawee (or Dsulawi), was baptized and changed his name to Andrew Fuller. He served for a time as Jones's interpreter and then, as an assistant missionary, began to preach on his own with a salary of ten dollars a month.[23] In the early 1830s five other interpreters and exhorters were appointed by Jones: Alexander McGrey, Oganaya (sometimes caller Peter), Dsusewala, David Foreman, and Jesse Bushyhead. All proved highly successful.

Of them all, Jesse Bushyhead was clearly the most outstanding. A mixed blood who rose to wealth and influence, he could read and write both Cherokee and English fluently (one of the few men in the nation with that ability). He had been converted after attending a white school in Tennessee in 1829 and began preaching among the people in his hometown, Amohee, on the western edge of the Great Smokies, before he had met any of the missionaries from the Baptist board. Amohee was sixty miles west of Valley Towns, too far for Bushyhead's converts to travel to join that mission church, so Bushyhead's followers formed their own church, an old Baptist tradition. His members, some of whom were white, chose him as their pastor in 1831, and he was ordained with the assistance of a Baptist minister from Tennessee in 1832. This was the first native Christian church formed in the Cherokee Nation. Its membership consisted of nineteen Cherokees, eleven whites, and one black slave.[24] When Evan Jones finally met Bushyhead in 1832, he was greatly impressed and requested the board to accept him as an ordained missionary with a regular salary as pastor and traveling evangelist. The board agreed. After 1833 Bushyhead managed to combine his missionary career with an outstanding political career in the nation, serving as a justice of the nation's Supreme Court (later its chief justice) and a member of several important delegations to Washington. When he could spare time, he assisted Jones in mastering Cherokee and then in translating the Bible into Cherokee, a task not completed until twenty years later.

Had the third removal crisis not started in 1829, just as the Baptists were launching their strong evangelistic effort with the help of these native preachers, there would undoubtedly have been a number of Baptist churches similar to Bushyhead's founded around the Cherokee nation under native Baptist preachers. This final crisis disrupted all missionary efforts.

After 1827, Jones (with one or more of his various assistants) began to itinerate widely and regularly around the nation. His circuit covered most of the North Carolina region of the nation, a large part of northern Georgia, and a small area in Tennessee. At various strategic towns or crossroads he

23. Minutes of the Baptist Foreign Mission Board, Vol. 2, pp. 325, 367.
24. *Baptist Missionary Magazine* 12: 324; Solomon Peck, *History of American Missions to the Heathen* (Worcester, Mass., 1840), p. 496.

established "preaching stations" at which he held services at appointed intervals. At each preaching station a log building was erected by the Cherokees in which to hold meetings in inclement weather. During the warmer months the Baptists preached out of doors just as the Methodist circuit riders did. There was continual rivalry between the two denominations in this region after 1831, when the Methodists first established a preaching circuit in North Carolina (claiming that the region was destitute of true religion).

In addition to circuit riding, Jones borrowed other methods from the Methodists. He and his assistants conducted "four-day," or "protracted," meetings, which were essentially camp meetings; they preached in the same direct, forceful manner, eliciting enthusiastic responses and shouts from the congregations. At the end of each sermon, the Baptists issued an "altar call," inviting "anxious inquirers" or "seekers" to come forward and sit on "the anxious bench" to be prayed for. The Baptists were not, however, so ready to encourage emotional behavior nor so quick to baptize "inquirers" and admit them to church membership. The numbers of their members lagged behind the total for the Methodists from 1825 to 1835. Nevertheless, after 1830 the Baptist denomination experienced a remarkable growth, and after 1835, when the Methodists decided to leave the old nation, the Baptists rapidly caught up with them in converts.

The Baptists had one important ritual which they did not take from the Methodists but which proved of inestimable value in winning the Cherokees to their denomination: the rite of baptism by total immersion in a stream or river as a seal of conversion. Baptists spoke of immersion as "burial from sin" and a symbolic resurrection or redemption "in the Saviour's liquid grave." From that watery grave the convert rose again cleansed of sin and reborn (regenerated or renewed) in spirit to start a completely different life. This baptismal ceremony resembled very closely the traditional Cherokee ceremony of purification called Going to Water. The Cherokees had always believed that rivers, like fire, wind, sun, moon, and smoke, were of spiritual significance. They were a river people, and Going to Water was a regular source of spiritual renewal to them. Thus the Baptist movement struck another responsive chord in the traditionalist Cherokee. Whenever a number of converts were deemed ready for baptism, the Baptist missionary dressed them in clean clothes (preferably white robes) and marched them to the water's edge. A crowd of singing and praying Christians followed. Then, like the Cherokee conjuror, the preacher entered the water and led them all in prayer to the Great Spirit and his son, Jesus Christ, the Savior of all humankind. Next, one by one, the converts entered the stream to be immersed, as the faithful stood on the shore shouting praises to God. The ritual was very satisfying to those making the transition from the old religion to the new, and it was employed by no other denomination.

Although Baptist membership began to surge upward after 1830, in the 1820s it appeared that no other denomination could possibly equal the astonishing success of the Methodist Episcopal Church. The Methodists were the last of the four major denominations to send missionaries to the Cherokees (if we exclude a lone evangelist for the Disciples after 1832). Although some Methodist ministers had preached there occasionally after 1815, the first official assignment of a missionary (a teacher) among the Cherokees did not occur until November 1822. The first circuit riders were not appointed until November 1823. William Shorey Coody, a whiteman married to the sister of John Ross and living near him at Ross's Landing (Tennessee), had asked the itinerants who served circuits in the white settlements north of the nation to come into the nation to preach at his house in 1821. Coody became a convert and by 1822 was the "class leader" of a group of Methodist "seekers" who met regularly at his home for prayer and exhortation. Jeremiah Evarts of the American Board, who visited the Cherokee mission at Brainerd in April 1822, took note of the meetings at Coody's, not far from Brainerd, and reported that "if the Cherokee converts are not attended to, they will probably become Methodists. The preachers of that denomination find no insuperable difficulty in coming over from Tennessee forty miles to preach here" and "in consequence of the preaching of the Methodists" there was "quite an attention to religion" in the neighborhood.[25] Apparently he wanted American Board missionaries to recruit among those seekers at Coody's whom the Methodists had awakened to Christian truth. By 1823 the Tennessee Annual Conference of the Methodist Episcopal Church reported that there were 80 converts meeting at Coody's home.[26]

Meanwhile, Richard Riley, the son of a whiteman and a Cherokee, had taken similar initiative in northeastern Alabama at his home in Guntersville. Riley's father, Samuel, was an official interpreter at the Cherokee Agency in the 1790s and early part of the nineteenth centry. Samuel Riley had raised his children by white standards and most of them were baptized. Richard Riley became a trader, a manufacturer of saltpeter, and the owner of a sizable plantation worked by black slaves. In 1819, however, the land on which he and his father had lived, just north of the Tennessee River, was ceded to the United States and he moved south of the river with his family and resettled within the nation at Guntersville. Having been friendly with the Methodist circuit riders north of the Tennessee, he invited one of them, Richard C. Neely, to preach at his home in Guntersville in 1822. Riley agreed to pay ferry fare for any trips which Neely or his colleague, Robert Boyd, would make to his home. They added Riley's house to their circuit on their own initiative. During the course of 1822, Neely made 33 converts at "Riley's station" and placed them in a Methodist "class" under Riley's leadership. A number of white and mixed-blood families living near Riley then asked

25. Jeremiah Evarts, "Memorandum," April-May 1822, ABCFM.

26. Bangs, *Methodist Missions*, pp. 141–42; Anson West, *History of Methodism in Alabama*, pp. 383–88; Wade C. Barclay, *History of Methodist Missions, 1769–1844*, vol. 2, pp. 126–28.

Neely whether he could persuade the Tennessee Missionary Society (an auxiliary of the Tennessee conference and of the National Missionary Society, organized in 1819) to take advantage of the Education Fund and establish a school at Guntersville.[27]

At Neely's request, the Tennessee Annual Conference agreed in November 1822 to send Andrew Jackson Crawford to start a school. Crawford met with the local chiefs in December and with their consent opened his school at Riley's plantation on December 30. But like most Methodist missionaries, Crawford preferred preaching to teaching. "Our Missionary has been more successful in his attempts to preach the gospel than in teaching the children," the chairman of the Tennessee Missionary Committee reported a year later. "At first he met with some opposition in preaching, but through the influence of Mr. Riley, this was removed."[28] Whether the opposition came from Cherokee traditionalists or from chiefs who wished Crawford would stick to teaching, the records do not say. The opposition may have followed an enthusiastic camp meeting organized near the school in July 1823 in which 31 Cherokees were converted or "seriously impressed." By November 1823 Crawford reported 108 converts at his station. This success persuaded the Tennessee Conference to initiate two regular circuits within the Cherokee Nation in November 1823. Richard Neely was assigned that winter to start a circuit in the vicinity of Guntersville, and Nicholas D. Scales was to start a circuit in the vicinity of Coody's home near Chattanooga. Crawford remained at the school despite his limited success as a teacher. Scales started a second school at Coody's plantation. Within two years the Tennessee conference claimed almost 300 Cherokee converts—more than all the other denominations combined.[29]

The Methodists' evangelistic system greatly annoyed the missionaries of the other denominations. "Their manner of receiving members is directly calculated to lead souls to hell," said the Reverend Isaac Proctor of the American Board.[30] Methodists admitted to their "societies" or "classes" any whom they considered to be seriously seeking further instruction in or understanding of Christian faith, and then listed these totals (often including many whites and black slaves) as "converts" within the Cherokee Nation. Commenting on a report by Nicholas Scales in 1828 that the Methodists had now made 700 converts among the Cherokees, Proctor declared "no more than one out of twenty of their members was a real christian." Furthermore, "not one-fourth of them are Cherokees and of this fourth, not forty full Cherokees. There are seven of this 700 in this place [Carmel]," Proctor wrote to his board, "and but one of them is a Cherokee," and he was a whiskey dealer. "The remaining six are Negroes and whites and surely you

27. Bangs, *Methodist Missions*, pp. 137–40.
28. *Methodist Magazine* (sometimes *Methodist Review*) 7 (1824): 192.
29. Barclay, *History of Methodist Missions*, Vol. 2, p. 128.
30. Isaac Proctor to Jeremiah Evarts, July 10, 1828, ABCFM.

could hardly find in any part of Boston more filthy and degraded characters
. . . . [H]ow liable Christians abroad are to be deceived" by such statistics.
In Proctor's opinion, the advent of the Methodists into the nation was "a
calamity to this people." While this and other similar comments from the
missionaries of other denominations indicates a certain envy of the
Methodists' success, it also indicates how different the Methodists' approach
was.

Most Methodist circuit riders considered baptism merely an indication
of a sincere desire to inquire further into Christianity and not a sign of
conversion. Hence many of those listed as "members" of classes or societies
(and sometimes described in official reports as "converts") were in fact
"seekers" or "inquirers" or persons "seriously impressed" by the Holy Spirit
with a sense of their sinfulness and their need for salvation. They were
baptized, registered as members of a Methodist class, and then they met
weekly with more advanced Cherokee Christians (like Riley or Coody), who
were called "class leaders" but who were not ordained or even licensed to
preach. Class leaders were laymen whom the circuit rider believed to be truly
converted and capable of helping others to increase their faith, piety, and
understanding of doctrine until they reached a state of full conversion and
were able "to evince the sincerity of their profession [of faith] by an upright
walk and conversation." This process of learning to be a good Christian
might be long and arduous or it might be rapid and easy, depending upon the
individual and the work of the Holy Spirit in his or her heart. Methodists
believed that people "grew in grace" and hence placed less emphasis upon the
initial experience of "divine transformation" of the soul.

In other denominations the path to baptism and church membership
was very different. Baptism (except of children) for the Moravians, American Board (Congregationalists and Presbyterians), and Baptists was the "seal
of grace," the ritual which confirmed a completed work of God's grace in the
heart of the convert. Persons merely "awakened" or "impressed" or "inquiring" for more light after a revival meeting were not yet ready for baptism. A
long period of training and spiritual counseling must precede that ritual, and
another long period of doctrinal instruction might follow before the individual was admitted to church membership and the ritual of communion.
Evangelical Christians generally held that churches could only properly
consist of truly "gracious" or converted (regenerated) persons. The
Methodists, by establishing "classes" or "societies" as preliminary organizations to churches, blurred the line between probation and church membership. Periodically the ordained Methodist circuit rider came to every class on
his circuit and spoke with the class leaders and with those who felt they were
ready for communion and full membership. But technically the Methodists
had no "churches" with settled ministers until there were sufficient communicants available to support such an institution financially. At that point
the conference appointed a pastor for them and they were taken off the

circuit. No class or society ever reached the church stage in the Cherokee Nation up to the time of their removal, hence there were no Methodist churches with settled pastors comparable to those at the mission stations of the other denominations.

Methodists, being Arminians, did not believe in predestination, the limited atonement, or the perseverance of the saints as the Calvinists did. Salvation was open to all, and by acting on their own free will sinners had the power to repent and believe; with the help of the Holy Spirit, this action was confirmed and the soul was regenerated through the grace of God. To Arminians conversion was thus a cooperative effort. The preacher conveyed God's Word, which, through the power of the Holy Spirit, acted upon the heart; the sinner, awakened to his sinfulness by "the Word" and "the Spirit," then repented and expressed his or her willingness to believe; then God, by his gracious mercy, pardoned and regenerated the soul, cleansed it of sin and rebellion against the divine will, and offered his power to strengthen the will of the sinner to live henceforth according to God's commands as revealed in Scripture (and applied to specific circumstances by the Methodist church discipline). But man's will was weak and Satan's power of temptation was strong. Some who expressed this faith or "hope" during the excitement of a revival and who accepted baptism as the first step in their salvation later might yield to some sinful temptation and lapse from their pledge to serve God. Such persons were called backsliders or scapegraces. They lost their standing in the Methodist class until they repented of the lapse and rededicated themselves to following God rather than Satan.

This ambivalent or ambiguous attitude toward salvation annoyed the members of other denominations because it seemed to leave people in confusion. That was Proctor's point. Many Cherokees might think they were truly saved if they were enrolled in a Methodist class when in fact they had not fully grasped what faith was. Many might accept the rite of baptism as a proof or seal of their conversion (as it was among Calvinists) when in fact they were still far from it. Methodism thus seemed to mislead Cherokees rather than to enlighten them to the true meaning of Christianity and church membership (by Calvinist standards). The Reverend William Chamberlain (or Chamberlin) of the American Board summed it up in 1824:

> Our Methodist brethren have established meetings among us. Some [Cherokees] have joined them of whom I have a very favourable opinion, and others who give no evidence of a change of heart . . . . Many of these people have no idea of any other religion than joining a society and as soon as they become a little serious [about religion], they will go join the Methodist[s] and they feel safe [from damnation] . . . . They think they have done all that is necessary. If you say anything to them about a new heart, they will appear surprised and invariably answer, 'Why, I have joined the Methodist[s].' One woman very seriously asked me the other day if they always had the jerks and

fainted away when their hearts were renewed. She said the [Methodist] people
told her that was the way they were born again.[31]

But those aspects of Methodism which seemed its great failing to those in
other denominations were the very aspects which constituted its great appeal
to many Cherokees. Christianity was a new and complex religion. The
feelings of the Cherokees toward becoming a Christian were ambivalent and
even when they took a first, hesitant step toward it, they remained uneasy in
their hearts and minds as to whether they could truly accept it. Methodism
provided them with a convenient solution to this dilemma. It tolerated a
period of spiritual indecision, ambivalence (or liminality) when the seeker
was between the old ways and the new. The Methodist system made it far
easier for a Cherokee because it allowed him to move more slowly through
this transition, at his own pace, and offered him help along the way. Though
it demanded repentance for sin, Methodism did not demand total abasement;
it did not destroy so utterly the self-worth of those who occasionally "fell
from grace." Methodists emphasized God's love and not the fear or wrath of
God. The Methodists always gave the seeker the benefit of the doubt.
Backsliding was of course "disgraceful," but it was not irremediable, unfor-
givable. To the Calvinist a backslider demonstrated that he had been a
hypocrite, claiming to be among the predestined elect when he was not. To
the Methodist, a backslider simply demonstrated that human nature was
weak and temptation was strong. Consequently, along the white frontier and
among the Indian nations, Methodist Arminianism was far more com-
prehensible and comforting than Calvinism in any of its forms, and over the
next generation most Calvinist theologians and ministers gradually modified
(in the direction of Arminianism) the harsher aspects of their creed in order
to attract and hold followers.

The Methodist circuit riders wished to meet the Cherokees halfway.
They considered the rigid doctrines and exalted membership standards of the
other denominations cruel and unreasonable. They also felt that the highly
charged emotional atmosphere of a camp meeting was necessary to arouse
"the heathen Indian," to shock him out of his complacent, unthinking
commitment to the old religion and to give him the courage to consider the
new. The Methodists' manner of preaching was nondoctrinal. Their missionaries recognized that the Cherokees knew little of the theology of Christianity. But they believed the Indians, like all men and women, possessed an
inner moral sense or conscience which could feel guilt, doubt, spiritual
anxiety. Indians also possessed the ability to make the decision to accept
Christ on faith. The circuit riders preached so as to awaken guilt, inspire
repentance, and hold out hope: "Our plan of preaching to them was to
convince them of their guilt, misery, and helplessness by reason and experience; not appealing to the Scriptures as the law by which they were

31. William Chamberlain to Jeremiah Evarts, July 8, 1824, ABCFM.

condemned but to their own knowledge of right and wrong. The gospel proffering them an immediate change of heart, was seized by them as Heaven's best blessing to ruined man."[32] When Cherokees came forward to the Methodist anxious bench after a camp meeting sermon, they did not say they felt they were now Christians; usually they "requested the preachers to instruct them." They admitted they had done bad things and that they did not know how to prevent themselves from being or doing bad. They asked "how they could obtain favour of the Great Spirit and be happy like their [Christian] brethren who were praising God," shouting and singing in ecstatic enthusiasm and joy.[33]

The Methodists had another advantage over the more staid denominations. Their camp meetings resembled in tone and excitement the all-night dances of the Cherokee religious tradition. Sometimes their camp meetings lasted all night. At a camp meeting the Cherokees recognized the same feelings of exhilaration or uplifting and sensed the same strong emotional force at work that they felt when their own people gathered to shout, dance, and sing in unison to the Great Spirit hour after hour. The Methodists' enthusiastic revival style out under the trees was a familiar mode of worship to the Cherokees. The fainting fits, the falling exercise, "the jerks," and other emotional outbursts which took place at Methodist meetings and which so annoyed the ministers of the American Board from New England did not faze the Cherokees. They expected and wanted a direct relationship between their spiritual and their physical feelings. Religious worship for them was a participatory action, not a passive absorption of theological doctrine.

Usually each circuit rider held four camp meetings (and "love feasts") each year on his circuit. Like Cherokee festivals, they provided occasions when friends and relatives gathered from distant parts to break the routine of daily life and to enjoy the pleasure of a common activity which would give a spiritual lift to their lives and inspire them with new energy and hope. The Methodists were singularly successful in recruiting as circuit riders dedicated young whitemen from the frontier areas who had experienced conversion at a camp meeting and enjoyed spreading the word and sharing their experience. Several of these young missionaries became so closely identified with the Cherokees that they married among them and took their side against white injustices. For some Cherokees this proved that Christianity contained the power to break through national, racial, and cultural barriers. It seemed odd that other missionaries were not interested in mingling with them if they were truly "brethren," and even more strange when a missionary said he loved them but he could not become involved in their social and political problems.

Starting with two circuits in November 1823, the Tennessee Annual

---

32. *Christian Advocate*, March 13, 1829.
33. *Methodist Magazine* 7 (1824): 192–93.

Conference had established seven circuits within the Cherokee Nation by 1829. These seven circuits, crisscrossing throughout the nation, competed with the other denominations everywhere. So much friction had developed by this time among the missionaries of the four denominations that any pretence of Christian unity or fellowship was demolished. The Cherokees could now see that they had various modes of conversion to choose from within the Christian fold. The older missionary societies, threatened by the serious inroads into their territories, accused the Methodists of breaking an unwritten rule which had divided the nation into spheres of interest. Each denomination was supposed to avoid impinging upon the other's territory or engaging in unseemly competition for converts. This rule had been generally observed by the Moravians, the American Board, and the Baptists, each of which had centered its activities in different parts of the nation. The Methodists ignored this. In their view religious competition was healthy. Besides, the other denominations were making so little headway against heathenism that most of the nation was still virtually destitute of Christianity so far as the Methodists were concerned.

Methodists were also accused of conducting unruly meetings, of "sheep stealing" (that is, luring away members or potential members from other mission stations), of conducting slipshod schools, and of preaching erroneous doctrines. Cherokees who had attended the staid religious services of the Moravians and American Board were at first astonished at the extravagant emotionalism encouraged at the Methodist camp meetings. One Moravian convert, William Hicks, came to the Moravian mission at Oochgelogy in 1829 to speak with Henry Clauder "respecting the curious custom prevalent in Methodist meetings of jumping and tumbling about like persons bereft of sense."[34] Clauder of course deprecated such behavior as an appeal to the animal emotions rather than to the spiritual affections. The Cherokee was told that this was not true Christianity.

Clauder also found that some of the students at his school at Oochgelogy had left to attend a new Methodist school started only two miles away in 1828. He reconciled his loss by reporting to his board that these were his worst students: "Two of our scholars have been persuaded into the Methodist school kept about two miles from here; they are both very stupid creatures and the Methodists are welcome to them, however, as their school is to continue but six months in this neighborhood, it is to be expected that the children will be sent hither again" when it closes.[35] After conversing with the circuit riders who had invaded his neighborhood, Clauder conceived an intense dislike for them. They were immature young men, crude, bold, uneducated, and militant. Speaking of one of their "native exhorters" in his diary, Clauder wrote, "He is like most Methodists, a violent partisan."[36]

34. Clauder, Diary, March 7, 1829, MAB.
35. Clauder, Diary, January, 7, 1829, MAB.
36. Clauder, Diary, March 1, 1829, MAB.

Some of what Clauder called unchristian partisanship was simply Methodist zeal, but part was self-righteous conviction that the Methodist form of education and evangelism was superior to those of all other denominations. Because they held that Christianization must precede civilization, the Methodists took comparatively little interest in schooling. When a committee of the Missionary Society of the Tennessee Annual Conference was asked to report to the conference in 1824 regarding the best means of evangelizing among the Cherokees, its chairman, Thomas Douglas, wrote: "Your committee are of opinion that a great parade about Missionary establishments and the expenditure of thousands of dollars to give the heathen science and occupation without religion, is of but little advantage." In other words, the approaches of the Moravians, Presbyterians, Baptists, and American Board were entirely misguided. There was no need for boarding schools and model farms. The committee recommended primary emphasis on itinerant preaching, the same plan the Methodists used on the white frontier. The opposite of "savage" was not "civilized" in the Methodist lexicon, it was "Christian." "For after all their acquirements, they are still savages unless their hearts be changed by the grace of God." Education was secondary; it was "the power of the gospel" which "makes [a] man a new creature and fits him for his place in society."[37] Or, as the Reverend Nathan Bangs wrote in his history of Methodist Indian missions in 1832: "Instead of waiting for the slow process of learning the language of the natives in order to instruct them in the truths of Christianity, God takes a short method by awakening and converting the souls of the natives and then putting His Spirit upon them, qualifies them to instruct their brethren in their own language."[38] Methodists considered every conversion of a non-English-speaking Cherokee to be a confirmation of this truth. "This man," said a missionary describing the conversion of Turtle Fields in 1826 (who became one of the most successful Methodist exhorters), "with hundreds of others, stands as demonstrative evidence that the gospel is capable of exerting its renovation and sanctifying energy over the hearts and lives of men before human science and the arts of civilized life have prepared its way."[39]

Nevertheless, the Methodists were forced to make some concessions to the persistent demands of the Cherokees that they provide some education. Their response was the establishment of what they called itinerating schools. Each itinerant Methodist missionary chose a spot on his circuit where there was a Methodist class or group of interested families and for six months (in addition to his preaching duties) conducted classes for several hours a day in the fundamentals of reading, writing, and arithmetic. Usually the Cherokees themselves constructed a rough log cabin for the school, and the circuit rider relied heavily upon bilingual children to assist him in the teaching. When

37. *Methodist Magazine* 7 (1824): 193–94.
38. Bangs, *Methodist Missions*, p. 147.
39. *Methodist Magazine* 11 (1828): 79.

the six months were up, the school was abandoned and another constructed somewhere else along the circuit. To the American Board, the Moravians, and the Baptists this system was frivolous and useless. Nevertheless, it appealed to the Cherokees, who did not want their children to be away from home for long periods, who recognized that their children did not like the rigid schedules and work chores imposed in the elaborate boarding schools, and who were concerned only with their children's obtaining the minimal knowledge of a grammar school. The Cherokees had come to realize that other denominations considered schools a means for the total transformation of their children into models of the whiteman, and in choosing the Methodists they were rejecting that total transformation. While the impermanence of these schools prevented the Methodists from obtaining subsidies from the federal Education Fund, they also avoided the suspicion of the Cherokees that they were out to get some of their land. Furthermore, the Methodist schools went to where the Cherokees were, rather than demanding that the Cherokees come to them. In all likelihood, they also served a very different clientele, although the failure to keep any records of these schools prevents detailed analysis. Where the Moravian and American Board schools catered primarily to the well-to-do, the Methodists, like the Baptists, reached the ordinary and the poor.

Nicholas Scales displayed typical Methodist zeal when he wrote a letter to the *Cherokee Phoenix*, the national newspaper, in 1828, describing the four schools which his denomination had started at Creek Path, Chattooga, Oochgelogy, and Pinelog: "None of these stations are permanently fixed," he said: they were "itenerating [*sic*]." "Itenerating schools of this character are, in my opinion, the best possible means to improve and enlighten and effectually to civilize and christianize the rising generation." He went on to deprecate the "antiquated permanent establishments with their concomitant appendages" (the model farms, dormitories, missionary residences), although he added ingenuously, "It is not my design in this remark to reflect upon the well meant exertions of other denominations."[40] The Cherokee editor of the *Phoenix*, Elias Boudinot, a product of the Moravian school and translator for the American Board, felt called upon to defend their system against Scales's aspersions:

> We are inclined to think that the writer is here incorrect, or at least, this assertion is not supported by facts or experience. It is not from Schools of this nature that an ignorant child will derive permanent benefit. In 'itinerating Schools' children may be taught to speak the English language (in neighborhoods where the Cherokee only is spoken even this will hardly be acquired). . . . [y]et all this will but poorly qualify them as instructors to others; for the complete civilization of this people must depend in great measure upon the instrumentality of their own Citizens.[41]

40. *Cherokee Phoenix*, November 12, 1828.
41. *Cherokee Phoenix*, November 12, 1828. Scales became so annoyed at Boudinot's criticism that he did his best to have him removed from his post as editor.

The issue was indeed related to "permanent benefit" and "complete civiliza-tion," terms and goals upon which the Cherokees as well as the missionaries disagreed. Thinking of his own higher education at Springplace and Corn-wall Academy, Boudinot reflected the elitism he had imbibed from the American Board. He expected the Cherokees to rise over the long haul through the efforts of their "talented tenth." The Methodists were simply interested in giving the bare rudiments of English and arithmetic to everyone for their immediate use.

The most persistent complaint by the other denominations against the Methodist missionaries was that they pushed into areas where other denomi-nations had already been at work for years and stole the ripening fruits of their labor by offering them a looser form of Christian commitment. Charles Hicks, devoted to the Moravians but by no means hostile to the spread of Christianity by other denominations, protested in 1826 when he found that the Methodists were establishing circuits, schools, and preaching stations in areas where other denominations were at work. He wrote to the Reverend Francis A. Owens, the superintendent of the Methodist mis-sionaries that year, and "stated to him my objections in [his] establishing a school near brother Gambold's" at Oochgelogy, "and desired him at the same time to inform Mr. Neeley [the Methodist teacher at Oochgelogy] that it was my wish that he preach at Neu-ope-ta or elsewhere." However, the Methodists had ignored his recommendations. Thus, Hicks went on, it "plainly appears that these circuit riders goes emmediately in[to] the neigh-bourhood where the most light has beeng [*sic*] given to the people by the preaching of the Gospel where others are [already] labouring." In Hicks's view, this "looks too much like an opposition" rather than a supplement to the efforts of other Christians. He protested that while crowding in on other denominations, "they leave those dark places where they ought to go to enlighten the dark minds of the ignorant Cherokees to bring them to the light of the Gospel."[42]

Clauder claimed that the Methodists near his mission "have en-deavoured to keep persons from attending our church on the sabbath and that successfully; they have persecuted a young female because she united herself with our little brood and endeavoured to draw her away from here before she was baptized." Clauder found such "sheep stealing" abominable. "Notwith-standing this," he noted, "they pretend to be friendly when we meet. . . . [S]uch infernal hypocrisy I abhor. . . . I cannot with confidence visit them."[43]

Isaac Proctor of the American Board had a similar experience. One of the members of his mission church, he wrote in 1828, "has gone off to the Methodists and is trying to do us much harm by telling [them] that we want the land and persuading the Cherokees who are members of our church to

42. Charles Hicks to Johann Schmidt, January 9, 1826, MAS.
43. Clauder, Diary, October 15, 1830, MAB.

join the Methodist[s], etc." Any who were offended by the American Board or by board missionaries who criticized whiskey selling and other wicked actions deserted as soon as the Methodists became available, Proctor found.[44]

Evan Jones, the Baptist, was astonished and angry when the Methodists entered his area of the nation in North Carolina in 1830 and then announced in their missionary journal that the Valley Towns were a "dark and uncultivated waste" so far as the Gospel was concerned. Their circuit riding and preaching in North Carolina, they said, was "the first as such that ever sounded the thrilling note of salvation along these long neglected valleys."[45] Jones had recently preached in one of the Valley Towns called Desyhohee and had aroused considerable interest in the Gospel. He returned there in May 1830 to see whether his inquirers were ready for baptism. He discovered that "the Methodists were here a few days ago and took seventeen of the inquirers into their Society. Some of them made objections to joining them on the ground that they were under the instructions of this Mission. The [Methodist] preachers removed their scruples and received them into the [Methodist] church."[46] The Methodists' method of removing the scruples of those Cherokees at Desyhohee who assumed that they would become Baptists was simply to tell them that the members of all Protestant denominations were brethren who worshipped the same God. A few of the inquirers at Desyhohee pointed out that the Baptists were different because they baptized by total immersion while the Methodists only poured or sprinkled water upon them. The Methodist circuit rider, Greenberry Garrett, then "agreed to immerse them rather than let them join the Baptist church," Jones reported.[47] Jones was proud of one Cherokee who held out against this perversion of truth and said he thought the Cherokee inquirers "have been deceived about the nature of church membership; the Methodists having first represented it as a matter of perfect indifference what church they should join" in order to acquire them and then, having baptized them into a Methodist society, Garrett "afterwards endeavored to extort a promise from them that they should not change" denominations.

Jones had already met and argued with Greenberry Garrett about the proper mode of baptism before this happened. "Mr. Garret agrees that in the primitive churches Baptism was administered by immersion, but he does not like the notion of the Baptists' refusing to admit the validity of Sprinkling or pouring."[48] To Jones, of course, there could be only one true form of baptism.

Much as the other denominations deplored the aggressive, partisan, perverse, or uncooperative proselyting techniques of the Methodists, they

44. Isaac Proctor to Jeremiah Evarts, February 29, 1828, ABCFM.
45. *Christian Advocate*, September 10, 1830.
46. Evan Jones, Journal, May 16, 1830, BFMB.
47. Evan Jones, Journal, July 29, 1830, BFMB.
48. Evan Jones, Journal, April 15, 1830, BFMB.

could not deny their obvious success. In 1827 they claimed 400 converts; in 1828 they listed 700; by the end of the decade the figure reached 1,028 persons in Methodist classes or societies within the Cherokee Nation.[49] The other three denominations combined had fewer than 300 converts in 1830, although among them they had had seven or eight times as many years of missionary work among the Cherokees. Because of their firm belief that the Holy Spirit could transform Cherokee hearts through preaching by an interpreter, and because they found sufficient Cherokee converts willing to preach in their own language, the Methodist circuit riders made little effort to learn Cherokee themselves. Nor were they particularly interested in translating the Bible or religious tracts into Cherokee. To this extent their anti-intellectualism worked against them. In part this was necessitated by their lack of money. The Tennessee Annual Conference operated on a shoestring compared to the budgets of the other denominations, and they sacrificed everything else to itinerant preaching. Missionaries with families received a salary of $350 a year; missionaries without families, $150; interpreters and exhorters, $10 per month.

While the Methodists in theory had a hierarchical polity in which bishops made the decisions which the circuit riders had to obey, the circuit riders themselves were plain and simple people. Their idealism and their eagerness to help the Cherokees were evident in their style. Most of them were young, poor, barely literate themselves, but eminently pious and enthusiastic about their mission. They were paid little and had to find room and board by living among the Cherokees as they rode their circuits. One unforeseen advantage which came out of this familiar intercourse between the circuit riders and the Cherokees was the decision of several of them to court and marry Cherokee women. Richard Neely married a Cherokee named McNair in 1825; James J. Trott married Sally Adair in 1828; and Nicholas D. Scales married Mary Coody, the niece of John Ross, in 1827. All these marriages were solemnized in Christian form. The women were daughters of mixed bloods of considerable influence in the nation. The young missionaries took this matrimonial connection seriously, and, as was traditional, the Cherokee Nation gave full and equal rights of citizenship to them.[50] The fact that the Methodist preachers were willing to throw in their

49. John B. McFerrin lists 1,028 "Indian members" in 1831 and says this marked a gain of 839 since the fall of 1824, when there were 189 Indian members: *History of Methodism in Tennessee*, vol. 3, pp. 374–75. Other Methodist historians cite the figure 1,028 for the year 1830; see Marion E. Lazenby, *History of Methodism in Alabama and West Florida*, p. 177.

50. Neely died in 1827. Scales remained in the nation with his family after leaving the mission in 1832 and lived at Lookout Mountain, where he owned a few slaves and ran a small farm. Trott also continued to live in the nation at Etowah after leaving the mission in 1831; after his first wife died he married her sister and became an evangelist for the Disciples of Christ. He owned no slaves. See the "List of Whitemen who have Indian families" compiled by the Cherokee agent Hugh Montgomery, September 13, 1830, Letters Compiled and Transcribed under the direction of Mrs. J. E. Hays, part 1, p. 231, typescript, Georgia State Archives.

lot personally with the Cherokees, to marry and raise families among them, to be adopted members of their nation contributed to the feeling that this denomination was truly egalitarian and earnestly committed to the nation's welfare. No missionary of any other denomination married a Cherokee woman; when they wished to marry they went back East to find a wife or married another member of the mission family.[51]

To a greater extent than the other missionaries (with the possible exception of the Baptists) the Methodists needed and welcomed Cherokee assistants and gave them important roles to play. Within four years of starting their first circuit, there were ten Cherokees on the conference payroll actively engaged as interpreters and preachers. From the beginning, the Methodists had made immediate use of any Cherokee convert willing to work with them in the process of evangelization. Some, like Richard Riley and William Coody, were put at the head of Methodist classes or societies, a position similar to that of an exhorter or Sunday school teacher in other denominations. Those who were bilingual, like Edward Gunter and John Brown, became interpreters. But the most important converts were those who became licensed itinerant preachers. The first of these was Turtle Fields in 1826. Fields had fought with the Cherokee volunteers in the Creek War; he spoke no English, but after his conversion he felt a call to preach to his people. The Tennessee Annual Conference appointed him a traveling exhorter "on trial" in 1826. He worked first near Creek Path, but in 1828—29 he itinerated in the Georgia area of the nation and after 1830 in North Carolina. The superintendent of the Cherokee mission in 1827 reported, "Our worthy brother Fields has been exceedingly useful in his itinerant labours; he has formed a circuit and returned 140 members most of whom have professed religion" and not simply "inquired" for more knowledge. "He was received into the travelling connection at the last Tennessee annual conference."[52]

John Fletcher Boot, converted in 1828, began itinerating that same year and he was ordained a deacon in 1832. Other "traveling exhorters" licensed by the Methodists included Young Wolf, Joseph Blackbird (sometimes called J. B. Bird), John (Jack) Spears, and Arch Campbell. Several Cherokees were paid by the conference as interpreters and accompanied different circuit riders on their rounds: Edward (Ned) Graves in 1829; William McIntosh in 1829; John Spears in 1830. All of these Cherokee Methodists played a major role in the rapid growth of their denomination. It does not appear, however, that the conference ever formally licensed them to

51. Milo Hoyt, the son of Ard Hoyt of Brainerd did marry a Cherokee, but he was not an official member of the mission. Delight Sargent, a female teacher of the American Board, married a Cherokee. But I have found no record of a male missionary marrying a Cherokee except among the Methodists. Robert S. Walker, *Torchlights to the Cherokees*, p. 134.

52. Turtle Fields continued to spread the Methodist faith even after he left the old nation in 1837 to move to the western part of the nation.

perform marriages or communion services, although they probably all performed baptisms.

A Methodist circuit covered from 200 to 400 miles and included 30 to 40 "preaching stations" along the route. John B. McFerrin said he covered his complete circuit in the nation once every four weeks, or about twelve times a year. At many of the preaching stations the Cherokees built crude log houses in which they held their classes and conducted their services or schools. Some of the preaching stations were dignified with the name of *meetinghouse* if a class or society met there regularly. While there were never enough interpreters and exhorters to meet all the demands, their number increased from one in 1824 to eight in 1830. The number of white circuit riders rose in the same period from two to eleven. From 1822 to 1829 the Methodists considered the Cherokee Nation a part of the Huntsville (Alabama) District under the Tennessee Methodist Conference. In the fall of 1829, the Annual Conference constituted the Cherokee Nation a separate district with its own superintendent. The constant turnover of personnel (a Methodist tradition) added variety to Methodist preaching but robbed it of stability and continuity. The Tennessee Annual Conference not only altered the routes of the circuit riders every year but changed the circuit riders from place to place. Seldom did an itinerant remain more than three years among the Cherokees. The Methodists were good at generating participatory activity and a sense of excitement among the Cherokees, but their system lacked the stability necessary for permanence. On the white frontier the denomination relied upon the local settlers to build a church and support a regular pastor after a few years, but the Cherokee societies lacked the surplus wealth to do this, especially among the poorer Cherokees to whom the Methodists appealed most.

Methodism achieved one of its most notable triumphs in October 1829 when two of the leading Cherokees, John and Lewis Ross, came forward and signed their names as "seekers" following a revival meeting conducted near their homes by the Reverend John B. McFerrin. John Ross was at this time principal chief of the Nation and by all odds its most influential leader and spokesman. His brother was one of the wealthiest men in the nation and a close advisor to John. Because both men lived near Brainerd and had expressed strong gratitude toward the American Board for its help to the nation during the second removal crisis, the missionaries of that denomination fully expected that if these men ever joined any church it would be theirs. They were dismayed when they learned that the Rosses had joined the eccentric Methodists. Politically, however, it seemed a wise move, for the Methodists in 1829 appeared to be sweeping the nation. Moreover, John Ross had good reasons for wanting to support a denomination which believed in civilizing the Cherokees from the bottom up.[53] He needed mass support.

53. *Christian Advocate*, November 13, 1829, p. 42. The event took place on October 5, 1829.

Despite the tremendous success of the Methodist circuit riders and their native assistants in making Christianity a viable alternative to the old religion, there seems to have been a disconcerting lack of understanding of what was taking place in the Cherokee Nation among those who edited the Methodist journals and wrote their missionary reports. The gap between the missionary publicists and the missionaries in the field was great in every denomination, but it seemed to be even greater among the Methodists. For example, the publicists were obsessed with the notion that conversion to Methodism was capable of working miracles—transforming "savages" into civilized farmers overnight. They consistently portrayed the Cherokees and other Southeastern Indians as stereotypical forest hunters except for those being brought into the Methodist fold. "Seven years ago," said Nathan Bangs, speaking of a group of Cherokee converts in 1827, these Indians "were as wild as the game they chased."[54] The editor of the *Methodist Christian Advocate* reported in 1829 that "the spirit of industry is universally awakening" among the Choctaws, and "the chase is abandoned for the farm," as though prior to the coming of the Methodists in 1824, the Choctaws were the most primitive of people—or if not primitive, certainly inveterately shiftless and lazy: "So soon as they [the Indians] obtain a change of heart, they evince the most anxious wish to be informed and, complaining that they are not at ease in mind when idle, as heretofore, they immediately turn their attention to their houses and farms, that their situation may be rendered more comfortable."[55] This illusion of instantaneous and miraculous transformation in economic as well as spiritual status ran counter to the average Indian hater's belief that the Indians were by nature unchangeable, uncivilizable, and always a threat to peace on the frontier. Why should Methodists have been more sanguine about civilizing the Indians than the average white? Methodist missionary efforts among the Cherokees came from the westerners, not, as in the other three denominations, from the East. The western Christian preacher needed to believe (perhaps more than the easterner) that his religion could work miracles among the "savages" or he would never have supported the missionary movement (as the antimission Baptists in Kentucky and Tennessee refused to support it): "No sooner do they bow a willing obedience to the command of Jesus Christ, and their hearts and lives are brought under the salutary restraints and precepts of his gospel, than their docility in submitting to be taught the arts of agriculture, of domestic economy, and all the social duties becomes manifest to all . . . . When this is effected what harm or danger can be apprehended from their proximity to the white population?"[56] Implicit in such miraculous claims was a self-serving and subconscious guilt. If the westerner wanted the In-

54. Bangs, *Methodist Missions*, p. 145.
55. *Christian Advocate*, May 15, 1829, p. 145.
56. *Christian Advocate*, December 19, 1828, p. 62.

dians' land but feared to take it because the unpredictable Indian might yet rise up and attack their settlements in the night, then it would be comforting to know that Methodism was not only making them industrious and agricultural but also docile and submissive. A good Christian was always submissive to God's will; if it was God's will that the whiteman should take over the Mississippi Valley, then it would be very helpful to persuade the Indians to accept that fact (and perhaps some Cherokee converts felt the same way). One Methodist missionary to the Choctaws, Alexander Talley, who ultimately helped the government to write the fraudulent treaty which removed them to the west, wrote in the *Christian Advocate* in 1829, "Christianity removes that distant, shy, reserved carriage" so common among the Indians, "bringing them to feel the warmth and brotherly friendship for their white brethren."[57] Furthermore, Talley noted, converted Indians learned to accept their lot with "an entire reliance upon their Father above." If Indians were Christians and all Christians were brothers, then brothers would not turn against each other. The younger brother would accept the will of the older. Methodists did not make these connections overly explicit. They did not say that religion was the opiate of the "savage" class, but behind their faith in miracles seems to have been that hope. The sweeping of Methodism through the Cherokee Nation was the prelude to sweeping the Indians out of the valley. The miracle of Christianity (the missionaries believed) was that this would all take place painlessly.

Gradually some conservative Cherokees came to suspect that Christianization was double-edged. It gave hope and encouragement, but it also denigrated their heritage, confused their identity, and created deep social fissures. While missionary journals of every denomination praised the rapid expansion of Christianity among the Cherokees from 1819 to 1829, they failed to mention the growing factionalism among the Cherokees and the emergence after 1824 of serious antimission sentiment among them. The missionaries themselves could hardly believe that those whom they had sacrificed so much to help could turn against them. But sooner or later an aggressive Christian evangelism was bound to produce a reaction among the adherents of the traditional Cherokee religion. The reaction eventually climaxed in 1827 as White Path's Rebellion, but this movement began as early as 1824.

57. *Christian Advocate*, May 15, 1829, p. 145.

CHAPTER EIGHT

The Rise of Cherokee Nationalism and Antimission Sentiment, 1824–1827

Can any white man catch thunder? Can any white man catch lightning? Can any white man catch the wind?

Cherokee questions to an itinerant missionary, 1826

Although antimission sentiment was always present among the Cherokees in some degree, the development of a concerted movement against missionaries and acculturation after 1824 was different. It stemmed from sources larger than local antagonism toward aggressive itinerant evangelism within the nation. In part, it was a result of the general success of the missionary effort. Prior to 1824 the missionaries were as much a source of help and hope as of fear and dislike. But as the new religion and its educational establishments grew in popularity, and as more and more of the mixed bloods (who played such an important role in tribal economic and political affairs) accepted the attitudes and behavior (if not always the doctrine) of the missionaries, the Cherokees who held to the traditional ways and cosmology became increasingly estranged from their leaders. In turn, some of the acculturated Cherokee leaders, embarrassed by the cultural resistance of the fullbloods, began to make patronizing remarks about "the backward," "the ignorant," and "the superstitious" members of the tribe who were "holding back" the nation's progress.[1] Prior to the mid-1820s,

1. It is surprising how frequently the mixed-blood chiefs expressed their disdain for their own culture. John Ross, George Lowery, and Elijah Hicks told John Quincy Adams in 1825 that they would "willingly see the habits and customs of the aboriginal man extinguished," and the sooner, the better. ASP II, 651–52. John Ridge told Albert Gallatin in 1826 that those conjurors who still believed they could call upon spiritual power for "making rain, allaying a storm or whirlwind, playing with thunder and foretelling future events" were now "generally living monuments of fun to the young and [sources of] grave ridicule for those in maturer years." John Ridge to Albert Gallatin, February 27, 1826, Payne Papers, VIII, 110–11. In conversations with missionaries, these acculturated Cherokee leaders frankly joined them in deploring the superstitious, ignorant, and backward "lower class." For a statistical effort to identify the Cherokee elite, or ruling class, in the years 1825–35, see W. G. McLoughlin and Walter H. Conser, Jr., "The Cherokees in Transition," *Journal of American History* 64, no. 3 (December 1977): 678–703.

this internal conflict was muted by the effort to sustain Cherokee unity against the constant efforts of the United States to destabilize their community and force them to move West. But as the Cherokees' prosperity increased, and their tenure in the East seemed secure, the ambitious desires of the mixed bloods for progressive reform produced sharper differences between them and the great mass of ordinary Cherokees. These differences—evident in the growing gap between the rich and the poor[2]—were exacerbated by the rapid centralization and bureaucratization of Cherokee political authority in the 1820s.

The first step in this consolidation of power occurred during the removal crisis in 1817, when the Council voted that "The affairs of the Cherokee Nation shall be committed to the care of the Standing Committee."[3] Although the elected town chiefs retained the right to review the actions of this committee of thirteen "head chiefs," they in effect delegated most of their authority to it. The National Committee (as it was called) was elected for two-year terms by the Council and consisted principally of those well-to-do, English-speaking mixed bloods who knew how to cope with the complex machinations of the federal and state officials of the United States. In this capacity the National Committee served the nation well. However, these well-to-do leaders also dominated the internal affairs of the nation, persuading the Council to adopt laws designed primarily to meet the economic needs of the nation's large farmers, plantation owners, traders, and entrepreneurs. The National Committee controlled the nation's annuity and thus its financial affairs. All legislation was drafted in the committee and presented to the town chiefs in the Council for concurrence. Very often the laws presented were so complex and so far from the commercial experience of the average fullblood in the Council as to be unintelligible. Such laws were passed primarily on faith, on the assumption that the members of the National Committee were patriots and knew what was best for the development and security of the nation as a whole. So long as the town chiefs managed local affairs in their town councils, they were willing to leave national affairs to the "head chiefs." However, an increasing number of laws passed after 1820 began to encroach on the authority of the local chiefs. Some of these laws were also offensive because they seemed designed primarily to please the missionaries—such as the laws honoring the Sabbath and prohibiting cardplaying and polygamy. The mixed-blood elite appeared to be forcing a redefinition of the traditional way of life from the top down rather than allowing for the gradual evolution of change from the bottom up.

In 1820 the National Committee pushed through the Council a complex series of laws affecting the judicial and electoral system. This legislation drastically curtailed the traditional powers of the chiefs in the fifty-four towns and villages of the nation. The first of these laws divided the nation into eight

2. Evidence of the socioeconomic divisions among the Cherokees after 1820 can be found in McLoughlin and Conser, "The Cherokees in Transition."

3. This and other laws discussed below are available in *Cherokee Laws*, pp. 4–20.

judicial districts (comparable to counties) upon geographical lines which seemed arbitrary to the average Cherokee. Within each of the eight districts there was henceforth to be only one official council house (or courthouse) for the administration of local affairs. "District judges" appointed by the National Council were to decide all cases of law according to national precedents but using Anglo-Saxon procedures (such as jury trials) and keeping records in English. A "circuit judge" (also responsible to the Council) was to preside over these district councils. Most of the actions taken in these circuit courts had formerly been taken in town councils under the jurisdiction of locally chosen chiefs. Another law then constituted these judicial districts as electoral districts and stipulated that elections to the National Council were no longer to be from the towns (each of which had formerly sent anywhere from three to eight local chiefs to represent them) but from the districts.[4] Each district was to elect four representatives. This significantly reduced the size of the Council (from over one hundred to thirty-two) and also its representation of different interests. The National Council now became a bicameral legislature, which meant that the National Committee of thirteen was the upper house and had the power to veto the actions of the lower house and vice versa. The whiteman's system of majority rule was replacing the redman's tradition of consensus, and bureaucracy was replacing egalitarianism.

Then in 1821, the National Committee persuaded the Council to establish salaries for all government officials. This in turn required laws to lay taxes because the annuities from the federal government were no longer adequate to sustain the mounting bureaucracy. Taxes required tax collectors as well as punishments for the delinquent payment of taxes. A year later, in 1822, a National Superior Court was established at New Echota, the new national capital. It dealt with all appeals from the district courts and completed a tripartite system of government with checks and balances like that of the American states. The National Superior Court (later renamed the Supreme Court), like the district courts, employed lighthorse sheriffs and marshalls to arrest criminals and execute orders; it impaneled juries, followed English procedures, and employed a clerk to keep written records in English. By 1825, the Cherokee Nation was said to be more efficient and honest than many of the white counties surrounding it, but it had moved a long way in a short time from the easy-going, decentralized town government which the Cherokees had always known.

During the tense negotiations with Governor Joseph McMinn in 1818, at the height of the second removal crisis, the Cherokee Council had defiantly declared, "We consider ourselves a free and distinct nation and that the

---

4. I have not been able to locate this electoral law. It is not included in the compilation of 1852. However, it was clearly described by John Ridge and Elias Boudinot in 1826 and probably was passed in October 1820, when the eight districts of the nation were defined. See John Ridge to Albert Gallatin, February 27, 1826, Payne Papers, VIII, 106–07, and Elias Boudinot, *Address to the Whites*, p. 11.

government of the United States has no policy over us further than a friendly intercourse in trade."[5] Few Cherokees at that time had expected that within six years their old form of government would be so completely transformed. Confusion over the rapidity of change as well as over the goals toward which their leaders were pushing them worried the local chiefs and conservative citizens. They began to dig in their heels, to ask questions, and to express dissent. Such actions were taken slowly at first, for the traditional emphasis upon harmony, their patent need for unity, and the obvious patriotism of their leaders in negotiating with the United States placed a grave burden upon those who dissented.

The ambivalence of the fullblood majority toward their mixed-blood ruling class was heightened by their respect for their achievements. In three separate negotiations between 1823 and 1825, the Cherokee leaders had successfully refused to yield another foot of Cherokee land for sale or exchange to the government of the United States; they also refused on several occasions in the 1820s to allow the states of Tennessee and Georgia to conduct surveys in the Cherokee nation to find routes for canals and horse-drawn railroads for interstate commerce. Not only did the Cherokee negotiators firmly withstand the pressures brought to bear by a steady stream of white negotiating commissioners, but they inspired everyone by their eloquent defense of the nation's treaty rights and by exposing for all to see the blatant efforts of the federal government to bribe some of the Cherokee chiefs.[6] In the past, white negotiators had successfully bullied the Cherokees into cession after cession, often finding willing recipients for their bribes, but in the 1820s all treaty commissioners sent to the Cherokees returned to Congress empty-handed and embarrassed.

Pride in the nation's achievements was further enhanced after 1821 when a Cherokee discovered a means of writing the Cherokee language. This remarkable feat was accomplished, moreover, by a Cherokee who could not read or write English, who had no connection with the missionaries or the ruling class, and who espoused the conservative position of the traditionalists. George Guess (Sequoyah) was, it is true, born of a white father and a Cherokee mother, but his father had deserted the family, and Sequoyah grew up among the fullbloods in the Lower Town region.[7] When

5. Statement by the Cherokee Council at Oostenali, June 30, 1818, OSW, M−221, roll 79, #0060.

6. Chief William McIntosh of the Creeks was instructed by the United States treaty commissioners in October 1823 to offer thousands of dollars in bribes to Charles Hicks, John Ross, and Alexander McCoy, but they publicly exposed his efforts. Duncan Campbell to Joseph McMinn, October 27, 1823, BIA, M−208, Gary Moulton, *Cherokee Chief John Ross* (Athens: University of Georgia Press, 1978), p. 25. One of the first items printed in the *Cherokee Phoenix* in 1828 was a detailed account of their chiefs' successful resistance to these negotiations, obviously to instill national pride.

7. Sequoyah's life is still shrouded in mystery and racked with controversy. He deserves a new scholarly appraisal. For opposing interpretations, see Grant Foreman, *Sequoyah*, and Traveller Bird, *Tell Them They Lie: The Sequoyah Myth*.

in 1811 or 1812 he began his effort to find a way to write Cherokee, no Indian nation in North America had a written language. Many Cherokees believed that the Great Spirit had not meant the Indians to learn to write. Some creation myths said the Great Spirit had freely bestowed "the Great Book" on the first whiteman; some said the whiteman chose the book while the first redman chose the bow and arrow; some said the first whiteman stole the book from the redman. In any case, writing did not seem to be part of the redman's destiny, and many of Sequoyah's friends ridiculed his efforts. Some (including Sequoyah's fullblood wife) even accused him of trafficking in witchcraft for trying to uncover such a dark secret. But Sequoyah wanted to prove that a Cherokee could do anything a whiteman could do. Furthermore, he said, "many things were found out by men [Indians] and known in the world, but . . . this knowledge escaped and was lost for want of some way to preserve it."[8] If the Cherokees (and other tribes) could write down their discoveries, they would preserve and build up their own knowledge and be able to compete with white Americans on an equal basis as the nations of Europe did. Sequoyah hoped that his discovery, which he finally perfected and made public in 1821, would be a major force for the preservation of the Cherokee heritage, traditions, and religion. He consistently supported Cherokee separatist nationalism and was bitterly disappointed when his syllabary was appropriated by the missionaries to translate the Bible and other Christian works. In 1822 Sequoyah took up permanent residence among those of his people who had migrated to the west rather than adopt the assimilationist program.

Sequoyah's achievement brought great satisfaction and self-respect to all Cherokees. He had achieved what no whiteman had been able to do, though whites had been trying for years to find a way to transcribe Cherokee into roman letters for missionary purposes. A medal which the National Council ordered struck in his honor was delivered to him in Arkansas. However, Sequoyah's discovery came too late. Acculturation had proceeded so far that the nation could not adopt it. The mixed-blood leaders of the nation spoke English better than Cherokee, and English remained the official language of the nation.[9] Although the Council paid to have the laws translated into Sequoyan form, little else of the Cherokees' culture was ever printed on the nation's printing press. In 1828 the American Board provided for the nation's press fonts of type in the Sequoyan syllabary, cast in Boston, but they were used primarily to promote Christianization.[10]

8. Foreman, *Sequoyah*, p. 28.
9. For example, John Ross, the leading figure in Cherokee resistance to removal from 1817 to 1839 and principal chief from 1828 to 1866, spoke Cherokee so poorly that he had to deliver all of his talks to the Council through interpreters. He never used the Sequoyan syllabary.
10. The two bilingual Cherokees who were best able to translate English into Sequoyan symbols were Elias Boudinot and Jesse Bushyhead. The former devoted most of his efforts as a translator to assisting Samuel Worcester to translate the Bible; Bushyhead assisted Evan Jones in

Nevertheless, at the grass roots level the Sequoyan syllabary played a crucial role in creating a nationalist identity and in promoting the antimission sentiment which culminated in White Path's Rebellion. The eighty-six symbols of the syllabary could be learned with relative ease by anyone who spoke Cherokee, and once the symbols were mastered, anyone could write messages in the language. Within a year or two after Sequoyah released his discovery to his people, Cherokees throughout the nation were using it to communicate privately with each other. "A great part of the Cherokees can read and write in their own language," the Reverend William Chamberlain wrote from Willstown in October 1824; "The knowledge of Mr. Guess's Alphabet is spreading through the nation like fire among the leaves."[11] A short time later, the Reverend Isaac Proctor, living in the heart of one of the most traditionalist parts of the nation, noted that "letters in Cherokee are passing in all directions" and nothing is in "so great demand as pens, ink, and paper."[12] Proctor was convinced that the new invention boded no good for missionary work: "all the scholars" in his school, "as well as all the neighborhood, have become conversant with this new mode of writing," he reported in July 1825. "This, no doubt, more than anything else, has operated against English schools."[13] Some Cherokees felt they no longer needed help from the supercilious missionaries with their patronizing attitudes toward Cherokee culture. Almost overnight the Cherokees had moved from an illiterate to a literate people; miraculously a dying culture sprang to life again.

Against their will the missionaries were forced to make use of the Sequoyan syllabary for their own purposes. Their reluctance sprang not only from the difficulty and expense of translating but also from the fact that Sequoyan would keep alive a language which they thought might better die out.[14] But for the Cherokees, the use of Sequoyan was a great liberation. It

translating the Bible. The *Cherokee Phoenix*, though bilingual, devoted most of its Sequoyan pieces to Christian literature. The American Board was allowed to use the national press for Christian publications when it was not being used to publish the *Cherokee Phoenix*. The board provided hymnbooks and catechisms in Sequoyan to the other missionary societies.

11. William Chamberlain, Journal, January 25, 1825, ABCFM.

12. Isaac Proctor to Jeremiah Evarts, January 25, 1825, ABCFM. By February 1828 it was "the general opinion of the missionaries that two-thirds of the men and probably more than one-half of all the Cherokees can read in the new character." David Greene to Jeremiah Evarts, February 4, 1828, ABCFM.

13. Isaac Proctor to Rufus Anderson, March 27, 1826, ABCFM.

14. The ABCFM had, through the efforts of John Pickering at Harvard, almost succeeded in finding a system for transcribing Cherokee into roman letters when Sequoyah's discovery became known, and a long debate took place over whether it was worth using Sequoyah's syllabary instead of Pickering's method. The board thought that use of Sequoyan would lead to a disinterest in learning English. Samuel Worcester noted that Sequoyan would make Christian literature more immediately available to the fullbloods, and he noted astutely that "national feeling" or pride in Sequoyah's accomplishment was too strong to be ignored. Samuel Worcester to Rufus Anderson, March 27, 1826, ABCFM.

also had the important consequence of giving the traditionalists a secret form of communication entirely their own. So few whitemen and so few of the educated mixed bloods spoke Cherokee that Sequoyan became virtually a code to sustain the traditionalist community beyond the perception of the authorities, red or white. During the rebellion (and later during the third removal crisis) letters in this syllabary provided the basic cohesion for the antiacculturation majority not only throughout their homeland but between Cherokee traditionalists in the East and their friends and relatives who had migrated west. Sequoyah's invention thus provided a powerful impetus after 1821 to the growing division between the acculturated and the unacculturated, the rich and the poor, the Christians and the traditionalists, though we shall probably never know how it operated, for virtually none of the letters and other writings of the common Cherokees written in Sequoyan in these years have survived. What did survive were the sacred myths and rituals written down by the Cherokee conjurors and medicine men for their private use; this in itself was a major contribution, strengthening the antimission movement as well as preserving the Cherokee world view and its practice.[15]

One other important source of antimission and antiacculturationist sentiment in the years preceding White Path's Rebellion was provided by forces totally outside the Cherokee nation. Historians have not ascribed any particular date to the demise of Enlightenment Republicanism and the rise of Romantic Nationalism in American history, but most would agree that it occurred between 1815 and 1830 as Thomas Jefferson passed from the scene and Andrew Jackson rose to power. The first official signs that no Cherokees—that no Indian people—would be allowed to share equally in the manifest destiny of "the chosen people" of the United States were the forthright statements by various governors of the old Southwest that they would never accept even the most acculturated and Christianized Indians as equal citizens. Governor McMinn of Tennessee had said in 1816 that Indians would never be entitled in his state to any privileges beyond those of freed blackmen. In 1824, Governor George M. Troup of Georgia said the same thing to Secretary of War John C. Calhoun when Calhoun asked whether that state would adhere to George Washington's Indian policy. Troup replied, "The answer is that if such a scheme were practicable at all the utmost rights and privileges which public opinion would concede to the Indians would fix them in a middle station between the negro and the whiteman, and that as long as they survived this degradation, without the possibility of attaining the elevation of the latter, they would gradually sink to the condition of the former—a point of degeneracy below which they could not fall."[16] By 1830, President Jackson was to make racial segregation

15. Between 1888 and 1890 James Mooney of the Bureau of Ethnology in Washington acquired several of these manuscripts from Cherokee conjurors and through his translations and analysis of them he provided by far the best insights we have into the sacred myths, rituals, legends, and medicinal cures that we have for the Cherokees. See Mooney, *Myths.*

16. ASP II, 475—76. Fully aware of the danger of being classed with blacks as "people of

of the Indian the new national policy, though he masked it under the "benevolence" of removal.

The Cherokees had always known that white frontier people considered them an innately inferior race, but they had expected the more enlightened views of eastern whites to prevail. Cherokees thought they saw in the missionaries, particularly those from the North, a clear repudiation of all such racist positions. Christian orthodoxy seemed to preclude hereditary racial distinctions because all men were descendants of the same original parents, and the whiteman's Great Book said explicitly, "God hath made of one blood all nations." But between 1821 and 1827 the Cherokees discovered that "their friends at the North" shared the same racial prejudices as the whites of the South and West. The shock was all the more devastating because it was brought to light by leading ministers and laymen of the American Board in reaction to the proposed marriages of two of the most highly educated and pious Cherokee youths attending the Cornwall Academy in Connecticut. John Ridge, son of Major Ridge, and Elias Boudinot, son of David Watie, both attended Cornwall in these years and both fell in love with young women in the town who reciprocated their affection.[17] In both cases, the families of the women did all they could to throw obstacles in the way of these marriages, and when the parents finally capitulated, their relatives and the local townspeople engaged in riotous scenes, burning the offenders in effigy on the village green. Worse than that, the local newspaper editors wrote scathing editorials against "intermarriage with Indians and blacks" which in turn so frightened the managers of the school (including the local Congregational minister and the most famous clergyman in New England, Lyman Beecher) that they too issued public statements repudiating the marriages and blaming the parents for allowing them. After being put off for three years, John Ridge was married in Cornwall in 1824; Elias Boudinot married there in 1826. By 1827 the public outrage was so great that the American Board decided to close Cornwall Academy lest any further such incidents embarrass the missionary cause.

The Cherokee elite were more unnerved by this episode than the ordinary Cherokee. They had a much greater stake in sustaining the belief that white Christians were above that sort of prejudice. The years 1824 to 1827 were awkward for everyone. Of course some missionaries had not considered the marriages desirable (and neither, it must be said, did the parents of the bridegrooms at first), but the intensity of the racial animosity in Cornwall and the capitulation of the American Board to it were a source of profound

---

color," the slaveholders in the Cherokee Council persuaded it to adopt an elaborate black code similar to those in the neighboring slaveholding states in order to demonstrate that they saw the necessity for a caste system for Africans. See Theda Perdue, *Slavery and the Evolution of Cherokee Society*.

17. The details of these marriages and the reactions to them in New England can be found in Ralph H. Gabriel, *Elias Boudinot*, and Thurman Wilkins, *Cherokee Tragedy*, p. 148.

embarrassment to its missionaries and of great disillusionment to their Cherokee supporters. The scandal grew steadily from the day of John Ridge's proposal of marriage in 1821 until it reached its ignominious conclusion in 1827. During these years the American Board missionaries in the field kept hoping in vain that their colleagues in Cornwall and Boston would rise to the occasion. When they failed to do so, irreparable cracks developed in Cherokee—missionary relations. No group of whites, it now appeared, could be trusted to support the Indians in their aspirations for equality within the white nation. Individuals might be trusted, but no institution could, not the Congregational churches of New England nor the American Board.

There are no extant comments from the Methodist or Baptist missionaries about this incident, although the continued intermarriage of Methodist missionaries with Cherokee women in these years spoke eloquently to their views. The Moravian John Gambold at Oochgelogy, near the homes of the Ridges and Waties, had strongly urged Mrs. Ridge to oppose the marriage when he learned of John's proposal. Johann Schmidt, Gambold's assistant, had written to the Moravian board in Salem, North Carolina,

> John Ridge has asked his parents to permit him to marry the daughter of a Cornwall innkeeper. His mother is beside herself. Br. Gambold has written on behalf of his parents regarding the matter and expressed his own opinion in the affair. My God! Is it [Cornwall Academy] supposed to be a training school of the Holy Spirit where evangelists and apostles are reared [or a place] . . . for the encouragement of such liaison and the encouragement of affairs of this world and its lusts?[18]

When Mrs. Ridge asked Daniel Butrick of the American Board whether she should permit the marriage, he told her "that a white woman would be apt to feel above the common Cherokees, and that . . . her son would promise more usefulness to his people were he connected with them in marriage."[19] However, after John Ridge had persuaded his mother to relent, Butrick accepted the marriage and expressed profound disgust at the reactions of the townspeople of Cornwall and of the academy's managers:

> I believe that he [Ridge] was shamefully abused by some northern editors, and I think that the directors of the Cornwall school might have treated their objections with deserved contempt. But instead of this, they seem to justify the objections by excusing themselves as not having been accessory to the marriage and by expressing their confidence that such an event would not be likely to occur again. This is placing the Cherokee youth in a very delicate situation. They must not look at a young woman lest they should conceive an affection for her which could not be gratified. . . . They must be viewed with suspicion as a grade of inferior beings.[20]

18. Johann Schmidt to Van Vleeck, May 16, 1822, MAS.
19. Cited in Wilkins, *Cherokee Tragedy*, p.133.
20. Daniel Butrick to Jeremiah Evarts, October 26, 1824, ABCFM.

Eventually the matter reached such a pitch that Charles Hicks, the second principal chief, felt obliged to ask whether the Congregationalists and Presbyterians in the nation would publicly repudiate the action of the Cornwall directors. Samuel Worcester, residing at Brainerd, wrote to his board in October 1825, explaining the reaction of the southern Presbyterians with whom the American Board missionaries had allied themselves:

> I am told that affairs in Connecticut relative to Boudinot's marriage have very much excited the minds of the Cherokees. Charles Hicks sent a letter to the [Presbyterian] Synod of Marryville [to which many of the board's missionaries belonged] proposing to them some questions relative to the subject and requesting an answer for publication which, by a majority vote they granted. Whether it will actually appear in print I know not. I suppose the Synod generally agreed on disapproving the course of the Board of Agency of the Foreign Mission School (as are the good people of Tennessee generally) though they did not all see what concern they, as a Synod, should have with it.[21]

Whatever the synod said, it was never published. Evidently it was not sufficiently supportive to persuade Hicks that it would bolster confidence in the missionaries. Jeremiah Evarts of the American Board wrote to Worcester from Boston, explaining that he should convey apologies to Boudinot, but ultimately the board acquiesced in the closing of the school on the grounds that its usefulness had ended.[22] Worcester said that in these years Boudinot and many of the students who attended Cornwall had become very cool toward Christianity. It was reported in 1825 "that nearly all the Indian youth educated at Cornwall had turned back to their heathen ways."[23] Although some of them, including Ridge and Boudinot, returned to the faith and continued their close connection with the missionaries of the American Board, the whole incident was a severe blow to those favoring acculturation, while it confirmed the views of those opposing it.

The division within the Cherokee nation between promission acculturationists and traditionalist conservatives was in many respects a product of the same forces which drove the white citizens of the United States away from the original Indian assimilation policy of George Washington. The revolutionary ideology was founded upon the Enlightenment theory that all men are created biologically equal—that differences within the human species were simply external and environmental, not hereditary and ineradicable. By 1840, a new school of "American Ethnology" had arisen, claiming to have incontrovertible empirical evidence (cranial capacities, facial angles, distinctive hair shapes, statistics of infertility and insanity) that the

---

21. Samuel Worcester to Jeremiah Evarts, October 24, 1825, ABCFM.

22. Jeremiah Evarts to William Chamberlain, September 16, 1825, ABCFM. Evarts refers here to his letter to Worcester.

23. Daniel Butrick, Journal, February 24, 1825, ABCFM.

white, or Caucasian, race was innately superior to all others.[24] A romantic concept of national identity led the Anglo-Americans to believe that by Nature and by Nature's God, the United States was destined to be ruled by the white, Anglo-Saxon, Evangelical Protestant people who constituted its majority.[25] They were a specially chosen people because they were not like the Indians, the Africans, the Celts, and the Asians. Those other races were social deviants from the white norm who might earn some rights and privileges by conforming to the standards of the majority, but, not being of the chosen "race," they could never attain complete equality. In fact, their presence might well deflect the nation from its destiny. This was to be a whiteman's country; North, South, East, and West could agree on that by 1830. Consequently, as a more specific definition of what it meant to be an "American" developed in these years, so did a more precise definition of what it meant to be a "Cherokee." The division between assimilationists and traditionalists which fatally fractured the Cherokees thus had its roots in the crisis of white American nationalism. As the two kinds of nationalism grew stronger each year, the missionaries among the Cherokees were painfully torn between them.

As always, when their problems grew heavy and the world seemed out of harmony, the Cherokee people turned to their conjurors for help. Dreams received more attention, and some had visions offering solutions. One of the more dramatic incidents of this spiritual and psychological tension occurred at Springplace in June 1824. It was recorded by the Moravian missionaries. In symbolic form it foretold the cultural turmoil which was to evolve over the next three years. An elderly Cherokee prophet came to Springplace bringing to the students of the mission school a message he had received from the spirit world.[26] Not wanting the missionaries to see him, he slipped into the boys' dormitory after dark to tell them of his vision. The students listened all night as he explained the crisis facing their people. He began by telling them "he did not know why the white teachers came into [their] country; their doctrine was false, at least it was not suitable for the Indians, who had derived from their ancestors quite different and correct teaching." Then he said that he had recently been very ill, so ill that he "had been dead to all appearance for four days. At that time he had visited heaven where everything was beautiful, where the welschcorn grows without work and where the deer are plentiful and grow to the size of oxen. The Indians there were in very good health and had faces as round as the full moon and spent their time with constant diversions, like dances, etc. He had seen there

24. See William Stanton, *The Leopard's Spots* (Chicago: University of Chicago Press, 1960).

25. See Reginald Horsman, *Race and Manifest Destiny*. Undoubtedly it was the heightened awareness of the racial question which led the Cherokees in 1828 to place the motto "Our rights, our country, our race" under the name *Cherokee Phoenix* on the masthead of their newspaper.

26. Springplace Diary, June 1, 1824, MAS.

Indians who had died a long time ago, but had met no white people there." The fact that there was a special place for Indians to go after death clearly indicated that they did not have to follow the new and confusing ways of the whiteman.[27] In fact, to be in harmony with the Great Spirit they must follow the ways of their ancestors on earth as they would in heaven. The next world being an idealized model of how this world ought to be, the message of the prophet was the message of national separatism. "The white people," he reminded the young Cherokees, "always say that the way to heaven is far; he, however, found that it was a scant mile from here."

Missing the symbolism, the missionaries, when they heard the story from the boys the next morning, considered the vision ridiculous. The Cherokee prophet had left the mission at dawn without being seen by the missionaries. He had entered the enemy's camp to warn the younger generation that they were being led away from truth and peace by following the crooked path of acculturation. In the next few years many other prophets and conjurors appealed to the Cherokees, young and old, to cling to their own ways and reject the will-o'-the-wisp of assimilation into the whiteman's millennial destiny.

The antimission or, more accurately, the antiassimilation movement began slowly after 1820 and proceeded through a number of stages before it produced a leader and a program. First came political efforts in the Council by conservatives to regulate the rapidly expanding mission movement. When this failed, the conjurors tried to counter the aggressive proselyting by opposing itinerant missionaries whenever they came into the traditionalists' areas. When the conjurors proved inadequate in public debates with the missionaries, some of the traditionalists tried to strike back by violently abusing the Christian invaders. By 1824 vehement opposition to Christianization had developed even among Christian converts who found that the regimen of Christian orthodoxy was far more rigid than they had imagined.

The American Board bore the brunt of the antimission sentiment because its missionaries were the first to develop a nationwide network of permanent mission stations. The Moravians felt it the least because they were the least aggressive. Letters from the Moravian missionaries John

27. It is difficult to know precisely what the Cherokees believed about life after death before they met Europeans, but they had some concept of another world where the spirits of the dead lived on. Path Killer told the missionaries that when he was a child, in the 1750s, his elders told him "we went to another country when we died — that there were many people there and great towns and villages." Brainerd Journal, May 7, 1823, ABCFM. One old Cherokee woman said that before she became a Christian she had thought "that there was nothing in religion, at least, that Indians would get to heaven without it, and that christianity was necessary for white people only." Report of the Visiting Committee at Brainerd, May 29, 1818, ABCFM. Given their strong clan and family ties, the Cherokees apparently found it unpleasant to think that Christian converts were separated from their relatives after death and that "heaven" for them would be peopled chiefly by whites while their "heathen" kinfolk were consigned to hell.

Gambold and Johann Schmidt in the summer of 1824 stated that "it appears that some of the Cherokees have become hostile to the Presbyterian [American Board] missionaries and want to drive them out."[28] To overcome the deep-seated distrust of whites and the fear that the missionaries were entering their country for ulterior purposes, the chiefs who favored missions had asked the American Board to follow some simple guidelines when they began their work. They suggested that they concentrate upon education rather than evangelism; that they make no charges for schooling; that they put less emphasis upon one large mission and more upon dispersing their stations; and that they accept the right of the Council to regulate their growth. (After 1819, when the Cherokees thought they would soon have their own education fund, the Council expected to assert more direct control over schooling in partnership with the missionaries by the dispersal of its own funds, but in this the Cherokees were unsuccessful.) By 1825 the board had, one way or another, broken most of these rules. Yet they were constantly surprised that the Cherokees were not grateful for their efforts.

In August 1821, Charles Hicks told the missionaries at Brainerd that "the more ignorant class of the Nation" were convinced by the rapid increase of mission stations that "the missionaries are about to take large tracts of land as pay for teaching the children . . . that heavy charges are laid against the nation for the expense of these schools and soon the President [of the United States, who had come to encourage the expansion of Brainerd] will compel their payment in land." Hicks said such rumors came from the more backward elements in the nation, but he did not underestimate their force. He therefore informed the missionaries that it was "necessary to proceed with great caution" in expanding their work.[29] Henceforth, he said, the superintendent of the mission should inform the Council, and obtain its permission, whenever he wished to add new members to the staff of any of the stations. In January 1822, Butrick learned that Hicks "thinks the school at Brainerd had better be smaller if by that measure more schools could be established through the country."[30]

But the superintendent at Brainerd, Ard Hoyt, misunderstood Hicks's instructions. He could not believe there would be any objection to the expansion of their benevolent work, and he failed to ask permission of the Council when the board in Boston sent additional members to Brainerd. In May 1822, Hicks again warned the board that "the people were displeased that so many persons had arrived at Brainerd; they said the intention was to build a town" of white people in their midst.[31] In addition, some Cherokees were angry at an article in the board's journal, *The Missionary Herald*, because "it contained an estimate of mission property at Brainerd, including

28. Fries, 8 (1823–27): 3704.
29. Brainerd Journal, August 2, 1821, ABCFM.
30. Daniel Butrick, Journal, January 3, 1822, ABCFM.
31. Jeremiah Evarts, "Memorandum," May 9, 1822, ABCFM.

improvements of land, to a considerable amount." Boasting of their expanding establishments in their missionary publications to the church people who had donated to them, the missionaries failed to realize the bad effect this would have upon the Cherokees when they read about it. Hicks said "that although *he* might understand it and be satisfied, yet the Cherokees generally could not but consider it as a claim on the land and say, 'This is what we always told you, that these missionaries would claim the land for themselves.' "32

Similar misgivings arose toward the Baptists when Evan Jones tried to make a census of the region around Valley Towns in 1821—22 in order to determine how many Christians might have children to be educated. "The measure excited much jealousy" and suspicion for fear that it was a prelude to their removal.33 The missionaries could not even draw maps of their stations or preaching cricuits without arousing more fears: "I would endeavor to draw a map," Butrick wrote to the board in 1823. "were it not for fear of continuing among the Cherokees an idea" they hold "that we intended ultimately to get their land. I was told last Sabbath at Coosewaytee that the people there (the full Cherokees) still object to Mission Schools from the supposition that they will at some period claim their country, or part of it."34 Some Cherokees accused Hicks and other pro-Christian chiefs of being in league with the missionaries in order to enrich themselves. They said "that Mr. Hicks spoke well of it [Brainerd] because he got money for everything that was done here—that the boys would be sent away among the white people and never returned—that Mr. Hicks had a summ of money for every boy that was thus sent away."35 (The boys referred to were those going to school in Cornwall, Connecticut.)

The failure of the American Board to accept the request of Hicks that they submit to the Council their plans for increasing their stations and staff led to the first overt criticisms of missions in that body. In 1824 several chiefs (probably led by White Path) asked the Council to censure the Brainerd missionaries for failing to ask the Council's permission whenever it added a new member. Hicks told Hoyt that "As there is now a very powerful opposition to Missions among the Chiefs," it would be necessary for the superintendent to appear before the Council in October to defend the Board's actions. The Reverend William Chamberlain (who became acting superintendent in May of that year) explained to the board the division he saw taking place within the nation:

> Mr. Hicks is unshaken in his confidence in the Prudential Committee and more than ever convinced of the utility of their mission among his people. This, I believe, is the case with all the enlightened chiefs. But Pathkiller and Speaker

32. Daniel Butrick to Jeremiah Evarts, January 22, 1823, ABCFM.
33. Jeremiah Evarts, "Memorandum," May 1, 1822, ABCFM.
34. Daniel Butrick to Jeremiah Evarts, June 11, 1823, ABCFM.
35. Ard Hoyt to Jeremiah Evarts, August 4, 1824, ABCFM.

[both later supporters of White Path's Rebellion] are violently opposed, and as they have great influence among the common people and the unenlightened chiefs, it is very probable that there will be a very powerful opposition to the mission in the next council.[36]

Chamberlain also noted that at the previous Council in 1823, "some of the chiefs were calculating to deliver speeches against the missionaries, but Major Ridge took the advantage of them and delivered a very long and animated speech in favour of the missions," thereby making it difficult for the dissidents to act without causing a heated confrontation.

At the Council in October 1824, Ridge again managed matters with a high hand in an effort to forestall opposition to the missionaries. It was at this meeting that he asked the Council to allow a minister to open the session with Christian prayer. Chamberlain was then permitted to give a long sermon. Ridge's son John, just returned from Cornwall with his white wife, interpreted it to the Council. The next day the Council honored the Sabbath by holding no session. On Monday, John Ridge, still hoping that the opposition to his marriage was atypical, and David Brown, also just back from Cornwall, made strong speeches in support of Christianization and then asked the Council to vote money from the national treasury to have the Bible translated into the Sequoyan syllabary. [37] Then, during a short break in the Council session, a Cherokee convert, Alexander Saunders (or Sanders), was allowed to give a testimonial statement to those in attendance regarding the marvelous way in which God had transformed him from a wicked way of life to one of sobriety, industry, and honesty. By the time the American Board representatives finally made their presentation in defense of their work, the opposition had been pretty well silenced, though not convinced.[38]

Chamberlain and two of his colleagues took a very high tone in explaining their activities to the Council. They noted that their mission board had already spent $32,000 to educate the Cherokees while the Council had spent nothing. They detailed the immense personal sacrifice of the missionaries, who had left comfortable homes and loving families to live among them and uplift them. They detailed the generous support of white Christian churchgoers in the North, who supplied the schools with funds and the children with books, clothing, and supplies. They stressed the vocational training given to Cherokee boys and girls at Brainerd. If the mission took land for farming it was for the sake of raising food for the students and giving them training to be farmers and farmers' wives and not simply for the missionaries. Finally, Chamberlain said that while it would considerably add to

36. William Chamberlain to Jeremiah Evarts, August 11, 1824, ABCFM.

37. Charles Hicks was the prime mover behind translating the Bible into Sequoyan. He asked David Brown to do it with the help of George Lowery, but in the end Daniel Butrick did the bulk of the work. Daniel Butrick to Jeremiah Evarts, February 22, 1825, ABCFM.

38. Ard Hoyt, "Report on Questions from the Council," October 12, 1824, and William Chamberlain, Journal, October 24–26, 1824.

his work and might slow down the board's efforts to help the nation, he would hereafter seek prior approval for every new individual added to any mission station. He then presented a request to add another farmer (lay missionary) to the station at Brainerd.

To his surprise, and that of the pro-Christian chiefs, the Council turned down the request. It was the only way the fullbloods and ordinary Cherokees could express their frustration. Hicks, Ridge, and Ross later said, in embarrassment, that this rejection would be reconsidered later; they did not explain why the majority had been so uncooperative.[39] They also reminded Chamberlain that the Council expected at any time to obtain money from the tract it had laid aside for a school fund in the treaty of 1819 which it expected to use to supplement the contributions of the board.[40]

A somewhat more subtle but no less significant expression of opposition to the American Board can be seen in the declining proportion of fullblood students enrolled at Brainerd mission. In 1821, the number of fullbloods registered there came to 65 percent of the total. Thereafter the number and proportion of fullbloods steadily declined until it amounted to only 40 percent. The popularity of Sequoyah's mode of writing may have accounted for some of this decline, but so did the feeling that the missionaries were partial to those of mixed ancestry, or at least, that these had a much easier time of it at the school.[41] Isaac Proctor, whose mission school was located in the predominantly fullblood town of Etowah (Hightower), notes in 1825: "The novelty has ceased. Daily attendance has become wearisome and the restraints painful" to the students.[42] Evan Jones reported the same situation among the fullbloods of the Valley Towns in 1827: "As respects the full Indians, the time and expence required to teach them the English Language and through the medium to instruct them in useful knowledge, is out of all proportion to the good produced. Five years is as short a period as a full Indian ten years old would take to acquire an English education that would be of benefit. . . . [N]ot one in fifty of those who commence have the resolution to go through."[43]

Partly because of this failure successfully to educate fullbloods (a failure blamed essentially upon the students and their parents by the missionaries

39. Daniel Butrick, Journal, November 6, 1824, ABCFM. Evarts wrote in May 1822 of "the expenses of the Cherokee mission up to this time, amounting to $50,000 in money and $10,000 in articles of clothing." "Memorandum," May 1822, ABCFM. Chamberlain may have been referring simply to the expenses at Brainerd.

40. The government had failed to survey the original tract designed for the school fund before white settlers moved onto it and claimed preemption rights. Another tract, twelve miles square, in Alabama had to be found to replace this.

41. See Morey D. Rothberg, "The Effectiveness of Missionary Education among the Cherokees," seminar paper, Brown University, 1973.

42. Isaac Proctor, "Annual Report from Hightower Mission," July 20, 1825, ABCFM. Proctor attributed the decline to lack of parental discipline and the spread of Sequoyan.

43. Evan Jones to Lucius Bolles, March 27, 1827, BFMB. Jones attributed the decline to the failure of parents to compel their children to remain in school.

and not on any shortcomings in their mode of instruction), partly because of the great expense of running schools and model farms, and partly because of the successful competition of the Methodist circuit riders, both the American Board and the Baptist board drastically revised their missionary work between 1824 and 1827. This was done unilaterally in both cases; the Cherokees were never consulted. The Prudential Committee voted in 1824, "as the instruction of the heathen in Christian knowledge and true piety is the great object of missions . . . that our main reliance must be placed on the plain doctrines of the gospel for any permanent melioration of the character and condition of any heathen people"; therefore "the secular labors of each station . . . should be as few and simple as possible" and "the natives should get mechanics to live among them unconnected with any missionary stations," while all schools should be "kept small to enable closer instruction." No longer could Cherokees come to the missionary blacksmith to obtain repairs or new horseshoes or to obtain help from a wheelwright, miller, or carpenter. Furthermore, "Mr. Chamberlain [is] to be principally employed as an evangelist, in making circuit of the Cherokee nation," while "Mr. Potter and Mr. Butrick [are] to spend some part of their time alternatively in evangelical labors."[44] In other words, missionaries were to do less teaching and more preaching, primarily because this cost less and promised quicker results in Christianization.

Not only did the board drastically curtail the number of students it would teach at each station, but as early as 1823 the missionaries in some stations had started to ask that the parents share part of the expense of the schools. Chamberlain had started a school at Willstown in the summer of 1823, and acting on instructions from the Prudential Committee, he told the parents of his students that they must agree to furnish some support for the school in produce or in cash. They "fixed upon the quantity of food which should be furnished by the parents for each schollar that should be put into our [mission] family. viz. one bushel of corn meal per month, 30 pounds of pickled beef, or 22½ pounds of pickled pork or 15 pounds of bacon."[45] However, the parents could not meet this fee, nor did they like the alternative of having the students board at home and walk to school each day. Ard Hoyt reported the reaction to the board's new policy a year later: "There is reason to believe that increasing the number of [mission] stations, requiring the children to board with or at the expense of their parents . . . greatly lessening the number of scholars at [Brainerd] where the board is [still] free, [and] stopping the gratuitous supply of clothing to the poorer, is construed into a fulfilment of this prediction" that the missionaries had only got a foothold in order to enrich themselves.[46] Proctor wrote from Hightower in

44. Joseph Tracy, *History of the American Board of Commissioners for Foreign Missions* (New York, 1842), pp. 146–48.
45. William Chamberlain to Jeremiah Evarts, June 11, 1823, ABCFM.
46. Ard Hoyt to Jeremiah Evarts, August 4, 1824, ABCFM.

1825, "Several things operate unfavorable to schools among this people," one of which was "the inability of most parents to clothe and feed their children."[47] The burden fell most heavily upon the poor, most of whom were fullbloods. The parents began to remind the missionaries that "It was a school that was asked for and not preaching." "Nearly all in the nation can probably see that there is some advantage, and most of them great advantage, to be derived from school education," Hoyt reported, "but there is reason to think very few comparatively see any good to be derived from preaching."[48] However, the American Board had embarked upon its new policy and did not intend to retreat from it.

The board of managers of the Baptist Foreign Mission Society adopted the same revision in its program in 1827, and Evan Jones fully endorsed this "radical change." "As regards the half breeds," he said, "Most of them could just as well be boarded and clothed at home," while the fullblood children almost never stayed long enough to really benefit from the school. The expenses of boarding them at Valley Towns mission "could be very profitably applied to aid in the support of a preacher," and the energies of the missionaries "could be much more profitably employed in the spiritual business of the Mission."[49] The truth was, as Butrick said, that the great majority of the missionaries loved to preach and hated to teach; teaching was a dreary, routine occupation as they did it, and it often had disappointing results, while preaching, with the aid of the Holy Spirit, was apt to work miracles.[50] Teaching was prosaic; preaching, romantic. Preaching, furthermore, was the vocation they had selected in volunteering for missions. To be able to report scores of heathen souls saved from perdition was glorious; to report that a handful of students after a hard year's work had advanced from the first grade to the second grade in spelling and arithmetic was uninspiring.

While few of the Baptist or American Board itinerant preachers were able to report anything like the totals of conversion that the Methodists reported in the 1820s, they nevertheless traveled far and wide through the nation trying to reach those Cherokees who had not yet heard the Gospel. In 1823–24, Butrick and his interpreter rode 3,400 miles on horseback, held 171 meetings, baptized 18 adults and 25 of their children[51] As a result of this increasing itinerancy, the conjuror-priests were finally forced to come forward to defend the old religion among their followers. The missionaries enjoyed searching out these "sorcerers" and engaging them in spiritual battles. (This was the religious equivalent of the face-offs between frontier

47. Isaac Proctor to Jeremiah Evarts, January 25, 1825, and postscript. February 9, 1825, ABCFM.
48. Ard Hoyt to Jeremiah Evarts, June 17, 1824, ABCFM.
49. Evan Jones to Lucius Bolles, March 27, 1827, ABCFM.
50. Daniel Butrick, Journal, November 6, 1824, ABCFM.
51. Ibid., September 3, 1824, ABCFM.

sheriffs and outlaws in the expansion of civilization along the wild frontier.) They reported with delight their successes in confuting and confusing them. Much of the romance of mission work lay in this battle between the forces of God and the forces of Satan. Fortunately for the missionaries the conjurors were ill-equipped for this kind of theological warfare. The old religion had not articulated a systematic theology or the kind of doctrinal precisianism needed for oral debate. The stories and legends of the Cherokees were believed simply because the people had always believed them; their rituals had been practiced for centuries without any need for rational justification. The formulas chanted by the medicine men to ward off evil or heal the sick were not even known to the common people, who trusted to their efficacy. The art of these priests and doctors lay essentially in its mystery and secrecy known only to those trained in the profession. Insofar as any of the conjurors had worked out a rationalized system to explain their system of belief, it was syncretic, an adaptation of the old ways to the new, a conflation by 1824 of the traditions of the Cherokees and the half-understood theology of the Christians.

The Cherokee ministers spoke from a totally different perspective in religious cosmology from their Christian counterparts. They saw no difference between science and religion, historical fact and oral legend, man and nature, nature and the supernatural. Nor did they separate church and state. Religion was not a matter of individual belief but of collective belief, not of personal rebirth but of social cohesion. Religion did not exist apart from the community of believers and their common understanding of the cosmos. It was not objectified in a written revelation. Daniel Butrick realized the connection between preaching the Gospel of personal salvation and explaining to the Cherokees the cosmology of Galileo and Newton:

> The Cherokees are peculiarly inquisitive, and although they discover much grandeur in the works of God, yet the book of nature is to them in many respects sealed. And a minister not well versed in Geography, Natural Philosophy, Astronomy, and mathematics generally labours under many and great disadvantages among them. . . . Last summer when at Creek Path, in answer to various enquiries of the Cherokees, I was led to make remarks relative to the figure, motions, etc. of the earth, the bulk, relative situations, distances etc. of several planets, causes of eclipses, etc. A gentleman living in the nation, considered by the Indians a very learned man, told them that I spoke entirely wrong—that no one could tell the size of any planet nor shew its distance from the sun; that the earth was a plane—that the sun, moon and stars moved round it as it appears to them. . . . [A] complete knowledge of these subjects is necessary in order to explain them to the understanding of the Indians.[52]

He did not think how sealed to himself was the book of nature as the Cherokees knew it.

52. Ibid., August 31, 1821, ABCFM.

In response to such discussions of natural philosophy with a conjuror named William at Valley Towns—a man "much attached to his old ways" and "one of the great Doctors of the region"—William told Butrick that thunder came from a cave in Raccoon Mountain and that a council of spiritual beings above had created men, women, and death a very long time ago. He then tried to explain to Butrick the mysteries of healing by pointing out that the Cherokees were not pantheists or idolators but "that when they call on Eagles, butterflies, etc. etc. to help them perform cures, they do not mean such Eagles etc. as we see but beings above to whom they give these names."[53] But to Butrick this sealed book was not worth opening. The conjuror concluded that Christianity was not talking about the same spiritual power that the Cherokees understood and were in communion with. Their discussion no doubt confirmed the old conjuror's view that the Cherokees and the Christians lived in different worlds. Nevertheless, the Indians realized that educated white men did know some important things which they did not. "The people [Indians] in former times," one conjuror told Evan Jones, "possessed a great deal of knowledge of which the moderns are destitute." He then had recourse to the tradition that the whites stole the Great Book "first offered to the Indians by the Creator. . . . And having the Book in their possession, were not liable to forget as the Indians were."[54]

Another way the conjurors had of coping with the threat to their own system of religion was to add to it those aspects of Christianity which seemed to make sense. But this did not always strengthen the popularity of a conjuror with his followers. Jones met such a man who "some years ago had great influence among the people. His popularity is now declining." He had been trying to provide some answer to the questions the missionaries kept raising about sin and the origin of evil. "On the origin of man, he said, 'Man was created good and the Creator set the good way before him. Evil was afterwards created and men had now their choice.'" He then had to form an answer to the problem of free will and the rewards and punishments for choices. "Those who [are] bad," he said, "chose evil and were plunged into error and darkness and [are] driven headlong with sin and misery.'" Jones noted, however, that "His system affords no remedy for evil. He makes the future state to consist of Four Divisions: first, the Good; second, those who die in war; third, the wicked, and fourth, wicked and lewd women. All these are treated according to their deeds," said the old man.[55] Such efforts to synthesize the old and the new beliefs were bound to be unsatisfying to both sides, and the conjuror who debated on such grounds with an itinerant missionary seldom helped his cause. Most conjurors tried to avoid such confrontations. There was no way to agree upon the terms of the debate. When forced by their people to stand up for the old religion, the stress

53. Ibid., November 8, 1824, ABCFM.
54. Evan Jones to Lucius Bolles, April 1, 1828, BFMB.
55. Ibid.

became unbearable. "A few days ago an orator came 50 miles to urge the people to hold on in their old ways," Evan Jones reported. "He was to have made a great speech at a town meeting." Jones went there to hear him and to confute his teaching. "All the people assembled to hear what he [the conjuror] had to say, but unfortunately the old man met with some spirits, got drunk, and failed to make his appearance and his adherents were a good deal discomfited."[56] The orator was able to move his followers when he spoke to them on their own terms, but he did not want to compete on alien ground.

As Butrick said, the Cherokees were an inquisitive people. They were also very polite. When first invited to attend a sermon by an itinerant evangelist, they would assemble quietly, listen patiently, ask questions, and go away. But when the new religion began to make converts, it could seriously split families and disrupt local communities. Husband was pitted against wife, children against parents, the old community against the apostates. A chief known as the Big Half-breed drove his eighty-year-old wife, Qualiucka, from his home in 1827 when she told him she was going to join the Moravian church.[57] Indian masters whipped their slaves for going to hear Christian preaching. Butrick preaching at Coosewatee lamented over "the poor blacks who have been so abused lately for their attention to religion."[58] Butrick also reported that Chief Big Cabin (or Cabbin Smith) had "a little Creek girl" captured in the Creek War "who is kept much like a slave"; he refused to let her attend Christian meetings at Turkeytown. Sometimes, Butrick said, she tried to attend secretly, but "when he discovers she is gone [he] will whip her on her return."[59]

Adherents to the old religion expressed their opposition to Christian evangelism in many ways. Occasionally missionaries or native exhorters were threatened with personal harm. In 1825, the Reverend Frederick Elsworth, the American Board minister at Haweis, asked Sally Ridge, the thirteen-year-old daughter of Major Ridge, to assist him by intepreting for him at a preaching service. An old chief in the audience named Noisy Water considered it inappropriate that a child should be given the role of instructing her elders. He came to the front of the room and told Sally to sit down because he would interpret the sermon. But Noisy Water was not a Christian nor was he familiar, as Sally was, with Christian theological terms. "I told him," Elsworth reported, "that I did not consider him a proper person to interpret." Noisy Water took great offense. He had been embarrassed in front of his friends when he had only wanted to be of assistance and do what he considered proper and fitting. He left the meeting threatening angrily "to come again and whip me," Elsworth said.[60] Another missionary, David

56. Evan Jones to Lucius Bolles, December 11, 1830, BFMB.

57. Schwarze, *Moravian Missions*, pp. 162−63.

58. Daniel Butrick to Jeremiah Evarts, July 29, 1823, ABCFM. George Martin and a man named Robertson were the owners of the slaves.

59. Daniel Butrick, Journal, January 18, 1822, ABCFM.

60. Frederick Elsworth to Jeremiah Evarts, March 1, 1825, ABCFM.

Greene, noted the same problem when he tried to turn young converts into exhorters. There was "a difficulty in making use of any of their young men" as exhorters, he said, because "the natives feel that their old men should be the teachers."[61] To the Cherokees, the missionaries seemed to lack respect for the aged, yet the missionaries felt that it was generally the young who were more willing to try to make the change to the new religion.

One of the more tense confrontations occurred at the American Board's mission at Carmel, where the Reverend Moody Hall had determined to stamp out the Cherokees' hospitality ethic. Hall was convinced that the ethic had deteriorated into a form of systematic begging by the idle, lazy, and dissolute. Ignoring the fact that there was a severe shortage of food in the spring of 1824, Hall refused to share any of the mission's supplies with hungry Cherokees who came to his door. One night in April a Cherokee named Pritchett decided to confront Hall with his inhumanity and hypocrisy. He appeared at Hall's door stark naked and demanded something to eat. Hall refused. Pritchett became angry and burst into the house swinging at Hall with a knife. Others present disarmed him, and he left.[62] Believing that he and his wife were in danger, Hall fled from the mission. His church members were astonished at his cowardice and his desertion of their cause. He had preached to them about the duty of standing up to abuse for Jesus' sake; now he failed to heed his own words. Some concluded that he had an ulterior motive in leaving; he wished to embarrass the Cherokees by reporting that they had attacked Christian missionaries and thus provide an excuse for the whites to dispossess them. He fled, some said, "merely to disgrace them" and to promote the removal policy of the land speculators.

The superintendent of the American Board missions sent one of their most responsible native preachers, John Arch, from Brainerd to investigate

61. David Greene to Jeremiah Evarts, September 19, 1828, ABCFM.

62. Jeremiah Evarts to Moody Hall, August 20, 1824; Moody Hall to Jeremiah Evarts, September 18, 1824, ABCFM. Hall was at Carmel from 1820 to 1826. This incident occurred on April 26, 1824. Pritchett may have heard Hall preach from the text, "For I was an hungered and ye gave me meat . . . naked and ye clothed me." See also William Chamberlain, Journal, July 30, 1824, and Daniel Butrick, Journal, May 5, 1825, ABCFM. See John Arch to Jeremiah Evarts, June 20, 1824, in Robert S. Walker, *Torchlights to the Cherokees*, pp. 210−11. The Moravians complained often of the number of begging Indians they had to feed, and in 1827 there was some consideration given to ending the practice, but in a letter from Johann Schmidt that year, it is evident that they feared repercussions if they did so:

They are not to be blamed for the problem of hospitality. . . . [I]t is difficult to pull in the reins . . . . [S]ince the Nation is already so much in commotion, and one does not know how it will come out . . . one could cause harm to the Mission. Mr. Kingsbury among the Choctaws wanted to do away with this problem and almost undid the whole Mission. Mr. Hoyt tried the same several years ago at Brainerd and that was the reason that all their members except 4 persons turned to the Methodists . . . . It is the custom of the country that people think that no matter how little you have, still every one who is present must have a share . . . . We just have to see patiently how we can reduce this problem from time to time (Johann Schmidt to Schulz, June 5, 1827, MAS).

this incident. Arch found Pritchett and after talking to him reported that Pritchett had merely lost his temper and had no grudge against Hall: "Mr. Hall's life was no more in danger than mine would be," he told the superintendent.[63] The pro-Christian chiefs sent the lighthorse to arrest Pritchett and bring him to trial. Later Hall returned sheepishly to the mission. The Prudential Committee in Boston comforted him: "I do not wonder that you are greatly alarmed at the attack of Pritchett. . . . I do strongly hope you will not be driven to precipitate measures. This whole interrupting [of our work] I consider to be the work of the devil to prevent the salvation of souls, and I exhort you not to give place to the devil."[64]

However, six months later another incident occurred which confirmed Hall's fears. "A son of Mr. George Sanders, having drunk to excess, took his gun and dirk and started toward our house" one dark night in October, Hall said. "His purpose, he said, [was] to kill me." But Sanders's friends disarmed him before he got into the house.[65] Two months later a third Cherokee was found lurking near the house with a gun. Hall was now certain that the heathen at Carmel were plotting to assassinate him. "The opposition and hatred many express to the Gospel," he wrote in April 1825, "and the boldness of many in this, gives reason to expect that missionaries will not long be safe in this land unless the government of the United States interferes."[66] His last letter from this station stated that "two Indians, sons of Thomas Pettit, waylaid" him and one of them "threatened my life."[67] That was in October 1825. Shortly thereafter he left and never returned.

Not only the missionaries but the native exhorters were sometimes threatened. John Huss, one of the more active and effective of the American Board's converts, visited Turkeytown in the spring of 1827 and after preaching to a crowd promised to return for further evangelizing. "Before the time arrived" for his return, "he received a letter from the head man of the town threatening him if he came again." The headman said "he would put out his eyes."[68] Unlike Hall, Huss refused to be intimidated. He kept his appointment, and the headman did not carry out his threat. Only occasionally did the Cherokees actually resort to violence. One of the few such acts during the years of controversy was taken not by the antimission Cherokees but by those who belonged to a mission church against their non-Christian neighbors. It occurred in Taloney (where Carmel mission was located), and it undoubtedly contributed to the hostility there toward Moody Hall. Prior to his departure in 1825, Hall had been denouncing the heathen practices of the community which took place at the town council house. Some of Hall's

63. Walker, *Torchlights*, p. 210.
64. Jeremiah Evarts to Moody Hall, August 20, 1824, ABCFM.
65. Moody Hall to Jeremiah Evarts, October 24, 1824, ABCFM.
66. Moody Hall to Jeremiah Evarts, April 25, 1825, ABCFM.
67. Moody Hall to Jeremiah Evarts, October 4, 1825, ABCFM.
68. William Chamberlain, Journal, August 13, 1827, ABCFM.

converts, led by Alexander Saunders, decided to carry the battle into Satan's territory. Saunders gathered some friends and burned down the town council house. He then boasted of the act, saying that to a Christian, the council house was nothing but "the Devil's meetinghouse." Moody Hall reported that "the wicked are very much enraged and threaten to burn our School house" in retaliation."[69] But they never did so.

Sometimes antimission sentiment took the form of ridicule or taunting. At one mission a group of Cherokees who disliked the missionary for constantly denouncing the sin of ball playing "assembled in plain sight of the Mission house, stripped themselves entirely naked, and for some time played Ball" in order to display their contempt. The missionary, Isaac Proctor, was particularly annoyed because the young men who thus mocked his preaching were "the sons of professors" of religion at the mission church and students at the school "who have a good education." They were not unenlightened fullbloods, yet like them they could not see why participation in their native sport should be an offense against the Christian religion.[70]

The missionary doctor, Elizur Butler, while preaching at Haweis in 1826, encountered heckling questions from some in the groups who gathered to hear him (a notable departure from customary Cherokee courtesy). The questions were designed to challenge the whiteman's supercilious assumption that he knew the answers to all human questions and had solved all the secrets of nature and the supernatural. "Can any white man catch thunder?" one asked. "Can any white man catch lightning? Can any white man catch the wind?"[71] Others in Butler's audience challenged the miraculous and mysterious aspects of Christian teaching: "Who made the Saviour? Why did not God make man holy? He is a good Being; He is our Father; why did he let Satan tempt Eve?" Some let it be known that in Christian theology, as they understood it, God was the author of sin: "If you had an orchard and you told your children they might go into it and eat of the fruit of every tree but one, you would be very careful no wicked man should go and tell your children they might disobey you." Yet God was unable to keep Satan out of the Garden of Eden.[72] The questioners seemed eager to show that they had listened to the whiteman's preaching, but that they found it inconsistent, illogical, and less satisfying than their own sacred legends. They also wished to let the evangelists know that there were forces in nature which they could not control any better than the Cherokee conjurors, and perhaps not so well. Conjurors often had brought rain for their parched fields or prevented hailstorms from destroying their harvests.

Antimission sentiment was not always a confrontation between Chris-

69. See Moody Hall to Jeremiah Evarts, August 20, 1825, July 16, 1825, August 22, 1825, November 21, 1825, ABCFM.

70. Isaac Proctor to Jeremiah Evarts, December 11, 1827, ABCFM.

71. Elizur Butler to Jeremiah Evarts, September 13, 1826, ABCFM. They also asked him, "When did God begin to live?"

72. Ibid.

tians and non-Christians. Some of the most severe problems arose within mission churches when Cherokee converts discovered that there was more to being a Christian than repenting of one's sins and turning to Jesus for help in leading a good and pious life. Admission to a mission church brought a commitment to live by the whole behavioral code of white Christians. Brothers and sisters in the mission church were required to "keep watch" over each other's moral and spiritual lives and to report infractions of Christian behavior for church censure. The most common causes for church censure (which in turn could lead to the disgrace of expulsion or excommunication from the church) were, according to one missionary, "drunkenness, fornication, sabbath-breaking, gambling in various ways, fighting, conjuring, lying, cheating, faithlessness in fulfilling bargains, ingratitude for favors shown them, and profane swearing."[73] Not included in this particular list were the sins of attending ballplays and the customs of infanticide and polygamy. The missionary who made up this list, William Holland, did not hold out much hope that the Cherokees would ever make very good Christians. The converts of his church, he said, "may be styled ungrateful, dishonest people" who did not take their religious commitments seriously. What this meant in fact was that the missionaries were unable to make it clear to their converts that Christianity demanded a total abnegation of everything that gave the Cherokees an identity of their own; it left no aspect of their lives unchanged.

The Cherokees who were censured by their fellow church members for these sins could accept in most cases the principle, if not always the rigor, of the penalty. However, it was often difficult for them to comprehend why participation in sports, rain dances, or medical cures conflicted with their profession of belief in Christianity. Did not whitemen pray for rain, attend sporting events, go to doctors? Similarly, they could not comprehend the sinfulness of "conjuring" when it was done simply to find lost objects, solve romantic or marital problems, interpret dreams, predict the outcome of a ballplay, or stave off harmful consequences in some venture. Nothing in Christian practice seemed applicable to these kinds of everyday problems. The urge to combine old ways with new where they made for better ordering of life was obviously strong, but the holistic aspect of evangelical Protestant conversion was hard to accept. Missionaries spoke of ballplays, rain dances, and conjuring as "polluting customs"; the convert could see that drunkenness, lying, and stealing were sins, but he could not see the sinfulness in attending a Green Corn Dance to thank God for a good harvest.

One of the first sources of conflict arose over the practice of polygamy. Cherokee men of standing and importance often had two and sometimes three wives. When such a man decided to adopt Christianity, he found that he was required to put aside all but one wife—a difficult emotional choice as

---

73. William Holland, "Report on Candy's Creek Station," April 1828, ABCFM.

well as one insulting to the other wife and her clan. Polygamous wives were commonly sisters who had been taken in marriage on the same occasion. Charles Reece had married three sisters and had children by all of them. One of these died before he asked for baptism at Brainerd, but he wished to keep his relationship with the other two. The Reverend Ard Hoyt was convinced that Reece was truly converted, but he put off baptizing him until he could ask the board in Boston for advice: "Where a native is converted who has and lives with two or more wives, shall he be required to put away either?" The Prudential Committee replied: "A convert who has more than one wife should be required to separate himself from all but his first wife." Hoyt wrote back that Reece had married the three sisters simultaneously and "we should not know which to have him put away."[74] Somehow Reece resolved the difficulty and was admitted to the mission church, but all such choices created moral dilemmas which the missionaries failed to resolve. The Moravian answer was to allow polygamous converts to keep both their wives.

Nor was the resolution of the sin of conjuring any better. Few of the missionaries took the trouble to distinguish, as the Reverend William Chamberlain did, between the useful and the polluting aspects of Cherokee medicine. Conversing with an old Cherokee near Willstown in 1822, Chamberlain discovered that "she had been in the habit of doctoring in the Cherokee manner (which is conjuring) and she had begun to question in her own mind whether it was right or not. . . . I told her it was very good for her to administer medicine to the sick, but it was not good to use the art of conjuring."[75] But it was impossible to distinguish between the two in practice. Medicine required the use of spells, ceremonies, and divinations to diagnose the sickness, to find the remedy, and to drive out the evil spirit which caused it. Medicine administered without rituals was useless. The Cherokee world did not allow for the simple division between nature and the supernatural. The science of healing was the spiritual understanding of the connection between the seen and the unseen worlds. In explaining the work of the Holy Spirit in converting the human heart, the missionary spoke within the realm of Cherokee understanding; in explaining the totally material causation of illness, he did not.

"Some of the dear Cherokee [church] members the year past," reported the Reverend Daniel Butrick, "were at one time very much dissatisfied on account of the sermons I preached on conjuring, rain-making, etc." In fact, "My preaching respecting idleness, sabbath-breaking and especially conjuring, and my determined public opposition to them, has excited some feeling against me."[76] An old Cherokee woman expressed typical surprise when she learned that conjuring was considered improper by Christian missionaries: "A woman, probably ninety years old, who had received [religious] instruc-

74. Ard Hoyt to Samuel Worcester, September 25, 1818, Cyrus Kingsbury, Journal, January 25, 1817, Samuel Worcester to Ard Hoyt, November 19, 1818, ABCFM.
75. William Chamberlain, Journal, June 29, 1822, ABCFM.
76. Daniel Butrick, Journal, May 6, 1828, and November 28, 1828, ABCFM.

tion from Mr. Huss came twenty miles expecting to be baptized. She appeared well [that is, sincerely converted] in every respect excepting she expressed unwillingness to renounce conjuring. She had for years been a conjuress."[77] For this woman, and other conjurors, joining the Christian church may well have been a pragmatic effort to gain the support of the strong spiritual powers of that faith system to add to those of the Cherokee system.[78] Furthermore, conjuring was a professional skill which provided influence and standing in the community as well as an income. For a conjuror to give up conjuring would require forsaking an honored and perhaps lucrative professional training acquired through years of hard work.

Even in those communities where mission schools were established upon request of the local chiefs, the cause of Christianization and civilization began to suffer losses after 1824 as a result of religious conflicts. The fullblood chiefs at Taloney had asked for a school in their district, but when the Reverend Isaac Proctor also formed a mission church and then used it to attack the wicked customs of the region, his welcome wore thin. One of Proctor's converts, named Zacharias, had been a conjuror before joining the church. In July 1827, Proctor reported that he had had to criticize brother Zacharias in front of the whole congregation because he "has lately tried to make it rain and to cure a member of the church by conjuration." "Zacharias, the aged," as he was known, did not take kindly to this public criticism and continued to practice his professional skills when asked. He "lately instructed Charles Moore of Hightower in the art of conjuration, and that too on Monday after we had a Communion Season at which both had been" participants. Proctor could not comprehend such inconsistency; it was an affront to his teaching. "Their conjuring is as purely heathen as almost anything to be met with on the River Ganges. When conjuring they pray to almost every creature—such as white dogs, butterflies, turtles, etc. etc."[79]

Proctor had formerly been the missionary at Hightower, several miles away. He was succeeded there by Daniel Butrick, who became involved in the same kind of problem. "We have had many severe trials," he wrote, "some especially on account of conjuring. Once, on going to Carmel to administer the Holy Communion, our dear brother Moore and sister Eleanor, his daughter, accompanied me. Sister Eleanor was unwell and her father, on Sabbath morning, got brother Zacharias, a member of Carmel Church, to conjure for her and tell her whether she would recover. This, however, was unknown to me at the time. But on visiting Carmel again, the members of the church told me what Brother Zacharias had done." Butrick

77. Daniel Butrick, Journal, August 3, 1829, ABCFM.

78. Raymond D. Fogelson found that while conjuring remains important among the Cherokees today, "all of today's conjurors consider themselves to be good Christians and feel that their work is completely consistent with Christianity." See Raymond Fogelson, "Change, Persistence and Accommodation in Cherokee Medico-Magical Beliefs," in Symposium on Cherokee and Iroquois Culture, ed. William N. Fenton and John Gulick, p. 219.

79. Isaac Proctor to Jeremiah Evarts, July 28, 1827, ABCFM.

called Zacharias in and began to upbraid him through an interpreter, John Sanders. Sanders, "thinking me too severe, I suppose, told me he could talk better himself." Sanders was also a member of the mission church. He was caught in the middle. What Butrick had asked Sanders to say about conjuring was this:

> I told brother Zacharias that it was only the black waters of heathenism, designed and calculated to keep their thoughts entirely from the true God. The people in all their wants applied only to their conjurors, and these applied their petitions to some fictitious, imaginary being who had no real existence in the universe. So that the true God was neither an object of fear or reverence or gratitude. Of course, brother Zacharias was to renounce it forever.[80]

Butrick was evidently unaware that Proctor had said the same thing to old Zacharias three years before. Nor were Zacharias and his fellow church members any more willing to accept Butrick's censure. A few weeks later Butrick returned to Carmel and found "that brother More [Moore] had been conjuring to make rain and sister Rowe had sent to a woman and employed her to conjure and tell her where some cloth was which had been lost." Butrick made further inquiries and found that "a great part of the church [was] involved in the evil." To them it was not sin to take Christian communion on Sunday and on Monday to ask help from their own priests for private matters totally unrelated, in their minds, to the ceremonies and worship at the mission church. Having failed to convince them by individual admonition, Butrick proceeded "publicly to reprove and instruct them," thus holding them up to public shame. The result was to turn his whole congregation against him. "Our dear brother More became very angry," Butrick reported, because he knew of no other remedy for his son's illness. He appeared before Butrick after the meeting with his son and "held out to me the arm of his little boy covered almost with sores, saying 'There, those [sores] may be there till he dies; I shall not doctor them." The others took Moore's side, and "the whole church forsook me."[81]

Similar angry confrontations took place when missionaries denounced their church members for attending ballplays and dances. Proctor was astonished to find that his converts at Etowah in 1827 "still retain their grossest vices. Those that are the most heathenish are their Ball Plays, all-night Dances and Eagle Dances." In part, his objection was to the immoral activities which he believed accompanied these affairs. "At their

80. Daniel Butrick, Journal, September 8, 1830, ABCFM.

81. Ibid. It is difficult to say what proportion of the Cherokee converts retained some or all of their views about conjuring, but the evidence indicates that most converts did rely upon conjurors in times of sickness. The Reverend Isaac Proctor, speaking of his mission church members in 1827, remarked, "it seems exceedingly difficult for them to forsake entirely their heathenish habits. Many of their old practices will be resorted to in time of sickness, and I have known but one instance where a native Christian was unyielding when requested [by relatives or friends] to employ a Cherokee doctor." Proctor to Jeremiah Evarts, December 11, 1827, ABCFM.

Ball play the players are literally *naked* and yet a large proportion of the spectators are females. The all-night dances are attended by wives without their husbands and husbands without their wives, and as they are held during the night, we may safely infer that all the deeds of darkness are committed."[82] In addition, the practices themselves were sacrilegious. "As to the Eagle dance, I possess no information," Proctor said, "but have lately been informed that it is more heathenish than either of the others."[83]

When asked to explain their objections to conjuring, missionaries said that it broke the First Commandment by placing other gods or supernatural beings on a par with the Great Jehovah. Some missionaries dismissed Cherokee religion as "zootheism," or the worship of birds and animals, because they were ignorant of the spiritual symbolism of the prayers used. Forced to choose between the personal consolations of a mission church and the concrete advantages of their traditional religion, many Cherokees chose the latter, even though they would have preferred to have both. Missionaries reported after 1824 that their adherents were beginning to lose interest and were dropping away. "Two or three who were called promising Christians," said the Reverend Frederick Elsworth of Haweis mission in October 1825, "have openly renounced their pretensions to religion." Apostasy brought guilt and bitterness with it. "The people in general manifest a spirit pretty far from friendly and would doubtless be well pleased to have no school" or church in the town to remind them of their conflicting allegiances.[84]

That same year the Reverend William Chamberlain visited the Etowah converts, who had no pastor at that time. He found that many were "in a most deplorable situation" spiritually. They seemed unable to sustain their belief and practice without the regular supervision of a minister: "they had concluded to leave the service of God and turn back to their old ways; one of them said he thought the service of Satan as sweet as the service of God." Hearing this, Chamberlain called together as many of the church members as would come and announced the immediate excommunication of six apostates.[85] Three years later, when the American Board sent a representative from Boston to inspect the mission at Etowah, he reported, "One half of all who have been added to the church have been suspended," and at the nearby Carmel mission, "out of fifty, twenty have been excluded from membership" for returning to their old religion.[86]

Even at New Echota, the nation's capital and the showplace of Cherokee acculturation, some of the leading families left the church in the mid-1820s. "The two principal families of Mr. Elijah Hicks and Mr. [Alex] McCoy care nothing for religion," reported an American Board

82. Isaac Proctor to Jeremiah Evarts, December 11, 1827, ABCFM.
83. Ibid.
84. Frederick Elsworth to Jeremiah Evarts, October 13, 1825, ABCFM.
85. William Chamberlain, Journal, July 9, 1825, ABCFM.
86. David Greene to Jeremiah Evarts, July 28, 1828, ABCFM.

visitor in February 1828.[87] Elijah Hicks was the son of Charles Hicks and had been educated in mission schools by the Moravians. Alex McCoy was the chief clerk of the National Council. Both had previously been strongly pro-Christian. To be a leader of the Cherokees one had to be sensitive to the feelings of the majority, and many of the influential leaders grew as resentful of missionary evangelism as did the poorer, ordinary Cherokees. "The state of religion is almost melancholy," said the Reverend William Potter of the American Board in 1827. "The enemy appears to be coming in like a flood."[88]

Although all of the missionaries felt some of this antimission sentiment, the American Board missionaries bore the brunt of it. Their New England Calvinism was particularly strict and made heavy demands upon their converts. They had made a sharp shift in their tactics between 1824 and 1827. And they were obviously the most wealthy, most closely connected with the government, and the most politically influential with the chiefs who favored rapid acculturation. The American Board received the most criticism because it was trying, in its way, to do the most for the Cherokees. The complexity of its position was revealed in an antimission incident which took place in Etowah in 1824. Etowah was the largest town in the nation at this time; it contained over two hundred families, about 1,200 people, and its homes and farms stretched in a continuous line along the thirty-mile valley of the Etowah River.[89] Though primarily populated by fullbloods, the town had its share of mixed bloods eager for schools. The headmen of Etowah were Chulioa, Shoeboots, Cannutohee, Esannoo, Colenawa, Conullahee, Cachitanue, and Nautatagut. On May 26, 1824, these chiefs signed a letter to the second principal chief, Charles Hicks, complaining that the American Board missionary there and the missionary blacksmith were causing so much trouble that they must be removed. Proctor and his teachers "are complained of very much by the young people [who] are under their care for Education," wrote the chiefs. The blacksmith, hired by the mission, proved to be a bad workman who charged "extravagant" prices. In addition, some of the converts of the mission had harassed the nonconverts in the town, taunting them for being unenlightened heathen and singing at them, "You will die, you will die." These converts also told their friends that the "red physic" (the communion wine) used in Christian ritual was a more powerful spiritual drink than "the black physic" (brewed from holly leaves) used in the sacred rituals of the Cherokees. So powerful was it, they claimed, that it "would make the Heathen faint if present" when it was taken by believers in the new religion. In short, the Christian Cherokees boasted that they had more powerful medicine and more powerful spiritual forces on their side and

87. David Green to Jeremiah Evarts, February 4, 1828, ABCFM.
88. William Potter to Jeremiah Evarts, March 2, 1827, ABCFM.
89. Ard Hoyt et al. to Jeremiah Evarts, March 8, 1822, ABCFM

issued spiritual threats against the nonbelievers which the non-Christians took to be evil spells or curses.

The headmen said that this friction was bad for harmonious relations in their community, and they wished to have the mission closed. They found the Christians the aggressors. When Charles Hicks received their message, he refused to act upon it. He pointed out that the mission had been started at the request of the headmen; he said that Cherokee children always complained when they first began going to school; and he pointed out that the songs of the Christian converts were not meant as harassment but were simply expressions of Christian faith—the belief that true believers would have eternal life while non-Christians would not. The words "you will die," he explained, meant only that because of Adam's sin, "the soul of the unbeliever in the next life" would suffer; it would be "banished from the presence of God." As for the talk about the superior power of communion wine over the black physic, Hicks dismissed this as nonsense.[90]

He was equally insensitive, being himself a thoroughgoing Christian, to the complaint that antagonism between the two religious groups was destroying the political harmony of the community. Hicks gave short shrift to the headmen's complaints that the missionaries were promulgating many "strange rules" for those under their sway. They would not allow them to attend religious ceremonies at the council house or dances or ballplays. The missionaries "are trying to doe away [with] our common custom of meeting in our townhouse" for local business. The meetings at the town house were opened with a religious ceremony conducted by a conjuror who prepared the black physic for all present (the drink being used to purify the mind and spirit of those who were about to conduct the affairs of the local council). Hicks did not seem to understand or care. He had long since given up such customs and to him the affairs of church and state were now entirely separate. "I am confident," he told the chiefs, "that the society [the missionary church] to which they have joined, do not forbid our people to Exercise their publick authority which any of them may be vested with." This was technically true. Any Cherokee convert was free to carry out his specific public duties. But in fact, the secular and spiritual life of the community were integrally related, and if the mission church prohibited the converts from participating in the religious ceremonies of the council (or the Green Corn Dance of the community) it was in effect prohibiting their being an effective part of the governing process. The people of the United States, and especially of New England, had only recently emerged from a system which united church and state, and one might have thought the missionaries would appreciate such a dilemma. At the root of White Path's Rebellion lay this vital issue of political and religious unity.

90. Charles Hicks to Johann Schmidt, June 5, 1824, MAS. See W.G. McLoughlin, "Cherokee Anti-Mission Sentiment," *Ethnohistory* 21, no. 4 (Fall, 1974): 361–70. For a discussion of "the black physic," or "black drink," and its role in the affairs of the town councils, see Charles Hudson, *The Southeastern Indians*, pp. 226–29.

While Hicks was unquestionably a Cherokee patriot, he seemed unaware that he had uprooted himself from his role as spiritual leader of his people. As a pious Christian, Hicks had heard the criticism "that I was more mindful of prayer meetings than [of] my National duties."[91] In effect, he had chosen a new kind of civil religion for his people. But to many of his people he had almost ceased to be a Cherokee.

One further feature of the antimission movement was hinted at in the confrontation between Hicks and the headmen of Etowah in 1824. They reported that as a result of having become converted and admitted to the mission church, some of the black slaves were no longer obedient to their masters. The chiefs were losing the respect not only of their people but of their servants. Hicks considered this complaint ridiculous. He owned slaves himself, and he knew that Christianity did not in any way alter the political status of the slave or his duty to obey his master. The missionaries of every denomination in the nation either owned slaves or hired them to work for them. The mere fact that a slave was admitted to a mission church and allowed to take communion with other Christians, even the fact that in ecclesiastical affairs a slave member might be addressed as "sister" or "brother," did not alter his or her social status. "The Gospell requires Servants to be faithful to their masters," Hicks told the headmen of Etowah. Christianity, in fact, supported slavery. If the Christian slaves of Etowah refused to obey their masters, he said, the master should whip them just as he did his own disobedient slaves.

Once again Hicks had missed the point. In the Cherokee religion, slaves were not equal participants; they were never "sisters" or "brothers." No slave was a member of a clan, and a recent law had specifically forbidden intermarriage between any Cherokee and a person of African descent. If Christian slaves were truculent toward their Cherokee masters, this resulted from constantly hearing the missionaries say that Christians were infinitely superior to heathens. Why then should a black Christian be humble or obedient to a red heathen? Furthermore, most blacks could speak and understand English. They therefore understood the Calvinistic doctrine of "the elect" and "the reprobate"; they understood that the elect had a special relationship to God that the reprobate could never have. Added to this, the missionaries praised the superior morality of Christians to those who followed pagan customs. And of course it was praiseworthy for Christian slaves to preach Christianity to other slaves. Inevitably, then, some slaves began to feel a spiritual contempt for their masters. Having a more powerful God on their side (as well as the white missionaries), the slave had an advantage, and some masters might have hesitated to whip them.[92] Certainly the Christian

91. Charles Hicks to John Gambold, April 3, 1819, MAS.
92. Some Cherokees, when they wished to learn English, turned to their slaves for help. Ard Hoyt recorded that Catherine Brown, one of the early converts at Brainerd, was taught to read the Bible by one of her slaves. See Brainerd Journal, June 7, 1818, ABCFM.

slaves had the missionaries on their side in demanding humane treatment.[93] Although all missionaries at this time studiously avoided saying anything that might be construed as antislavery preaching, the problem (especially for northern Christians) was real.

While missionary magazines in the 1820s almost entirely ignored these antimission conflicts and gave their readers a sense of steadily and harmoniously expanding Christianization, the fact was that antimission sentiment was rampant in the Cherokee Nation from 1824 to 1827, and so was the rebellion against continued rapid acculturation. In the year 1827 the conflict could no longer be avoided. A political rebellion unified the opponents of the ruling elite. Influential but disaffected leaders united the dissidents and offered an alternative to the political structure and policies of the duly elected council. At the height of their progress as a civilized nation, the Cherokee people were radically split.

93. In the Creek Nation in 1827–28, when several Creek chiefs whipped their slaves to prevent their attending worship at a Baptist mission, the Reverend Lee Compere took the case to the secretary of war on the grounds that it was an infringement of religious liberty and Christian missionary work. The secretary of war upheld him. See the letters of Lee Compere to Lucius Bolles, BFMB. Evidently no missionary to the Cherokees took this view when they heard of similar situations.

White Path's Rebellion and the Cherokee Constitution, 1827–1828

Since the death of our departed Brother [Charles] Hicks, the whole Nation here is in the greatest turmoil. The greater part wants to have the new laws abrogated and are voting also that missions shall be discontinued. . . . Nightly there are dances organized and during the whole day they have Council. . . . Houses are being set on fire by the Negroes.
Letter from the Moravian missionaries, Springplace, May 16, 1827

It is much to be regretted that the idea of Sovereignty should have taken such a deep hold of these people.
Thomas L. McKenney, director of the Office of Indian Affairs, 1827

White Path's Rebellion in 1827 culminated six years of rising antimission sentiment and growing Cherokee nationalism. As the Christian mission movement grew, so did the resentment against it. The traditionalists had tolerated missionaries when the nation needed their help, but with rising prosperity and self-confidence many thought their help was unnecessary. Furthermore, the initial deference and compliance of the missionaries had changed into smug and patronizing complacency. The rebellion was an assertion of national pride against white arrogance. It was not a reactionary movement seeking simply a return to a lost past but rather an effort to keep faith with their own heritage and identity as a people. The Cherokee nation had its own religion; it did not need that of the whiteman. The rebels were not opposed to all acculturation, but they resented the constant missionary assault upon their "polluting customs" and "heathen superstitions." To some extent the movement pitted fullbloods, poorer Cherokees, nonslaveholders, and older people against English-speaking, mixed-blood, and wealthier Cherokees.[1] It never denied

1. Though no one in the Cherokee Nation lacked land to cultivate because vacant land was open to any Cherokee who wanted to settle on it, the increasing gap between the rich and the poor can be measured to some extent by how much land a man cultivated. In 1835 the average Cherokee family farmed 14.1 acres and in the poorer parts of the nation, 9.7 acres. But some of the richer Cherokees had farms of 600 to 1,000 acres and with their black slaves were able to grow large surpluses of corn, wheat, and cotton for sale. See W. G. McLoughlin and Walter H. Conser, Jr., "The Cherokees in Transition," *Journal of American History* 64, no. 3 (December 1977): 678–703. The poor were often so strapped for cash that they could not pay the fifty-cent poll tax levied by the Council in 1820 upon "each head of a family . . . and each single man under the age of sixty." The tax was laxly enforced for this reason. See *Cherokee Laws*, p. 13.

the patriotism of the elite, only its excessive eagerness to ape the whiteman. The goal of the rebellion was to achieve tolerance toward and self-respect for the majority who still adhered to the religion and traditions of their culture. "The dissident party," as it was called by the federal agent, felt that the Cherokee culture was reaching a point of no return. It rankled them to see their mixed-blood, English-speaking leaders giving so much credit for Cherokee survival to the whiteman and so little to the intelligence, tenacity, and skill of the Cherokees.

In answer to the complaints of the rebellious, the Cherokee elite tried to explain how important rapid acculturation was. By carefully reading the American newspaper and congressional reports, the educated Cherokees understood that the rapid rise of the western states to national power under the leadership of Andrew Jackson and the Democratic Party after 1820 was of momentous consequence to the Indian nations. Cherokee security rested with the National Republican Party of John Quincy Adams, Henry Clay, Theodore Frelinghuysen and upon the goodwill of those pious northern churchgoers committed to the support of missions and of federal over states' rights. The Cherokee leaders considered the missionaries their most important allies. Jacksonian frontiersmen were justifying their removal policy by stressing the need to give the "backward" Indians more time to catch up to white civilization; in the meanwhile, Jacksonians said, their removal would enable Christian whitemen to cultivate the soil and use the resources which the "savages" east of the Mississippi were incapable of developing properly. The Cherokee leaders told their people that whites who would be willing to remove to reservations in the west a tribe of nomadic, pagan hunters might hesitate to uproot a republican society of Christian, churchgoing, Bible-believing farmers tilling their own fields and supporting their own families by their industry. Thus the closer the Cherokees came to assuming the identity of whites, the better off they would be. It was precisely this necessity for apparently totally transforming their identity which the Cherokee rebels repudiated. They already had a respectable identity, and it was sufficiently progressive and productive, the rebels believed, to convince any honest observer that the Cherokees should be treated as an equal and self-governing nation.

White Path's name was given to the rebellion of 1827 because he was one of the first chiefs to oppose publicly the rapid acculturation, and he was the rebels' first martyr. After trying to obstruct the passage of a number of laws passed by the National Council in October—November 1825, White Path was "broken," expelled from his seat, disgraced. The Council majority, still under the sway of the assimilationist chiefs, voted for his expulsion even though many undoubtedly sympathized with him. One and one-half years later, White Path had the majority on his side and became one of the leaders of the rebel council formed in opposition to the elected council.[2] When this rebel

2. For White Path's removal from the Council, see *Cherokee Laws*, p. 67. For his rebellion, see Mooney, *Myths*, pp. 113—14. Mooney dates the rebellion in 1828.

council seemed about to take control of the nation in the spring of 1827, the missionaries were stunned. Fearful for their safety, they waited anxiously for the elite to reassert control. They heard rumors that Christian converts were being persecuted and that Christian missionaries would be driven from the nation. Attendance at mission churches and evangelistic services fell off sharply. Christian converts recanted. All around them the old dances and ceremonies revived.

White Path (Nunnatsunega) was born about 1763.[3] He was one of the most respected old chiefs, a headman of Turniptown near Ellijay. As a youth he had fought in the guerrilla warfare against the frontier whites in Tennessee. In middle age he fought against the Creeks. Andrew Jackson had cited him for valor in that war, and he had served on the Council for many years. Now approaching sixty-five, he owned a small farm in the southeastern part of the nation. He owned no slaves and spoke no English, but he could read and write in Cherokee.

Precisely what pieces of legislation he objected to in the crowded session of the Council in October—November 1825 is not known, for no explanation for his expulsion exists. He may simply have been offended by the sheer number of new rules and regulations. Thirty-one bills—the largest and most complex body of legislation ever considered by a single session—were presented to the Council by the National Committee for concurrence between October 14 and November 14. Most of these laws were designed to assist the growth of the market economy for the ambitious and the acculturated. A tabulation of the printed laws of the nation from 1808 to 1827 indicates the rapid increase of such legislation in the 1820s:

Number of laws passed annually by the council[4]

1808 — 1	1820 — 8	1824 — 20
1810 — 1	1821 — 8	1825 — 31
1817 — 1	1822 — 11	1826 — 15
1819 — 6	1823 — 4	1827 — 4
		plus the constitution

Or, to put it more simply, from 1808 to 1820 the Council passed a total of only nine laws, while in the seven years from 1820 to 1827, a total of ninety-seven laws was passed. The number and intricacy of these laws confused, frustrated, and angered the fullbloods. Beyond that, the vast majority of the laws concerned the economic, legal, and contractual aspects of entrepreneurial activities which had little bearing upon the daily lives

3. Mooney, *Myths*, p. 528. In the federal census of 1835, White Path's household at Ellijay is listed as consisting of two fullbloods, one weaver, one spinner, and one reader of Cherokee. At his death in 1838, his age was estimated at seventy-five.

4. This tabulation includes only those laws printed in the codification of 1852. Many others which are not in this codification were probably passed or debated.

of most Cherokees. They demonstrated how far removed the average Cherokee dirt farmer was from the wealthy traders and plantation owners. Some of the laws were directly opposed to Cherokee political traditions and some were specifically pro-Christian. The thirty-one laws presented to the Council in 1825 concerned such matters as proper fencing of property, the regulations for employing white mechanics, the evidence for claims against the national treasury, the making of wills, the regulation of the police, the appointment of judges, the ownership and sale of private property, the management of the treasury, the laying of taxes, and the payment of debts. Typical of these laws was one passed on November 12, which filled a whole page in the law book. Its first paragraph read,

> Resolved by the National Committee and [concurred in by the] Council: That all lawful contracts shall be binding and whenever judgment or judgments shall have been obtained from any of the Courts of justice in the Cherokee Nation against any person or persons whatsoever on a plea of debt, it shall be lawful for such person or persons to stay such judgment or judgments by giving bond with sufficient security within five days after such judgment shall have been issued; and the stay shall not exceed for all sums under ten dollars, twenty days; for all sums from ten and under thirty dollars, sixty days; for all sums . . .[5]

This law, vital to the growth of the nation's economy, meant little to most fullbloods, who were barely able to scratch a living from the soil and seldom had ten dollars in cash. It was probably incomprehensible to older chiefs like White Path and to many other non-English-speaking Cherokees even when translated into Cherokee. Such rules and regulations had no connection with traditional Cherokee concepts of community, harmony, and sharing. They were designed to promote individualistic free enterprise. A long and complex law passed on November 5, 1825, explained how educated Cherokee traders and businessmen might obtain money from the national treasury to provide capital for new private ventures:

> Resolved by the National Committee [and concurred in by the] Council: That the treasurer of the Cherokee Nation be, and he is hereby, authorized to loan out on interest at six per cent per annum, such surplus public monies as may be in the treasury, after ample appropriations have been made to meet the annual expenditures for the support of government, to such citizen or citizens of the Cherokee Nation as may desire a loan; *Provided* such person or persons may be fully able to repay the sum or sums so loaned and also shall give bond and two good and sufficient securities . . .[6]

Other laws passed at the session of 1825 dealt with the centralization of political authority, protected the borders from white intruders, asserted the Cherokee Nation's control over its own mineral deposits, proposed the establishment of a "national academy" (or classical seminary) and a national printing press.[7] There was probably no objection by White Path and his

5. *Cherokee Laws*, p. 59.
6. Ibid., p. 50.
7. Ibid., p. 47.

friends to the law stating that "the children of Cherokee men and white
women living in the Cherokee Nation as man and wife, be . . . equally
entitled to all the immunities and privileges" of Cherokee citizership, for
this had long been accepted in practice.[8] But there were other laws presented
by the National Committee which ran counter to Cherokee tradition. For
example, on November 10, the National Committee brought in a bill making it unlawful "hereafter for any person or persons whatsoever to have more
than one wife."[9] This was an amendment to the law of 1820 "recommend-
ing" the end of polygamy. Now it was to be prohibited. Many of the old
chiefs had more than one wife. (White Path may have had more than one.)
If objections were made to this ancient custom they were probably from the
missionaries. Significantly, no penalty was attached to this law, so the mixed
bloods could assure its opponents that it was more prescriptive than regula-
tive. It probably passed with the understanding that it would not be strictly
applied.[10]

The law against polygamy was just one in a series of Christianizing
laws affecting social affairs passed during these years. In 1819 a law required
Cherokee women who married whitemen to do so "by a minister of the
gospel or other authorized person"; a law of 1820 required parents to pay
costs when they withdrew their children from a mission school; a law of
1822 prohibited the import of whiskey; that same year a law forbade "gam-
ing at cards"; the next year the Council voted to suspend its own sessions on
the Sabbath; in 1824 ardent spirits were prohibited "at ball-plays, all night
dances, and other public gatherings"; in 1824 all "intermarriages between
negro slaves and indians or whites" were prohibited.[11] Probably each of these
laws came in response to claims that the practices condemned were harmful
to the general welfare. But taken together they marked, step-by-step, a
march away from traditional Cherokee culture toward white Christian
practices.

White Path and his friends may also have raised questions over the new
law governing wills. It made even more emphatic that shift from matrilineal
to patrilineal inheritance which had begun with the first written law in
1808. The law of 1825 required that if a person died intestate "the property
of the deceased shall be equally divided among his lawful and acknowledged
children, allowing the widow an equal share."[12] Most Cherokees died without wills and had little to leave their heirs. Only the educated or Christianized property owners were concerned that their children and not the older
brothers of the deceased (or the brothers of the mother) should inherit their
property. Other conservatives on the Council may have been surprised to

8. Ibid., p. 57.
9. Ibid.
10. The only known case brought under this law (against Thomas Petti) ended in
acquittal. Cherokee Supreme Court Docket, October 28, 1829, Tennessee State Archives,
Nashville.
11. Ibid., p. 38.
12. Ibid., p. 52.

find that the nation now required a strict law punishing any man "who shall lay violent hands upon any female by forcibly attempting to ravish her chastity contrary to her consent."[13] Rape had been almost unknown in former times when sexual relations for all men and women were considered natural upon reaching puberty and when divorce was simple. Now a woman had become the private property of the man who married her; marriage was expected to be for life, and chastity became a measure of a woman's worth upon marriage and afterward. Under a matrilineal clan system the natural father of a child was of less concern; in a patriarchal, monogamous, and patrilineal society fatherhood and husbandhood became of great importance. The National Committee was not proposing laws simply for good order, prosperity, and protection of their homeland; it was proposing laws which substituted new cultural norms for the traditional ones. Although the missionaries believed that White Path's movement constituted a rebellion against law and order, the traditionalists believed that they were trying to prevent a revolution. To White Path, the acculturationists were the rebels, intent upon forcing the whole tribe to adopt the whiteman's way of life and to abandon their own.

Probably most offensive to the conservatives was an oath of office adopted at the legislative session of 1825. Its conjunction with a law removing White Path from the Council provides circumstantial evidence that this may have been the immediate cause of his expulsion. The oath, though undated, was used to install George Hicks as marshall of Coosewatee District, the district in which White Path and several other leading conservatives lived and where they had, by tradition, authority as town chiefs to uphold law and custom. Hicks was a Christian convert and the nephew of Charles Hicks. He was appointed marshall by a law which is listed immediately following the law expelling White Path from the Council. The expulsion law states only that "the Committee have elected W.[illiam] Hicks [brother of Charles Hicks] as a member of Council for Coosewatee in place of White Path, removed."[14] William Hicks was not only a Christian but a leading acculturationist. The oath installing George Hicks (William's son) as marshall for Coosewatee reads: "You do solemnly swear, by the Holy Evangelists of Almighty God, that you, as Marshall of Coosewatee district, will strictly support and observe the laws of the Cherokee Nation and to execute the decisions of the Courts and make collections [of taxes, debts, court fines] without favor or affection to any person, to the best of your knowledge and abilities, so help you God."[15] Circumstances seem to indicate that White Path was removed because he had said he would not enforce some of the new laws in his district and that George Hicks, a Christian, was

13. Ibid., p. 54.
14. Ibid., p. 67. The law does not say how or why White Path was removed. The *Cherokee Phoenix*, in reprinting the laws in 1828–29, omitted this one.
15. *Cherokee Laws*, p. 68.

specifically chosen to assert the centralized power of the Counc l over a district where local chiefs were unwilling to obey the new laws. White Path's rebellion may have been a last-ditch effort against tightening centralized authority over a people who, from long past, had honored the right of local towns and chiefs to go their own ways regardless of the National Council. This seems confirmed by the fact that the nationwide rebellion burst into the open in the spring of 1827, when the Council proposed adoption of a national constitution that would formally abolish all remnants of decentralized town government.

One of the most unpopular laws enacted in 1825 laid a poll tax upon every Cherokee to raise revenues for the expanding bureaucracy of the central government. While the conservatives had never opposed the idea of "speaking with one voice" against the whiteman, they may have felt that the poll tax, like the treasury loans to wealthy traders, was a manifestat on of a different kind of centralization, one which favored the rich over the poor. Furthermore, the fullbloods saw little need for the law of November 12, 1825, creating a new Cherokee capital (called New Town and later New Echota) with streets fifty feet wide and official buildings—to be erected at public expense—mapped out in a series of building lots around the main square; the lots were to be sold at auction.[16] The wealthy could bid high for these lots and thus be close to the seat of power. Similarly, the new printing press to be purchased with tribal funds would be in the hands of Christian converts and subject to missionary influence in what was printed (few traditionalists had the bilingual skill needed to edit the newspaper). That the Cherokees were divided into a wealthy upper class and a poor majority was not a new discovery in 1827, but the growing insensitivity of the rich toward the poor seemed new. In many respects the dirt farmers among the Cherokees faced the same problems as the poor whites in the Cotton Kingdom around them. They were tied to the rich by loyalty and politics but separated from power by a great social and economic barrier.

The missionaries, who in 1819 had been heroes to rich and poor in the nation for helping to stave off compulsory removal and for bringing free education to all, had within a decade become villains to the traditionalists by dividing the nation. Mission schools trained the sons of the rich to rise to power but failed to serve the sons of the poor. The missionaries preached self-reliance and "God helps those who help themselves," but the new political and economic order enabled the rich to pass laws to help them get rich while leaving the poor to pay taxes and help each other.

White Path's expulsion from the Council in 1825 did not trigger any widespread protest at that time, probably because the need for unity in the face of pending treaty negotiations was so great. Moreover, the action was against White Path only. The majority of the lower house still consisted of fullbloods. So the questions raised by White Path's impeachment smoldered

16. Ibid., pp. 62–63.

for another eighteen months until experience with the new laws and the decision to write a new constitution finally brought resentment to a head. This began when the Council voted in November 1826 to hold an election the following spring in order to choose delegates to a convention which would draft "a Constitution for the future Government of said Nation."[17] There is no record of the debate over this controversial issue. To win over the conservatives, the National Committee added a clause to this act stating that "the Constitution to be adopted by the Convention shall not in any degree go to destroy the rights and liberties of the free citizens of this Nation or to effect [sic] or impair the fundamental principles and laws by which the Nation is now governed."[18] According to the Moravians, the idea for a constitution arose because "it came to the attention of the last Council from many sides that many of their laws were contradictory and not only with one another but also with the laws of the United States" and this convinced the Council "of the need of a Constitution on which all their laws must be grounded."[19] Yet in another sense, the constitution was a natural consummation of the revitalization that had started in 1810. Some of the Cherokee elite may well have seen it as a more effective form of national separatism, an assertion of national sovereignty. But to most conservative Cherokees it seemed likely that the new constitution would create a Christianized Cherokee nation based on the principles of Anglo-American society and obliterating Cherokee traditions forever.

According to the director of the Office of Indian Affairs, Thomas L. McKenney, the adoption of a constitution was close to a declaration of independence. "They seek to be a People," he said.[20] He meant by this that the Cherokees had been only an inchoate group of "savages" doing their best to become civilized in order to merit integration into the American republic as individual citizens. He feared the constitution would prevent this. "It is much to be regretted," he told the secretary of war, "that the idea of Sovereignty should have taken such a deep hold of these people."[21] Most frontier whites agreed and thought the adoption of a constitution was a Cherokee bid for national independence, for in their own national experience, the United States Constitution had become a symbol of their successful establishment of independent nationhood. "They deserve to be respected and to be helped," McKenney said, in their effort to become civilized and Christianized, "but with the kindest regard to them . . . they ought not to be encouraged in forming a Constitution and Government within a State of the Republic to exist and operate independently of our laws. The sooner they

17. Ibid., p. 73.
18. Ibid., p. 76.
19. John Gambold to Schulz, April 14, 1827, MAS.
20. Thomas L. McKenney to James Barbour, November 29, 1827, BIA, M-21, roll 4, p. 153.
21. Thomas L. McKenney to James Barbour, February 20, 1827, BIA, M-21, roll 3, p. 390.

have the assurance that this cannot be permitted, the better it will be for them. If they will agree to come at once under our laws and be merged as citizens in our privileges, would it be objected against? But if they will not, then" let them "go into a Territory," like the area west of Arkansas, and live as they wish among other Indians.[22]

The Cherokee ruling elite, led essentially by John Ross, Charles Hicks, Elijah Hicks, Major Ridge, William Hicks, John Martin, Alexander McCoy, John Ridge, George Lowery, and Elias Boudinot, apparently believed that the establishment of a constitution based on that of the United States would be solid evidence of Cherokee maturity. If it was not an outright rejection of integration (or incorporation) into the United States (the denationalization program of the federal government), it was certainly a move to postpone that step indefinitely. Ross and Hicks had, like White Path, become national separatists, but they approached this solution by trying to show white Americans that the Cherokees were fully as capable as those in any state in the United States to be civilized, Christian, republicans, farmers, and capitalist entrepreneurs. The Cherokee elite did not see the issue as "sovereignty," for by treaty they had always been self-governing while they acknowledged the right of the United States to regulate their affairs with other nations. What the elite wished to prove was that the Cherokees were of right an independent state within the Union, just as Georgia or Tennessee were. In that respect, the Cherokee constitution was like a territorial constitution, the first step toward statehood. To some, this action was the shrewdest step the nation could take; to others it was its worst political blunder. Clearly the Cherokee elite hoped it would forestall the mounting effort of Jacksonians for the compulsory removal to the west.

Virtually all the missionaries considered the drafting of a constitution to be a logical and wise step toward stabilization, maturation, and the unification of this confused and divided tribe. Since the death of Colonel Return J. Meigs in 1823, the federal agency had ceased to play any significant role in the civilization process. During the futile negotiations for a land cession in October 1823 the federal commissioners, Campbell and Meriwether, had offered the Cherokees the possibility of "your becoming a Territory of the United States with the right of representation in Congress."[23] The Cherokees had then rejected that option because the commissioners insisted that such territorial status could be granted only after they removed as a nation from the East to land set aside for them in the West. Over the following three years, and especially after the near election of Jackson in 1824, the Cherokee leaders had obviously concluded that they should make their stand for territorial status on their homeland.

A groundswell of opposition to forming a constitution developed during

22. Thomas L. McKenney to James Barbour, November 28, 1827, BIA, M-21, roll 4, p. 153.
23. ASP II, 464–72.

the winter of 1826/27, and then a double misfortune befell the Cherokees, plunging them into an orgy of confusion. On January 6, 1827, Path Killer, the principal chief since 1811, died. Charles R. Hicks succeeded him and within two weeks he also died. With the election of delegates to the constitutional convention only four months away, the nation was suddenly shorn of its two oldest, most experienced, and trusted chiefs. Path Killer, born in 1749, had fought for the nation in the Revolutionary Era on the British side. In the guerrilla wars from 1783 to 1794 he had fought with Dragging Canoe and the Lower Towns. Then he had joined with James Vann and Charles Hicks in 1807 to oppose Doublehead and those ready to sell their land and move west. With the death of Black Fox in 1811, Path Killer assumed his role as chief of the reunited nation. He spoke no English and was trusted by the conservative, poor fullbloods to be their voice in the Council. So long as Path Killer was principal chief, the majority felt that their views were ably and firmly represented.

Charles Hicks was equally trusted and had always respected the views of Path Killer. He belonged to the transitional generation of chiefs who had led the nation in the first removal crisis, fought in the Creek War, successfully fought off the second removal effort. Though Christian, bilingual, wealthy, and the owner of twenty slaves, Hicks was unquestionably a patriot. Now with his death, an immense political vacuum prevailed at the very top, just when strong and steady leadership was needed most. From what faction among the current generation of younger chiefs would the new leadership emerge?

The Moravians, though sorry at the death of Hicks, their most famous and loyal convert, were convinced that God's hand lay in the death of Path Killer, for he might have sided with White Path. "It seems Providential to me that old Pathkiller was unharnessed at the same time as Bro. Hicks," wrote John Gambold, the head of the Moravian mission, "for the otherwise worthy man would, at his age—he must have been near to 80 years old—and because of his complete ignorance [lack of education] and because of the loss of support which he had in Bro. Hicks for many years, surely have been a poor instrument in the guidance of a new type of government, and his old co-chiefs, many of whom do not want to submit to changes in any way, would have made him still more unfit."[24] Gambold, like the missionaries of the other denominations, hoped that leadership would now fall to a younger generation of chiefs who were sympathetic to rapid acculturation and Christianization. According to law, until a new election was held, John Ross, as head of the National Committee, became principal chief protem; Major Ridge, as speaker of the lower house, became second principal chief protem; John Martin, a judge of the Supreme Court, took over Hicks's duties as treasurer protem. Because a constitution would soon alter the form of government, the elite argued that it was neither wise nor necessary to hold any

24. John Gambold to Schulz, April 14, 1827, MAS.

new national election. New chiefs would be formally elected under the new rules of the constitution, which it was hoped would be adopted in July 1827.

But to the fullblood majority, this interim government marked a serious threat to their effort to block the constitution, and if it were adopted, they might never again have a significant voice in shaping the nation's destiny. In this state of confusion, White Path and some of his friends issued a call for an extralegal council in February 1827: this act launched the rebellion. John Ross, though he was the chief architect of the proposed constitution, tended to be a cautious and pragmatic leader of the legitimate government. He evidently realized that White Path's frustrations reflected a widespread malaise too powerful to be put down by force. To the consternation of the missionaries, Ross refused to confront the rebels directly, as Major Ridge advised him to do. "John Ross, who should take the matter in hand," said the Moravian Johann Schmidt "has withdrawn completely. The other day he was asked by Major Ridge and other wise chiefs to make a motion that a general Council should be convened, but he declines to take any initiative."[25] The traditionalists proceeded to send delegates from all over the nation to the rebel council in Ellijay, and that council began to assert its own plans for the nation's future.

"Since Mr. Hicks' death," wrote the Reverend Samuel Worcester of Brainerd mission on March 29, 1827, "a dissatisfied party have held a Council at which they are said to have had some [representatives] from every district except one (not, however, *chiefs* from all)."[26] Worcester did not mention any attacks upon missions or Christian institutions by this dissatisfied party. He saw the extralegal council as an internal Cherokee quarrel over laws and policies. The council, he said, "took it upon themselves to say what should be and what should not be in regard to the affairs of Government and to repeal and enact laws." He provided no details as to what laws they repealed or enacted, but had they been directed against the missionaries he would certainly have reported them to his board. To him the resolutions of this council were essentially manifestoes of discontent, for the dissidents "took no measures to secure the execution of their laws." That is, he did not believe the rebels wanted to overthrow the existing government, even though in Worcester's opinion the protests represented the views of a large proportion of the Cherokees: "Though perhaps the majority of the people are dissatisfied with some features of the laws, yet for want of system and energetic leaders, I presume the faction is not to be dreaded." Why representatives of the majority of the people should be dismissed as a "faction," he did not explain.

Many years later, in the 1880s, James Wafford, a Christian Cherokee who had lived through the controversy, was asked by James Mooney to describe the significance of the rebellion. Wafford called it "a rebellion

25. Johann Schmidt to Benade, May 16, 1827, MAS.
26. Samuel Worcester to Jeremiah Evarts, March 29, 1827, ABCFM.

against the new code of laws" and said that White Path "preached the rejection of the new constitution, the discarding of Christianity and the whiteman's ways, and a return to the old tribal law and custom."[27] But Wafford's memory was faulty in several respects. First of all, he dated the rebellious council as having taken place in 1828; second, he implied that Charles Hicks was instrumental in putting it down, or at least so Mooney understood him; third, there is little contemporary evidence that the rebels wanted to drive out Christianity, though they undoubtedly wished to prevent its becoming the official or predominant religion of the nation. Samuel J. Mills, a close Cherokee friend of Samuel Worcester, attended the rebel council and signed its resolutions, but he evidently said nothing to Worcester of any attack upon Christianity. Mills was a Cherokee Christian exhorter for the American Board, and Worcester was shocked that he had participated in the rebellion; but though a rebel against the laws and constitution, Mills evidently made no effort to abandon his church connection at Brainerd mission nor did the members of that church take any steps to censure his behavior.[28] It does not seem, therefore (as Wafford implied), that one had to denounce Christianity in order to join White Path's Rebellion, at least, not initially.

Worcester, of course, was hardly privy to what went on at the council, though Mills could have told him. He may have been reassured by the behavior of John Ross. He reported that while the dissident movement was producing "much commotion in some parts of the nation," John Ross "appears to have very little apprehension" about it. Ross would naturally have played down the dangers of the movement in conversations with missionaries. Worcester concluded in March 1827 that the rebellion was a tempest in a teapot. "The party, though not small, is without a head and without system, and it appears to me probable that the attempt to form a system would at once destroy it." Possibly, he concluded his report to Boston, "it may excite so much of a spirit of opposition to the [Cherokee] Government as to occasion a serious difficulty in the execution of the laws" if the dissidents refused to obey those they disliked, but he saw no signs at that moment of a violent overthrow of the duly elected authorities.[29]

Significantly, Worcester did not identify White Path as the leader of the movement. From other accounts it appears that Kelechulah (or Ki li tsu li) may have been a more important figure and that Rising Fawn, Big Tiger, Cabbin Smith (or Big Cabin), Katchee, and Terrapin Head may have been equally prominent.[30] Moravian accounts of the rebellion also fail to mention White Path; they speak of Rising Fawn, Drowning Bear, and Big Tyger as

27. Mooney, *Myths*, pp. 113–14, 237.
28. Samuel Worcester to Jeremiah Evarts, March 29, 1827, ABCFM.
29. Ibid.
30. Others whose names were mentioned then and later as prominent among the dissidents were Ahchatoueh, Frying Pan, George Miller, Atosotokee, Wausasey, Amakelah, and Alexanders Sanders; see Payne Papers, VII, part 1, 70.

the leaders. The Moravians' account of the rebellion to their board was made in May 1827, and by that time the situation was more alarming. The rebels' extralegal council continued to meet, and Johann Schmidt now heard definite statements of antimission sentiment. The "sorcerers," or conjurors, were playing a more prominent role in the rebellion; Cherokee religious ceremonies were increasing the fervor of the dissidents, and new prophets were preaching about their visions, dreams, and spiritual messages from their ancestors or from the Great Spirit. One of the more "terrible" miraculous events about which the Moravians heard told of a woman who "was [recently] delivered of three children [triplets] which brought all their teeth with them into the world; when the first one was born, it is supposed to have spoken and called her to account for her godless way of life, etc." In this case "godless" meant lack of respect for the spirits and ceremonies of the old Cherokee religion and the term "etc." carried the implication that the new-born children were ready to bite or attack their mother for her failure to observe the rituals of the Cherokee religion.[31] How the new prophets interpreted the event Schmidt did not say, but clearly it symbolized a revolt against perverted maternal authority.

The Moravians also reported that "nightly there are dances organized and during the whole day they have Council" sessions to discuss their grievances. "No one trusts anybody any more" and some had threatened the lives of those who supported the new laws and norms. Judge Martin, the treasurer protem, "is being threatened with death and with having his house burned down." George Hicks, the marshall of Coosewatee District, was "being blamed for murder" (possibly in connection with law enforcement). One of the Moravian converts, "Brother Joshua," was mistreated by dissidents. There was even a rumor that Charles Hicks, before his death, had received a letter "in which he was told to turn over [to the traditionalists] all Christian Indians in the land in order to hang them."[32] According to Schmidt, the nation was close to anarchy in May, and some of the slaves were in revolt. "Houses are being set on fire by the Negroes and others are supposed to have poisoned one another." There were many runaway slaves and a number of murders. The dissidents, according to Schmidt's information, had "made Big Tiger the king" of the new extralegal council; "he is a sorcerer," the Moravians reported, "and an arrant thief and so also his sons." When the clerk of the National Committee, Alex McCoy, wrote to "the rebellious Council" seeking a conference with the elected chiefs, one of the rebel leaders, Rising Fawn, "who is the chief instigator among them . . . stepped on it" as a sign of contempt for the duly constituted rulers. "The whole Nation here is in the greatest ferment. The greater part wants to have the new laws abrogated and are for having the missions dissolved." Not one out of fifteen Cherokees was in favor of the new laws, Schmidt reported.

31. Johann Schmidt to Benade, May 16, 1827, MAS.
32. Ibid.

Most striking of all, some of the leading mixed-blood Christians were joining the conspiracy. "Elijah Hicks, the natural son of our departed Brother, C. R. Hicks, sent a piece of tobacco for smoking to the disaffected party, together with a promise that he was willing to become their leader."[33]

With due allowance for the fact that information reported by Schmidt came from frightened Cherokees sympathetic to the mission, it seems fair to conclude that by May 1827 the rebellion had developed antimission ramifications which Worcester was unaware of in March. Two weeks after his alarming letter in May, Schmidt again told his board that "the Nation is already so much in commotion" that he did not know "how it will all come out."[34] The Moravians had been complaining about the immense drain upon their time and supplies made by the expectation of traveling Cherokees that the mission would provide them with free meals, lodging, and feed for their horses; they were contemplating refusing such services in future unless paid for them. But because of the "commotion" Schmidt urged the board to take no action on this matter. To curtail this hospitality at the moment would simply exacerbate the antimission sentiment.

Opposition to the new constitution was also mentioned in the missionary letters, and as the time neared for the election of delegates to the convention which was to draw up the document, there was apprehension that efforts would be made to disrupt the voting. The election was scheduled for the end of May, and by May 10 the Reverend Isaac Proctor at Carmel mission was as frightened as Schmidt. "There is now existing in *this* nation a most *fearful* division among the Cherokees. The full Cherokees have risen up against the laws of the Nation and appear to desire their old form of Government."[35] Proctor, who had faced disturbances in his mission for several years, was convinced that "the old party are rather opposed to Missionaries" and "we have great reason to fear that something like what was witnessed in the Creek Nation [in their civil war in 1813] will be witnessed here." Proctor's estimate of the scope of the movement agreed with those of Worcester and Schmidt, that the rebels spoke for the majority. "This party is much the largest" part of the nation. However, he noted that "the other party are about to call a National Council to see if a reconciliation cannot be brought about." Evidently after three months of confusion among the ruling elite, Major Ridge had finally prevailed upon John Ross to act.

Writing two weeks after Proctor, Worcester believed that the tension was still mounting as the election of delegates neared. "There has been still greater alarm since I wrote respecting the opposition party," he said on May 28, but he saw signs that it would dissipate because "the leaders of this party have begun to quarrel with each other."[36] The Reverend William Chamber-

---

33. Ibid.
34. Johann Schmidt to Schulz, June 5, 1827, MAS.
35. Isaac Proctor to Jeremiah Evarts, May 10, 1827, ABCFM.
36. Samuel Worcester to Jeremiah Evarts, May 28, 1827, ABCFM.

lain wrote in May that the dissidents could be called "the heathen party" because they were made up of fullbloods opposed to Christianization. "At this time," he alleged, this party was "making a grand and united effort to destroy the government and drive [true] religion and all improvements from the Nation." He had faith, however, in God's providential care of his church: "As it is darkness fighting against light, we trust they will not prevail."[37] Probably by this time it was evident that the rebel council had specifically attacked some of the pro-Christian laws in its manifestoes, but none of the rebels' own statements survive. If written at all, they were probably written in Sequoyan.

Despite the missionaries' fears, the election of delegates to the constitutional convention took place at the end of May without violence. Perhaps the dissidents simply boycotted the election or perhaps the offer of the elected Council to hold a reconciliation meeting following the election had produced a temporary truce. One important aspect of the election deserves mention. The Council of October 1826 had nominated slates of candidates from each of the eight elective districts to run as delegates. The nominees were predominantly persons of education, mixed ancestry, and speakers of English. The convention would do its business in English and the constitution would be written in English. These nominations may themselves have been one of the major causes of the unrest. In any case, those elected in May 1827 were preponderantly from the upper, educated class. Only four of the twenty-four were fullbloods. All but nine could at least write their names in English. The most spirited contest took place in Coosewatee District, where White Path lived. Here Kelechulah ran against John Ridge. Kelechulah was an aged chief, a fullblood married to a fullblood, a man who owned no slaves and spoke no English. He had long service on the Council and was several times chosen as a delegate to serve in treaty talks for the nation. The result of this district election was a tie vote. Worcester reported that Kelechulah "has been considered as the head of the opposition party." He also reported the important fact that Kelechulah "denies having thought of a rebellion."[38] Evidently he considered it just a protest by the majority against an unrepresentative minority. Because the fullbloods dominated the Coosewatee District it would appear that the tie vote between Kelechulah and John Ridge resulted from the failure of many citizens to vote. However, the election law required a *viva voce* vote and this may have inhibited some rebels from voting. Nevertheless, in the runoff election Kelechulah defeated John Ridge.

Kelechulah is not known to have ever publicly opposed missions, but a number of those elected as delegates had expressed hostility toward them in recent years. Some were apostates from mission churches. Their apostasy may have accounted for their election. John Beamer, a delegate elected from Etowah District, was a wealthy headman of that town; he had joined the

37. William Chamberlain, Journal, May 3, 1827, ABCFM.
38. Samuel Worcester to Jeremiah Evarts, July 4, 1827, ABCFM.

mission church but left it when the minister attacked conjuring, ballplays, and all-night dances.[39] John Martin, elected as a delegate from Coosewatee, was a wealthy slaveholder; he had first welcomed the missionaries to his home and sent his daughters and a niece to the mission school at Carmel. But in 1826 Martin "was quite opposed to missions and [to the] minister" there; he withdrew his children from the school and hired a tutor for them.[40] Thomas Foreman, elected as a delegate from Amohee District, had been very friendly to the missionaries until the fall of 1825, when he and his brother Stephen became "inveterate enemies of the gospel, and were it not for the benefit their children are deriving, they would have doubtless used all their influence to remove missionaries from their vicinity."[41] Thomas Pettit, a delegate from Etowah District and a headman of Etowah, was among a group who were decidedly "unfriendly" to the mission there and disturbed the church meetings at Hightower in 1825.[42] Moody Hall reported in 1825 that two of Pettit's sons had threatened his life in an effort to drive him out of Carmel.[43] Even John Ross, elected as a delegate from Chickamauga District and chosen president of the constitutional convention, was reported by the missionaries at Brainerd in 1825 to have "manifested great coldness" toward them. The Reverend Frederick Elsworth said that Ross "is not friendly to the mission" and accused Ross's brother Lewis of being equally hostile.[44]

The election of these men who had turned cool toward Christianization or at least toward the American Board's version of it—even though all of them had been part of the Council for many years and instrumental in passing the new laws as well as supporters of the constitution—seems to indicate two things about the rebellion. First, it was of sufficient strength to cause some efforts by the mixed-blood leaders to reexamine their own zeal for Christianization. Second, the antimission sentiment that had begun in 1824 had influenced members of the mixed-blood elite as well as the fullblood common man. Perhaps most important, election of these men who had been part of the Council for so long indicated that the rebels were not opposing individual leaders but the general policy they had adopted. They were still willing to trust the elite provided they adhered more closely to the will of the majority. In any case, it is not adequate to describe the rebels simply as "fullbloods," "pagan," "antimission," or "ignorant poor." No single label will suffice. The Cherokee people were, by 1827, too complex a society to be described in terms of the simplistic factionalism between a

39. Isaac Proctor to Jeremiah Evarts, July 28, 1827, ABCFM.
40. Isaac Proctor to Jeremiah Evarts, February 12, 1827, ABCFM.
41. William Holland, "Report on Candy's Creek Mission," April 1828, ABCFM.
42. Isaac Proctor, "Annual Report for Hightower Mission," July 20, 1825; Daniel Butrick, Journal, May 11, 1825, ABCFM.
43. Moody Hall to Jeremiah Evarts, October 4, 1825. ABCFM.
44. Frederick Elsworth to Jeremiah Evarts, February 7, 1827, ABCFM.

"pagan party" and a "Christian party." And in different respects both sides were patriots and nationalists; they differed over means more than ends.

The reconciliation meeting of the rebels and the elected council members took place on June 25, ten days before the convention was to start. Worcester noted on June 12 that "the commotion among the people is subsiding"; he thought there was hope for "conciliating the disaffected."[45] Ard Hoyt reported somewhat overoptimistically a month later:

> [God] has settled the tumult of the people in this nation. A special council was called last month with reference to the defections. The chiefs of the old school [the dissidents] all succumb[ed] and have pledged themselves in an open council to do all in their power to still the people and pursue civilization. The delegates directed by the [last] fall's Council to be appointed to prepare and propose to the next fall's council a constitution or form of government, have been appointed [elected?] and are now in convention pursuing their business without interruption. Thus this portentous cloud appears to have carried over without destructive wind or hail, and we do hope it has done something toward clearing the political atmosphere of this struggling people.[46]

But it was not quite so simple. What had happened at the meeting between the rebellious council and the duly elected council was that some of the dissident leaders had "succumbed" or given in while others had not. "A committee of conference" had been appointed by the two groups. John Ross, Major Ridge, Going Snake, Elias Boudinot, and Alex McCoy had represented the legitimate council; it is not known which members of the dissident council were on this committee. After wrestling with the matter for five days, the committee issued a long resolution which was signed by nine of the dissidents: Kelechalah, Cabbin Smith, Terrapin Head, Ahchatoueh, Katchee, Frying Pan, George Miller, Atosotokee, Tyger. It was notably *not* signed by White Path, Rising Fawn, and Drowning Bear among other dissidents. "Whereas dissatisfaction at some of the public laws of the nation has been manifested in the proceedings of certain individuals who did call meetings at Eh,la,chay,e [Ellijay] Town for the object of supporting the view of their party," the resolution of this conference committee began, and whereas these meetings resulted in actions "calculated to produce party feelings injurious to the public welfare," therefore it was agreed to confer upon the problems. As a result of that conference, "the undersigned" members of "the dissatisfied party" had made three agreements: first, "that harmony and unanimity be strongly recommended to the people in supporting the public laws of the nation"; second, "that all meetings of opposition be discouraged;" and third, that "if any of the laws should be considered unwholesome, it shall be the duty and privilege of those wishing amendments respectfully to petition the General Council" or to "instruct their immediate representatives" to work for reform within the established system.[47]

45. Samuel Worcester to Jeremiah Evarts, June 12, 1827, ABCFM.
46. Ard Hoyt to Jeremiah Evarts, July 16, 1827, ABCFM.
47. Payne Papers. VII, part 1, 69–70.

However, the depth of resentment aroused over the past three years and the disquiet over the new constitution were not so easily allayed. The Moravians noted that this reconciliation council was only sparsely attended: "A council is being held in Newton since June 28, but up to the present only very few have come for it." Johann Schmidt believed "the prospects are bad" for a resolution of the schism.[48] Apparently the old elite triumphed in the end because the rebels were divided.

The constitutional convention was to meet at New Echota on July 4, a date obviously chosen for its symbolic value. Evidently to alleviate the continuing animosities, the legitimate Council met and voted on July 3 to certify that those members of the dissatisfied party who had been elected delegates would be given their rightful places as delegates. "Keelechuleeh and Katchee are duly elected members of the National Council and the Little Turtle is duly elected as a member . . . from Chattoogee District."[49] Nevertheless, the next day John Ridge told Worcester that the future of the convention was still in peril and "expressed doubts whether the Convention would be deferred."[50] General John Cocke, who had been appointed by John Quincy Adams to try to negotiate a new treaty in the fall of 1827 ceding more land or agreeing to removal, decided that it would be useful to visit the nation to discover whether he could take advantage of its divisions. On July 1 he wrote in his journal, "I learn considerable excitement now exists among the Indians as to what policy should be persued; the mixed blooded are now, and have been for some time, at the head of affairs and passed laws so contrary to ancient customs that the native Indian is ready to revolt."[51] Always ready to fish in muddy waters to the government's advantage, Cocke went to New Echota and began nosing around. On July 7 he wrote in his journal, "Learned from E. Boudinot, Clerk of the late National Convention, that the Council adjourned without settling their business amicably and that some of the old Indians are very much dissatisfied and intend to raise opposition to their new mode of Government by Constitution."[52] Clearly the council of reconciliation had not wholly settled the problem. As anxiety increased, rumors circulated to the effect that the elected authorities might use force against recalcitrant rebels. The Moravians heard early in July that the legitimate council had decided "that every leader of an extra council should be punished with a hundred lashes."[53]

Nevertheless, the constitutional convention met on July 4 and it continued to meet until it completed its work on July 24. Apparently three of

48. Johann Schmidt to Schulz, July 2, 1827, MAS.
49. Payne Papers, VII, part 1, 70.
50. Samuel Worcester to Jeremiah Evarts, July 4, 1827, ABCFM.
51. John Cocke, Journal, BIA, M-234, roll 72, #0245−0262.
52. John Cocke, Journal, BIA, M-234, roll 72, #0246.
53. Johann Schmidt to Schulz, July 18, 1827, MAS. The rumor was not entirely untrue, for in July 1828, as a result of continuing rebellion, the Council did pass such a law, though it was not signed by the principal chief until November. *Cherokee Laws*, p. 117.

the twenty-four delegates elected resigned in opposition, or never appeared, for only twenty-one signed the document. This seems to indicate a struggle within the convention, but the Cherokees were careful not to let this become known. On July 31, Schmidt optimistically told his mission board, "The Cherokee Nation completed its counseling last Sunday; all the dissension has been put aside and they have a written Constitution according to the form of the United States Constitution."[54] Trying to explain to the board how such a frightening event could have been so peacefully concluded, John Gambold wrote, "[T]he dissatisfied parties, which had almost threatened a Revolution, allowed themselves to be convinced and solemnly joined in the position on maintaining the existing laws. Therefore at the next Council in October, there will be correct discussions."[55] Gambold was probably right that most of the dissidents had "allowed themselves to be convinced." We have no record of what arguments convinced them. No doubt the fact that General Cocke was planning to push a new federal removal effort in the fall had much to do with pulling the factions back together. It was also likely that the governing elite had made some concessions to the dissidents and explained more clearly the reasons why they were trying so hard to convince white Americans that the Cherokees were the most civilized tribe in America. The new laws, they may have said, were designed for the outside world and should not be taken at face value within the nation. Promises were probably made by the ruling elite to the effect that the missionary aggression would be checked and that the religious practices of those who held to the old ways would not be hindered. Concessions were essential in order to avoid a division which might lead to a new migration westward by those dissatisfied with acculturation or, worse, to a disgruntled faction which General Cocke might take advantage of to obtain a treaty of some kind.

Examination of the constitution drafted and signed by twenty-one delegates on July 26, 1827, indicates some of the compromises.[56] For example, the constitutional oath of office made no mention of God, the holy evangelists, the Bible, or religion. It simply required adherence to the constitution and loyalty "to the interest and prosperity of the Nation." The constitution prohibited ministers of the Gospel from holding any political office. In addition, no whiteman (and no black or descendant of "the African race" by either parent) could hold office: "No person except a natural born citizen shall be eligible to the office of Principal Chief," and the chief was to have three counselors to assist him in decision-making—an effort to indicate that experienced fullbloods would be part of the decision-making process. A bill of rights within the constitution guaranteed "free exercise of religious worship," and the preamble expressed "humility and gratitude [to] the goodness of the Sovereign Power of the Universe." No specific reference

---

54. Johann Schmidt to Schulz, July 31, 1827, MAS.
55. John Gambold to Schulz, August 3, 1827, MAS.
56. The constitution is printed in *Cherokee Laws*, pp. 118–27.

was made to Christianity or to any preference for Christianity over the old religion. Studied ambiguity allowed outsiders to interpret the constitution as moving in the direction of "a Christian nation" while allowing the majority of Cherokees to sustain the old religion as the religion of the nation.

One of the most controversial clauses in the constitution concerned the need for public schools. This paragraph was modeled on Article III of the Massachusetts Constitution, and Massachusetts at that time still retained the remnants of the religious establishment inherited from the Puritans. The clause began, "Religion, morality and knowledge being necessary to good government, the preservation of liberty and the happiness of mankind, schools and the means of education shall forever be encouraged in the Nation." However, nothing required that these be religious schools or that they be sustained by missionaries, and some years later (after removal) the Cherokee Nation established a secular public school system which was under the direction of the Council, not the missionaries.

The clause which may have annoyed the fullbloods most stated that "No person who denies the being of God or a future state of rewards and punishment shall hold office in the civil department of this Nation." However, the "speakers," or translators, in translating the document into Cherokee, probably rendered the word "God" as "Great Spirit." The Cherokees had accepted the notion that one God governed all people, and they could reconcile the concept of rewards and punishment after death with their own belief in the wandering ghosts who had offended the Great Spirit in some way. In any case, there is no known case where this clause ever disqualified any traditionalist from office even though missionaries cited it to demonstrate that the Cherokees accepted the basic tenets of the Christian faith.

The constitution was modeled closely upon that of the federal and state governments of the United States; judged as a measure of Cherokee political maturity, it was a sound and workable document. It lasted the Cherokees until the Civil War and grew out of a generation of political experience. In most respects it simply codified existing statutes and practices. Despite the "near revolution" that year, the Cherokees remained sufficiently united to withstand the government's treaty negotiations in the fall of 1827. Cocke returned to Washington empty-handed, to the great discomfort of John Quincy Adams. Though the rebellion died down, it never wholly ceased; certainly, the revival of the old religion continued. When the Baptist missionary Evan Jones was asked by the marshall of the Valley Towns region to "attend at the town house tomorrow to read the New Constitution to the people" and explain it to them, he arrived to find "a great part of the inhabitants attending the Adoneeskee or Conjuror. They were just going to [the river] to bathe, it being the first day of their new year, i.e., of eating new food, the produce of the present season."[57] He was not pleased by this conjunction of events.

57. Evan Jones, Journal, July 25, 1827, BFMB. Jones read and answered questions about the constitution at a series of meetings from July 25 to August 12. He reported no

Some indication of the still rankling feelings of the rebels and the uneasiness of the ruling elite can be found in the statements by the first candidates who stood for election to office under the new constitution. Though adopted in October 1827, the constitution did not go into effect until October 1828. It may mark some censure of John Ross and his strong stand for acculturation that when the Council met in the fall of 1827 to choose an interim chief until the first elections took place under the new constitution, it chose William Hicks, the brother of Charles, to be principal chief. Ross was demoted to second principal chief. Elijah Hicks was named president of the National Committee.[58]

The elections to the first legislature under the constitution did not take place until August 1828. By that time the *Cherokee Phoenix*, the official national newspaper, had begun publication. Its first issue appeared on February 28, 1828; some of its columns were printed in English and some in the Sequoyan syllabary. Several leaders used the paper to express their views on the direction the nation should take and the kinds of persons who should be elected to office. These statements indicate that the debate over acculturation was far from settled. Utaletah, apparently a mixed blood, wrote on May 6, 1828, that for him the overriding concern was national "unity." The Cherokees must combine with "one object, the preservation of ourselves as a free and sovereign people, observing strictly our relations with the United States with whom alone we are connected by solemn treaties." He noted that unity was now difficult because of the sharp divisions within the nation. "The art of legislation is little understood by a majority of the nation." The laws were numerous and complex. Utaletah proposed that "the Committee [the upper house] should be composed of men of education and good knowledge in the affairs of our nation, while the Council [the lower house] should be composed of full blooded Cherokees known for their love of country, the land of our forefathers, and also celebrated for their good natural sense, justice and firmness." Confident of the ability of his people to combine the interests of the ordinary citizens with those of the "men of education," Utaletah spoke with optimism of the future: "Our nation as a political body has reached an important crisis and bids fair for rapid progress in the path of civilization, the arts and sciences, while at the same time we can say with no ordinary degree of exultation, that agriculture is gradually gaining an ascendancy amongst us equalled by no other Indian tribe."[59] The critical issue of

---

dissatisfaction with the constitution in this fullblood area of the nation, but over the next five years he, as an itinerant evangelist, encountered continued opposition to evangelism and so did his native assistants. See his letters of December 11, 1830, and March 17, 1831, to Lucius Bolles, BFMB, for examples.

58. The election of Elijah Hicks (brother-in-law of John Ross and son of Charles Hicks) as president of the National Committee in October 1827, given his overtures to the rebels in May 1827, also seems significant. The elected authorities may also have decided to delay implementation of the constitution for a year in order to ease the disquiet over the transition to the new form of government.

59. *Cherokee Phoenix*, May 6, 1828.

the election was to combine the interests of those ready to push on with civilization and those satisfied with things as they were. Utaletah felt this could be done by giving each interest control of one part of the bicameral legislature and forcing them to cooperate.

John Huss, a fullblood Christian convert who served as an exhorter for the American Board, wrote to the *Phoenix* to say he disagreed with Utaletah. Such a partisan division of the legislature "would be a great evil, for it would appear like creating a division among the people, and we know the remark often made by the unlettered, that those who talk English are overbearing." The upper and lower houses would be continually at odds. "Dissensions" would increase. While there were two different perspectives in Cherokee affairs, Huss argued, "it would be well that they should be mixed" in both houses, for then both factions would learn better how to understand one another's views and to cooperate. "If we be divided into parties, we shall be liable to lose our territory." Some did not like the new constitution, he noted, but it could be a force for unity: "Wherever a people preserve a regular system of government that community is firmly established. So let it be with the Cherokee."[60]

Elijah Hicks, president of the upper house, in a letter printed in July 1828, took another position. No longer sympathetic with the dissidents, he insisted on the unqualified leadership of the acculturated. Not only did he intend to "support strenuously the election of a Principal Chief who shall be a learned man," but also he wished the second principal chief to be of the same caliber. There was no need for a balance between the educated and uneducated. "Our advanced situation requires a learned man at the head of our government," and as many learned men as possible to work with him in every department of the government. However, Hicks took care to say that such men must not be simply the tools of the missionaries nor cater to their demands. He found serious fault with the missionaries; their twelve mission stations were "splendid establishments on the choicest lands," but they were not providing the best form of education. Many of their schools were small and inadequate; others were located in the wrong places. He proposed a closer supervision of the missions in order to control their size and location, to regulate their curriculums, and to inspect their effectiveness: "We have permitted them to settle on our land without a special understanding of the duration of time for their continuance." Hicks implied that a learned chief would be better able to cope with and regulate the missionaries in order to make certain that they served national ends, but he considered that a general assault upon missions by ignorant men would only cause trouble.[61]

Major Ridge, aware of the continuing strength of the opposition to

60. Ibid., July 2, 1828.

61. Ibid., July 21, 1828. The editor headed this letter "Address to the Citizens of Coosewatee District," so it may have been written to Hicks's constituents and then copied for the paper by the editor.

acculturation, wrote to the *Phoenix* urging the people to choose their representatives with great care, "for to elect hastily such men as will be too speedy imitators of white people would not be well." It should be remembered, he said paternalistically, that "many are yet without knowledge" and were not ready to adopt the whiteman's ways. "It is not right to proceed hastily and form laws which people do not understand." In homely images he explained the danger they faced: "If a child beginning to walk attempts to run, he soon falls and cries. And if a man working in the field does not perform his work thoroughly, he goes over much ground indeed, but the field which he has passed over is still full of weeds." So it would be if the Cherokees moved ahead too fast. Ridge would not turn the nation over to the learned men, who were overly eager to adopt new ways. Some balance must be kept between the old ways and the new. Federal treaty "commissioners will probably be here at the time of the next Fall Council," he warned, and they would try to get their land from them. They would try, as in the past, to use their divisions against them. This must be avoided at all costs.[62]

It is difficult to tell what effect these counsels printed in the *Phoenix* (and no doubt repeated in many general discussions) had upon the voters, but when the election took place in August 1828 a number of the dissidents were chosen to the Council. White Path was elected from Coosewatee (Kelechulah had died in February 1828). Thomas Foreman and George Sanders entered the lower house with White Path. John Martin became chief justice of the Supreme Court. Alex McCoy remained as clerk of the National Council. Nevertheless, a surprising number of those elected were strongly promissionary. The Reverend Isaac Proctor was pleased to note that "there are forty legislators elected in all and more than one-fifth are pious."[63] By "pious" he meant that they were Christian converts. In the nation as a whole, less than 6 percent of the people were converts at this time, most of them women (who could not vote). On the other hand, the Reverend William Potter noted that "many of the members" of the new legislature were ignorant men, "entirely unacquainted with public business." He expressed to his mission board serious doubts that the new constitution could work with such uneducated men in office. "Permit me confidentially to say to you that I have never viewed the nation in as much danger as at present."[64]

Though outward unity was achieved in the face of external threats to national security, antimission activity had by no means ceased. Two days after the constitutional convention adjourned, Johann Schmidt wrote that "Adversaries of the Gospel are not lacking" and that in the district of Chatooga "old Drowning Bear . . . tries to convince everyone that the teaching of the white people is not suitable for Indians."[65] In April 1828,

62. *Cherokee Phoenix*, June 24. 1818.
63. Isaac Proctor to Jeremiah Evarts, September 3, 1828, ABCFM.
64. William Potter to Jeremiah Evarts, September 29, 1828, ABCFM.
65. Johann Schmidt to Schulz, July 30, 1827, MAS.

Dr. Elizur Butler reported that the traditionalist Cherokees near Haweis mission sometimes "threaten our lives but more frequently [threaten] to whip us."[66] In June 1828 a Cherokee convert named Downing was exhorting some Cherokees twenty miles from Haweis when he "was stoned" by auditors amidst "considerable disturbance."[67] Two years later the Reverend Daniel Butrick stated that at the town of Running Water some of the Cherokees threatened to meet him with loaded guns if he appeared to keep a preaching engagement. He came anyway but was not disturbed.[68]

As a result of such efforts to curb Christian evangelism and prevent freedom of worship, one of the first acts of the new government, adopted November 12, 1828, was to pass a law fining "any person or persons [who] shall interrupt by misbehaviour any congregation of Cherokee or white citizens assembled at any place for the purpose of Divine worship." The fine was ten dollars upon conviction; slaves who interrupted a meeting were to receive thirty-nine lashes.[69] The law did not deter such actions, however, and there is no evidence of its being enforced. Six days after this act, John Ross approved an act passed on July 3, 1828, to punish with one hundred lashes "any person or persons whatsoever who shall be found guilty of forming unlawful meetings with intent to create factions against the peace and tranquility of the people or to encourage rebellion against the laws and Government of the Cherokee Nation."[70] This was the last act in White Path's Rebellion.

At this same Council extensive debates took place over a proposal by John Gunter to restrict and regulate the missionaries. "Mr. Gunter moved that missionary establishments be placed on the same grounds as [any business of] citizens of the nation and [be] required to obtain permits." He believed that it was "inconsistent" to allow missions to bring whitemen into the nation at will when citizens of the nation had to obtain permission of the legislature to bring in a whiteman to work for them. As things stood, for example, parents who wanted to start a secular school and hire a white tutor or teacher would be regulated by the Council, but mission stations had no regulations. Apparently the effort in 1823—24 to impose such regulations upon the missionaries had never been enacted into law. Gunter's motion was

66. Elizur Butler to Jeremiah Evarts, April 7, 1828, ABCFM.

67. Elizur Butler to Jeremiah Evarts, June 5, 1828, ABCFM; Downing was preaching inside a house and the house was stoned. Butler also reported, "My family is occasionally assaulted by those who are intoxicated which makes it necessary to spend most of my time at home." At Haweis, where he preached, people "on the outskirts of the congregation were inclined to make disturbances" and "showed their opposition to the work of the Lord." In general, he noted, there was "considerable disturbance made by our enemies."

68. Daniel Butrick, Journal, September 8, 1830, ABCFM. He also said that at Hightower "we have many severe trials, some especially on account of conjuring."

69. *Cherokee Laws*, p. 107.

70. Ibid., p. 117. It is not clear why this law was passed in July but not approved until November. Perhaps the Council in July was not considered an official session of the legislature or perhaps Ross hoped the dissidence would subside and the law would not be necessary.

opposed by Richard Taylor and Joseph Vann (of Coosewatee), who "argued on the blessing of education and the good which has been produced by mission establishments." The motion was tabled pending an investigation of what privileges in general had been granted to mission agencies when they were first allowed into the nation. Apparently it was never brought up for further discussion.[71] However, the Council did act upon a recommendation made to it by the first and second principal chiefs suggesting the appointment of visiting committees to inspect the mission schools and make a report to the Council each year on their effectiveness: "[T]here shall be appointed by the Principal Chief of the Cherokee Nation, two committees, of two members each, one in each judicial circuit, whose duty it shall be to visit the different schools in the Nation . . . once a year and to report to the General Council annually on the number of scholars, progress of education, etc."[72] This initial effort of the Cherokees to gain some control over the mission schools would have led to efforts to regulate their size, location, and curriculums had not the third removal crisis interfered. Though unsuccessful, the fact that the effort was made was probably the result of White Path's Rebellion.

It might seem that the election of John Ross as first principal chief and George Lowery as second principal chief by the new legislature on October 17, 1828, constituted a final victory for the party of acculturation. Both men favored the policy of competing with the whites on their own terms. Yet they had also learned something from the rebellion. Ross's coolness toward the American Board after 1824 was an effort to dissociate himself from the most aggressive of the mission agencies. When his niece Mary Coody married a Methodist itinerant, the Reverend Nicholas D. Scales, Ross had an excuse to join that more democratic, easygoing denomination.[73] His decision in 1829 probably reflects a change of perspective toward the notion of total transformation through Christianization. But it was not a full conversion. When Elizur Butler made some discreet inquiries about the

71. This scrap of legislative debate is in the Payne Papers, VII, part 1, 91–92, dated November 4, 1828. Evidently, detailed records were kept of this and perhaps other Council debates, but they have not been preserved. For the act regulating the licensing of whites admitted to the nation (to which Gunter was proposing this amendment), see *Cherokee Laws*, p. 110.

72. The message of William Hicks and John Ross to the new legislature suggesting the creation of visiting school committees (dated October 13, 1828) is in the *Cherokee Phoenix*, October 22, 1828. In the same message they recommended "suitable provisions for the erection of a National Academy at New Echota" and a committee to investigate why the federal government had not yet sold the land set aside by the nation in 1819 for a school fund. See *Cherokee Laws*, p. 94.

73. For the Rosses' decision to become Methodists, see *Christian Advocate*, 4 (November 13, 1829): 42. Ross's hostility toward the American Board was also symbolized, in the opinion of the missionaries, by his decision to appoint William Coody (a Methodist) to replace himself as postmaster in the area of Brainerd (when Ross moved to Georgia in the spring of 1827). Ross knew that the missionaries hoped to have one of themselves appointed because it would have saved them postage costs. Ross also seems to have forced a Methodist printer to be hired for the national printing press at New Echota over the recommendation of a man whom Samuel Worcester recommended and who, in Worcester's opinion, had superior competence.

significance of Ross's action, a relative said he "made no pretensions to a change of heart" when he joined the Methodist altar call; "he only joined the Society as a Seeker." Probably, Butler concluded, "he never will experience a change of heart, and as his publick conduct is as moral as most methodist members, will continue a regular member of the church during his life."[74] It never occurred to the American Board that there might have been some political significance to this decision, or that Ross may have wished to keep a little more of his Cherokee identity than a conversion to Congregationalism and Calvinism would have allowed him. In addition, because the Methodists received no federal money to support their work, he may have thought they would be less acquiescent to government policy and more free to side with the Cherokees against removal. Certainly it seemed advisable to have a relationship with a southern and a frontier mission agency rather than to rely solely on a New England agency whose members and supporters were notably anti-Jackson.

With respect to the Methodist circuit riders in the nation, Ross's hunch proved right. But with respect to the Tennessee Annual Conference, he was very wrong. When the third removal crisis began in 1829, the Cherokees discovered that none of the mission agencies could hold out for long against their own ethnocentric and nationalistic feelings. Somewhat ironically, Ross's strongest support in his strenuous effort to save his country between 1829 and 1839 came from those ordinary Cherokees, and especially from the fullbloods, who had supported White Path's Rebellion. But of course these rebels had always considered themselves the real patriots.

74. Elizur Butler to David Greene, February 27, 1830. Ross did remain a Methodist all his life and attended church regularly. When his first wife died, however, he married a Quaker from Pennsylvania. There is no evidence that Ross's first wife, a fullblood named Quatie, ever became a Christian. Why Ross, who was only one-eighth Cherokee, married a fullblood is one of the many mysteries of his life. For Ross's decided preference for the Methodists after 1824, see Elizur Butler to David Greene, February 27, 1830, ABCFM, in which Butler said, "Formerly his influence was exerted in favor of the ABCFM but for six years it has been in favour of the Methodists. I mean by this he now gives preference to the methodist society."

The American Board and the Removal Crisis, 1829—1833

I had rather suffer with and for the Cherokees than to discourage them by having it said that the Board and its missionaries could not trust the Supreme Court of the United States.

Rev. Samuel A. Worcester, New Echota, January 28, 1831

The New York Observer denominates us martyrs in the cause of *liberty*. If we are not suffering for the sake of righteousness, let us yield the contest.

Rev. Samuel A. Worcester from his jail cell in Milledgeville Penitentiary, Georgia, November 14, 1831

The collision course between the forces of white American nationalism and those of Cherokee nationalism in the 1820s caught the missionaries unprepared. Under George Washington's original national policy of civilization and integration of the Indians, the missionaries had no difficulty justifying their activities, but once white Americans doubted the feasibility of integration and the Cherokees countered by moving toward a separatist position, the missionaries were placed in a painful dilemma. If they had abandoned their schools and vocational training entirely and concentrated on saving souls, they might have solved this, but their government subsidies were for education and not for evangelism, and they considered the subsidies necessary. Furthermore, they could never separate their zeal for Indian Christianization from the necessity of Indian civilization. And civilization had social as well as political implications. The first inkling they had of a conflict between their work and the political interest of the voters of America (whom they assumed to be favorable toward both Christianization and civilization of the Indians) came in 1824, when the Georgians forced a congressional inquiry into the value of continuing the Education Fund which supported Indian missions. The Georgians believed that the fund was working against the compact they had made with Thomas Jefferson in 1802 to remove all Indians from within Georgia's boundaries and give their land to Georgia "as soon as the same can be peaceably obtained on reasonable terms."[1] But this crisis passed when the House

---

1. See Ulrich B. Phillips, *Georgia and State Rights* (Washington, 1902), p. 34. This compact was part of the price Jefferson willingly paid to obtain for the federal government Georgia's cession of her western territory.

Committee on Indian Affairs, chaired by Congressman John McLean of Ohio, reported that the law was "judicious," "benevolent," and reflective of the "high sense of moral duty" which Americans felt toward civilizing the Indians.[2] Congress declined to repeal the law, and the missionaries relaxed. But it proved to be only the first of many efforts by the Georgians to undermine the missionary effort.

The missionaries received a more devastating shock to their self-image as dedicated redeemers of a benighted people in November 1828, when John Quincy Adams's secretary of war, Peter B. Porter, publicly denounced Indian missionaries in a message to Congress. Porter described them as self-interested opponents of the president's Indian colonization (that is, removal) plan. Using (or misusing) government funds, they had created, Porter said, a small faction of "half-educated" Indians who loudly and maliciously opposed this benevolent plan. Porter described the missionaries as "agents [who] are operating, more secretly to be sure, but not with less zeal and effort, to prevent such emigration." Their opposition did not arise so much from pious concern for the Indians' welfare, Porter said; it arose because "missionaries and teachers with their families . . . having acquired, principally by the aid of this [education] fund, very comfortable establishments, are unwilling to be deprived of them by the removal of the Indians."[3]

The Adams—Porter colonization bill never came to a vote in Congress because Andrew Jackson's election made Adams a lame-duck president. Most advocates of Indian removal realized that Jackson would have his own plan and preferred to let him bring that forward. The difference between Adams's answer to "the Indian question" and Jackson's was clear. Adams was willing to give the Indians a choice and to protect their treaty rights while at the same time exerting every possible inducement and pressure to negotiate a removal treaty. Jackson, who had long since said the federal government ought not to bother making treaties with "savages" defeated in just wars, was prepared to force the Indians to remove and would deny them any protection under their treaty rights so long as they refused to sign an agreement to do so. Adams, through the efforts of Thomas L. McKenney, had negotiated a treaty with the Western Cherokees in Arkansas in May 1828 which McKenney believed would effect removal of that tribe if properly managed (and perhaps help Adams win reelection). Between 1780 and 1828, some 4,000—5,000 Cherokees had voluntarily left their homeland to live in Arkansas Territory.

2. ASP II, 437—39, and R. Pierce Beaver, *Church, State and the American Indians*, pp. 75—76. Beaver states that it was in response to this inquiry that the American Board, under the influence of the Reverend Jedidiah Morse, petitioned Congress in favor of colonizing the Indians west of the Mississippi, a plan Morse had advocated in his *Report to the Secretary of War*, written in 1820 (published in 1822); but in this petition no particular Indians were specified, and Morse had implied that the civilized Southeastern Indians might be an exception. The board did not push this matter and later declined to join the Baptists in a similar petition in 1827.

3. Porter's speech was printed in the *Cherokee Phoenix*, January 7, 1829.

But in 1824 Arkansas had surveyed its western border, and its citizens wanted all the Indians east of that border removed. McKenney's treaty granted the Cherokees in Arkansas a new tract of land one hundred miles further west (in what is now Oklahoma) in exchange for what they owned in Arkansas, and he tucked into this treaty a clause stating that in order "that their [Cherokee] Brothers yet remaining in the States [east of the Mississippi] may be induced to join them," the federal government agreed "that each Head of family" now residing in the East "who may desire to remove West, shall be given, on enrolling himself for emigration, a good Rifle, a Blanket, a Kettle, and five pounds of tobacco" as "just compensation for the property he may abandon." Furthermore, "the cost of emigration" as well as of "provisions for twelve months after their arrival" was to be "borne by the United States."[4]

Had Jackson not been elected, this "induced" emigration plan of McKenney's would have amounted to little, but the strong pressures which came to bear on the eastern Cherokees after Jackson's inauguration in March 1829 caused a number of them (including probably some still-dissatisfied followers of White Path's Rebellion) to consider the option seriously. Jackson sent agents into the Cherokee Nation to cajole or frighten as many as possible into "enrolling" for emigration. From 1829 to 1835 "enrollment" or "regis-tration" of emigrants by Jackson's agents became a major problem to the Cherokee leaders, and it had a disastrous effect upon the nation's political and economic affairs. The Council considered anyone who enrolled a traitor to the new nationalistic movement. The missionaries were thrown into a quandary. Hitherto they had supported the government's Indian policy; now they doubted both its wisdom and its justice. As their Christian converts and others who trusted their judgment came to ask their advice about emigration, the missionaries tried at first to be neutral. They said that they were not in the nation to meddle in political affairs but only to provide spiritual assistance and enlightenment. However, because they were subsidized by the government (and could be considered agents of the government) their silence was construed by some Cherokees as acquiescence to removal. Jackson's administration made support for removal both a national and party issue (while the Whigs opposed it). Picking up where Porter left off, Jacksonian officials said that the refusal of the missionaries to encourage the new plan of emigration actively and vigorously was an indication of opposition to the government. Missionaries from the North in particular were considered opponents of national policy, tools of (Whig) party interest, and abettors of sectional division when they refused to support emigration.

4. Charles C. Royce, *The Cherokee Nation of Indians*, pp. 101–21; and McKenney to Porter, July 9, 1828, OSW, M-221, roll 106, #7290. McKenney told Porter that he viewed this as essentially a treaty to remove the Cherokees in the East and to comply with the Georgia Compact. "You will see," he told the Cherokee agent, "one of its principal objects is . . . to induce the Indians in Georgia especially to remove." McKenney to Peter Porter, July 9, 1828, BIA, M-21, roll 5, pp. 32–35.

The only way the missionaries could respond to this dilemma and keep their self-respect (and the respect of the Indians and many white American churchgoers) was to rise above politics. They had to evaluate "the Indian question" upon strictly moral terms; that is, in terms of abstract social justice, higher law, revealed truth, or, as some of them put it, "righteousness." They had to ask not whether removal was expedient, feasible, desirable as a matter of national welfare or the welfare of the Cherokees, but whether it was right or wrong. The efforts of the individual missionaries and of their mission boards to answer this question constitute a study in personal conscience and ecclesiastical gymnastics. Basically the matter became a problem of defining what was Caesar's and what was God's. Most missionaries insisted that they were the servants of God and not of Caesar (even though they were dependent on Caesar's money for their work). But this did not go far toward a solution. To decide whether Jackson's removal policy was right or wrong required delicate judgments about the rights and wrongs inherent in the very nature of the American political and social system. Did the power of Caesar rest in the federal (or General) government, the state governments, the validity of treaties, the supremacy of the Constitution over states' rights, the sovereignty of Indian nations? How did one define the word *nation* and the term *civil rights,* especially when applied to Indians? Those who turned to Scripture found texts which said that Christians must "obey the powers that be" and must support those ordained of God as rulers. But within the conflicting jurisdictions of the American system, who or what was the ruling power? Did their treaties give the Cherokees the right of self-government over Indian land within state boundaries and thus make the federal government the power ordained of God in this case? Or did the Constitution make each state the ruling power within its own jurisdiction, as Jacksonians claimed? Which branch of government was to make the decisions on Indian policy—the president? Congress? the Supreme Court? the will of the white majority (assuming the voice of the people to be the voice of God)? Could the government treat the Indians as children ("wards of the State") and as their guardians (acting "in loco parentis") order them to emigrate "for their own good"? Or did the sovereign states in which the Cherokee Nation was located (Georgia, Alabama, Tennessee, North Carolina) each have the right to assert its jurisdiction at will over that portion of the Cherokee Nation within their own borders and appropriate that land to their own state uses regardless of Congress or the Supreme Court? (This turned out to be Jackson's solution.)

Looked at from the viewpoint of the individual missionary, there were further complications. Was he really free to decide for himself or was he only the employee of his mission board? Should he remain silent until his board spoke and then accept its will or should he follow his own conscience and either support or oppose the government for himself? If he chose to "obey the powers that be," was he free to select among those claiming power or should he simply obey the first authorized civil force that confronted him (be that tribal authority, state authority, or officials of the War Department)? Solomon himself could not have answered these questions with any assurance of righteousness. Merely the effort to defend themselves against charges of self-interest by government officials and to protest their neutrality or innocence of meddling was bound to offend one side or another. Jacksonians pretended that any opposition to the removal policy was wrong; the Cherokees concluded that those who were not for them were against them. In the end the missionaries could not make the neat separation between Church and State, God and Caesar, which they desperately wished to make. Their uncertainties and inconsistencies could not help but hurt the cause of missions and Christianization. Where now was the assurance of righteousness with which they had first entered the Cherokee Nation? The missionaries, like the Cherokees, were caught in the flux of events surrounding America's transition in its national identity. It did not mean the same thing to be an American in 1830 as it had in 1800.

Publicly most missionaries preferred to abdicate from any choice and leave the matter to the will of God. Dr. Elizur Butler of the American Board wrote to his Moravian friend the Reverend Gottlieb Byhan in October 1831, "Our blessed Saviour has never promised to secure us our rights in this World, nor can we, as missionaries to the heathen, engage to defend their temporal interests. By divine Assistance we will love them and pray for them, that all the dealings of divine Providence may be subservient to their good. But our heavenly Father governs the temporal and political interests of the world by another set of men over whom we as missionaries cannot control."[5] Yet one year later, Butler found himself sitting in a penitentiary in Georgia starting a four-year term at hard labor for his actions in the crisis. Butler, a Connecticut Yankee, was the most honest and kindly of men—none was more truly dedicated to being a good citizen and a faithful missionary. Nevertheless, he could find no simple way out of his dilemma. Historically Butler has emerged as the hero and Andrew Jackson the villain of the removal conflict. What troubled some missionaries at the time was that the public considered Andrew Jackson the great national hero and by opposing him, they became villains. Before 1828 missionaries were greatly admired by the public, and they had thought of themselves as heroic figures—men and women who sacrificed family, friends, home, and comfort for the sake of advancing God's cause in the wilderness. After 1828 they became ordinary citizens caught in the flux of political issues they had helped to create but could not solve.

On the other hand, Jacksonians and Georgians did not have an easy task in reversing a policy started by George Washington, carried on by every succeeding president, guaranteed by scores of treaties, written into the Trade

5. Elizur Butler to Gottlieb Byhan, October 8, 1831, MAS.

and Intercourse Acts, upheld by the United States Constitution, and which, so far as the missionaries to the southern tribes were concerned, had been eminently successful in civilizing and Christianizing the Indians. Even though the tide of public opinion, economic development, and expansionism was flowing strongly in Jackson's favor, the success of his removal program depended upon his convincing the American voters that they were not sacrificing their ideals, laws, or institutions when they compelled 125,000 friendly Indians to move hundreds of miles from their homes to the westernmost frontier. The president was given considerable assistance in his removal effort by the dramatic emergence of the nullification problem of 1828–33, when South Carolina refused to obey the tariff laws of Congress. Jackson was able to plead that by assisting Georgia and the other southern states to rid themselves of Indians, he was in fact strengthening the power of the Union to defeat the nullifiers (while refusal to remove the Indians might well put the Deep South in the camp of South Carolina). Jackson could also quote Scripture to his purpose, noting that God commanded Adam (and the white sons of Japheth in particular) to inherit the earth, to replenish it and subdue it by cultivating the soil, while most Indians (according to the prevailing stereotype) were hunters who did nothing with America's God-given resources and so were poor stewards of it. He could, and did, argue that despite a generation of missionary efforts the vast majority of the Indians east of the Mississippi were still heathens. But Jackson's strategy at bottom was much more simple. He told Americans what they wanted to believe, namely, that they could carry out their benevolent plan of helping the Indians much more efficiently if they removed them than if they left them where they were. To move them west, Jackson said, would put them beyond the reach of those oppressive, wicked whites who cheated them and plied them with liquor and intruded on their land; to remove them would enable "the real Indians," the fullbloods, who were slow to acculturate, more time to benefit from the pious work of the missionaries and the nurturing assistance of the federal government. To remove them would gather up the fast-perishing, small fragments of tribes and place them in areas contiguous with other more advanced and stable tribes, where they could mutually assist each other; to remove them would thwart the selfish aims of corrupt, half-educated, and ambitious "half-breeds" who had become rich by cheating their brethren and, having built large homes and farms and trading posts for themselves in the East, now intimidated the "backward" members of their tribe from acting in their own best interest. It was taking much longer to civilize and Christianize the Indians than the Founding Fathers ever imagined. Were the founders still with us, Jackson argued, they would applaud this slight alteration in their policy for the sake of the Indians as well as for the good of the republic.[6]

6. Jackson's public rationalization covered a variety of less palatable aspects of his policy. For these, see Michael P. Rogin, *Fathers and Children* (New York: Knopf, 1975), pp. 165–205.

Though about seventy Indian tribes were included in Jackson's removal policy, the Cherokees became the center of the controversy. For Jacksonians and for philanthropic, churchgoing voters, the Cherokees were the test case for a major reexamination of "the Indian question." They were the prime example of how far a tribe of heathen hunters could progress under benevolent guidance within one generation. Their nation contained more mission churches, more schools, more farms, more Christians than any other. They had the most stable and republican form of government. They were the most prosperous and economically self-sufficient. If one needed proof of the potential of the Indian to become a white American in everything but the color of his skin, the Cherokees provided it. For the people of Georgia, the Cherokees were a test case precisely because they were so successful. Did a handful of Indian Christians and farmers have the right to monopolize 6,200,000 acres of corn, cotton, timber, and mineral land in the sovereign state of Georgia just because a few missionaries (most of them from the North) supported by public funds claimed that the Cherokees were the most civilized tribe in America? Not so openly spoken of by Georgians and the frontier whites in other southern states were the arguments centering on the alleged racial inferiority of the Indian.[7] As the South moved toward its racial justification for black slavery after 1820, so it moved toward a decision to classify Indians as "people of color" within its caste system. In addition, Nat Turner's Rebellion in 1831 gave point to an old fear that the presence of armed "people of color" in the Indian nations was also a threat to the peace of the South.[8]

With so many forces working against the Cherokees, it is no wonder that many missionaries believed that fate (Satan or Providence) was conspiring to remove them. David Greene, corresponding secretary of the American Board, wrote in 1831, "It seems to be the Lord's will that everything shall work against the Indians."[9] But if the missionaries were flabbergasted at the turn of events after 1828, the Cherokees were not. They had learned to expect the worst in their dealings with the whiteman. In the end, it was their able, determined, and courageous efforts on their own behalf which made the Cherokees the focus of national attention during the removal crisis. Their leaders proved extremely skillful in manipulating white public opinion and the white political and legal structure. They made regular trips to Washington, cultivated congressional support, drew up and published force-

7. For the changing racial attitudes of white Americans in this era, see William Stanton, *The Leopard's Spots* (Chicago: University of Chicago Press, 1960).

8. George Fredrickson argues that 1820 was the date after which white Americans developed a true concept of "racism." See *Black Image in the White Mind* (New York: Harper and Row, 1971), pp. 1−2. The Cherokees were fully aware of this racial issue and did their best in these years to show that they held the same view of Africans and of slavery as white southerners. See Theda Perdue, *Slavery and the Evolution of Cherokee Society*. The missionaries did their best to ignore the racial problems involved and tried hard in their missionary journals to avoid mentioning the fact that the Southeastern Indians owned black slaves.

9. Quoted in Althea Bass, *Cherokee Messenger*, p. 253.

ful and eloquent memorials, circulated their views in the *Cherokee Phoenix,* and even sent some of their fluent young orators to the cities of the Northeast to speak at protest meetings where they obtained signatures for petitions and funds for their lawyers. As the wealthiest of the Indian nations, the Cherokees were able to hire the best lawyers in America to try their cases in the state and federal courts. Even Jackson's efforts to cut off their annuities did not stop them, though it put their nation heavily in debt.

For the Cherokees the battle began as soon as Jackson was elected. Elias Boudinot, editor of the *Cherokee Phoenix* in New Echota, reported the possible consequences to his readers on December 10, 1828: "It is now certain that General Jackson is elected," and so the whiteman, "with republican tyranny" drives the Indian from his homeland. Two weeks later the Georgia legislature spelled out in a carefully worded law of eight sections just how it would compel the Cherokees (and the Creeks) within Georgia's borders to accept Jackson's "benevolent" removal program. They voted to denationalize the Cherokees, to take their land, and to make them second-class citizens as of June 1, 1830, if they were so foolish as to still be there at that time. Entitled "An act to add the territory lying within the limits of this state and occupied by the Cherokee Indians, to the counties of Carroll, DeKalb, Gwinnett, Hall, and Habersham and to extend the laws of this state over the same and for other purposes," the law said that all whitemen within the Cherokee Nation were immediately subject to Georgia's laws and that after June 1, 1830, "all Indians then and at that time residing in said territory . . . shall be liable and subject to such laws and regulations as the legislature may hereafter prescribe." Another section of the law stated that as of that date "all laws, usages and customs made, established and enforced in the said territory by the said Cherokee Indians, and the same are hereby . . . declared null and void"; finally, that "no Indian or descendant of an Indian residing within the Creek or Cherokee nations of Indians shall be deemed a competent witness or party to any suit in any court created by the constitution and laws of this state to which a white man may be a party."[10] In effect, the Cherokee Nation would disappear on that date and all the Indians still living in Georgia would become "people of color" unable to vote, to testify in court, to serve in the militia, or to send their children to public schools. It was assumed that the Cherokees, being too proud or frightened to accept such status, would shortly leave for the Indian Territory (then called "the Arkansaw" but really west of Arkansas Territory in what is now Oklahoma) to join the Western Cherokees. Under another law, passed in December 1830, the Georgia legislature arranged to send teams of surveyors into the Cherokee Nation to divide it into lots of 160 acres; these plots were then to be put in a lottery and distributed among the white citizens of Georgia. Technically the Cherokees who did not emigrate were to be allowed to retain the 160 acres on

10. These laws are printed in the appendix of Richard Peters, *The Case of the Cherokee Nation.*

which they lived, but as it turned out, most of them were driven off by whites if their land and improvements were of any value. Even the land on which the mission stations had been built was ultimately placed in the lottery.

Although the Cherokees' land was guaranteed to them and protected from white intruders by treaties, the Georgians fully expected President Jackson to support the supremacy of the state over the Indians' claim to federal protection. Before John Quincy Adams left office, the Cherokee Council sent a delegation to consult with him about Georgia's actions, but he could say only that every president was sworn to uphold the Constitution. The delegation waited for Jackson to arrive and shortly after his inauguration it met with his secretary of war, John Eaton. Chief John Ross asked Eaton what Jackson intended to do about Georgia's "defiance of the Laws of the United States and the most solemn treaties existing" between the federal government and the Cherokees?[11] On April 18, the Cherokees received their answer. President Jackson had decided, Eaton told the delegates, that the federal government would never assert its authority against the sovereign rights of the state of Georgia. Did the Cherokees really expect, Eaton asked, that the federal government would

> step forward to arrest the constitutional act of an independent state exercised within her own limits? Should this be done and Georgia persist in the mainte-nance of her rights and authority, the consequences might be that the act would prove injurious to us and in all probability, ruinous to you. The sword might be looked to as the arbiter of such inteference. But this can never be done. The President cannot and will not beguile you with such an expectation. The arms of this country can never be employed to stay any state of this Union from those legitimate powers which attach and belong to their sovereign character.[12]

If they were wise, Eaton concluded, the Cherokees would immediately take steps to enroll and emigrate to the land on which their western brethren already lived. Shortly thereafter the Cherokees learned that the states of Alabama and Mississippi had passed laws similar to those of Georgia, and four years later the state of Tennessee passed such a law. In his first message to Congress on December 8, 1829, Jackson said he had "informed the Indians inhabiting parts of Georgia and Alabama that their attempt to estab-lish an independent government would not be countenanced by the Executive of the United States and advised them to emigrate beyond the Mississippi or submit to the laws of those States."[13] Because he believed that the Indians were not ready for citizenship in Georgia, he urged Congress to provide him with funds and power to negotiate treaties which would assist the Indians to remove to a territory in the West where they could have more time to

11. Thomas L. McKenney to Cherokee Delegation, BIA, M-21, roll 5, pp. 391–92 (April 4, 1829), 402 (April 11, 1829).
12. John H. Eaton to Cherokee Delegation, April 18, 1829. BIA, M-21, roll 5, p. 408.
13. Dale Van Every, *Disinherited*, p. 112.

improve their condition. "Humanity and national honor demand that every effort should be made to avert so great a calamity" as would occur if a primitive, backward people were forced to try to compete with the white, Anglo-Saxon race in Georgia.[14]

The congressional bill providing this money to Jackson was known as the Indian Removal Bill, and by a close vote it was passed in May 1830; by that act the American public more or less washed its hands of the Indian question. Though the missionaries kept up the debate for another two years and carried a case to the Supreme Court, and though the Cherokees stubbornly refused to emigrate, there was no going back on the will of the majority. The strategy of the Cherokees was to wage a patient effort at passive resistance, hoping that public opinion would change, that the Whigs would win the next election, that their treaty rights would be upheld against Georgia and Alabama. They hoped that the missionaries would side with them in their difficult struggle for justice.

The public responses of the various Cherokee missionaries to the removal policy depended to a great extent upon the attitudes taken by the mission boards. Privately, among the missionaries in the field, there was virtual unanimity in their sympathy for the Cherokees' resistance and outrage at the behavior of the Georgians. There was also virtual unanimity that removal of the Cherokees would be "ruinous" to the progress of that nation toward civilization and Christianization and that it would be utterly demoralizing with regard to their faith in the government of the United States. But there was sharp disagreement over how missionaries should respond officially to the crisis. Those missionaries who resided at mission stations within the boundaries of Georgia and Alabama—where, after June 1, 1830, they were subject to arrest and expulsion for opposing state jurisdiction—had a somewhat different problem from those who resided in Tennessee and North Carolina, where missionaries were still free to act openly on behalf of the Cherokees. If their mission boards were supportive of moral or political protest, the missionaries tended toward such action, but if their boards were neutral or hostile toward protest, the missionaries generally obeyed these wishes. Only two missionaries left their denominations because their boards required them to be silent; only one signed an oath of allegiance to the state of Georgia.

There were, in 1829–30, about fifty-six resident "missionaries" among the Cherokees, excluding native preachers, native exhorters, and interpreters.[15] However, this total includes all white persons (farmers, teachers, mechanics) sent by or supported by mission boards as well as the

14. In his annual message in December 1833, Jackson frankly declared that the Cherokees could not survive in the East because they were an inferior race "in the midst of another and a superior race." Congressional Serial Set, *House Executive Documents*, 23d Congress, 1st session, vol. 234, doc. #1, p. 14 (Washington, D.C.: Gales and Seaton, 1833).

15. The figures cited here are taken from the annual reports of the various mission agencies for the year 1830. This was probably the peak year for Cherokee missions.

wives of these people and of the missionaries. Technically speaking, the number commonly referred to by the public as missionaries (that is, the ordained preachers and teachers) was much smaller, only about one-third of this total. Most boards did not include wives or daughters in their lists of missionaries even though many of them taught school or otherwise played major roles in running the mission stations. The number and importance of women in the Indian mission field has been greatly underestimated. Of the total of fifty-six whites supported by mission boards in the seventeen mission stations in the Cherokee Nation in 1830 (including the five Methodist schools) at least one-half were women. Only the Methodists had no women on the circuits or teaching in their schools. The other three boards had as many, or more, women than men at the stations. No women were specifically called missionaries because that title seems to have been reserved for ordained ministers; but several were listed as assistants. Many of them were called teachers, but wives often taught without being designated as teachers; all of the women, in addition to managing the chores of cooking, sewing, mending, washing, and managing the women's dormitories, also tended (with student help) the vegetable gardens, the chickens, and the pigs, churned the butter, and made the cheese. While women missionaries were sometimes consulted in deliberations at each station, the decisions were always made by the males. Because the farmers, millers, and mechanics at the missions were considered essentially as hired hands, when a mission station reported decisions made by "the brethren" they really meant the decisions made by those designated officially as "missionaries." However, when they referred to "the mission family" they meant all the whites living at the mission. Of the total number of whites who managed the mission in the Cherokee Nation in 1830, only eighteen were officially designated as missionaries: two Baptists, two Moravians, five of the American Board, and nine Methodist circuit riders. The American Board designated Dr. Elizur Butler, a physician, as "Physician-Catechist" with regular missionary status; it also gave missionary status to some whom it designated simply as "Teachers" (although they were not ordained). For a time the board's superintendent in the Cherokee Nation was a man who was not ordained; his title was "Superintendent of Secular Affairs." In most denominations the senior missionary was the superintendent, although the Methodists specifically designated a new superintendent each year. Among the other categories were "assistant missionary," "farmer," "catechist," "teacher," and "miller." The American Board listed thirty-four persons at its eight mission stations in 1830, some of them simply as Mrs. so-and-so (the wife of a missionary, farmer, or teacher). It included that year only five officially titled "Missionary," one designated "Superintendent and Teacher," one "Physician and Catechist," four listed as "Assistant" (all women), eight as "Teachers" (five of these women). Five of the nine Methodist circuit riders (officially called missionaries) also taught "itinerating schools" on their circuits. The Moravians had seven persons at their two missions, only two of whom were missionaries; two were women teachers, one was a farmer, the other two included a wife and the widow of a missionary. The Baptists had one missionary at each of their two mission stations, but the wife and daughter of Evan Jones were teachers and so was Duncan O'Briant's wife. O'Briant conducted a school at Hickory Log and a church at Tinsawattee; in addition, he was assisted by two ministers from the Sarepta Baptist Association in Georgia, who preached at his mission stations at regular intervals and more or less supervised his work for the Sarepta Baptist Missionary Society. In addition to managing the mission stations at which they resided, a number of the Baptist and American Board missionaries were, by 1830, also itinerating around the nation in imitation of the Methodists.

In the end, the responses of the missionary boards to the removal issue seem to have depended in part upon the historical traditions of the denominations they represented, in part on how the boards were structured, and in part on their regional location. The Moravians chose a quietist response in keeping with their separatist tradition and their marginal place in American society. The American Board favored an activist role stemming from its Puritan heritage. The Methodists faced a conflict between the privately determined moral ideals of their missionaries (some of them married to Cherokees) and the regionally determined interpretations of their "discipline" or ecclesiastical code by their board in Tennessee. The Baptists were divided by the sectional feelings of the delegates to their national missionary association (the Triennial Convention). Furthermore, the political inclinations of the persons in charge of mission affairs played a significant role in all the decisions of the boards. One either admired or disliked Andrew Jackson and what he stood for. The ideals of a transcendent Christian faith were frequently at odds with mundane political sentiment, regional attitudes, and pragmatic denominational interests. Because most of the members of the American Board were Whigs, they had little trouble making their decision. Because most of the members of the Tennessee Annual Conference (which supervised the Methodist missionaries) were Jacksonians living on the frontier around the Cherokee Nation, they had little difficulty resolving their dilemma. The Baptists, being the most broadly national in the makeup of their supervisory structure, suffered the most serious internal strife. The Moravians, trying to remain apolitical, wrestled essentially with their sense of conflicting duties toward evangelizing the heathen under God's command and remaining obedient to the powers that be; they were the most effectively neutral or neutralized.

The sense of crisis developed slowly among the missionaries following Jackson's election.[16] It reached a climax during the early months of 1831,

16. The best discussions of the political side of the removal crisis on a national scale are contained in Van Every, *Disinherited*; Rogin, *Fathers and Children*; Ronald N. Satz, *American Indian Policy in the Jacksonian Era*. For attacks on the missionaries by southern congressmen and defenses of them by Whig congressmen, see *Speeches on the Passage of the Bill for the Removal of the Indians* (Boston: Perkins and Marvin, 1830), esp. pp. 148 and 256.

when Georgia prepared to enforce a new law (the Oath Law) designed to drive them out of the Cherokee Nation (or that part of it within the boundaries of Georgia). The most active and nationally important role in the crisis was played by the American Board. It had always thought of itself as the spiritual vanguard of the republic. In many respects its actions represented the essence of the dilemma as most Americans saw it. The board's shift from a position of moralistic outrage to one of pragmatic acquiescence between 1829 and 1833 fairly represents the shift in American public opinion, particularly in the North. Ostensibly interdenominational, the board continued to be dominated by New England Congregationalists. After its incorporation by the state of Massachusetts in 1812, its board of directors chose its own successors, and the board selected a Prudential Committee to manage day-to-day affairs. Most of the board's members were prominent political leaders, businessmen, and clergy who were heirs of the Federalist tradition and National Republicans (or Whigs) in political affiliation.

From the moment the board decided to include American Indians as part of its foreign mission field in 1816, it had engaged in politics. During the removal crisis of 1817—19, the board had no hesitation about engaging in political activity on behalf of its own and the Cherokees' interest, and it had kept a close eye on the politics of Indian affairs ever since. It had petitioned the government in 1824 on behalf of Jedidiah Morse's colonization plan, and it had sent its corresponding secretary, Jeremiah Evarts, to Washington in January 1829 to keep an eye on the Porter—Adams bill for Indian colonization. Evarts's lobbying at the lame-duck session of Congress in January and February of 1829 made him aware of the more serious efforts which Georgia and Jackson would make after the new administration came into office. Because the American Board had so much more at stake in any reversal of the old Washingtonian Indian policy, Evarts returned to Boston with a warning that concerted action would be needed to stop the plans for compulsory total removal of all the Indians. To alert and arouse the public to the unconstitutionality of the Georgia—Jackson removal plan and to point out its injustice toward the Cherokees in particular, Evarts prepared a series of intensively researched articles which were published in the *National Intelligencer*, a Washington periodical. To avoid directly implicating the American Board in this publicity effort, Evarts signed the articles with the pen name William Penn, but soon after the first one appeared, in July 1829, his authorship became an open secret. The articles were very popular and provided the first thorough analysis of the Indian question; to make them more useful, Evarts later published them in a separate volume. The articles were also reprinted in over forty other newspapers during the course of the long debate. Having alerted the general public to the problem, Evarts then distributed copies to congressmen, editors, and other influential molders and shapers of public opinion.[17]

17. See Jeremiah Evarts, *Essays on the Present Crisis*. Samuel Worcester wrote to Evarts congratulating him on his William Penn letters and telling him how much they pleased John

The next step was to commence active lobbying against Jackson's removal bill as it moved through Congress between January and May 1830. Evarts again went to Washington to inform Senator Theodore Frelinghuysen, Congressman Edward Everett, and other opponents of the bill of the interests of the board and the Cherokees. Equally important, the members of the Prudential Committee, the board, and various churches associated with them began to hold protest meetings throughout the Northeast and Midwest. Petitions were signed and memorials published in local papers and sent to Congress. Funds were donated to assist in the effort. *The Missionary Herald* and the annual reports of the board kept the churchgoing public informed of the harassments the Christian missionaries were experiencing. The board itself sent a petition to the president and to Congress opposing compulsory removal. Thanks largely to the American Board the Indian removal issue became one of the first major efforts in American history in which private citizens were mobilized nationally by a voluntary reform society on behalf of a specific political cause. All of this was noted and deeply resented by the Jacksonians, who believed that they represented the popular will. The Georgians countered the protests by declaring them the work of misguided philanthropists, northern hypocrites who had shown no mercy to their own local Indians, bleeding hearts, and political partisans; and of course they insisted more vehemently than ever that justice was on their side. The battles over this issue were to become a very common part of the American political scene after 1830.

During the debate on the bill, Congressman Wilson Lumpkin from Georgia (soon to become governor of his state) rose to denounce "the wicked influence of designing men veiled in the garb of philanthropy and christian benevolence" who excited "the Cherokees to a course [of resistance] which will end in their speedy destruction."

> Where do you find one solitary opponent of President Jackson in favor of the [removal] measure? . . . Upon this question our political opponents have availed themselves of the aid of enthusiastic religionists to pull down the administration of President Jackson. . . . Who compose this "christian party" in politics? . . . [T]he fanatics . . . from these philanthropic ranks, flocking in upon the poor Cherokees, like the caterpillars and locusts of Egypt.[18]

The passage of the Removal Act by a narrow margin was a bitter blow to the board and its supporters, but they were far from giving up. The board was particularly upset when Jackson instructed his secretary of war to curtail all further expenditures of the Education Fund for missionary activities east of

---

Ross and the other Cherokee leaders. They "have had much effect towards removing prejudices against missionaries from the minds of this people and creating attachment towards us and the Board." November 25, 1829, ABCFM.

18. Van Every, *Disinherited*, p. 118.

the Mississippi. Announcing this decision in June 1830, Secretary John Eaton stated that "the Government by its funds should not extend encouragement and assistance to those who, thinking upon this subject, employ their efforts to prevent removals."[19] The loss of this subsidy meant either that missionary activities had to be curtailed or that extra funds would have to be raised. The Cherokees were in no position to take up the financial slack. The government still had not sold the land it set aside in 1819 for the Cherokee education fund. In addition, Jackson effectively cut off the Cherokee annuity at this same time by arguing that since Georgia had denationalized their tribe as of June 1, 1830, there was no longer any Cherokee treasury or treasurer to accept the annuity in a lump sum; therefore the $6,666.66 due to the Cherokees in payment for past sales of land would have to be paid to each individual Cherokee at the rate of 44 cents per person per year. The Cherokee people steadfastly refused to apply for this pittance from the agent and consequently the annuity remained untouched in a bank in Nashville for the next five years. When the Prudential Committee learned of these developments, Evarts wrote to Samuel Worcester at New Echota, "A series of efforts will be made to awaken the public to defend the Indians."[20]

At the annual meeting of the board in Boston in October 1830 the Prudential Committee presented a series of resolutions on behalf of the Cherokees and in defense of their missionaries which were enthusiastically adopted. One of these called for a memorial to be addressed to Congress asking it to uphold the nation's treaty obligations. Another stated that it is "our indispensable duty . . . to express our sympathy" with the Southeastern Indian nations "in their distressed condition" and also "our deep sense of the solemnity of the obligations which treaties, superadded to the claims of natural justice, have imposed on the government of our country in their behalf." A third called for the board to implore the blessing of Almighty God to guide the authorities in Washington "so as to secure the just rights of the Indians and preserve the faith and honor of the government." Finally, the board supported the right of its missionaries to express their own views on this moral issue by noting that while "it is not expedient for religious societies to take part in any questions merely political, and the missionaries under their [the board's] direction have been manifestly instructed not to interfere with the political, commercial, or municipal affairs of the natives," nevertheless, "it has not been thought a violation of these principles . . . for the missionaries among the Cherokees to assure them that they might rely upon the justice of the United States and that all the treaty stipulations with them would be honorably fulfilled." Georgia, in other words, had no right, in the board's opinion, to assert its jurisdiction over the Cherokees, and Jackson was abrogating his responsibilities as chief executive by allowing

19. Francis P. Prucha, *American Indian Policy in the Formative Years*, p. 246.
20. Jeremiah Evarts to Samuel Worcester, November 18, 1830, ABCFM.

them to do it. "In [our] judgment," the board said, "no Indians should be compelled to leave the lands which they derived from their ancestors, of which they are in peaceable possession, and which have been repeatedly guaranteed to them by ancient treaties." The board made no mention of the compact Jefferson had made with the Georgians to remove the Indians. So far as the board was concerned, the proceedings of Georgia were "altogether unjustifiable and such as should never be expected from a Christian people"—a statement which cast censure upon many Christians in the South and Northwest who sincerely believed that removal was not only justifiable but would be beneficial to the Indians.[21]

The American Board was trying to give support to its missionaries, who were being criticized for having injected themselves into the political controversy. Samuel Worcester, the leader of their Cherokee mission, had twice taken it upon himself to assist the Cherokees and to inform the public about the situation in Georgia. In March 1830 a delegation of Cherokees went to Washington to try once again to persuade Jackson and Congress to prevent Georgia's usurpation of their land. Worcester, at their request, provided the delegates with a long and informative statement of Cherokee progress in civilization and Christianization; his report was designed to show that it was a gross imposition upon such highly acculturated people for the Georgians to call them savages, to give them second-class citizenship, abolish their tribal government, and curtail missionary efforts for their further progress. In this statement Worcester said, "Many of the heathenish customs of the people have gone entirely or almost entirely into disuse." He then listed the number of converts to Christianity in each denomination and said, "I believe the greater part of the people acknowledge the Christian religion to be the true religion."[22] Worcester's statement was presented to the secretary of war by the Cherokee delegation and reprinted in *The Missionary Herald* in May 1830. It also appeared in the *Cherokee Phoenix*. Politically the statement implied that white Americans could not allow such injustice to civilized, Christian Indians. Also in May 1830 Worcester wrote an even stronger statement to the Reverend Ezra Stiles Ely of Philadelphia, attacking his misrepresentations of the Cherokees in a newspaper he edited entitled *The Philadelphian*. Ely was a noted Presbyterian leader and not a Jacksonian, but he had accepted the general stereotype of the Indians as savages dominated by a few ambitious half-breeds. What was worse, in speaking of the Cherokees, he emphasized that they were slaveholders. Worcester retaliated, "You speak of 'Those Indians, generally half-Indians, who have built their houses and cultivated lands by their slaves' " as though all Cherokees owned slaves. "Sir, the mass of the Cherokee people have built their own houses and

21. Twenty-First Annual Report, ABCFM (1830), p. 18.
22. Robert S. Walker, *Torchlights to the Cherokees*, p. 254; *Cherokee Phoenix*, May 8, 1830. Worcester listed the converts as follows; Presbyterians (American Board), 180; United Brethren, 54; Baptists, 50; Methodists, over 800.

cultivated lands with their own hands." (The *Cherokee Phoenix* printed Worcester's letter in the same issue in which its editor attacked a new organization which Thomas L. McKenney had formed in July 1829 called the Indian Board for the Emigration, Preservation, and Improvement of the Aborigines of America. McKenney had been aided by the Reverend Eli Baldwin, a leading minister of the Dutch Reformed church in New York City, but, as McKenney wrote to his superior in the War Department, John Eaton, the thirty members of this board were "the most thorough-going Jacksonites in the nation.")[23]

For taking these actions Worcester was criticized for stepping out of his role as a missionary and entering the political realm, but he denied that he was doing anything more than throwing light upon a subject of which the public was woefully ignorant and misled. Once his board had issued its own antiremoval resolutions in October 1830 Worcester felt free to seek endorsement of the board's position by other missionaries in the Cherokee Nation. On November 30, 1830, Worcester issued a call to the missionaries of all four of the denominations at work in the nation to come to his home in New Echota on December 22 to consider issuing a public statement about the situation. Thirteen missionaries from the four denominations attended the meeting and, after reading and amending the draft of a manifesto which Worcester had prepared, twelve of them signed it.[24] Some of them did so because the manifesto claimed to exonerate them from unjust accusations of influencing the Cherokees to resist the authority of Georgia. Others signed because they believed that they knew the Cherokee people better than anyone else and that, as honest and impartial observers, it was their duty to clear up some of the false information which had been given to the public. But the manifesto was hardly neutral. It clearly expressed a negative attitude toward removal and strong sympathy for the Cherokees' resistance to it. Their statement is important because it was the first, and only, joint action taken by the missionaries of the four denominations. About one-half of it provided a detailed picture of Cherokee civilization and refuted the claims of Jackson and the Georgians that the fullbloods really wanted to emigrate but were intimidated by their "half-breed chiefs." "The people require patriotism of all whom they elect to office," said the manifesto, and "the very touchstone of patriotism is 'Will he sell his country?' " The rest of the manifesto offered a defense of the missionaries and expressed their opinions on removal. They

23. Herman J. Viola, "Thomas L. McKenney," Ph.D. diss., Indiana University, 1970, pp. 250–52 (since published as *Thomas L. McKenney, Architect of America's Indian Policy 1816–1830*, Chicago, 1974).

24. The first day for this meeting was set as December 16, but it was postponed due to inclement weather. Daniel Butrick said that he felt Worcester had created a situation in which the missionaries present at the meeting had little choice but to sign the manifesto: "We must sign the Document prepared or be censured as unfriendly to the Cherokees, whereas in my opinion, the Cherokees should never have been taught to expect political aid from missionaries." Payne Papers, IX, 1.

said that they had "not acted the part of advisors nor would, nor could, have influenced the views of the people or their rulers." But, "if we withheld our opinion [as individuals] when called for, we could not hold up our heads as preachers of righteousness among a people who would universally regard us as abettors of iniquity." They believed that removal would have "the most unhappy results" in terms of Cherokee progress. The success of removal (or of the Cherokees' coming under Georgia's jurisdiction permanently) "would drive them to despair," destroy their faith in the United States, and "goad many to ruinous excesses of vice." The chances of uplifting them further might be lost forever: "Hard is the task of that philanthropist who would attempt to elevate or even to sustain the character of a broken hearted people."

The manifesto's eight resolutions called for the prayers and aid of "all benevolent people," disavowed any missionary influence "in directing the political affairs of this nation," asserted the missionaries' rights to "free and public expression of our opinion," viewed "the removal of this people to the West of the Mississippi as an event to be earnestly deprecated," asserted that "the whole mass of the Cherokee people . . . are totally averse to a removal," and declared that "the establishment of jurisdiction of Georgia and other states over the Cherokee people" would be "an immense and irreparable injury" and that it was "no more than an act of justice to the Cherokee Nation that we publish" this manifesto. It was signed by Evan Jones for the Baptists, Henry Clauder and Gottlieb Byhan for the Moravians, and Samuel Worcester, Elizur Butler, Daniel Butrick, William Chamberlain, William Potter, John Thompson, Isaac Proctor, J. C. Elsworth, and William Holland for the American Board. The Methodist who attended, Dickson C. McLeod, fully sympathized with the manifesto but did not sign because he had been warned by his board against political meddling.[25]

On January 1, 1831, the *Cherokee Phoenix* published an extra edition containing the full manifesto, and three months later the *Missionary Herald* did the same. The Baptist *Missionary Magazine* published only a brief account of it. Elias Boudinot said in his editorial comments in the *Phoenix* that the manifesto was accurate, impartial, and designed to "counteract many base falsehoods and base misrepresentations." Speaking for his people, Boudinot added, "We believe no one can now remain neutral—there is no halfway ground on this momentous question—each individual in America must either be for the Indians or against them." Boudinot was especially pleased by the united action of the missionaries in asserting that the Indian question was "not merely of a political but of a moral nature, inasmuch as it involves the maintenance or violation of the faith of our country." If the people of the United States agreed with Jackson that treaties with "savages"

25. Clauder, Diary, December 29, 1830, MAB, mentions that Dickson McLeod was the Methodist present at this meeting. The actions of the Moravians, Methodists, and Baptists in the removal crisis are discussed in the next chapter.

were foolish, or if they agreed with Governor Forsyth of Georgia that treaties were mere expedients to be dispensed with as soon as the "savages" were no longer a threat to peace, then the United States was not, as it claimed, a country of laws but of men. The editor of the *Missionary Herald* prefaced the manifesto with a defense of the missionaries' right to speak out on two grounds: first, "no persons possess so ample means as the missionaries of knowing what the present condition and prospects of the Cherokees are . . . and what their wishes respecting removal are" and also what effect removal would have upon them. Second, and more important, "The mere fact that men are Christian missionaries cannot deprive them of the right to have an opinion and to express it publicly on an important moral question, though the question may involve the civil rights of the people among whom they reside and affect their political as well as their moral welfare. . . . [T]hey could not maintain their character as preachers of righteousness without stating their views freely upon [the removal issue]."[26] Yet what seemed so obvious to Christians of the Congregational and Presbyterian persuasions in the North did not seem so obvious to other Christians in the North or in the South.

On the very day that the Cherokee missionaries were assembling at Worcester's house to consider their manifesto, the legislature of Georgia (totally unaware of their actions but fully cognizant of the statements of the American Board at its annual meeting in October and its efforts to arouse public opinion against Georgia's plan) enacted a law declaring that all white males "residing within the limits of the Cherokee nation on the first day of March next . . . without a license or permit from his excellency the governor . . . and who shall not have taken the oath hereinafter required" of allegiance to the state of Georgia, "shall be guilty of high misdemeanor and upon conviction thereof shall be punished" by four years at hard labor in the state penitentiary.[27] While the law seemed to imply that licenses or permits would be granted to those who took the oath, and while it seemed to apply to all whitemen (traders, mechanics, sharecroppers) and to all missionaries within the Cherokee nation, it was specifically designed to drive out the missionaries of the American Board. Furthermore, the governor had no intention of granting a license to any missionary even if he did take the oath.[28]

The missionaries learned of this "oath law" in January 1831 when they each received a copy of it from the state of Georgia. They did not reassemble as an interdenominational group, but the missionaries of each denomination did consult among themselves. Four of the American Board's mission stations were within Georgia's boundaries: those at New Echota, Carmel, Hightower, and Haweis. The missionaries of these four stations met soon

26. *Missionary Herald* 27 (March 1831): 79; *Baptist Missionary Magazine* 11: 127.
27. Walker, *Torchlights*, p. 38.
28. George R. Gilmer, *Sketches of Some of the First Settlers of Upper Georgia*, p. 301; *Missionary Herald* 27:248−54.

after receiving notice of this law and, as Worcester wrote to the Prudential Committee, unanimously concluded that "taking an oath of allegiance is out of the question."[29] As the board informed the public, there were seven reasons for the missionaries' decision to flout the law: first, "because they believed that [Georgia's extension of] jurisdiction was an invasion of the rights of the Cherokees and highly unjust and oppressive"; second, because "they could not easily consent to abandon their work"; third, because "they supposed the constitution of the United States gave them, being citizens of other states, a right to remain there unmolested"; fourth, because "if the Cherokee country was not rightfully under the jurisdiction of Georgia, they could not of course be justly ordered away"; fifth, because "abandoning their stations, it seemed to them also, would be attended with considerable sacrifice of property"; sixth, because "it would also be likely to have a very unfavorable effect on the Cherokees," causing them to "doubt whether the missionaries were really as desirous to promote their welfare" as they professed to be; and seventh, because "they could not feel that their duty to the Head of the Church would permit them to abandon that work for slight reasons." Therefore, they felt "called to suffer persecutions . . . for the sake of Christ and the gospel."[30]

The missionaries consequently remained at their posts until the March 1 deadline had passed. They did so with the full permission of their board, which, however, said that while it could not advise them to take such risks, it would fully support any of them who chose to do so.[31] While awaiting their inevitable arrest, the missionaries carefully worked out their strategy for the confrontation with Georgia. With the support (moral and financial) of the board, they hired lawyers in Georgia, and, when arrested, planned to carry a test case to the United States Supreme Court. "We trust that we are in the path of duty," Worcester wrote to the Prudential Committee in Boston, "and we cheerfully leave the event to God."[32] It was one of the finer moments in missionary history.

The Prudential Committee was sanguine about this strategy because the Cherokee Nation had itself already brought one case to the Supreme Court, *Cherokee Nation v. Georgia*, which was heard in the spring term, 1831. While the Court had ruled that the Cherokee Nation did not have standing in the court and could not therefore obtain an injunction against Georgia's laws, nevertheless John Marshall let it be known that he fully sympathized with the Cherokees' arguments about federal supremacy and that if a suitable case could be brought, the Court would be happy to decide the issue on its merits.[33] Writing to Worcester in January 1831 about the prospect of his

29. Samuel Worcester to David Greene, January 18, 1831, ABCFM.

30. *Missionary Herald* 27 (May 1831): 166.

31. Jeremiah Evarts to Samuel Worcester, February 1, 1831, ABCFM.

32. Samuel Worcester to David Greene, March 14, 1831, ABCFM.

33. See Edwin A. Miles, "After John Marshall's Decision," *Journal of Southern History* 39, no. 4 (November 1973): 520–44.

being the person to bring the suit, Evarts encouraged him toward civil disobedience. Such action was "clearly the path of duty," and no one could accuse him of "violating any law of God." "By standing firm in this case and being willing to suffer for righteousness' sake, you will do much to encourage the Cherokees."[34] He then indicated that, sympathetic though he was with the Cherokees, he believed that they were, as a race, incapable of standing up to the oppression by legal means: "Courage is the thing they want; i.e., long continued courage or fortitude; it is the very point, in my judgment, where they will lose their country and their earthly all. . . . I have always feared for them on this point. I have often said, 'White men, in a high state of civilization, are alone competent and expect deliverance by the slow process of law.' "[35] This was certainly one of the low points in Indian mission history. Despite their loyalty to the Cherokees as a suffering people, the New Englanders could not help expressing their ethnocentric and racial prejudice. "These things I have said many months ago," Evarts continued, to indicate that this was not simply a passing remark. "Now God is likely to bring this trial upon white men of a select character who went out for a holy purpose; that is, to give their labor and their lives, if need be, to the Cherokees." Without the missionaries' help, the Cherokees could not hope to win. "If you leave, I fear the Cherokees will make no stand whatever." Self-exaltation mingled with the concern for social justice. "If Georgia should carry some of you to prison, the fact would rouse this whole country in a manner unlike anything which has yet been experienced." Petitions would flood into Congress and the president and even "to the governor of Georgia." Worcester's sacrifice would shake the world. "You would do good to the poor and oppressed everywhere." In one sense Evarts was right; the imprisonment of white missionaries pursuing their religious duty aroused far more vehement reactions from the general public, North and South, East and West, than any oppression of the red man.[36]

On March 12, 1831, three of the American Board's missionaries (Worcester, Proctor, and Thompson), along with the printer, Wheeler, and two other whitemen, were arrested by the Georgia guard and taken to jail in Lawrenceville, Georgia. The missionaries' lawyers immediately applied for a writ of habeas corpus and argued in the Superior Court of Georgia that its laws were unconstitutional. Judge Augustin Clayton denied this defense but released Worcester, Proctor, and Thompson because as missionaries supported in part by federal funds they were in his opinion "agents" of the federal government and thus not subject to the law. Wheeler and the other whitemen, however, were required to return for trial in September. Clayton also pointed out that Worcester, being postmaster at New Echota, was exempt from the oath on that ground as well. Governor George Gilmer of

34. Jeremiah Evarts to Samuel Worcester, February 1, 1831, ABCFM.
35. Ibid.
36. See Gilmer, *Sketches of the First Settlers*, pp. 330–31.

Georgia was irate and wrote at once to the postmaster general, William T. Barry, and to John Eaton, secretary of war. His letter to Barry reveals the position of the Georgians on this issue:

> [These missionaries] have exercised extensive influence over the Indians and been very active in exciting their prejudices against the Administration of both the General and State Governments . . . . The object of this communication is to request that you dismiss Samuel Worcester from the office of postmaster. If Worcester is not now removed, he will, without doubt, consider himself authorized to continue his seditious conduct . . . . It is due to the State, however, that those who, under the cloak of religious ministry, teach discord to our misguided Indian people and opposition to the rulers, should be compelled to know that obedience to the laws is both a religious and civil duty.[37]

Barry immediately dismissed Worcester from his post office position while Eaton assured Gilmer that the government did not consider missionaries to be in any sense its agents. The missionaries were informed of this on June 1 and were given ten days to sign the oath or leave the limits of Georgia. At this point some of the board's missionaries began to have second thoughts about going to jail. Isaac Proctor and Daniel Butrick had written to Elias Boudinot on April 15 that they thought Judge Clayton was right that missionaries were "here by authority and the protection of the United States Government" but "if the President should decide that we are not under the protection of the general government and we were again ordered to limits of the State, we should do so."[38] Ten days later Butrick told the Prudential Committee that he was going to leave Georgia and establish residence at one of the missions in Tennessee because "it has appeared to me more like suffering in a political contest, from motives of worldly policy, than in the spirit of Christian meekness." The missionaries, as he saw it, had been admitted to the Cherokee Nation by the president (under the Trade and Intercourse Act), and if Jackson now chose to transfer his authority in this matter to the state of Georgia, then Georgia became "the powers that be" and had a right to expel them.[39] When Butrick left, Proctor and Thompson went with him. Because women were not included under the oath law, these missionaries left their wives behind to manage the schools at their stations.[40] Butrick and others who thought they could continue to serve their mission congregations by itinerating from outside Georgia were mistaken. Un-

---

37. See ibid., p. 304. He took the liberty in this letter to suggest a loyal Georgian as a replacement for Worcester.

38. Daniel Butrick and Isaac Proctor to Elias Boudinot, April 15, 1831, Payne Papers, IX, 3−4.

39. Daniel Butrick to David Greene, April 25 and May 12, 1831, Payne Papers, IX, 5−9. See W.G. McLoughlin, "Civil Disobedience and Evangelism among the Missionaries to the Cherokees," *Journal of Presbyterian History* 51, no. 2 (Summer, 1973): 116−39.

40. While this was only a temporary measure in most cases, it entitles the women missionaries to more credit than they have been given for their role in trying to help the Cherokees in this crisis.

licensed itinerants were also arrested, even though the law spoke only of whites who "resided" in Georgia. As Governor Gilmer said, "White persons who continue to move about from one place to another among the Cherokees are considered as much within the mischief which the law intends to remedy as if stationary and will be arrested in like manner."[41] But Gilmer did not make this clear until September.

Late in May 1831, Worcester wrote to Evarts, "I cannot but view it as a matter of regret that our ranks are broken. I mentioned last week the view of Mr. Butrick and I am informed by Mr. Thompson that he and Mr. Proctor have written a long letter" explaining that they agreed with him.[42] Thompson "thinks that perhaps the President of the United States has lawful authority to order us out of the nation, and if so, the intimation in Gov. Gilmer's letter is a virtual order from the President which, if we would be " 'subject to the higher power,' we must obey." Worcester could not accept their arguments. It was prejudging the whole case to assume either that Georgia or the president was the legitimate "higher power" or rightfully constituted authority in that situation. Worcester believed that within their borders the Cherokees were the "higher power" because the treaty gave them the authority to govern themselves according to their own laws.[43] He therefore concluded, "I am willing to bear the burden alone. Only let not God forsake me." He did add, however, that Dr. Elizur Butler was still of his opinion and also was willing to suffer for the cause.[44] Worcester proved prescient on one point:

> My wish that the Committee may be found of the same mind as before in regard to our staying does not depend on my hope of triumphing in the trial before the Supreme Court. I do not indeed see how that court can well decide against me, but I think it very likely, if in my favor, to be an inefficacious decision of 'the mere question of right' which will not take me out of prison unless there be a new administration of the Executive Government. I apprehend there is danger of my having to suffer the full penalty of the unrighteous law.[45]

Worcester expected the board to make the most of his case in arousing public support for the Cherokees. "Let an address be written to the good people of the State of Georgia setting briefly before them the true state of the case as to the Indian rights and especially presenting the subject in its moral aspect, reminding them that they have been looking at the subject too much as a mere political question." The general public must also be aroused. He felt that there was a terrible "apathy of the people" and that "something ought to

41. Gilmer, *Sketches of the First Settlers*, p. 325; he wrote this on September 8, 1831.
42. Samuel Worcester to Jeremiah Evarts, May 31, 1831, ABCFM.
43. See Worcester's statement in the annual report for 1833, p. 98. As he put it, "The Cherokee government was of rightful authority," and he accepted it as the power ordained of God in that situation.
44. Samuel Worcester to David Greene, May 31, 1831, ABCFM.
45. Samuel Worcester to David Greene, June 2, 1831, ABCFM

be done to direct the attention of christians" to do their duty and vote Jackson out of office. They must assert "the right which they possess in the choice of rulers to save our country from the guilt of covenant-breaking and oppression and robbery," for if injustice were permitted without protest, God would surely punish his chosen people. "Have not ministers and private christians felt so much that politics belonged not to them as to withhold their votes when they ought to have been given" on the side of righteousness?[46] This perhaps was the most extreme statement by any missionary regarding the Christian's duty to use political power to correct social injustice toward the Indians.

On July 5, still awaiting imminent arrest, Worcester asked the board if his wife should remain at the mission with their children. "Mrs. Worcester is perfectly ready to run the risk of being forcefully removed."[47] Two days later he was arrested along with Butler. Mrs. Worcester remained at her post, though ill herself and nursing a dying child. A Methodist minister, James J. Trott, was arrested with them, and when another Methodist, Dickson McLeod (who did not reside in Georgia as Trott did), protested, he too was arrested; a third Methodist missionary was beaten over the head with a stick by the Georgia guard for protesting the arrest. Those arrested were treated with great severity, forced to walk sixty miles to prison, chained at night, abusively pushed, and profanely shouted at. Later they were released on bail and told to leave the state until their trial in September. When Worcester's sick child died and he reentered the state from Tennessee to comfort his wife, he was arrested again, but this time the commander of the guard allowed him to return to Tennessee without imprisonment.

The Prudential Committee published all the vivid details of these "relentless persecutions" of God's workers and did its best to stir up public resentment. Many other missionary and religious journals carried stories and shocked editorials. The trial took place on September 16, 1831. The jury took only fifteen minutes to find the defendants guilty. "The judge," Worcester said, "in pronouncing sentence reiterated the accusations against us and against missionaries in particular and urged upon us those laws of God in regard to obedience to laws and to rulers which we have violated."[48] Then the judge offered to release any of those convicted who would sign the oath or agree to leave the state. Nine of the eleven whitemen convicted took one or the other alternative; Worcester and Butler would not. They were taken to Milledgeville Penitentiary to start serving their four years at hard labor while their lawyers began the long process of appeal to the United States Supreme Court.

The editor of the *Missionary Herald* said that the state had produced no evidence of the crimes they were accused of, namely, "opposing the policies

46. Samuel Worcester to David Greene, June 29, 1831, ABCFM.
47. Samuel Worcester to David Greene, July 5, 1831, ABCFM.
48. Samuel Worcester to David Greene, September 16, 1831, ABCFM.

of Georgia," influencing the Cherokees "to refuse to abandon their country," opposing "the extension of state laws," and appealing to "the general government for redress." "The missionaries solemnly deny" these accusations. As for failing to uphold " "the powers that be," as the judge in the case accused them of doing, "the missionaries cannot be considered as resisting the 'powers that be' in the sense of the New Testament unless it is admitted that the apostolic injunction requires Christians to submit to any and every government which may assert authority over them." If the state of Pennsylvania tried to assert its authority over the ministers in Delaware and to require them to take an oath of allegiance to Pennsylvania, would anyone assert that "the state of Pennsylvania was the power to which the people of Delaware were bound to be in subjection?"[49] To the editor the issue was one of the civil rights of all decent, churchgoing citizens: "Is a religious man . . . bound to submit quietly to every law which may be enacted without inquiring whether it invades or not his rights as guaranteed to him by constitutions and treaties?"

The harsh treatment of the missionaries, their trial and imprisonment caused a wave of indignation around the country. A new avalanche of letters, petitions, and memorials was sent to the authorities. However much southern Christians might support the removal of the Indians or the states' rights policy of Georgia, as Christians they were indignant at the arrest of ministers of the Gospel guilty of no civil crime. Worcester reported that even the Georgians showed concern: "From what we gather respecting public sentiment in this state, we are led to believe that a good deal of sympathy is excited in our behalf among the pious who, while they do not approve the course we have taken, give us credit nevertheless for the uprightness of our motives."[50] In his memoirs, Governor Gilmer wrote, "No official act of mine occasioned so much abuse at the time . . . as the punishment of religious missionaries by imprisonment. . . . The subject excited great interest throughout the country" and brought great "mortification" to the people of Georgia.[51] The Union Presbytery of Eastern Tennessee issued a public protest. So did the Northern Alabama Presbytery and the Presbytery of Rockingham, Virginia.[52] The North Carolina Presbyterian Synod called the arrest "shameful and shocking"; it had "disgraced the annals of our free institutions." The synod also denounced the new secretary of war, Lewis Cass, who had excused Georgia by saying that "the missionaries of the different religious societies stationed among the Indians had found their situations too lucrative to give them up willingly."[53]

The Cherokees were equally upset over the government's treatment of

49. *Missionary Herald* 27 (November 1831): 364–65.
50. Samuel Worcester to David Greene, November 8, 1831, ABCFM.
51. Gilmer, *Sketches of the First Settlers*, p. 330.
52. Ibid., p. 331.
53. *Missionary Herald* 28 (February 1832): 47.

the missionaries. The loyal support given by the American Board to the nation's interests had transformed the previous coolness toward it into warm admiration. Cherokees sent letters to Worcester and Butrick at the prison, donated money to provide them with comforts, and told Mrs. Worcester they were sorry they could not do more: "They are suffering for us."[54] Feelings toward the American Board, which had been so negative in 1827, were now extremely positive.

The audacity of the Georgians seemed at last to have played into the hands of their most determined opponents. The case was argued before the United States Supreme Court in February 1832. The chief attorneys for Worcester and Butler were William Wirt, former attorney general of the United States and that fall to be a candidate for the presidency on the Anti-Masonic ticket, and John Sergeant, an eminent Washington attorney who that fall would be the vice-presidential candidate on the Whig ticket with Henry Clay. Daniel Webster was also consulted for his views. Marshall's decision, rendered on March 3, 1832, was everything Worcester, the board, and the Cherokees could have hoped for. He held the treaty power supreme, declared the laws of Georgia over the Cherokee Nation null and void, and ordered the immediate release of the two missionaries. Victory seemed at hand. But the celebrations proved short-lived. Georgia's Superior Court refused to accept Marshall's order for the release of the prisoners on the grounds that the United States Supreme Court had exceeded its authority; its ruling had no standing in the sovereign state of Georgia. Senator George M. Troup of Georgia stated, on March 5, after the Court's decision, "The people of Georgia will receive with indignant feelings, as they ought, the recent decision of the supreme court, so flagrantly violative of their sovereign state. . . . The jurisdiction claimed over one portion of our population [the Indians] may very soon be exerted over *another* [the African], and in both cases they will be sustained by the fanatics of the north."[55] Thus antislavery agitation was, by 1832, linked in the minds of many southerners with the antiremoval agitation. "If, in the last resort," Troup continued, "we [slaveholders] need defenders, we will find them everywhere." Andrew Jackson, who had already intimated that he would do nothing to execute Marshall's decision, wrote to his friend John Coffee, "The decision of the supreme court has fell stillborn."[56] He said nothing and did nothing.

Still there was one final legal step that Worcester and Butler could take before the game would be played out. They could instruct their attorneys to report to the Supreme Court when its next session opened in January 1833 that the Superior Court in Georgia had refused to honor Marshall's mandate. When the Court certified this and notified the chief executive, Jackson

54. Ibid., p. 45.
55. Van Every, *Disinherited*, p. 148.
56. Rogin, *Fathers and Children*, p. 218.

would be required to force Georgia to do what it had refused to do voluntarily. Or at least he would have to explain why.

From March through December 1832 the Cherokees' situation became increasingly tense and so did the pressure upon Worcester and Butler. Jackson, having won immense popularity across the nation by vetoing the charter of the Bank of the United States, was easily reelected in November. John Ridge, Elias Boudinot, and several other leading Cherokees had become so discouraged that they were seriously considering the possibility of removal.[57] Meanwhile a number of very distinguished citizens of Georgia visited Worcester and Butler in prison and seriously urged them to seek a pardon. They argued that it was fruitless to press Jackson to the wall by asking Marshall for a writ. Moreover, a serious national crisis was approaching in which the two missionaries would play a critical role. South Carolina had decided in November 1832 to declare the tariff of abominations null and void within its borders. President Jackson wished to enforce the tariff and put down the notion of nullification, but he dared not act against South Carolina until the question of Georgia's claims against the Indians was settled. There was imminent danger, these eminent visitors told Worcester and Butler, that Georgia, Alabama, and Mississippi might join forces with South Carolina, especially if Jackson were required to carry out Marshall's decision against Georgia. For the sake of the Union, to avoid a possible civil war, Worcester and Butler were begged to give up their case, request a pardon (which the visitors said the governor was eager to grant), and thus allow Jackson to proceed against South Carolina and save the nation. Once Georgia felt that the Indians would be removed, it would support Jackson (and so would Alabama and Mississippi) and thus South Carolina would be isolated and have to yield. These were arguments which weighed heavily with conscientious believers in the Union like Worcester and Butler.[58]

On the other hand, the majority of the Cherokees, bolstered by the determination of John Ross and the patriot leaders, urged equally strongly that Worcester and Butler carry through their heroic action. To do otherwise would be to abandon the Cherokees and everything the missionaries had worked for. The fate not only of the Cherokees but of all other Indian nations was at stake. Would not seeking a pardon be an admission that the missionaries had been wrong and Georgia right? Would not this be tantamount to a victory of the states' rights theory, which was every bit as dangerous to the Union as South Carolina's nullification proclamation? Somehow, what had started out as a simple act of Christian duty and morality had placed Worcester and Butler at the center of a major national crisis, perhaps the most momentous crisis since the founding of the nation.

57. Thurman Wilkins, *Cherokee Tragedy*, pp. 228–31.

58. Miles, "After John Marshall's Decision," pp. 526–27; Samuel Worcester to David Greene, November 14, 1831, ABCFM.

CHAPTER ELEVEN

Baptist, Moravian, and Methodist
Responses to Indian Removal, 1829 — 1833

This is a specimen of Republicanism—of Liberty and Equality! O,
America—Thou Land of Liberty, where are thy boasted 'People's Rights!'
Alas! it's all a mere name.
      Rev. Henry G. Clauder, Moravian missionary, January 30, 1829

W hile the American Board struggled with its crisis of conscience, the other missionary organizations in the Cherokee Nation were also trying to come to grips with the removal crisis. Next to the American Board, the most actively concerned was the Baptist Foreign Mission Board. Formed in 1814 by the General Convention of the Baptist Denomination in the United States for Foreign Missions (later called the General Missionary Convention or the Triennial Convention), it was designed originally for overseas mission activity in Burma and India. The convention elected a twenty-one member managing board to take care of the work between conventions. The day-to-day management of mission affairs was conducted by a small executive committee (located after 1826 in Boston). The managing board met annually to hear reports from its executive committee, and triennially the convention set the general policies within which the board operated. Any local Baptist mission societies throughout the country which contributed more than $100 a year to the treasury of the board were allowed to send two delegates to the Triennial Convention, which set overall missionary policies.[1] Being a national rather than a regional organization, the Baptist Foreign Mission Board was not so homogeneous in outlook as the American Board of Commissioners for Foreign Missions. It also tended to operate more from the bottom up than the top down, in keeping with Baptist tradition. Support from the southwestern states (particularly Tennessee and Kentucky) was slight because of the hyper-Calvinist, antimission views of the Baptists in that area. However, mission support was strong from the southern states on the East Coast and in the Middle Atlantic states as well as New

---

1. Robert G. Torbet, *A History of the Baptists* (Chicago: Judson Press, 1963), p. 250.

England and the Middle West (the old Northwest). Ultimately the board had difficulty reconciling regional interests on the Indian question, but until the Triennial Convention of 1829, the Baptist denomination was virtually unanimous in support of gradual, voluntary removal of the Indians and the establishment of a "permanent home" for them in an Indian Territory in the West. Consequently, during the early years of the removal crisis, the Baptist Foreign Mission Board proved to be the most formidable opponent of the American Board, although the two managing committees lived in Boston and occasionally consulted on common problems. Eventually the executive committee of the Baptist board came to agree with Jeremiah Evarts and the Prudential Committee of the American Board about the unnecessary harshness and cruelty of Jackson's compulsory removal plan, and when it did, there was a very sharp controversy within the denomination.

Much of the sympathy for Indian removal among the Baptists was generated by the indefatigable Reverend Isaac McCoy, one of the first of the board's Indian missionaries and considered by many people in the 1820s to be the outstanding authority on Indian missions in the country. McCoy lobbied in Washington as extensively and effectively as Jeremiah Evarts did for the American Board, and while they took opposite sides on the removal question, they knew and respected each other. Born in Pennsylvania in 1784, McCoy moved to Kentucky with his parents at the age of six. In 1810 he was ordained by the Baptists, and from 1816 to 1826 he served as a missionary among the Miami, Potawatomi, Ottawa, Wea, Chippewa, and other small tribes in Indiana, Illinois, and Michigan.[2] By 1824, McCoy had concluded that it was impossible to produce a stable, self-subsistent community among these small tribes on isolated reservations where they were surrounded, cheated, harassed, and debauched by unconscionable frontier traders and riffraff. By 1827, he had developed an elaborate scheme for the "collocation" of all these "perishing" tribes in a single reservation or "permanent home" in the area west of Arkansas and Missouri. That year he published his plan under the title *The Practicability of Indian Reform, Embracing Their Colonization*.[3] His program called for a careful survey of a large, suitably fertile tract to which all the tribes would be removed and settled contiguously; here, under the "guardianship" of a government superintendent and his aides, they would be protected, educated, and civilized. The federal government would constitute this an Indian Territory forever; it would appoint white commissioners, give each tribe its own county and each Indian family its own plot of land. Suitable laws would be passed by Congress for their governance, and reliable Indians would be appointed in each county (that is, each Indian nation within the territory) as

2. For McCoy, see George A. Schultz, *An Indian Canaan*, and Robert F. Berkhofer, Introduction to Isaac McCoy, *History of Baptist Indian Missions* (New York: Johnson Reprint Corp., 1970).

3. Schultz thinks McCoy may have adopted the notion of "colonization" from his earlier interest in the colonization of freed slaves in Africa. For a long and favorable contemporary review of McCoy's plan, see *Baptist Missionary Magazine* 8: 147–55

sheriffs, constables, and other law enforcement agents. Missionaries would be invited to provide the schools, which would be subsidized by the government and taught in English. Gradually, the Indians would become acculturated and homogenized under this benevolent, paternalistic protectorate, and ultimately the territory might be admitted to the Union as an Indian State.

McCoy became an ardent advocate of his "collocation" plan of Indian reform, and he found a receptive hearing not only among the Baptists but in the War Department and the White House. He provided just the kind of "disinterested" religious support which political leaders needed for the removal program. McCoy came to think of himself as the country's foremost expert on Indian policy and fully expected that he would be appointed the superintendent of the Indian Territory once Congress adopted his plan. As a result, he spent less and less time among the Indians as a missionary and more and more as a lobbyist, government surveyor, and "conductor" for Indians who voluntarily agreed to move West. After 1827, he received no salary from the Baptist board but supported himself by government contracts as surveyor and conductor, but he insisted on retaining his honorary title and position as "missionary" of the board until 1836, and the board felt honored to give it to him. Though sincere in his dedication to the welfare of the Indians, McCoy had little respect for their abilities and little regard for their treaty rights or their tribal integrity. His approach was thoroughly paternalistic; the Indians were "wards of the state" and should be told by experts like himself to do what was best for them. His outlook was colored by his unsuccessful efforts among the smaller tribes in the old Northwest; he had no experience among the large, stable, more acculturated southeastern tribes, though in his book he held them up as an example of what he expected to accomplish in the Indian Territory. These more acculturated tribes, like the Cherokees, were also to be relocated in the west in order to provide leadership and examples to their less acculturated brethren. In some respects McCoy pushed himself and his plan upon those in high office; in other respects he unwittingly allowed them to manipulate him for their own ends.

At the Triennial Convention of 1826, the delegates were persuaded by McCoy to instruct the managing board to prepare a memorial to Congress on behalf of the Baptist denomination in support of Indian removal. The board also passed a resolution in June 1826 releasing McCoy from his mission station so that he could explore the west "to look out a country for Indian Colonization." After the convention, Lucius Bolles, the corresponding secretary for the board, wrote to Thomas McKenney at the Office of Indian Affairs, "The Board will act at their next meeting" on the subject "of a Memorial to Congress in favor of Colonizing the Indians.[4] The memorial was not drafted until 1827. In it, the board asked that if Congress did enact a

---

4. Lucius Bolles to Thomas McKenney, May 26, 1827, BFMB. The Baptists thought they could also enlist the American Board to support colonization with them, as Bolles indicates here.

colonization plan, McCoy might be appointed to find and survey the appropriate tract for it.[5] Obviously the Baptists hoped that through McCoy their denomination would come to play a major role in the new civilization program in the West, perhaps snatching from the American Board the leadership in Indian missions and the lion's share of federal subsidies for Indian education.

The memorial drafted by the board and sent to Secretary of War James Barbour spoke of colonizing "the Indians who remain on small reservations in New England and the States of New York, Ohio, and Indiana, together with those bordering the frontier settlements" who were "rapidly decreasing in numbers and, as a people, perishing."[6] The board was confident "that colonizing these unfortunate people in some suitable section of country would not only preserve them from extinction but elevate them in social life." Based upon the trip McCoy had taken for the board in 1826–27, the memorial asked Congress to start such a colony "on the Elkhorn River, westwardly of Council Bluffs on the Missouri River or elsewhere north of the Territory of Arkansaw." If and when this place was selected, the board planned "to invite our pupils among the Brothertown, Shawnese, Chippewas, Otawas, Putawatomies, and Miamies" to be among the first settled and thereby encourage other Indians to relocate there. The petition concluded with the remark, "our views in relation to Indian reform are in perfect accordance with those of the Government."

While this memorial said nothing about removing the southeastern tribes, the board had no objection to their joining the exodus. The memorial was designed to assist in the passage of Barbour's colonization bill, and Bolles went to Washington in the spring of 1828 to help Barbour and McCoy lobby for it. They worked closely with Wilson Lumpkin, congressman from Georgia, but the bill failed.[7] However, Congress did pass a bill appropriating $15,000 to explore the Great American Desert west of the Missouri to ascertain the feasibility of establishing an Indian Territory there. Bolles was certain that McCoy would be appointed to make this survey. He therefore wrote to him on June 2, 1828, explaining the delicate problem raised by the fact that the southeastern tribes owned black slaves: "The opponents [of removal] with whom I laboured the point, professed to view it on political

5. Lucius Bolles to Thomas McKenney, November 27, 1827, BFMB.

6. Ibid.

7. Wilson Lumpkin, who was a member of the House Committee on Indian Affairs, had met McCoy in Washington some years earlier. "From my first acquaintance with this good man," Lumpkin later wrote, "to the day of his death, I found him an able auxiliary in the cause of Indian reform." When James Barbour's removal bill came before Congress in 1828, Lumpkin supported it in a speech, February 20, 1828, and noted the Baptists' support for it: "One respectable denomination of Christians have memorialized the present Congress on this subject and urged with much earnestness and ability, the results of their labors and experience, in favor of the emigrating plan, which is the only plan by which the Indians can ever be considered permanently located and settled. Sir, these opinions of wisdom, experience, and piety, I present in reply [to my opponents]." Wilson Lumpkin, *A Sketch of His Life* (Athens, Georgia, 1852), pp. 46, 51.

grounds and were specially averse to that feature of the Bill which left it indefinite as to degrees of Latitude within which the settlement should be made, and fearing that it might be fixed north of the point which was settled at the admission into the Union of the State of Missouri for the boundary of slavery."[8] To avoid this problem when the matter came up again, Bolles suggested that in his explorations McCoy should seek a spot below "the point which was settled at the admission into the Union of the State of Missouri for the boundary of slavery," that is, 36°30'. This was particularly important "as the Southern Indians own slaves" (an indication that the Baptists expected these Indians to be removed as well as those named in their memorial).

That same month the board indicated that it had in mind particularly the removal of the Creek Indians because they had obstructed the activities of its missionary, the Reverend Lee Compere. Some chiefs had entered Compere's mission station and whipped a number of their slaves who were attending a Sunday worship service. "The Creeks as a Tribe," Bolles wrote to Compere, "have taken so little interest in the Mission from the beginning and have lately exhibited so much hostility to it, that were it not for the prospect of a change by removal of a part or all of them to the West, where they may be placed under a better influence . . . we should doubtless think it best to give it up."[9]

McKenney did give McCoy the job of exploring the area west of Arkansas in 1828. He returned from this task in time to lobby early in 1829 for the removal bill presented by Peter B. Porter, who had replaced Barbour as secretary of war. Once again, the Baptist board sent one of its staff, Heman Lincoln, to lobby with McCoy. "It is our anxious wish," Lucius Bolles wrote to McCoy in Washington, "to find a permanent home for the Indians" in the West.[10] Jeremiah Evarts was there lobbying against the bill for the American Board. McCoy tried to persuade Evarts to change his mind, but failed.[11] The bill did not pass, but McCoy stayed in Washington for Jackson's inauguration and met with him and John Eaton to discuss the next move. The moment had at last arrived when McCoy felt certain of success. Jackson read his tract on colonization and said he would endorse it if McCoy published a new edition.[12] McCoy asked Eaton for money to support another exploring trip: "He appeared well-disposed towards the plan," McCoy said,

8. Lucius Bolles, to Isaac McCoy, June 2, 1828, BFMB.

9. Lucius Bolles to Lee Compere, June 17, 1828 and to Thomas McKenney, July 2, 1828, BFMB. When Peter B. Porter replaced Barbour as secretary of war in July 1828, Bolles again urged the desirability of removing the Creeks and said that Compere was ready to lead the way West with his congregation if the government would pay for their transportation. Lucius Bolles to Peter Porter, July 8, 1828, BFMB.

10. Lucius Bolles to Isaac McCoy, March 3, 1828, BFMB.

11. Isaac McCoy, *History of Baptist Indian Missions*, p. 377.

12. Schultz, *An Indian Canaan*, p. 106.

"but said he had no funds" for that purpose yet.[13] McCoy found himself very popular with the southern politicians and Jacksonians, and his hopes were high when he suddenly discovered that some of the members of the Baptist board in Boston were beginning to have second thoughts about removal, probably because they realized that under Jackson's aegis, it would be a compulsory removal that would abrogate treaty guarantees. The removal plans the Baptists had hitherto supported required the voluntary cooperation of the Indians. But McCoy attributed the change of attitude in his board to the machination of Jeremiah Evarts and the American Board; in his opinion, the shift came "because the acting members of our board of missions [Bolles, Lincoln, Sharp], though they acted [most of the time] with dignified independence, were not a little influenced by theirs [the acting members of the American Board]. This was natural because both societies were in the same neighborhood [Boston] and both were in a country [Massachusetts] where they" had little true understanding of Indian conditions. "Therefore some of the more active members of the Baptist board were made to doubt the eligibility of the plan."[14] It seemed clear to him that he must now mobilize his friends within the denomination to counteract the waning zeal of the managing board in Boston.

With the help of the Reverend Spencer H. Cone, a leading Baptist of New York City, the Reverend John L. Dagg of Philadelphia, and the Reverend Elon Galusha of Whitesboro, New York, he began "a correspondence with . . . distant members whose wishes, reaching the active members, produced decisions in accordance with what were supposed to be the views of a large majority."[15] In short, he rallied the Baptists with pro-Jacksonian views of removal to make their influence felt upon the executive committee in Boston. McCoy was convinced that those who opposed removal were misinformed and probably tools of the National Republican (Whig) Party: "They who worked the wires stood behind the political curtain and adroitly aggravated opposition to the administration."[16] McCoy left Washington in April 1829 to go to Boston himself to use his influence with the board and to persuade it to finance a new edition of his colonization tract. The board said it was willing to support a reprinting, but not if it included a new appendix written by McCoy which "contained some sentiments relative to the management of missions not in strict accordance with those of the board." McCoy indignantly refused to be muzzled and published the new edition out of his own pocket. The Reverend S. H. Cone saw the manuscript through the press for him in New York.[17]

13. McCoy, *History of Baptist Missions,*, p. 377.
14. Ibid., p. 378.
15. Ibid.
16. Ibid. p. 380. Spencer Cone was a Jacksonian Democrat and also a "general agent" for the Baptist Foreign Mission Board; Bolles and Lincoln were Whigs.
17. Ibid., p. 382.

The division within the Baptist denomination over Jackson's plan for Indian removal first came to a head at the Triennial Convention in Philadelphia in April 1829. McCoy was there to voice two complaints: one, that the board was not sufficiently zealous in support of colonization, and two, that insufficient attention was being given to Indian missions in general. McCoy was correct on the second point. All foreign mission boards devoted their principal attention toward overseas missions, and while Indian missions were placed within the control of foreign mission boards, these boards found that the public was much more interested in the more romantic work in exotic lands overseas and so were those who volunteered to serve as missionaries. McCoy noted with astonishment that the committee appointed to draft a report on the best means to promote foreign missions had "wholly omitted" any mention of Indian missions. One prominent Baptist who edited a religious journal, *The Columbian Star,* told McCoy "there were so many appalling circumstances connected with the business of Indian improvement that he had a thought of introducing into the convention a resolution declaring the belief that their reformation was impracticable."[18] It is much more likely that many Baptists in 1829 realized that the removal question had become such a highly partisan political issue that it might well split their denomination. The convention delegates would have preferred to move cautiously on the Indian question so as not to give offense to either side in the controversy. McCoy, however, considered that silence on the issue was a cowardly desertion of the Indian cause, which the Baptists had so long supported (on his terms). He therefore used his influence to have another committee appointed to look into the question of Indian missions. His friend the Reverend John L. Dagg was made chairman of it, and its report was much more satisfactory to McCoy. It began by noting the lack of "any great advance" among the Indian missions over the last three years despite "all the toils and anxieties that have been endured on account of this wretched people" by the missionaries. So long as the Indians remained in their present locations "they must perish." After commending McCoy for his work and reiterating the Baptists' commitment to civilization and Christianization, the committee concluded that "no measure which has yet been proposed is so likely to accomplish these objects as the settling of the Indians in a permanent home upon our western lands. . . . [W]e contemplate with pleasure the movement which the Government of our country appears to be taking toward this object."[19] In effect, this constituted an endorsement of Jackson's removal policy. The convention then voted: "That the Board of Managers be requested to prepare . . . and to lay before Congress at their next session, and at their subsequent sessions if necessary . . . a memorial in favor of granting to the Indians, as a permanent possession, a portion of our western lands

18. Ibid., p. 383; Schultz, *An Indian Canaan,* p. 128.
19. *Baptist Missionary Magazine* 9: 210–11.

suitable for their settlement and future home." But the executive committee of the board of managers was not so easily outdone. It decided to give the narrowest possible interpretation to this vote. In designing the memorial to Congress, they asked simply for congressional provision of "a permanent home" but did not specifically endorse Jackson's plan for getting them there.[20]

McCoy felt betrayed, and when he met Heman Lincoln in Washington in December 1829 it became clear that the breach between his views and those of the executive committee were wider than ever. In pursuance of the vote of the Triennial Convention, McCoy had taken the liberty of drafting a memorial for the board's approval for which he had already solicited signatures among the Baptist missionaries in the Northwest. His draft constituted an ardent endorsement of Jackson's program for total, compulsory removal of all the Indians east of the Mississippi regardless of their treaty rights: "The interest of the Indians imperiously requires their collocation in the West"; their claims to "independent national character and legal claim to the soil" were meretricious and wrongheaded; "from the very nature of things" they would be "harassed" and go "to ruin" if they remained "in the South" or the North: the board, he said, "view the rights of Indians in the light of those of minors. . . . Justice as well as humanity require that the ward be provided for according to the better judgment of the guardian."[21]

When Heman Lincoln read this, he was shocked. He believed McCoy's draft had gone far beyond what the Triennial Convention voted and that it would give great offense to many northern Baptists. On the other hand, when Lincoln spoke to McCoy about the kind of memorial the board proposed to submit to Congress when debate on Jackson's removal bill began, McCoy declared that the board was refusing to carry out the wishes of the delegates at the convention. "It appeared to me," McCoy wrote later, "that the tenor of the memorial [which the board proposed to make] was such as would produce an impression that we were receding instead of advancing on the matter of colonization."[22] McCoy was so intent on instituting his colonization program that he cared little how Jackson got the Indians to the west. Lincoln wrote at once to Boston. Bolles convened a quorum of the managing board, which then voted a very stern rebuke of McCoy. Agreeing that the convention had voted in May 1829 to submit a memorial, the board insisted that it was to be the same as the one submitted in 1827; it should "not solicit the *removal* of the Indians," but only the creation of a permanent home in the West for those who might choose to go there of their own free will. "Foreseeing that the Executive [Jackson] and leading members of Government were determined on a general removal of Indians, they deemed

20. McCoy, *History of Baptist Missions*, pp. 384–85.

21. McCoy Papers, draft of memorial, December 5, 1829; McCoy to Lucius Bolles, October 21, 1829.

22. McCoy, *History of Baptist Missions*, pp. 395–96.

it unnecessary to do more at this time than ask that in said removal, our Indians (as I may call them) should be provided for"; that is, the board's Indian students should be allowed to go west. "We should avoid augmenting a zeal in some merely political men which [is] already ardent." This letter to Lincoln instructed him to present the memorial the board had agreed upon and to inform McCoy that "they will exceedingly regret any measure on the part of McCoy (such as presenting to Congress a petition for the removal of the Indians in his own name) tending to show his disagreement with their counsel." The board warned McCoy on December 22, 1829, that "should he act in opposition to the Board in any respect by presenting another memorial or otherwise, the Board will feel itself compelled to dissolve the connection between him and them."[23] In a covering letter to Lincoln, Bolles assured him that the board would support him against McCoy and his Jacksonian friends: "Shall their judgment [the board's] always be treated by McCoy as of no weight when thrown in the scale with his?" "What has he shown of prudence, judgment or economy, that we should follow him?" "Do not let your heart fail you, my brother, in this day of trial." Obviously the board felt that a great deal was at stake for the Indians, as well as for those who feared sectional division in the denomination or in the nation. Although the board was not ready to openly oppose Jackson's program, neither did it wish to encourage it.

McCoy decided to fight back. He and Spencer Cone circulated a letter among prominent Baptists (including those on the board) protesting that the executive committee, or "Acting Board," in Boston had not properly carried out the vote of the Triennial Convention. When the executive committee learned of this letter, it printed a response on March 2, 1830, which it sent to all those who had received McCoy's and Cone's letter. This began by quoting the resolution of the Triennial Convention in May and then noted that "this resolution does not require the Board to ask Congress to remove the Indians." It then provided the wording of the memorial which the board had written for Congress and asked rhetorically whether it was not in accord with the resolution. Then the board made a confession:

> While, therefore, the Board feel that they have fulfilled the letter, as well as the spirit of the resolution of the Convention, they admit freely that they purposely employed a more guarded phraseology in their Memorial than some of their brethren might think needful, or than they themselves would have thought necessary at the time the Convention assembled. Events have since occurred [for example, the Georgians' behavior toward the Cherokee Nation] which have awakened a general and deep feeling in the community. An alarm has been spread through the nation that the Government were determined to remove the Indians by force. The President of the United States has stated officially that the Indians must be removed or become subject to the state laws. Many of the friends and supporters of our Convention are apprehensive of wrong to the Indians.[24]

23. Lucius Bolles to Heman Lincoln, December 22, 1829, BFMB.
24. McCoy Papers, roll 7 (1829–32), #00408–9.

In view of this heightened feeling, the board felt that it had to act carefully in its claim to represent "the Baptist community." Their memorial was designed to be evenhanded. It informed Congress "that the Indians ought, for their own safety and happiness to remove, and at the same time" it tried to "give no countenance to the idea that the Indians ought to be, or could rightfully be, compelled to leave their lands or forfeit their rights." Baptists should be aware "that large and powerful bodies of Christians are petitioning Congress against the removal of the Indians." Caution dictated that the Baptists' memorial should not "furnish occasion for placing our denomination in array against other Christians on a question of the utmost importance whether viewed as a measure of Christian benevolence or of national policy." The board, in short, was only trying to maintain denominational harmony, national harmony, and harmony among philanthropic Christians of all denominations. But looked at in another light, the letter also seemed to indicate that the northern Whigs on the board seemed at last to have discovered that McCoy's maneuvers were pushing the denomination into the Jacksonian camp.[25]

In the end McCoy was prevented from presenting his own memorial, but he remained free to lobby as he chose, and he proved very adept and determined in this respect.[26] He had started in December 1829 to discuss the removal bill with members of the administration and Congress who were preparing to push for its passage the following spring. "I have visited with the President and Secretary of War," he wrote to his son on December 21, "both of whom appear full of the Spirit of colonizing the Indians."[27] He also visited his friends Wilson Lumpkin of Georgia and John Bell of Tennessee, chairman of the House Committee on Indian Affairs and sponsor of the administration's bill.[28] Because Evarts and the American Board had by this time generated so much opposition to removal, and the National Republican Party clearly planned to make it a partisan issue, McCoy was instructed by the bill's supporters to do all he could to generate enthusiasm for the bill in the North to counter Evart's work. McCoy wrote to his friend Spencer Cone in New York about his troubles with the board. Cone replied in January that Lincoln and Bolles were "afraid to squint at the Poor Indian least they should lose their reputations by the bare suspicion of leaning towards any of the measures of General Jackson."[29] Cone also told him to work closely with Lumpkin. McCoy spent the early months of 1830 helping John Bell and the Indian Affairs Committee to answer all the petitions flooding in

25. See also the effort of the board to further separate itself from McCoy in an editorial on Indian removal in the *Baptist Missionary Magazine* 10: 158.

26. For the memorial, see Lucius Bolles to Thomas McKenney, December 22, 1829, BFMB.

27. McCoy Papers, Isaac McCoy to Rice McCoy, December 21, 1829.

28. Lumpkin in his autobiography states that *he* drafted the Removal Bill for Jackson but persuaded Bell, from Jackson's home state, to introduce it; *Sketch of His Life*, p. 52.

29. Spencer H. Cone to Isaac McCoy, January 29, 1830, McCoy Papers.

from opponents of removal.[30] "Among the hundreds of petitions there was [not] one in favour of any [tribe] except the southern tribes," McCoy noted; "and even among these, the Choctaws, Chickasaws, and Creeks were almost wholly overlooked. The burden of the prayer of ten thousand voices was 'Spare the Cherokees!' "[31] McCoy found this intensely annoying. The Cherokees were in his view totally atypical, and he saw no reason why they should be an exception to a general removal which would benefit every other tribe. Besides, he believed that even the Cherokees "would inevitably perish" where they were because of Georgia's and Alabama's extension of jurisdiction over them—actions which he was now convinced were totally within the rights of the sovereign states; Georgia and Alabama, he said, were simply following the previous examples set by all of the northern states when, at an early date, they took their Indian affairs into their own hands.[32]

"In order that those in Congress who opposed the measure might not have all the arguments to be drawn from memorials" in support of the cry "Let them remain where they are," McCoy said, "I wrote to friends in divers places, setting forth what I deemed to be the true state of the case and requesting them to forward memorials in *favour* of the plan under consideration."[33] Among those to whom he wrote were Elon Galusha, John L. Dagg, S. H. Cone, William Colgate, David Jones, Adiel Sherwood. He also planned trips to Philadelphia, New York, Hartford, and Boston to generate meetings and petitions in support of removal. He instructed his friends to send the petitions they collected to Wilson Lumpkin, who was leading the fight for Georgia in the Congress.[34] Jeremiah Evarts had met his match. In addition, McCoy said, "Some of us made considerable efforts to enlist in the cause we espoused, public prints which had a wide circulation" (such as Duff Greene's *New York Telegraph*) and "some of us" personally appeared "before the public in defence of the scheme in both political and religious prints, but in the former, commonly under a fictitious name."[35] Like Evarts, McCoy "worked the wires behind the political curtain" without apology in the name of benevolence toward the Indians. But McCoy had only part of his denomination behind him, and his mission board continued to walk a narrow line between the advantages of removal and the disadvantages of compulsory removal. When the Baptist Board held its annual meeting in May 1830, a committee headed by S. H. Cone reported on the subject of Indian missions that "as the question of Indian Emigration is now before Congress, it would be premature and imprudent to adopt any positive meas-

30. "Remarks Submitted to Hon. W. Bell," McCoy Papers, January 11, 1830. He meant *John* Bell.
31. McCoy, *History of Baptist Missions*, p. 380.
32. Ibid., pp. 378—80.
33. Ibid.
34. Isaac McCoy to Elon Galusha, February 5, 1830, McCoy Papers.
35. McCoy, *History of Baptist Missions*, pp. 381, 397.

ures in anticipation of their removal." However, the committee was convinced that there should be "but little, if any, enlargement" of its missions to the Indians in the East; on the other hand, "the period has arrived when missionary operations should be commenced by us west of the State of Missouri and the Arkansaw Territory," where more and more eastern Indians were arriving daily.[36]

McCoy's friend and supporter Wilson Lumpkin, himself a devout Baptist, presented the Baptist memorial on the floor of Congress.[37] However mildly worded, its introduction by Lumpkin gave it the appearance of endorsing the position of Jackson and Georgia. In his speech in support of the removal bill on May 17, Lumpkin led Congress and the public to believe that however the Congregationalists of New England might stand, the Baptists of the nation were solidly behind the removal bill:

> Our most enlightened superintendents and agents of Indian affairs have all become converts to Indian emigration; our most pious and candid missionaries. One of the most devoted and pious missionaries (the Rev. Isaac McCoy) with whom I am acquainted, has [supported removal] . . . . The Baptists have, through their organs and associations, for years past, at every session of Congress, reminded you of the interest they feel and the labours they have bestowed towards the great object of Indian civilization. Moreover, they have expressed their convictions that your emigration plan affords the best and most permanent prospect of success to their missionary efforts.[38]

The passage of the removal bill on May 26, 1830, brought praise from McCoy and an editorial in the *Baptist Missionary Magazine* which said, "The act contemplates no coercive measure for their removal and requires a faithful observance of existing treaties." The editor ignored the fact that the act in effect endorsed the states' rights policy of Georgia and the president's withdrawal of treaty protections and thus permitted enormous indirect compulsion upon the Cherokees and other southeastern tribes either to remove or become second-class citizens. "If the governments of the States within whose limits they are included oppress them," the editor wrote, "they must answer to their country and to the tribunal of Jehovah." But he concluded ambiguously that while it might be "inexpedient" for the Cherokees to remove, it nevertheless was expedient for many other tribes.[39]

By December 1830 the plight of the Cherokees and other southeastern tribes had aroused so much concern among Baptists in the North that the *Baptist Missionary Magazine* printed a long letter signed "Roger Williams" trying to dissociate the Foreign Mission Board from any complicity in the persecution of the Cherokees. The author noted that "the Cherokees, Creeks and some other southern tribes, who have become practically civilized, have

36. *Baptist Missionary Magazine* 10: 162.
37. McCoy, *History of Baptist Missions*, p. 396.
38. Ibid., appendix, p. 591.
39. *Baptist Missionary Magazine* 10: 215.

instituted governments and are practising agriculture and the mechanic arts
. . . . There is consequently a less urgent necessity for these Indians to
remove" than for the northern tribes. Although the board had supported
McCoy's colonization plan, "they have specifically referred in their memorials to the government to these northern tribes and to other Indians in a
similar situation. . . . They have expressed no opinion respecting the civilized Indians at the south" and especially "the Baptists have uttered no
opinion respecting the Cherokees. Neither the Convention nor the Board has
intimated a wish that they should remove."[40] It was a little late in the day,
however, for the Baptists to start calling attention to the difference between
"the civilized Indians" and "the perishing tribes." The writer of this article
claimed that "the States within whose limits the Indians reside have no right
to extend their laws over them and that, consequently, the President of the
United States is bound by his oath to protect the Cherokees and guarantee to
them their rights." He also found that McCoy, in the first edition of his
tract on colonization, had specifically stated in speaking of the Cherokees,
"Force is not to be used in this case. All righteous men agree that their lands
cannot be forced from them." Whoever "Roger Williams" was, he probably
spoke for most New England Baptists.

As a reward for his services on behalf of the removal bill, Jackson
offered to place McCoy in charge of distributing the Education Fund.[41] But
he did not want a desk job in Washington. John Eaton, the secretary of war,
then offered him a post as teacher in the Choctaw academy in the West.[42]
He was not interested in teaching. Finally Eaton offered him the job of
surveying a tract onto which the Delaware Nation could move in the West.
McCoy accepted. "I am appointed to survey an assignment of lands to the
Delawares," he wrote to his wife. "This is such business as I have long
desired, and although the job is small, yet it may prepare the way for other
business. It will also enable me to give some business to two of my sons" as
assistant surveyors.[43] Later that year McCoy moved his residence from the
Potawatomi reserve in Michigan to a spot on the western edge of Missouri,
and for the rest of his life he remained in the West.[44]

The changing position of the Baptist board of managers after 1830 was
motivated by several factors. Not only did it become increasingly convinced
that Jackson's and Georgia's treatment of the Cherokees was unconstitutional
and inhumane, but it feared that it might lose the goodwill of the Cherokees.
Lucius Bolles wrote to Spencer Cone in September 1830 explaining why the

40. *Baptist Missionary Magazine* 10: 363.

41. McCoy, *History of Baptist Missions*, p. 40; Schultz, *An Indian Canaan*, p. 134.

42. Berkhofer, Introduction, p. xvi.

43. Isaac McCoy to his wife, June 3, 1830, McCoy Papers.

44. In 1842 McCoy broke with the Baptist Board entirely and founded the American
Indian Missionary Association and established its office in Louisville, Kentucky. It was
supported almost wholly by southern Baptists after the schism of 1844. Schultz, *An Indian
Canaan*, pp. 201–02.

board had continued to support its mission to the Cherokees in the East but was reluctant to start a major effort among the Cherokees in the west: "Efforts to the improvement of the Indians now present themselves in two aspects, one as connected with their removal to the West, the other as purely evangelical. . . . If our views were confined to the latter exclusively, we should feel no difficulty [in supporting western missions] . . . but as we are so identified in operation with the plans for their removal, we find it not a little embarrassing."[45] To promote missions west of the Mississippi at that time the board would have had to apply for government funds, and that would have meant expressing its support of removal. The board preferred, it said, to "hazard nothing by anticipation." It would not move its missionaries from the Cherokees in the East to the Cherokees in the West on the assumption that the Cherokees would all have to remove eventually. It seemed better to wait and "*follow* them" westward when, and if, they decided to go. Furthermore, Bolles said, the board now wondered whether "we should continue to have any connexions with the government."

When the matter came before the next Triennial Convention in 1832, there was a sharp debate over whether the Baptists should commence missionary activity among the Indians who were moving (or had been moved) to the West. But despite the best efforts of McCoy, Cone, Dagg, and others who favored such action, the convention decided that to do so would be construed as supporting "a political measure" (supporting Jackson) and not a Christian measure.[46] The denomination as a whole had decided to remain neutral, though McCoy and his friends interpreted the decision as anti-Jackson. In a sense this was a victory for the executive committee in Boston, for it enabled them to continue to support their mission at Valley Towns in the Cherokee homeland for as long as the Cherokees could hold out there. The Baptist Board had not consulted their Cherokee missionaries on this matter at any time during the controversy because the board was the servant of the Baptist convention and its missionaries took their orders the same way. Whether or not to support removal was a general policy to be made by the parent body. There is nothing in the board's correspondence with the Reverend Duncan O'Briant at the Tinsawattee station nor with the Reverend Evan Jones at Valley Towns concerning the whole debate prior to 1832. In many respects this was greatly to their advantage, for they were able to tell the Cherokees that they were not involved in the board's action or in McCoy's. In the long run, however, their work was bound to be associated with the position of their board, and it was with some relief that Evan Jones learned in 1832 that the board would not support Jackson's policy by asking federal support for Indian missions in the West.

45. Lucius Bolles to Spencer Cone, September 16, 1830, BFMB.

46. For the debate in the Triennial Convention of 1832, see Schultz, *An Indian Canaan*, p. 137; McCoy, *History of Baptist Missions*, pp. 447–48, 595–98.

Jones had acted entirely on his own when he attended the interdenomi-national meeting called by Samuel Worcester at New Echota in December 1830 and signed the manifesto opposing the actions of Georgia. The Baptist Board took no notice of his action, and the small excerpt from the manifesto published in the *Baptist Missionary Magazine* merely described the religious progress of the Cherokees.[47] From this account the readers would not have known that Jones had taken a stand opposing that of his denomination. Jones, as it turned out, was not only strongly opposed to colonization and removal so far as it applied to the Cherokees, but he did his best to support the Cherokees in their resistance. However, because he was located in the North Carolina region of the nation and that state did not extend its jurisdic-tion over the Cherokees, he did not run the risks of those missionaries who lived in the Georgia area of the nation, at least not in the early stages of the crisis.

With Duncan O'Briant the matter was entirely different. His mission church at Tinsawattee and his school at Hickory Log came within the jurisdiction of Georgia, and he himself was a Georgian, hired by the Sarepta Baptist Missionary Society of that state.[48] Because his mission stations were located close to the nation's eastern border, the Cherokees there were subject to continual intrusions and harassments by frontier whites.[49] O'Briant had been successful in his work and the Cherokees liked him.[50] It is not clear why he did not come to the interdenominational meeting at New Echota, but perhaps Worcester did not think of him as a member of the Boston board; or perhaps he suspected that O'Briant's sympathies lay with Georgia. In any case, O'Briant proved to have no interest in taking any moral or political stand on the removal question. In November 1829 four of the leading families in O'Briant's mission church decided that life was too unpleasant for them around Tinsawattee, and they enrolled to go west to Arkansas under the individual emigration scheme McKenney had written into the treaty with the Western Cherokees in May 1828.[51] Seven months later, when Georgia extended its jurisdiction over the nation, life became even more difficult for

47. *Baptist Missionary Magazine* 11: 127.
48. In a letter to Jesse Mercer of the Sarepta Baptist Missionary Society in 1828, Lucius Bolles referred to the "Committee at the South" as the agency which supervised O'Briant's work. This was evidently composed of ministers appointed by the Sarepta Baptist Association. It was to this committee. headed by Mercer, that O'Briant sent his reports up to 1832. It appears that the Sarepta Mission Society raised the funds for the Tinsawattee mission, though it sent them to the board in Boston. Bolles to Mercer, November 28, 1828, BFMB.
49. See O'Briant, Journal, September 5, 1830, BFMB, discussing the problems with white gold diggers in the Cherokee Nation.
50. In 1830 O'Briant had thirty-six students at Hickory Log and thirty-one church members at Tinsawattee. *Baptist Missionary Magazine* 10 (June 1830): 176, 182. Samuel Aldrich, who succeeded O'Briant as pastor of this church in 1834, spoke of its members as being "white Indians," which apparently meant whites married to Indians or Indians of mixed blood; none of them, he said, spoke Cherokee. Aldrich to Lucius Bolles, July 27, 1835, BFMB.
51. *Baptist Missionary Magazine* 10:182.

O'Briant's church members, and more of them began to talk about going West. When Georgia passed the law requiring all missionaries to sign an oath of allegiance to the state, O'Briant, as a citizen of Georgia, had no qualms about signing it.[52] Whether or not he then received a license from Georgia to continue to preach is not known, but because of his compliance he was treated very differently by the Georgia guard from any other missionary. Evidently he had decided by the summer of 1831 that he would join with his church members and emigrate to the West. Most of the members apparently were of mixed ancestry or whites married to Cherokees. The Reverend Jesse Mercer of the Sarepta Baptist Missionary Society wrote to the Baptist board in August 1831 that "Col. Nelson [of the Georgia guard] gives me a good account of Mr. O'Briant, and says he is doing more good in giving instruction and reforming the Indians than any other missionary in the nation." Nelson's reason for giving this praise, Mercer said, was that O'Briant "would be able to unite about eighty families in a removal."[53] O'Briant wrote a letter to Mercer in August stating that virtually all of his church members wished to enroll for emigration, but whether he had urged them to go or whether the initiative came from them Mercer did not say. Mercer and the Sarepta Baptist Association, however, were thoroughly in accord with Georgia's effort to compel the Cherokees to go and may even have put some pressure upon O'Briant to that end.[54]

When O'Briant said he was willing to emigrate, Mercer wrote to Lucius Bolles to ask him to write to the secretary of war to find out whether the government would "pay for their improvements" at the mission stations and "bear the expenses of removal." He told Bolles that O'Briant "is a good man, and if approved by Government would make a suitable leader or Agent of an emigrating party." Bolles wrote to Lewis Cass about this, noting that "as the Cherokees are not likely as a Tribe to agree to go," perhaps the departure of a church and its minister to the west might aid "such as are disposed to transfer themselves" to make up their minds. "The example of one village might affect another materially and so on till the emigrating spirit infected the whole mass."[55] Bolles said that if O'Briant and his church

52. George R. Gilmer, *Sketches of the First Settlers of Upper Georgia*, pp. 304, 344. Gilmer states that O'Briant had signed the oath by April 19, 1831, and presumably before the deadline of March 1, 1831.

53. Lucius Bolles to Lewis Cass, August 13, 1831, BFMB. Eighty families with an average of six in each family seems a large number, but if they all were, as Aldrich said, "white Indians," this would confirm the claims made at the time that it was primarily the whitemen with Indian families who were the first to enroll for emigration.

54. In June 1832, Jesse Mercer wrote a letter to Elizur Butler deploring the resistance of the American Board missionaries to Georgia's oath law: "I think," he told Butler, "you have taken a very mistaken (and to yourselves and country a most ruinous) course." Georgia had every right to assert its jurisdiction over the Cherokee land, Mercer said, and consequently was within its rights in imprisoning Butler and Worcester for disobeying its authority. Mercer to Butler, June 18, 1832. Payne Papers, IX, 19–22.

55. Lucius Bolles to Jesse Mercer, August 13, 1831, BFMB.

and school left the Cherokee Nation, the board would abandon the mission stations at those places and not try to send a replacement for him. He asked whether the government would reimburse the board for the money it had laid out to build the two stations and whether it would pay O'Briant's travel expenses. Cass wrote back that O'Briant should make all arrangements through the federal agent in the nation, Colonel Hugh Montgomery. The board assumed that once O'Briant arrived in the West "a permanent provision could be obtained for Mr. O'Briant as their teacher," thus continuing the school abandoned at Hickory Log. They expected that the funds for this would come from the government "independent of us." "The Government will derive sufficient advantage from Indian lands to afford them instruction," Bolles told Mercer.[56] Apparently Bolles was unaware that if the Cherokees left, their land would revert to Georgia and not to the federal government. O'Briant talked to Montgomery and understood him to say that funds would be available for himself and his church members. They left Tinsawattee in November 1831 and, after spending the winter in Tennessee, embarked on boats at the agency in March as part of a larger emigrating party of 382 Cherokees, all of course considered traitors by those who remained to uphold their homeland.[57] They arrived in what is now northeastern Oklahoma via the Arkansas River in May 1832. To O'Briant's surprise, he discovered that he was not going to be paid for his transportation nor was he given a salary as a schoolteacher. The board had to pay his salary of $250 a year as it had in the East.[58] Needless to say, this effort of the Sarepta Baptists and the managing board to promote Cherokee emigration did not ingratiate them to the antiremoval Cherokees; nor did their continued efforts to obtain reimbursement for their mission stations from the government.[59] In 1833, Joseph B. Adams, a preacher for the American Board at Haweis, heard an influential Cherokee say that O'Briant was "bad because he went over the river," and that to become a Christian was to become, as O'Briant's members became, enemies to the nation. As Adams reported, the Cherokees told him "that Mr. O'Brien, a Baptist preacher . . . formerly talked kindly and well, just as I did, but that he and every member of his church emigrated and that none but the religious did go from that neighborhood." Adams said, "This is true."[60] O'Briant's action was a serious blow not only to the Baptist cause but to missions in general.

Gradually the Baptist Board became more sympathetic to the Cherokee resistance to emigration. They were shocked by the arrests of the missionaries of the American Board, the Methodists, and the Moravians. An

56. Ibid.

57. *Baptist Missionary Magazine* 12: 182; 13:16. See also the letters from O'Briant and Aldrich to Bolles regarding the difficulties the Tinsawattee church and school had trying to get established in the West; BFMB.

58. Lucius Bolles to Duncan O'Briant, August 8, 1832, BFMB.

59. Lucius Bolles to Lewis Cass, October 22, 1832, BFMB.

60. Joseph B. Adams to David Greene, May 2, 1833, ABCFM.

unsigned editorial on this subject in the *Baptist Missionary Magazine* in December 1831 described the imprisonment of Worcester and Butler as "disgraceful"; it aroused "feelings of the most decisive disapprobation in the breast of every Christian patriot!" "Perhaps no event has occurred in the country which has excited greater surprise and displeasure among good men."[61] Jesse Mercer took exception to this editorial, and Daniel Sharp of the board's executive committee had to apologize for the magazine's injecting itself into politics.[62]

Evan Jones in Valley Towns had always taken a totally different view of the removal crisis from O'Briant and Mercer. Shortly after the first arrest of the missionaries in Georgia, he wrote to Bolles, "How far despotism and oppression will go the Lord only knows."[63] The board finally decided, in February 1832, that it ought to ask Jones what his views were on the Indian question. It seems likely that O'Briant's unfortunate experience and Jones's response to their inquiries played an important part in revising the thinking of the board on this whole issue. "With regard to the case of brother O'Briant," Jones wrote, and "the painful subject of Indian Emigration . . . I have strong fears that the plan is not a happy one." It "has had the effect to bring into question among the less informed [Cherokees] the friendly feelings of our denomination towards the Indians. I have been challenged on the subject repeatedly." To him it was so obvious that forced emigration was cruel, unjust, and oppressive that he was surprised to find the board and so many other whites still confused about the subject. "There is evidently a strong tendency in the reporters [on Indian affairs] so to frame their relations as to suit the views of men in power" rather than to convey the truth. The whole subject has been "transformed, colored and magnified to favor the side of emigration." Nevertheless, having now spent a dozen years among the Cherokees, Jones could say without qualification that it is "the decided, constant, unvarying voice of the whole body of the people . . . that they have no disposition to remove." Yet this obvious fact was treated by the public, and often by missionaries, as of "no regard and is suppressed and misrepresented." The War Department thought in 1828 when it opened its agency office to enroll emigrants and offered to pay their way that "one-half or two-thirds . . . would eagerly" sign up to go. But despite "threats and promises," despite "the Georgia Guard at the point of the bayonet" throughout the nation only "300 Emigrants have been obtained out of a population of 16,000 or about fifty families." "Most of these are White men with Cherokee families. . . . Some of the emigrants are Cherokees of mixed blood. . . . No more than ten or eleven full Cherokees have enrolled in all." Jones lived in that part of the nation where 96 percent of the people were fullbloods. In conclusion, he told the board, emigration had become by 1832

61. *Baptist Missionary Magazine* 11: 381.
62. Lucius Bolles to Jesse Mercer, May 22, 1832, BFMB.
63. Evan Jones to Lucius Bolles, March 15, 1831, BFMB.

the touchstone by which a Cherokee differentiated a patriot from a traitor, a friend from an enemy: "I am fully persuaded that nothing short of positive coercion would induce them to think of such a measure. Such a proposition to a Christian or Pagan Cherokee from a Missionary would be regarded with indignation and his influence and usefulness would be utterly destroyed."[64] By and large Jones was right, and after 1832 the Baptist Foreign Mission Board, and especially its executive committee in Boston, accepted and supported his strong antiremoval position. His activist position on this question was to make him the most successful missionary among the Cherokees over the next six years. It was at the opposite pole from the Moravian response to the crisis.

The Moravians were by long tradition apolitical. They were also small in number, lacking in political influence, and limited in funds. The board of managers or directors of the Society of the United Brethren for the Propagation of the Gospel among the Heathen obtained most of its funds from the contributions of Moravian congregations in Salem, North Carolina, and Bethlehem, Pennsylvania.[65] It had been hoped that the missions among the Cherokees would sooner or later become self-supporting, but they never did. Expenses at Springplace were small, however, less than $500 a year (excluding the $200 to $300 provided by the government for its school after 1809). With the formation of the second mission station at Oochgelogy in 1822, the expenses doubled. Georgia's decision to assert its jurisdiction over the Cherokee territory within its borders greatly worried the Moravians. Privately they were appalled at the actions of the Georgians and sympathetic to the plight of the Cherokees. But they had no inclination to challenge the government of Georgia or the president of the United States. After a century in America, the Moravians still conducted their affairs in German; they were American citizens but they thought of themselves essentially as Christian pilgrims, not as voting citizens. They had always believed in submission to the powers that be, and their approach to problems of this kind was one of patient resignation to the will of God. Still, like other missionaries, they had to decide precisely who were "the powers that be" in this situation.

The Reverend Henry Gottlieb Clauder, who took charge of the Oochgelogy mission in 1828, offered a typical response for his denomination when one of his more prominent church members, Elijah Hicks, asked him in January 1829 what he thought about Georgia's law to denationalize the Cherokees. "To an inquiry he made respecting the opinion of the Missionaries about the Cherokee Land question," Clauder wrote in his diary, "I answered him that Missionaries have no cause to trouble themselves about local affairs—that as their labours were to be confined to spiritual things only, the *place* where their labours were to be expended must necessarily

64. Evan Jones to Lucius Bolles, April 26, 1832, BFMB.
65. See Schwarze, *Moravian Missions*.

remain immaterial to them."[66] Hicks was not satisfied with this evasive answer; he "appeared to be anxious about a missionary's opinion" as to whether the Cherokees should try to hold on to their native land or emigrate; "I answered that not being in possession of the necessary information, I was unable to form a just opinion whether the Indians should remain in possession of their Lands or emigrate."

Three weeks later, when George Hicks and some other converts came to him with the same question, Clauder said, "I endeavoured to recommend to them absolute reliance upon the Lord whose ways, however mysterious to us, are always best."[67] Despite this outward submission to God's will, Clauder was privately very upset by Georgia's actions. The day before he spoke to George Hicks he had written in his diary regarding Georgia's law denying the Cherokees the right to testify in their own defense in court: "This is a specimen of Republicanism—of Liberty and Equality! O, America—Thou Land of Liberty, where are thy boasted 'People's Rights!' Alas! it's all a mere name."[68] Six months later, after Jackson had announced his support of Georgia, Clauder was even more upset with Georgia's and Jackson's "appalling" assault upon the Cherokees' rights. "The United States and Georgia will heap upon their guilty heads the just imprecations of thousands of this generation and of generations yet unborn.'[69] His sympathy for the Cherokees around his mission was profound: "The present is a gloomy time with the poor Indians who are to be deprived of their lands which they possessed by inheritance for centuries past—the sorrow, pain and despondency which is depicted on the countenance of every Cherokee is readily calculated to awaken the sympathy of the stoutest heart—even the hearts of their enemies would become softened were they witness [to] their misery."[70] Yet he did not know what he could do for them.

The missionaries at Springplace, Gottlieb and Nathaniel Byhan, were equally distressed but also unwilling to offer any public judgments. When the Indians came to Springplace in January 1830 "to ask us what we think of the relations between the Cherokees and Georgia, we answered that we knew no more than we read in the papers from time to time . . . that the entire matter is in the hands of the Lord. He would do what was best. He had permitted them to be confronted with this situation to bring them to Him and to teach them to entrust their affairs to Him."[71] When two elderly Cherokees, Canandoah and his wife, received an equivocal answer from him, Gottlieb Byhan was surprised at their firm response to him: "We will not go West, for God has given us this land and we wish to spend the rest of our short lives here."[72]

66. Clauder, Diary, January 9, 1829, MAB.
67. Clauder, Diary, January 31, 1829, MAB.
68. Clauder, Diary, January 30, 1829, MAB.
69. Clauder, Diary, June 16, 1829, MAB.
70. Clauder, Diary, June 28, 1829, MAB.
71. Springplace Diary, January 14, 1830, MAS.
72. Ibid.

The official journal of the Moravian Board, *The Missionary Intelligencer and Religious Miscellany,* provided the only public indication of the denomination's position on removal. As early as 1827 the board believed that sooner or later the Cherokees would have to go westward. Their annual report that year stated,

> It might appear doubtful to some, at the present crisis which renders it uncertain, how long the Cherokee nation may be suffered to retain their present places of residence, and how long in consequence, our missionary establishment there can be maintained, whether it is altogether proper to attempt to supply them with new missionaries. In fact, we cannot help entertaining a belief that finally their removal from the territories of Georgia will be brought about.[73]

The crisis of which they spoke in 1827 was the furor aroused among the Georgians over the refusal of the Cherokees to sell any more land to the federal commissioners and over the rising Cherokee nationalism which had produced their constitution. The annual report of 1829 offered a more pessimistic appraisal of the Cherokee predicament. It noted that an inevitable conflict had arisen between Georgia's claims under the Compact of 1802 and the civilization program of the federal government, which made the Cherokees unwilling to part with any more land. Describing (as the Georgians also did) the Cherokee constitution as a declaration of "national independence" which had established "an independent community and government within the state of Georgia," the Moravians' mission board asserted that "circumstances may render it imperatively necessary" for the Cherokees to choose either removal or submission to denationalization. It was "greatly to be wished," the board went on, "that the endeavours of government may succeed" in convincing the Cherokees of the necessity of choosing one or the other, for they could not cling to such an *imperium in imperio.* This report noted that the board's missionaries within the Cherokee Nation found "the case peculiarly delicate" because "several of the Indians belonging to the missions of the Brethren are among those to whom both their countrymen and the government look up for an influential decision." Consequently the missionaries "strive to abstain from any interference" or expression of opinion lest they be accused of trying to influence these tribal leaders. All that their missionaries could offer to do was to preach the Gospel to them wherever God destined them to be: "On the part of the Brethren there is no doubt that every thing possible will be done, not to abandon their little flock, even if obliged to emigrate. Let us hope that these severe trials are to be considered the means through which the Lord shall the more perfectly obtain his purpose, however little we can understand his ways."[74] The Moravians made no attempt to arouse public opinion to support the Cherokees and no effort to participate in the debate over Jackson's removal bill. They sent no petitions or memorials to Congress, held no protest meetings, issued no

73. *Missionary Intelligencer* 2:562.
74. *Missionary Intelligencer* 3:378–79.

statements. The board held strictly to its policy of political neutrality throughout the decade 1828–38, neither supporting removal nor opposing it. The only public action taken by the Moravians during the crisis was the decision made by Clauder and Byhan in December 1830 to join in signing the interdenominational manifesto drawn up by Samuel Worcester. They did so without asking the advice of the board in Salem, and Worcester expressed surprise at their signing. Clauder referred briefly to the action in his diary: "Br. Byhan and myself went to New Echota according to invitation to attend a meeting of the Missionaries of the American Board to adopt certain resolutions on the present crisis of the Indian affair. . . . Much love prevailed throughout our deliberations which were all signed by us and ordered for publication in the *Phoenix*."[75] However, the Moravian board did not publish anything about this manifesto in its journal and probably regretted the impulsive gesture, which had compromised the denomination's strict neutrality.

Neutrality became impossible, however, after December 1830, when Georgia passed its oath law. Clauder was astounded at "this tyrannical law of a state styling itself free and independent—of one too that has already raised the flag of rebellion against the union."[76] Like the missionaries of the other denominations, he did not want to sign the oath nor did he want to leave his mission station. "It caused me much trouble in my mind. I can't think of fleeing from the poor Cherokees in this perilous time—yet the thought of leaving my wife and child and consenting to be confined in a penitentiary is also enough to chill my blood."[77] Gottlieb and Nathaniel Byhan at Springplace were also astonished: "We fear its detrimental effect on the mission."[78] Early in January 1831 Clauder rode the twenty miles from Oochgelogy to Springplace to consult with his brethren. The three of them concluded "it would be against our conscience to take an oath of allegiance to the laws of Georgia."[79] Then they talked it over with the Cherokees in their mission church and "they agreed that we and they were in a similar predicament."[80] The three missionaries wrote to their board for instructions. Meanwhile they decided that Clauder and Nathaniel Byhan should move eighteen miles north, across the Georgia border, to live with a Cherokee friendly to the mission, Captain David McNair, who had a plantation at Connesauga, Tennessee. McNair was not a Moravian convert but his wife and daughter were. Gottlieb Byhan decided to remain at Springplace because he was the postmaster there and believed his status as a federal employee made him exempt from the law.[81] Because the law did not apply to women, Clauder's

75. Clauder, Diary, December 29, 1830, MAB.
76. Clauder, Diary, January 29, 1831, MAB.
77. Clauder, Diary, January 21, 1831, MAB.
78. Springplace Diary, January 9, 1831, MAS.
79. Springplace Diary, January 25, 1831, MAS.
80. Springplace Diary, January 31, 1831, MAS.
81. Springplace Diary, February 21–22, 1831, MAS.

wife and Anna Gambold remained at Oochgelogy to continue the school, while Byhan's wife remained at the Springplace school.

When the board in Salem received their letter, it wrote to approve their decision against signing the oath. To avoid further trouble, the board instructed Gottlieb Byhan to resign his position as postmaster.[82] The board preferred to have all its missionaries move out of the jurisdiction of Georgia rather than face any conflict with the authorities. It wrote to Governor George Gilmer expressing its regret that its missionaries could not sign the oath and its willingness to have the missionaries remove after March 1, asking only that he give them timely warning so that they could be gone before the Georgia guard came to arrest them for noncompliance. Gilmer wrote back politely saying, "I regret that your Missionaries should have found any difficulty in complying with the requirements of the laws of the State. The principal object of those laws has been to remove from the Cherokees white men of bad character and those who, from mistaken views of the rights and powers of the state have been engaged in exciting the Indians to sedition and opposition to the policy of the Government."[83] When the Georgia guard arrested the American Board missionaries in March, the Moravians were fearful. But after Judge Clayton released them on the grounds that they were "agents" of the federal government, Clauder and Byhan returned to their posts in Georgia. Nevertheless, the Georgia guard arrested Clauder at Oochgelogy on May 31. He escaped imprisonment by agreeing to leave at once for Salem. Governor Gilmer, however, was far more magnanimous toward Byhan than toward Worcester. When he wrote to the postmaster general asking for Worcester's dismissal, Gilmer praised Byhan: "Mr. Byhan is said to be a respectable man and I have no doubt will hereafter, under the direction of the pious men who employ him, confine himself to his duty. I have no objection to his continuing in his present office. . . . We ask only for the removal of political incendiaries."[84] As a result, Byhan was not bothered by the guard so long as he remained at Springplace.

Clauder, acting on instructions from his board, prepared to shut down the Oochgelogy mission permanently and to move out all of his and Mrs. Gambold's property. He requested the Georgia guard (which he privately referred to as the Georgia Bloodhounds for their constant harrying of the Cherokees) to grant him forty days' grace so that wagons could be sent from Salem to carry their belongings. Colonel Nelson, the subcommandant of the guard, wrote to reassure him: "I have no doubt that Col. Sanford will without the least hesitation grant to each of you the fullest time so that you may make your arrangements to leave the Territory. Our object is not to

82. Schwarze, *Moravian Missions*, p. 194.

83. George Gilmer to the Directors of the [Moravian] Board, April 13, 1831, MAS, and Gilmer, *Sketches of the First Settlers*, p. 305.

84. Gilmer, *Sketches of the First Settlers*, p. 304.

oppress any who manifest a determination to comply with our Laws. Your conduct, so unlike others who professed no other motives than yourselves in locating in the Country, has created within us the most hearty Reciprocity of feelings."[85] Gottlieb Byhan continued at Springplace until March 1832, when he asked to be relieved. Clauder, his family, and Dorothea Ruede, a schoolteacher, then returned from Salem. Jackson's postmaster general allowed Clauder to succeed Byhan as postmaster at Springplace. Clauder remained for a year, itinerating once a month to Oochgelogy to preach while he and Dorothea Ruede sustained the school and mission church at Springplace. At the end of 1832, however, Clauder was forced out of Springplace by the arrival of the Georgia citizen who had won the plot on which it stood in the land lottery. Thus ended the Moravian presence in Georgia, although Clauder (and later other Moravians) continued to itinerate occasionally to Oochgelogy from Connesauga, Tennessee, where he went back to live on David McNair's plantation.[86]

The policy of neutrality in the end had led the Moravians to make some promises they could not really fulfill. They had promised their converts that they would never desert them. But as their reports indicate, once they had left Georgia, their converts were left essentially without spiritual leadership and their students had no schools. Some converts tried for a time to carry on at Oochgelogy with native exhorters, but without regular missionary direction, the Moravian churches collapsed. Only those converts who followed them to Tennessee continued to have their spiritual needs and their schooling cared for with any regularity.

The Methodist missionaries responded to the removal effort with activities that fell somewhere between the neutrality of the Moravians and the activism of the American Board. Like the Baptists, they were divided among themselves, but it was a different kind of division. It pitted the antiremoval missionaries in the field against a neutral board in Tennessee. The Methodist Episcopal Church, the fastest growing denomination in early-nineteenth-century America, was the last to found a missionary society. The Methodist General Conference established the Missionary Society of the Methodist Episcopal Church in 1819,[87] but it had very little authority over missionary activity. Its primary task was to raise funds and keep records. The task of Indian missions was delegated to the annual conferences in each state because they were considered part of home mission work. The Tennessee Annual Conference was the first southern conference to send circuit riders to the Cherokees, although a few from the Alabama conference occasionally went into the nation. The Tennessee Annual Conference established its own missionary society to raise funds locally, but the conference set the

85. This letter is enclosed in one from Gottlieb Byhan to Schulze, July 16, 1831, MAS, and is dated July 15, 1831.
86. Schwarze, *Moravian Missions*, pp. 198–202.
87. Wade C. Barclay, *History of Methodist Missions*, vol. 1, p. 205; vol. 2, p. 112.

policies, assigned the circuit riders, and supervised Cherokee mission activities. Because the Tennessee Annual Conference received no financial
subsidy from the government for its Cherokee missions and because it made
almost no financial investment in buildings or schools, the Methodists were
less worried about offending the War Department than the other three
denominations and had almost no contact with it or with various state
officials. Ultimately, however, the logic of the Methodists' regional control
over mission policy was to work against them with the Cherokees. Although
the Methodist circuit riders were sympathetic to Cherokee interests, those
who appointed and supervised them spoke primarily for the interests of the
white frontier settlers on the borders of the Cherokee Nation who raised the
funds for the mission.

When Georgia extended its jurisdiction over the Cherokees and Jackson
withdrew federal protection of their civil rights, the Methodist itinerants did
not hesitate to express their sympathy for the Cherokees and to exhibit their
chagrin at the barbarous behavior of white authorities. Not only did they
express themselves privately on these points but they sometimes used their
sermons as vehicles for their feelings. The Reverend Daniel Butrick of the
American Board chanced to overhear a Methodist sermon in September 1830
and was amazed at its blatant political character. It started, he said, as an
ordinary evangelical appeal to sinners, and "I was tolerably well pleased with
the fore-part of the meeting" but "near the close of the discourse the speaker
imagined a council held in hell—which extended to some of the state
legislatures—and also included the President of the United States—all for
the purpose of rob[b]ing the Cherokees of their country and breaking them
up as a Nation." The Methodist preacher "also imagined a council held by
Christians, by holy angels, and finally by the Father, Son, and Holy Ghost
for the purpose of saving the Cherokees; and he predicted the Salvation of the
Nation. This much affected the minds of some, even produced groaning and
tears."[88] Methodist circuit riders were not educated men; they spoke extem-
poraneously and they were judged by their zeal and their results. If this was
typical of the preaching of their circuit riders among the Cherokees, it is easy
to see why they were so popular and why John Ross would join them. They
were in effect the spiritual arm of the patriot movement. Methodism pro-
claimed that the powerful God of Christianity was on the side of social and
political justice for the Indians. After the sermon, Butrick reported that a
crowd of tearful, groaning Cherokees surged forward by the score to express
their interest in learning more about the Father, Son, and Holy Ghost; they
were enrolled as "seekers" and assigned to Methodist societies. Butrick
was "disgusted" with the whole performance, but the Cherokees were overwhelmed with feeling. Here were white missionaries who truly cared for
their national concerns as a people and not simply for their souls and sins and
status in the next world. Because as an oppressed people they felt the need for

88. Daniel Butrick to Jeremiah Evarts, September 22, 1830, ABCFM.

solidarity and supernatural assistance, they found the Methodist version of Christianity tremendously appealing.

In the same month that Butrick overheard this sermon, the Methodist missionaries called a special meeting at the Chattooga campground in the Cherokee Nation in order to draw up a set of resolutions asking their denomination to support justice for the Cherokee people in their crisis. Eight of the ten circuit riders attended and signed a statement expressing their firm support for the Cherokee Nation and their indignation and concern at the "oppressed condition of our brethren, the Cherokees, and the future of the mission cause among them." These missionaries did not speak of the Cherokees as "the children of the forest" or as "the poor, wretched race of perishing aborigines." Nor did they distinguish between the spiritual aspect of the missionary cause and the social circumstances within which evangelization occurred. They did not even wrestle with the abstract problems of obedience to "the powers that be" and of whether they were letting their political feelings interfere with their spiritual calling. To them there was a direct connection between the salvation of Cherokee souls and a concern for the welfare of the Cherokee community.

The eight missionaries who signed the resolutions on September 25, 1830, were James J. Trott, Dickson C. McLeod, Nicholas D. Scales, Jacob Ellinger, Joseph Miller, William McFerrin, Greenberry Garrett, and Francis Owen—the last was the superintendent of the mission that year.[89] The missionaries pledged themselves to set forth a description to the public of the progress the Cherokees had made in civilization and Christianization and to inform the public that "the Cherokee nation is firmly resolved not to remove from their present home." Furthermore, they resolved that "it is the unanimous opinion" of the Methodist missionaries that removal would be "ruinous" to the Cherokees. They also denied emphatically the allegation of the secretary of war and various southern politicians that the missionaries were "under the controlling influence of the principal men of the nation merely in order the more effectually to extend our missionary operation." They concluded by calling upon "the Christian community of the United States" to express its sympathy for the "aggrieved condition of the Cherokees" and to interpose its opinion against the current policies of Georgia and of the federal government in the name of "humanity and justice."[90]

The resolutions were sent to the *Methodist Christian Advocate* and the *Cherokee Phoenix* for publication and to the Tennessee Annual Conference for action. The signers hoped to persuade their mission agency to issue "a public and official expression of sentiment" opposing the cruel oppressions of their brethren, the Cherokees. This Methodist proclamation was the model for the interdenominational manifesto which Samuel Worcester per-

89. The two who did not sign were G. M. Rogers and Robert Rogers. There is no indication that they would not have signed had they attended.
90. *Christian Advocate*, October 26, 1830, and *Cherokee Phoenix*, October 1, 1830.

suaded the twelve missionaries of the other three denominations to sign three months later in New Echota. The *Methodist Christian Advocate,* which printed these resolves on October 29, 1830, was one of the quasi-official organs of the Methodist Episcopal Church. It had gone on record two years before in defense of the denomination's missionaries against Peter Porter's claim that missionaries opposed removal because they did not want to give up a life of luxury subsidized for them by the taxpayers: "If comfortable establishments were the only inducements presented to these self-denying men to persuade them to remain in their present stations," said the editor, "we venture to predict that they would soon abandon them 'to the moles and the bats.' " Methodist missionaries, the editor continued, worked in conditions of great deprivation to bring the Gospel to the heathen: "in the prosecution of their benevolent designs [they] are reduced to all the privations and hardships peculiar to half-civilized society, and are obliged from their scanty allowance to unite the most rigorous economy with the most patient industry." Paid only inconsequential salaries, they in fact lived essentially upon the hospitality of the Cherokees; the Cherokee people fed them, housed them, and built their schools and churches for them with their own tools and labor.[91]

The *Methodist Christian Advocate* was published in New York City, and its editor had no qualms about attacking the Georgians and defending the Cherokees against Jacksonian injustices; he may well have been a National Republican in politics. In any case, speaking as a Christian and a philanthropist, he deplored this reversal of the original Indian policy and the effort to "compel them" to sell their country "either by direct coercion or by the intrigues which too often disgrace state policy or by the cupidity which so frequently characterizes mercantile and speculating operations"—especially where Indians were concerned.[92]

When the *Cherokee Phoenix* published the Methodist resolves on October 1, 1830, Elias Boudinot added an editorial praising the Methodists for being the first missionaries to speak out for his people's rights. He urged others who professed benevolent concern for the aborigines to follow their noble example: "The time has come when it is the duty of every friend of justice and humanity to speak out and express his opinion and raise his voice in favor of oppressed innocence. Why should not missionaries, the true friends of the Indians, who toil day and night for their spiritual good, be permitted to exercise the sacred right of freemen—the liberty of free speech and freedom of inquiry?"[93] The Tennessee Annual Conference met at Nash-

91. *Christian Advocate,* December 19, 1828. The *Advocate* in this editorial drew attention to increasing racism as a cause for the removal program. Pointing out that the Cherokees and other tribes were fast becoming Christianized and civilized, so that their savagery could no longer be held against them, the editor asked, "Is the mere circumstance of the different colour of their skin to make them to be abhorred forever by the white man? Is this characteristic peculiarity alone sufficient to entail upon them the malediction of our government, that it must adopt measures to push them to the utmost of our western territories?"
92. Ibid.
93. *Cherokee Phoenix,* October 1, 1830.

ville on November 12, 1830. The missionaries were present to accept their assignments for the next year. By Methodist custom, ministers, particularly circuit riders, held only annual appointments subject to renewal for two or three years. Indian mission work was a starting point from which the young preachers worked up to more important work for the denomination. When the resolutions of the Cherokee missionaries came before the conference for discussion, it became apparent that the conference as a whole (consisting of ministers, circuit riders, and bishops) had a very different perspective from their circuit riders and from the editor of the *Christian Advocate* in New York. By and large those who conducted the affairs of the conference were frontier people whose fathers and grandfathers had fought against the Cherokees and other Indians for the land they now lived upon; the circuit riders, most of them in their early twenties, had not known the fears of the Creek War in 1812–14 and had forgotten the Indian raids and scalping parties of the 1780s and 1790s. By tradition and locality, the people of Tennessee shared the views of Andrew Jackson and the Georgians on the Indian question, even though they held back about extending their state's jurisdiction over the Cherokee Nation within their borders until 1833. They fully supported compulsory Indian removal to the west, though some Tennesseans thought the Georgians were a bit rough about it.[94] There were no antiremoval protests in Tennessee. As Christians, the members of the Tennessee Annual Conference tried not to let party politics control their lives, and they wanted to keep evangelization separate from worldly concerns. They believed in the separation of church and state and thought it was dangerous for the church to meddle in politics. Their denomination had been badly burned in this regard when, thirty years earlier, it had tried to stand up against the sin of owning and selling black slaves. The denomination had been forced to back down from that stand between 1800 and 1820; the view now prevailed among southern Methodists that slavery was a political and not a moral or religious issue. So they thought removal should be. Consequently the vast majority of the delegates at the conference in November 1830 were disconcerted to find that their young circuit riders among the Indians were trying to drag them into a new confrontation with public racial and political issues. It was not good for the church. The delegates found a rule in their ecclesiastical polity which enabled them to point this out to the incautious and headstrong circuit riders. Article Six of the Methodist Discipline was (or seemed to the majority) perfectly clear on the matter: "As far as it respects civil affairs, we believe it is the duty of Christians and especially all Christian ministers to be subject to the supreme authority of the country where they may reside, and to use all laudable means to enjoin obedience to the powers that be."[95] The Methodists had never considered the Indians part of

94. See St. George Sioussat, "Tennessee and the Removal of the Cherokees," *Sewanee Review* (July 1908): 1–8.

95. Quoted in John B. McFerrin in his discussion of this confrontation; *History of Methodism in Tennessee*, vol. 1, pp. 373–74.

their foreign mission field, but still it was not clear whether Cherokee missionaries who were to be subject to the "supreme authority of the country where they may reside" were subject to the Cherokee Nation in which they lived, to the state of Georgia, or to the federal government. Simply by making a judgment on this vexed question, the Tennessee Annual Conference was entering into politics. But, like Butrick among the American Board missionaries and like the Moravian board, the Tennessee Annual Conference readily accepted the notion that if Andrew Jackson acquiesced in the assertion of Georgia's jurisdiction, then Georgia was the supreme authority. There was no need for the United States Supreme Court to rule on the matter or to worry over treaty rights as "the supreme law of the land." The conference therefore flatly rejected the plea of its missionaries that it express its concern over the oppression of the Cherokees in the name of humanity and Christian justice. Instead, it administered a stern rebuke to the missionaries for thoughtlessly and imprudently trying to push the denomination into an area where it did not belong: "Whatever may be our private views and sentiments as men and free citizens relative to the sufferings and privations of the aboriginal nations of our country . . . or of the policy adopted and pursued by the State authority or General Government, yet as a body of Christian ministers, we do not feel at liberty . . . to depart from the principle . . . of our Church in carefully refraining from all such interference with political affairs."[96] The conference expressed official "regret" at the precipitous actions of its missionaries. As individuals they "sincerely sympathized with our Cherokee brethren in their present afflictions" and assured them of their "unabating zeal for the conversion and salvation of their souls." Yet they felt they must express their "confidence in the wisdom and integrity of our rulers." Georgia's legislators and Jackson's administration had rightful charge of the Cherokees' civil rights; the only proper concern of the Methodists was for the souls of individual Cherokees. In the end, then, the circuit riders' efforts came to naught; if anything, they had produced from the Methodists an endorsement of Jackson's removal program.

Elias Boudinot, in publishing these negative results of the conference on January 8, 1831, accused the Methodists of taking too narrow a view of Christianity: "We sincerely regret that so respectable a body as the Tennessee Conference should call the *Indian question* merely a *political question*. It is exactly the way enemies of the Indians blind the people. . . . Perhaps nothing has a greater tendency to prejudice the cause of the Indians. . . . [I]n approbating the present policy in regard to the Indians . . . they have as much interfered with *political* affairs as the Missionaries." This was the beginning of the end for Methodist progress among the Cherokees. There could be no political neutrality from the Cherokees' viewpoint.

96. Cited in ibid., vol. 1, pp. 370–73. See also W. G. McLoughlin, "Cherokees and Methodists," *Church History* 50 (March 1981): 44–63.

Despite the inaction of the conference, the circuit riders remained loyal to the Cherokee cause. Having instructed its missionaries to cease all political activity, the conference reassigned them to circuits in the Cherokee Nation. When Georgia passed its oath law, the conference gave no instructions to the circuit riders. Four of them who resided within the limits of Georgia discussed the matter and then sent their decision to the *Methodist Christian Advocate* to be printed: "Having every reason to believe that our taking the oath prescribed by the Georgia legislature would be attended with ruinous consequences to the missionary cause here, and being ourselves conscientiously opposed to the measure, we shall be compelled to move our residences from this disputed ground in order to avoid the fearful penalty of the law."[97] It was signed by Scales, McLeod, Trott, and J. W. Hanna. Trott, however, changed his mind and refused to leave. He and his Cherokee wife and their two children lived in Etowah. He said, "Believing that the law was unconstitutional and knowing that it was passed for the purpose of stripping the Cherokee of religious and educational privileges, by driving the Missionaries from the field of their labors in order to force the Nation into a treaty with the United States, I could not conscientiously take such oath."[98] On March 12, 1831, he was arrested along with Worcester and several others but released when Judge Clayton declared missionaries to be agents of the federal government. When Eaton declared that missionaries were not agents, he was arrested again on May 29. McLeod, hearing of the arrest, went to the Georgia guard to protest; they arrested him too, even though he was now living in Tennessee. A third Methodist missionary, the Reverend Martin Wells, who also protested, was beaten by the guard. The Georgians took the action of the Tennessee conference as an endorsement of its authority and a repudiation of their missionaries' politics. The officer in charge when Trott and McLeod were arrested described Trott as a preacher "who had been discountenanced by his own Conference for his officious and over-zealous interference in Indian politics."[99] Trott was forced to march 110 miles on foot: "I was chained four nights in succession and compelled to lie on the floor." He was arraigned, charged, and released on giving a bond of $500 to appear for trial in September. Meanwhile he was to remain outside of the state of Georgia. When Trott asked the commander of the guard, Colonel Sanford, if he could itinerate from Tennessee in order to minister to his converts in Georgia, the commander "stated to me that he did not suppose the missionaries would be allowed to itinerate and preach in the territory of Georgia [even] provided they were to remove their residence, for it was the determined policy of the state to expel from her charter [limits] all white persons who refused to obey her laws and pursue a course detrimental to her interest." Trott wrote a detailed account of his arrest for the *Methodist*

97. *Christian Advocate*, March 11, 1831.
98. Quoted in J. Edward Moseley, *Disciples of Christ in Georgia*, p. 127.
99. *Cherokee Phoenix*, October 29, 1831.

Christian Advocate, noting, "It is now clear as noon day that they [the Georgians] designed to destroy missions in that part of the nation which they so confidently claim."[100]

Trott was arrested a third time on July 6 when he went to visit his wife; he was released after twelve days' confinement. The Tennessee conference issued no complaint about this treatment of its missionaries and made no offer to assist them with attorneys. The *Christian Advocate,* however, was outraged. "Why was Mr. Trott, the Methodist minister put in chains?" the editor asked. "The conduct of the authorities of the state of Georgia toward the missionaries stationed among the Cherokee Indians . . . is a barbarous outrage. . . . Has it come to this? Is a missionary, peaceably pursuing his calling, for no other crime alleged than a refusal from conscientious motives to take an oath of allegiance to a particular state, to be suddenly apprehended, bound in chains, and incarcerated in prison? Are these inquisitorial transactions to be tolerated in a Christian land?"[101] The only southern Methodist to come to Trott's defense was the Reverend John Howard of Milledgeville, Georgia, who wrote a letter to Governor Gilmer on August 29, 1831, asking why the Georgia guard had treated a minister of the Gospel with such great severity and requesting an investigation of the conduct of the guard. Gilmer replied that he had full faith in the guard's officers and that he thought that missionaries who refused to take the oath or leave the state should "feel the full weight of the law."[102]

Trott returned from Tennessee to stand trial on September 15 and was found guilty, as were Worcester, Butler, and eight others (who were not missionaries). Because his wife was very ill, Trott did not accept his sentence but took the alternative offered by the judge of leaving the state. His wife died a week later. Frustrated and angry, Trott underwent a new religious conversion after reading the works of Alexander Campbell. He was baptized by immersion into the Disciples denomination on October 29, 1831. He had ceased to be a Methodist.[103]

The other Methodist itinerants continued their work but found it increasingly difficult. Writing to the *Methodist Christian Advocate* in February 1831, the circuit riders assigned to the Georgia area said that "the disagreeable excitement produced by the operation of the laws of that state in

100. *Christian Advocate,* July 29, 1831; *Cherokee Phoenix,* July 2, 1831.
101. *Christian Advocate,* July 8 and July 29, 1831, May 20, 1831, August 12, 1831; among Samuel Worcester's letters to his board is one from John Williams of Knoxville, August 23, 1831, in which Williams expresses hope that the Tennessee Annual Conference might petition President Jackson to "rescue their clerical brethren [Trott and McLeod] from their coming doom in the Georgia penitentiary." If such a petition was ever sent, I have not been able to find it. See ABCFM, August 23, 1831.
102. Gilmer, *Sketches of the First Settlers,* pp. 322–24.
103. See Trott's letter, signed "Cherokee," in *The Millennial Harbinger* 3 (February 1832): 85, and (August 1832): 389; and 4 (September 1833): 472. Also see Moseley, *Disciples in Georgia,* pp. 123–24.
104. *Christian Advocate,* February 12, 1831.

opposition to those of the nation, are wholly indescribable. . . . [A]ll white men in this part of the nation are placed in very unpleasant and precarious circumstances."[104] Nevertheless, they were determined to do all they could "for the spiritual benefit of these disheartened and injured people. Never will we give over our united efforts for the salvation of the Cherokees until we are called off by proper authorities or driven away by the propelling edicts of a republican state." A year later a short history of Methodist missions was published by the Reverend Nathan Bangs in which he printed a letter from Dickson McLeod dated February 14, 1832. McLeod reported that the Cherokee Nation was being invaded by Georgians who had won tracts of land in the lottery and many others, "lewd fellows of the baser sort," who had made the country a scene "of villainy, stealing and intemperance . . . indescribable and shocking to humanity. Tears of grief are wrung from the very heart of a missionary while beholding this exceedingly unpleasant state of things." Still, he found the Cherokee converts faithful: "If their fiercest oppressors could but once witness, as I often have, the heavy sighs, flowing tears and mournful complaints which their distressed condition and threatening calamities draw from their inmost souls, they would doubtless tremble through fear of incurring the displeasure of God . . . who will most assuredly punish the adversaries of His people either in time or in eternity."[105] It is significant that for McLeod, God's chosen people included the Indians. This was not a common view among white Americans at that time or among missionaries. Nathan Bangs summarized his account of Methodist missions among the Cherokees (as of 1832) without much assurance about the future of that people: "What will be the end of these things we cannot tell, but it must be evident to every one that such a state of political excitement cannot be otherwise than unfriendly to the interests of religion. Our only consolation is that God rules."[106]

The missionary response to the removal crisis of 1829—32 reached its climax in the final months of 1832. After a year in prison, Worcester and Butler contemplated their final appeal to the Supreme Court. In addition to the eminent educators, clergymen, lawyers, and statesmen of Georgia who visited them to urge the desperate consequences for the United States if they persisted, they had evidence that some of the most influential Cherokee leaders were weakening in their resistance. They were aware of Jackson's popular victory at the polls and knew that his next step must be to persuade Congress when it met in January to give him the power to force South Carolina to obey the laws of the Union. Nevertheless, on November 26, 1832, they instructed their lawyers to inform Governor Wilson Lumpkin (who had defeated Gilmer in the state election that fall) that they intended to ask the Supreme Court to take the final step to compel Jackson to his duty. Lumpkin had met with Worcester's wife in September and urged her to ask

105. Bangs, *Methodist Missions*, pp. 149—50.
106. Ibid., p. 149.

her husband to seek a pardon, which he said he would gladly give. But she said the decision was his.[107]

Worcester and Butler were not easy over their decision to pursue their case and wrestled with their consciences over their respective duties to the Cherokees, to their government, and to the cause of missions. Then, at the end of the first week of December, they gave up. On December 7, they wrote to the Prudential Committee explaining that they no longer saw anything to be gained by persisting with the case. The board met in Boston on December 25 and voted, over the objection of Evarts's successor, David Greene, to advise them to withdraw their final appeal. The committee resolved "that in view of the change of circumstances, it is in the opinion of the Committee inexpedient for Messrs. Worcester and Butler to prosecute their case further before the Supreme Court of the United States."[108] Worcester and Butler received the letter from the board on January 7, 1833. The next day they wrote to their lawyers telling them to withdraw their final appeal. In the long letter they wrote to the public explaining their reasons for abandoning the case, they offered seven arguments which had persuaded them: first, they noted that Georgia's legislature had repealed the oath law in December 1832 and thus, "We no longer had to contend for the right of laboring among the Cherokees without restraint in the work of the gospel"; second, because eminent jurists had told them that Jackson would not enforce the writ, "there was no longer any hope, by our perseverance, of securing the rights of the Cherokees or preserving the faith of our country"; third, because the Georgians still believed they were right, "the State had placed herself in an attitude of resistance which it appeared evident that nothing but force could overcome"; fourth, "it was not so clear that it was *our* duty to insist on this course"—a course leading to force—because given the danger of Georgia's armed resistance, "it is no sacrifice of the authority of the law for an individual to yield his lawful right rather than that blood should be spilt in his defense"; fifth, because the nullification crisis was still awaiting settlement, "the political aspect of our country was in other respects such as to render it doubtful . . . whether the public would not sustain injury by the prosecution of our appeal" (that is, the threat of secession and civil war seemed real); seventh, "We had the assurance of an unconditional release" by the governor in which they would not have to acknowledge any crime or error on their part for their act of civil disobedience.[109] There seemed in this complex reasoning a greater emphasis upon prudence and political expediency (not to mention defeatism) than had been evident in their former pronouncements; spiritual righteousness and national honor had

107. Ann Worcester to David Greene, October 4, 1832, ABCFM. See also Edwin A. Miles, "After John Marshall's Decision," *Journal of Southern History* 39, no. 4 (November 1973): 535–36.

108. Benjamin Wisner to Samuel Worcester, December 26, 1835, ABCFM.

109. Annual Report, ABCFM (1833), pp. 99–100.

somehow been displaced by practical necessity, national security, and "changing circumstances."

Although the governor had promised to make it easy for them to obtain a pardon once they had withdrawn their case, he rejected their first appeal because he thought it implied that Georgia was somehow to blame for their imprisonment. They wrote a second letter in which they threw themselves upon "the magnanimity" of the state. Lumpkin took this to be an acknowledgment of their guilt and issued an order to the warden of the penitentiary on January 14 to release them.[110] Two days later, Andrew Jackson sent to Congress a request for an act empowering him to force the state of South Carolina to give up its absurd notion that it could decide which acts of the federal government it would obey and which it would not. Jackson "had wit enough," said the editor of *The Telescope*, a South Carolina paper, "to take no step like 'the military force bill' till he had got the Georgia case out of his way."[111] Certain now that Georgia and the other southern states would side with him (for he had won their case for removal of the Indians), Jackson was free to act against nullification.

In the long run, the effort to uphold Indian treaty rights and to prevent removal fell mainly upon the Cherokees themselves. The missionaries had too many reasons for siding with their white brethren to persist in defense of their red brethren. Blood was thicker than water; ethnocentrism was stronger than righteousness. After 1832 the missionaries withdrew from the struggle (with a few notable exceptions). They did not, in their opinion, "desert" the Cherokees, because some missionaries in all the denominations continued to live and work among them during the next six years. But after January 1833 they confined their work to preaching and teaching school. Had the Cherokees followed the advice of the missionaries after this date, they would have made a treaty and removed to the West immediately. So the American Board advised them when it wrote John Ross that Worcester was withdrawing his appeal.[112] Some would argue that the Cherokees made a grievous mistake in not taking that advice. But to them, only the use of force to eject them from their homeland would finally make clear the choice white America had made for its destiny. Some missionaries thought they were right and did their best to strengthen the Cherokees' resistance.

110. See Samuel Worcester to David Greene, January 14, 1833, ABCFM, with copies of his letters to Lumpkin seeking release from prison.

111. Miles, "After John Marshall's Decision," p. 541, n. 51. According to Ulrich B. Phillips, not more than one-third of the voters of Georgia ever showed any sympathy for South Carolina's nullification notions. U.B. Phillips, *Georgia and State Rights* (Washington, D.C., 1902), p. 133.

112. Ross wrote to Elizur Butler in March 1833, saying he thought the Prudential Committee had acted "prematurely" in advising him "that they think in the present posture of affairs in this Nation, it would conduce to the best good of the Cherokees for them to accept terms proposed to them by the Government of the United States and remove to the Country west of the Mississippi." Ross's letter is included in one from Elizur Butler to David Greene, March 18, 1833, ABCFM.

CHAPTER TWELVE

Missionary Responses to the Final Phase of Cherokee Resistance, 1833—1838

The Georgians and, I found, most of the other white settlers, had a decided antipathy to him [the Reverend Evan Jones] on account of the advice which he gave to the Cherokees which had frequently enabled them to baffle the machinations of the persons who are plotting to get their lands.
George W. Featherstonhaugh, English
visitor to the Cherokee Nation, 1837

As the missionaries dwindled in number after 1833 and tried to practice neutrality in the final phase of the Cherokees' struggle to remain in their homeland, many Cherokees in the mission churches found it difficult to sustain their Christian faith; some lost all interest in religion and, gripped by a terrible despondency, turned to drink. But the great majority of the Cherokees stubbornly refused to admit defeat. As the Baptist missionary Evan Jones had said, "nothing short of positive coercion" would induce them to emigrate, and because that was also the position of their chief, John Ross, they followed him loyally to the bitter end. The missionaries faced difficult times and were unable to find consistent roles to play in the crisis. The Cherokees were greatly upset that the mission boards, after 1832, ceased all efforts to defend their rights against the Jacksonians; the studied neutrality of the mission boards from 1832 to 1838 was considered proof that white Christians believed the Cherokee cause was hopeless. Missionaries therefore became associated in the popular mind with that group of Cherokee chiefs (led by John Ridge, Major Ridge, Elias Boudinot, Stand Watie) who, after 1832, were called the Ridge Party or the Treaty Party because they thought the Cherokees had better make a treaty with Jackson and obtain all the money they could for their country before they were forced off it. Those who opposed this plan and followed John Ross were known as the Patriot, or Antiremoval, Party. They hoped by their opposition to stall off removal until 1838, when they thought that the Whig Party would win the presidency and reverse Jackson's policy. While the Ross Party, which was the overwhelming majority of Cherokees, was not antimissionary in these years, their relations with them were generally cool, distant, and formal. Some Cherokees believed that the missionary effort was subverting the antiremoval cause; others in the Ross Party identified those Cherokees who were voluntarily emigrating to the West with mission converts (as in the case of Duncan O'Briant's church). Many Cherokee patriots simply said that Christianity itself was the cause of all their troubles. Chief John Benge of Creek Path, who had previously been friendly toward missionaries, told the Reverend William Potter of the American Board in 1835 that all those who oppressed the Cherokees were Christians. "I observed," Potter said, "that he ought not to suppose all the white people christians. All did not approve what had been done." But Benge replied, "O, yes, all christians. The government of the United States is a Christian government and is upheld by christians. All alike. The government does it and the people uphold the government. All are christians." Potter was nonplused. Like most missionaries Potter had always believed and preached that the United States was a Christian nation and that its people were a Christian people: "What reply could be made to such reasoning?" he asked. "I attempted one, but it neither satisfied him nor myself."[1]

Missionaries had promised the Cherokees that the surest way to save their country was to become civilized and Christianized—to give up heathen ways and join mission churches. Jeremiah Evarts had used such an argument in 1824 when trying to persuade David Brown, a recent Cornwall graduate, to pursue his theological training so that he could become a minister to his people. "The prevalence of the Christian religion among your people," Evarts had said, "is the only thing that will secure the public opinion of this country strongly in their favor, and if public opinion is strongly in their favor, our national government will treat you all with kindness and attention . . . and the public indignation would be aroused by any open and flagrant acts of injustice towards your countrymen."[2] The missionaries were now hoist with their own petard; their optimistic faith in their own country's philanthropic concern for the heathen and their faith that the Cherokees' rapid progress in acculturation would enable them to share in—become equal participants in—the progress of God's chosen nation had been betrayed. Somehow despite all their efforts the Cherokees had failed to overcome the whiteman's prejudices. Yet even after the missionaries were ready to advise the Cherokees to emigrate, they still insisted that God would give them help if they only worked harder. Daniel Butrick had a heated discussion with Andrew Sanders, a convert at Carmel mission in 1832, in which Sanders said he was tempted to go West but "thinks it would only prolong the evils, as the whites would soon trouble them there as they do now here." Butrick's answer was simple: "I told him it would doubtless depend entirely on themselves should they remove to a new country—be industrious, clear and improve the land [and] they would keep it, otherwise it would be taken from them. Because God, the Great disposer of all events, would have people industrious and would give the earth to those who would till it."[3] Butrick

1. William Potter to David Greene, May 27, 1835, ABCFM.
2. Jeremiah Evarts to David Brown, January 6, 1824, ABCFM.
3. Daniel Butrick, Journal, August [n.d.] 1832, ABCFM.

then noted in his diary, without any sense of irony, "Were all [Cherokees] as industrious as this dear man and his family, such remarks would be needless." On the one hand, the missionaries preached the Protestant ethic of individualistic hard work as the key to the Cherokee problem, and on the other, they insisted that the Cherokee people as a whole must be held responsible for their fate. The irony was heightened by the continual observation by the Cherokees, corroborated by all the missionaries, that the whitemen to whom their land was being turned over under Georgia's lottery system were the offscouring of American society. Butrick himself had written this in his journal only a few months before: the Cherokees, he said, "cannot live with such wretches"—and therefore

> They must go to the more virtuous Comanches of the West. . . . If American citizens were not insensible to shame, they would blush . . . but now they glory in their shame. . . . Yes, American citizens are so much worse than the Indians that the latter cannot live near them without being robbed, corrupted, and debauched. . . . Let France and England know it. Let Spain know it, and be told the hands of her Cortes and Pizarro are white when compared to those of American citizens. . . . Let Italy know it. Let the Pope of Rome be told. . . . Let inmost Africa hear of it. O, how inoffensive is the tiger of the torrid zone compared with the covetous citizens of the United States.[4]

Butrick acknowledged that it was the wickedness of whitemen intruding into their country which was leading many of "the poor Indians to swear eternal enmity to religion as well as to those who profess to be its followers."[5] All of the missionaries (particularly those of the American Board) reported after 1832 that they "were never in so low estimation among the Cherokees as at the present time" and that "though they do not directly censure us, yet they rather set us down as useless." As Butrick put it, "They evidently put too much confidence in us."[6] But there was more to it than that.

If the Cherokees were disillusioned with Christianity and with the missionaries, the missionaries were disheartened that the Cherokees failed to appreciate their efforts and expected miracles. In their thirty odd years among them, the missionaries believed that they had done much to uplift and enlighten these primitive people. The American Board believed that in 1817–19 it had helped to save the nation from the second removal crisis. From 1828 to 1833 many missionaries and mission supporters had fought vigorously for Cherokee rights. But God, fate, and public opinion had been against them. Now it was necessary for the Cherokees to face up to the hard realities of American politics and not to turn against those who were still their best friends and well-wishers. The Prudential Committee of the American Board reported sadly on this situation to its supporters in 1835:

4. Daniel Butrick, Journal, January [n.d.] 1832, ABCFM.
5. Daniel Butrick, Journal, January [n.d.] 1832, ABCFM.
6. Daniel Butrick to David Greene, September 28, 1834, ABCFM.

"With respect to this [the Cherokee] mission . . . it should be remarked that during the past year, as during the two or three preceding years, the political affairs of the Cherokee have been in such a state as to render the situation of the missionaries extremely perplexing and discouraging." But the committee admitted it was not only the actions of the Georgians which produced this state of affairs: "The [Cherokee] people, believing themselves to be oppressed and spoiled of their dearest rights by a nominally Christian nation, have, to a great extent, imbibed a deep prejudice against our religion and nation and against Christian missionaries as citizens of the United States."[7]

To many Cherokees the Christians' god seemed to be, as their conjurors and old men had warned them, a god whose power worked for the whiteman only. Some therefore turned back to their old religion, practiced their sacred dances and rituals, performed their purification ceremonies, listened to the revelations of new prophets. If the new way had failed, perhaps the old way could be revived. After 1832, however, the Cherokee revival seemed more truly a Ghost Dance movement, a recognition that only supernatural intervention could save them. Or, at least, if they were to be destroyed, they would prefer to die being true to their old ways than to the new ones which had raised and then dashed their hopes.

However, not all Cherokees felt this way. For some, Christianity still seemed a source of strength and hope in their time of trouble. But now it was a different side of Christianity which appealed to them—not the progressive, activistic, optimistic postmillennialism of the missionaries but the consolative hope of the premillennialists waiting patiently for ultimate justice by divine judgment upon their oppressors. This side of Christian teaching came to them less from the white missionaries than from their own native preachers and exhorters, to whom Christianity offered a different message from the one they had learned in mission schools and churches. The Methodist missionaries who remained among them noticed this aspect in those converts who still remained faithful: "They seem perfectly resigned," wrote the Reverend Dickson McLeod in 1832, "to the merciful disposal of the all-wise Being, firmly believing that if they trust in Him, He will glorify His great name in their deliverance from political and spiritual thraldom."[8] Deliverance from thraldom, not inclusion within the whiteman's manifest destiny, was a spiritual theme perfectly compatible with Cherokee patriotism.

Some Cherokee converts, however, adopted a more otherworldly or world-rejecting type of premillennialism. They saw no hope in this world but looked for a better home, a finer country, in the next. "In the midst of numerous and strong temptations," McLeod noted, "and trials of a very afflicting nature, the most of our established members still remain steadfast and are seeking a 'better country.' They say that they have no intention to

7. Annual Report, ABCFM (1835), p. 89.
8. Quoted in Bangs, *Methodist Missions*, p. 149.

give up their [church] religion nor relinquish their title to the promised heavenly country."[9] If God had turned their homeland and the United States over to the wicked, then he must have intended the Cherokees for a better country on high. Baptist missionaries too reported revivals of interest in Christianity of this kind after 1833. What Christianity had failed to achieve in the halcyon days of Cherokee progress in acculturation, it might yet attain in their days of adversity. This form of Christianity was peculiarly adapted to an oppressed, powerless people in an alien, hostile world; the dispossessed poor whites in the clay hills and pine barrens of the rural South had adopted the same world-rejecting religious outlook to explain their position in America in these same years. "They were concerned," as Dickson D. Bruce, Jr., puts it, "with an ontological God rather than a functional one, for the mode of existence which they attributed to Him was symbolic of the ultimate hope they had for themselves."[10] Those whom the world rejected, God would honor, not here, perhaps, but hereafter.

The most striking feature of Cherokee life in the hectic years 1833 to 1838 was the patient endurance of the ordinary people and their unwavering loyalty, unity, and faith in their chief, Cooweescoowee (John Ross, or "Little John"). He became their prophet and eventually their Moses. The average Cherokee did not comprehend the complex details of his battle with the courts, the state legislatures, the Congress, the election campaigns; they left the stratagems to Ross and meanwhile bore patiently the harassments of the Georgians. Whenever Ross returned from Washington or called them into council to hear his reports and to vote on his recommendations, they wholeheartedly gave him their support. After Jackson withheld their annuities, they had to give up publication of their newspaper, the *Cherokee Phoenix* (in 1834). Thereafter they relied upon oral communication or letters written in the Sequoyan syllabary to spread and exchange information. When Ross needed to get out special news in a hurry, he sent runners to every town to give the local chiefs his message, and they passed it on to their people in local councils. The key to Ross's success as a leader was his ability to keep in close touch with the ordinary people and to express their determination to hold on to their land. In every town loyal chiefs or headmen kept him informed of the mood and needs of the people. The missionaries existed now only on the periphery of national life.

The handful of missionaries who continued to preach among the Cherokees were demoralized and subdued. "The present state of our mission," Henry Clauder told the Moravian Board in 1836, "like that of the American board among the Cherokees, is discouraging to a higher degree from causes with which you are doubtless familiar and which are alike mortifying to every sense of justice and equity as they are disgraceful to a civilized and enlightened government."[11] Though pleased by the faithful-

9. Ibid.
10. Dickson D. Bruce, Jr., *And They All Sang Hallelujah* (Knoxville: University of Tennessee Press, 1974), p. 105.
11. Henry Clauder to John Howard Payne, Payne Papers, V, 34−37.

ness of those who remained in their churches and by sporadic conversions, the missionaries felt inadequate to the needs of the Cherokees. "The Nation is entirely broken up and split into divisions among themselves and their minds are so occupied about their situation as a people that it is very difficult to make them think anything on the subject of religion. Some that we have thought were very promising, have turned back," wrote William Chamberlain of the American Board in 1834.[12] To make matters worse, the white intruders did their best to turn the Cherokees against the missionaries: "The country is full of white people," the Reverend William Potter noted in 1835, "who have brought iniquity like a flood and say a great deal to prejudice the Cherokees against the missionaries."[13] As a result, "many of those who formerly attended quite regularly our meetings on the Sabbath, now absent themselves almost altogether. . . . [S]ome even of our church members have been led far astray."[14]

Because the mission agencies did not own the land on which their stations were built, the Georgia legislature included those tracts among the vacant Cherokee land thrown into the land lottery and available for immediate occupancy by white citizens of Georgia. The drawings for the lottery began in October 1832, and in January 1833 the first lucky winners began to arrive in the Cherokee Nation to claim their plots.[15] The Moravian mission at Springplace was among the first to go. On January 1, 1833, twenty people in five wagons arrived at the mission door and demanded immediate occupancy. Clauder held them off for a few days, but the Georgia guard arrived to enforce their claims. Clauder, his wife and child, and Dorothea Ruede packed their things again and moved to David McNair's farm in Tennessee. One by one the other missionary stations in Georgia and Alabama were yielded up by the missionaries to white lottery winners. Most of the missionaries in the American Board moved into the Brainerd, Red Clay, or Candy's Creek mission stations in Tennessee and for a time itinerated on horseback to their former stations to meet and worship with their distracted congregations. In some cases Cherokee converts followed their missionaries to Tennessee. Some missionaries resigned from the work; some were told they could no longer be supported.

More and more white families moved into the Cherokee Nation, dispossessing hundreds of Cherokees from their farms until by 1835 there were over 15,000 whites—more than there were Cherokees.[16] Still the Cherokees refused to sign a removal treaty.

When the various missionary boards concluded, after 1832, that it was useless to fight any longer against Jackson's removal policy, they faced a

---

12. William Chamberlain to David Greene, January 29, 1834 ABCFM.
13. William Potter to David Greene, May 27, 1835, ABCFM.
14. William Potter to David Greene, July 9, 1835, ABCFM.
15. See Thurman Wilkins, *Cherokee Tragedy*, pp. 241–42.
16. *Missionary Herald* 31: 22.

number of serious decisions. The central problem for the missionaries was how to avoid alienating one faction or the other among the Cherokees. At the same time, they had to avoid angering the War Department. Neutrality, though desirable, was impossible. For example, as whites moved into the nation and Cherokees moved to different places to escape them, it was difficult to sustain the mission schools. Yet to close a school, even if only a handful of students still attended, offended the Cherokees and seemed to imply a lack of faith in their ability to hold out in their homeland. On the other hand, if the missionaries decided to open a school in another part of the nation to compensate for one it closed, the federal government accused them of trying to thwart emigration and encouraging the Cherokees to remain in the East. Furthermore, since federal annuities were cut off for Indian schools east of the Mississippi after 1832, to open a new one required a large expenditure of mission funds. The government offered generous subsidies for mission schools in the West, and because most mission boards thought removal was inevitable (as well as because more and more Indians were moving West) it seemed logical to open schools there. But if they did this, the Cherokees again accused them of betraying their cause. In an effort to solve this dilemma, the mission boards tried to devote more time to evangelism and preaching services, but this annoyed those dedicated to the old religion and seemed to deny Cherokee children the opportunity to obtain the skills they needed to cope with the whiteman. One solution was to abandon the expensive boarding schools and operate day schools or "neighborhood schools." When the American Board asked its missionaries what they thought of this plan, they received very negative answers. Samuel Worcester wrote, "I cannot think of a single instance in which a child who could not speak English or did not acquire it from some other source than the school, has derived any manifest advantage from attending a neighborhood school."[17] Laura Potter, who assisted her husband, William, at Creek Path mission, wrote that boarding schools were far superior. In them the students had "the constant example of their Teachers," whereas "in a neighborhood school the children are constantly under the influence of their Heathen parents. . . . Their sabbaths are spent in idleness and dissipation. In a boarding school they are constantly under the influence of pious example and instruction, are led daily to the family altar, and on the sabbaths to the House of God and are in various ways restrained from evil." The only place where a neighborhood school might work would be "where nearly all the families speak English," for they were the more acculturated.[18] Worcester came up with the most felicitous solution when he suggested that the board start schools which would teach the children to read and write in Cherokee and hire good Christian Cherokees to run them. The board agreed in 1834 to pay John Huss and a convert named Jesse to establish such schools, and for two

17. Samuel Worcester to David Greene, July 12, 1833, ABCFM.
18. Laura Potter to David Greene, August 30, 1833, ABCFM.

years they were highly popular, teaching the Sequoyan script to Cherokees from four to eighty years old in different parts of the nation.[19] Nevertheless, the board still had to keep as many of its boarding schools open as it could.

An even thornier problem arose whenever a mission was closed (by compulsion or expediency) and the mission board had to decide whether to ask the federal government to reimburse it for the expenditures it had made—the so-called improvements on the land, including not only buildings but cultivated fields, fencing, and corncribs. This problem became even thornier after December 1835, when a handful of chiefs who favored emigration to the West negotiated a fraudulent treaty with Jackson's emissary.

The Emigration, or Removal, Party, later known as the Treaty Party or the Ridge-Boudinot Party, consisted of a small group of prominent mixed-blood chiefs who concluded as early as 1832 that there was no hope of stopping Jackson's policy of Indian removal. John Ridge and Elias Boudinot were the leaders of this group.[20] They had come to this decision in April 1832, when Worcester and Butler were still in prison considering an appeal to the United States Supreme Court to force Jackson to carry out its decision in *Worcester v. Georgia*. Ridge spoke at that time with Associate Justice John F. McClean and Senator Theodore J. Frelinghuysen in Washington. Both of them had been supporters of Cherokee treaty rights, but Ridge discovered that neither of them now thought there was any hope of persuading Jackson to carry out Marshall's decision. Ridge and Boudinot concluded that rather than wage a long, costly, and useless battle to remain in the East, the Cherokees should make the best possible treaty to obtain a fair price for their homeland, for remuneration for all of their improvements and for transportation costs to the West. Ridge's father, Major Ridge, agreed and so did Boudinot's brother, Stand Watie; William S. Coody (a nephew of John Ross), Andrew Ross (a brother of John Ross), William Hicks (brother of Charles Hicks), John Walker, Jr., David Vann, John Fields, William Rogers, and James Starr later joined their efforts. Through Jackson's new secretary of war, Lewis Cass, treaty proposals were made to the Council in the summer of 1832. Overwhelmingly they were turned down. So vehement was the objection to capitulation that Ridge and his friends were called traitors to the nation. When they urged emigration, threats were made on their lives. But the Removal Party persisted in its efforts and, though they never represented as much as 10 percent of the chiefs (and less than that among the fullbloods), they ultimately succeeded. A small extralegal council met at New Echota in December 1835 with Jackson's treaty commissioner, the Reverend John F. Schermerhorn, and signed the infamous Treaty of New Echota.

19. See William Chamberlain to David Greene, July 17, 1834, ABCFM. Of course, the items used in this teaching were translations of Christian works.
20. The best account of the signing of the Treaty of New Echota in 1835 is in Wilkins, *Cherokee Tragedy*, pp. 254—78.

By this treaty, a small group of mixed-blood chiefs, claiming to act for the whole nation but in fact acting from the paternalistic view representative of their conquerors, agreed to sell their homeland to the United States for $5 million. In addition, the United States agreed to provide in exchange for it an equivalent tract of land in what is now the northeastern corner of Oklahoma. Furthermore, the government offered payment for all improvements and for transportation costs. Ridge considered it a good bargain and praised Jackson for his generosity. But the treaty was so transparently illegal by Cherokee law and so overwhelmingly repudiated by the vast majority of chiefs and Cherokee citizens that the Ross Party foolishly believed that the United States Senate would never ratify it. When the Senate did so in May 1836 the Cherokees still refused to accept it.

Jackson had demonstrated some shrewdness in appointing a Calvinist, Dutch Reform minister from New York to negotiate the treaty. Although Schermerhorn had retired from the ministry and was never a missionary, he was seen by many American Christians as a representative of the clergy and a man who must therefore have the best interests of the Cherokees at heart. His support of removal countered to some extent the behavior of Worcester and Butler and seemed to demonstrate Jackson's claim that good churchmen, North and South, were divided on the complex issue. From the point of view of the Cherokees, Schermerhorn was another example of Christian hypocrisy. They nicknamed him the Devil's Horn (probably a term which in Cherokee had derisive sexual overtones) and displayed utter contempt for the bullying manner in which he conducted negotiations. Several times prior to December 1835 he had tried to force the duly elected chiefs to act on his treaty, but they had flatly refused.

Schermerhorn's most Machiavellian trick was to include in the treaty a clause which would reimburse all mission boards for their buildings and improvements. He knew that the boards were eager to avoid a total loss and that they wanted money to establish new mission stations among the Cherokees once removal was effected. This clause further split the Cherokees from the missionaries and even some of the missionaries from their managing boards. Naturally the application by a mission board for remuneration under the Schermerhorn treaty meant acknowledgment of the validity of the treaty and placed the missionaries in the camp of the traitorous Ridge—Boudinot Party. Furthermore, Schermerhorn worded this clause so as to require that any funds paid to remunerate mission boards were to be deducted from the $5 million paid for the Cherokees' homeland. He did so on the ground that the Cherokees had benefited from the missions and therefore they, not the federal government, should reimburse the mission boards for their benevolence. Patriotic Cherokees—Christian converts as well as traditionalists—once again felt betrayed. The missionaries had originally promised them that use of their land for mission schools would cost the nation nothing. Here was one more proof that Christians could not be trusted. Some of the missionaries in the field felt obliged to protest to their boards over their applications for reimbursement. William Potter told his board, "[T]here is . . . very much dissatisfaction respecting the Board receiving pay for its improvements in the way provided in the so-called Treaty" and "I am decidedly of the opinion the Board had better receive the sum and pay it directly to the Nation" so that the Cherokees could use it for defense of their homeland.[21] The American Board did not take Potter's advice.

The American Board ran into a peculiar problem at Brainerd, where it had the most efficient gristmill and sawmill in the region. As white intruders moved into this area after 1835, they constantly came to Brainerd to have their corn ground and their logs sawed into planks to build their new homes on the Cherokees' land. The missionaries were paid for this and admitted making a good deal of money from it. But it was galling to the Cherokees to find the mission station giving aid and comfort to those who were oppressing and displacing them. Yet on what grounds could the mission refuse to do so?[22]

Under these circumstances it is not surprising that the reactions of the missionaries and the mission boards to the Cherokee resistance to removal often seemed equivocal, timorous, or self-serving. Missionaries quarreled with each other about these issues as well as with their boards. Unable to resolve their dilemma, it seemed easier to some missionaries to retire; to others, it seemed best to emigrate to the west. When this happened, the boards were faced with the problem of whether or not to replace them. Most boards preferred to cut their losses, yet in some cases, where it meant closing an effective school, they were reluctant to do so. When a mission board did decide to replace a departing missionary, it discovered that it was no longer easy to find recruits willing to go to the Cherokee Nation. The Georgians had let it be widely known that missionaries were no longer welcome. William Chamberlain of the American Board made a trip to Pennsylvania in 1835 to try to hire a new teacher for his mission school at Haweis. He was unsuccessful: "I found it more difficult to procure suitable help than I had before imagined." Those pious people apt to volunteer were also the ones who had been reading of the trials of the missionaries in their mission journals. "It requires a stronger call," Chamberlain concluded, "than can be given from the present broken state of the Cherokees to induce them" to come.[23]

The result was a steady decline in mission stations, schools, and personnel after 1832. Of the four stations of the American Board in Georgia, Hightower was given up in April 1831, Haweis in February 1834, New Echota in March 1834, and Carmel, though vacant in 1831, reopened under

21. William Potter to David Greene, April 23, 1837, ABCFM. There are many other letters on this subject in the files of the ABCFM.
22. John C. Elsworth to David Greene, November 2, 1835, and Daniel Butrick to David Greene, March 31, 1836, ABCFM.
23. William Chamberlain to David Greene, October 26, 1835, ABCFM.

Daniel Butrick in 1832 and then closed in December 1835. The board's stations in Alabama, at Creek Path and Willstown, continued until 1837; Candy's Creek in Tennessee was abandoned in 1837. Brainerd stayed open until removal took place in the fall of 1838. To accommodate the missionaries and converts who left Georgia, two new mission stations were established by the board in Tennessee, one at Amohee in 1832 and one at Red Clay in 1835. However, the Amohee station closed after one year. The large staff of American Board missionaries, which had totaled thirty-four in 1830, was reduced by 1837 to three missionaries, one physician, five women assistants, one farmer, and four "wives." The government made matters more difficult by ruling that any indemnities to be paid by the government for improvements made by mission agencies would be evaluated as of their status in 1830; any additions made to them after that date, or any new stations opened after that date, were totally at the expense of the mission agency and nonremunerable. Given this and other problems, the American Board always felt that it had done more than its share to assist the Cherokees in those trying times. Most of its funds and manpower after 1832 went into building up new mission stations in the eastern part of what is now Oklahoma to which the Western Cherokees and other Southeastern tribes were being removed. By 1833 the board had established three mission stations for the Western Cherokees, and several of the board's missionaries (including Samuel Worcester) left the eastern Cherokees to join those in the West between 1835 and 1838. Samuel Worcester's departure in April 1835 had, said the Prudential Committee regretfully, "strengthened" the belief among the Cherokees "that all the missionaries were, as they termed them, 'treaty men' and desirous that the nation should cede their country and retire beyond the Mississippi." "Never before," said the board's annual report in 1835, "has the Board or those laboring under its patronage been so little esteemed by the Cherokees or had so little influence with them."[24] Because Worcester, Chamberlain, and several other of the American Board's missionaries were closely associated with Elias Boudinot (who assisted Worcester in translating the Bible), John Ridge, Major Ridge, and Stand Watie, they were accused by many Cherokees of encouraging this Treaty Party to make the infamous Treaty of New Echota. Worcester, who had left before the treaty was made, denied the charge, but there is little doubt that he and other American Board missionaries had privately urged these Cherokee leaders to try to persuade the Cherokee people that removal was in their best interest and their only choice.[25]

24. Annual Report, ABCFM (1835), p. 89.
25. When Worcester returned to New Echota from prison he asked Elias Boudinot, "Cannot you get your people together and persuade them to remove?" See Samuel Worcester to James Orr, February 8, 1839, John Ross Papers, Gilcrease Institute, Tulsa, Oklahoma. For the Prudential Committee's suggestion to John Ross that he agree to removal, see Benjamin Wisner to John Ross, December 27, 1832, ABCFM.

The suspicion of some Cherokees that the American Board's missionaries had all become their enemies was not fair. The Reverend Daniel S. Butrick was the last of the board's missionaries to give up his station in Georgia. He remained at Carmel until December 1835, and when forced out, moved to Brainerd station.[26] Butrick, who had disagreed with Worcester over the necessity for civil disobedience to the Georgia oath law because he believed he could fulfill his job just as well on horseback from Tennessee, had returned to Carmel in May 1833, after Georgia repealed the law. Although he had insisted to Worcester in 1831 that missionaries were forbidden by their calling from ever meddling in politics, Butrick was gradually drawn into the controversies which developed after 1835 following Schermerhorn's New Echota treaty. Virtually all of the missionaries in the field considered the treaty a fraud, but after the United States Senate ratified it, they resigned themselves to it. By the terms of the treaty, the Cherokees now had two years to move West. The Reverend John C. Elsworth, who was at Brainerd when he heard of the treaty, not only declared it a fraud but said that the Reverend Schermerhorn was a disgrace to religion: "It is a pity that he was ever known here as a minister of the Gospel or even as a professor of religion."[27] Butrick fully agreed, and he set out to persuade John Ridge and Elias Boudinot, two of the treaty's principal architects, of the enormity of their sin against the Cherokee Nation.[28] Because they were members of a mission church, he asked them to publicly confess and repent of their sinful behavior. When they refused to admit any guilt, Butrick persuaded the members of his mission church to pass a resolution stating "that it will not be our duty to unite in Christian fellowship with any members of Presbyterian [American Board] or Methodist churches who voted for the New Echota Treaty, or signed it, or assisted as a committee in executing it, inasmuch as they acted by usurped authority."[29] Butrick justified this on the grounds that as a result of this treaty the whole Cherokee Nation was exposed "to be taken by armed soldiers, dragged with all the insult and suffering of prisoners of

26. "Our friends and co-workers, Mr. and Mrs. Butrick," reported the Moravians on October 22, 1834, "told us in a letter that they were the only missionaries still in the Georgia part of the Cherokee Nation. They are living with an Indian family and therefore cannot be expelled." Springplace Diary, October 22, 1834, MAS. The Butricks were, nevertheless, forced to leave the Indian's house a year later.

27. J.C. Elsworth to David Greene, November 2, 1835. Schermerhorn was a Dutch Reformed minister from New York appointed by Jackson. He was never a missionary and when appointed had retired from the ministry. For the details of this treaty see Thurman Wilkins, *Cherokee Tragedy*, pp. 254—78.

28. For Butrick's views of the New Echota treaty and those involved in it, see Payne Papers, IX, 1—17, 93—94, and W. G. McLoughlin, "Civil Disobedience and Evangelism among the Missionaries to the Cherokees," *Journal of Presbyterian History* 51, no. 2 (Summer, 1973): 116—39. Worcester privately deplored the treaty and told Boudinot of his disapproval, but he said nothing publicly.

29. Daniel Butrick to John Howard Payne, October 31, 1838, entry in his Journal, Payne Papers, IX, 93—94.

war from house and home and everything of an earthly nature but the clothes
they might have on—hurried at the point of bayonets to forts and then to
filthy and polluted boats or goaded on by land to faint and die by the way."[30]
Butrick was describing here precisely what happened to the Cherokees in
1838, when the government finally sent the army to compel removal. In
addition, Butrick's church declared that Schermerhorn "has forfeited the
confidence of the church of Christ . . . by his abusive conduct toward the
principal chief and council . . . by taking advantage of our national distress .
. . [by] making a treaty with a small minority." When Butrick was accused
of having changed his position on missionary neutrality by these actions and
of having dragged his mission into politics, he denied it. "I have not censured the signing of that treaty from any political or party motives, but for
the same reason that I would censure any other course of conduct which
seemed directly opposed to the dictates of [divine] inspiration." He wrote
personally to John Ridge, saying that he thought Ridge and the other signers
had broken the law of their own nation and that they could not "expect
forgiveness in thus acting." In a letter to Elias Boudinot, he said, "Now,
though I have disclaimed all interference with political affairs, yet I have
considered it my duty to strengthen the hands of the chiefs, not merely
because they were deserving it personally, but also because it was my duty to
God."[31] In this case, he was clearly making known his support for the
Patriot Party.

Butrick further added to his status among the Patriot Party by denouncing his own mission board in 1836 when it asked the government to appraise
its mission property and was awarded the sum of $28,683.25. Because this
was to be taken out of the sum paid by the government for the Cherokee
homeland,[32] Butrick considered this "blood money" and did not believe the
board should soil its hands with it. Moreover, Butrick reminded the board
that the first missionaries from the board to come among the Cherokees (at
Brainerd) in 1817 had given them a written assurance "that we never should
call on them for land or anything else as pay for what we were doing." If the
board went back on its word, the Cherokees "will honestly class us among
other white men who have manifested duplicity—such double dealing as to
forfeit forever their confidence."[33] The board denied his charge. He had a
"wholly distorted view" of the situation, wrote the corresponding secretary.

30. Ibid.
31. For Butrick's letters to John Ridge and Elias Boudinot on this subject, see Payne
Papers, IX, 24—40.
32. Daniel Butrick to David Greene, June 24, 1836, and September 5, 1836, Payne
Papers, IX, 41—48. For the evaluation of the mission stations, see Annual Report, ABCFM
(1837), p. 103. Inasmuch as the government had paid for two-thirds of the cost of the buildings
in the first place, it is strange that so much remuneration was necessary unless the government
was trying to accelerate missionary departure and hoped to buy the goodwill of the board (at the
expense of the Cherokees). See R. Pierce Beaver, *Church, State and the American Indians*, p.
67.
33. Payne Papers, IX, 37.

The Cherokees had benefited from the schools and the board planned to use this indemnity to build new ones in the West for them. Butrick then pointed out that the "mission improvements were valued at nearly, or quite as much again as they were worth," evidently an effort by the government to win approval for the treaty. "Whether the Indians think of this, I know not," Butrick wrote, "as it is dangerous making enquiries, yet I presume they do, and will ever remember it" as a fraud against their treasury.

Butrick was doing his best to dissociate the American Board from the Treaty Party, but it was impossible. Worcester, upon his release from prison, had asked the board to hire Elias Boudinot to assist him in translating the Bible and other religious works into Sequoyan, knowing full well that Boudinot was already deeply involved in trying to undermine Ross's leadership and promote emigration. Sophia Sawyer, the doughty American Board schoolteacher who had stood up to the Georgia guard in 1832 when they berated and threatened her for teaching black children to read (contrary to Georgia law), left the American Board in December 1834 to become a private teacher for the Ridge family at John Ridge's plantation, Running Water. Delight Sargent, who served the board as a teacher at Brainerd, Creek Path, and Red Clay until 1837, married Elias Boudinot that year (a year after his first wife's death). William Chamberlain, though he remained as head of the mission station at Willstown, Alabama, until 1838, publicly advised the nation to cease its resistance and emigrate to the west; and in 1836 Chamberlain personally purchased in Alabama the horses, wagons, and carriages which the Ridges and Boudinots used to emigrate to the west.[34]

Except for Butrick, Dr. Elizur Butler probably was the only American Board missionary who supported John Ross and the antiremoval party after 1832. Butler, who had heard Worcester urge Boudinot to promote removal in 1833, was so angry at this that he reported it to others as a gross betrayal of the Cherokees.[35] When a Georgian tried to force Butler out of the house he lived in at Haweis mission in 1833, he consulted John Ross, and on his advice obtained an injunction against the intruder in a Georgia circuit court.[36] To his surprise, Elias Boudinot opposed his effort, and "Mr. John Ridge also spoke against it and said he hoped I should be defeated" in the effort to retain the mission property. They wanted no support for Cherokee resistance to removal. In May 1837 Butler decided that the American public should be better informed of the continuing mistreatment of the Cherokees by Georgia and by Jackson. He wrote a letter to the journalist John Howard Payne about it and urged Payne to form a voluntary society in New York or Philadelphia to devote itself to defending the rights of the Indians.[37] Butler also won the respect of the Cherokees for his untiring efforts to provide them with medical care not only during the devastating epidemic of 1838, but

34. William Chamberlain to David Greene, October 25, 1836, ABCFM.
35. Samuel Worcester to James Orr, February 8, 1839, Ross Papers.
36. Elizur Butler to David Greene, January 30, 1833, ABCFM.
37. Payne Papers, V, 61.

through the whole long march from their homeland to the Oklahoma area in 1838–39—a trip which he and Butrick made on horseback with the Cherokee people.

Despite the division among its missionaries over removal and reparations, the American Board managed to sustain a working relation with the Cherokees during their final years in the East. However, the number of Cherokee converts in American Board churches barely held its own from 1830 to 1838. In 1830 the board claimed 167 Cherokee members; in 1832 at the height of Worcester's and Butler's martyrdom, the figure rose to 213; by 1837 it was back at 167, and it probably declined some after that.[38]

The status of the Tennessee Annual Methodist Conference among the Cherokees fell even more precipitously after 1830 than that of the American Board. So long as the young circuit riders who had supported the Cherokees' resistance in the Chattooga Resolves of 1830 remained in the field, there was considerable support for the Methodist version of Christianity. Even Trott's defection to the Disciples in 1832 did not lessen interest in the camp meetings; the work of the numerous native class leaders and preachers was always successful, though it is difficult to know whether or not they mixed politics with their evangelism. Dickson McLeod continued to itinerate among them until 1834, but the confusion within the Georgia area of the nation seriously impeded his work. "It is lamentable," he wrote in 1832, "to see how the cause has suffered and is impeded within the Georgia dominions from the disorders, strife, and contention which the late policy of that state has introduced among the Indians."[39]

Dr. Alexander Talley, a highly successful and much-publicized Methodist missionary among the Choctaws, dealt a heavy blow to the Methodist cause among the Southeastern Indians in 1830 when he helped to push through the infamous treaty of Dancing Rabbit Creek.[40] Talley had been an ardent advocate of removal for some time before the federal commissioners arrived among the Choctaws to negotiate such a treaty. He made himself immediately available to them, helped to draft the document, and persuaded a handful of chiefs to sign it over the strong objections of the great majority of the council and people. Talley was the Schermerhorn of the Choctaw removal. Nevertheless the Senate had ratified his treaty, and he was among the first to lead a band of Choctaws to their new home in the west.[41] His

38. Although the *Missionary Herald* and the annual reports contain some general statements about church members in these years, and though occasional individual church figures are mentioned in the ABCFM papers, there are no good overall totals which break down the mission church members among whites, Cherokees, and blacks. From the ABCFM letters it appears that there were perhaps ten to twelve black members, some of whom were freed slaves but most of whom were Cherokee slaves.

39. Bangs, *Methodist Missions*, p. 149.

40. See Angie Debo, *The Rise and Fall of the Choctaw Republic* (Norman: University of Oklahoma Press, 1934), pp. 52–57, 63–67, and Arthur H. DeRosier, Jr., *The Removal of the Choctaw Indians* (New York: Harper, 1972), p. 130.

41. Isabelle G. John, *Handbook of Methodist Missions*, pp. 120–21; Wade C. Barclay, *History of Methodist Missions*, vol. 2, pp. 137–38.

actions were well known among the Cherokees and deplored at the time even
by those who later led the Cherokee Removal Party.

Statistics regarding the Methodist church members among the
Cherokees are unclear and those which survive show considerable discrep-
ancy. Most authorities agree that the peak of Methodist success came in
1830–31, when one report gave 1,028 as the total number "in society" or
"seekers." But this total included white and black seekers as well as
Cherokees. The figures were turned in by the circuit riders, and totals
reported did not always specify the date at which they were taken. In any
case, the available figures for the years after 1830 all agree in recording a
sharp drop in members. By 1835 half of the converts or seekers had deserted
their societies: only 521 remained.[42]

In 1834 the Tennessee Annual Conference decided to curtail all missionary activity among the Cherokees, and it assigned no circuit riders after
that date. The conference concluded, as other missionary boards had by then,
that removal of the Cherokee Nation was both desirable and inevitable. The
best way to encourage them to emigrate was to transfer schools and
evangelism to the Indian area west of Arkansas. This meant that the
Methodist mission to the Cherokees had to be transferred to the Missouri
Annual Conference (later the Arkansas Annual Conference). The Missouri
Annual Conference already had several itinerants preaching among the
5,000 Western Cherokees in 1834.[43] Furthermore, the Tennessee Conference did not want to encourage the idea that to join the church was to save the
country. It had never supported resistance to Georgia or Jackson, and it did
not believe that God and the Gospel should be used for that purpose. Finally,
the Methodists were influenced by the fact that the people of Tennessee
concluded that if Georgia was going to acquire Cherokee land for its citizens,
they should acquire the land occupied by the Cherokees in their state. In
1833 the legislature of Tennessee enacted a law extending the state's jurisdiction over the Cherokee land within its borders, and soon white Tennesseans
were pouring into the Cherokee Nation. While Tennessee did not pass an
oath law or otherwise try to discourage missionary efforts, the Methodists'
Tennessee Annual Conference took this act as a sign that they should cease to
encourage the formation of Cherokee societies and schools in the East. This
did not mean that the Methodist denomination totally deserted the Eastern
Cherokees. In 1836 the Holston Conference in northeastern Tennessee sent
three itinerants into the nation, D. T. Fulton, David B. Cumming, and
David King. Although their mission circuits extended into Georgia, the
Moravians spoke of the Cherokee Methodists they saw in Georgia from
1835 to 1838 as being "deserted," which seems to indicate that the Holston

---

42. Enoch Mudge gives a figure of 930 members for 1830; Enoch Mudge, "History of
the Missions of the Methodist Episcopal Church," in *History of American Missions to the
Heathen* (Worcester, Mass., 1840), p. 539. John gives the figure 1,028 for the year 1829: see
John, *Handbook*, p. 115; she gives the figure 855 for the year 1830.

43. Barclay, *History of Methodist Missions*, vol. 2, p. 171.

circuit riders seldom visited them.[44] It may also mean that the Holston itinerants were more interested in evangelizing among the whites who were rapidly filling up the Cherokee Nation and that Indians would not attend meetings where the white invaders formed the bulk of the congregation. It seems unlikely, given the tense relations between Cherokees and whites in those years, that the Methodists could have formed effective classes or societies in which Indians and white intruders united. The Moravians noted that many former members of Cherokee Methodist societies preferred to join their mission churches or those of the American Board, where the Indians constituted the overwhelming majority of members. However, David Cumming seems to have had a special interest in the Cherokees, and, perhaps at his request, he was assigned to the Arkansas Methodist Conference in 1838 so that he could march with his converts (and others from previously organized Methodist societies) to northeastern Oklahoma and continue to minister to them there.[45] Although the official minutes of the Holston Conference registered a zero for the number of Methodist converts within the Cherokee Nation in 1838, this was simply a way of indicating that the conference no longer kept any records of Eastern Cherokee societies: henceforth they were reported to the Arkansas Methodist Conference. Cumming, in his account of the march westward, reported that he found 480 Methodists among the Cherokees in the East in 1837, and there were probably about the same number there in 1838.[46]

The Moravians tried to minister to the needs of the Cherokees from 1833 to 1838 from makeshift mission stations on David McNair's plantation in Tennessee and at Red Clay, Tennessee. Henry Clauder, his family, and Dorothea Ruede lived in two small cabins on the McNair plantation from 1833 to 1836.[47] Here some of their converts followed them from Oochgelogy and Springplace. Ruede opened a small day school in one of the cabins. Clauder tried, by itinerating to Georgia, to preach occasionally to the remnants of the congregations at Oochgelogy and Springplace, but there were so many whites at these places by 1835 that most of the Cherokees had moved elsewhere: "At Oochgelogy, where Brother Clauder can only visit occasionally," said a report in 1835, there were now "only five or six" members of the "small but once thriving flock"—"the rest being thus, for

44. For accounts of former Methodists converted to Moravianism after 1834, see Springplace Diary, March 23, and June 15, 1834; January 6 and April 5, 1835, MAS, and *Missionary Intelligencer* 5: 435.

45. For David Cumming and the work of the Holston Conference among the Cherokees, see Mary T. Peacock, *The Circuit Riders and Those Who Followed*, pp. 40–43. For Moravian comments on the work of David Cumming, see Springplace Diary, April 12 and April 26, 1835, MAS. Henry Clauder mentions the work of Craige, Davis, and other Methodists in the area of Red Clay, Candy's Creek, and Cleveland, Tennessee, in 1837 but does not mention Cumming. Journal, April 23, 1837, MAB.

46. Peacock, *Circuit Riders*, p. 43. Mudge, "Missions of the Methodist Episcopal Church," p. 539, reports the figure of 525 Methodist members in the Cherokee Nation in Indian territory in 1939–40, after the removal had taken place.

47. Schwarze, *Moravian Missions*, p. 201.

lack of spiritual nourishment returned to the husks of the world."[48] In August 1836 David McNair said that he needed his cabins for some relatives who had been forced out of Georgia. For a time Clauder and Ruede returned to Salem, North Carolina, but Clauder came back to the Cherokee Nation in March 1837 and stayed for eight months, doing what he could at Red Clay and elsewhere to preach to the remaining Moravian converts and to admit some "deserted" Methodist converts into the small congregation. In June 1837 the Moravian mission board sent Miles Vogler, a schoolteacher, to work among the Cherokees. After teaching a short time at McNair's, he was asked by the American Board if he would conduct their school at Brainerd, for they no longer had a teacher there. Vogler agreed and in August 1837 he began; he remained at Brainerd until May 1838.

While the Moravians had some followers, like David McNair and George Hicks, who were staunch supporters of Ross and the Patriot Party, far more of their leading supporters and converts over the years ended up in the Removal, or Treaty, Party—Major and John Ridge, William Rogers, William Hicks, Stand Watie. The mission at Oochgelogy had been started specifically at the request of the Ridges and Waties. It was difficult, especially after the Treaty of New Echota in December 1835, for the Moravians to avoid being identified with the Treaty Party. Clauder remained on friendly terms with the Ridges and Waties and frequently dined at their homes. In addition, the Moravian mission board, like the American Board, annoyed many Cherokees by asking the government to appraise its missionary stations and remunerate them (out of Cherokee funds) for their property losses. They promised the Cherokees that they would use this money ($7,554.50) to open a new mission and school in the west (and kept that promise), but nevertheless it was not taken as a friendly act.[49]

The Moravians appear to have concluded by 1834 that removal was inevitable and for the best. A statement in the annual report of their mission board that year noted that "the tendency to emigration" among the Cherokees was increasing and "this, in the opinion of the Missionaries would be the better alternative."[50] The missionaries were specifically requested by the government agent and other officials to urge their converts and members of their congregations to enroll for Arkansas, but they firmly refused to give such advice (at least publicly). They would not put any pressure of their own upon the Cherokees. In December 1833, Hugh Montgomery, the federal agent, told Clauder that he expected nine hundred Cherokees to leave soon for Arkansas and offered to pay his way and that of his congregation if they would join this party.[51] Clauder knew that few of his congregation in Tennessee were willing to go, and he declined to ask them or to go himself.

48. *Missionary Intelligencer* 5: 426.
49. Schwarze, *Moravian Missions*, p. 202.
50. *Missionary Intelligencer* 5: 244–45.
51. Springplace Diary, December 20, 1833, MAS, and Schwarze, *Moravian Missions*, p. 205.

Though publicly silent about the Cherokees' troubles in these years, Clauder filled his diary with trenchant criticisms of the cruelty of the Georgians and the inhumanity of Andrew Jackson. In April 1837 he wrote that it was common even in Tennessee for soldiers to arrest Cherokees whom they considered troublemakers and forcibly put them on boats for Arkansas: "this is the usual cry among the whites here. Every Indian who happens to look cross (for which everybody knows they have reason) is put down as a hostile, bloodthirsty dog and must forsooth be caught, secured and dragged off like a Galley slave, on board the boats and sent to Arkansas to be made happy and civilized under General Jackson's *human* policy for the preservation of the Indian tribes."[52]

Despite their best efforts, the Moravians did not escape being associated with the Treaty Party. They could not avoid indicating, if asked, that they thought the Treaty of New Echota, however unfairly obtained, was in their opinion a generous settlement and one that the Cherokees should accept. In its annual report of 1835, the Moravian Board stated that the Cherokees "appeared determined to reject the apparently favorable terms again offered by the General Government"—a reference to the rejection of Schermerhorn's first attempt to get his treaty signed in October 1835.[53] In 1836 some Cherokees accused Clauder of supporting removal because he made a fatal mistake in urging the starving Cherokees in Tennessee to accept food offered to them by the government. Chief Ross had told the Cherokees not to accept it. Clauder wrote in exasperation: "The Indians refused to accept this kindness for they believed that this was payment for their land and that by receiving this gift they would be considered as having agreed to the treaty."[54] A few days later he wrote, "I learned of their dissatisfaction [with me] from all sides; they complained that I had gone over to their enemies, the white people, and that I was trying to be helpful to them [the whites] and to do them out of their land." All of this, he concluded, "gave us a clear indication of their lack of confidence in us and how little love they really feel for us."

Miles Vogler nearly came to grief the same way at Brainerd. Some of the Moravian congregation were determined to emigrate in April 1838, before John Ross had agreed that their cause was hopeless. They asked Vogler to go with them. He was tempted to do so, which would have been a serious mistake. But in the end he "declined for the reason that his presence among them might again be interpreted to mean that the Moravians were in sympathy with the Ridge Party."[55] In the winter of 1837/38 the Moravian Board in Salem had appointed three missionaries to go to the Western

52. Clauder, Journal, April 3, 1837, MAB.
53. *Missionary Intelligencer* 5: 426. See also Springplace Diary, July 10, 1836, MAS.
54. Springplace Diary, August 14, 1836, MAS. Schwarze dates this event as occurring in November 1837, but I think he is mistaken. Schwarze, *Moravian Missions*, p. 213
55. Schwarze, *Moravian Missions*, p. 215.

Cherokees and establish a mission. Vogler, Herman Ruede, and Johann R. Schmidt were chosen to go. In May 1838 they were given a wagon and supplies at Salem, North Carolina, and drove to Brainerd. The United States Army had now entered the nation, and the Cherokees were ordered to prepare to emigrate. John Ross had to concede. He told the Cherokees the struggle was over and received from the army commander permission to direct the eight-hundred-mile trek of 14,000 Cherokees to the west. George Hicks, one of the Moravian converts and an influential leader of the Patriot Party, was appointed by Ross to lead one of the thirteen contingents of Cherokees on the march. Vogler, Ruede, and Schmidt decided to go with this contingent. The contingent was supposed to leave early in September 1838 but was delayed. The three Moravians went ahead on their own. No Moravian missionary accompanied the Cherokees on the Trail of Tears.

Like the American Board, the Moravians barely held their own in terms of converts between 1830 and 1838. In 1830 they gave their total as 45. In December 1833 there were 36 adult converts at Springplace (including one black slave) and 10 at Oochgelogy. They made no estimate of how many were left of these in 1838, but Clauder reported 35 communicants at his Easter service in Red Clay in March 1837. With some additions from the Methodists, the Moravians may have had 45 to 50 converts in September 1838.[56]

While the Methodist denomination lost over half of its members between 1830 and 1838, and while the American Board and Moravians barely held their own, the Baptist denomination increased by over 500 percent. In 1830 they reported 90 members, about half of whom left for Arkansas with Duncan O'Briant the next year. But by 1835 they had increased their total to 244 members, and in 1838 over 500 (some reports say 700) were among those who made the march to the west.[57] The explanation for this remarkable success lies in part in the fact that the Baptists preached primarily in the mountainous region of North Carolina and northern Georgia, where there was the least disturbance from intruding whites and where the 5,000 inhabitants of that region were almost all fullbloods. In part it stemmed from the fact that the Cherokees in this area were not split between the Removal and Patriot parties but were almost solidly behind John Ross. Nor were they split between rich and poor, educated and uneducated, slaveholders and nonslaveholders. By and large it was a homogeneous region of small, nonslaveholding, one-horse dirt farmers. But undoubtedly the most significant fact in the Baptists' growth was the dynamic personality of the Reverend Evan Jones and the work of his dedicated native preachers.

Jones and the Baptists had several important assets. First of all, by 1833 Jones had been at the Valley Towns mission station for over a decade.

56. For 1833, see *Missionary Intelligencer* 5: 245; for 1837, see Schwarze, *Moravian Missions*. p. 207.

57. *Baptist Missionary Magazine* 19: 64.

Second, he was one of the few white missionaries (perhaps the only one) who learned to speak Cherokee with sufficient confidence to preach in it as well as to write it in Sequoyan. Third, he assembled a group of native interpreters, exhorters, and licensed preachers who were remarkably successful in winning converts by itinerating throughout the mountain region. And finally, Jones was so wholeheartedly in support of John Ross and the resistance to removal that he became a member of Ross's inner circle of political confidants and assistants. As a result, there was much less conflict between loyalty to Christianity and loyalty to the Nation in the Baptist mission churches than in any others. Of course, Christianity was still the whiteman's religion, and Jones could not overcome that stigma; he reported in his daily journal several confrontations with conjurors and other advocates of the old religion who were particularly influential in this fullblood region and who did their best to thwart his evangelism in these years. But no one could ever accuse Jones or his coworkers of trying to aid Georgia or Jackson. Moreover, some of the Baptist converts were among the most eminent leaders of the Patriot Party in the Council. Jesse Bushyhead, for example, one of the three licensed Cherokee Baptist preachers, was a confidant of John Ross and went with him to Washington on several occasions to plead for the nation's rights. Nevertheless, Bushyhead maintained his role as a minister to his church at Amohee whenever he could.

Whatever stigma had attached to the Baptists prior to 1832 because of Isaac McCoy's success in identifying the denomination with removal was erased after that date by the board's dissociating itself from McCoy and by Jones's becoming the symbol of the Baptist cause in the Cherokee nation. In a sense, the Baptists picked up the cause of Christian nationalism among the Cherokees just when the Methodists and the American Board were dropping it. Like the Methodists, they had the benefit of a democratic ecclesiastical system, a willingness to make use of native preachers, a lack of concern for an educated ministry. Jones adopted the Methodist practice of itinerant circuit riding and made regular use of the camp meeting (sometimes called four-day meeting or protracted meeting), which enabled the Cherokees to gather from long distances at prearranged meeting places under the trees to combine religious and social activities. While Baptist meetings were not quite so enthusiastic as those of the Methodists, they included the important ritual of baptizing in the river. Unlike the other boards, the Baptist Foreign Mission Board decided to increase rather than decrease its staff in the 1830s. In 1832 it sent Leonard Butterfield and his wife along with Sarah Rayner to assist Jones. The Butterfields remained until 1835 and Rayner till 1836. They were assigned to teach in the schools at Valley Towns, thereby leaving Jones free to preach along his 150-mile circuit through the mountains.

Though Jones did not write much about it in his letters to the managing board in Boston, he spent a good deal of his time at Cherokee national and town councils and in conferences with John Ross and other Cherokee leaders dealing with political affairs. He was well informed on the activities of the

Patriot Party, passing on political information as he made his circuit, collecting information for Ross, gathering signatures for petitions to Congress, and assisting in drafting official documents for the chiefs. Some insight into the social activism of Jones's ministry and of his rapport with his congregations can be gathered from a description given by Sophia Sawyer of a visit to Valley Towns. Jones had been to New Echota to learn the results of a recently returned delegation to Washington; Sawyer accompanied him back to Valley Towns, where, she said, as he entered the mission area, Cherokees flocked around him to learn the news "They had been waiting with anxiety to learn from Mr. Jones what return the delegation brought from Washington." He had only bad news, and when he told them, "they said, 'How can we trust them when they are breaking the most solemn treaties?' " Sawyer, who was accustomed to the views of the Removal Party, was surprised at the determination of these fullbloods to hold on to their country: "They cling to the graves of their fathers and say, 'Let us die with them. If we leave this country, these hills and valleys, and mountain air, we shall sicken and die. What can we have in exchange? Perhaps war [with the Osage] on our arrival [in the West] or, if we remain [there], a few years of peace and cultivate the land [until] the white man will [come again and] trade our rights. . . . [W]e may as well die here.' "[58] Jones agreed with them.

Sawyer happened to be in Valley Towns on a day which Chief Ross had appointed as a day of humiliation and prayer for the nation. Jones celebrated it with his congregation, but instead of turning their attention to personal sins of intemperance, profanity, failure to observe the Sabbath, he emphasized the social sins of the nation: "If Providence does not favor a nation, it cannot prosper." In the discussion afterward about what kinds of national sins might have brought God's anger against them, Sawyer found that the Cherokees in Valley Towns agreed it was probably the sin of black slavery. "God cannot be pleased with slavery," said one of them. There followed "some discussion respecting the expediency of setting slaves at liberty." When one of them said this might cause more trouble than good, a native Baptist preacher told him, "I never heard tell of any hurt coming from doing right." Their choice of slavery as the preeminent national sin for which their people were suffering may well have reflected the social antipathy of these poorer, nonslaveholding Cherokees toward the wealthy, mixed-blood, plantation-owning Cherokees to the south. Nevertheless, the point was that Jones encouraged such discussions whereas most missionaries would have avoided them.

No Baptist converts signed the fraudulent Treaty of New Echota (though some members of the other three denominations did). Nor did any of the local chiefs in North Carolina sign it. When Schermerhorn came to this mountain region to try to persuade some of the chiefs there to sign it so that it would seem more representative of the general will, he could find

58. Robert S. Walker, *Torchlights to the Cherokees*, pp. 298–99.

none to oblige him. Schermerhorn placed the blame for this squarely upon Evan Jones: "I visited the North Carolina Indians in order to explain the treaty to them and obtain some of their signatures to it, but through the influence of the Baptist Missionary, who was under the influence of Ross, I did not succeed in getting any of them to sign."[59] In May 1836, Jones wrote to his board that news of the ratification of the treaty was "spreading gloom and consternation through the community."[60] The secretary of war, fearing that there might be an armed uprising among the Cherokees similar to those occurring among the Creeks and the Seminoles over removal, sent General John E. Wool into the nation with a contingent of 2,000 United States troops. His task was to take away all the guns from the Cherokees. Coming to North Carolina during one of the chronic periods of famine, when hunting small game was one of the few means of feeding Cherokee families, Wool was bound to arouse considerable hostility by trying to take away their guns. Jones faced a delicate decision when he was asked to assist Wool in this task. "On his arrival at Valley Towns," Jones told his board, the general "was informed by some person that my influence among the Cherokees was very extensive and that it might be of great advantage in forwarding his designs" if Jones were to cooperate with him. Wool had a second mission. He was supposed to try to persuade the Cherokees to accept the Treaty of New Echota and to enroll for emigration. Jones was not willing to be a party to either of these pursuits:

> When I was introduced to him he used many arguments to induce me to advise the Indians to submit to the treaty. I took the liberty, respectfully, to state to him the plain truth with regard to the injustice practised on the Cherokees in the making of this Treaty and that the whole body of the Cherokees were opposed to it. He agreed to the truth of all this, but said the Treaty was ratified and must be executed. I, however, declined taking any part in the business.[61]

He did agree to call the Cherokees to assemble and listen to Wool's proposals. They came and listened politely "but utterly refused to recognize the treaty." Wool then called a second meeting and harangued them some more, "with the same results." When Wool called a third meeting, Jones refused to attend. At this meeting Wool demanded that they turn in all of their rifles, but few Cherokees were present and none brought their rifles. Wool held Jones and some of his assistants to blame and arrested, in Jones words, "four Indian men and two of their wives, one white man married to a native, and myself." The detainees were taken to Wool's headquarters near Valley Towns on August 5. Wool discharged all of them but Jones and his native

---

59. Duane King, "The Origin of the Eastern Cherokees as a Social and Political Entity," in *The Cherokee Indian Nation*, ed. Duane King (Knoxville: University of Tennessee Press, 1979), p. 168.

60. Evan Jones to Lucius Bolles, May 23, 1836, BFMB.

61. Evan Jones to Lucius Bolles, February 6, 1837, BFMB.

assistant, David Foreman. "The General said he should take us through the mountains to collect the Indians' arms." They had no desire to be co-opted into this work, and "to prevent this disagreeable route, I consulted with some of the Old Cherokees and advised them to bring in their arms to the order of the General, which they did."[62] Jones feared that trouble might start if the soldiers went into people's homes or tried to seize their guns while they were hunting. It also probably occurred to him and the old chiefs that if they were left to turn in their guns voluntarily, they could choose which ones to hide and which ones to offer up as token compliance with the order. Jones suspected that Wool would soon try to use his services for other unpleasant duties and rather than submit to this, he decided to leave the nation until the troops had departed. "It was believed by the Government officers that the Cherokees in the mountains were altogether guided by my advice." Jones also learned that "threats had been made to drive us [the Baptists] out of the Nation" by members of the Treaty Party.

In August 1836, Jones put his family and belongings into a wagon and moved to a place called Four Mile Branch near Madisonvile, Tennessee, on the western side of the Great Smokies. There he rented a place for his family after giving his students at Valley Towns a vacation until his return. He sent Sarah Rayner home. By November, he believed it would be safe to return to Valley Towns, and he sent a wagon ahead with his belongings in it. But "just at this time [November 3] I received an order from General Wool . . . forbidding our return, at least for the present." Jones then rented a farm with several cabins in the nearby community of New Columbus just on the edge of the Cherokee Nation in Tennessee. Here, he and his wife opened a school and invited the Cherokees to send their children. As Jones read the order against his returning to North Carolina, it referred to his residing in that state and did not prevent his itinerating and preaching in the nation. So as soon as his wife and daughter got the school under way in New Columbus, he returned to preaching around his circuit. On one preaching tour early in 1837, he and Bushyhead reported to the board that they had preached twenty-six times, administered communion once, had six conference meetings, received twenty-nine candidates for baptism and after examining them baptized twenty-two as follows: at Coosewatee, four males and two females; one black woman; at Still's place, one male and four females and one black woman; at Long Swamp, one male and one female; at Deganeetla, three males and four females.[63] "Just before we started on this tour," he reported to his board in June, "the commander of the troops issued an order for my arrest, threatening at the same time to arrest my [Cherokee] associates and send them off to Arkansas."[64] Jones and Bushyhead had simply ignored the

62. Ibid.

63. See letter of Evan Jones to Lucius Bolles dated June 28, 1837, in the *Baptist Missionary Magazine* 18: 17.

64. *Baptist Missionary Magazine* 18. The letter from Jones is dated June 28, 1837.

threat. Occasionally Jones sent to the board a letter written by Bushyhead about his own work and that of his brother, Beaver Carrier: "I have the pleasure of baptizing thirteen cherokees since my return from Washington," Bushyhead wrote in 1837. "Brother Beaver and myself have formed a circuit this last fall over about two hundred and thirty or forty miles round. It is interesting to see the people flocking in to hear the word of God preached or read."[65] Bushyhead and Beaver Carrier of course preached in Cherokee.

On the one hand, Jones was a preacher and evangelist, but on the other, he was a political agitator. In March 1836, Ben F. Currey, who was appointed by the War Department to get the Cherokees to enroll for Arkansas, wrote to Elbert Herring, the commissioner of Indian Affairs, saying that Jones was heavily involved in coordinating Cherokee resistance to emigration in North Carolina. Currey's interpreter had attended a council near Valley Towns where he heard "part of what had been translated into the Cherokee language as he believes by the Revd. Evan Jones which was full of abuse against Mr. Schermerhorn and those who made the Treaty at New Echota and which I suppose was intended to inflame the minds of the ignorant Indians against the Treaty."[66] This council had been called by James Wafford, a Baptist convert and exhorter who worked closely with Jones. The council had collected money to send "runners to other parts of the nation bearing copies of a letter supposed to have been addressed by Ross to Jones." Currey told Herring that Jones tried to conceal the fact that he was in regular correspondence with Ross and with Bushyhead about political affairs: "Inflammatory communications received from Ross and his coadjutors," like Jones, were seriously impeding the government's work, Currey said.

Among the Ross papers are some clear indications that Currey was right. In one letter, dated November 20, 1837, Jones told Ross that he had just returned from Valley Towns, where Currey and other government agents "are urging on the execution of the Schermerhorn Treaty by every means, force and fraud, but altogether without success." Jones reported the names of four Cherokees who had been cajoled into enrolling for Arkansas, thus keeping the chief informed of those who were disloyal to the government. He also reported that "Tennessee is about to grant occupant rights to the intruders who have violated the supreme laws of the land" by moving onto Cherokee land claiming it was now "under the jurisdiction" of Tennessee and therefore free to whoever wanted it. In this same letter, he denounced the activities of W. H. Thomas in North Carolina. Thomas, he said, was "a very busy little man" who claimed to be acting by authority of the Cherokee Council and who was trying to persuade the Cherokees in Valley Towns to join the settlement of Cherokees at Lufty, outside the boundaries of the nation so that "he may have the management of their

65. Evan Jones to Lucius Bolles, October 24, 1836, BFMB.
66. Ben F. Currey to Elbert Herring, March 7, 1836, Grant Foreman Papers, Indian Archives, Oklahoma Historical Society, Oklahoma City, IV, 245.

property."[67] An Englishman who happened to visit the nation at the time of the national council at Red Clay which Jones attended in August 1837 reported, "In the course of the evening I attended at the Council-house to hear some of their resolutions [against removal] read by an English missionary named Jones who adhered to the Cherokees; a man of talent, it was said, and of great activity, but who was defeated by the Georgians" in his efforts to uphold the Cherokees' rights:

> After breakfast I made myself acquainted with Mr. Jones, the Missionary, whom I found to be a man of sense and experience and who must have received a tolerable education for he was not even ignorant of Hebrew. He was exceedingly devoted to this nation. . . . The Georgians, and, I found, most of the other white settlers, had a decided antipathy to him on account of the advice which he gave to the Cherokees which had frequently enabled them to baffle the machinations of the persons who are plotting to get their lands.[68]

Typical of the kinds of machinations which Jones found time for in the midst of his evangelistic labors was the drawing up and circulating of petitions for Ross. In a letter to Ross on December 29, 1837, he said, "Will another protest from the people be of any avail? If so, let me know the principal points to be dwelt on, and the kind of stile or tone rather—whether confident or submissive or both mixed." Evidently Ross later wrote from Washington that a protest signed by as many of the people as possible would be helpful in pleading his case to rescind the Treaty of New Echota. For the next two months Jones and the Ross Party circulated such a protest, obtaining signatures from almost every man, woman, and child in the nation.[69]

Elias Boudinot published a pamphlet defending the Removal Party in 1837. Entitled *Letters and Other Papers Relating to Cherokee Affairs: Being a Reply to Sundry Publications Authorized by John Ross*, it was used in Congress by Senator Wilson Lumpkin to defend the validity of the New Echota treaty. Ross's inner circle decided that it was important to answer Boudinot's charges against Ross. Evan Jones was chosen to draft the response.[70] Jones also kept Ross informed of the movements of the United States troops in the nation and of their plans for "catching the Indians and chaining and handcuffing them" to take them to stockades for shipment to Arkansas. "Anything you may wish that I can do," he wrote to Ross, "make no hesitation in commanding my feeble efforts."[71]

Although the Baptist board in Boston did not know, and did not want to

67. Evan Jones to John Ross, November 20, 1837, Ross Papers.

68. George W. Featherstonhaugh. *A Canoe Voyage Up the Minnay Sator* (London, 1847), vol. 2, pp. 150–53.

69. Evan Jones to John Ross, December 29, 1837, and February 26, 1838, Ross Papers.

70. Evan Jones to John Ross, February 24, 1838, Indian Archives, Oklahoma Historical Society, and February 26, 1838, and March 20, 1838, Ross Papers.

71. Evan Jones to John Ross, February 24, 1838. Indian Archives, Oklahoma Historical Society, and February 26, 1838, Ross Papers.

know, about this side of Jones's missionary work, it was more than pleased with the tremendous increase in Baptist converts from year to year. The board would have considered his political actions totally inappropriate for a missionary. But to Jones, they were two sides of the same coin. One could not in sermons express serious spiritual concern for the oppressed without also demonstrating some interest in alleviating that oppression. Naturally Jones's political activity was deeply resented by the Treaty Party, the federal agents, and the United States Army. "Jealousy has grown to a high pitch at the Agency," Jones wrote to Ross in March 1838: "If a dog should bark [at] the treaty, he would no doubt be put in the guard-house for his temerity. I presume Mr. L[ewis] Ross has informed you of my adventure with the Honorable Commissioner. He ordered me to depart in ten minutes on pain of being put in the guard-house. I was not allowed to answer a word." By March 1838 the two years allowed for the emigration of the Cherokees under the terms of the New Echota treaty were almost up, and the agency was in feverish activity expecting the army to send troops any day to compel the Cherokees to go. Jones did not wish to be jailed. "I feel no disposition to provoke the old Gentleman," he told Ross, referring to the commissioner, "nor do I feel at all disposed to surrender my liberty to his tyranny. And as long as I believe I can be of any service to the Cherokees, he may rest assured that nothing short of physical force will prevent my visiting them."[72] Jones tried to hide his political activism behind his role as a missionary, claiming that any interference with his free travel in the Nation would be tantamount to interference with his constitutional freedom of religion.

When Ross accepted failure in May 1838 and divided the Cherokees into thirteen separate detachments for the march westward, he designated Jesse Bushyhead, the Baptist preacher, to lead one of them. Another was to be led by Situagi, an elderly fullblood from Valley Towns who could not read or write English; Ross chose Evan Jones as second in command to Situagi. Jones was the only missionary to be given such responsibilities upon the Trail of Tears, though he was not the only missionary who went with the Cherokees on that march. Jones reported to the *Baptist Missionary Magazine* that in his detachment and Bushyhead's combined there were over five hundred Baptists; throughout the long trip they held regular services and sang their hymns in Cherokee to keep up their spirits.[73]

The only minister besides Evan Jones to demonstrate such intensely activistic political and religious concern for the Cherokees after 1832 was James J. Trott. Trott did not give up evangelism when he left the Methodists to become a Disciple. He remarried (his new bride was the sister of his

72. Evan Jones to John Ross, March 20, 1838, Ross Papers.
73. *Baptist Missionary Magazine* 19: 64. After Jones arrived in the western area of the Cherokee Nation (northeastern Oklahoma), the members of the Treaty Party managed to persuade the federal agent to prohibit him from taking up residence as a missionary. It took John Ross a year to get this decision overruled.

former wife) and continued to live in Etowah with her and his two children.
He also preached his new faith to the Cherokees and undoubtedly converted
some to it. Because he was a Cherokee citizen by marriage, Trott was
appointed to a Cherokee delegation which went to Washington in 1835 to
plead for Cherokee rights. The next year he served on a committee appointed
by Ross which traveled through the nation gathering data and evaluations of
depredations against Cherokee property by white citizens of Georgia. The
Cherokee Nation hoped to present the federal government at some future date
with a detailed list of spoliations for remuneration. When the Georgians
discovered this, he was arrested. They released him only after he promised to
desist from his work.[74] Explaining to John Howard Payne the reasons for
his support of the Cherokees in 1836, Trott said, "The most puissant
weapons of the day, and perticulary the present administration in the Indian
Department, are wielded against the Cherokees—*lying, money, and physical
force*—while the Cherokees are panoplied with truth, justice, innocence and
unexampled forbearance."[75] For Trott, the Cherokees exemplified the virtues of true Christians, and their oppressors, the traits of the Devil. Trott
continued to help and preach to the Cherokees until they were forced to
emigrate, but remained in the South to evangelize for the Disciples until
1859. Then he moved to Indian Territory and once again preached to
them.[76]

Active participation in the Cherokee efforts to resist removal was pursued by only a handful of the missionaries. Nevertheless it indicated to the
Cherokees that Christianity could stand for more than personal salvation and
premillennial hope. In the long run it was the wide variety of uses to which
Christian teaching and symbols could be put that gave the new religion its
continued appeal. Even after they had lost faith in the citizens of "the
nominally Christian nation" which persecuted them, some Cherokees could
still find hope and strength in Christian faith.

It is difficult to say, in the end, who was more frustrated by their long and
difficult relationship, the Cherokees or the missionaries. Certainly neither
got out of it what they expected. The Cherokees had hoped for secular
schools to teach them the basic skills they needed for a new way of life;
instead, they got religious schools to convert their children into model
Christians.[77] The missionaries expected to find a simple, childlike people,

74. James J. Trott to John Howard Payne, Payne Papers, VII, 242–44, 293–302. J.
Edward Moseley, *Disciples of Christ in Georgia*, pp. 123–31. Trott's second wife was Rachel
Adair.
75. James J. Trott to John Howard Payne, Payne Papers, V, 11–12.
76. Moseley, *Disciples of Christ*, pp. 123–31. Moseley states that Trott made
seventy-five converts to the Disciples denomination among the Cherokees before the Civil War
interrupted his work. There appears to be no record of how many he converted before removal.
77. At a more mundane level one might argue that the Cherokees' hope for secular
schools was thwarted by the chronic shortage of labor in America. In 1793, Henry Knox had

grateful for their services and eager to adopt their superior beliefs, values, and manners; instead, they found a proud, self-willed, resolute people deeply committed to their own ways and beliefs. The missionaries thought they represented a benevolent effort to lift the Indians out of barbarism and admit them as full and equal citizens into the republic; the Cherokees considered the missionaries haughty, paternalistic, and patronizing—too ready to undermine their sense of self-worth and too likely to prevent them from joining the republic by making impossible demands for their conformity to white standards. Robert Berkhofer's final assessment of missionary work among Native Americans from 1787 to 1862 seems all too applicable to the Cherokee mission effort: "Although the modern analyst can see only the inevitable failure of the missionary enterprise given the participants' cultural assumptions . . . the religious observers of the time never saw clearly the extent of their failure."[78]

The blame for failure, however, did not lie wholly with the missionaries in the field; they acted within (or were acted upon by) forces quite beyond their control. In the first place, while few missionaries shared the growing racism of white Americans, they could not escape its consequences. Frontier whites generally considered the whole missionary enterprise a waste of time, and the federal Civilization Fund for the Indians a waste of money; they did their best to undercut and oppose the missionaries so that they could get on with the business of utilizing the Indians' land as they saw fit. Second, the missionaries were constantly hampered by their cautious, conservative, cost-conscious mission boards, which ranked salvation of Native American souls at the bottom of the foreign mission effort. Mission boards were timid about opposing the government or the public, even when they disagreed with their actions; often the boards succumbed to the same stereotypes of the "savage Indian hunter" or "child of the forest" as those who despised the Indians. Third, the missionaries were frustrated by the mounting sectional divisions (North and South, East and West) in the United States, which produced mounting political friction over the Indian question after 1815. The Indian question had never been high on the political agenda of most politicians, and the welfare of the voteless Indians was easily sacrificed by them to the importunings of frontier whites. When missionaries and benevolent societies voiced opposition to mistreatment of the Indians, it was denigrated as the work of moralistic fanatics or political partisans. In the final clash of sectional interests after 1828, the unsettled

---

tried to create secular schools among the Iroquois and found money to support them, but, according to R. Pierce Beaver, "teachers and farm mechanics who had the right character and sufficient motivation to participate in the scheme could not be found. Only strong missionary motivation, it appeared, could induce the right kind of persons to devote themselves to the Indians with sufficient permanency and with their welfare in view." Secular schools were thus impossible to staff, and missionary staffs were committed to Christianization as their primary goal. See Beaver, *Church, State and the American Indians*, p. 66.

78. Robert F. Berkhofer, Jr., *Salvation and the Savage*, p. 152.

constitutional problem of states' rights overrode all commitments ever made to the Indians (by treaties, civilization programs, or missionary support). Circumstantially, nullification was the overriding issue; Indian rights the minor one. To preserve the Union, it seemed logical to sacrifice the latter to the former. "O, they are not going to war—much less for the Indians," commented Elias Boudinot to Samuel Worcester in reference to the nullification crisis.[79] In a broader sense, the missionaries fell victims to the rise of a new American definition of nationalism which ruled out a multiracial, integrated (at least for red and white) republic such as Washington and Knox had envisaged.

In addition to the invincible racism of most whites there were fundamental flaws and ambiguities in George Washington's Indian policy which became evident when the missionaries tried to implement it. The policy nowhere stated when or how the determination would be made to admit Indians as full and equal citizens. The missionaries tried to define what it meant to be Christian and civilized, but their definition was almost impossible to attain. Furthermore, missionaries preached as though integration could not take place until every single Cherokee met their high standards —standards which the missionaries frankly admitted were met by few of those frontier whites in the communities surrounding the Cherokee Nation. Missionaries offered no explanation for this double standard. Furthermore, Washington's policy never said what, if anything, could be done if the states into which the Cherokees were integrated chose only to allow them second-class citizenship; missionaries too gave little thought to this embarrassing question, and when faced with it, could only wring their hands and shake their heads. Finally, Washington's policy, again with full missionary support, called for every Cherokee to have his own fee-simple tract of land before he could become a citizen; but the Cherokees (like most Indians) quickly recognized that their only basis of resistance to detribalization and the loss of self-government was to maintain tribal land ownership; once the land was parceled out to individuals to dispose of as they saw fit (or once it could be transferred by cash, force, or fraud from a Cherokee owner to a white owner) the foundation of Indian nationhood would be eroded bit by bit. Yet missionaries consistently urged "division of the land in severalty" on the grounds that without individual land ownership, there could be no sense of personal independence and responsibility.

Most of the missionaries were also hindered by their commitment to a Calvinist interpretation of Christianity when the rest of the country was rapidly moving toward the Arminianism of the Methodists. They told the Cherokees that God could immediately convert "even the wretched savage" into a rational Christian, but their doctrines of predestination and election (for those Cherokees who tried to understand them) clearly implied that only

79. Samuel Worcester to David Greene, March 18, 1833, ABCFM.

a few of the Cherokees were predestined for salvation. God, it seemed, was an elitist. What hope then was there for the whole Cherokee Nation to meet the standards set for integration as equal citizens? Not only was it hard to get into a mission church, but it was easy to get put out. Those of mixed ancestry seemed best able to meet the standards of "visible sainthood." They had more self-discipline, found rewards in hard work, prospered in the world (being "diligent in business" as the Bible commanded). They did not so often "backslide" into those heathen practices (ballplays and conjuring) which marked the presumed convert as a "hypocrite"—a person claiming to be one of the elect, entitled to church membership, but in reality still a reprobate and unfit for Christian fellowship. The logic of this was that if few were destined for church membership, few were destined for full citizenship. In white America the poor were poor because they deserved to be; they were wicked, lazy, intemperate, irresponsible, or otherwise ineradicably tainted with original sin. Better then, the Cherokees concluded, to be poor and unchurched in their own nation, for by their traditions the poorest and richest were still equal—there were no property qualifications for office; the hospitality ethic applied to all as a right, not a "charity"; respect was based upon age, experience, loyalty to tribal traditions, and personal abilities, not on wealth. The brotherhood and sisterhood which the missionaries fostered among the predestined elect in the church, was, in the Cherokee Nation, accorded to everyone through kinship.

Given all this, the poignant question remains: did the missionaries, given their obvious sincerity and benevolence, do more to help or to harm the Cherokees? Why, for example, did they unilaterally alter their own program for civilization and Christianization after 1824 by curtailing their schools and increasing their proselytism? Was it simply cost-efficiency? Were they admitting that their schools were failures? Or had the schools only been an excuse for proselyting in the first place? Once again forces outside the missionaries' control lay behind the decision, namely, those evangelical energies unleashed by what historians call the Second Great Awakening—that continuous series of revivals and religious organizations which flourished throughout the nation from 1800 to 1835. The missionaries to the Indians wanted to be participants in this movement. What worked so effectively among unchurched white Americans should work among red Americans. The Holy Spirit was loose in the land; showers of blessing were falling everywhere. How could the missionaries fulfill the desire to share in that ultimate rapport with God's power except by getting on their horses and riding out to preach the Word?

Perry Miller has argued that the Second Great Awakening was a major force leading toward patriotic national unity, defined, of course, in Evangelical terms.[80] But as America moved "from the covenant to the revival" (as

80. See Perry Miller, *The Life of the Mind in America* (New York: Harcourt, Brace, 1965), pp. 66–70.

Miller put it) it also moved from gemeinschaft to gesellschaft, from a sense of corporate community to one of intense, competitive individualism. The Puritans held that God had made his covenant with a whole people; after the Awakening, Evangelicals believed it was the decisions of countless individuals (made of their own free will) which created and sustained the necessary covenant with God. Contrary to Jefferson's hope that the separation of church and state would lead the nation to a Unitarian religious ideology, the voluntaristic principle led to a revivalistic, evangelical ideology. But the Cherokees did not want to give up their sense of community; their identity rested upon an involuntary, birthright, traditional concept of religion. To abandon that communal commitment was to abandon their sense of being a Cherokee. Only a person of mixed ancestry was prepared to cut himself off from tribal identity and accept the self-reliant individualism which the missionaries preached (that is, God helps those who help themselves). When some of the more self-reliant mixed bloods (like the Ridges, Waties, Hickses, Rosses) realized that their skin color was more important to the average whiteman than was their civilized, Christian character, they too had second thoughts about assimilation and veered toward national separatism (at least until such time as the whiteman could learn to practice his professed belief in equality). All along the line the missionaries to the Cherokees were fighting against American cultural developments which they sometimes misapplied, misunderstood, and at other times ignored or disagreed with.

Finally, the missionaries worked against themselves by their inconsistent positions in regard to the critical issues of political action and social justice. Some, like the Moravians, were less inconsistent than others; political neutrality was ingrained in their ideology. Yet even they considered themselves agents of the War Department, bound in return for the subsidies to implement government policy (or at least never to challenge it), and equally bound to give advice to the War Department on how best to promote its goals. By contrast, the missionaries of the American Board were obviously the most inconsistent about politics. They came to the South eager to monopolize not only the program for civilizing all of the Indians there but also the Civilization Fund. They freely told the government that they would act as its agents and that they had the bureaucracy to be the most effective missionary agents. At the same time, they told the Cherokees that they were men of great influence in Congress, and to prove it, they went to Washington to assist them in making the treaty of 1819. The board remained committed to this politically activist role (allegedly on behalf of Cherokee rights) until 1832. Thereafter, when the Cherokees' rights ceased to coincide with the board's own interests (it had more far-ranging goals than it wished to stake on the Cherokees), the board suddenly adopted a pose of righteous neutrality, insisting that its only purpose was to save souls. The Cherokees rightly found this to be hypocritical; how could the missionaries one day espouse their Christian concern for social justice in America and the next day argue that Christians cared only for salvation in the world to come? The influence of the Methodists and the Baptists, who were caught in this same dilemma, was weakened by the quarrels that took place between the missionaries in the field and their mission boards at home. The left hand and the right hand worked against each other. The Bible, the Great Book of the whiteman, proved to have no answers (or too many different answers) to the most important questions facing the Cherokees and the missionaries: What is God's and what is Caesar's? Who in America are "the powers that be"? When is civil disobedience justified in the name of a higher law of justice? What proportion of Christian effort should be given to saving souls and what proportion to promoting a just society?

The anguished breast-beating of the missionaries, eloquently revealed in their diaries and letters, indicates the spiritual confusion into which the mission cause fell after 1832, when all of these inconsistencies began to come to light. In their frustration, many missionaries turned upon one another and against their equally ambivalent and torn mission boards. Powerless to attack the government (having lost their bearings on social justice), they vented their anger upon one another—Butler against Worcester, Heman Lincoln against Isaac McCoy, Butrick against his board, James J. Trott against the whole Methodist denomination. Others took a worse course, berating the Cherokees, blaming the victims because they were so slow to acculturate. Still others complacently believed that they had expected too much of these feckless heathen; perhaps, they said, Jackson's new policy was more benevolent than the old one, for out in the West, free from the barbarous white citizens of the frontier, these simple people might have more time to acculturate. Some even professed to believe that God, for his own good reasons, might have destined the Indians to perish. When John Thompson of the American Board reneged on his decision to support Worcester and Butler in civil disobedience to Georgia's oath law in May 1831, he said, "It may be part of God's plan in promoting the interests of His church, to destroy the Majority of the Cherokees. . . . [T]he Redeemer's cause may, for aught I know, be promoted in the end by such an event."[81] For a missionary to say that God might destroy the redman to promote the Christian church was surely the nadir of missionary thought. But it was obviously not unthinkable.

However, it was not only the false hopes and inconsistencies of the missionary effort which limited the success of Christianization among the Cherokees. The cultural persistence of the great majority of Cherokees was far stronger than the whites had imagined; Cherokee loyalty to the old ways was not to be broken by empty promises. In fact, many Cherokees were hardly touched by the missionaries' ideology. The belief in the old cosmology remained strong, as the continual reliance upon conjuring demonstrated. Most Cherokees continued to believe that the earth, the woods, the waters,

81. John F. Thompson to David Greene, May 25, 1831, ABCFM.

the animals and birds, the sun and the moon were animated by spiritual forces with whom they had daily contact. They still looked for portents in their dreams and expected visions or messages from their ancestors. Man, nature, and the supernatural were in reciprocal harmony; their attachment to their Mother, the earth, and their Father, the Great Spirit, "the giver of breath," remained. They still felt it important to perform their dances of thanksgiving at harvest time and their Purification rituals at the start of the new year. Their ballplays remained exciting rituals and their all-night dances a source of exhilaration, spiritual communion, and emotional release.

But these religious practices grew less regular with each new generation. The attachment to the old cosmology weakened slowly but surely between 1789 and 1839. The old ways had given meaning and order to a different set of tribal patterns, a different economic, social, and political order. In that half century, if not the preceding one, the rhythm of the old ways was irretrievably broken. The old people still remembered them, but the young found it difficult to understand the symbols imbedded in their sacred rites and myths; the symbols did not elicit a spontaneous emotional response. If they wanted to know, they had to ask. The Cherokee religion was no longer imbibed unconsciously from infancy, as naturally as their mother's milk. Each new generation—that born in 1789, in 1810, in 1831—grew up in a different order of relationships to nature, to one another, to the whiteman. First the communal villages broke up; then the clan ties waned; the family structure altered, and a new ethic of competition, hard work, barter, and trade for profit compelled a new orientation. The dominant culture had its way. Time was measured in weeks, not in "moons." Ballplays were sports to bet on, not surrogates for war. Violins and reels competed with drums and stomp dances. The whiteman stopped business for his holidays and so did the Cherokees who did business with him. The Council reshaped Cherokee political order to resemble the whiteman's order. With the passage of half a century much of the ideology of the elderly was a subject of sentiment and nostalgia rather than a reflection of reality. In times of political and social crisis, the young tried to revive their emotional links with the past in order to feel more deeply their identity as Cherokees. But it is the nature and necessity of the young to look forward. The old religion seemed forever behind them. And what was left of it was changing.

There was something symbolic about the conversion of Big Cabin (Cabbin Smith) to Christianity in 1831. He was then eighty years old. He had been a leader in White Path's effort to slow down the hectic pace of acculturation. Though his father was white, he was one of those whites who "turned Indian," and he raised Big Cabin as an Indian. Big Cabin never learned to speak English. According to Dr. Elizur Butler, who described his conversion, Big Cabin had been "intemperate, licentious, a conjourer and disturber of the peace." "He was once a Chief but was broken some years ago for attempting to hire a Cherokee to purjure himself. He had been an opposer to religion" in the past and on earlier visits "he would not speak to me" about Christianity. But in his old age he became ill and lonely. "I performed a small surgical operation on him which gave him much relief from pain, with which he was highly pleased." When Big Cabin asked to be taken into the mission church at Haweis, Butler baptized him and wrote, "we trust [he] is a real convert to Christianity."[82] What did it mean when an old chief like Big Cabin, worn out with efforts to preserve the past and corrupted by a system he did not understand and could not cope with, decided to become a Christian? Butler obviously was unsure. But if Berkhofer is right, that the missionaries "never saw clearly the extent of their failure," in another sense neither did they see the extent of their success. The Cherokees turned the missionaries' defeat into an unexpected victory, but on their own terms. They came to see that Christianity was not limited to the doctrines and practices of any particular denomination. When they heard it preached and interpreted in their own language by their own preachers they discovered how the power they had thought was within the Great Book could be made to work for them. But the message many Cherokees took from the Bible was not the message the missionaries preached.

---

82. Elizur Butler to David Greene, March 28, 1831, ABCFM.

EPILOGUE

The New Religion and the Old

The temper of the ancient adversaries of the gospel manifests itself in efforts to impede the progress of the truth. A priest or conjuror, an old man of some influence . . . sent messages through the country warning the people against us.

Rev. Evan Jones, Baptist missionary, June 28, 1837

O ne of the hardest tasks of the historian or ethnographer is to measure the impact or influence of Christianity upon any particular Indian people, especially within a limited timespan such as this study covers.[1] In the first place, it is almost impossible to know how much Christian ideology had worked its way into Cherokee thought, folklore, or sacred world view prior to the time this study starts (1789). In the second place, it is impossible to make generalizations for a people who, by 1839, were as diverse as they. And in the third place, there is far too little extant evidence among the Cherokee writings of the 1830s to make a conclusive evaluation of syncretism or borrowing. Robert F. Berkhofer's overall view of Indian resistance to the missionaries in the nineteenth century seems correct to me: "to fight them and the other forces of the dominant society, they borrowed elements from the culture they fought in order to resist effectively."[2] The greatest source of Cherokee resistance was the ancient tradition of harmony and community. Jacob Scudder, a white trader who lived among the Cherokees from 1807 to 1831, indicated this in his description of the outlook of the fullbloods he knew well in northwestern Georgia. He estimated that in 1831 there were about 3,000 Cherokees (or 750 families) living within the boundaries of Georgia, most of them near Etowah. Each family, he said, cultivated from four to five acres: "Their principal dependence for Support is from what Ground They Cultivate in Corn, pumpkins, potatoes & beans, etc." The only fullblood of any wealth in the

---

1. See Åke Hultkrantz, *Belief and Worship in Native North America*, pp. 187–90; see also the essays by A. F. C. Wallace, Raymond D. Fogelson, and Charles H. Holzinger in Symposium on Cherokee and Iroquois Culture, ed. William N. Fenton and John Gulick.
2. Robert F. Berkhofer, Jr., *Salvation and the Savage*, p. 159.

335

area was Major Ridge, Scudder said, whose property would not "eccede Eight or Ten Thousand dollars," mostly in "negroes, stock and Buildings" (since his land belonged to the nation, not himself). "The Larger portion are verry Poor and To persons unaccustomed To Indians, They would Seem miserably so. But To me, who has resided amongst them fourteen Years, They appear the most Contented and happy people on Earth. They reflect But Little on the future or the past. If their wants are Supplyed, They are Contented; if not, They Exhibit But Little uneasiness or regret, and it is allmost a pitty To disturb Their repose [by making them move West]."[3] Scudder may have idealized their contentedness, for they certainly suffered from poverty and resented the cultural impositions of the whites, but these Cherokees were not slaves; they had their own land, freedom, and self-government. If they were content with little, it was because they preferred to live by their former standards and values; they were not interested in exploiting those economic opportunities which ambitious men, like Major Ridge, took advantage of for private gain and to obtain the whiteman's approval. They simply did not share that restless urge to "get ahead in the world" which so animated white Americans and which was so fully reflected in the religious teachings of the missionaries.

The Cherokees had basically three ways to confront Christian evangelism: they could ignore it; they could embrace it; or they could adopt or borrow from it to suit their needs. To the missionaries, the only admirable Cherokee was the one who made the second choice and totally transformed himself or herself in thought and conduct into the whiteman's image of a "civilized Christian." Few indeed accomplished this almost impossible task. Many ignored Christian teaching altogether, insisting that it was for whitemen only. However, the economic breakdown of communal living seriously eroded the traditional pattern of religious and social ritual and behavior. The conjuring which survived most effectively out of the total religious configuration was that which was crisis oriented (the need for rain) or practiced primarily in family life (sickness and private relations). Most Cherokees borrowed from the Christian world view almost without realizing it, not in any specific theological or doctrinal sense so much as in acceptance of that broader perspective on science, geography, and human history which contact with the whiteman provided. If faith in the old cosmology waned, it was largely because closer contact with whites revealed so much that it could not account for. The world might still be flat and suspended from the arch of heaven, it might still be animated by all kinds of spiritual beings from above and below, but the Cherokee people were no longer at the center of it; it did not end at the shores of that terra firma the Indians occupied, nor did it respond solely to their prayers. Cherokee sacred myths could not explain those secrets

3. Jacob Scudder to the governor of Georgia, September 17, 1831, in Georgia Archives, WPA typescript, "Cherokee Indians" part 2, p. 316.

of nature which gave the whiteman such technological power to manipulate the world around him.

Just how much of Christianity or the civilized world view, moral values, and spiritual ideology beyond these necessary adjustments were accepted by any group of Cherokees rests upon such slim evidence that we can only speculate. How many Cherokees, for example, observed the Christian Sabbath? What did they make of John Ross's proclamations of national days of humiliation and prayer? Did they really accept the Christian view of the deity, of life after death, of heaven and hell as rewards or punishments for actions in this life? Though they spoke to whitemen of "the Creator," did they really define "the Great Spirit who made us all" as any Christian would define "God"? Was there any relation between their concept of evil spirits and the Christian concept of the Devil? When the federal agent to the Cherokees, Return J. Meigs, argued for the right of Indians to testify in white courts in 1802, he said, "The Indians believe in the being of a God and in the immortality of the soul; it is an instinctive idea with them."[4] However, another, and earlier, agent to the Cherokees, Silas Dinsmoor, said in 1803, "An Indian has no idea of the being of a God nor of future existence."[5] Who really knows what the Indians believed? What we can see with some clarity is that certain aspects of the whiteman's social and personal ethic and norms were more or less forced upon the Cherokees—their way of dressing and eating, their system of monogamy, patrilineal inheritance, law and order, bargaining for the necessities of a more technical economic system. But beneath these behavioral changes lie psychological patterns which are only dimly perceivable if at all.

Certainly the measure of missionary success (or failure) among the Cherokees can hardly be taken in terms of the number of converts, even if one could agree upon what constituted a convert. As we have seen, persons whom Methodists considered converts, Moravians did not; persons whom Baptists considered converts, Congregationalists did not. However, accepting the definitions of all four denominations on their own terms, we can say that in 1839, perhaps 8 per cent of the total Cherokee population, 1,250 out of 16,000, were officially listed as "members." (If they were heads of families, perhaps they persuaded their spouse and children to attend a mission church.) While that was about half that of the church membership figure for the United States as a whole at the time, the unchurched among the white Americans did not have an alternative religious tradition; white nonchurch members were often churchgoers; they gave at least nominal allegiance to the basic tenets, ethics, and values of the Christian tradition. Cherokee Christian converts, however, existed as outsiders in their own community, which is why Indian missionaries were classed with foreign and not domestic (or home) missions. The American Board of Commissioners

4. Return J. Meigs to Col. Overton, June 10, 1802, BIA, M-208, roll 1.
5. Silas Dinsmoor to Return J. Meigs, July 26, 1803, BIA, M-208, roll 1.

for Foreign Missions was so discouraged by its failure to spread the Gospel more widely among the Cherokees that in its annual report for 1838 it seriously questioned whether evangelization of the Indians should be continued: "Were it certain that these missions would, for ten years to come, remain in as unfavorable state as they have been for the ten years just past, it would hardly be wise to detain men in the field only to have their efforts paralyzed and, for all the labor, property and life expended to reap so little else than disappointment."[6] One aspect of this sense of failure derived from the apparent unwillingness of those who were converted to sustain their own churches (after the missionaries were driven out) without external aid from the mission agencies. The historian of the Moravian missions to the Indians, Edmund Schwarze, judged the work of his denomination among the Cherokees harshly: "Here was the weak point of the mission. . . . The mission did not need the support of the Christian Indians nearly so much as those Indians needed to support the mission. . . . [T]he Cherokee members themselves could have shouldered [the expense]. . . . Even the smallest contribution in money, produce, manufactures or labor on the part of an Indian member would make him a better Christian. . . . We failed to develop that sense of responsibility in our Cherokee Christians."[7] Samuel Worcester of the American Board made the same criticism of his denomination in 1833.[8] Attempts were made from time to time to force the Cherokees to contribute produce or cash for support of the mission schools, yet these all failed. Schwarze was aware of the argument that the Cherokees were too poor to sustain churches, but he noted sardonically that they always seemed able to raise plenty of money "in bets at a ball game"—sometimes as much as $3,000 in money, clothing, guns, and produce was bet on a single game. If the Christian converts had truly loved the Lord, Schwarze and other such critics believed, they would have made sacrifices to support his worship. However, a gambling bet is far different from a sustained commitment of regular support. In part this failure to contribute to church support did stem from poverty. The Cherokees, even at their most prosperous, had little surplus wealth for such voluntary institutions and, as in any frontier community, what wealth there was went first into more basic economic and political institutions—the development of roads, ferries, and manufactures, of police, courts, paid legislators, and administrators. But in part it stemmed from the consistent paternalism of the missionaries and their deep-seated conviction that even the best Cherokee converts were too childlike, fickle, and irresponsible to run their own churches.

The ultimate answer to sustained church support among the Indians lay in the creation of a native ministry. But here again both the unwillingness of most mission agencies to ordain Cherokee ministers and the missions' high

6. Twenty-ninth Annual Report, ABCFM (1838), p. 138.
7. Schwarze, *Moravian Missions*, pp. 203–04.
8. Samuel Worcester to David Greene, October 10, 1833, ABCFM.

educational standards for the ministry militated against them. Only in the last ten years that the Cherokees remained in the East were the missionaries beginning to see the importance of recruiting and licensing Cherokee converts to preach to their people in their own language. These native exhorters and licensed itinerants knew little theology, but they understood what the conversion experience had meant to them. They were highly dedicated young men willing to work for almost nothing. Furthermore, by preaching in Cherokee, they transformed biblical and Christian doctrine to fit Cherokee speech and thought patterns. They made Christianity understandable in a way that no white minister could. But in so doing they made subtle changes in emphasis and meaning. The ultimate success of Christianity among the Cherokees in the years ahead stemmed from this core of native preachers. The Baptists ordained four—Kaneeda (John Wickliffe), David Foreman, Jesse Bushyhead, and John Timson—between 1828 and 1838. They had employed fourteen exhorters and interpreters who made many converts: Wasadi, Dsulawi or Dsulawee (Andrew Fuller), Beaver Carrier, James Wafford, Alexander McGray (or McGrey), Oganaya (Peter), Lewis Downing, Desyohee, Gatogidsee, Tuquitty, Gunnee (Long Bullet), Galaneeya, Oodeluhee, Swimmer (Ayauduga)[9] and Astoo,eeste. Bushyhead, as pastor of his own church, gathered one hundred members and sustained the congregation until his death in 1844; after that it was strong enough to continue on its own. Several Methodist exhorters, Young Wolf, Joseph Blackbird, John Fletcher Boot, the Whirlwind (Akaluha), and Turtle Fields in particular, carried on as itinerant evangelists after the white circuit riders left the nation in 1834. They probably did not all baptize, marry, hold communion, or perform other ministerial duties, but some of them did, and all of them preached "the Word" in words the Cherokees could understand. The American Board exhorters, John Huss and Stephen Foreman, remained active for years. Foreman was licensed in 1833 and ordained in 1835; Huss was licensed in 1831 and ordained in 1834. After 1832, these native preachers were the backbone of the missionary effort. But the dislocations of the removal crisis made it impossible for them to form stable congregations and build meetinghouses. They were all itinerants.

Missionary journals and the annual reports of mission boards were obliged to provide statistical tables as corporate reports to their stockholders; but statistics were not the measure of successful missions. The missionaries and their Cherokee converts had other things in mind when they spoke about "Christianization." When David Brown, the Cornwall graduate, said in 1825 that "the Christian religion is the religion of the nation," he meant that "some of the most influential characters are members of the church," that mission schools "are increasing every year," that "the young class

---

9. It would be interesting to know whether the Swimmer, who was a Baptist exhorter, was the same Swimmer who in 1835 threatened to kill John Ridge for betraying his country by signing the New Echota treaty. Payne Papers, II, 93.

acquire English," that "the female character is elevated," that "indolence is discontinued," that "we are out of debt and our public revenue is in a flourishing condition," and that "our system of government [is] founded on republican principles."[10] In other words, a Christian nation was measured by some in terms of its conformity to white American standards of civilization. Many missionary journals emphasized similar standards—respect for the Sabbath, practice of Christian marriage, concern for temperance, adoption of white manners, the use of prayers at council meetings, the laws against polygamy, infanticide, gambling, billiards, theater, the constitutional prohibition against officeholding by atheists, the reliance upon Christian oaths for officeholding and legal testimony. All of these were by 1838 officially part of Cherokee life and as such could be held up as evidence of successful Christianization even though the observance of these standards varied considerably as one moved farther away from the highly acculturated communities.

When Samuel Worcester said in 1830 that the Cherokees could be considered a Christian nation, he meant that "the greater part of the people acknowledge the Christian religion to be the true religion" (an estimate he seems to have based upon conversations held primarily with the acculturated near New Echota and Brainerd). This was a very different kind of evaluation from Brown's, and Worcester qualified it by adding that "many who make this acknowledgment know very little of that religion and many others do not feel its power." In his view, a Christian nation both acknowledged the truth of Christianity and demonstrated its spiritual force as a constant part of daily life. He also put this another way: "Many of the heathenish customs of the people have gone entirely, or almost entirely, into disuse"[11] (another estimate based on very limited travel in the nation). By this standard, Christian spiritual power was to be measured by the declining power of heathenism. But "heathenism" was far from disappearing in 1830.

When John Ross spoke of the Cherokee Nation as "a rational and Christian community," he spoke in terms of the scientific and philosophical basis of Cherokee thought.[12] They were a rational people because they accepted the European laws of science and natural theology; they were a Christian people because they understood these laws within the Christian interpretation of moral philosophy—or their leaders did. God, the Great Architect of the Universe, had established the laws of nature which governed the world and human life; because he was a benevolent, merciful, just ruler, he ought to be worshipped. To those who honored the ideals of justice, truth, peace, goodwill, honor, he would provide rewards in this life and the next; to those who broke those laws, he would provide punishments. John Ross thought the Cherokees understood—had always understood—the laws of

10. ASP II, 651–52.
11. *Cherokee Phoenix*, May 8, 1830.
12. Schwarze, *Moravian Missions*, p. 192.

nature and social morality (however crudely they may have expressed these truths) and tried to carry them out in their deep commitment to personal honesty and social harmony. To add the knowledge of rational science through education would simply provide the Cherokees with a more consistent and far-ranging understanding of the world they knew. Ross understood that many Cherokees did not yet rationally understand Newtonian science or Christian theology, but he thought these were gaining ground through the spread of schools. How well he understood the strong hold which the traditional religion still held upon many Cherokees it is hard to say. He never experienced it in his own family or upbringing and never practiced it.

The alternative which their traditional religion offered the Cherokees took many forms and went through many changes between 1789 and 1839. Its hold weakened in some ways and became stronger in others. Some Cherokees who refused to join in any Christian activities also ceased to hold strong beliefs in the old religion. They were anti-Christian but not propagan. James Vann and some of the more sophisticated mixed bloods typified this skeptical view of the world. It was common among mixed bloods who felt at home with neither the old nor the new religion. Most fullbloods were brought up within the framework of the old religion and practiced at least occasional conformity to it. On the other hand, many fullbloods also, out of politeness or respect for the Council's laws, observed the Christian rules of the nation.

Despite the claims of the missionaries and acculturated leaders that the heathen rituals also were "dying out," they never did so. James Mooney found them intact in the 1890s, and they are still practiced today by some Cherokees. Throughout the 1830s the Green Corn Dance was celebrated annually in most communities by at least some of the people. Purification rituals were performed regularly in the more remote regions. All-night dances were common. Ballplays, though more secular, were always popular despite missionary opposition; even Council meetings stopped so that they could be attended. Some town councils continued to start with the black drink. The most pervasive aspect of the old religion was the continued regular appeal to conjurors and conjuresses for help with medical, meteorological, and personal problems. This in itself was strong evidence that "rational Christianity" had not supplanted the Cherokees' elder world view. However, the regular pattern of tribal rituals had altered; some rituals were combined (the Green Corn Dance and the Purification rite), and some dances had lost their relevance and were seldom performed. Probably too the original significance of the rituals had faded, especially for the young, who lived a different mode of life.[13]

Those Cherokees who remained practitioners of the old ways were

13. The works of James Mooney, based upon field research among the Cherokees in the 1880s and 1890s, point to the continuity of traditional religion throughout the nineteenth century.

described by the missionaries as the incurably superstitious. They continued to think and act in terms of the pervasive spiritual interaction between man, nature, and the spirit world which was imbedded in their sacred philosophy. Although the old religion became less visible to white observers after 1820, its constant resurgence in times of crisis vouched for its strong hold upon the Cherokee psyche. While the conjurors did their best to retain the purity of the old rituals and myths, keeping special notebooks in Sequoyan to preserve them, nevertheless changes inevitably crept in. The most striking change was the increasing politicization of the conjurors themselves. In part this was a natural response to the aggressive evangelism of the missionaries, but probably more important was the increasing fervor of Cherokee nationalism. One way to clearly identify oneself as a Cherokee was to be a practitioner of the traditional religion. Another was to be anti-Christian or at least antimissionary. Despite the best efforts of politically active missionaries like Evan Jones, James Trott, Daniel Butrick, or Elizur Butler to maintain that one could be a good Christian and a good patriot, this was never so convincing as the argument that a good Cherokee adhered to the old religion.

Many accounts by missionaries of the opposition to Christian evangelism in the 1830s indicate that a new upsurge of the old religion sprang directly from the antipathy to removal and the tendency to blame all Christians for the injustices being perpetrated on the Cherokees (and other Indian nations) as a result of Jackson's rejection of the original Indian policy. Sometimes Christian converts frankly expressed the polarization within themselves as they were torn between loyalty to Christianity and loyalty to the nation. "The troubles of this present time," said Henry Clauder in 1837, about the spiritual doubts of one Moravian convert, "seem to destroy his enjoyment of Christ."[14] Another convert, who had been a student at Springplace school, "complained bitterly of her various trials and seemed to lack patient submission to the ways of God," Clauder said.[15] More often the missionaries confronted this divided loyalty in the revival of all-night dances and ballplays, which claimed the attention of their congregations after 1832. In these ceremonies the Cherokees could express their solidarity and vent their emotions outside of the restraining confines of Christian worship under white supervision. "Today the Indians had a ball play in the neighborhood," Clauder wrote in July 1837 with obvious chagrin, "and several who attended our meeting, afterward went to the play. Satan is very busy opposing our efforts."[16] In previous years, such actions would have produced an immediate censure from the mission church, but after 1832 missionaries hesitated to heap coals on the fire. Their hold upon their converts was growing weak, and they told their mission boards that the rising popularity of heathen rites signified that the forces of Hell were taking control of the Cherokees

14. Clauder, Journal, May 4, 1837, MAB.
15. Clauder, Journal, May 30, 1837, MAB.
16. Clauder, Journal, July 2, 1837, MAB.

away from them. "For three nights the Indians held a Medicine Dance at old Julstaya's, and this was the fourth and last principal one of revelry. After dark we heard the quick beating of drums and the savage whooping of the dances . . . at daybreak it appeared as if the vaults of hell had let loose the raving furies; the woods resounded with whooping and yelling. Such are the scenes missionaries must look for upon heathen ground."[17] Clauder spoke of this as "revelry" (probably assuming that a great deal of whiskey was being consumed) but in fact it was the opposite. It was an effort to release in ritual form the stresses, frustrations, and deep-seated anger of a people forced during the day to appear quiet and submissive in the face of repeated aggressions against them. The Cherokees hoped they might call upon the spiritual powers of the Cherokee religion to assist them in defeating the whiteman or keeping themselves under control. They identified participation in "medicine dances" with commitment to Cherokee patriotism, and it became increasingly difficult for a convert to hang on to the new faith. Evan Jones and Jesse Bushyhead found this to be true even among those who had formerly been good Baptists and who well knew that these two Christians were among the most loyal supporters of the Patriot Party. After returning from a trip of 150 miles around the nation in June 1837, Jones reported that he was much less successful than he had hoped because of the concerted opposition of the adherents of the old religion: "The temper of the ancient adversaries of the gospel manifests itself in efforts to impede the progress of the truth. A priest or conjuror, an old man of some influence among the advocates of Indian paganism, had been along part of our route and had sent messages through the country warning the people against us and ordering them not to attend our meetings and especially not to become members."[18] A rumor had been spread all along the route that "all who unite with us will be sent off to Arkansas in the fall." Obviously now the old slogan was reversed; to save the country one had to eschew the church.

American Board missionaries found the same kind of resistance to their itinerants. In 1833, the Reverend J. B. Adams went to preach at a village called Six Towns some distance from his mission station, a place where, he said, the people had never enjoyed any Christian preaching (and *enjoyed* may have been the right word). "They are bitterly prejudiced against missionaries, thinking that they are friendly to emigration." The American Board having by this time assumed a stance of neutrality on removal, Adams endeavored to show the people of Six Towns that there was no connection between hearing the Gospel and taking sides in the political struggle within that nation. "I told them that there was nothing about Arkansas in the Bible, and that I came to deal with their souls."[19] But the absence of any statement about Arkansas in the Bible was the essence of the Cherokees' objection to it.

17. Clauder, Journal, March 25, 1837, MAB.
18. *Baptist Missionary Magazine* 17: 17. Jones's letter is dated June 28, 1837.
19. Joseph B. Adams to David Greene, May 2, 1833, ABCFM.

Moreover, they believed Adams was misleading them since other American Board missionaries, like Worcester, were now supporting removal. They told Adams they would believe nothing they heard from a whiteman. "Some said they would believe the gospel if Mr. Ross would tell them to do it," but not on the word of any missionary. Adams was shocked to hear that adherence to their political leader came before adherence to the revealed will of God or any concern for their own souls. He was astonished that Ross could have that kind of hold upon his people.

This was not surprising to the Ridges, Boudinot, the Waties, and other leaders of the Removal Party. They recognized a very close connection between the revival of the old religion and Ross's efforts to keep the Cherokees united against removal. To them Ross was a hypocrite, for, though ostensibly a Christian, he was willing to manipulate the ignorant and superstitious people of the nation by supporting the old religion as a kind of political or nativist fundamentalism. In 1835, John Ridge urged Governor Lumpkin of Georgia to instruct the Georgia guard to suppress all meetings between members of the Ross Party and adherents of the old religion. Ridge asked the governor to "organize a guard of thirty men to scour the range in their [traditionalist] fastnesses to search for them in their caves and to suppress their secret meetings close to all night dances where the leaders of the Ross party usually meet with them for consultation."[20] To save the country from Ross's policy, Ridge was ready to stamp out the old religion.

After 1832, the missionaries had to acknowledge that the Cherokees were right to doubt the sympathy for them of many allegedly Christian whites. The missionary movement was on the defensive. Missionaries had to be content with small achievements such as the conversion of Drowning Bear and Big Cabbin, who had formerly been leaders in White Path's Rebellion.[21] Formerly they expected large additions to their churches every year; now they were happy that so many of their former converts remained faithful and so few deserted. What the missionaries did not see, or scarcely welcomed if they did see it, was the syncretic process at work slowly melding the old and the new religions together. Of course some of the efforts to put them together caused considerable friction, as when mission church members went to conjurors to cure an illness or pray for rain on the assumption that the same Great Spirit worked for both sets of priests. Sometimes the merging of the old ways and the new was sad, as when a Cherokee convert told Clauder that he had to hunt on the Sabbath because "his children begged him to shoot as they had had no meat for several days" and he did not think God would mind his breaking the rules for that reason.[22] Sometimes it was,

20. Thurman Wilkins, *Cherokee Tragedy*, pp. 262–63. See John Ridge to Wilson Lumpkin, September [n.d.] 1835, John Ridge Papers, Georgia State Archives, Atlanta, Georgia.
21. *Missionary Herald* 29: 242.
22. Clauder, Journal, June 4, 1837, MAB.

to the missionaries at least, bizarrre, as in this strange version of Creation and the work of the Serpent in the Garden of Eden told by an old Cherokee as one of their sacred myths:

> It is also stated that anciently the Cherokee supposed a number of Beings—more than two—some have conjectured three—came down and made the world. They then attempted to make a man and woman of two rocks. They fashioned them, but while attempting to make them live, another Being came and spoiled their work so that they could not succeed. They then made a man and woman of red clay and being made of clay they were mortal, but had they been made of rock, they would have lived forever. Others, however, ascribed their mortality to another cause. Soon after the creation, it is said, one of the family was bitten by a Serpent and died. All possible means were used to bring back his life, but in vain. Being overcome in this first instance, the whole race were doomed to follow not only to death but to eternal misery.[23]

More significant aspects of syncretism had begun long before any permanent mission stations were established among the Cherokees. One of these was the readiness to link the concept of a Great Spirit with the concept of God the Creator of the universe and father of all humankind. While a polygenetic theory was also developed in the eighteenth century in order to explain red, white, and black men and the different continents they lived on, it was probably only when whites pushed too hard with Christianization and civilization that this hardened into a belief that God gave each color a distinct way of life which could not and should not be changed.[24] By 1826, Elias Boudinot on his lecture tour to raise money for a Cherokee printing press explained the close harmony between Cherokee and Christian perspectives, emphasizing what he took to be the merging of the best of the old religion with the new:

> They [the Cherokees] cannot be called idolators, for they never worshipped Images. They believed in a Supreme Being, the Creator of all, the God of the white, the red, and the black man. They also believed in the existence of an evil spirit who resided, as they thought, in the setting sun, the future place of all who in their life time had done iniquitously. Their prayers were addressed alone to the Supreme Being, and if written would fill a large volume and display much sincerity, beauty, and sublimity. When the ancient customs of the Cherokees were in their full force, no warrior thought himself secure unless he had addressed his guardian angel; no hunter could hope for success unless, before the rising sun, he had asked the assistance of his God and on his return at eve he had offered his sacrifice to him.[25]

---

23. Payne Papers, I, 18. The early volumes of the Payne Papers contain many examples of syncretic borrowings by Cherokees from Christianity gathered by Daniel Butrick.

24. While a polygenetic theory of creation could be used to oppose acculturation, it had not prevented the Cherokees from making a drastic reorientation in their way of life to accommodate themselves to the fur trade economy.

25. Elias Boudinot, *An Address to the Whites*, p. 9.

Boudinot may have thought his ancestors held this romantic view of God and "guardian angels"; he was in fact describing his own amalgamation of traditional and Christian concepts. He was depicting what during his youth (he was born in 1803) was already a syncretic position, a century beyond its precontact form. His family was not Christian in 1803, but they had imbibed much from the nation's long contact with Christians, and he was sent to the Moravian school at the age of eight.

An equally strained, but more ironic, linkage between the old and the new religions emerged when certain missionaries began to search for evidence that the Cherokees were the remnants of one of the lost tribes of Israel. Daniel S. Butrick spent considerable time at this task with the complete cooperation of Charles Hicks and John Ross (and the rather skeptical assistance of Major George Lowery, the second principal chief to Ross). By 1835 Butrick was convinced that he had found positive proof.[26] Some Cherokees thought this would be of great political advantage to them; it would make it harder for white Christians to throw them off their land like a herd of buffaloes. In one of his numerous appeals for the sympathy of white America in the 1830s, John Ross made use of this theory: "Some of you have said we were the wanderers of that peculiar people [the Jews] whence true religion sprang. If it be so, imagine how glorious the effort to secure those wanderers a home—and such a home as may realize the bright predictions which still exist unclaimed for the lost race of Israel. Who knows but our prayers may be the instruments to accelerate the fulfilment of that prophecy and should this prove so, how can we offer you a return more exciting?"[27] If the Cherokees were the lost Israelites, and if the white American Protestants gave them a permanent homeland (in the East), and if they were converted to Christianity, then one of the major biblical prophecies of the prelude to the Second Coming would be fulfilled—the conversion of the Jews. Ross knew just how to titillate Christian consciences.

On the other hand, Major Lowery was rather skeptical of this appeal to the Protestants. Having spent much time among the whites, Lowery was well aware that some of them were not overly friendly toward Jews, and, said Butrick in 1837, "Major Lowery began, evidently, to be a little suspicious that any evidence of their being Jews, would militate against their continuing in this country."[28] The Cherokees had enough prejudices to contend with without adding anti-Semitism.

But these were only the more superficial aspects of syncretism. Far more important were the results of the Cherokees' search for religious concepts and spiritual symbols in the whiteman's religion which they could

26. See Daniel Butrick, *Cherokee Antiquities*.
27. John Ross, "The Cherokee Nation to the People of the United States," Knoxville *Register*, December 2, 1835, Ayer Collection, #6247, Newberry Library, Chicago.
28. Payne Papers, IV, 125.

apply to their own private and public needs. For example, most of them could see that the Protestant ethic of sobriety, industry, thrift, and persistence was helpful in adjusting to the market economy and staple-crop agriculture they needed to survive. As a moral code of supernatural origin, it played a key role in Cherokee revitalization not only economically but personally, especially among the mixed bloods.[29] John Ridge explained to Albert Gallatin in 1826 that "the influence of Religion on the life of the Indians is powerful and lasting" by pointing to an illustration of its power within his own family: "I have an uncle who was given to all the vices of savages in drunkenness, fornication and roguery and he is now, though poorer in this world's goods but rich in goodness and makes his living by hard labor and is in every respect an honest, praying christian."[30] The Christian doctrine of personal redemption from sin and the power of the Holy Spirit dwelling in the heart of the believer to give him control over temptation was of great help to a people in a state of cultural confusion and personal stress. It promised to wipe the old slate clean, to provide a new birth, a new life, as well as the resolve to make that new life work for the believer—with the help of his friends and of the Great Spirit.

In the 1830s, as adversity replaced progress and prosperity, Christianity offered consolation, hope, and faith. Jesse Bushyhead, the Baptist pastor, stressed this aspect of Christianity when he wrote to his congregation from Washington, D.C., in 1836. After noting the depredations of the Georgians who had taken over their mission churches and camp meeting grounds, destroyed their temperance movement, and left many homeless and poor, he said, "But there is one great consolation amidst these trying moments with the Cherokees; they have believed unto salvation . . . are now manifesting their love to God. These troubles teach them that this world is not their home; these make them look forward to that city which hath foundations and whose builder and maker is God; these teach them that they are but strangers and pilgrims in this world. This is my consolation for my brethren in the Lord."[31] He did not describe that new home, but many Cherokee Christian exhorters did. It was a home that had all the security which this world lacked. In that home, if there were any whites, they would be the kind who would recognize them as equals, and God would reward the Cherokees above those whites who had not behaved toward them as Christians should. So could the religion of their oppressors be used against them.

There was also good use to be made of the millennial symbolism of Christianity and the belief that God's justice would not sleep forever. John Wickliffe and Oganaya, two Baptist exhorters, wrote to the Baptist Foreign

---

29. See A. F. C. Wallace's discussion of the same kind of borrowing in the Seneca revitalization movement in these years; *The Death and Rebirth of the Seneca* (New York: Random House, 1972).

30. John Ridge to Albert Gallatin, February 27, 1826, Payne Papers, VIII, 111.

31. *Baptist Missionary Magazine* 16: 202.

Mission Board on behalf of the church at Valley Towns in October 1837 in terms of this hope: "Our earnest desire is that you will pray for us that the kingdom of God may be established and extended among the multitudes of our people."[32] They may have meant only that they hoped the spiritual kingdom of salvation would be established among them, but it is more likely they meant their desire for the establishment of God's kingdom "on earth as it is in heaven"—a kingdom in which the last should be first and the world should be turned upside down. The Cherokees had not found this eschatological message in the optimistic, postmillennial sermons of the missionaries who had come to them with the progressive ideal of amalgamation with the manifest destiny of the whiteman. They had found it when their own preachers read out of the Bible what seemed to them appropriate for their own spiritual and temporal needs.

John Ross, in a Fast Day proclamation to the nation on July 3, 1830, spoke as though prayer and humiliation in their time of "tribulation and sorrow" might cause God to intervene in some miraculous way to thwart their enemies. He questioned whether the trouble that had come to them was intended by "the unsearchable and mysterious will of an all-wise Being" or "has been directed by the wonted depravity and wickedness of man." If it were the latter, if Satan was leading the Georgians, God might rise up in wrath and strike them down. Therefore, he asked the "community to bow in humiliation and prayer before Him who can alone relieve the afflicted and protect the fatherless, and there to implore His gracious pleasure to avert the dreadful evil." There was also a second purpose to this national day of prayer, and that was that the "people may be united in sentiment and action for the good of the Nation."[33] Prayer for national unity to a just God who could avert their ruin was always basic in Christian thought, and the Cherokee preachers and leaders found that idea to be a very powerful source of strength in the 1830s. It was doubly powerful when linked to the singing of hymns in the Cherokee language, which also uplifted their spirits. In these, and many other respects, the Cherokees were able to apply Christian theology, imagery, symbols, and spiritual power to their own meanings and uses.

Finally, it has to be noted that John Ross himself provided the charismatic leadership which held the advocates of the old and the new religions together under stress. After 1828 Ross united the roles of statesman and prophet, political head and spiritual leader.[34] Charismatic leaders of nationalistic movements in all countries have gained strength by merging these roles. Every visitor and missionary, all government officials, and especially Ross's most vindictive enemies in the Removal Party acknowl-

32. *Baptist Missionary Magazine* 17: 19.
33. Ross's Fast Day proclamation is printed in Schwarze, *Moravian Missions*, p. 192.
34. See Walter H. Conser, Jr., "John Ross and the Cherokee Resistance Campaign, 1833–1838," *Journal of Southern History* 44, no. 2 (May 1978): 191–211.

edged time and again "the remarkable hold" that he had over the people. Their trust in him was complete and so was their obedience. "They would believe the gospel, if Mr. Ross would tell them to do it," as the anonymous patriot of Six Towns had said. But when Ross used Christian myths or symbols he conveyed the feeling that the Cherokees had a religion which was neither Christian nor Cherokee but a combination of the best elements of both. Ross's religious message was in the best sense a civil religion, a syncretic adaptation of Christian symbols and ideals to Cherokee needs and understandings.

It is difficult to say just how committed Ross was to Christianity. He never went through an evangelical conversion experience; it is not known whether he was ever baptized. He was clearly not a practitioner of the traditional Cherokee religion, for his family brought him up to be a whiteman, yet his marriage to a fullblood was apparently happy and she never joined a mission church or Methodist society. Some have argued that it was through his wife that Ross sustained his hold over the fullbloods and understood their feelings, but there is no record of her ever having played any part in Cherokee politics. She became something of a patriotic symbol after her death, for she died on the Trail of Tears. Some years later, when Ross chose a second wife, he chose a white Quaker from Philadelphia.[35]

After 1832 Ross was seen as a Cherokee prophet as well as a chief by his people. For Christian Cherokees he may have been like Moses; for traditionalist Cherokees, like George Washington. In the distant past the Cherokees had had a double set of chiefs, a priestly caste for peacetime, a warrior caste for war.[36] Ross combined the two. If he had a biblical model it was that of an Old Testament king, not a New Testament apostle. He did not storm and thunder like an Old Testament prophet but on two occasions he did, like Jeremiah, call upon his people to repent and pray in national humiliation. However, he did not castigate the Cherokees for their sins; they were the ones sinned against. The best extant example of his syncretic faith is an address he delivered to the Cherokee Nation, probably in 1832, after one of his unsuccessful trips to Washington, D.C., to negotiate with Jackson. Like all his addresses, it was written beforehand and delivered in English. Ross's "talks" were always read in a quiet, deliberate, sober tone, though he sometimes indulged in sardonic humor at the expense of the whiteman, which brought spontaneous laughter from the crowd. His speeches were translated into Cherokee as he read them.

In this address he began by explaining that he had spoken to the president and to the secretary of war and that they had refused to heed his appeals for justice and adherence to treaty rights. "The Great Spirit above

35. Rachel C. Eaton, *John Ross and the Cherokee Indians*, p. 45; Gary Moulton, *John Ross, Cherokee Chief* (Athens: University of Georgia Press, 1978), pp. 12−13, 100−01, 247−48, 139−43.

36. See Fred O. Gearing, *Priests and Warriors*.

only knows what is best for us to do," he then said, "and it is he alone that is able to pity or protect us should we trust in him." Because he wrote in English, we know that he used the term "Great Spirit" and we can be sure he did so deliberately. He then told them a story which, in the tradition of Cherokee oratory, was a parable of the theme of the talk. There was once, he said, a very rich and respectable man called Job, who "believed that God would forgive those that put trust in him. This good man was unfortunate enough to lose all his property—in one day—taken from him by his enemies. This man, Job, said he came naked into the world and he must return naked; what he had, had been given to him by the Lord [again, Ross's choice] and it was taken away, and blessed be the name of the Lord. His misfortune did not bring him to make use of any violent language, nor did he blame the Great Spirit; for he was never known during his existence to sin against the Great Spirit. The Great Spirit, in consequence of his cheerfulness, caused him to gather again double the amount of property he had lost."

Having set the tone which he wished the Cherokee people to adopt toward the injustice of the whites and toward the Great Spirit, Ross then went on to give them the details of "the policy of the government towards the Cherokees in plundering them of their property." This, he said, was very wicked. He then explained his own policy and how they must all remain united behind it, for "when the people of a nation divides against itself, then their national existence becomes destroyed." In conclusion, he returned to the story of the man called Job. "If the President of the white people should cease to protect us and our rights and should rob us of our rights, then I say to you, as Job said, 'My mother brought me naked into the world, and I must quit it naked.' Such is the bidding of the great Creator. 'The Lord giveth and the Lord taketh away; blessed be the name of the Lord.' This is what Job said when he was robbed. Bear like Job. Like Job may you be rewarded."[37]

At no point in this talk did Ross refer to the Bible as such, and throughout he purposely blurred the distinction between the Lord of the Bible and the Great Spirit of the Cherokee religion. There was no mention of Jesus; he was not discussing a matter of individual salvation but of the injustice of a powerful (but wicked) people toward a weaker (but upright) people: "the people of the world are rejoicing at our misfortunes, and we are left to grieve and be sorrowful. What shall we do that will relieve us of our misfortunes?" The Great Spirit Ross invoked was not a personal Savior but the God of Righteousness, who had a special covenant with this special people (the red people were, in Ross's address, still the favorites of the Great Spirit).

Like many nineteenth-century Christians, Ross chose a text from the Bible as his personal motto and often used it in his writing. The text was from the prophet Isaiah, chapter 35, verse 1: "The wilderness and the

37. Payne Papers, II, 147–55.

solitary place shall be glad for them; and the desert shall rejoice and blossom as the rose." He may have believed that the Cherokees were a key part of that millennial kingdom on earth which Isaiah prophesied; though cast out by the whites, they would be blessed of God. In the fourth verse of that same chapter, Isaiah said, "Say to them that are of fearful heart, Be strong, fear not; behold your God will come with vengeance, even God with a recompence, he will come and save you." Any Cherokee preacher would have known the text and understood the applications Ross intended. There was similar symbolic ambiguity in the choice of the name for the Cherokee national newspaper. Samuel Worcester, the missionary, was said to have suggested "the Phoenix" because it was a bird which arose from the ashes of defeat to fly again—a bird that could never die. Worcester probably also had other meanings which would be explained later to the Cherokees—the Phoenix represented the rising of the sinner to sainthood, of the pagan people to a Christian nation, of the dead Jesus to the resurrected Christ. The Cherokee words which appear around the picture of the Phoenix on the masthead of the paper, literally translated, mean "He has risen again." The Cherokees undoubtedly read it, as Ross read Isaiah, to mean that the Cherokee people would rise again. In 1828, when *The Cherokee Phoenix* appeared, the Cherokees seemed to have risen from the cultural chaos of defeat in the American Revolution; in 1838, they would, Ross believed, rise from the defeat of removal. In Cherokee tradition the name which they had for themselves was Ani-Yun-Wi-Ya, which meant "the real people" or "the true people."[38] In a Christian tradition, that could easily become "the chosen people," "the preferred people."

In a strange and unexpected way, the Cherokees' last years of tribulation in their homeland effected what so many missionaries had longed for, a great religious revival. But it was not, as they wanted, a revival of orthodox Protestant evangelicalism. The symbols of the revival were sometimes scriptural (Old Testament more than New) and sometimes from Cherokee religious traditions and national feelings. The Cherokees did come out of Egypt, trek through the wilderness, and settle in a Canaan which the whiteman had mistakenly called the Great American Desert. Eventually they made that desert bloom like a rose with their new farms and homes. Ross built a large house near Tahlequah, Oklahoma, which he called Rose Cottage, and he surrounded it with rosebushes. The prophet had led his people, more reluctantly than Moses (and certainly they went less triumphantly than white Christian expansionists who were following what they called Manifest Destiny westward), to a new land which for a time seemed flowing with milk and honey. The Cherokee nation did rise again. It had a second renascence. The Cherokees once again enjoyed stability and prosperity in the West from 1846 to 1861. But John Ross's rose garden was carefully tended by his black slaves, and when the Cherokee people faced their next major crisis (though

38. Mooney, *Myths*, p. 510.

once again it was not of their own making), it was one in which they fully shared the problem of white Americans—what to do about slavery. The Cherokee nation split in 1861 on the same fault line as white America. Half the Cherokees fought with the South and half with the North. In trampling the grapes of wrath, as Evan Jones's Cherokee converts had predicted on the first great Cherokee national Fast Day in 1830, God punished both nations for the sin of slavery, the white and the red—so intricately had their ways become interwoven even while they thought they were growing farther and farther apart.

Bibliography

Five kinds of archival centers provided the basic primary sources for this study: missionary archives, state and historical society archives. Cherokee archives, the Newberry Library, and the United States archives. Each of these provided different pieces of the puzzle which had to be fitted together to shape the analysis. Each itself contained various parts.

The missionary archives are divided denominationally. The most copious of them, and the best indexed, are those of the American Board of Commissioners for Foreign Missions (ABCFM) at Houghton Library, Harvard University. These contain the letters of the Prudential (or Executive) Committee to the individual missionaries and the letters back from the field to the corresponding secretaries. They also include letters from the board to the War Department, senators, congressmen, and other influential supporters of missions; minutes of the board meetings; miscellaneous documents, and the very valuable diaries and day-by-day journals kept at each mission station. While many excerpts from these materials appeared in *The Missionary Herald,* the official journal of the board, scholars should be aware that these excerpts were carefully edited and sometimes altered in order to present the most positive record of the missions. The annual reports of the board provide useful summaries of each year's work, the names of the missionaries, and various statistical summaries of schools, converts, expenses, and other data.

The Moravians have two separate archives, one at Bethlehem, Pennsylvania, and one in Winston-Salem, North Carolina. Because the Cherokee mission of the Society of the United Brethren for the Propagation of the Gospel among the Heathen was delegated to the Moravian community in Salem, the great bulk of the Cherokee material is there. Almost all of the records of the Cherokee mission are in German script, and only a small fraction of the whole has been translated. However, it is well catalogued, and the archivist, Mary Creech, as well as Elizabeth Marx, assisted me in obtaining accurate translations. These archives contain letters sent to the missionaries with instructions, as well as letters and journals of the missionaries, and miscellaneous related documents of many kinds, including some letters from Cherokee leaders like Charles R. Hicks.

The Presbyterian archives in the Presbyterian Historical Society in Philadelphia do not contain much material on the Reverend Gideon Blackburn's missions of 1804–10, though they have ample records of later Presbyterian missions among the Native Americans. Under the Plan of Union adopted by the Presbyterians and Congregationalists in 1801, these two denominations agreed to cooperate in missionary activities. Thus when the ABCFM was formed in 1811, Presbyterians were included on the board. However, the overwhelming proportion of missionaries to the Cherokees sent by the ABCFM were Congregationalists from New England. Because many of these missionaries joined the Union Presbytery of Eastern Tennessee, the ABCFM was often described as a Presbyterian organization and its missionaries called Presbyterians. However, all of their papers are in the archives of the ABCFM at Harvard.

The Baptist missionary archives are located for the most part at the American Baptist Historical Society in Rochester, New York. The Cherokee missionary records are not indexed but are filed by the names of the missionaries in chronological order. Some of the original records of the managing board of the American Baptist Foreign Mission Society are kept at the headquarters of the American Baptist Convention at Valley Forge, Pennsylvania. Prior to 1826, when the mission headquarters were in Philadelphia, the records were not well kept and the papers for the early years among the Cherokees are therefore sparse. It is necessary to consult the various Baptist journals prior to 1826 in order to find the earliest letters from missionaries in the field. After 1826, when the board was located in Boston, the records are virtually complete. Baptist missionaries were not very regular in their correspondence, and the record of their work is consequently much less detailed than that of the American Board and Moravian missionaries.

Because the Reverend Isaac McCoy was so intimately associated with all phases of Baptist Indian missions in these years, it is necessary to supplement the records in Rochester and Valley Forge with the Isaac McCoy Papers in the Kansas State Historical Society in Kansas City, Kansas. McCoy never worked in nor visited the Cherokee Nation prior to removal, but his personal papers contain much evidence about the policy decisions of the Baptists and the War Department regarding the Cherokees.

Methodist Indian mission records prior to 1839 no longer exist in manuscript. Apparently they were burned during the Civil War in a fire which destroyed the Southern Methodist Archives in Nashville, Tennessee.

What little is available in the way of missionary material has to be culled from the various Methodist newspapers and periodicals of the period and from the published records and reports of the various Methodist Conferences and mission societies. Fortunately, some Methodist circuit riders among the Cherokees sent regular letters to their missionary newspapers, so that primary material is not entirely lacking, though it is impossible to know how much these published letters were edited. The best sources for early Methodist newspapers, journals, and official reports are the Dargan-Carver Memorial Library of the United Methodists in Nashville, Tennessee, and the Garrett Evangelical Seminary in Evanston, Illinois.

The state archives in Atlanta, Georgia, and Nashville, Tennessee, contain considerable material relating to official White—Indian relations but have very little about the daily lives of the Cherokees or the missionaries. These records are most copious for the removal period (1829–39) and do provide insight into the Jacksonians' attitudes toward the missionaries who opposed removal. In the Atlanta archives, the Hawkins and Currey Papers are very helpful; in the Nashville archives, the Penelope Allen Papers are very helpful. In 1939 the Works Progress Administration (WPA) compiled, copied, and bound all the "Letters, Talks and Treaties" between the Cherokees and Georgia (1786 to 1838) under the direction of Mrs. J. E. Hays; these provide easy access to the most important Cherokee material in the Atlanta archives. In 1964 the Georgia Department of Natural Resources and the State Department of Planning and Research commissioned Dr. Carl C. Mauleshagen to translate the "Diary of the Moravian Mission at Spring Place, 1801–1836"; unfortunately, Mauleshagen did not make a literal translation, often summarizing entries in his own words, and this typescript must therefore be checked against the original diary at Winston-Salem, North Carolina.

There are several valuable archival sources in Oklahoma: the most helpful for this study were the Oklahoma Historical Society in Oklahoma City; the Thomas Gilcrease Institute at Tulsa, and the Western History Collection at the University of Oklahoma in Norman. Except for the John Ross Papers at the Gilcrease Institute, most of the material in these archives concerns the period after 1839. However, a number of Cherokee scholars (notably Grant and Caroline Foreman, Frank Phillips, E. E. Dale, Emmet Starr, and T. L. Ballenger) have gathered materials and notes for these archives which supplement the original sources. Also helpful in Oklahoma are the Worcester-Robertson Papers and the Schleppey Collection at Tulsa University in Tulsa.

The Newberry Library in Chicago, Illinois, is important for four notable collections containing Cherokee material: the Ayer and Graff Collections of Western materials, the T. L. Ballenger Papers, and the John Howard Payne Papers. The Payne Papers are particularly important for what they preserve of early Cherokee national affairs and culture. Payne visited the Cherokee Nation several times in the 1830s with the intention of gathering material for a history of the Cherokees. He filled fourteen large notebooks with materials of all kinds, some of it copies of official records supplied by Chief John Ross, some of it obtained from personal interviews with other Cherokees, and some derived from correspondence with various missionaries. Because so much of the Cherokee national records was destroyed during the removal era and later, Payne's papers contain more primary material on the Cherokee Nation from 1789 to 1839 than any other source. However, Payne never organized it, and it remains in tantalizing fragments. The Payne Papers have been typed out and I have cited these transcripts, but scholars should check them against the originals for misspellings and typographical omissions.

The National Archives in Washington, D.C., provide the fullest details of official relations between the Cherokees and the War Department. For a list of the microfilms used in this study, see the List of Abbreviations and Short Titles, p. xi. The most useful for this study were the records of the federal agents to the Cherokees, which are microfilmed as Record Group 75, M-208. The reports of Colonel Return J. Meigs, the agent from 1801 to 1823, are particularly detailed. However, the federal agents' reports are biased because of their tendency to rely chiefly upon those chiefs they considered "progressive" or "forward-looking" (meaning, cooperative with federal acculturation policy). The agents spoke no Cherokee and consequently relied upon information supplied by the cooperative mixed bloods or whites intermarried with Cherokees. Still, their observations about the "backward" or "patriotic" factions as well as their discussions of cultural persistence and resistance to acculturation are very important.

A small but important group of Cherokee materials is located at the Pennsylvania Historical Society, Philadelphia, Pennsylvania, in the Daniel Parker Papers and the Robert Vaux Papers.

RELIGIOUS PERIODICALS

The following religious periodicals contain valuable primary material respecting missionary activities among the Cherokees:

> *The Baptist Missionary Magazine* (also *American Baptist Magazine*), Boston
> *Christian Watchman* (also *Baptist Christian Watchman*), Boston
> *Evangelical Intelligencer*, New Haven
> *Latter Day Luminary*, Philadelphia
> *Methodist Christian Advocate and Journal and Zion's Herald*, Nashville and New York
> *The Methodist Magazine*, New York
> *The Missionary Herald*, Boston
> *The New York Missionary Magazine*, New York

The Panoplist, Boston
The Religious Intelligencer, New Haven
United Brethren's Missionary Intelligencer and Religious Miscellany,
  Bethlehem

CHEROKEE PUBLICATIONS

The most important Cherokee publication prior to removal was the national newspaper, *The Cherokee Phoenix and Indian Advocate* (New Echota). Though it was published in the East only from 1828 to 1834, it is the best source of Cherokee attitudes on official tribal affairs and contains much other cultural material. In addition, Elias Boudinot and John Ross published works of importance prior to 1839:

Elias Boudinot. *An Address to the Whites* (Philadelphia, 1826)
_____. *Letter Relating to Cherokee Affairs* (Athens, Ga., 1837)
John Ross. *Letter from John Ross* (Washington, 1836)
_____. *Letter from the Principal Chief of the Cherokee Nation*
(Washington, 1838)

The most accessible compilation of Cherokee laws is *Laws of the Cherokee Nation* (Tahlequah: Cherokee Advocate Office, Cherokee Nation, 1852).

BIBLIOGRAPHIES

So much has now been written about the Cherokees that it is important for scholars to consult published bibliographies on specialized topics. The Newberry Library Center for the History of the American Indian has recently published two such bibliographies which are relevant to this study:

James P. Ronda and James Axtell. *Indian Missions: A Critical Bibliography*. Bloomington: Indiana University Press, 1978
Raymond D. Fogelson. *The Cherokees: A Critical Bibliography*. Bloomington: Indiana University Press, 1978

A good bibliography of the anthropological material relating to the Cherokees and other Southeastern Indians is available in Charles Hudson, *The Southeastern Indians* (Nashville: University of Tennessee Press, 1976). The most complete bibliography of Cherokee history for the period 1789 to 1839 is contained in Thurman Wilkins, *Cherokee Tragedy: The Story of the Ridge Family and of the Decimation of a People* (New York: Macmillan, 1970).

IMPORTANT PUBLISHED PRIMARY AND SECONDARY SOURCES

Because the general bibliographies listed above provide the broadest possible sweep of primary and secondary sources, it is necessary to list those secondary sources which have been of particular help in the preparation of this study. I have listed them by category rather than alphabetically because I believe this will be of more help to scholars in the field.

I. Primary Sources

Adair, James. *History of the American Indians.* Edited by Samuel C. Williams. 1775. Reprint. New York: Johnson, 1969.

Bartram, William. "Observations on the Creek and Cherokee Indians." *American Ethnological Society Transactions* 3 (1853): 1–81.

Evarts, Jeremiah. *Essays on the Present Crisis.* Boston, 1829.

Gilmer, George R. *Sketches of Some of the First Settlers of Upper Georgia.* New York: Appleton, 1855. Reprint. Americus, Georgia, 1926.

Hawkins, Benjamin. *A Sketch of the Creek Country.* Publications of the Georgia Historical Society, vol. 3 (1938).

Lumpkin, Wilson. *The Removal of the Cherokee Indians.* Wormsloe, Georgia, 1907.

McCoy, Isaac. *History of Baptist Indian Missions.* Washington, 1840. Reprint. New York: Johnson, 1970.

McKenney, Thomas L., and James Hall. *History of the Indian Tribes.* Philadelphia, 1836.

Morse, Jedidiah. *A Report to the Secretary of War.* New Haven, 1822.

Owen, Narcissa. *Memoirs.* Washington, 1907.

Peters, Richard. *The Case of the Cherokee Nation.* Philadelphia, 1831.

Ross, William P. *Life and Times of Hon. Wm. P. Ross.* Fort Smith, Arkansas, 1893.

Stuart, John A. *A Sketch of the Cherokee and Choctaw Indians.* Little Rock, 1837.

Timberlake, Henry. *Memoirs.* Edited by Samuel C. Williams. 1765. Reprint. Marietta, Georgia, 1948.

II. Cherokee Culture

Bloom, Leonard. "The Acculturation of the Eastern Cherokee: Historical Aspects," *North Carolina Historical Review* 19 (October, 1942): 323–58.

Brown, John P. *Old Frontiers.* Kingsport, Tenn.: Southern Publishers, 1938.

Butrick, Daniel. *Cherokee Antiquities.* Vinita, I. T.: Indian Chieftain Publishers, 1884.

Fenton, William N., and John Gulick, eds. Symposium on Cherokee and Iroquois Culture. Smithsonian Institution, Bureau of American Ethnology Bulletin 180. Washington, D.C.: Government Printing Office, 1961.

Fogelson, Raymond D. "The Cherokee Ballgame Cycle." *Ethnomusicology* 15 (1971): 327–28.

————. "On the Varieties of Indian History." *Journal of Ethnic Studies* 2 (1974): 105–12.

Fogelson, Raymond D., and Richard N. Adams, eds. *The Anthropology of Power*. New York: Academic Press, 1977.

Gearing, Fred O. *Priests and Warriors*. American Anthropological Association Memoir 93. Menasha, Wisc.: American Anthropological Association, 1962.

Gilbert, William H., Jr. *The Eastern Cherokees*. Smithsonian Institution, Bureau of American Ethnology Bulletin 133. Washington, D.C.: Government Printing Office, 1943.

Hudson, Charles. *The Southeastern Indians*. Knoxville: University of Tennessee Press, 1976.

————, ed. *Four Centuries of Southern Indians*. Athens: University of Georgia Press, 1975.

Hultkrantz, Åke. *Belief and Worship in Native North America*. Syracuse: University of Syracuse Press, 1981.

Kilpatrick, Jack F. *Sequoyah, of Earth and Intellect*. Austin: Encino Press, 1965.

————, ed. *The Wahnenauhi Manuscript*. Smithsonian Institution, Bureau of American Ethnology Bulletin 196. Washington, D.C.: Government Printing Office, 1966.

Kilpatrick, Jack F., and Anna G. Kilpatrick, eds. *New Echota Letters*. Dallas: Southern Methodist University Press, 1968.

Mooney, James. "The Cherokee Ball Play." *American Anthopologist*, o. s. 3 (1890): 105–32.

————. *The Sacred Formulas of the Cherokees*. Smithsonian Institution, Bureau of American Ethnology, 7th Annual Report. 1885–86. Washington D.C.: Government Printing Office, 1891.

————. *Myths of the Cherokees*. Smithsonian Institution, Bureau of American Ethnology, 19th Annual Report, 1897–98. Washington, D.C.: Government Printing Office, 1900.

————. *The Ghost Dance Religion*. Smithsonian Institution, Bureau of American Ethnology, 14th Annual Report, part 2, 1892–93. Washington, D.C.: Government Printing Office, 1896.

Reid, John Philip. *A Law of Blood*. New York: New York University Press, 1970.

Spicer, Edward H. *Perspectives in American Indian Culture Change*, Chicago: University of Chicago Press, 1961.

Strickland, Rennard. *Fire and Spirits*. Norman: University of Oklahoma Press, 1975.

Swanton, John R. *The Indians of the Southeastern United States*. Smithsonian Institution, Bureau of American Ethnology Bulletin 137. Washington, D.C.: Government Printing Office, 1946.

Wilms, Douglas C. "Cherokee Settlement Patterns." *Southeastern Geographer* 14 (1974): 46–53.

III. American Indian Policy

Abel, Annie H. "The History of Events Resulting in Indian Consolidation West of the Mississippi." Annual Report of the American Historical Association for 1906, vol. 1, pp. 233–450. Washington, D.C.: Government Printing Office, 1908.

―――――. "Proposals for an Indian State, 1778–1878." Annual Report of the American Historical Association for 1907, vol. 1, pp. 87–104. Washington, D.C.: Government Printing Office, 1908.

Dippie, Brian W. *The Vanishing American*. Middletown, Conn.: Wesleyan University Press, 1982.

Harmon, George D. "Benjamin Hawkins and the Federal Factory System." *North Carolina Historical Review* 9 (1932): 138–52.

―――――. *Sixty Years of Indian Affairs*. Chapel Hill: University of North Carolina Press, 1941.

Horsman, Reginald. *Expansionism and American Indian Policy, 1783–1812*. East Lansing: Michigan State University Press, 1967.

―――――. *Race and Manifest Destiny*. Cambridge: Harvard University Press, 1981.

McCoy, Isaac. *Remarks on the Practicability of Indian Reform*. 2d ed. New York. 1829.

Prucha, Francis P. *American Indian Policy in the Formative Years*. Cambridge: Harvard University Press, 1962.

Royce, Charles C. *The Cherokee Nation of Indians, A Narrative of their Official Relations with the Colonial and Federal Governments*. Smithsonian Institution, Bureau of Ethnology, 5th Annual Report, 1833–1884. Washington, D.C., 1887. Reprint. Chicago: Aldine, 1975.

Satz, Ronald. *American Indian Policy in the Jacksonian Era*. Lincoln: University of Nebraska Press, 1975.

Sheehan, Bernard. *Seeds of Extinction*. Chapel Hill: University of North Carolina Press, 1973.

Viola, Herman J. *Thomas L. McKenney, Architect of America's Indian Policy, 1816–1830*. Chicago: Swallow Press, 1974.

IV. Cherokee History, 1700–1840

Brown, John P. *Old Frontiers*. Kingsport, Tenn.: Southern Publishers, 1938.

Conser, Walter H., Jr. "John Ross and the Cherokee Resistance Campaign, 1833–1838." *Journal of Southern History* 44 (May, 1978): 191–212.

Corkran, David H. *The Cherokee Frontier, 1740–1762*. Norman: University of Oklahoma Press, 1962.

Cotteril, Robert S. *The Southern Indians*. Norman: University of Oklahoma Press, 1954.

Dale, Edward E., and Gaston L. Litton, eds. *Cherokee Cavaliers*. Norman: University of Oklahoma Press, 1939.

Eaton, Rachel. *John Ross and the Cherokee Indians.* Chicago, 1921.

Foreman, Grant. *Indian Removal.* Norman: University of Oklahoma Press, 1932.

_____. *Sequoyah.* Norman: University of Oklahoma Press, 1938.

Gabriel, Ralph H. *Elias Boudinot.* Norman: University of Oklahoma Press, 1941.

Goodwin, Gary. *Cherokees in Transition.* Chicago: University of Chicago, Dept. of Geography, 1977.

Govan, Gilbert E., and James W. Livingood. *The Chattanooga Country, 1540–1951.* New York: E. P. Dutton, 1951.

Halliburton, Rudi, Jr. *Red Over Black.* Westport, Conn.: Greenwood Press, 1977.

Haywood, John. *Civil and Political History of Tennessee.* Nashville, 1821.

King, Duane, ed. *The Cherokee Indian Nation.* Knoxville: University of Tennessee Press, 1979.

Malone, Henry T. *Cherokees of the Old South.* Athens: University of Georgia Press, 1956.

Perdue, Theda. *Slavery and the Evolution of Cherokee Society, 1540–1866.* Knoxville: University of Tennessee Press, 1979.

Pound, Merritt B. *Benjamin Hawkins.* Athens: University of Georgia Press, 1951.

Royce, Charles C. *The Cherokee Nation of Indians.* 1887. Reprint. Chicago: Aldine, 1975.

Starkey, Marion. *The Cherokee Nation.* New York: Knopf, 1946.

Starr, Emett. *Early History of the Cherokees.* N. p., 1917.

_____. *History of the Cherokee Indians and Their Legends.* Oklahoma City: Warden, 1922.

Traveller Bird. *Tell Them They Lie: The Sequoyah Myth.* Los Angeles: Westernlore Publishers, 1971.

Van Every, Dale. *Disinherited.* New York: William Morrow, 1966.

Wardell, Morris. *A Political History of the Cherokee Nation. 1838–1907.* Norman: University of Oklahoma Press, 1938.

Woodward, Grace. *The Cherokees.* Norman: University of Oklahoma Press, 1963.

Young, Mary. "Indian Removal." In *Indians of the Lower South,* edited by John Mahon. Pensacola: Gulf Coast History and Humanities Conference, 1975.

_____. *Redskins, Ruffle Shirts and Red Necks.* Norman: University of Oklahoma Press, 1961.

V. Missionary Histories

A. GENERAL

Beaver, R. Pierce. *Church, State and the American Indians.* St. Louis: Concordia, 1966.

Berkhofer, Robert F., Jr. *Salvation and the Savage*. New York: Atheneum, 1976.

Bowden, Henry W. *American Indians and Christian Missions*. Chicago: University of Chicago Press, 1981.

B. DENOMINATIONAL

Anderson, Rufus K., ed. *Memoirs of Catherine Brown*. Boston, 1828.

Andrew, John A., II. *Rebuilding the Christian Commonwealth*. Lexington: University of Kentucky Press, 1976.

Bangs, Nathan. *An Authentic History of the Missions Under the Care of the Missionary Society of the Methodist Episcopal Church*. New York, 1832.

Barclay, Wade C. *History of Methodist Missions*. 2 vols., New York: Board of Missions of the Methodist Church, 1949–50.

Bass, Althea. *Cherokee Messenger*. Norman: University of Oklahoma Press, 1936.

Bass, Dorothy C. "Gideon Blackburn's Mission to the Cherokees." *Journal of Presbyterian History* 52 (Fall, 1974): 203–26.

Coleman, Michael C. "Not Race but Grace: Presbyterian Missionaries and American Indians, 1837–1893." *Journal of American History* 67 (June, 1980): 41–60.

Faust, Harold S. "The Growth of Presbyterian Missions to the American Indians." *Journal of the Presbyterian Historical Society* 22 (1944): 82–123.

Fries, Adelaide L., trans. and ed. "Records of the Moravians in North Carolina." *Publications of the North Carolina Historical Commission*, vols. 23, 24, 25, 27. Raleigh, N. C., 1943, 1947, 1954.

Hamilton, Kenneth G., trans. and ed. "Minutes of the Mission Conference Held in Springplace." *The Atlanta Historical Bulletin* (Winter, 1970): 9–87.

————, trans. and ed. "Minutes of the Mission Conference Held in Springplace." *The Atlanta Historical Bulletin* (Spring, 1971): 31–59.

Harrell, David E. *Quest for a Christian America*. Nashville: Bethany Press, 1965.

John, Isabelle G. *Handbook of Methodist Missions*. Nashville, 1893.

Lazenby, Marion E. *History of Methodism in Alabama and West Florida*. N. p., 1960.

McCoy, Isaac. *History of Baptist Indian Missions*. Washington, D.C., 1840.

McFerrin, John B. *History of Methodism in Tennessee*. Nashville: Southern Methodist Publishing House, 1879.

Malone, Henry T. "The Early Nineteenth Century Missionaries in the Cherokee Country." *Tennessee Historical Quarterly* 10 (June, 1951): 127–39.

Moffitt, James W. "Early Baptist Missionary Work among the Cherokee." *The East Tennessee Historical Society's Publications* 12 (1940): 16–27.

Moseley, J. Edward. *Disciples of Christ in Georgia.* St. Louis: Bethany Press, 1954.

Mudge, Enoch. "History of the Missions of the Methodist Episcopal Church." In *History of American Missions to the Heathen.* Worcester, Mass.: Spooner & Howard, 1840.

Peacock, Mary T. "Methodist Mission Work among the Cherokee Indians before Removal." *Methodist History* 3 (1965): 20–39.

————. *The Circuit Riders and Those Who Followed.* Chattanooga: Hudson Printing Co., 1957.

Phillips, Clifton J. *Protestant America and the Pagan World.* Cambridge: Harvard University Press, 1969.

Routh, Eugene C. "Early Missionaries to the Cherokees." *Chronicles of Oklahoma* 15 (December, 1937): 449–65.

Schultz, George A. *An Indian Canaan.* Norman: University of Oklahoma Press, 1972.

Schwarze, Edmund. *History of the Moravian Missions among the Southern Indian Tribes of the United States.* Bethlehem, Pa.: Times Publishing Co., 1923.

Strong, William E. *The Story of the American Board.* Boston: Pilgrim Press, 1910.

Tracy, Joseph. *History of American Missions to the Heathen.* Worcester, Mass., 1840.

Walker, Robert S. *Torchlights to the Cherokees.* New York: Macmillan, 1931.

Washburn, Cephas. *Reminiscences of the Indians.* Richmond: Presbyterian Committee of Publication, 1969.

West, Anson G. *History of Methodism in Alabama.* Nashville, 1893.

Index